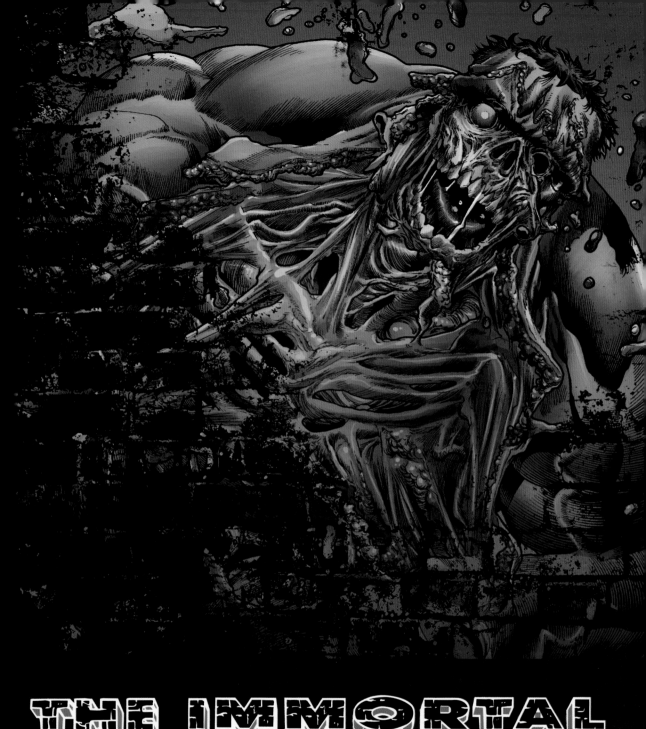

THE IMMORTAL HULK

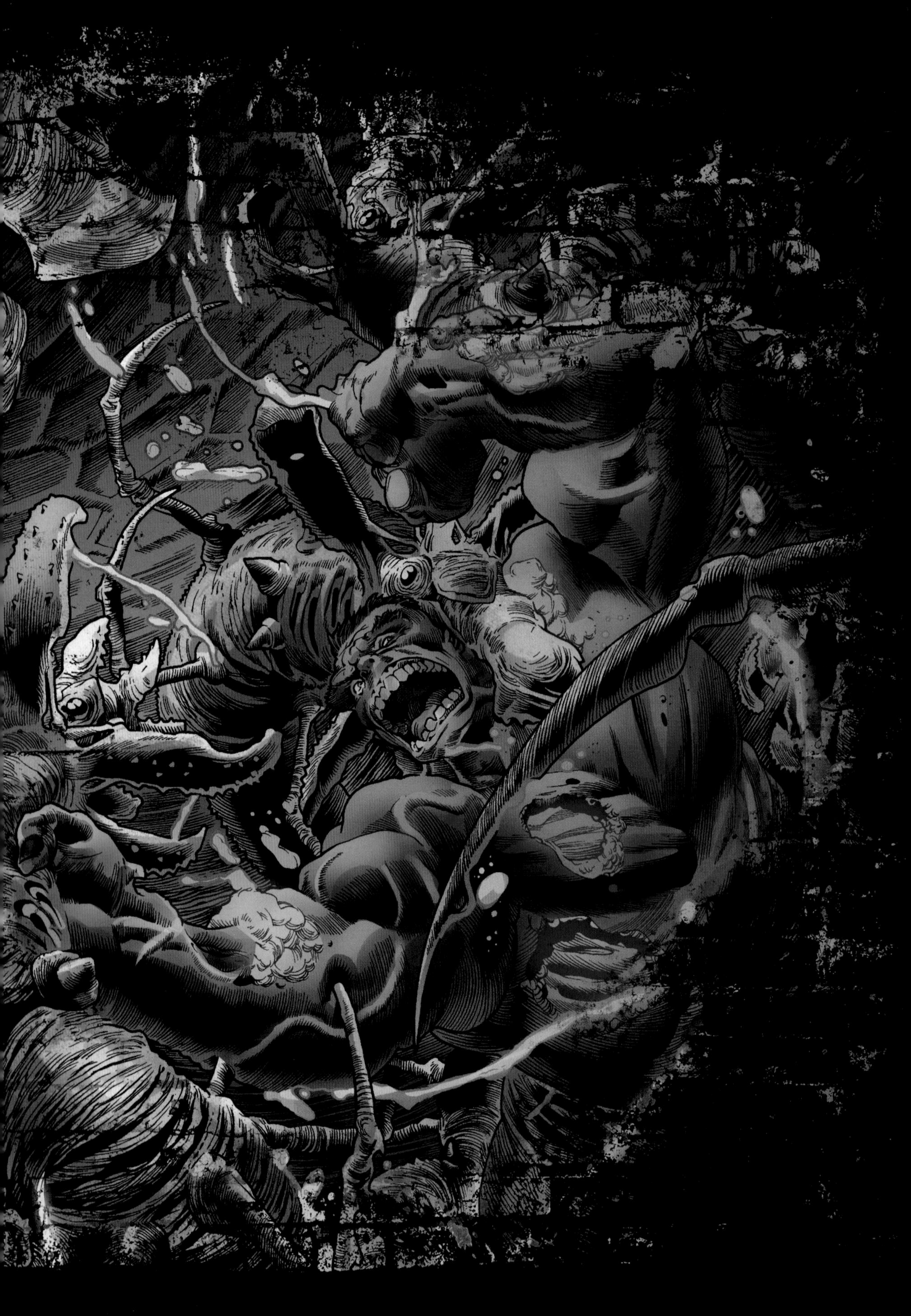

IMMORTAL HULK VOL. 3. Contains material originally published in magazine form as IMMORTAL HULK (2018) #21-30. First printing 2020. ISBN 978-1-302-92830-8. Published by MARVEL WORLDWIDE, INC., a subsidiary of MARVEL ENTERTAINMENT, LLC. OFFICE OF PUBLICATION: 1290 Avenue of the Americas, New York, NY 10104. **Printed in China.** KEVIN FEIGE, Chief Creative Officer; DAN BUCKLEY, President, Marvel Entertainment; JOE QUESADA,

THE IMMORTAL HULK

AL EWING
WRITER

ISSUE #21

RYAN BODENHEIM
ARTIST

PAUL MOUNTS
COLOR ARTIST

ISSUE #22-24, #26-27 & #29-30

JOE BENNETT
PENCILER

RUY JOSÉ & **BELARDINO BRABO** WITH **MARC DEERING** (#24, #27),
ROBERTO POGGI (#24), **BELARDINO BRABO** (#27, #29-30),
SEAN PARSONS (#27) & **CAM SMITH** (#29-30)
INKERS

PAUL MOUNTS
COLOR ARTIST

ISSUE #25

GERMÁN GARCÍA
PENCILER

RUY JOSÉ &
GERMÁN GARCÍA
INKERS

PAUL MOUNTS
COLOR ARTIST

ISSUE #28

OM REILLY & **MATÍAS BERGARA**
ARTISTS

PAUL MOUNTS
COLOR ARTIST

C's CORY PETIT
LETTERER

ALEX ROSS
COVER ARTIST

SARAH BRUNSTAD
ASSOCIATE EDITOR

WIL MOSS
EDITOR

TOM BREVOORT
EXECUTIVE EDITOR

COLLECTION EDITOR
JENNIFER GRÜNWALD
ASSISTANT EDITOR
DANIEL KIRCHHOFFER
ASSISTANT MANAGING EDITOR
MAIA LOY

VP PRODUCTION & SPECIAL PROJECTS
JEFF YOUNGQUIST
BOOK DESIGNERS
JAY BOWEN WITH **RODOLFO MURAGUCHI**
SVP PRINT, SALES & MARKETING
DAVID GABRIEL

HULK
CREATED BY
STAN LEE &
JACK KIRBY

21

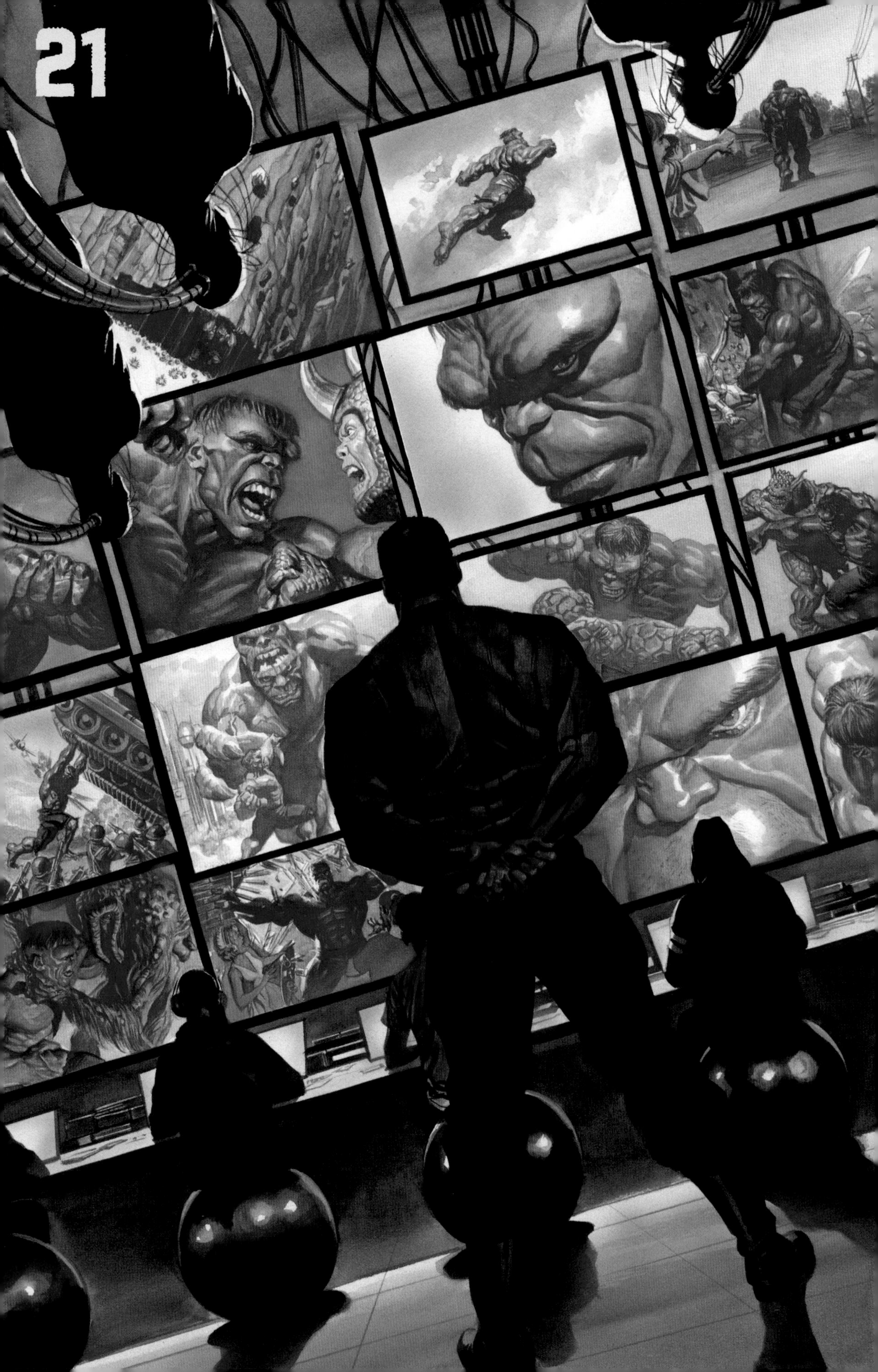

" ...IN ALL CHAOS THERE IS A COSMOS, IN ALL DISORDER A SECRET ORDER..."

– CARL JUNG
ARCHETYPES AND THE COLLECTIVE UNCONSCIOUS

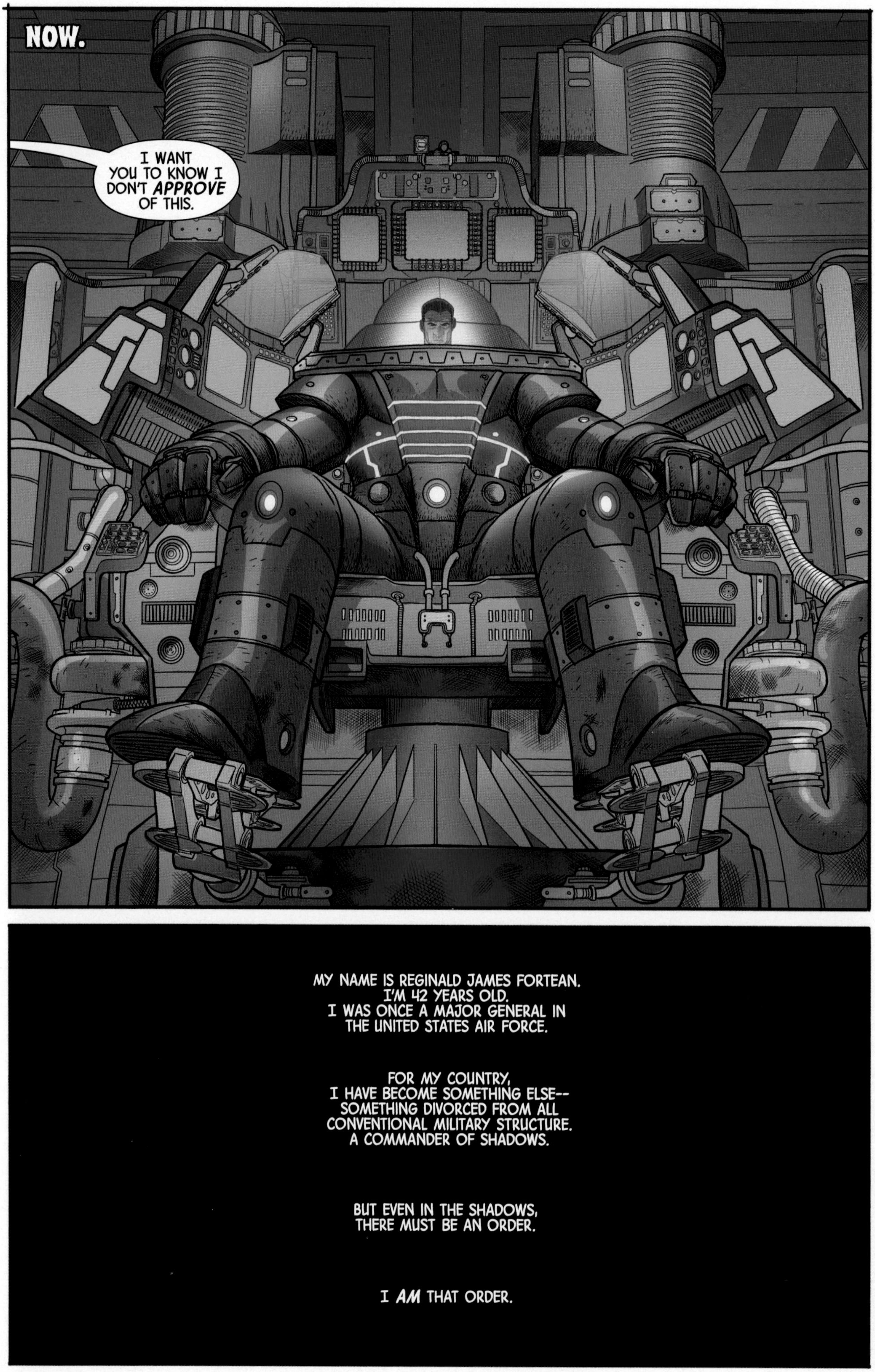
NOW.
I WANT YOU TO KNOW I DON'T *APPROVE* OF THIS.
MY NAME IS REGINALD JAMES FORTEAN.
I'M 42 YEARS OLD.
I WAS ONCE A MAJOR GENERAL IN THE UNITED STATES AIR FORCE.
FOR MY COUNTRY, I HAVE BECOME SOMETHING ELSE-- SOMETHING DIVORCED FROM ALL CONVENTIONAL MILITARY STRUCTURE. A COMMANDER OF SHADOWS.
BUT EVEN IN THE SHADOWS, THERE MUST BE AN ORDER.
I *AM* THAT ORDER.

SO YOU'VE SAID.

YOU DON'T SEEM TO APPROVE OF *MUCH* LATELY, DR. McGOWAN.

IF YOU MEAN THE *MURDER* OF *CIVILIANS*--

COLLATERAL DAMAGE.

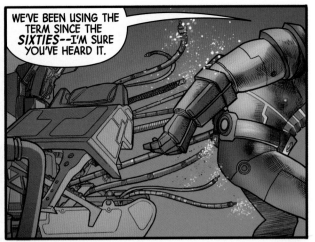

WE'VE BEEN USING THE TERM SINCE THE *SIXTIES*--I'M SURE YOU'VE HEARD IT.

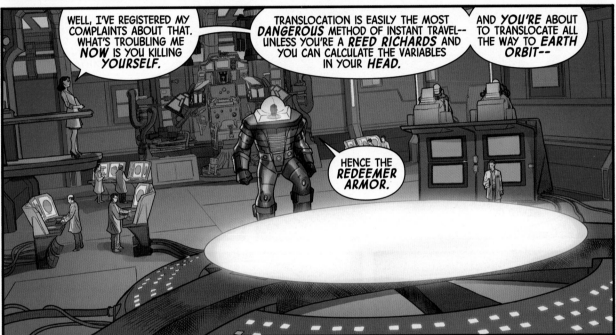

WELL, I'VE REGISTERED MY COMPLAINTS ABOUT THAT. WHAT'S TROUBLING ME *NOW* IS YOU KILLING *YOURSELF.*

TRANSLOCATION IS EASILY THE MOST *DANGEROUS* METHOD OF INSTANT TRAVEL-- UNLESS YOU'RE A *REED RICHARDS* AND YOU CAN CALCULATE THE VARIABLES IN YOUR *HEAD.*

AND *YOU'RE* ABOUT TO TRANSLOCATE ALL THE WAY TO *EARTH ORBIT*--

HENCE THE *REDEEMER ARMOR.*

IT'S SEALED AND OXYGENATED FOR VACUUM. IF I MISS THE *TARGET,* I CAN *SURVIVE* IN OPEN SPACE.

UH-HUH. WHAT ABOUT ARRIVING HALFWAY THROUGH A *BULKHEAD?*

IT WON'T COME TO THAT.

WILL IT, DR. McGOWAN?

... NOT ON *PURPOSE*, NO. BUT I CAN'T MAKE *PROMISES* HERE, SIR. THAT'S WHY WE NEED MORE *TIME.*

THERE ARE *RANDOM FACTORS* INVOLVED THAT NEED TO BE--

THAT'S WHAT IT'S ALL *ABOUT*, ISN'T IT?

THE RANDOM FACTORS. THE *HUMAN ERRORS.* THE *SHADOWS.*

CHAOS. DO WE RULE CHAOS, OR DOES CHAOS RULE *US?*

I KNOW WHAT *MY* ANSWER WOULD BE.

IF I *DON'T* COME BACK, PROTOCOL PLACES *YOU* IN COMMAND, DOCTOR. UNTIL THEN...THE FINAL DECISION IS *MINE.*

SIR-- *DON'T*--

BEGINNING TRANSLOCATION... *NOW.*

NO! SHUT IT *DOWN*, GENERAL!

WE NEED TO DOUBLE-CHECK-- *TRIPLE*-CHECK! IF THERE'S BEEN *ANY* ERROR AT *ALL*--

THAT'S THE DIFFERENCE BETWEEN US, DOCTOR. I CHOOSE NOT TO BE *COWED* BY THE RANDOM FACTORS.

WE *CAN* RULE OVER CHAOS.

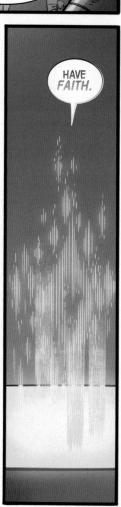

HAVE *FAITH.*

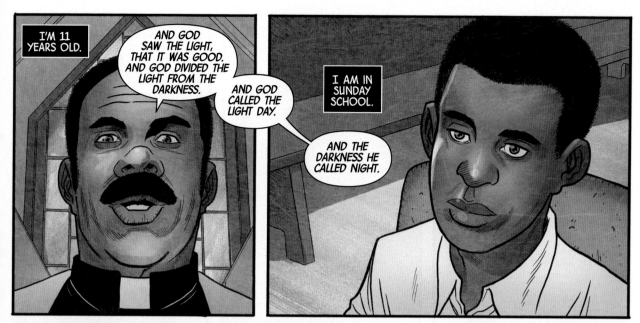

I'M 11 YEARS OLD.

AND GOD SAW THE LIGHT, THAT IT WAS GOOD. AND GOD DIVIDED THE LIGHT FROM THE DARKNESS.

AND GOD CALLED THE LIGHT DAY.

I AM IN SUNDAY SCHOOL.

AND THE DARKNESS HE CALLED NIGHT.

I AM LISTENING INTENTLY.

AND THE EVENING AND THE MORNING WAS THE FIRST DAY.

I WANT TO PAUSE THERE FOR A MOMENT.

WE'RE AT THE END OF THE FIRST DAY. THERE'S NO PEOPLE YET. NO ANIMALS--NOT EVEN PLANTS.

AND YET WHAT HAS GOD ALREADY DONE FOR US?

...

MADE THE LIGHT?

OF COURSE. BUT I'M THINKING OF SOMETHING EVEN MORE PROFOUND THAN THAT.

LET'S RETURN TO THE SECOND VERSE. THE EARTH WAS WITHOUT FORM, AND VOID.

WITHOUT FORM.

THINK ABOUT THAT.

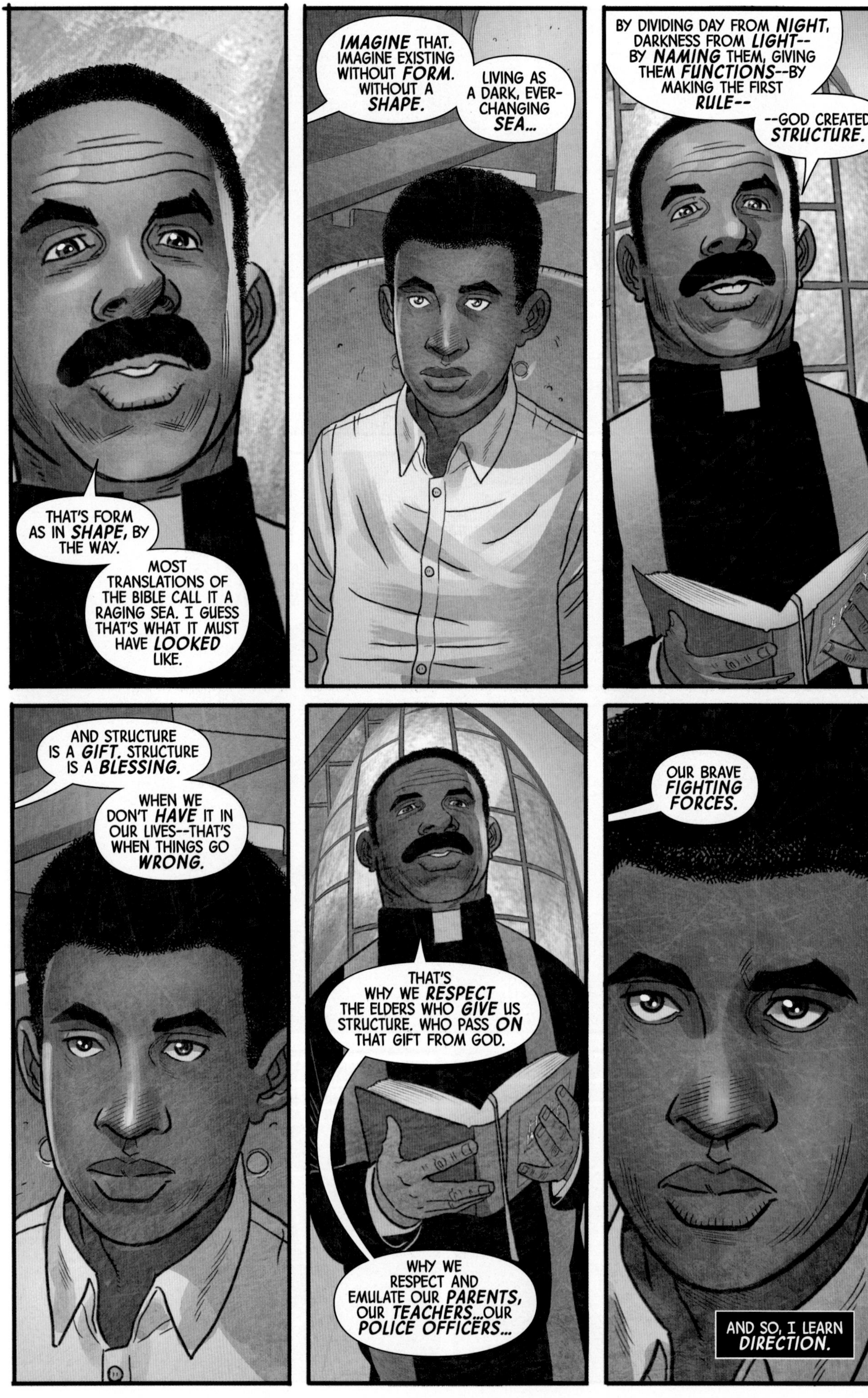
THAT'S FORM AS IN SHAPE, BY THE WAY.
MOST TRANSLATIONS OF THE BIBLE CALL IT A RAGING SEA. I GUESS THAT'S WHAT IT MUST HAVE LOOKED LIKE.
IMAGINE THAT. IMAGINE EXISTING WITHOUT FORM. WITHOUT A SHAPE.
LIVING AS A DARK, EVER-CHANGING SEA...
BY DIVIDING DAY FROM NIGHT, DARKNESS FROM LIGHT-- BY NAMING THEM, GIVING THEM FUNCTIONS--BY MAKING THE FIRST RULE--
--GOD CREATED STRUCTURE.
AND STRUCTURE IS A GIFT. STRUCTURE IS A BLESSING.
WHEN WE DON'T HAVE IT IN OUR LIVES--THAT'S WHEN THINGS GO WRONG.
THAT'S WHY WE RESPECT THE ELDERS WHO GIVE US STRUCTURE. WHO PASS ON THAT GIFT FROM GOD.
WHY WE RESPECT AND EMULATE OUR PARENTS, OUR TEACHERS...OUR POLICE OFFICERS...
OUR BRAVE FIGHTING FORCES.
AND SO, I LEARN DIRECTION.

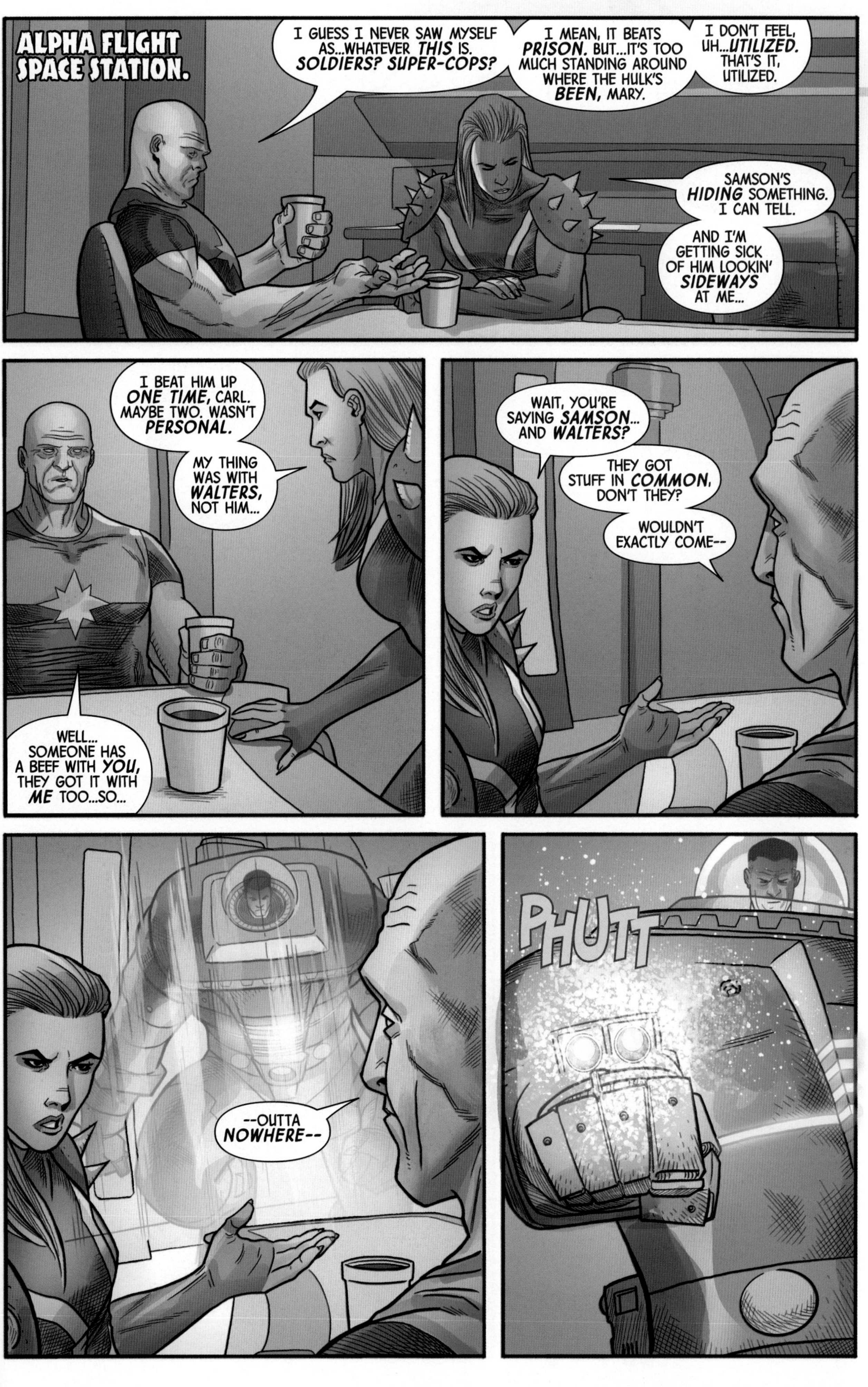
ALPHA FLIGHT SPACE STATION.
I GUESS I NEVER SAW MYSELF AS...WHATEVER THIS IS. SOLDIERS? SUPER-COPS?
I MEAN, IT BEATS PRISON. BUT...IT'S TOO MUCH STANDING AROUND WHERE THE HULK'S BEEN, MARY.
I DON'T FEEL, UH...UTILIZED. THAT'S IT, UTILIZED.
SAMSON'S HIDING SOMETHING. I CAN TELL.
AND I'M GETTING SICK OF HIM LOOKIN' SIDEWAYS AT ME...
I BEAT HIM UP ONE TIME, CARL. MAYBE TWO. WASN'T PERSONAL.
MY THING WAS WITH WALTERS, NOT HIM...
WELL... SOMEONE HAS A BEEF WITH YOU, THEY GOT IT WITH ME TOO...SO...
WAIT, YOU'RE SAYING SAMSON... AND WALTERS?
THEY GOT STUFF IN COMMON, DON'T THEY?
WOULDN'T EXACTLY COME--
--OUTTA NOWHERE--
PHUTT

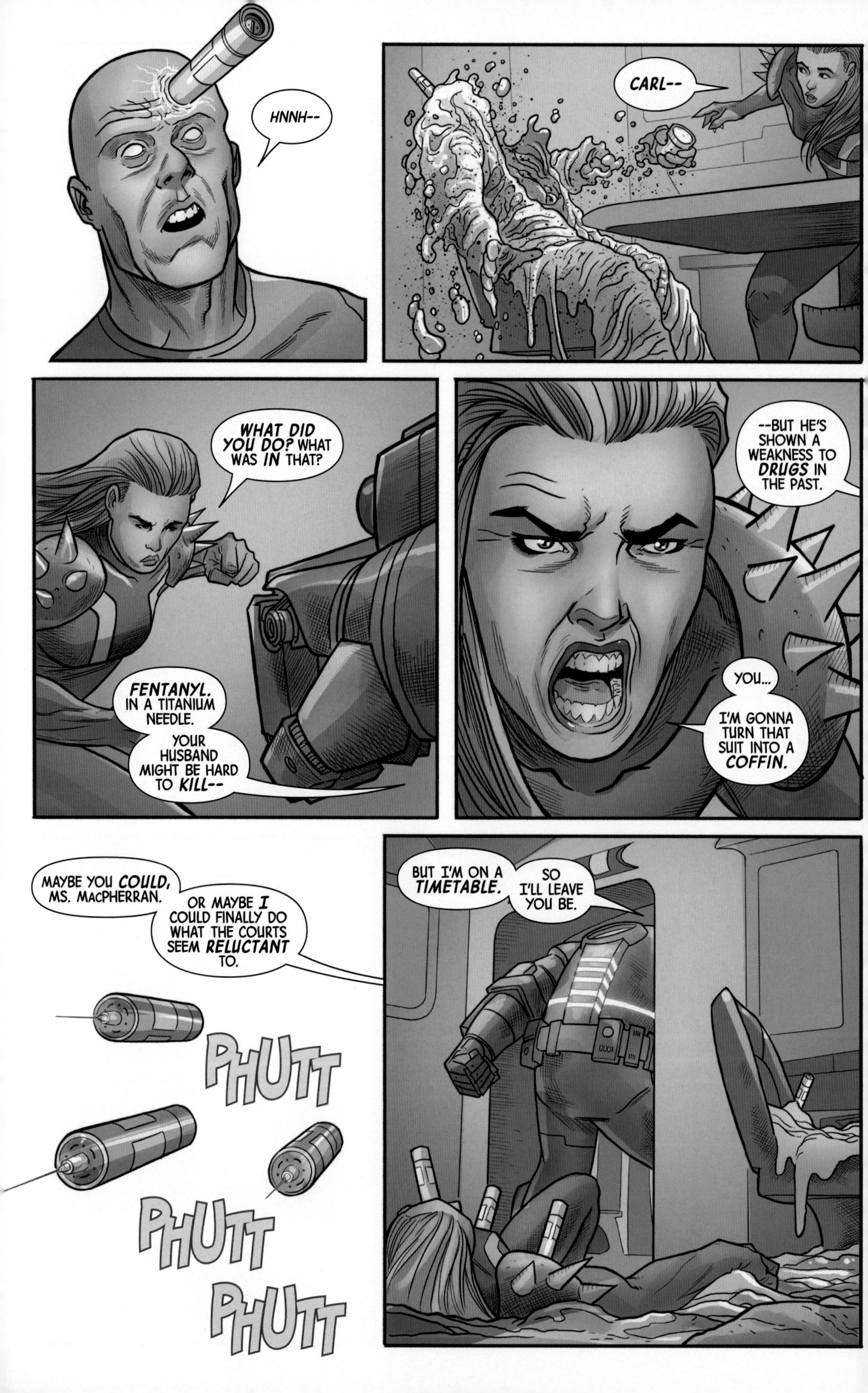
HNNH--
CARL--
WHAT DID YOU DO? WHAT WAS IN THAT?
FENTANYL. IN A TITANIUM NEEDLE.
YOUR HUSBAND MIGHT BE HARD TO KILL--
--BUT HE'S SHOWN A WEAKNESS TO DRUGS IN THE PAST.
YOU...
I'M GONNA TURN THAT SUIT INTO A COFFIN.
MAYBE YOU COULD, MS. MacPHERRAN.
OR MAYBE I COULD FINALLY DO WHAT THE COURTS SEEM RELUCTANT TO.
BUT I'M ON A TIMETABLE.
SO I'LL LEAVE YOU BE.
PHUTT
PHUTT
PHUTT

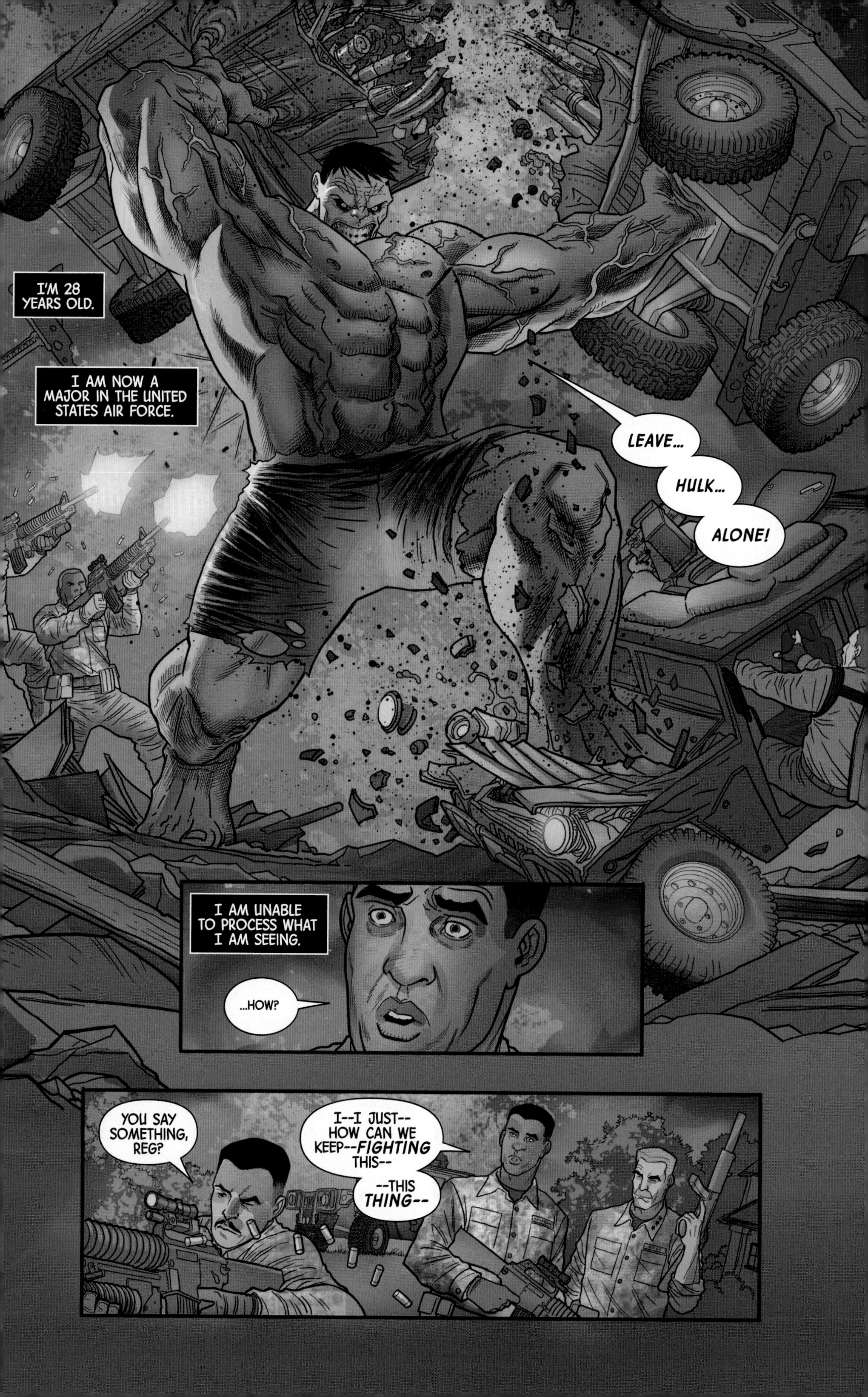
I'M 28 YEARS OLD.
I AM NOW A MAJOR IN THE UNITED STATES AIR FORCE.
LEAVE...
HULK...
ALONE!
I AM UNABLE TO PROCESS WHAT I AM SEEING.
...HOW?
YOU SAY SOMETHING, REG?
I--I JUST-- HOW CAN WE KEEP--*FIGHTING* THIS--
--THIS *THING*--

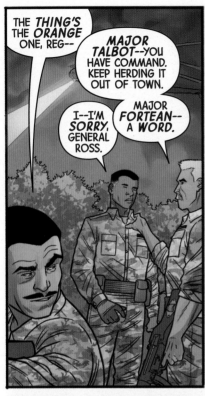

THE *THING'S* THE *ORANGE* ONE, REG--

MAJOR *TALBOT*--YOU HAVE COMMAND. KEEP *HERDING* IT OUT OF TOWN.

I--I'M *SORRY*, GENERAL ROSS.

MAJOR *FORTEAN*-- A *WORD*.

JUST--FOR A *MOMENT* THERE--

NEVER APOLOGIZE FOR BEING *HUMAN*, SON.

I'VE FELT IT *TOO*--WE *ALL* HAVE. THE *IMPOSSIBILITY* OF THIS... SITUATION.

BUT HERE'S HOW *I* HANDLE IT.

TAKE A *LOOK* OVER THERE. THAT *GIRL*.

SHE JUST LOST HER *HOME*, AND EVERYTHING *IN* IT. HER LIFE WILL *NEVER* BE THE SAME.

AND THERE ARE *HUNDREDS* LIKE HER. *HUNDREDS*. IN THIS ONE TOWN *ALONE*.

WHEN I HAVE MY MOMENTS OF...OF *DOUBT*, IN THE FACE OF THIS...I THINK ABOUT *THAT*. AND THEY *PASS*.

HOW ABOUT *YOU*, MAJOR?

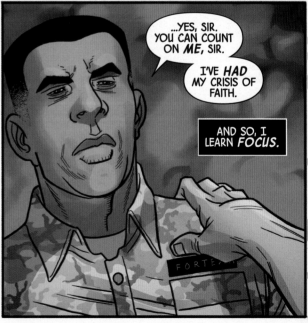

...YES, SIR. YOU CAN COUNT ON *ME*, SIR.

I'VE *HAD* MY CRISIS OF FAITH.

AND SO, I LEARN *FOCUS*.

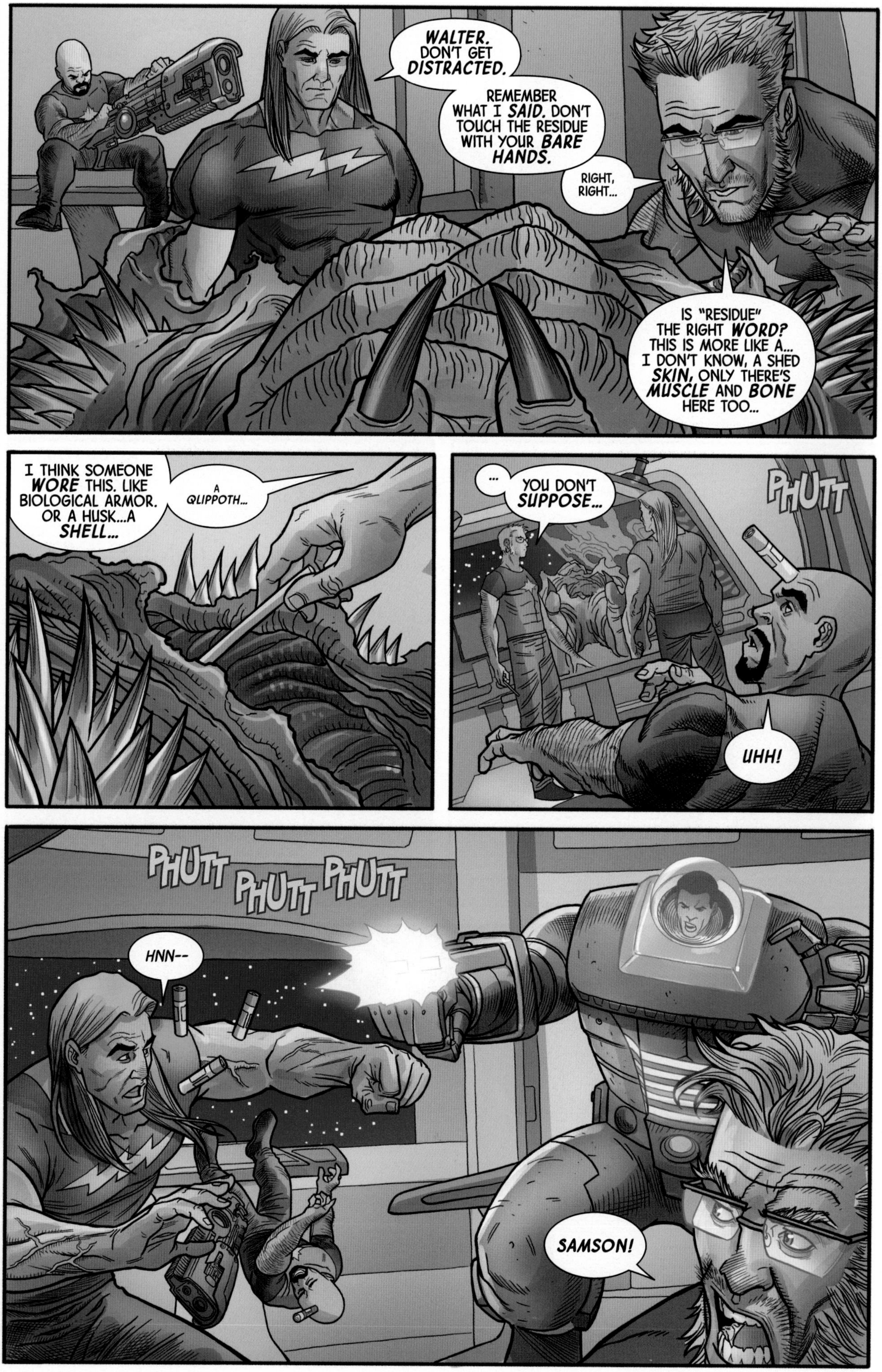
WALTER. DON'T GET DISTRACTED.
REMEMBER WHAT I SAID. DON'T TOUCH THE RESIDUE WITH YOUR BARE HANDS.
RIGHT, RIGHT...
IS "RESIDUE" THE RIGHT WORD? THIS IS MORE LIKE A... I DON'T KNOW, A SHED SKIN, ONLY THERE'S MUSCLE AND BONE HERE TOO...
I THINK SOMEONE WORE THIS. LIKE BIOLOGICAL ARMOR. OR A HUSK...A SHELL...
A QLIPPOTH...
...
YOU DON'T SUPPOSE...
PHUTT
UHH!
PHUTT PHUTT PHUTT
HNN--
SAMSON!

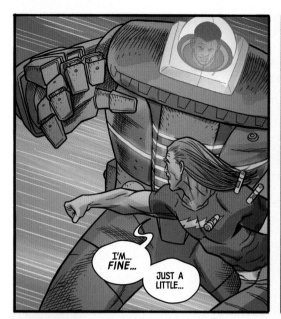

I'M... FINE... JUST A LITTLE...

A LITTLE...

DOC SAMSON. BACK IN THE WORLD OF THE LIVING *AGAIN*, I SEE.

EASY COME, EASY GO.

B-GHOOM

AS FOR *YOU*, DR. LANGKOWSKI...I STILL CONSIDER YOU AT FAULT FOR THE LIVES LOST IN *MINNESOTA*. AND THERE'S NO GAMMA IN YOU *NOW*.

I'D BEAR THAT IN *MIND*...

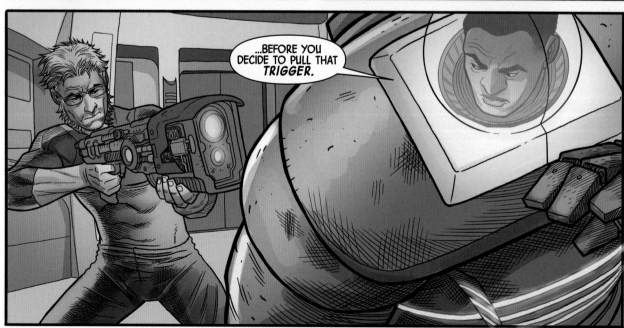

...BEFORE YOU DECIDE TO PULL THAT *TRIGGER*.

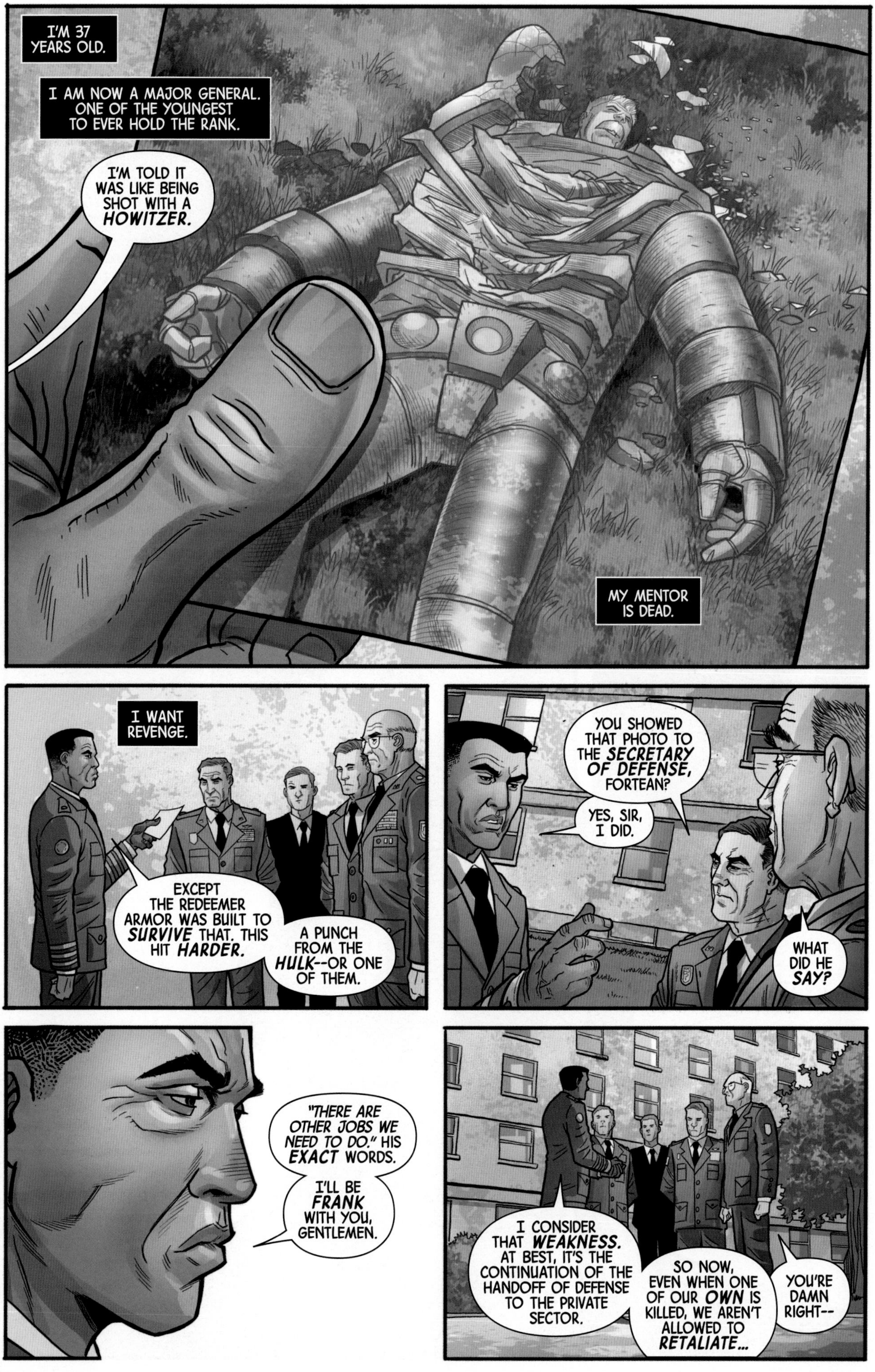

I'M 37 YEARS OLD.
I AM NOW A MAJOR GENERAL. ONE OF THE YOUNGEST TO EVER HOLD THE RANK.
I'M TOLD IT WAS LIKE BEING SHOT WITH A HOWITZER.
MY MENTOR IS DEAD.
I WANT REVENGE.
EXCEPT THE REDEEMER ARMOR WAS BUILT TO SURVIVE THAT. THIS HIT HARDER.
A PUNCH FROM THE HULK--OR ONE OF THEM.
YOU SHOWED THAT PHOTO TO THE SECRETARY OF DEFENSE, FORTEAN?
YES, SIR, I DID.
WHAT DID HE SAY?
"THERE ARE OTHER JOBS WE NEED TO DO." HIS EXACT WORDS.
I'LL BE FRANK WITH YOU, GENTLEMEN.
I CONSIDER THAT WEAKNESS. AT BEST, IT'S THE CONTINUATION OF THE HANDOFF OF DEFENSE TO THE PRIVATE SECTOR.
SO NOW, EVEN WHEN ONE OF OUR OWN IS KILLED, WE AREN'T ALLOWED TO RETALIATE...
YOU'RE DAMN RIGHT--

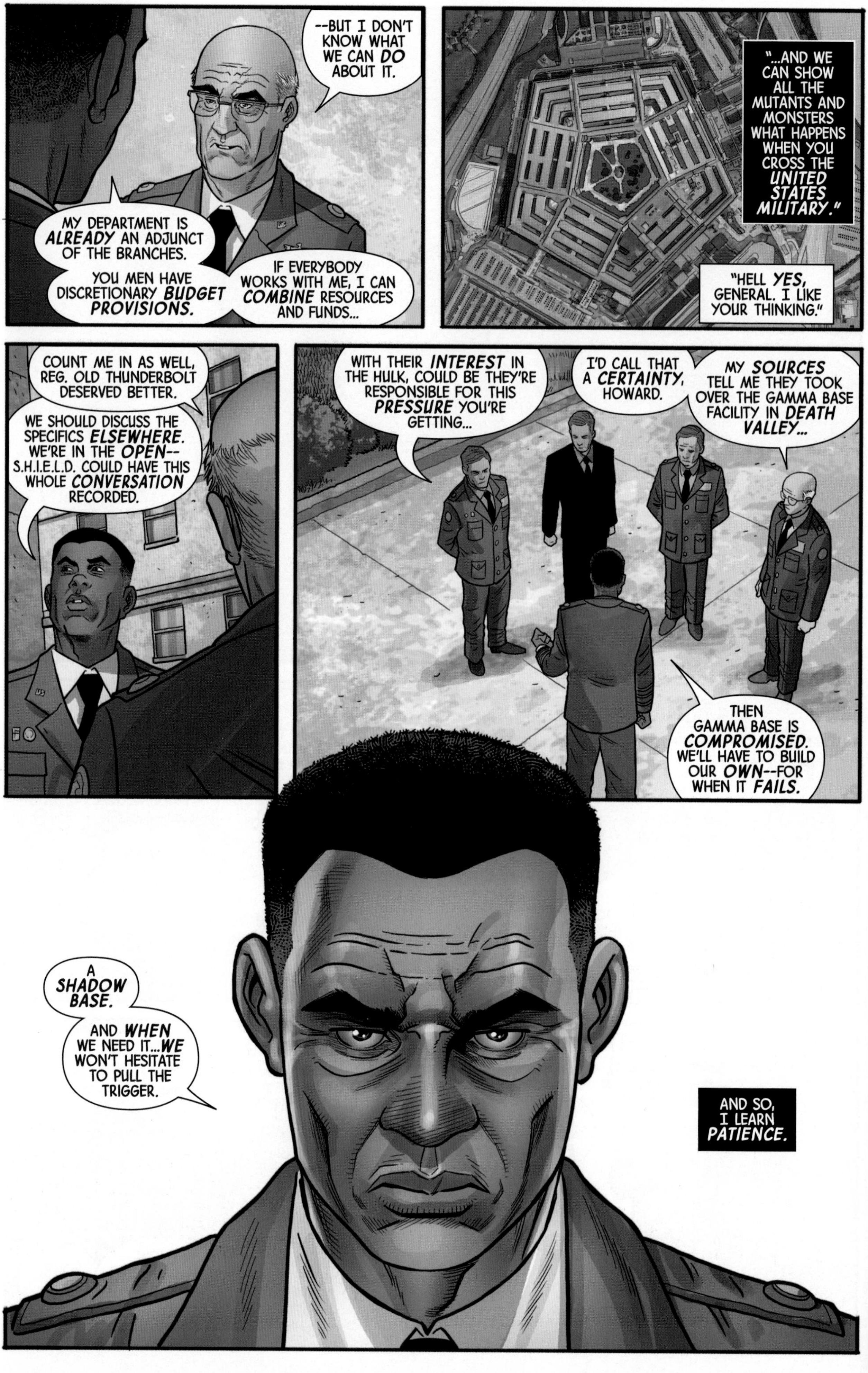
--BUT I DON'T KNOW WHAT WE CAN DO ABOUT IT.
MY DEPARTMENT IS ALREADY AN ADJUNCT OF THE BRANCHES.
YOU MEN HAVE DISCRETIONARY BUDGET PROVISIONS.
IF EVERYBODY WORKS WITH ME, I CAN COMBINE RESOURCES AND FUNDS...
"...AND WE CAN SHOW ALL THE MUTANTS AND MONSTERS WHAT HAPPENS WHEN YOU CROSS THE UNITED STATES MILITARY."
"HELL YES, GENERAL. I LIKE YOUR THINKING."
COUNT ME IN AS WELL, REG. OLD THUNDERBOLT DESERVED BETTER.
WE SHOULD DISCUSS THE SPECIFICS ELSEWHERE. WE'RE IN THE OPEN-- S.H.I.E.L.D. COULD HAVE THIS WHOLE CONVERSATION RECORDED.
WITH THEIR INTEREST IN THE HULK, COULD BE THEY'RE RESPONSIBLE FOR THIS PRESSURE YOU'RE GETTING...
I'D CALL THAT A CERTAINTY, HOWARD.
MY SOURCES TELL ME THEY TOOK OVER THE GAMMA BASE FACILITY IN DEATH VALLEY...
THEN GAMMA BASE IS COMPROMISED. WE'LL HAVE TO BUILD OUR OWN--FOR WHEN IT FAILS.
A SHADOW BASE.
AND WHEN WE NEED IT...WE WON'T HESITATE TO PULL THE TRIGGER.
AND SO, I LEARN PATIENCE.

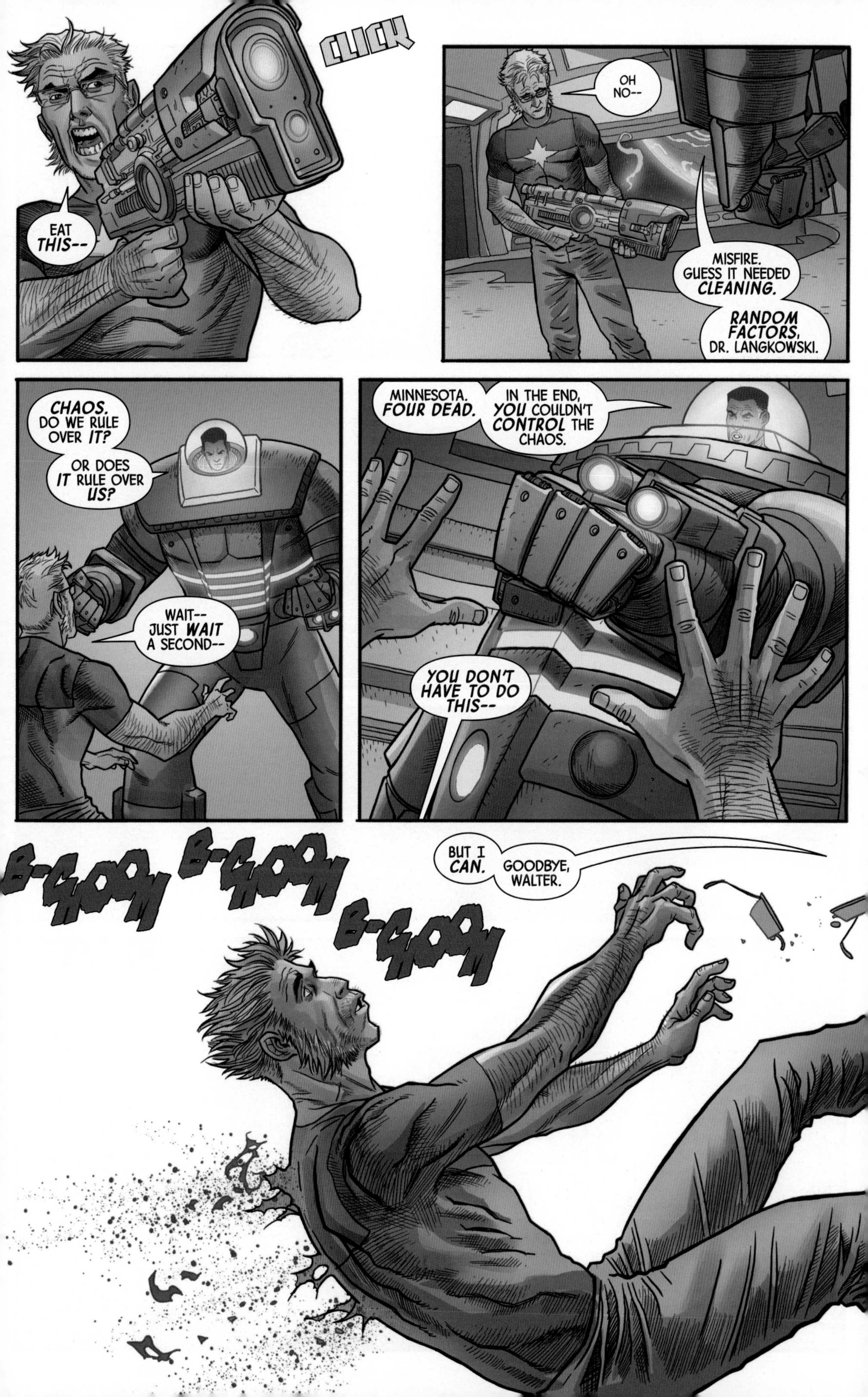
CLICK
EAT THIS--
OH NO--
MISFIRE. GUESS IT NEEDED CLEANING.
RANDOM FACTORS, DR. LANGKOWSKI.
CHAOS. DO WE RULE OVER IT?
OR DOES IT RULE OVER US?
WAIT-- JUST WAIT A SECOND--
MINNESOTA. FOUR DEAD.
IN THE END, YOU COULDN'T CONTROL THE CHAOS.
YOU DON'T HAVE TO DO THIS--
B-CHOOM B-CHOOM B-CHOOM
BUT I CAN.
GOODBYE, WALTER.

... FORTEAN TO *SHADOW BASE*.

RETRIEVAL OF THE SHELL IS *COMPLETE*.

NO HUMAN CASUALTIES.

...GENERAL?

NO HUMAN CASUALTIES? WHAT DOES THAT MEAN?

BEAM ME UP.

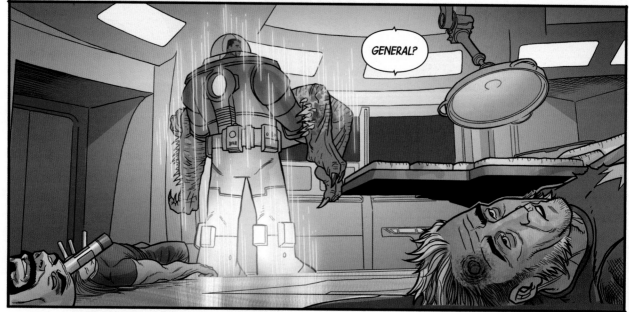

GENERAL?

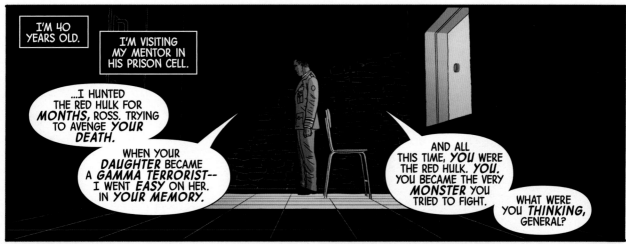

I'M 40 YEARS OLD.

I'M VISITING MY MENTOR IN HIS PRISON CELL.

...I HUNTED THE RED HULK FOR *MONTHS*, ROSS. TRYING TO AVENGE *YOUR DEATH.*

WHEN YOUR *DAUGHTER* BECAME A *GAMMA TERRORIST*-- I WENT *EASY* ON HER. IN *YOUR* MEMORY.

AND ALL THIS TIME, *YOU* WERE THE RED HULK. *YOU.* YOU BECAME THE VERY *MONSTER* YOU TRIED TO FIGHT.

WHAT WERE YOU *THINKING*, GENERAL?

I AM TRYING TO UNDERSTAND.

...DID YOU HEAR ABOUT THE *LAST* TIME I FOUGHT BANNER?

I DON'T SEE HOW THAT'S *RELEVANT*--

HE HAD *EXTREMIS* IN HIM. THAT NANO-JUNK *TONY STARK* MADE TO *PROGRAM* THE HUMAN BODY.

SAME STUFF BANNER USED TO TURN *ME* HUMAN FOR *KEEPS.*

HE'D USED IT ON *HIMSELF*-- TURNED THE HULK INTO A *GENIUS.* "DOC GREEN."

IT *WORE OFF* EVENTUALLY. BUT I TELL YOU, WHILE IT WAS *WORKING...*

...WHILE IT WAS WORKING, IT DID *NOTHING* TO HIM.

NOT A *DAMN* THING.

OH, HIS *VOCABULARY* WAS BETTER. HE *KNEW* MORE--LIKE A *HARD DRIVE,* FULL OF DATA.

BUT WHEN HE *CAME* FOR ME-- RANTING ABOUT HOW HE WAS THE *STRONGEST*-- I COULD SEE WHAT WAS *UNDER* ALL THE BIG WORDS.

A *CHILD.*

A RAGING, VIOLENT *CHILD*... WITH THE GENIUS OF THE WORLD'S GREATEST *SCIENTIST* AND THE POWER OF THE *ATOMIC BOMB.*

THAT'S WHAT I'M THINKING ABOUT *NOW.* AND I *GUARANTEE* I WAS THINKING SOMETHING LIKE THAT *THEN.*

BECAUSE *EVERY TIME* BANNER THINKS HE'S IN *CONTROL*... EVERY TIME *WE* THINK THAT...

...HE'S ABOUT TO *LOSE* IT.

HE BREAKS THE WORLD, REGGIE.

JUST BY BEING *IN* IT.

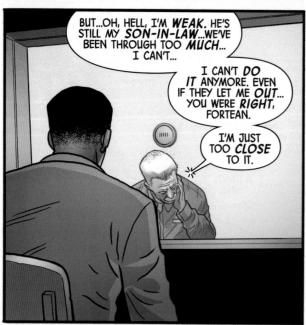

BUT...OH, HELL, I'M *WEAK.* HE'S STILL MY *SON-IN-LAW*...WE'VE BEEN THROUGH TOO *MUCH*... I CAN'T...

I CAN'T *DO* IT ANYMORE. EVEN IF THEY LET ME *OUT*... YOU WERE *RIGHT,* FORTEAN.

I'M JUST TOO *CLOSE* TO IT.

...I UNDERSTAND, GENERAL.

YOU CAN LEAVE IT WITH ME.

AND SO, I LEARN *PURPOSE.*

I'M 42 YEARS OLD.

I WAS ONCE A MAJOR GENERAL IN THE UNITED STATES AIR FORCE.

FOR MY COUNTRY... I HAVE BECOME SOMETHING ELSE.

SOMETHING DIVORCED FROM ALL CONVENTIONAL MILITARY STRUCTURE.

BRING IT HERE.

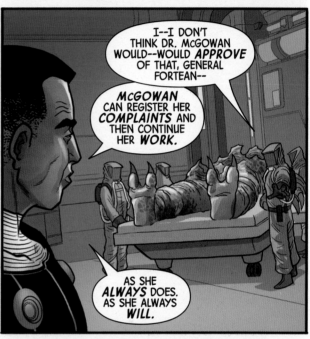

I--I DON'T THINK DR. McGOWAN WOULD--WOULD *APPROVE* OF THAT, GENERAL FORTEAN--

McGOWAN CAN REGISTER HER *COMPLAINTS* AND THEN CONTINUE HER *WORK.*

AS SHE *ALWAYS* DOES. AS SHE ALWAYS *WILL.*

NOW.

BRING IT *HERE.*

A COMMANDER OF SHADOWS.

BUT EVEN IN THE SHADOWS, THERE MUST BE AN ORDER.

SIR-- DON'T *TOUCH* IT--

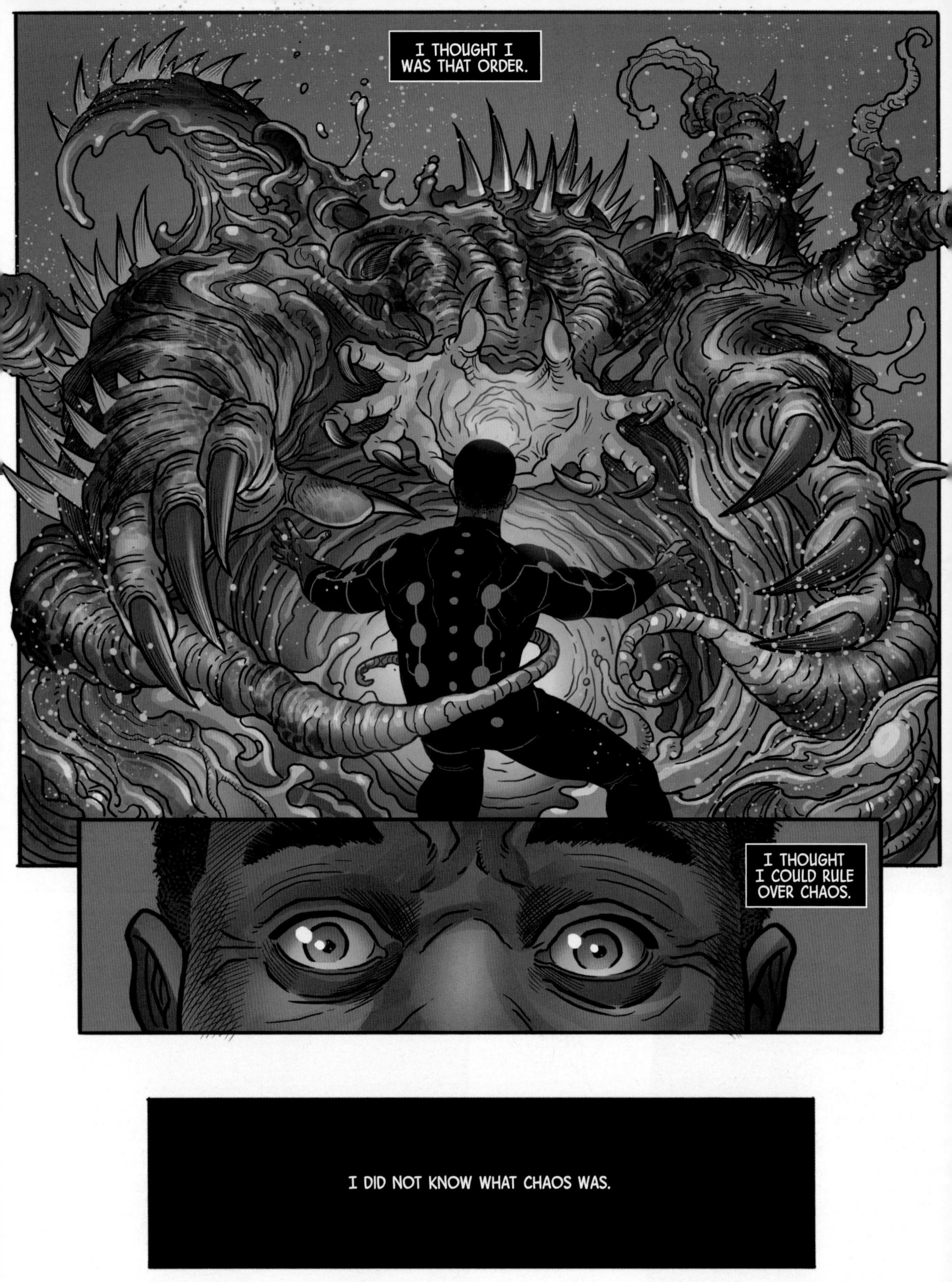
I THOUGHT I WAS THAT ORDER.
I THOUGHT I COULD RULE OVER CHAOS.

I DID NOT KNOW WHAT CHAOS WAS.

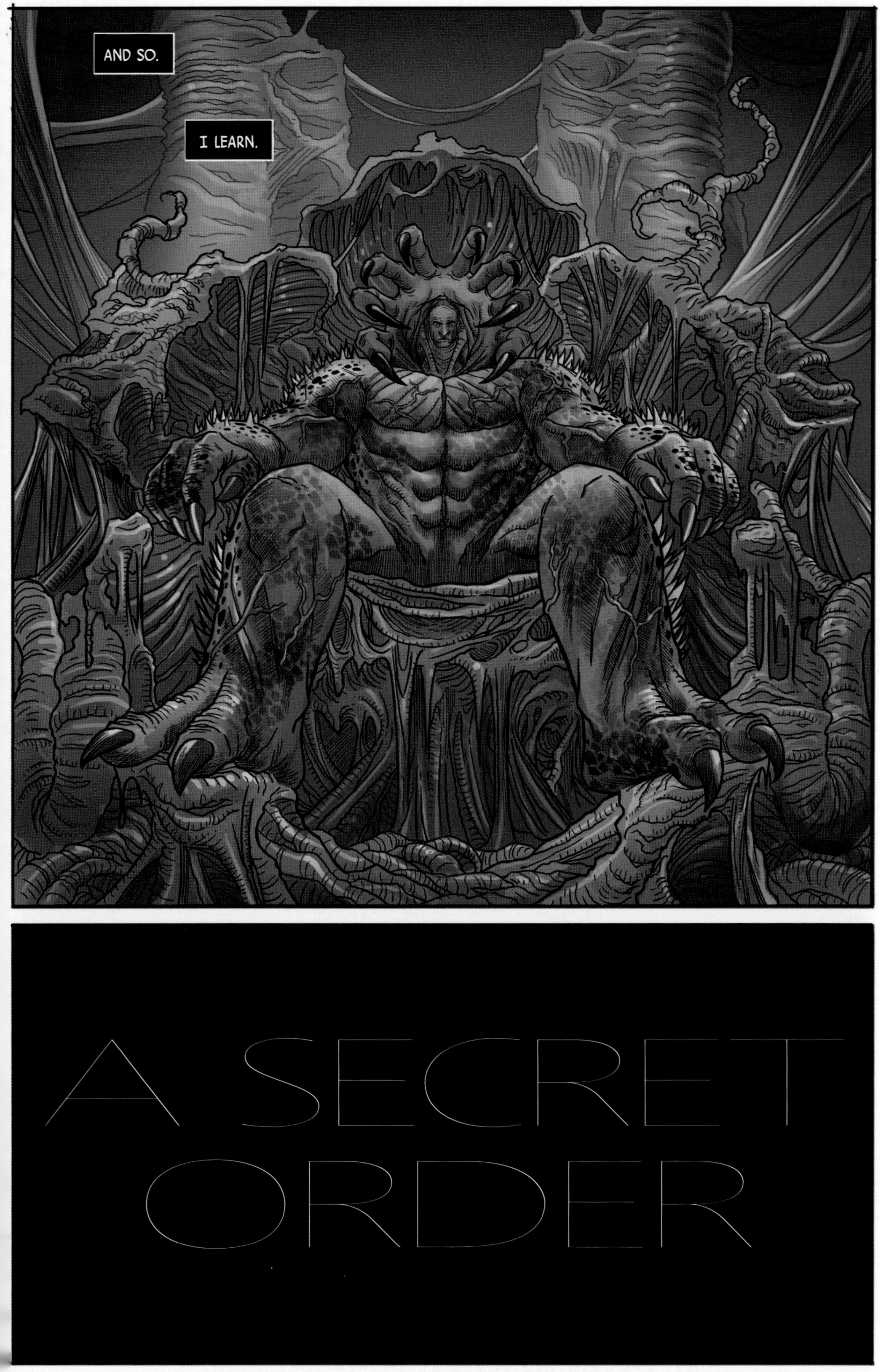
AND SO.
I LEARN.

A SECRET ORDER

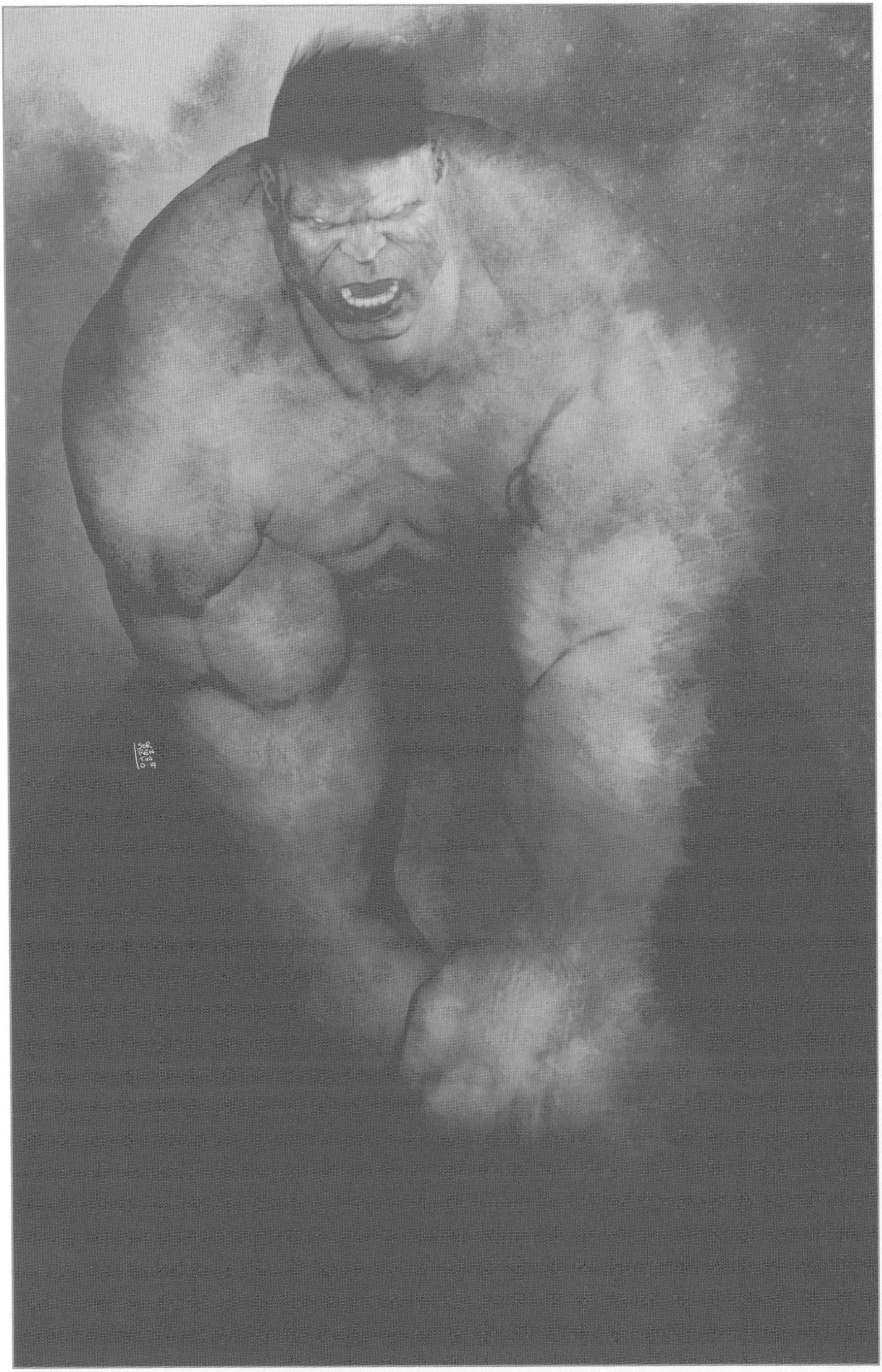

#21 2ND-PRINTING COVER BY ANDREA SORRENTINO

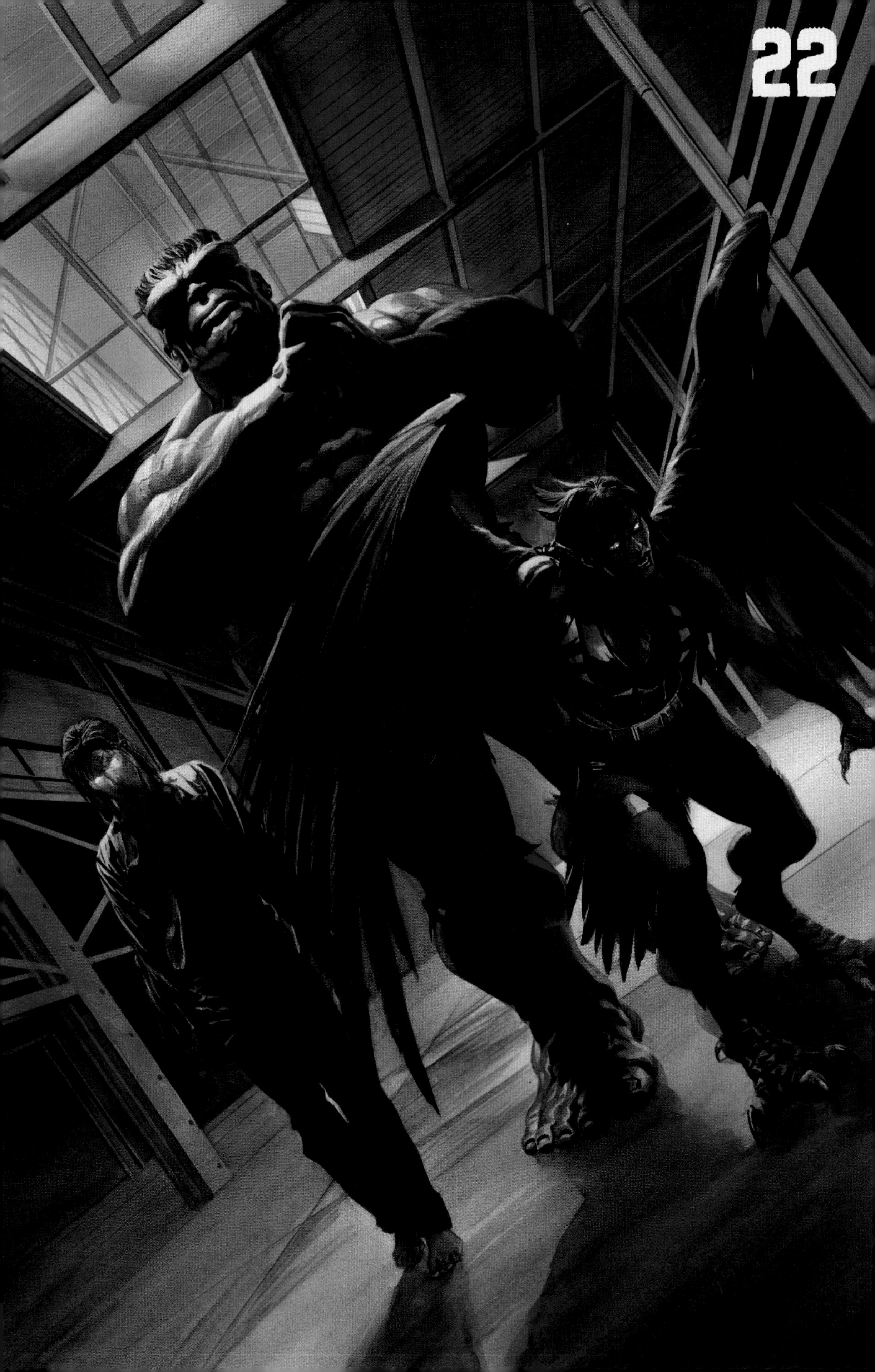
22

"HERE'S A KNOCKING INDEED! IF A MAN WERE PORTER OF HELL-GATE, HE SHOULD HAVE OLD TURNING THE KEY."

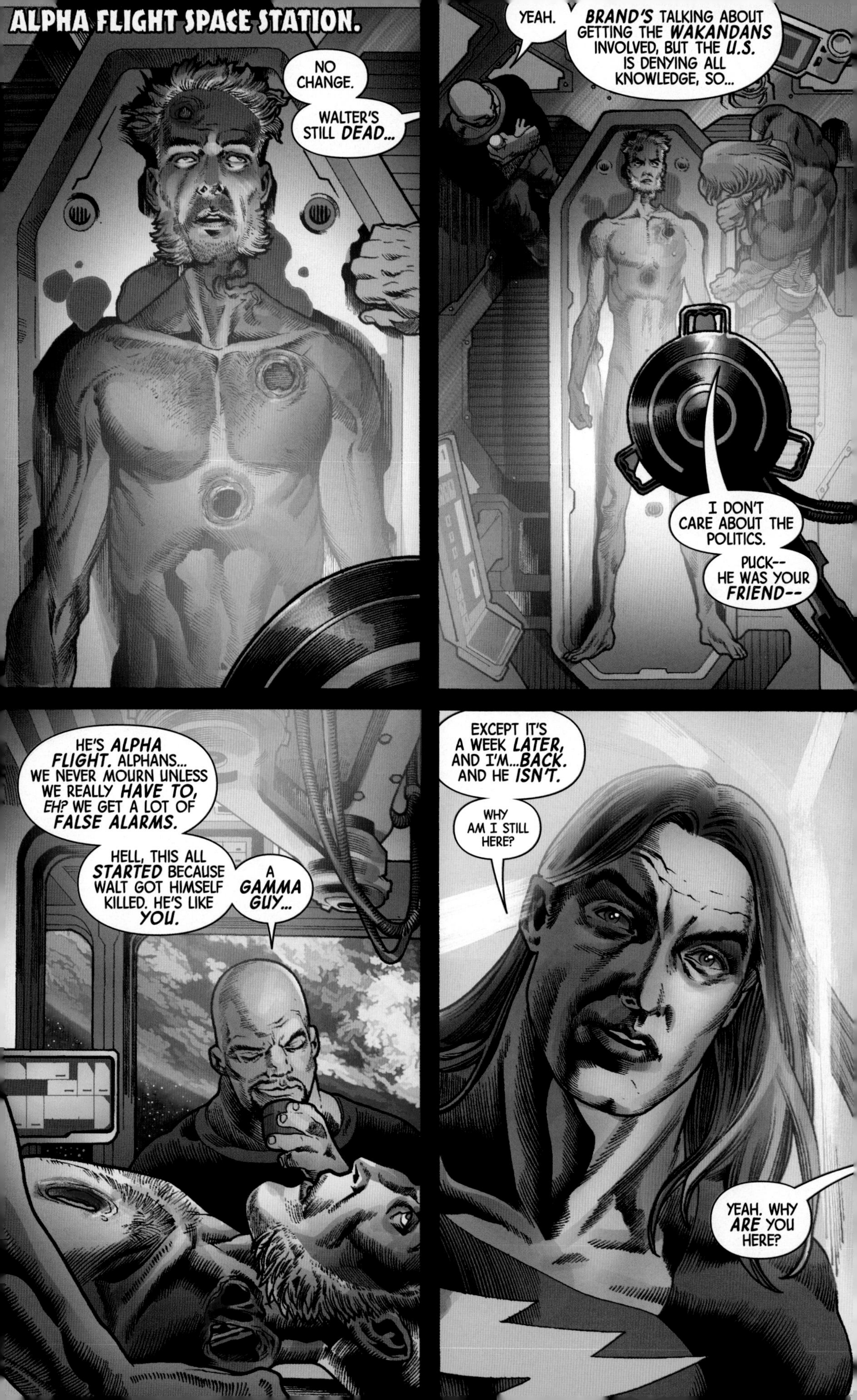
ALPHA FLIGHT SPACE STATION.
NO CHANGE.
WALTER'S STILL DEAD...
YEAH.
BRAND'S TALKING ABOUT GETTING THE WAKANDANS INVOLVED, BUT THE U.S. IS DENYING ALL KNOWLEDGE, SO...
I DON'T CARE ABOUT THE POLITICS.
PUCK-- HE WAS YOUR FRIEND--
HE'S ALPHA FLIGHT. ALPHANS... WE NEVER MOURN UNLESS WE REALLY HAVE TO, EH? WE GET A LOT OF FALSE ALARMS.
HELL, THIS ALL STARTED BECAUSE WALT GOT HIMSELF KILLED. HE'S LIKE YOU.
A GAMMA GUY...
EXCEPT IT'S A WEEK LATER, AND I'M...BACK. AND HE ISN'T.
WHY AM I STILL HERE?
YEAH. WHY ARE YOU HERE?

'CAUSE I DON'T SEE YOU HELPING US OUT WITH THE *HULK,* SAMSON.

AND I *TOLD* YOU--IF *WE* DON'T FIND HIM? *THIS IS WHAT HAPPENS.*

AND DON'T TELL ME YOU *CAN'T* FIND HIM. I KNOW YOU'RE *HOLDING OUT* ON US.

TITANIA--

YOU WANNA PROTECT YOUR *BUDDY,* YOUR *PATIENT*--YEAH, GREAT. NICE *ETHICS,* DOC.

BUT WE'RE *PAST* THAT NOW. FOLKS *DIED* IN THAT MOTEL. *CIVILIANS.*

A "*GOOD GUY*" WENT TO *WAR* WITH THE HULK--

--THE ONE WHO WANTS TO *END THE WORLD,* THE ONE YOU'RE *PROTECTING*--AND *PEOPLE DIED.*

AND THEN THAT SAME CREEP SHOWS UP *HERE?*

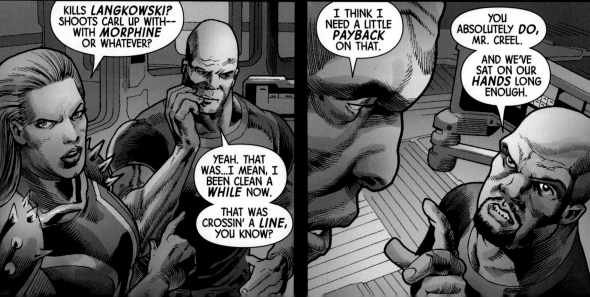

KILLS *LANGKOWSKI?* SHOOTS CARL UP WITH--WITH *MORPHINE* OR WHATEVER?

YEAH. THAT WAS...I MEAN, I BEEN CLEAN A *WHILE* NOW.

THAT WAS CROSSIN' A *LINE,* YOU KNOW?

I THINK I NEED A LITTLE *PAYBACK* ON THAT.

YOU ABSOLUTELY *DO,* MR. CREEL.

AND WE'VE SAT ON OUR *HANDS* LONG ENOUGH.

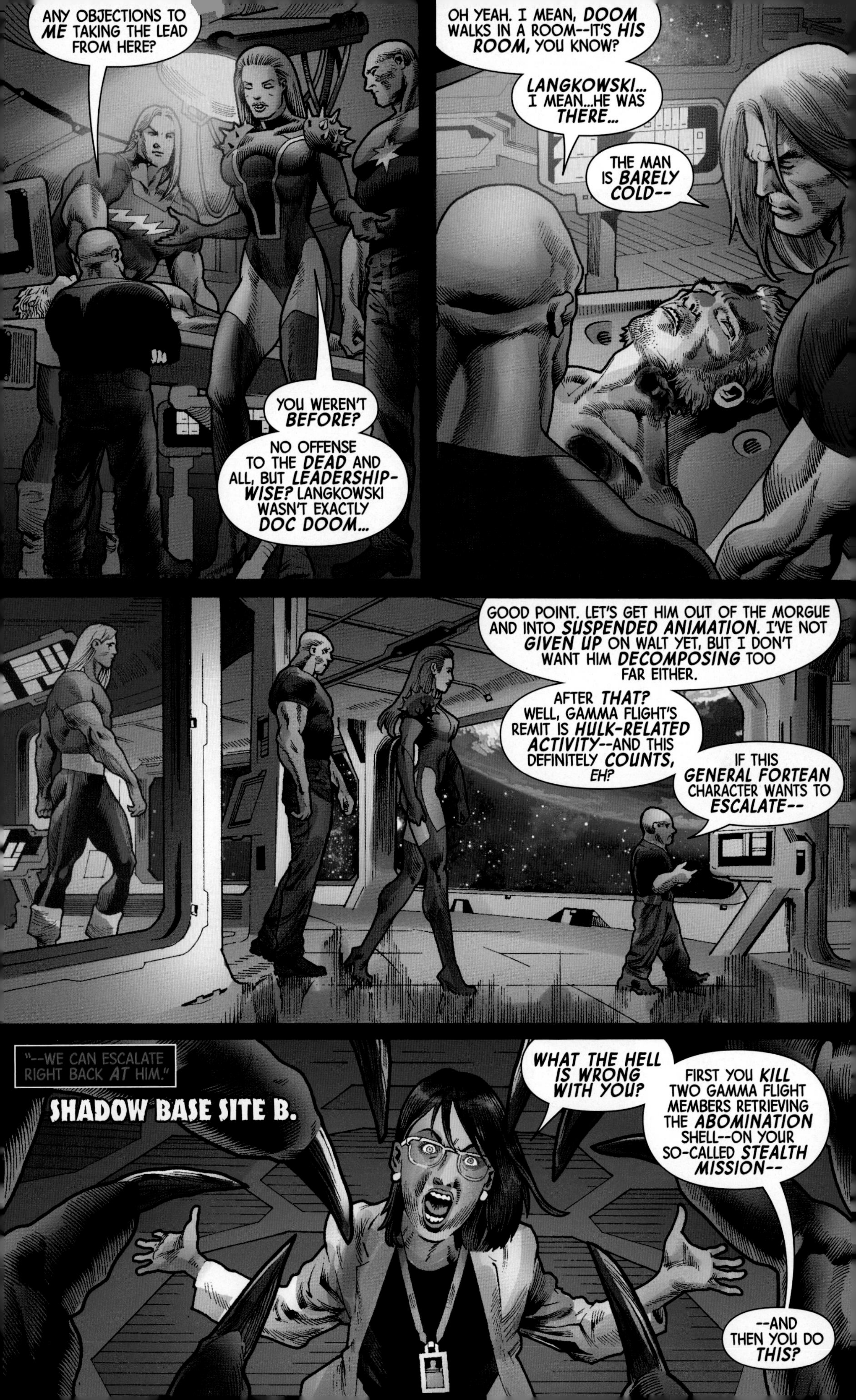
ANY OBJECTIONS TO ME TAKING THE LEAD FROM HERE?
YOU WEREN'T BEFORE?
NO OFFENSE TO THE DEAD AND ALL, BUT LEADERSHIP-WISE? LANGKOWSKI WASN'T EXACTLY DOC DOOM...
OH YEAH. I MEAN, DOOM WALKS IN A ROOM--IT'S HIS ROOM, YOU KNOW?
LANGKOWSKI... I MEAN...HE WAS THERE...
THE MAN IS BARELY COLD--
GOOD POINT. LET'S GET HIM OUT OF THE MORGUE AND INTO SUSPENDED ANIMATION. I'VE NOT GIVEN UP ON WALT YET, BUT I DON'T WANT HIM DECOMPOSING TOO FAR EITHER.
AFTER THAT? WELL, GAMMA FLIGHT'S REMIT IS HULK-RELATED ACTIVITY--AND THIS DEFINITELY COUNTS, EH?
IF THIS GENERAL FORTEAN CHARACTER WANTS TO ESCALATE--
"--WE CAN ESCALATE RIGHT BACK AT HIM."
SHADOW BASE SITE B.
WHAT THE HELL IS WRONG WITH YOU?
FIRST YOU KILL TWO GAMMA FLIGHT MEMBERS RETRIEVING THE ABOMINATION SHELL--ON YOUR SO-CALLED STEALTH MISSION--
--AND THEN YOU DO THIS?

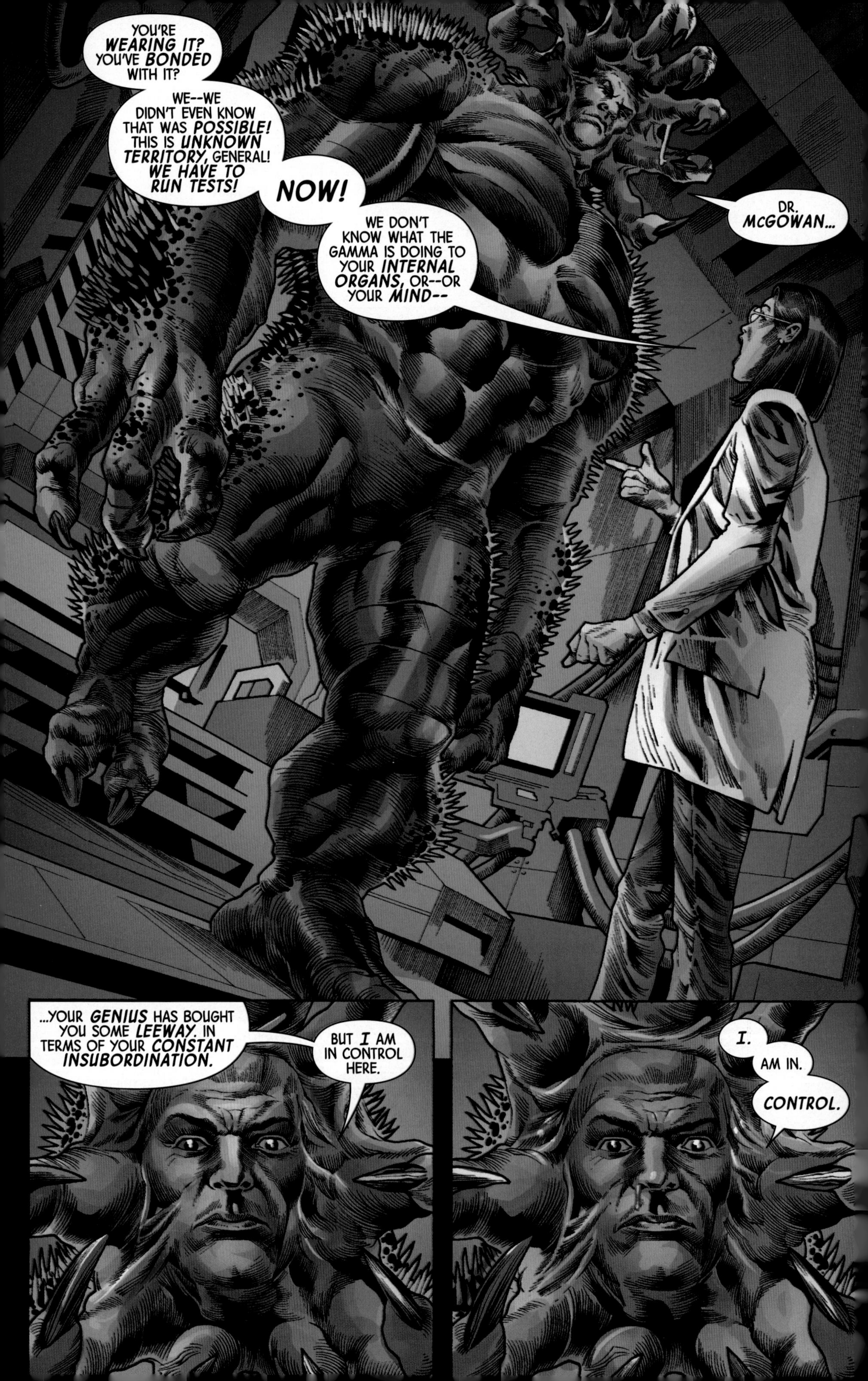
YOU'RE WEARING IT? YOU'VE BONDED WITH IT?
WE--WE DIDN'T EVEN KNOW THAT WAS POSSIBLE! THIS IS UNKNOWN TERRITORY, GENERAL! WE HAVE TO RUN TESTS!
NOW!
WE DON'T KNOW WHAT THE GAMMA IS DOING TO YOUR INTERNAL ORGANS, OR--OR YOUR MIND--
DR. McGOWAN...
...YOUR GENIUS HAS BOUGHT YOU SOME LEEWAY. IN TERMS OF YOUR CONSTANT INSUBORDINATION.
BUT I AM IN CONTROL HERE.
I.
AM IN.
CONTROL.

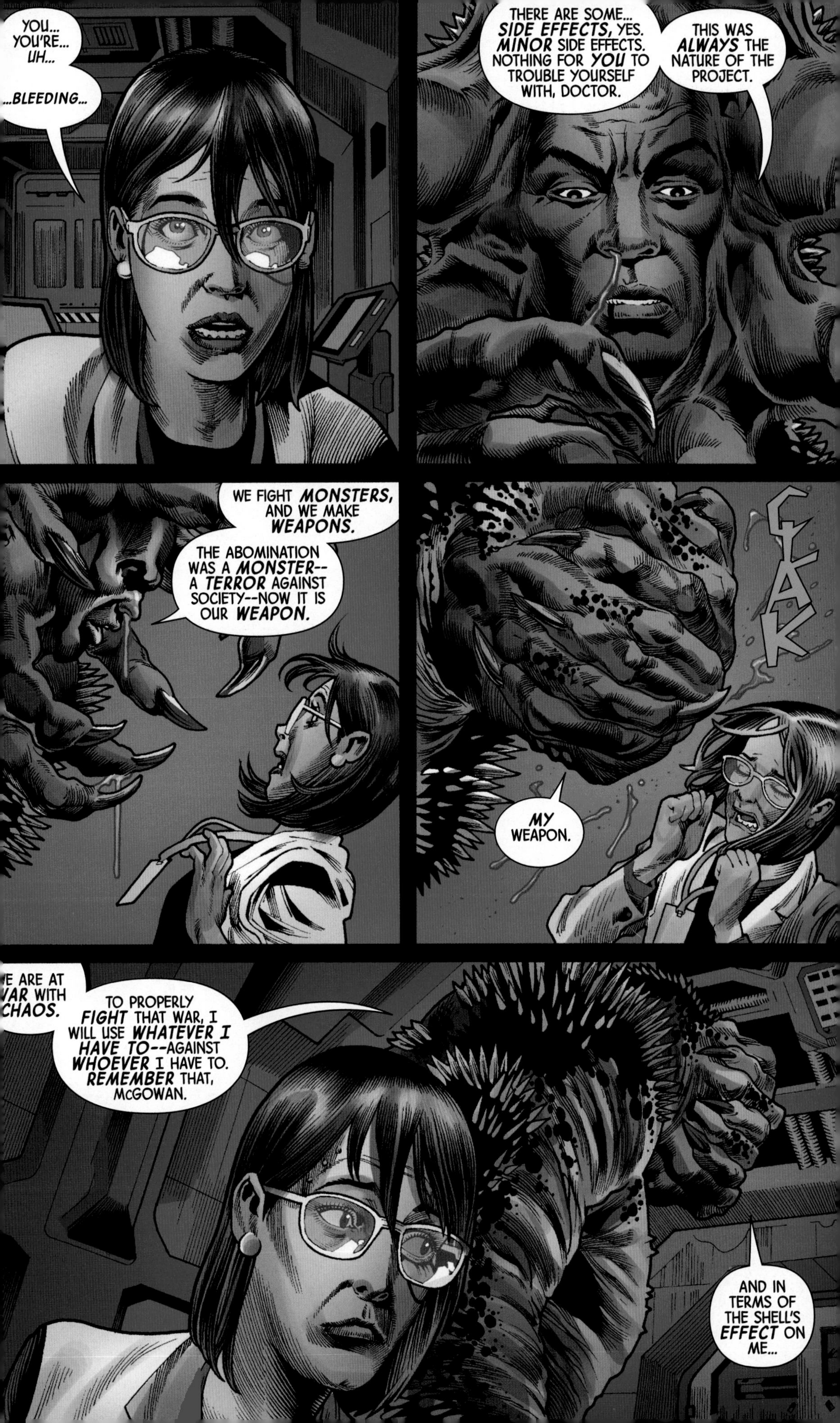
YOU... YOU'RE... UH...
...BLEEDING...
THERE ARE SOME... SIDE EFFECTS, YES. MINOR SIDE EFFECTS. NOTHING FOR YOU TO TROUBLE YOURSELF WITH, DOCTOR.
THIS WAS ALWAYS THE NATURE OF THE PROJECT.
WE FIGHT MONSTERS, AND WE MAKE WEAPONS.
THE ABOMINATION WAS A MONSTER-- A TERROR AGAINST SOCIETY--NOW IT IS OUR WEAPON.
CLAK
MY WEAPON.
E ARE AT VAR WITH CHAOS.
TO PROPERLY FIGHT THAT WAR, I WILL USE WHATEVER I HAVE TO--AGAINST WHOEVER I HAVE TO. REMEMBER THAT, McGOWAN.
AND IN TERMS OF THE SHELL'S EFFECT ON ME...

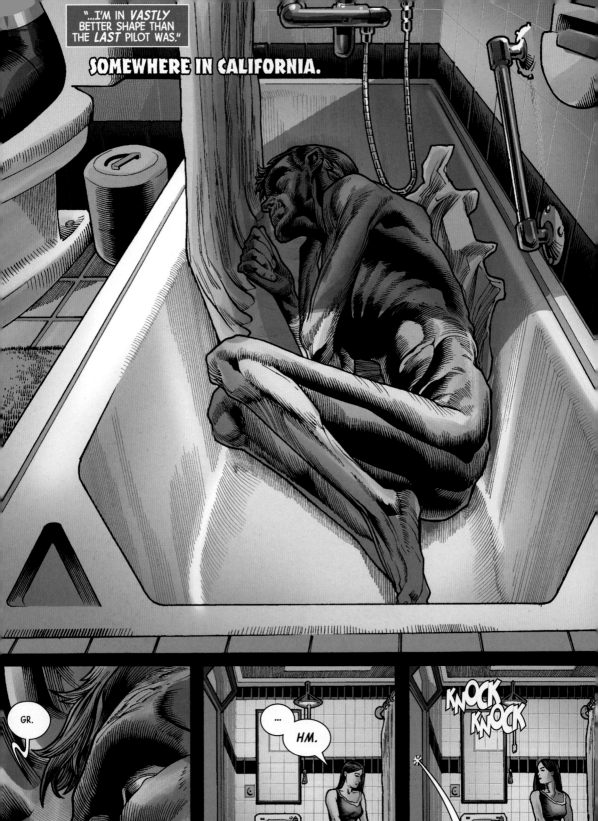

"...I'M IN *VASTLY* BETTER SHAPE THAN THE *LAST* PILOT WAS."

SOMEWHERE IN CALIFORNIA.

GR.

... HM.

KNOCK KNOCK

BETTY? ARE YOU OKAY?

YOU'VE-- YOU'VE BEEN IN THERE SINCE *DAWN*--

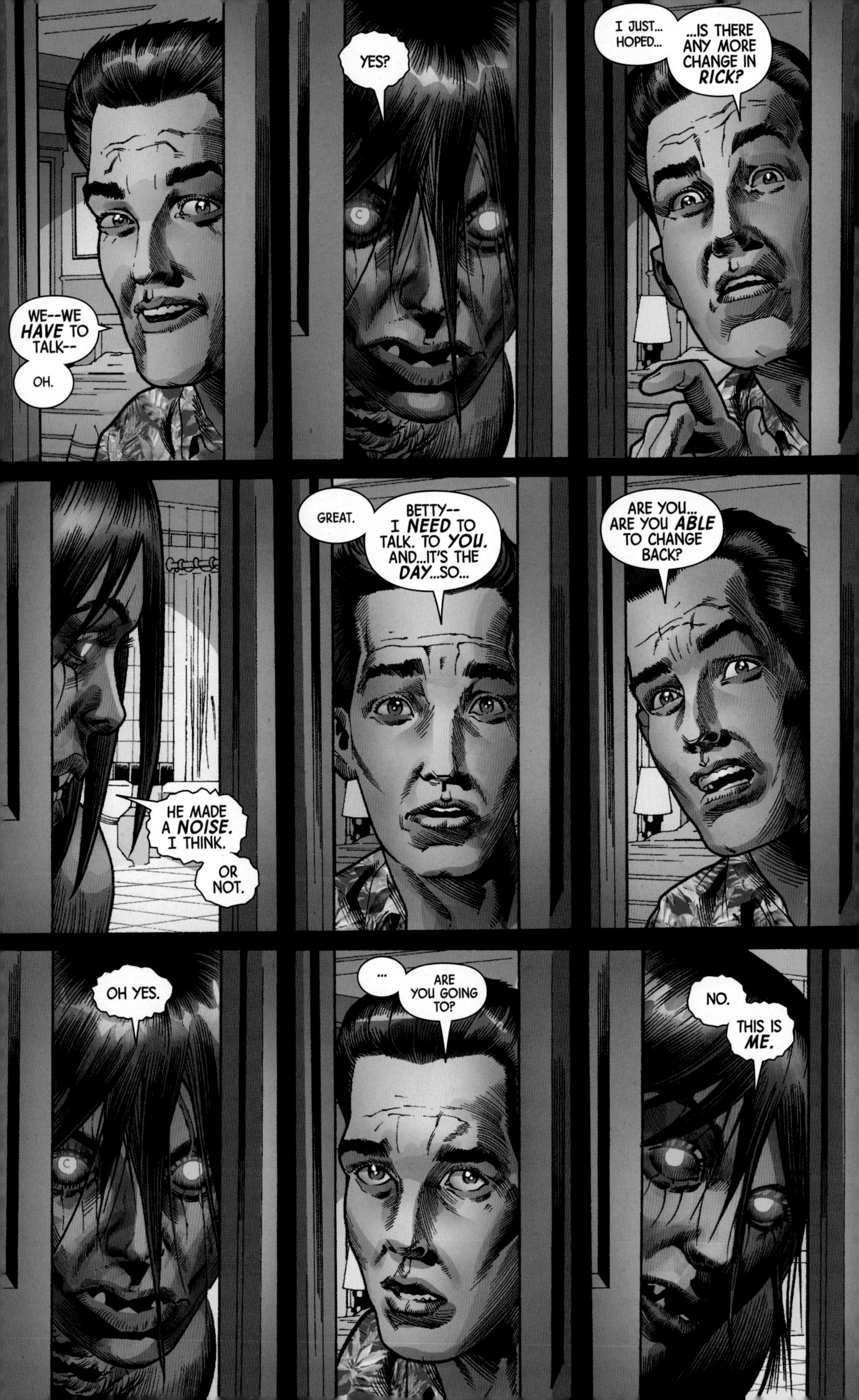

WE--WE HAVE TO TALK--
OH.
YES?
I JUST... HOPED...
...IS THERE ANY MORE CHANGE IN RICK?
HE MADE A NOISE. I THINK.
OR NOT.
GREAT.
BETTY-- I NEED TO TALK. TO YOU. AND...IT'S THE DAY...SO...
ARE YOU... ARE YOU ABLE TO CHANGE BACK?
OH YES.
...
ARE YOU GOING TO?
NO.
THIS IS ME.

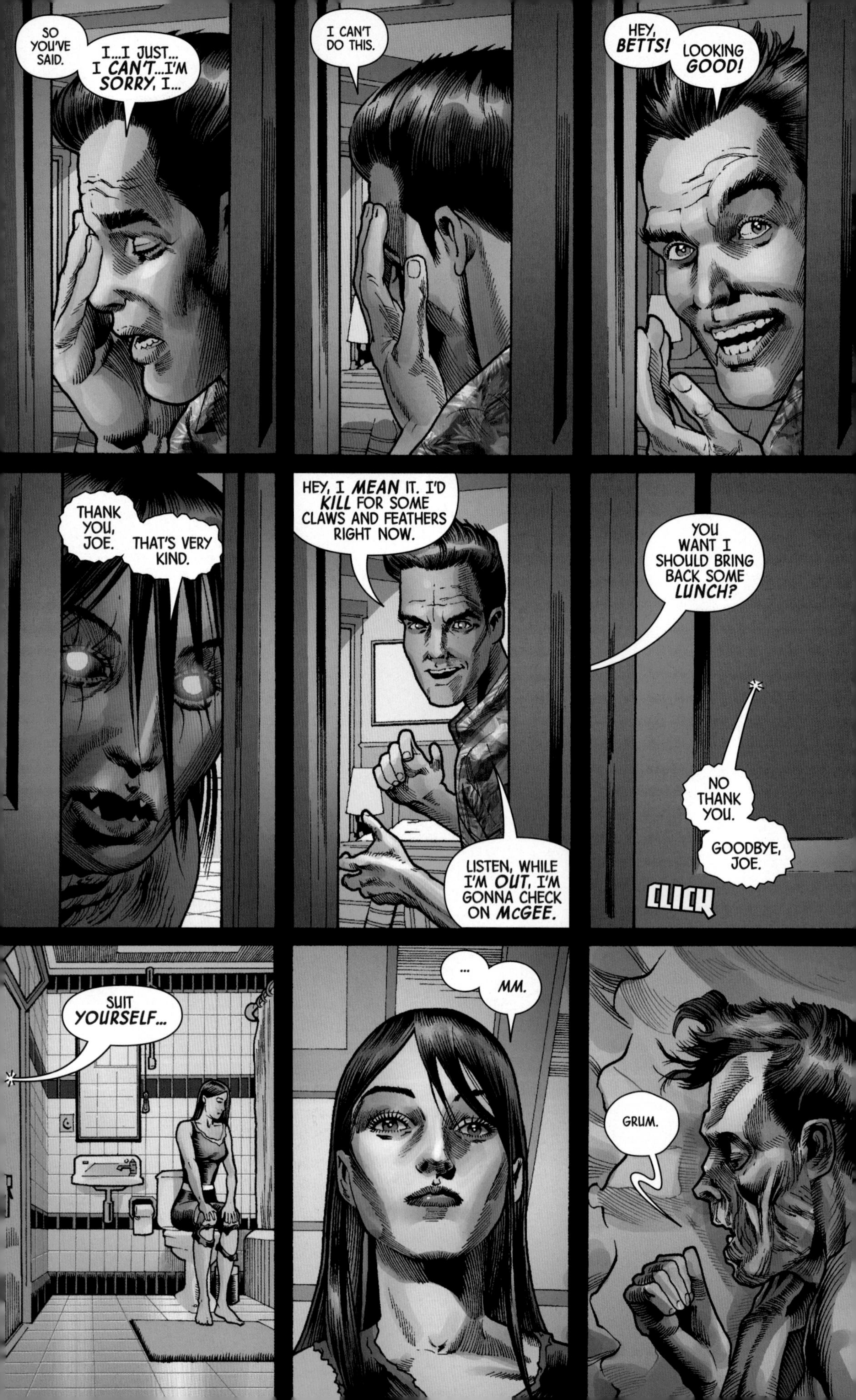
SO YOU'VE SAID.
I...I JUST... I CAN'T...I'M SORRY, I...
I CAN'T DO THIS.
HEY, BETTS!
LOOKING GOOD!
THANK YOU, JOE.
THAT'S VERY KIND.
HEY, I MEAN IT. I'D KILL FOR SOME CLAWS AND FEATHERS RIGHT NOW.
LISTEN, WHILE I'M OUT, I'M GONNA CHECK ON McGEE.
YOU WANT I SHOULD BRING BACK SOME LUNCH?
NO THANK YOU.
GOODBYE, JOE.
CLICK
SUIT YOURSELF...
...
MM.
GRUM.

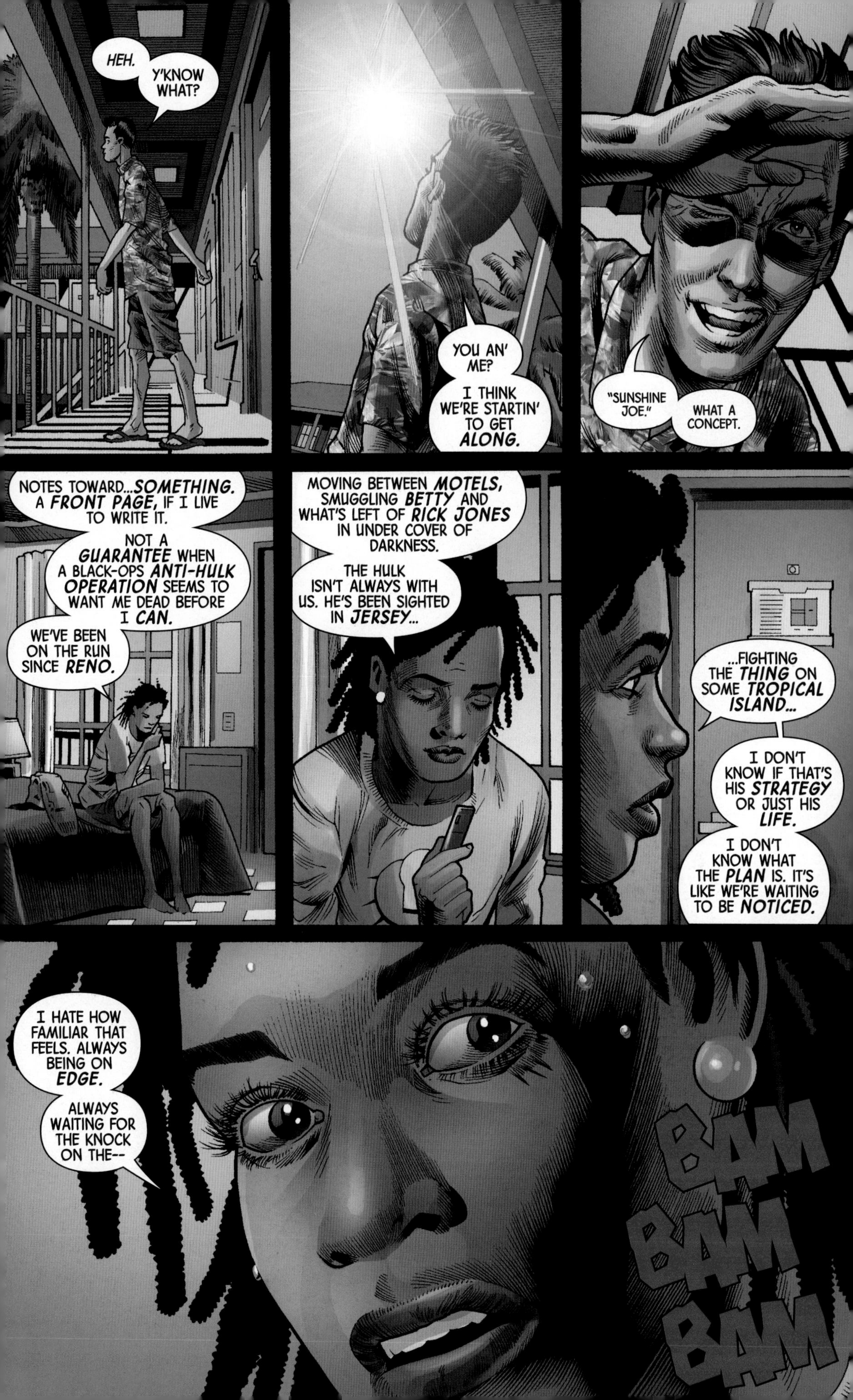
HEH.
Y'KNOW WHAT?
YOU AN' ME?
I THINK WE'RE STARTIN' TO GET ALONG.
"SUNSHINE JOE."
WHAT A CONCEPT.
NOTES TOWARD...SOMETHING. A FRONT PAGE, IF I LIVE TO WRITE IT.
NOT A GUARANTEE WHEN A BLACK-OPS ANTI-HULK OPERATION SEEMS TO WANT ME DEAD BEFORE I CAN.
WE'VE BEEN ON THE RUN SINCE RENO.
MOVING BETWEEN MOTELS, SMUGGLING BETTY AND WHAT'S LEFT OF RICK JONES IN UNDER COVER OF DARKNESS.
THE HULK ISN'T ALWAYS WITH US. HE'S BEEN SIGHTED IN JERSEY...
...FIGHTING THE THING ON SOME TROPICAL ISLAND...
I DON'T KNOW IF THAT'S HIS STRATEGY OR JUST HIS LIFE.
I DON'T KNOW WHAT THE PLAN IS. IT'S LIKE WE'RE WAITING TO BE NOTICED.
I HATE HOW FAMILIAR THAT FEELS. ALWAYS BEING ON EDGE.
ALWAYS WAITING FOR THE KNOCK ON THE--
BAM
BAM
BAM

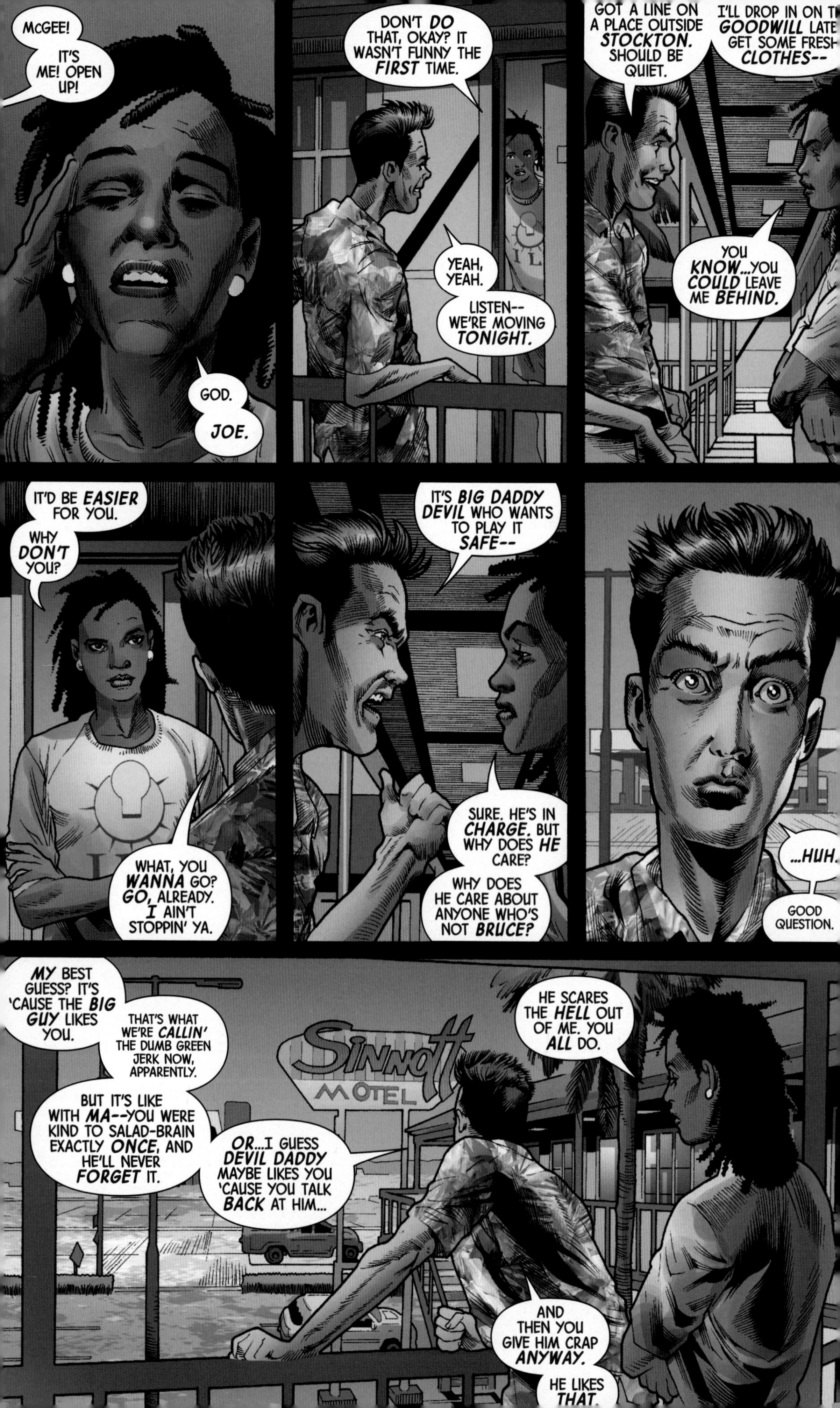
McGEE!
IT'S ME! OPEN UP!
GOD.
JOE.
DON'T DO THAT, OKAY? IT WASN'T FUNNY THE FIRST TIME.
YEAH, YEAH.
LISTEN-- WE'RE MOVING TONIGHT.
GOT A LINE ON A PLACE OUTSIDE STOCKTON. SHOULD BE QUIET.
I'LL DROP IN ON THE GOODWILL LATER, GET SOME FRESH CLOTHES--
YOU KNOW...YOU COULD LEAVE ME BEHIND.
IT'D BE EASIER FOR YOU.
WHY DON'T YOU?
WHAT, YOU WANNA GO? GO, ALREADY. I AIN'T STOPPIN' YA.
IT'S BIG DADDY DEVIL WHO WANTS TO PLAY IT SAFE--
SURE. HE'S IN CHARGE. BUT WHY DOES HE CARE?
WHY DOES HE CARE ABOUT ANYONE WHO'S NOT BRUCE?
...HUH.
GOOD QUESTION.
MY BEST GUESS? IT'S 'CAUSE THE BIG GUY LIKES YOU.
THAT'S WHAT WE'RE CALLIN' THE DUMB GREEN JERK NOW, APPARENTLY.
BUT IT'S LIKE WITH MA--YOU WERE KIND TO SALAD-BRAIN EXACTLY ONCE, AND HE'LL NEVER FORGET IT.
OR...I GUESS DEVIL DADDY MAYBE LIKES YOU 'CAUSE YOU TALK BACK AT HIM...
SINNOTT MOTEL
HE SCARES THE HELL OUT OF ME. YOU ALL DO.
AND THEN YOU GIVE HIM CRAP ANYWAY.
HE LIKES THAT.

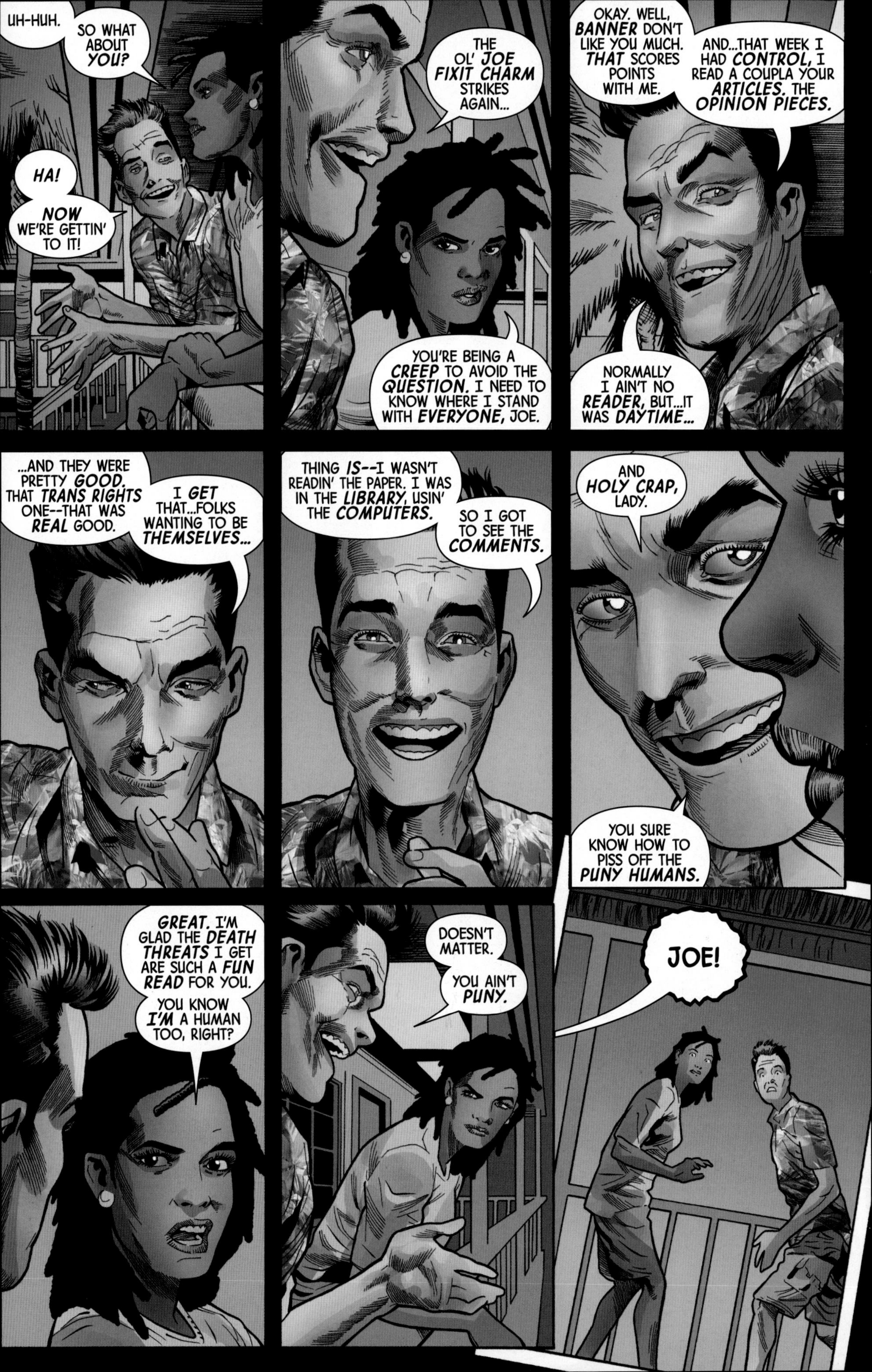
UH-HUH.
SO WHAT ABOUT YOU?
HA!
NOW WE'RE GETTIN' TO IT!
THE OL' JOE FIXIT CHARM STRIKES AGAIN...
YOU'RE BEING A CREEP TO AVOID THE QUESTION. I NEED TO KNOW WHERE I STAND WITH EVERYONE, JOE.
OKAY. WELL, BANNER DON'T LIKE YOU MUCH. THAT SCORES POINTS WITH ME.
AND...THAT WEEK I HAD CONTROL, I READ A COUPLA YOUR ARTICLES. THE OPINION PIECES.
NORMALLY I AIN'T NO READER, BUT...IT WAS DAYTIME...
...AND THEY WERE PRETTY GOOD. THAT TRANS RIGHTS ONE--THAT WAS REAL GOOD.
I GET THAT...FOLKS WANTING TO BE THEMSELVES...
THING IS--I WASN'T READIN' THE PAPER. I WAS IN THE LIBRARY, USIN' THE COMPUTERS.
SO I GOT TO SEE THE COMMENTS.
AND HOLY CRAP, LADY.
YOU SURE KNOW HOW TO PISS OFF THE PUNY HUMANS.
GREAT. I'M GLAD THE DEATH THREATS I GET ARE SUCH A FUN READ FOR YOU.
YOU KNOW I'M A HUMAN TOO, RIGHT?
DOESN'T MATTER.
YOU AIN'T PUNY.
JOE!

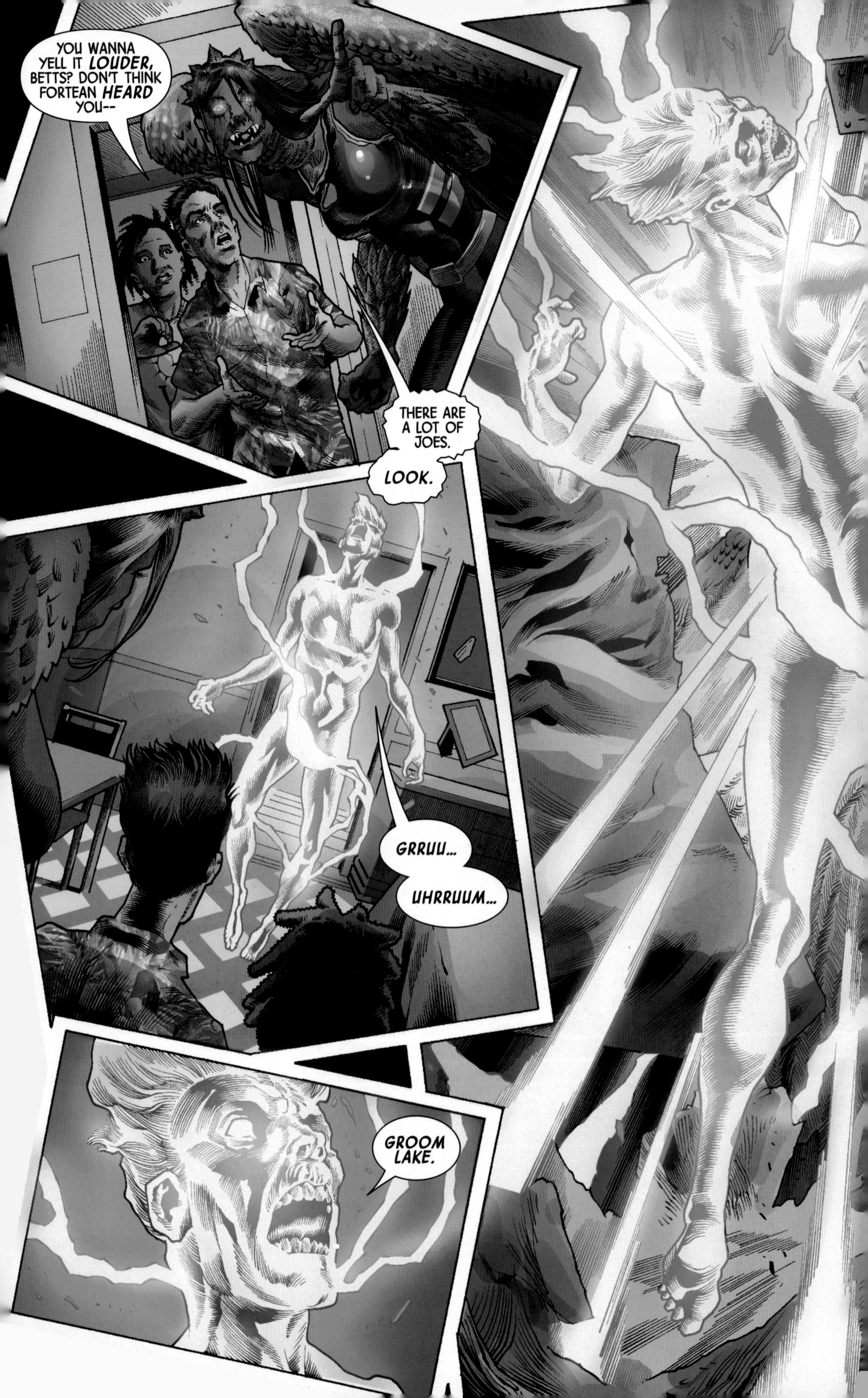
YOU WANNA YELL IT LOUDER, BETTS? DON'T THINK FORTEAN HEARD YOU--
THERE ARE A LOT OF JOES.
LOOK.
GRRUU...
UHRRUUM...
GROOM LAKE.

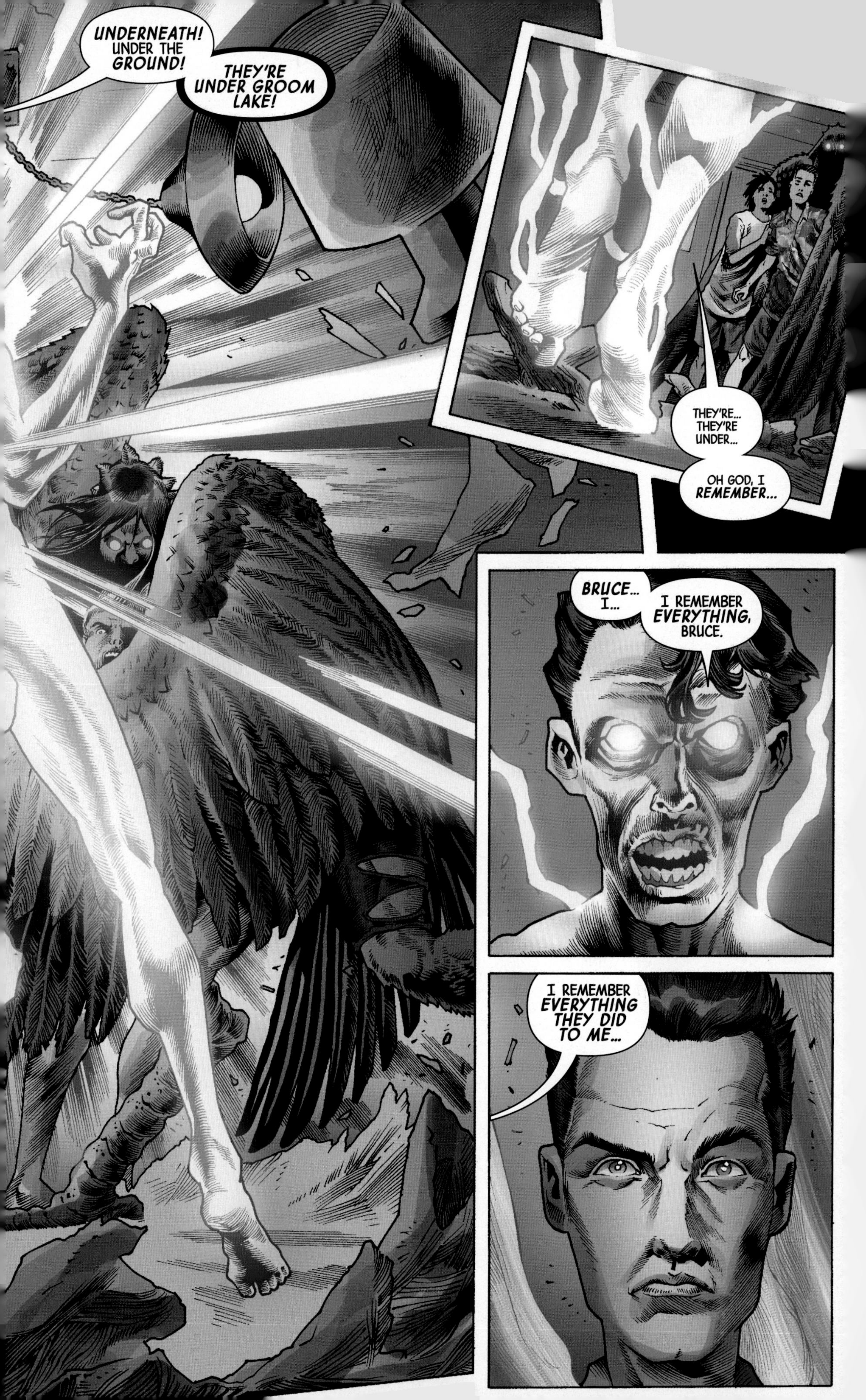
UNDERNEATH! UNDER THE GROUND!
THEY'RE UNDER GROOM LAKE!
THEY'RE... THEY'RE UNDER...
OH GOD, I REMEMBER...
BRUCE... I...
I REMEMBER EVERYTHING, BRUCE.
I REMEMBER EVERYTHING THEY DID TO ME...

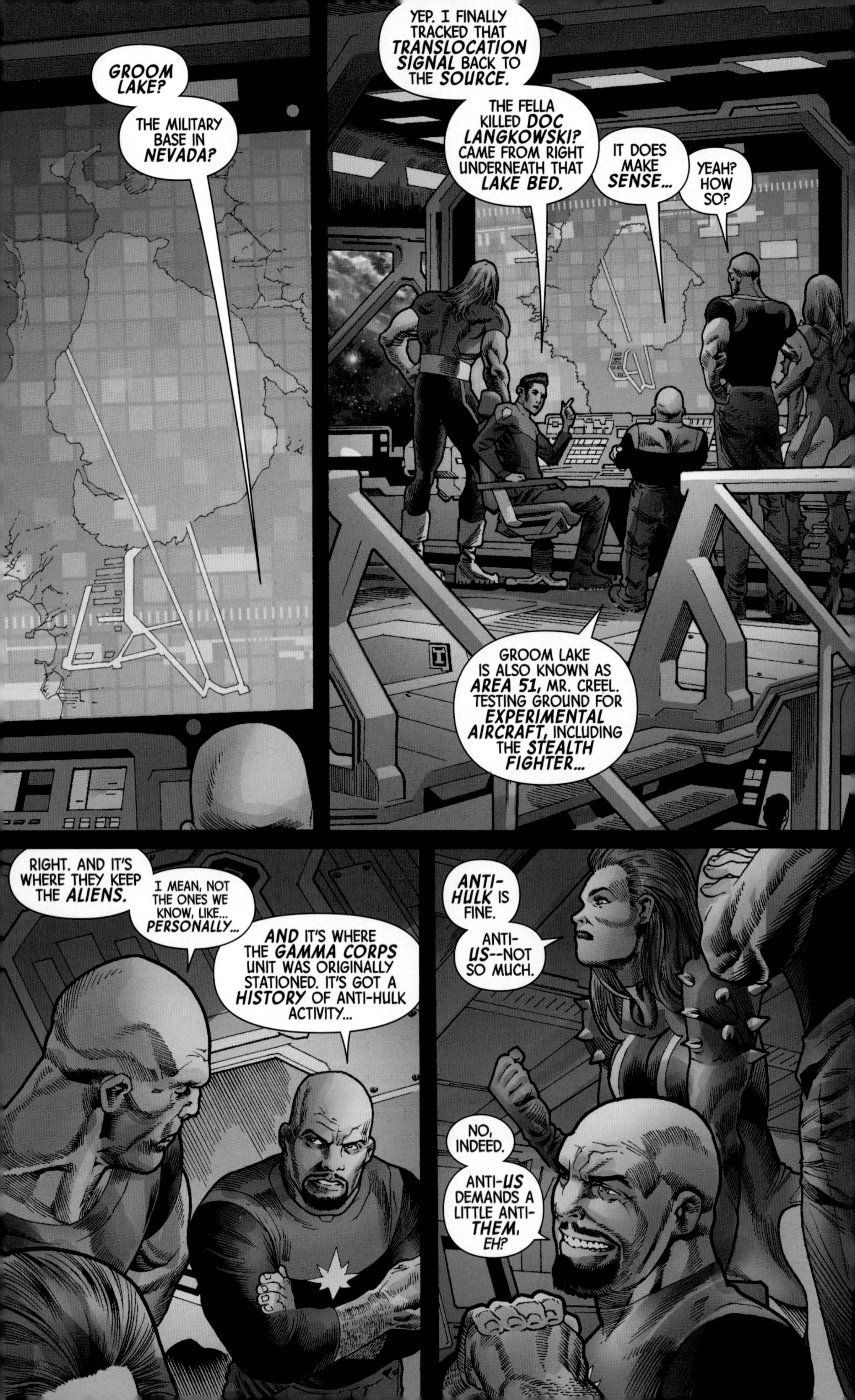
GROOM LAKE?
THE MILITARY BASE IN NEVADA?
YEP. I FINALLY TRACKED THAT TRANSLOCATION SIGNAL BACK TO THE SOURCE.
THE FELLA KILLED DOC LANGKOWSKI? CAME FROM RIGHT UNDERNEATH THAT LAKE BED.
IT DOES MAKE SENSE...
YEAH? HOW SO?
GROOM LAKE IS ALSO KNOWN AS AREA 51, MR. CREEL. TESTING GROUND FOR EXPERIMENTAL AIRCRAFT, INCLUDING THE STEALTH FIGHTER...
RIGHT. AND IT'S WHERE THEY KEEP THE ALIENS.
I MEAN, NOT THE ONES WE KNOW, LIKE... PERSONALLY...
AND IT'S WHERE THE GAMMA CORPS UNIT WAS ORIGINALLY STATIONED. IT'S GOT A HISTORY OF ANTI-HULK ACTIVITY...
ANTI-HULK IS FINE.
ANTI-US--NOT SO MUCH.
NO, INDEED.
ANTI-US DEMANDS A LITTLE ANTI-THEM, EH?

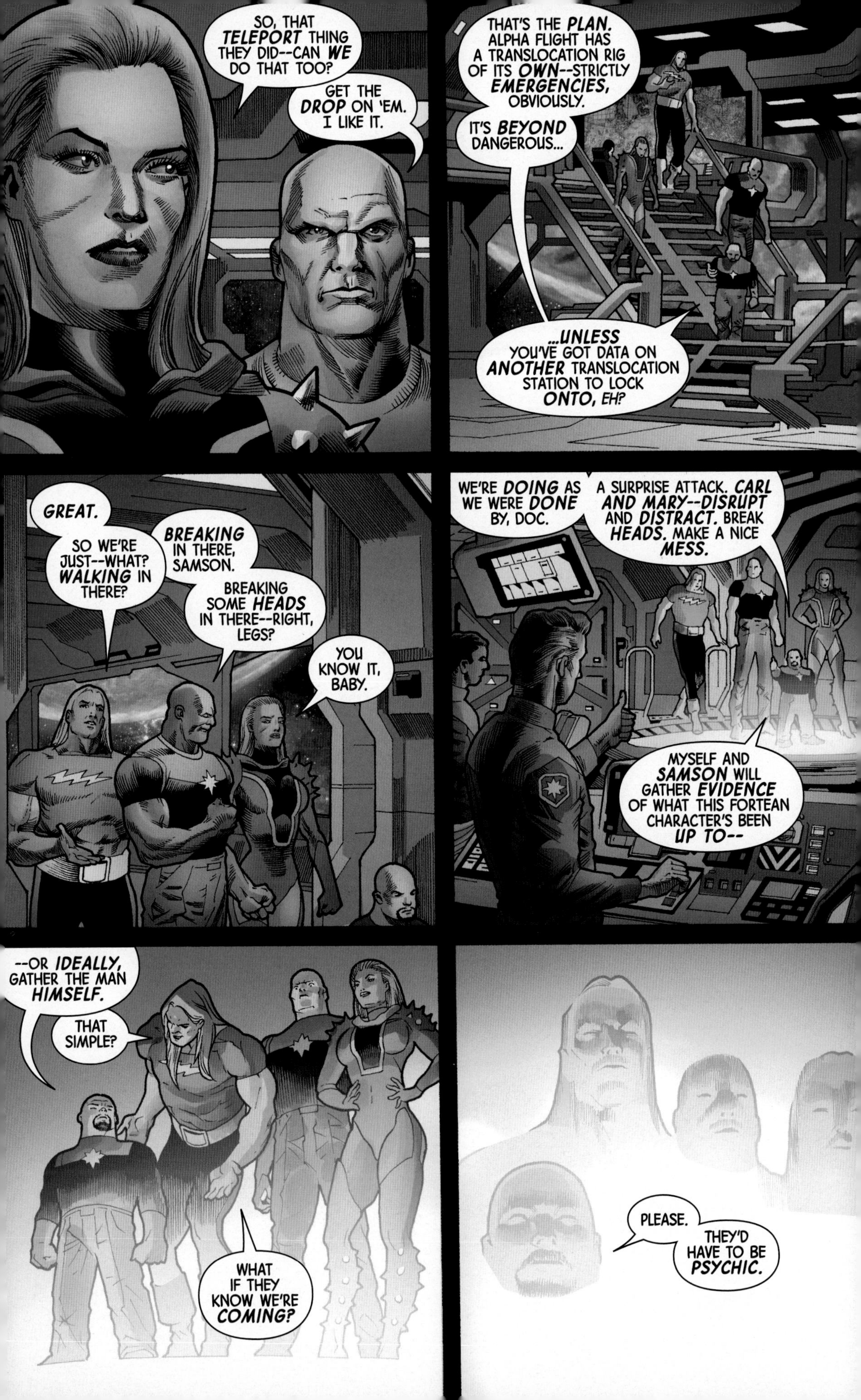
SO, THAT TELEPORT THING THEY DID--CAN WE DO THAT TOO?
GET THE DROP ON 'EM. I LIKE IT.
THAT'S THE PLAN. ALPHA FLIGHT HAS A TRANSLOCATION RIG OF ITS OWN--STRICTLY EMERGENCIES, OBVIOUSLY.
IT'S BEYOND DANGEROUS...
...UNLESS YOU'VE GOT DATA ON ANOTHER TRANSLOCATION STATION TO LOCK ONTO, EH?
GREAT.
SO WE'RE JUST--WHAT? WALKING IN THERE?
BREAKING IN THERE, SAMSON.
BREAKING SOME HEADS IN THERE--RIGHT, LEGS?
YOU KNOW IT, BABY.
WE'RE DOING AS WE WERE DONE BY, DOC.
A SURPRISE ATTACK. CARL AND MARY--DISRUPT AND DISTRACT. BREAK HEADS. MAKE A NICE MESS.
MYSELF AND SAMSON WILL GATHER EVIDENCE OF WHAT THIS FORTEAN CHARACTER'S BEEN UP TO--
--OR IDEALLY, GATHER THE MAN HIMSELF.
THAT SIMPLE?
WHAT IF THEY KNOW WE'RE COMING?
PLEASE.
THEY'D HAVE TO BE PSYCHIC.

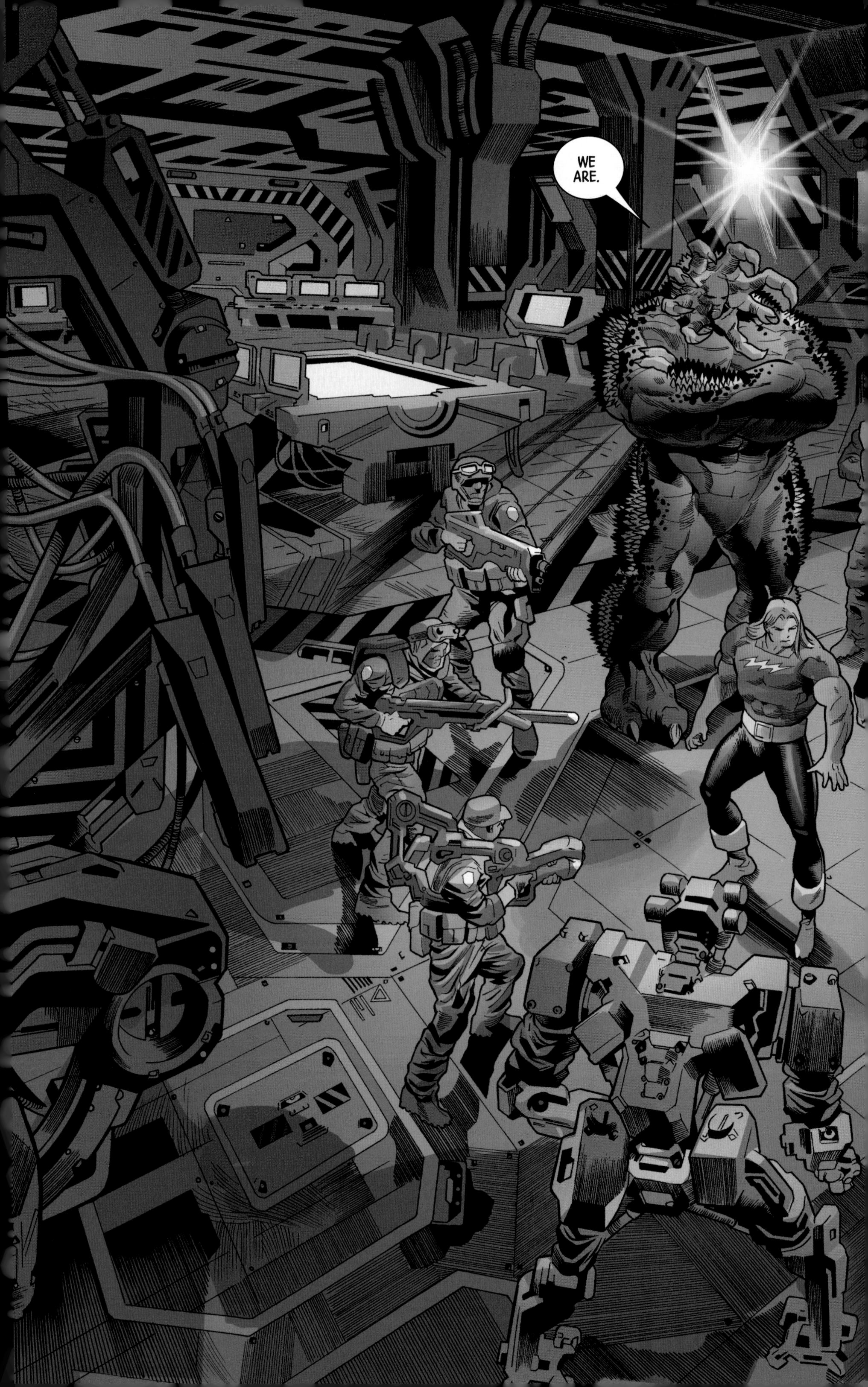
WE ARE.

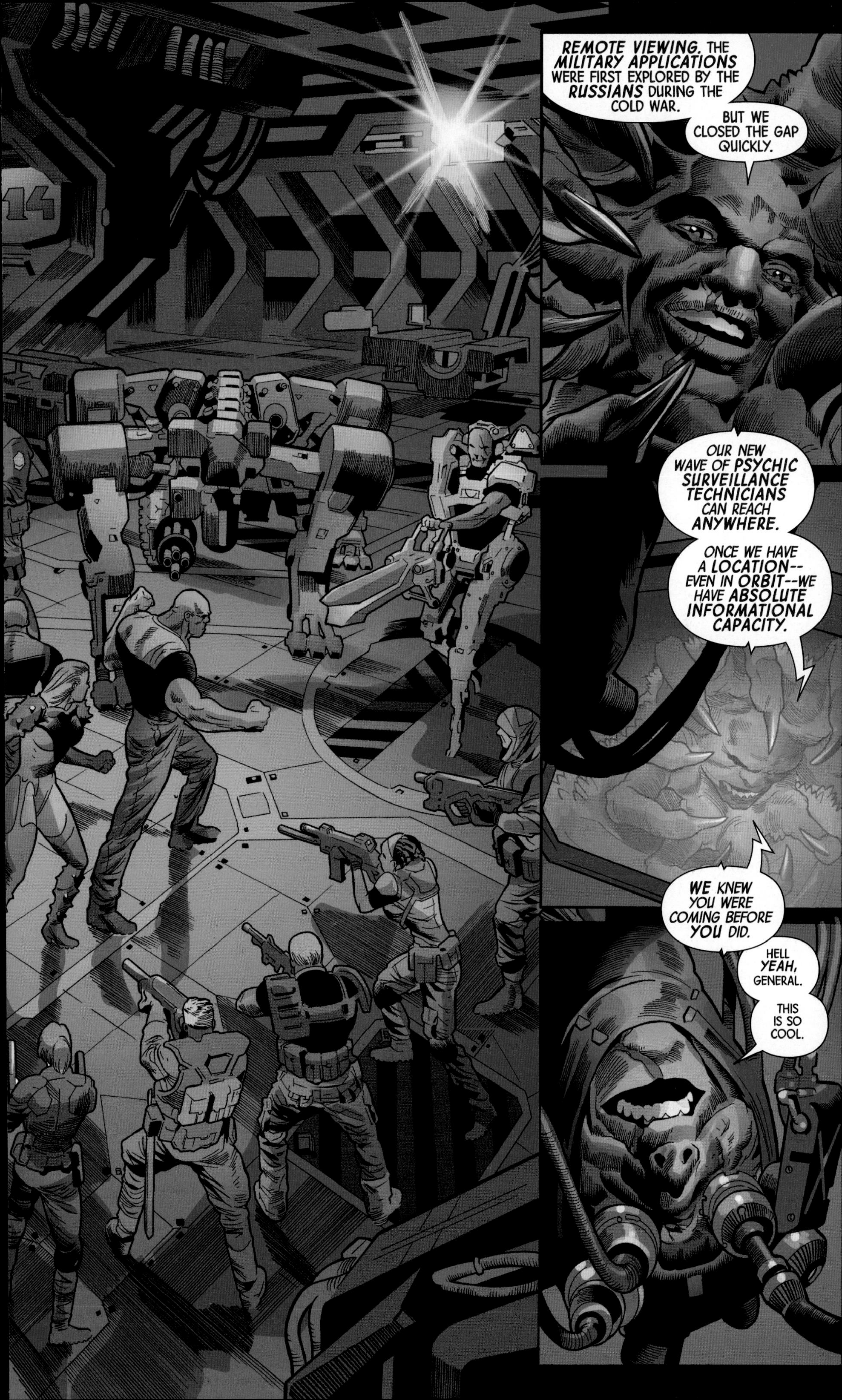
14
REMOTE VIEWING. THE MILITARY APPLICATIONS WERE FIRST EXPLORED BY THE RUSSIANS DURING THE COLD WAR.
BUT WE CLOSED THE GAP QUICKLY.
OUR NEW WAVE OF PSYCHIC SURVEILLANCE TECHNICIANS CAN REACH ANYWHERE.
ONCE WE HAVE A LOCATION--EVEN IN ORBIT--WE HAVE ABSOLUTE INFORMATIONAL CAPACITY.
WE KNEW YOU WERE COMING BEFORE YOU DID.
HELL YEAH, GENERAL.
THIS IS SO COOL.

INCIDENTALLY, *DR. SAMSON*-- IT'S *FASCINATING* TO SEE YOU UP AND ABOUT SO *QUICKLY.* YOUR RECOVERY PERIOD SEEMS TO GET *SHORTER* EACH TIME.

I'LL MAKE SURE DR. McGOWAN CONCENTRATES ON *THAT* ASPECT WHEN SHE *DISSECTS* YOU.

FORTEAN... FOR GOD'S SAKE, *LOOK* AT YOURSELF.

WHAT HAVE YOU *DONE?*

WHY... *WHY* WOULD YOU...?

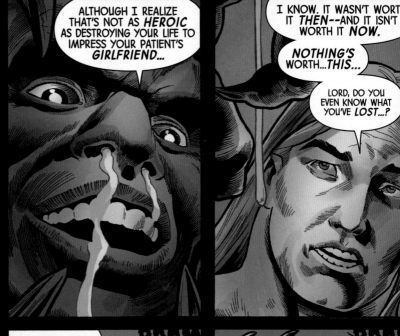

TO WIN A *WAR,* SAMSON.

TO BRING *ORDER* TO A WORLD *WITHOUT* IT.

ALTHOUGH I REALIZE THAT'S NOT AS *HEROIC* AS DESTROYING YOUR LIFE TO IMPRESS YOUR PATIENT'S *GIRLFRIEND*...

I KNOW. IT WASN'T WORTH IT *THEN*--AND IT ISN'T WORTH IT *NOW.*

NOTHING'S WORTH...*THIS*...

LORD, DO YOU EVEN KNOW WHAT YOU'VE *LOST*...?

I'LL KNOW ONCE MY *SCIENCE TEAM* GIVES ME THE *DATA.*

ONCE YOU'VE BEEN *TAKEN APART*... FILED AND *INDEXED* WITH ALL THE OTHER MUTATES.

AND ONCE WE'RE *READY,* WE'LL FINALLY BRING DOWN THE--

BOOM

BOOM

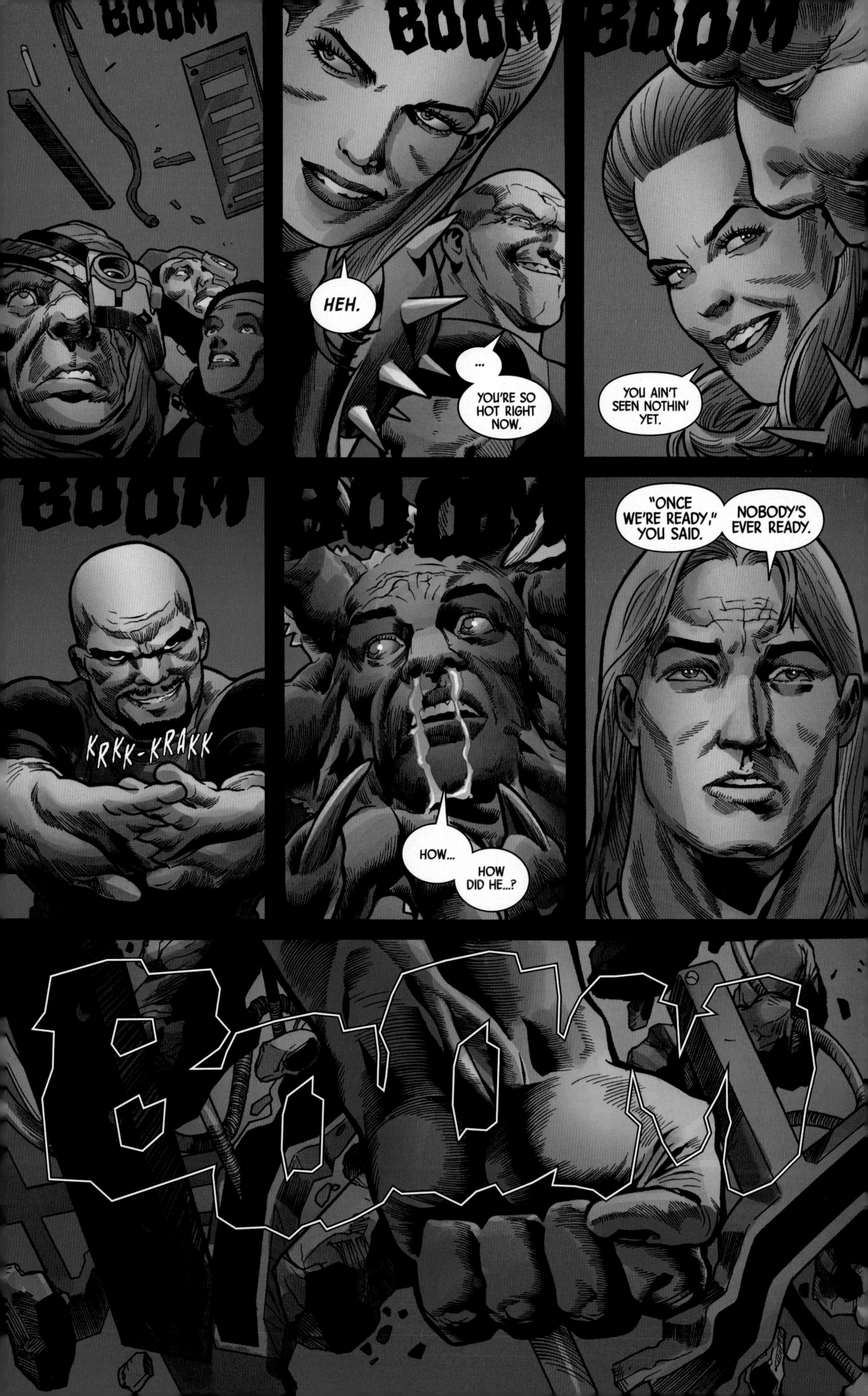
BOOM
BOOM
HEH.
...
YOU'RE SO HOT RIGHT NOW.
BOOM
YOU AIN'T SEEN NOTHIN' YET.
BOOM
KRKK-KRAKK
BOOM
HOW...
HOW DID HE...?
"ONCE WE'RE READY," YOU SAID.
NOBODY'S EVER READY.
BOOM

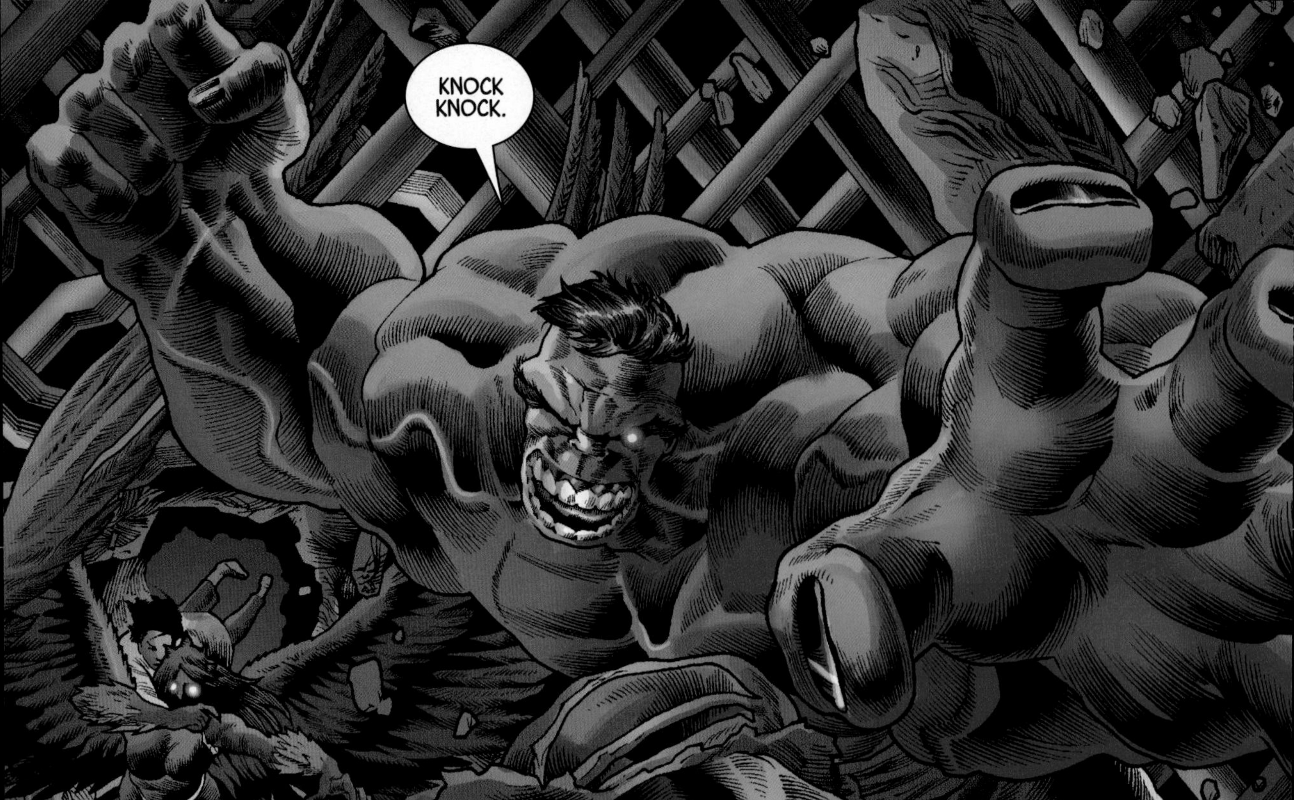
KNOCK KNOCK.

WHO'S THERE

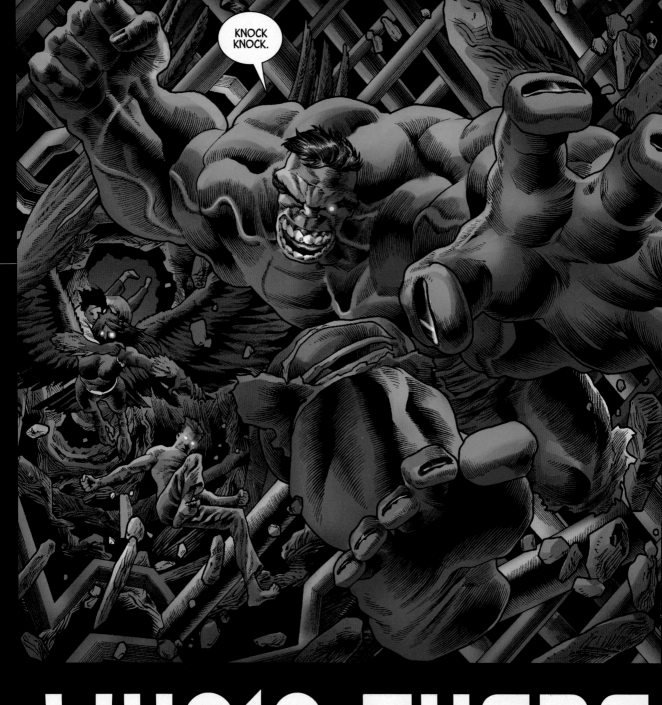

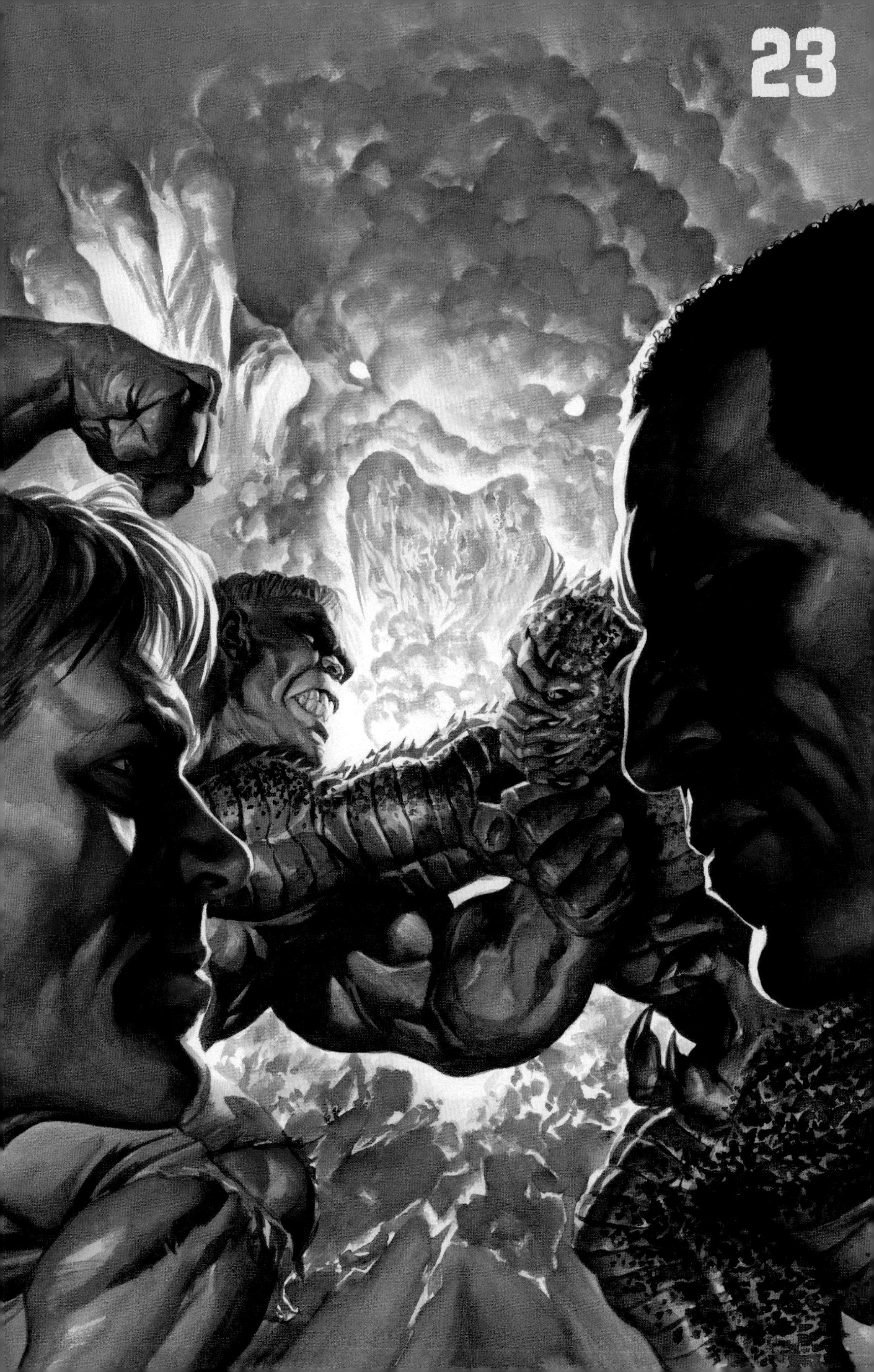
23

"LET YOUR PLANS BE DARK AND IMPENETRABLE AS NIGHT."

– SUN TZU
THE ART OF WAR

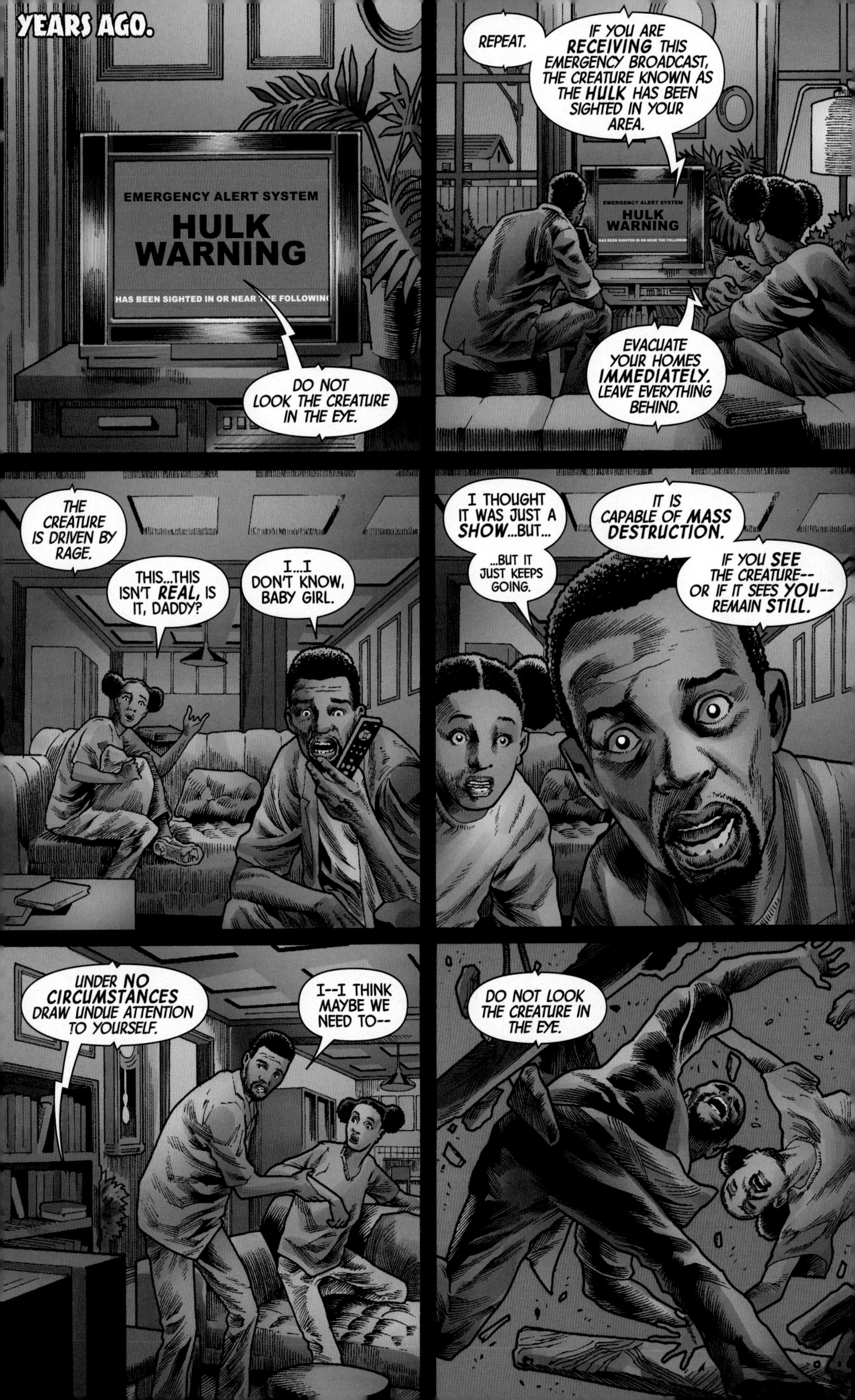

YEARS AGO.
EMERGENCY ALERT SYSTEM
HULK WARNING
HAS BEEN SIGHTED IN OR NEAR THE FOLLOWING
DO NOT LOOK THE CREATURE IN THE EYE.
REPEAT.
IF YOU ARE RECEIVING THIS EMERGENCY BROADCAST, THE CREATURE KNOWN AS THE HULK HAS BEEN SIGHTED IN YOUR AREA.
EVACUATE YOUR HOMES IMMEDIATELY. LEAVE EVERYTHING BEHIND.
THE CREATURE IS DRIVEN BY RAGE.
THIS...THIS ISN'T REAL, IS IT, DADDY?
I...I DON'T KNOW, BABY GIRL.
I THOUGHT IT WAS JUST A SHOW...BUT...
...BUT IT JUST KEEPS GOING.
IT IS CAPABLE OF MASS DESTRUCTION.
IF YOU SEE THE CREATURE-- OR IF IT SEES YOU-- REMAIN STILL.
UNDER NO CIRCUMSTANCES DRAW UNDUE ATTENTION TO YOURSELF.
I--I THINK MAYBE WE NEED TO--
DO NOT LOOK THE CREATURE IN THE EYE.

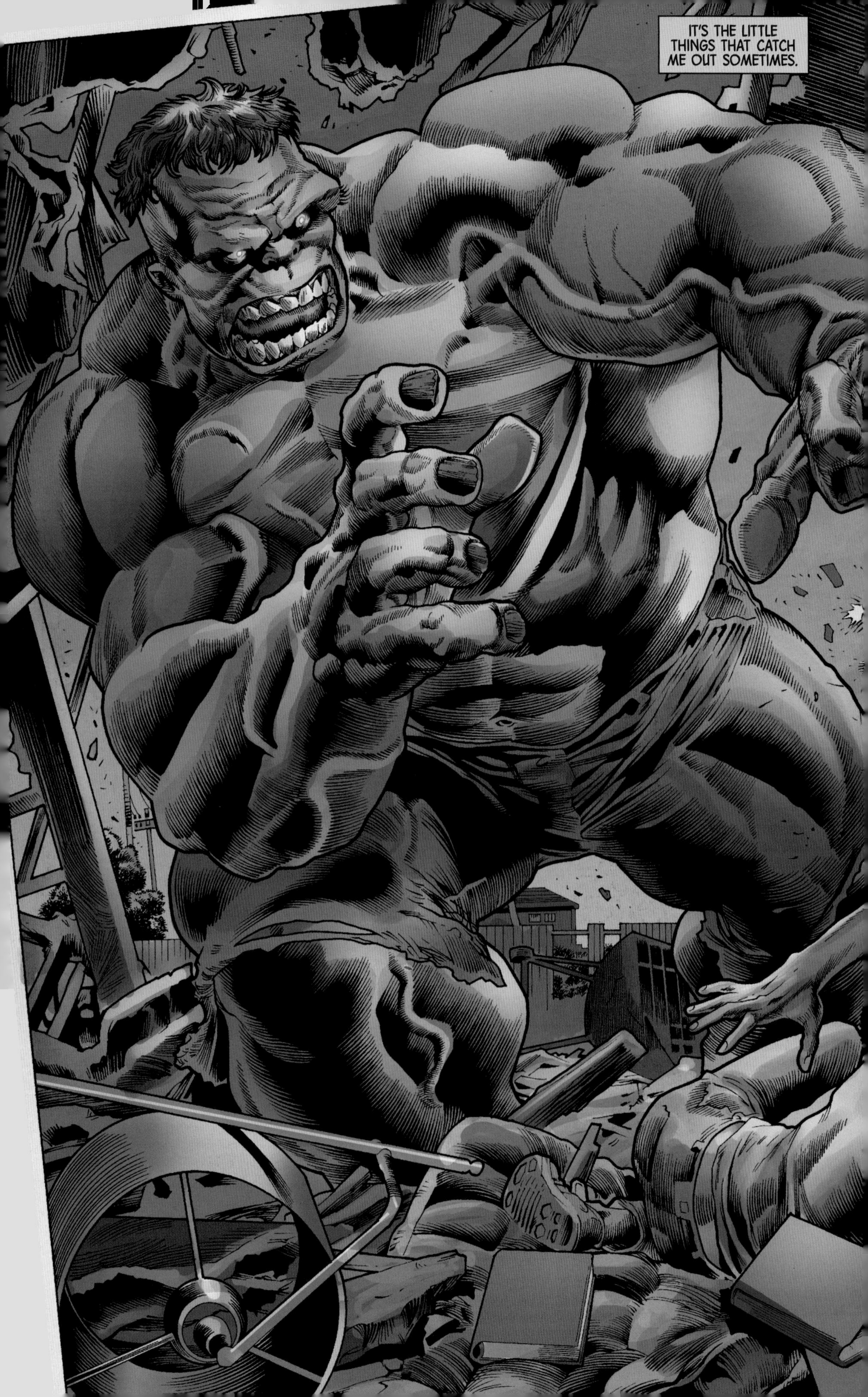
IT'S THE LITTLE THINGS THAT CATCH ME OUT SOMETIMES.

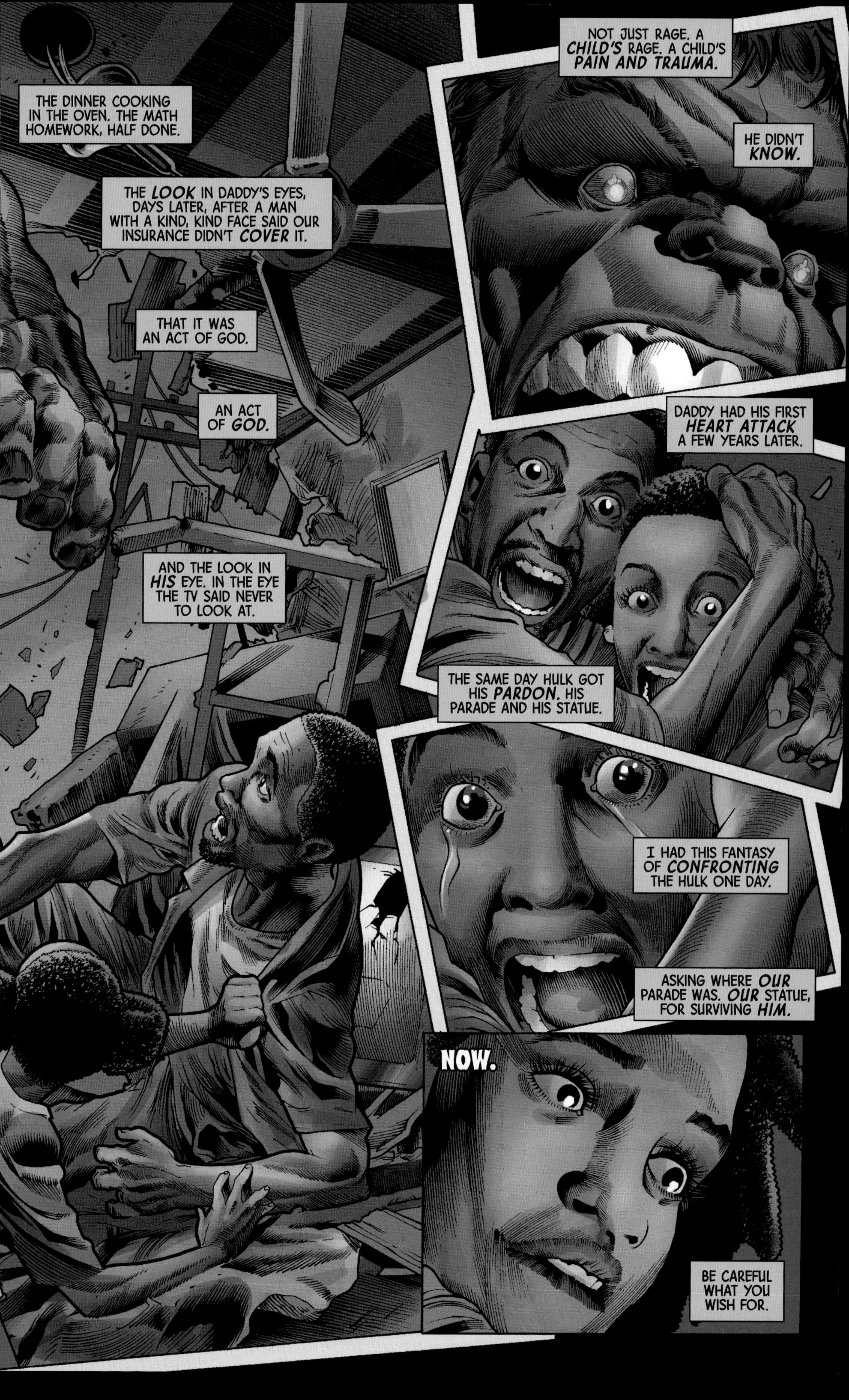

THE DINNER COOKING IN THE OVEN. THE MATH HOMEWORK, HALF DONE.
THE *LOOK* IN DADDY'S EYES, DAYS LATER, AFTER A MAN WITH A KIND, KIND FACE SAID OUR INSURANCE DIDN'T *COVER* IT.
THAT IT WAS AN ACT OF GOD.
AN ACT OF *GOD.*
AND THE LOOK IN *HIS* EYE. IN THE EYE THE TV SAID NEVER TO LOOK AT.
NOT JUST RAGE. A *CHILD'S* RAGE. A CHILD'S *PAIN AND TRAUMA.*
HE DIDN'T *KNOW.*
DADDY HAD HIS FIRST *HEART ATTACK* A FEW YEARS LATER.
THE SAME DAY HULK GOT HIS *PARDON.* HIS PARADE AND HIS STATUE.
I HAD THIS FANTASY OF *CONFRONTING* THE HULK ONE DAY.
ASKING WHERE *OUR* PARADE WAS. *OUR* STATUE, FOR SURVIVING *HIM.*
NOW.
BE CAREFUL WHAT YOU WISH FOR.

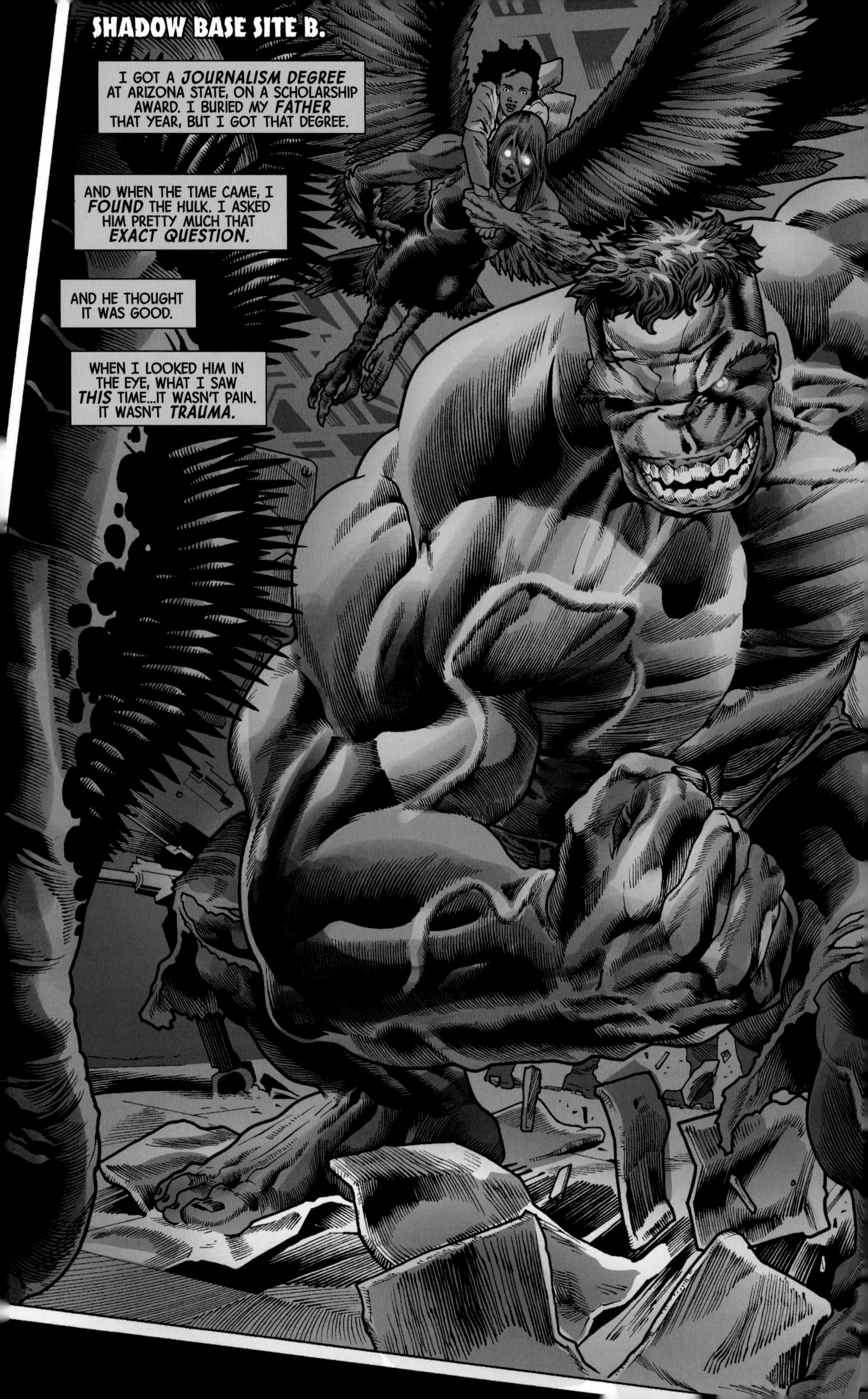
SHADOW BASE SITE B.
I GOT A JOURNALISM DEGREE AT ARIZONA STATE, ON A SCHOLARSHIP AWARD. I BURIED MY FATHER THAT YEAR, BUT I GOT THAT DEGREE.
AND WHEN THE TIME CAME, I FOUND THE HULK. I ASKED HIM PRETTY MUCH THAT EXACT QUESTION.
AND HE THOUGHT IT WAS GOOD.
WHEN I LOOKED HIM IN THE EYE, WHAT I SAW THIS TIME...IT WASN'T PAIN. IT WASN'T TRAUMA.

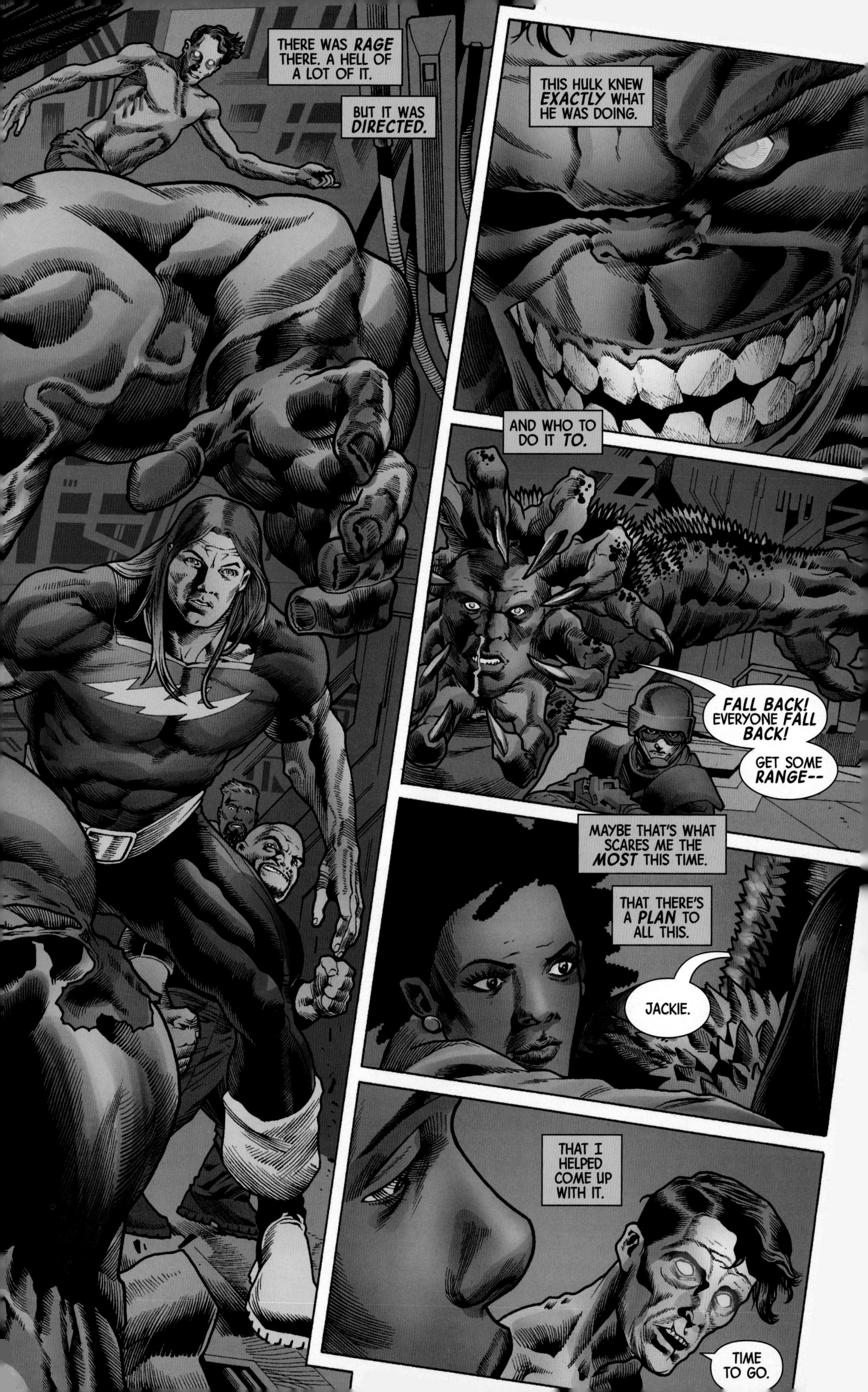
THERE WAS RAGE THERE. A HELL OF A LOT OF IT.
BUT IT WAS DIRECTED.
THIS HULK KNEW EXACTLY WHAT HE WAS DOING.
AND WHO TO DO IT TO.
FALL BACK! EVERYONE FALL BACK!
GET SOME RANGE--
MAYBE THAT'S WHAT SCARES ME THE MOST THIS TIME.
THAT THERE'S A PLAN TO ALL THIS.
JACKIE.
THAT I HELPED COME UP WITH IT.
TIME TO GO.

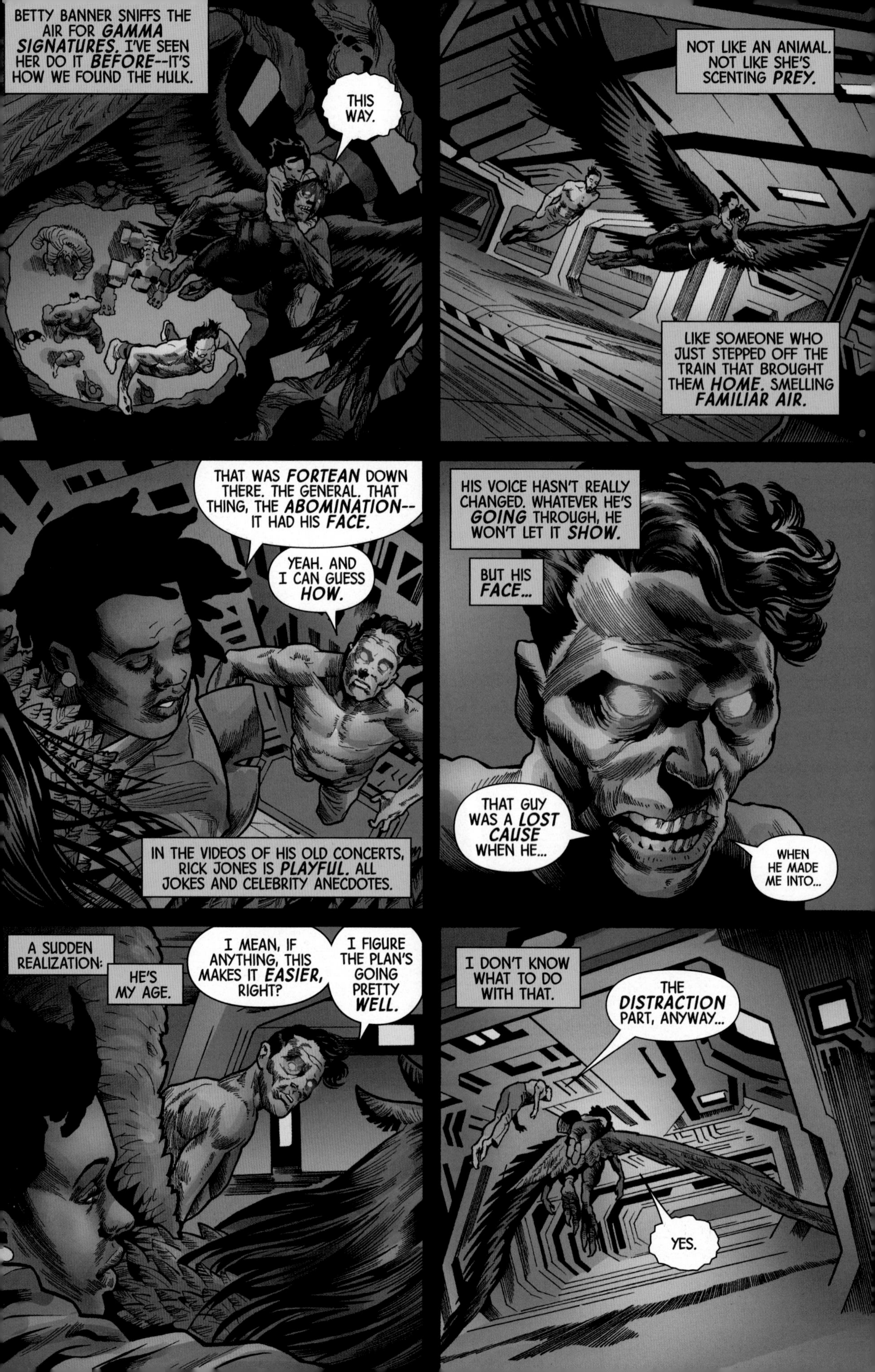

BETTY BANNER SNIFFS THE AIR FOR GAMMA SIGNATURES. I'VE SEEN HER DO IT BEFORE--IT'S HOW WE FOUND THE HULK.
THIS WAY.
NOT LIKE AN ANIMAL. NOT LIKE SHE'S SCENTING PREY.
LIKE SOMEONE WHO JUST STEPPED OFF THE TRAIN THAT BROUGHT THEM HOME. SMELLING FAMILIAR AIR.
THAT WAS FORTEAN DOWN THERE. THE GENERAL. THAT THING, THE ABOMINATION-- IT HAD HIS FACE.
YEAH. AND I CAN GUESS HOW.
IN THE VIDEOS OF HIS OLD CONCERTS, RICK JONES IS PLAYFUL. ALL JOKES AND CELEBRITY ANECDOTES.
HIS VOICE HASN'T REALLY CHANGED. WHATEVER HE'S GOING THROUGH, HE WON'T LET IT SHOW.
BUT HIS FACE...
THAT GUY WAS A LOST CAUSE WHEN HE...
WHEN HE MADE ME INTO...
A SUDDEN REALIZATION:
HE'S MY AGE.
I MEAN, IF ANYTHING, THIS MAKES IT EASIER, RIGHT?
I FIGURE THE PLAN'S GOING PRETTY WELL.
I DON'T KNOW WHAT TO DO WITH THAT.
THE DISTRACTION PART, ANYWAY...
YES.

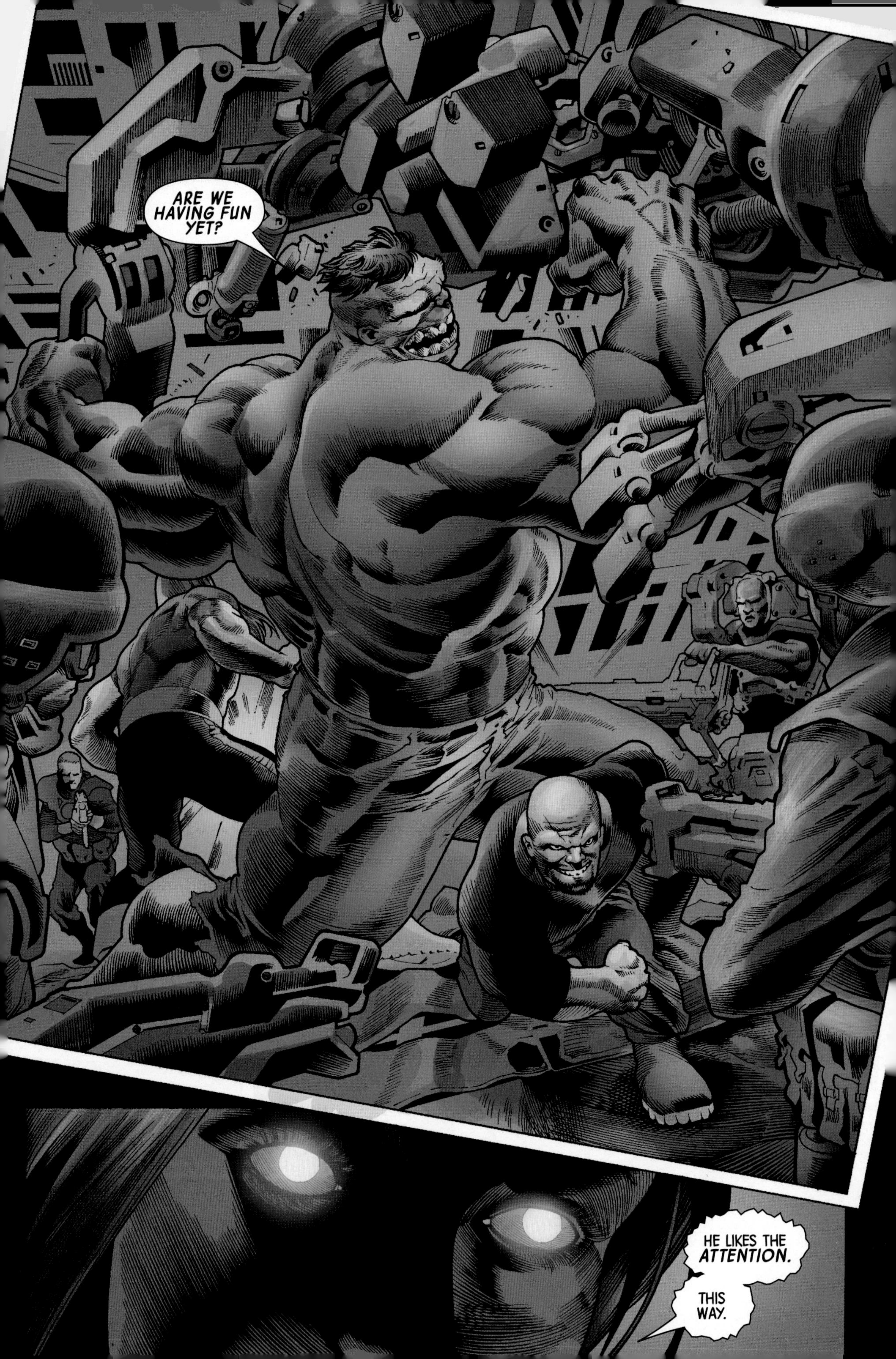
ARE WE HAVING FUN YET?
HE LIKES THE *ATTENTION.*
THIS WAY.

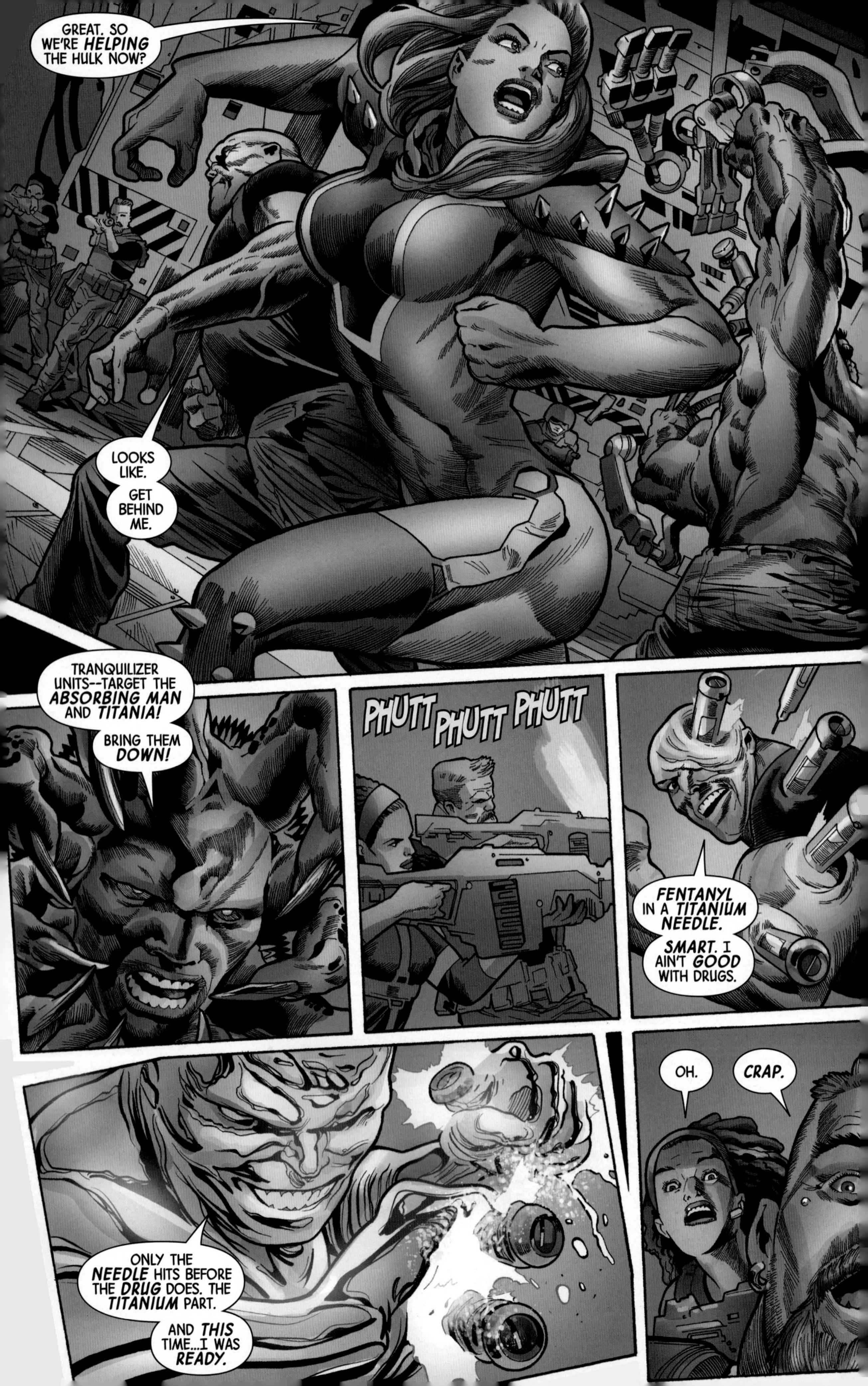
GREAT. SO WE'RE HELPING THE HULK NOW?
LOOKS LIKE.
GET BEHIND ME.
TRANQUILIZER UNITS--TARGET THE ABSORBING MAN AND TITANIA!
BRING THEM DOWN!
PHUTT PHUTT PHUTT
FENTANYL IN A TITANIUM NEEDLE.
SMART. I AIN'T GOOD WITH DRUGS.
ONLY THE NEEDLE HITS BEFORE THE DRUG DOES. THE TITANIUM PART.
AND THIS TIME...I WAS READY.
OH.
CRAP.

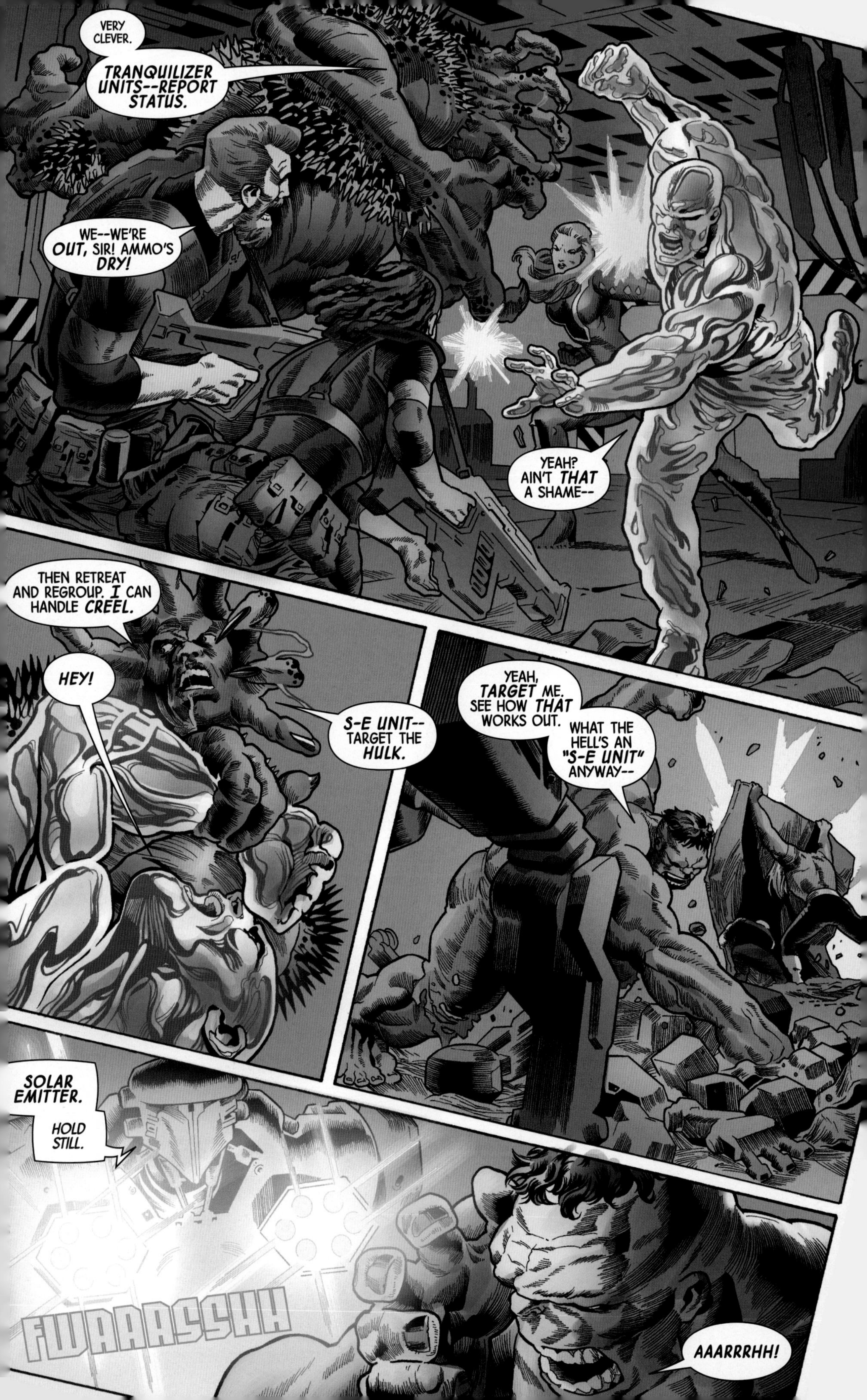
VERY CLEVER.
TRANQUILIZER UNITS--REPORT STATUS.
WE--WE'RE OUT, SIR! AMMO'S DRY!
YEAH? AIN'T THAT A SHAME--
THEN RETREAT AND REGROUP. I CAN HANDLE CREEL.
HEY!
S-E UNIT--TARGET THE HULK.
YEAH, TARGET ME. SEE HOW THAT WORKS OUT.
WHAT THE HELL'S AN "S-E UNIT" ANYWAY--
SOLAR EMITTER.
HOLD STILL.
FWAAASSHH
AAARRRHH!

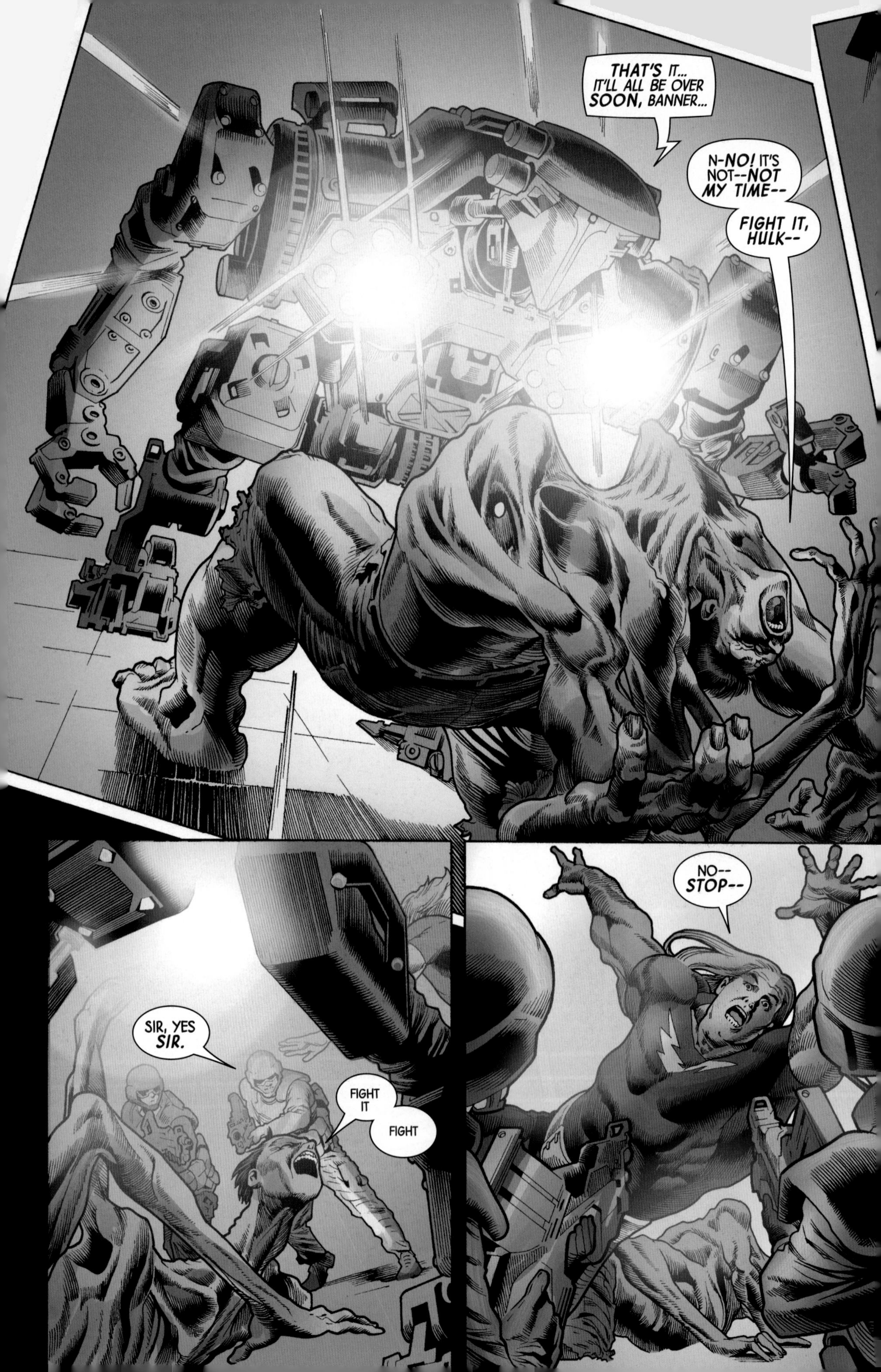
THAT'S IT... IT'LL ALL BE OVER SOON, BANNER...
N-NO! IT'S NOT--NOT MY TIME--
FIGHT IT, HULK--
SIR, YES SIR.
FIGHT IT
FIGHT
NO-- STOP--

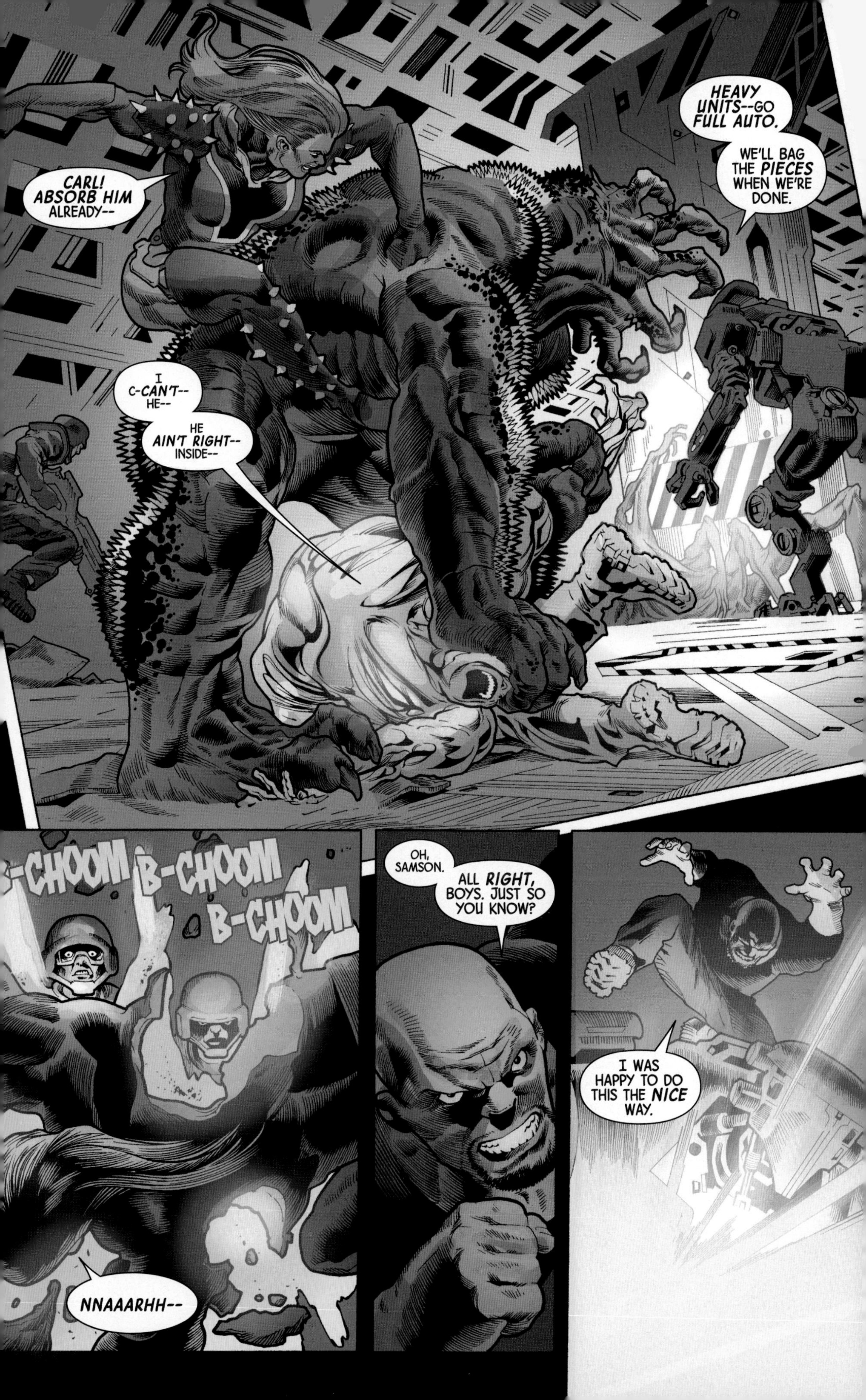
CARL! ABSORB HIM ALREADY--
HEAVY UNITS--GO FULL AUTO.
WE'LL BAG THE PIECES WHEN WE'RE DONE.
I C-CAN'T-- HE--
HE AIN'T RIGHT-- INSIDE--
-CHOOM B-CHOOM B-CHOOM
NNAAARHH--
OH, SAMSON.
ALL RIGHT, BOYS. JUST SO YOU KNOW?
I WAS HAPPY TO DO THIS THE NICE WAY.

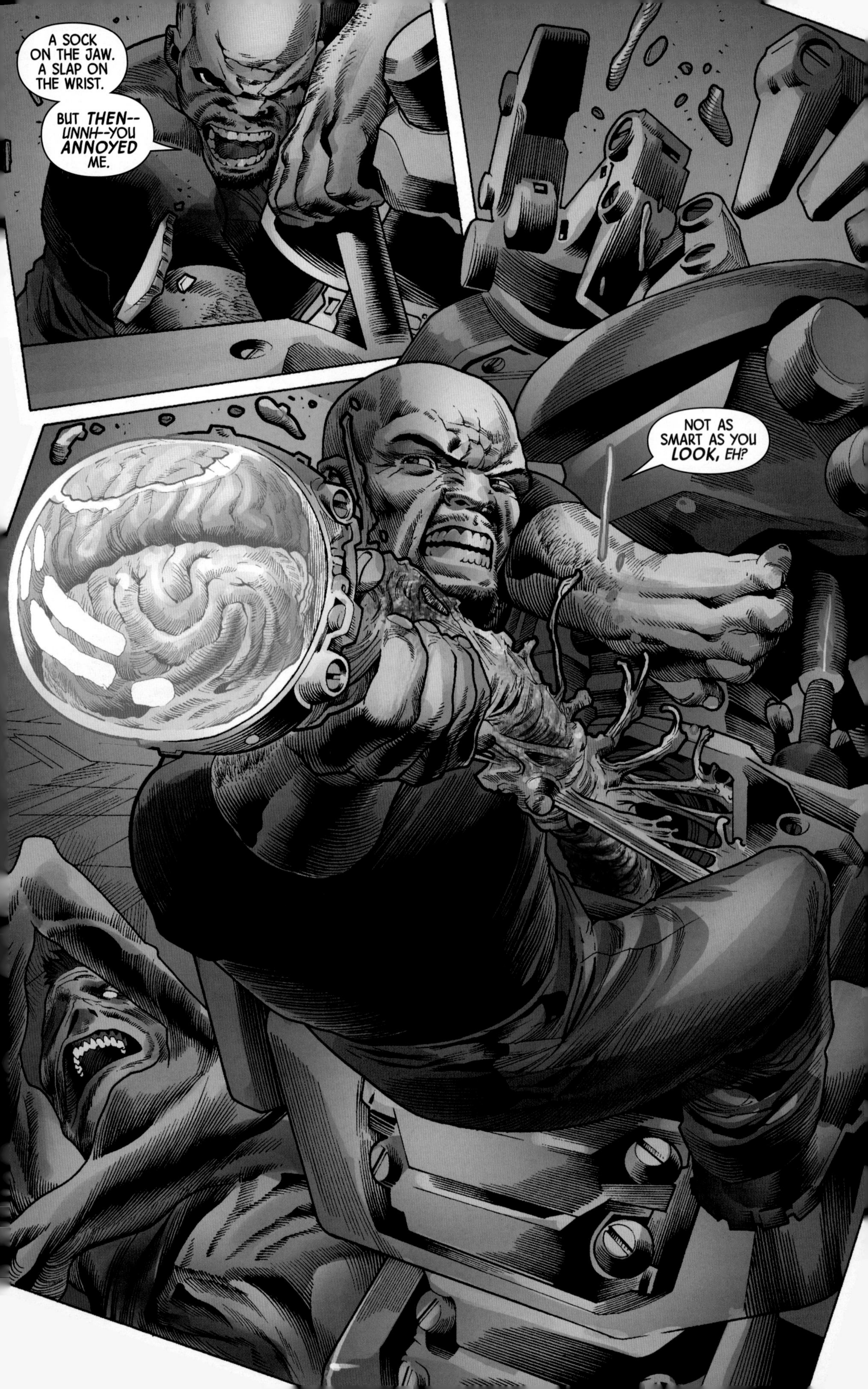
A SOCK ON THE JAW. A SLAP ON THE WRIST.
BUT *THEN*-- *UNNH*--YOU ***ANNOYED*** ME.
NOT AS SMART AS YOU ***LOOK,*** EH?

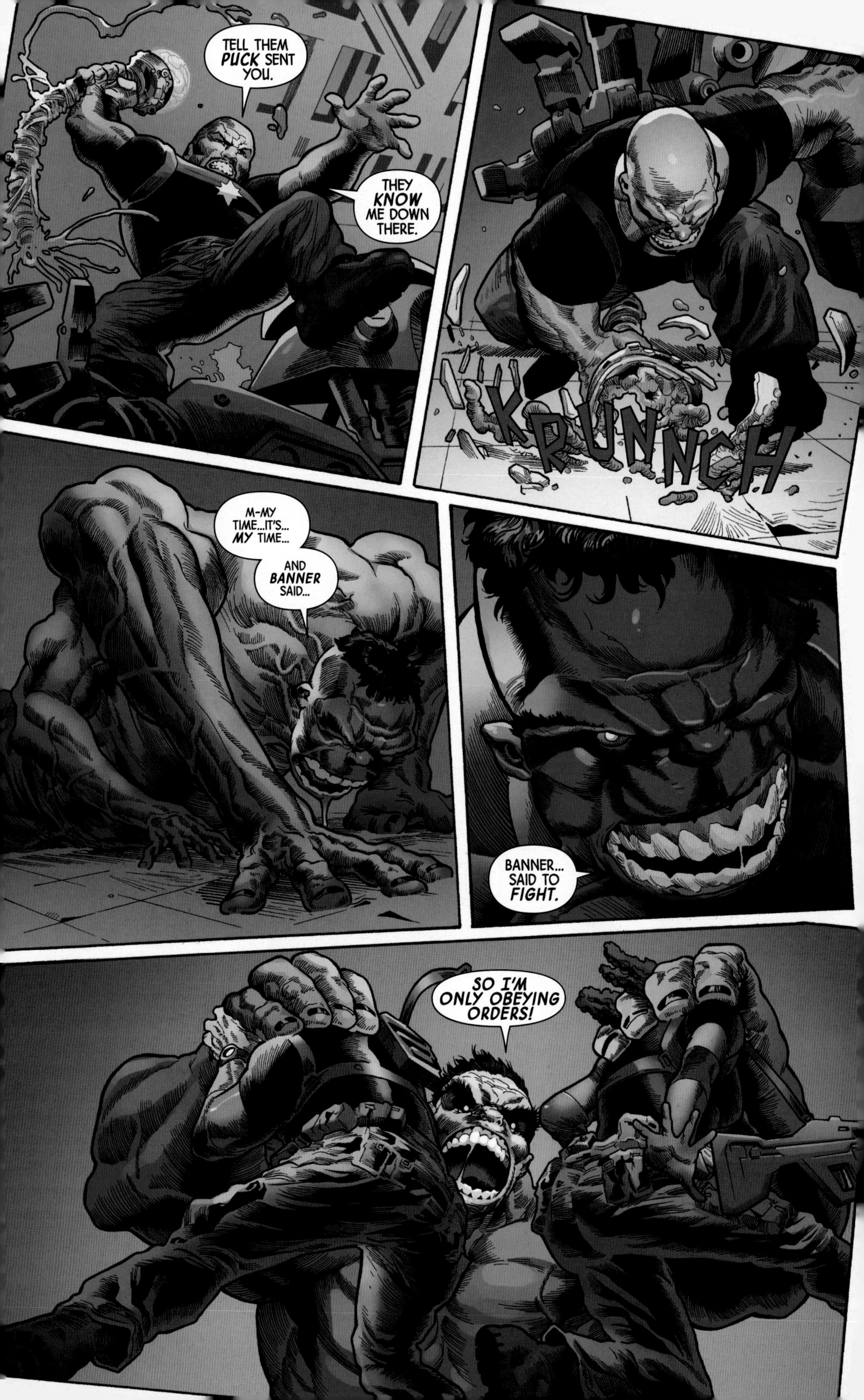
TELL THEM PUCK SENT YOU.
THEY KNOW ME DOWN THERE.
KRUNNCH
M-MY TIME...IT'S... MY TIME...
AND BANNER SAID...
BANNER... SAID TO FIGHT.
SO I'M ONLY OBEYING ORDERS!

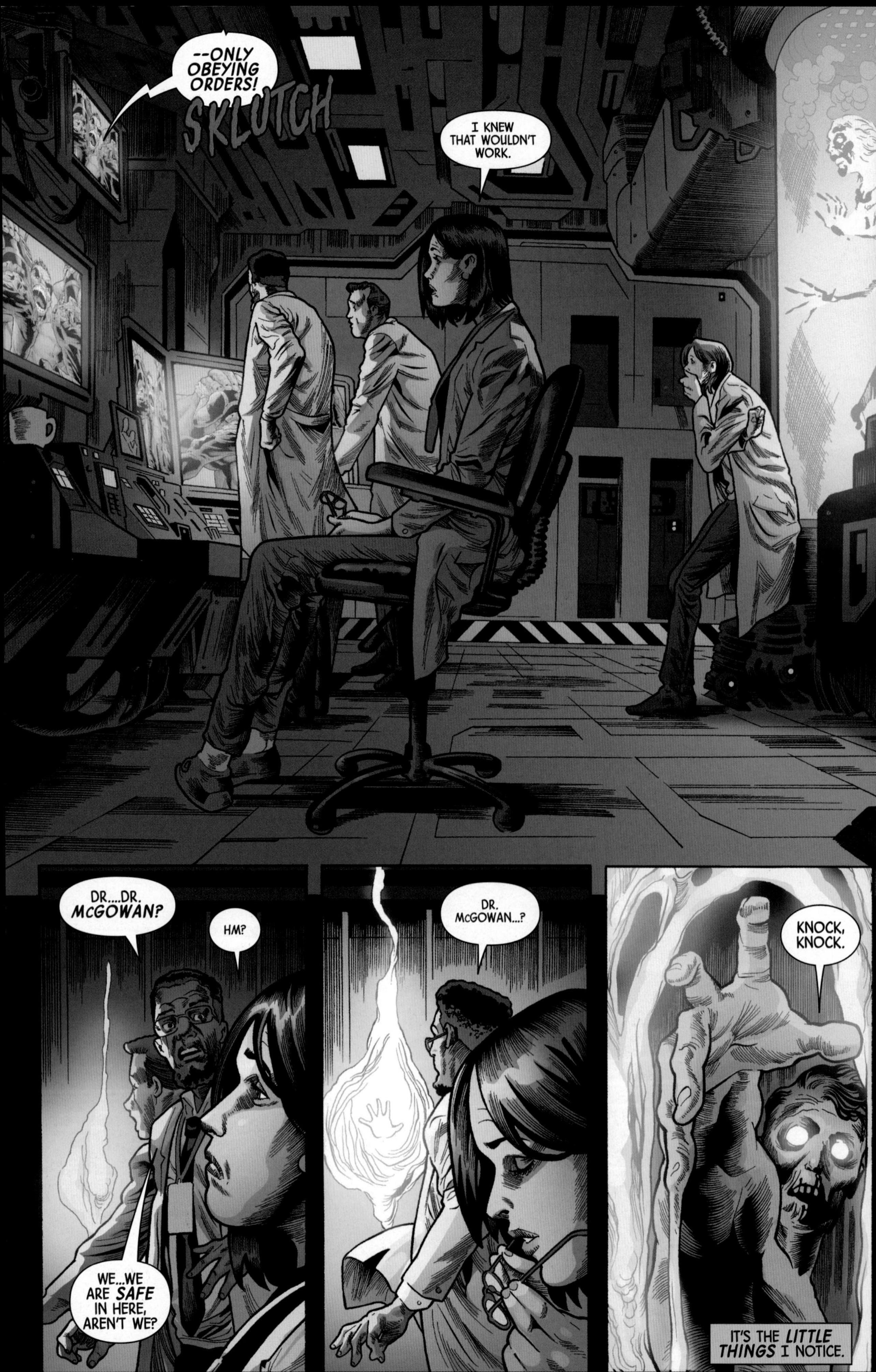
--ONLY OBEYING ORDERS!
SKLUTCH
I KNEW THAT WOULDN'T WORK.
DR....DR. McGOWAN?
HM?
WE...WE ARE SAFE IN HERE, AREN'T WE?
DR. McGOWAN...?
KNOCK, KNOCK.
IT'S THE LITTLE THINGS I NOTICE.

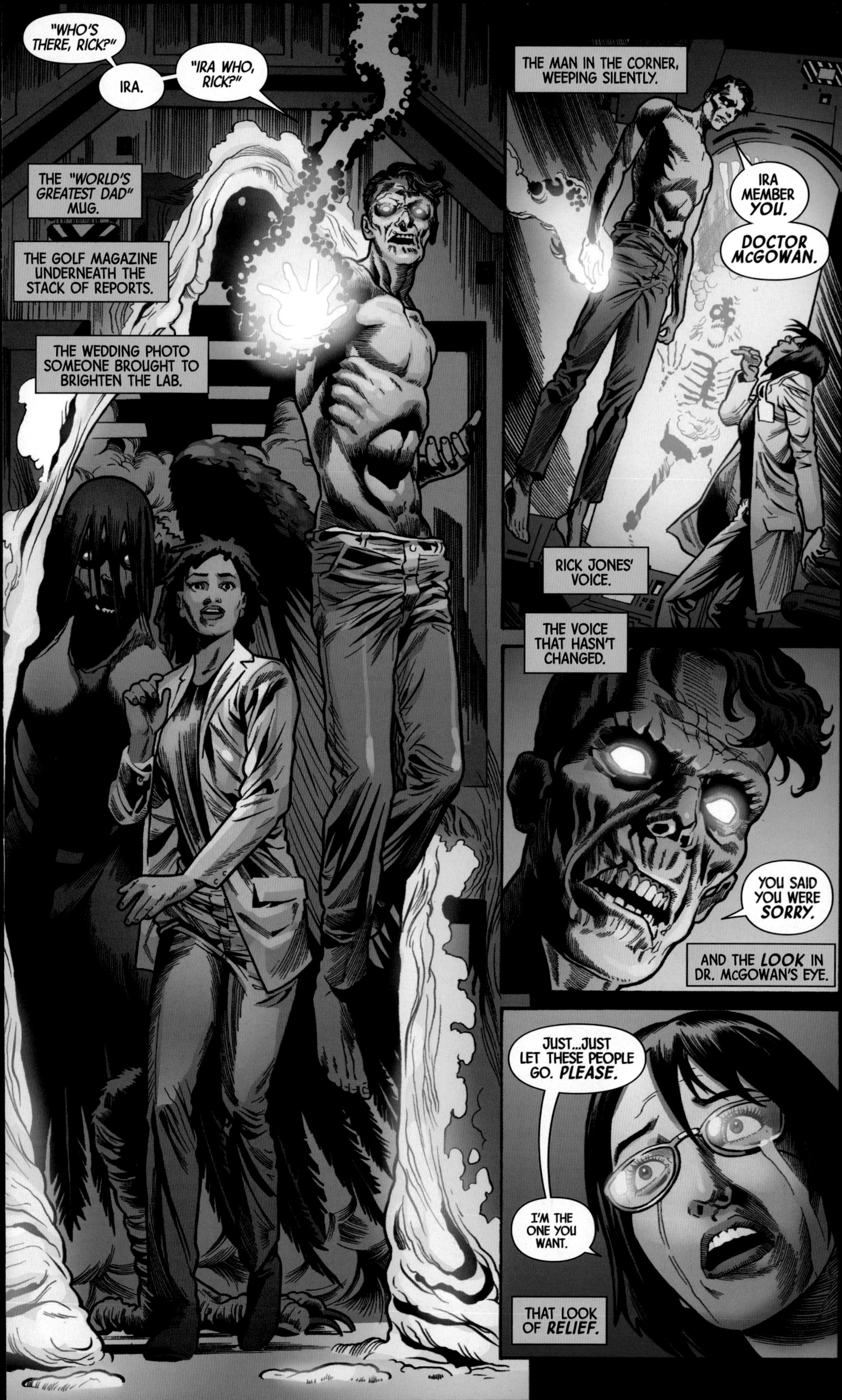
"WHO'S THERE, RICK?"
IRA.
"IRA WHO, RICK?"
THE "WORLD'S GREATEST DAD" MUG.
THE GOLF MAGAZINE UNDERNEATH THE STACK OF REPORTS.
THE WEDDING PHOTO SOMEONE BROUGHT TO BRIGHTEN THE LAB.
THE MAN IN THE CORNER, WEEPING SILENTLY.
IRA MEMBER YOU.
DOCTOR McGOWAN.
RICK JONES' VOICE.
THE VOICE THAT HASN'T CHANGED.
YOU SAID YOU WERE SORRY.
AND THE LOOK IN DR. McGOWAN'S EYE.
JUST...JUST LET THESE PEOPLE GO. PLEASE.
I'M THE ONE YOU WANT.
THAT LOOK OF RELIEF.

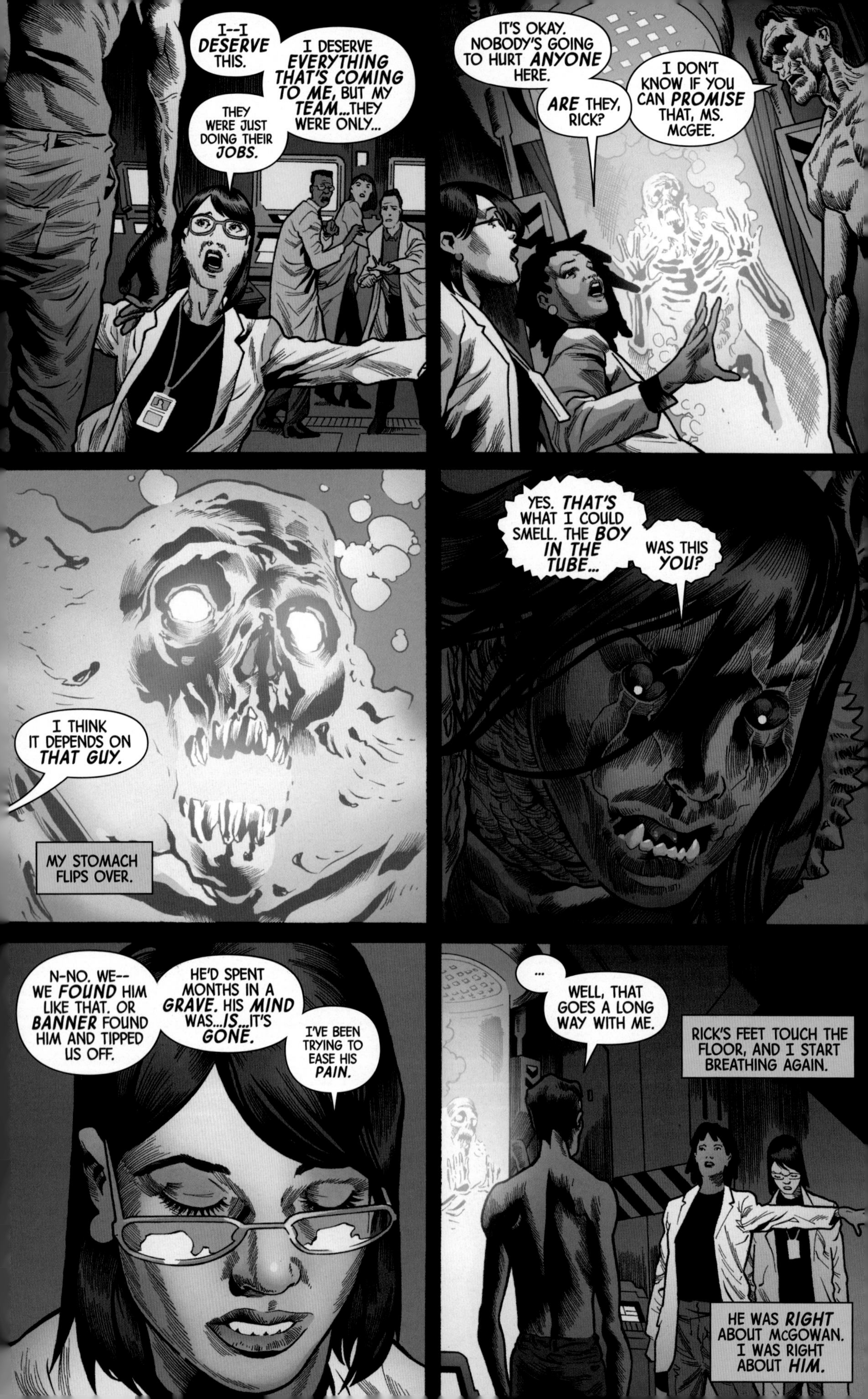
I--I DESERVE THIS.
I DESERVE EVERYTHING THAT'S COMING TO ME, BUT MY TEAM...THEY WERE ONLY...
THEY WERE JUST DOING THEIR JOBS.
IT'S OKAY. NOBODY'S GOING TO HURT ANYONE HERE.
ARE THEY, RICK?
I DON'T KNOW IF YOU CAN PROMISE THAT, MS. McGEE.
I THINK IT DEPENDS ON THAT GUY.
MY STOMACH FLIPS OVER.
YES. THAT'S WHAT I COULD SMELL. THE BOY IN THE TUBE...
WAS THIS YOU?
N-NO. WE-- WE FOUND HIM LIKE THAT. OR BANNER FOUND HIM AND TIPPED US OFF.
HE'D SPENT MONTHS IN A GRAVE. HIS MIND WAS...IS...IT'S GONE.
I'VE BEEN TRYING TO EASE HIS PAIN.
...
WELL, THAT GOES A LONG WAY WITH ME.
RICK'S FEET TOUCH THE FLOOR, AND I START BREATHING AGAIN.
HE WAS RIGHT ABOUT McGOWAN. I WAS RIGHT ABOUT HIM.

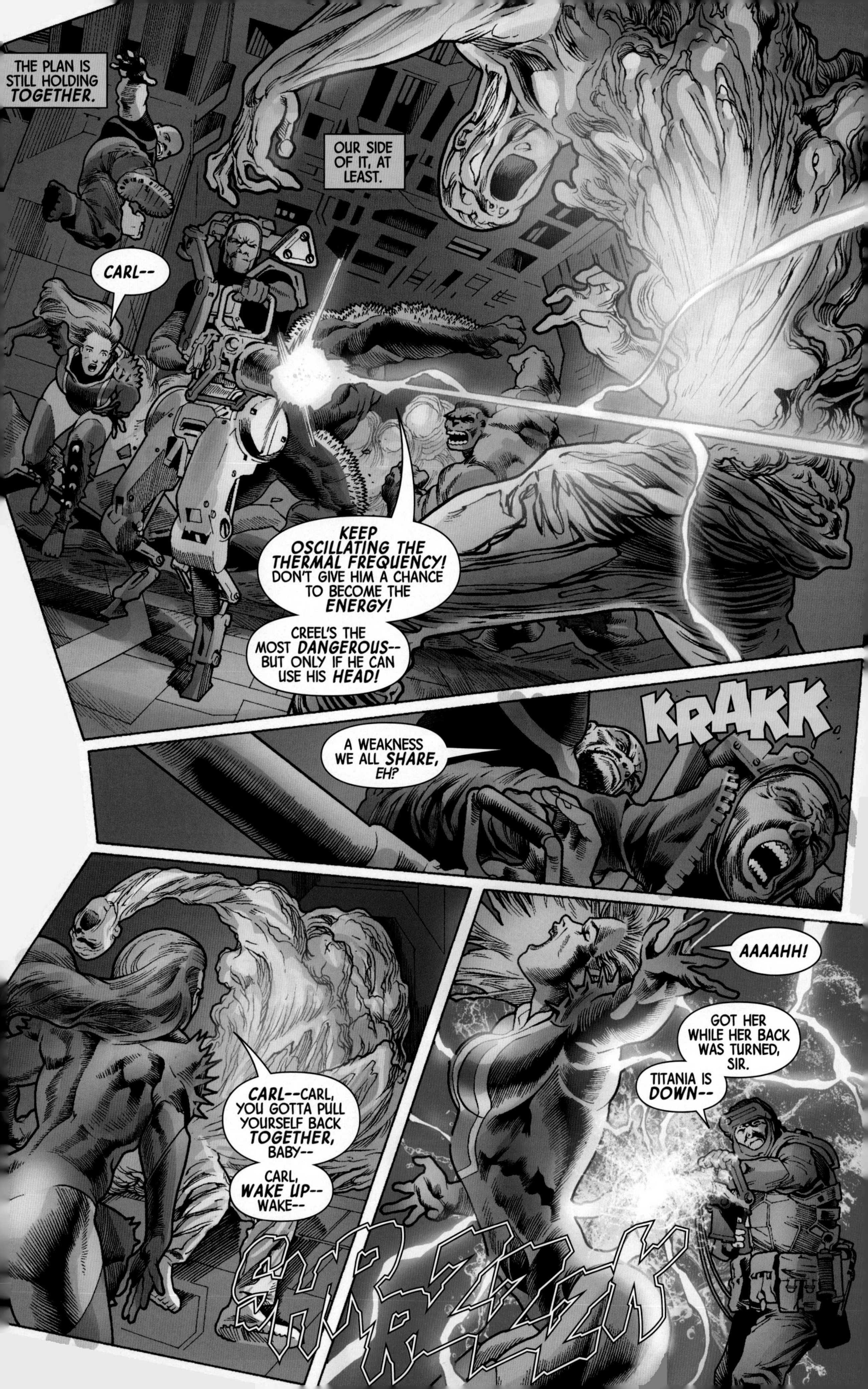
THE PLAN IS STILL HOLDING TOGETHER.
OUR SIDE OF IT, AT LEAST.
CARL--
KEEP OSCILLATING THE THERMAL FREQUENCY! DON'T GIVE HIM A CHANCE TO BECOME THE ENERGY!
CREEL'S THE MOST DANGEROUS--BUT ONLY IF HE CAN USE HIS HEAD!
KRAKK
A WEAKNESS WE ALL SHARE, EH?
CARL--CARL, YOU GOTTA PULL YOURSELF BACK TOGETHER, BABY--
CARL, WAKE UP--WAKE--
AAAAHH!
GOT HER WHILE HER BACK WAS TURNED, SIR.
TITANIA IS DOWN--

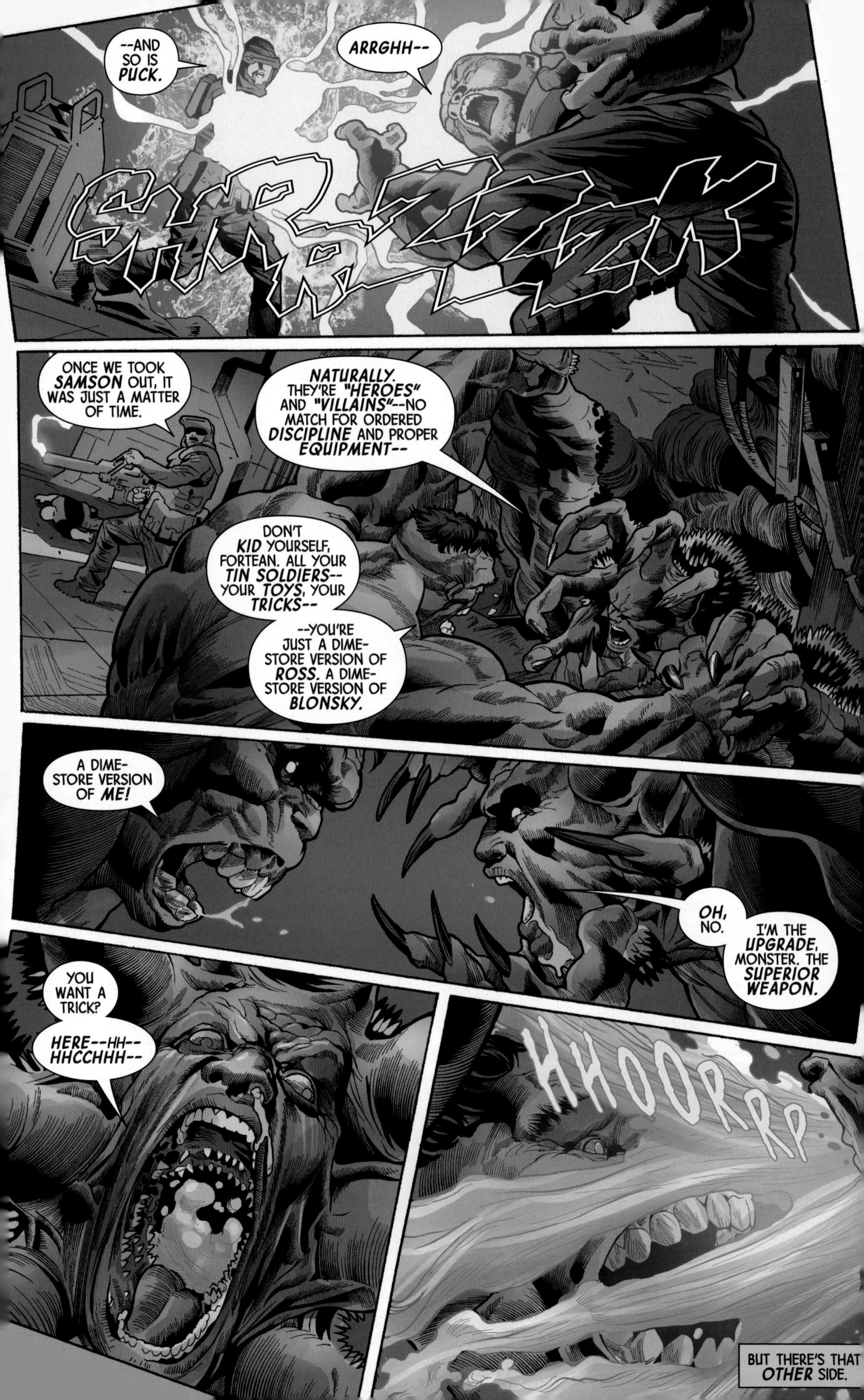
--AND SO IS PUCK.
ARRGHH--
SHRZZZZZK
ONCE WE TOOK SAMSON OUT, IT WAS JUST A MATTER OF TIME.
NATURALLY. THEY'RE "HEROES" AND "VILLAINS"--NO MATCH FOR ORDERED DISCIPLINE AND PROPER EQUIPMENT--
DON'T KID YOURSELF, FORTEAN. ALL YOUR TIN SOLDIERS-- YOUR TOYS, YOUR TRICKS--
--YOU'RE JUST A DIME-STORE VERSION OF ROSS. A DIME-STORE VERSION OF BLONSKY.
A DIME-STORE VERSION OF ME!
OH, NO.
I'M THE UPGRADE, MONSTER. THE SUPERIOR WEAPON.
YOU WANT A TRICK?
HERE--HH--HHCCHHH--
HHOORRP
BUT THERE'S THAT OTHER SIDE.

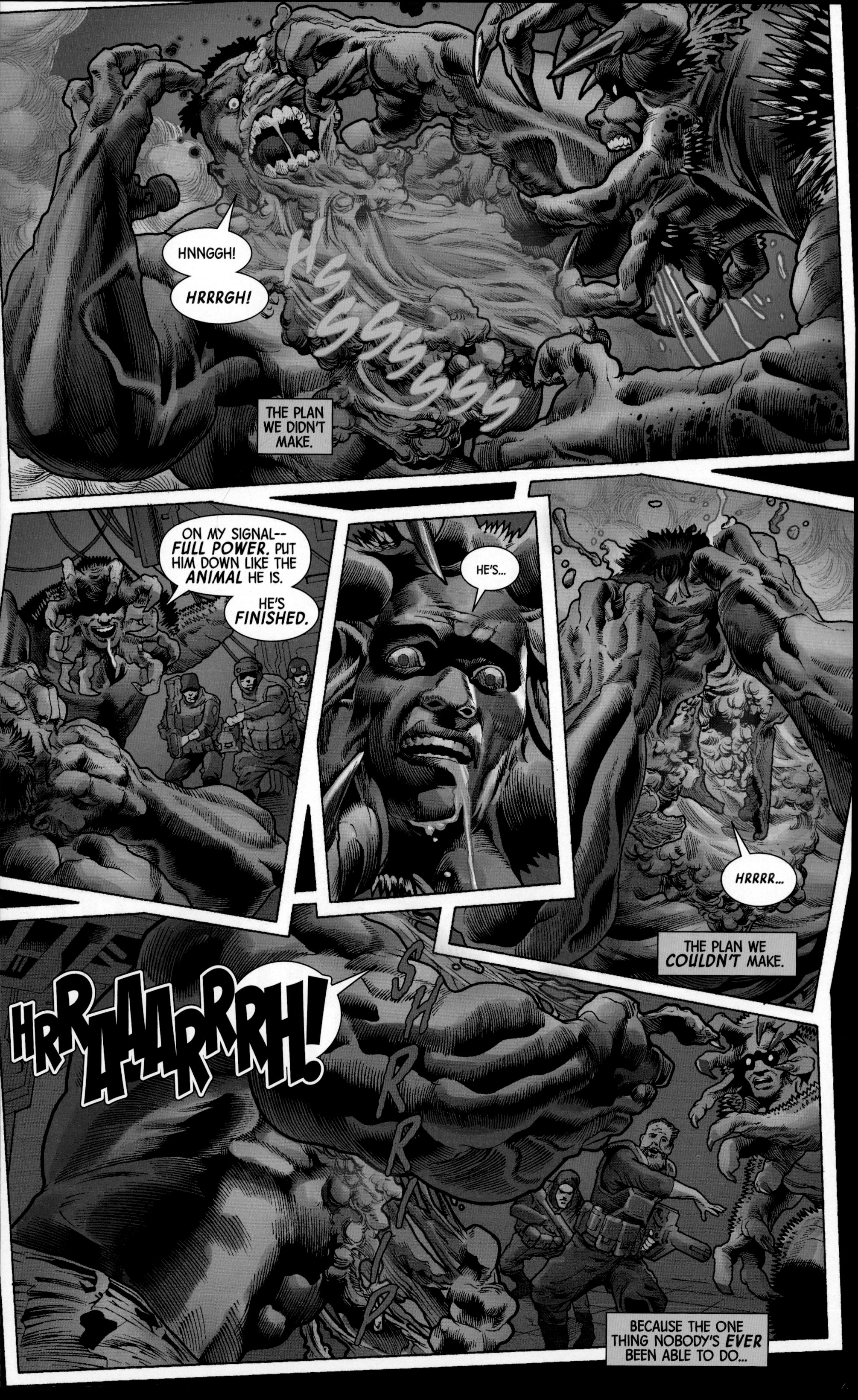
HNNGGH!
HRRRGH!
HSSSSSSSSS
THE PLAN WE DIDN'T MAKE.
ON MY SIGNAL-- FULL POWER. PUT HIM DOWN LIKE THE ANIMAL HE IS.
HE'S FINISHED.
HE'S...
HRRRR...
THE PLAN WE COULDN'T MAKE.
HRRAAARRRH!
SHRRIP
BECAUSE THE ONE THING NOBODY'S EVER BEEN ABLE TO DO...

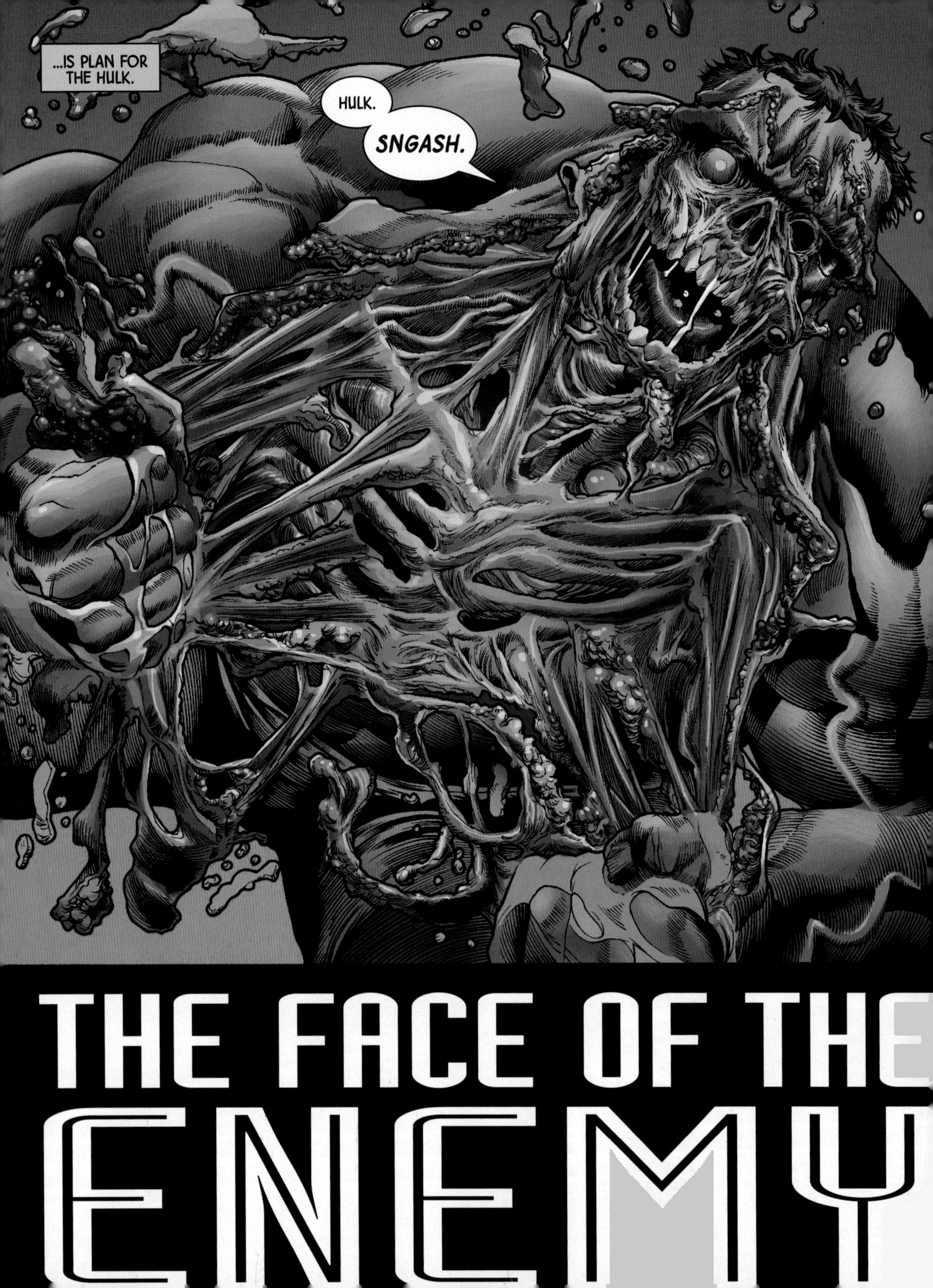
...IS PLAN FOR THE HULK.
HULK.
SNGASH.
THE FACE OF THE ENEMY

24

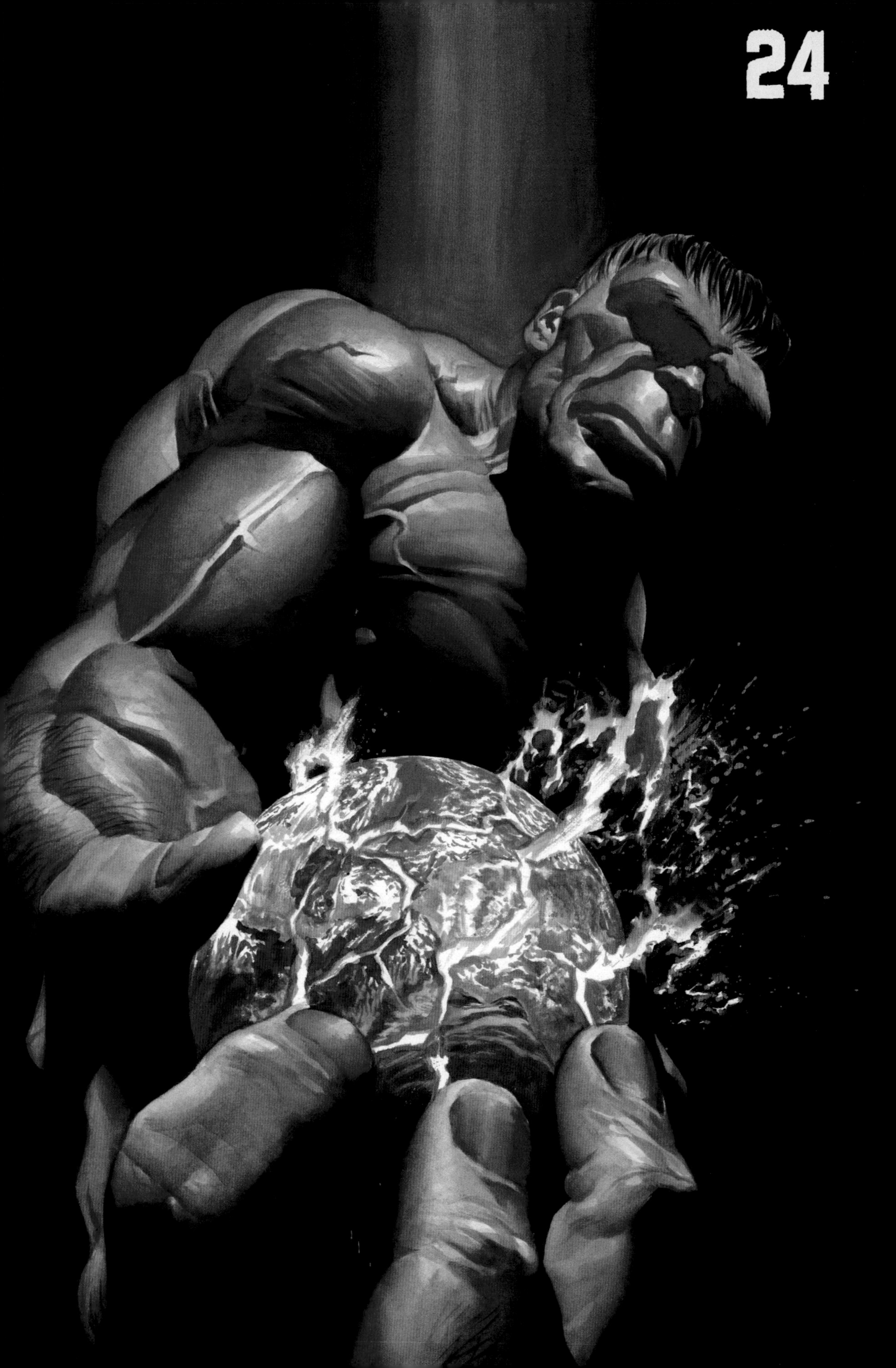

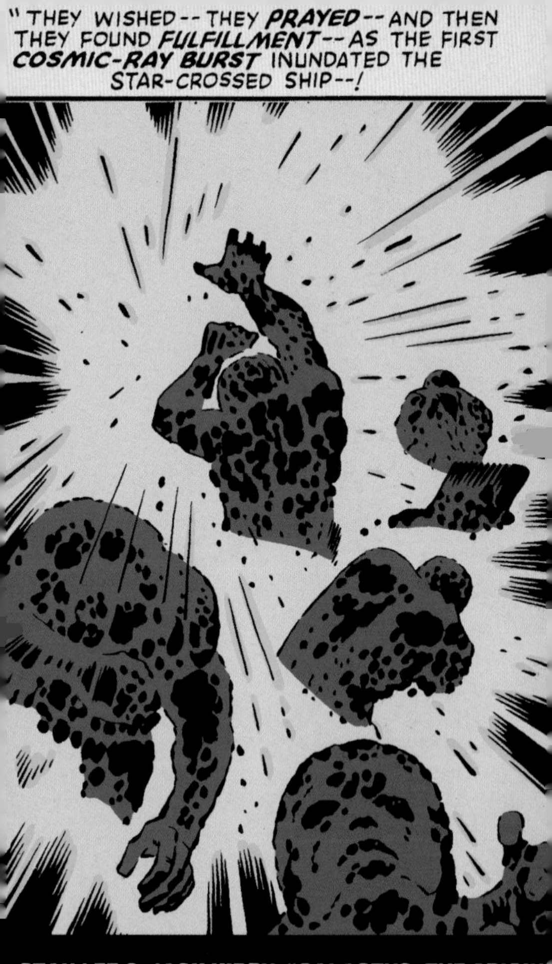
"THEY WISHED--THEY PRAYED--AND THEN THEY FOUND FULFILLMENT--AS THE FIRST COSMIC-RAY BURST INUNDATED THE STAR-CROSSED SHIP--!

- STAN LEE & JACK KIRBY, "GALACTUS: THE ORIGIN

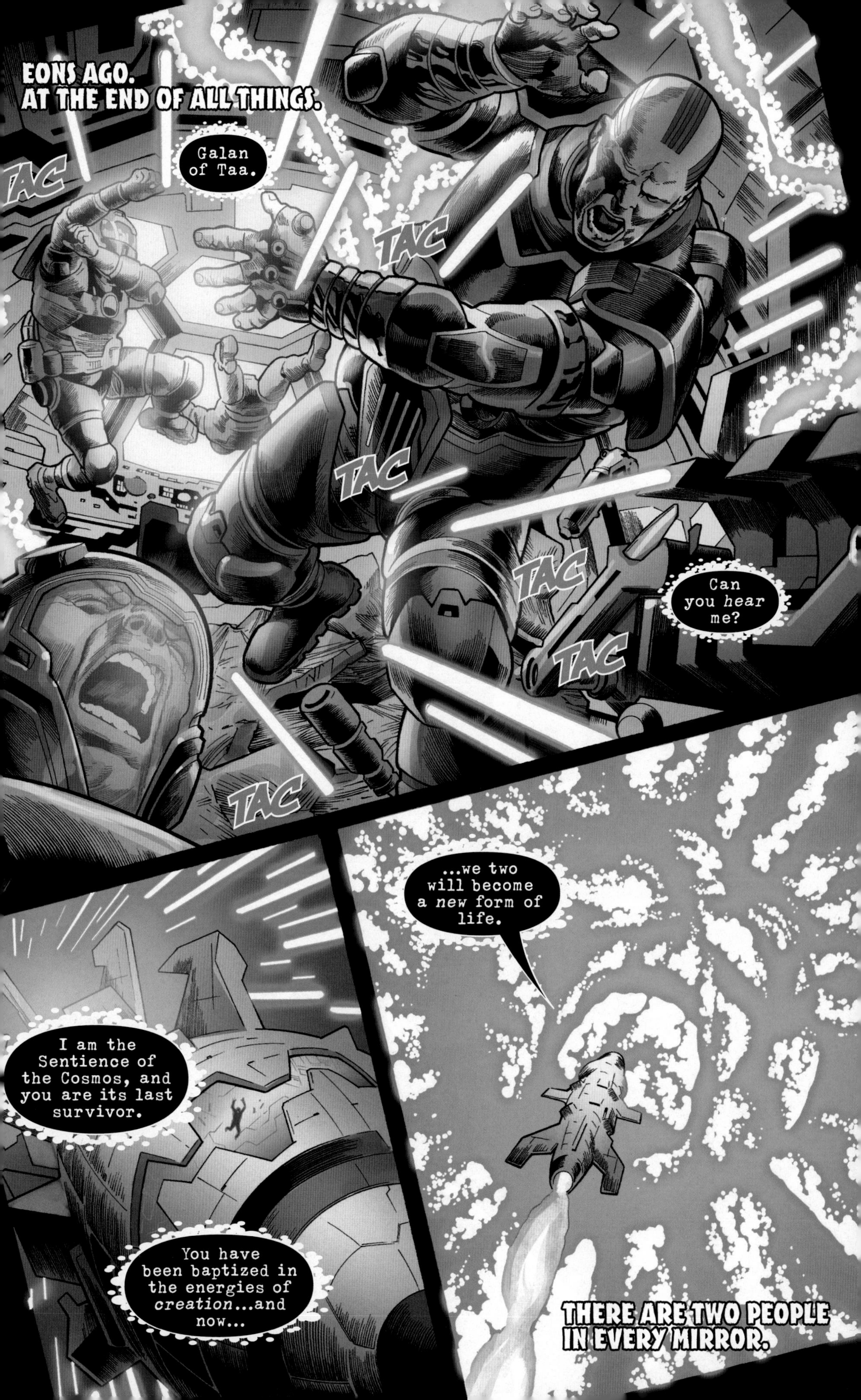
EONS AGO.
AT THE END OF ALL THINGS.
Galan of Taa.
TAC
TAC
TAC
TAC
Can you *hear* me?
TAC
TAC
I am the Sentience of the Cosmos, and you are its last survivor.
You have been baptized in the energies of *creation*...and now...
...we two will become a *new* form of life.
THERE ARE TWO PEOPLE IN EVERY MIRROR.

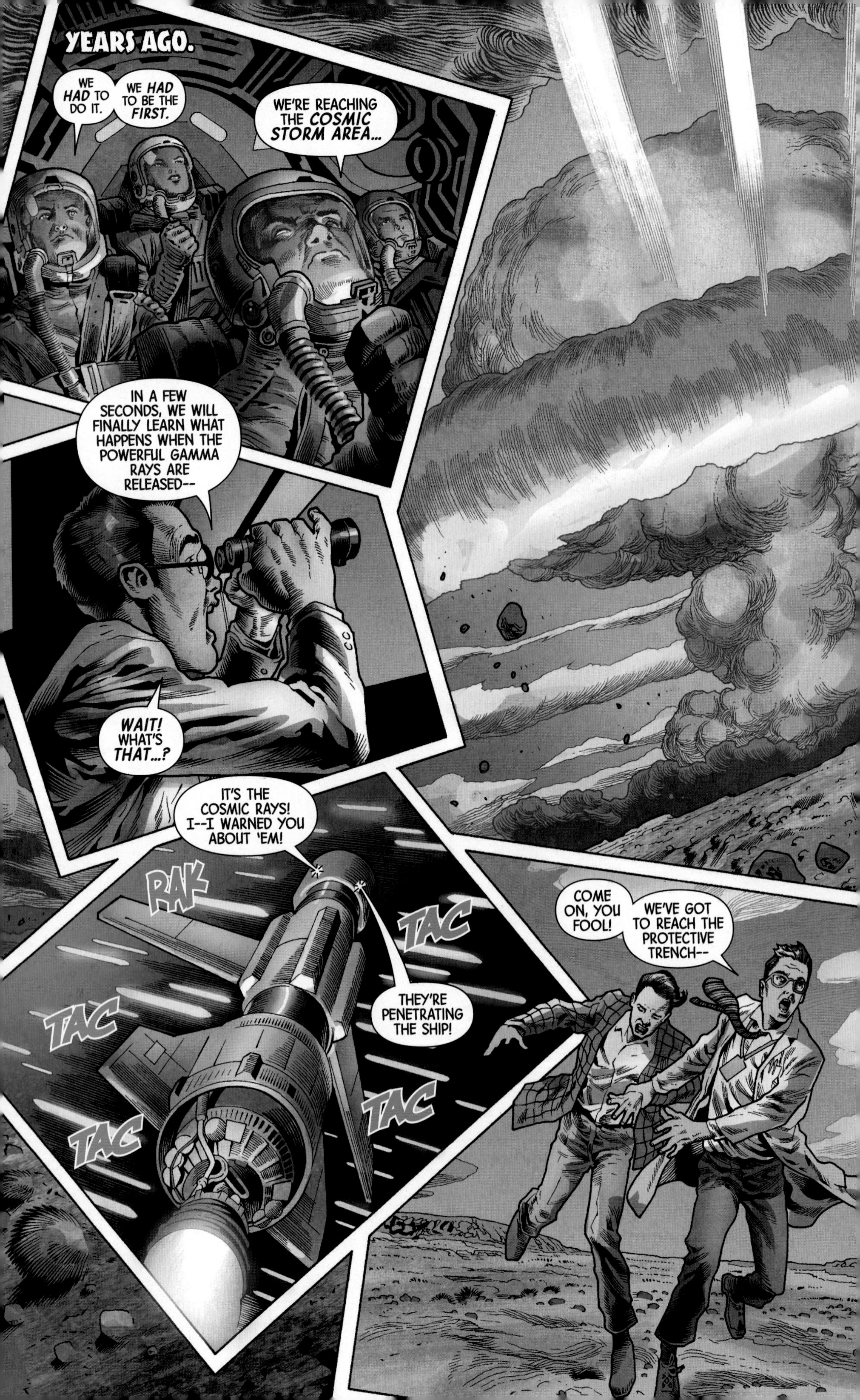
YEARS AGO.
WE HAD TO DO IT.
WE HAD TO BE THE FIRST.
WE'RE REACHING THE COSMIC STORM AREA...
IN A FEW SECONDS, WE WILL FINALLY LEARN WHAT HAPPENS WHEN THE POWERFUL GAMMA RAYS ARE RELEASED--
WAIT! WHAT'S THAT...?
IT'S THE COSMIC RAYS! I--I WARNED YOU ABOUT 'EM!
RAK
TAC
THEY'RE PENETRATING THE SHIP!
TAC
TAC
TAC
COME ON, YOU FOOL!
WE'VE GOT TO REACH THE PROTECTIVE TRENCH--

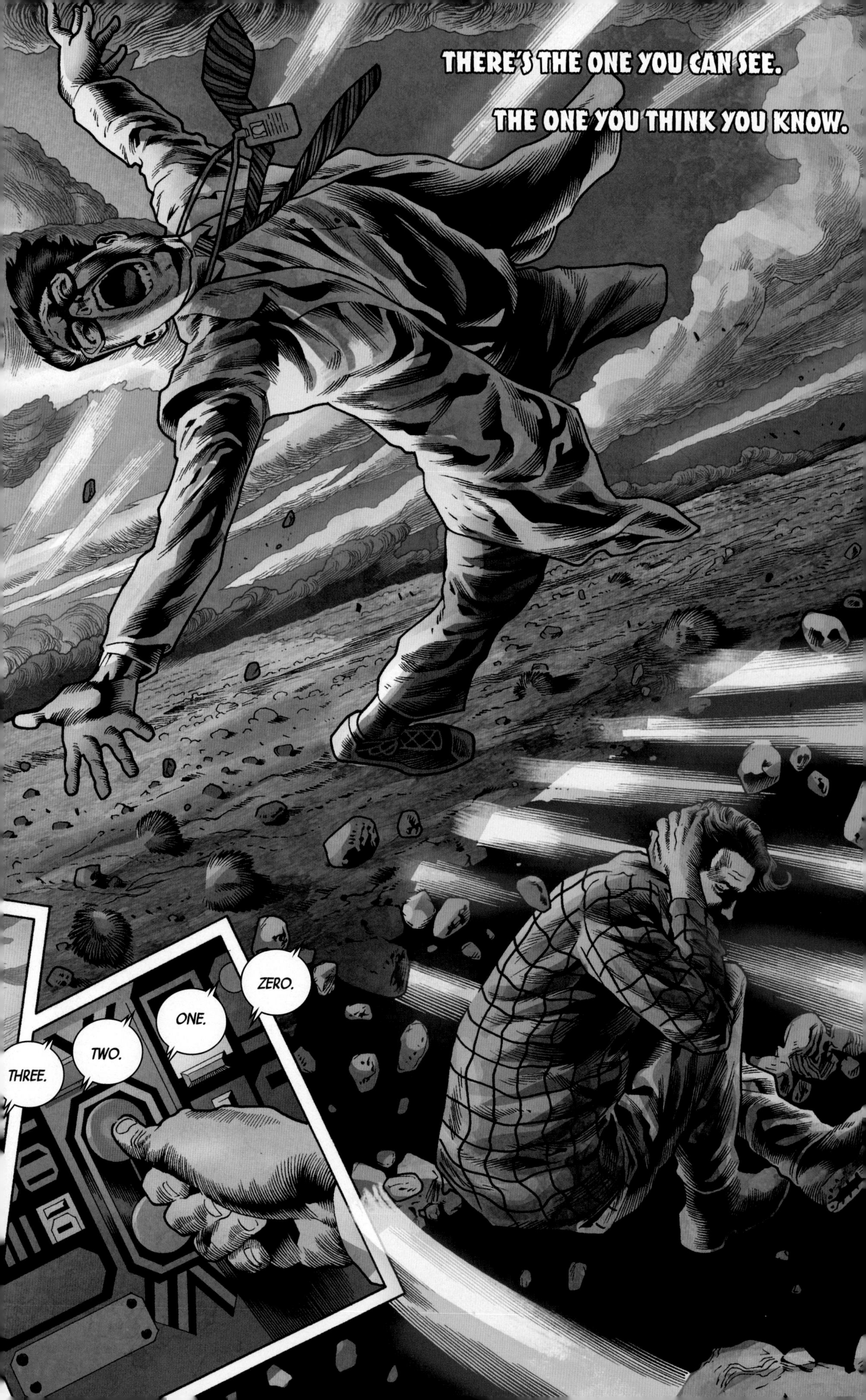
THERE'S THE ONE YOU CAN SEE.
THE ONE YOU THINK YOU KNOW.
THREE.
TWO.
ONE.
ZERO.

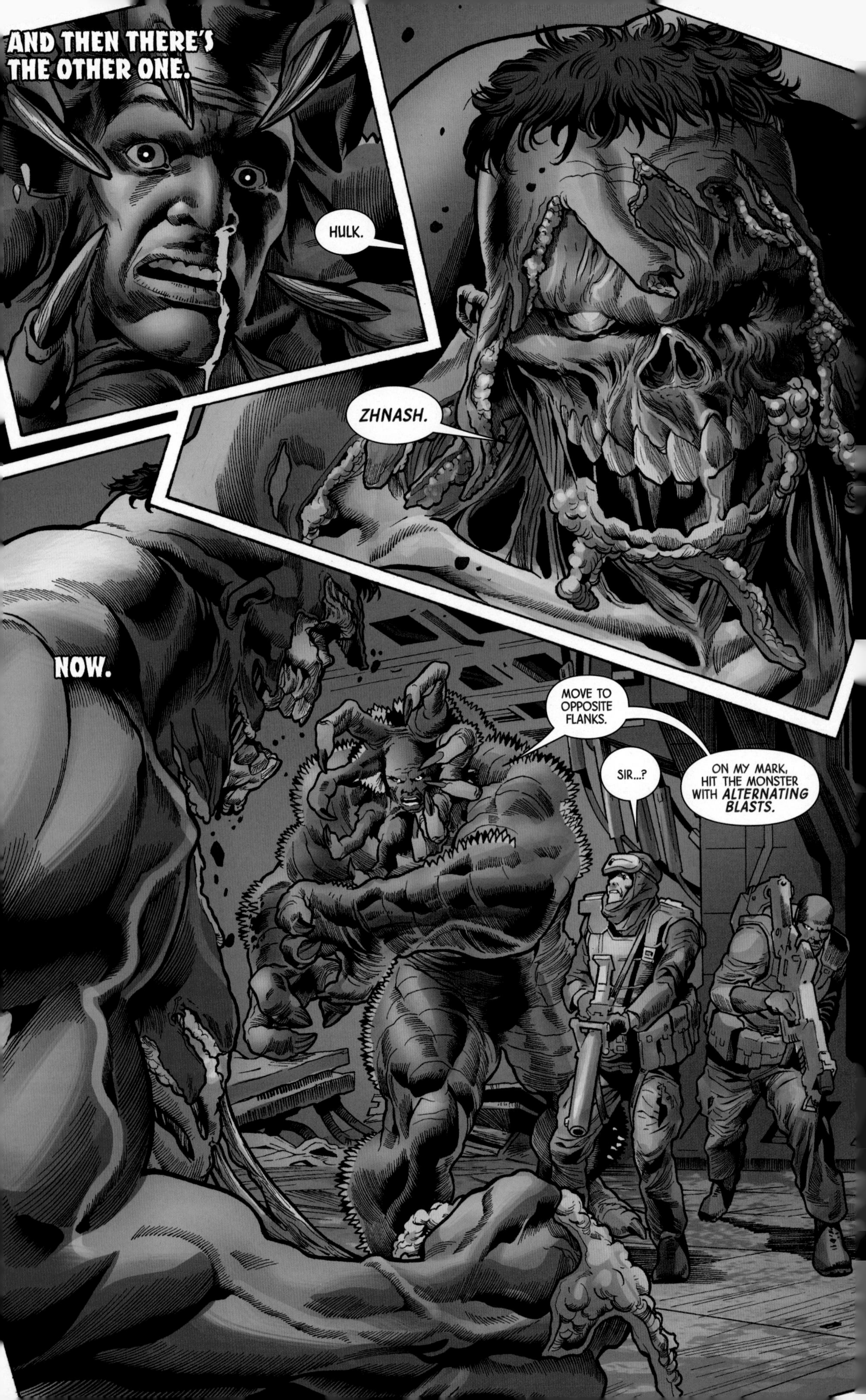
AND THEN THERE'S THE OTHER ONE.
HULK.
ZHNASH.
NOW.
MOVE TO OPPOSITE FLANKS.
SIR...?
ON MY MARK, HIT THE MONSTER WITH ALTERNATING BLASTS.

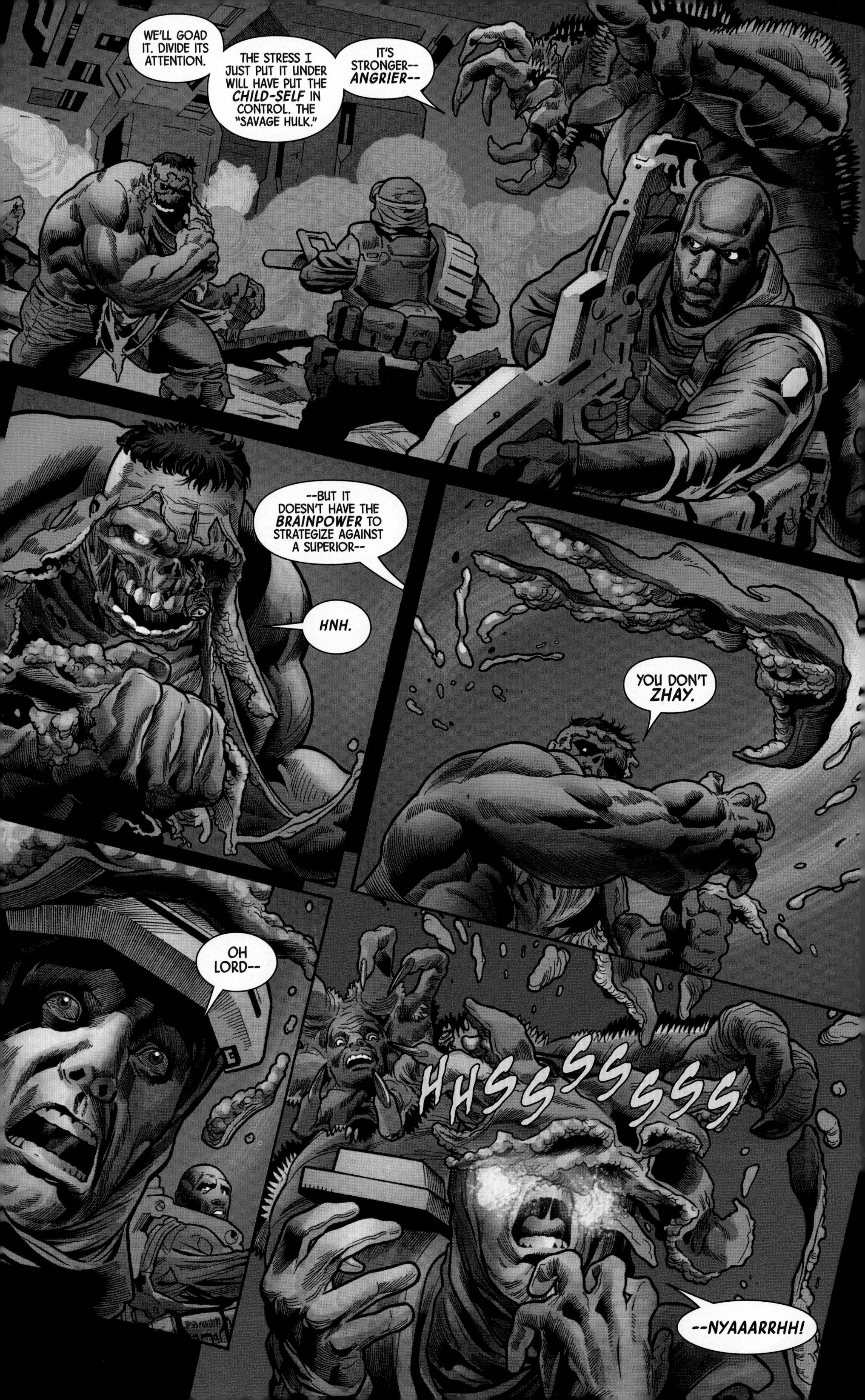
WE'LL GOAD IT. DIVIDE ITS ATTENTION.
THE STRESS I JUST PUT IT UNDER WILL HAVE PUT THE CHILD-SELF IN CONTROL. THE "SAVAGE HULK."
IT'S STRONGER-- ANGRIER--
--BUT IT DOESN'T HAVE THE BRAINPOWER TO STRATEGIZE AGAINST A SUPERIOR--
HNH.
YOU DON'T ZHAY.
OH LORD--
HHSSSSSSSSS
--NYAAARRHH!

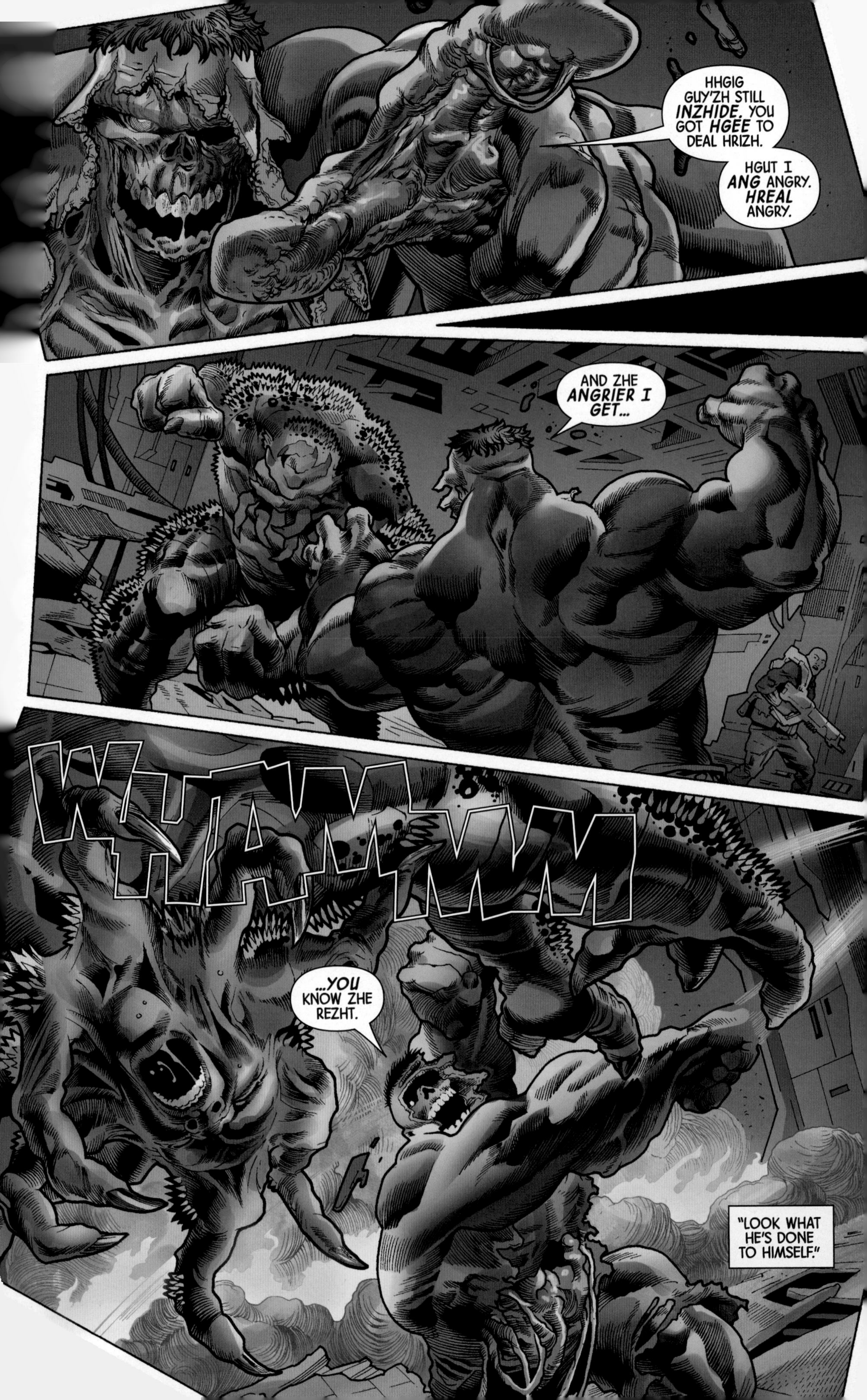
HHGIG GUY'ZH STILL INZHIDE. YOU GOT HGEE TO DEAL HRIZH.
HGUT I ANG ANGRY. HREAL ANGRY.
AND ZHE ANGRIER I GET...
WHAMMM
...YOU KNOW ZHE REZHT.
"LOOK WHAT HE'S DONE TO HIMSELF."

HE'S *DESTROYED* HIMSELF. AND NOW YOU WANT ME TO DESTROY HIM *AGAIN?*

I DON'T KNOW IF I CAN DO THAT.

WHEN THE GENERAL *FOUND* US-- THE SCIENCE TEAM, THE OPS TEAM, THE MONITORS, *ALL* OF US--

--HE PULLED US OUT OF SOME *BAD SITUATIONS. BAD DECISIONS.*

I...WAS FIRED FROM *CALTECH.* DRINK AND DRUGS. I ENDED UP WORKING IN AN *MGH* LAB.

IT WAS *UGLY* WORK, BUT...ONCE YOU'RE *IN,* THERE'S NO OUT.

THEN *DAREDEVIL* HAPPENED, AND I WENT TO *JAIL.*

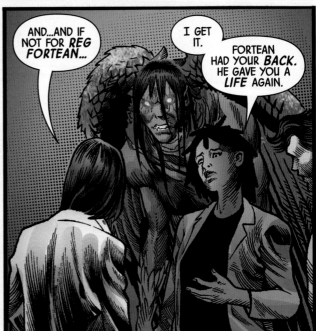

AND...AND IF NOT FOR *REG FORTEAN...*

I GET IT. *FORTEAN* HAD YOUR *BACK.* HE GAVE YOU A *LIFE* AGAIN.

YOU STILL *TRUST* HIM.

MORE THAN YOU TRUST A COUPLE OF *MONSTERS* AND THE WOMAN YOU TRIED TO *KILL...*

I'M SORRY.

THAT WASN'T MY DECISION.

NO.

IT WAS *REG FORTEAN'S.*

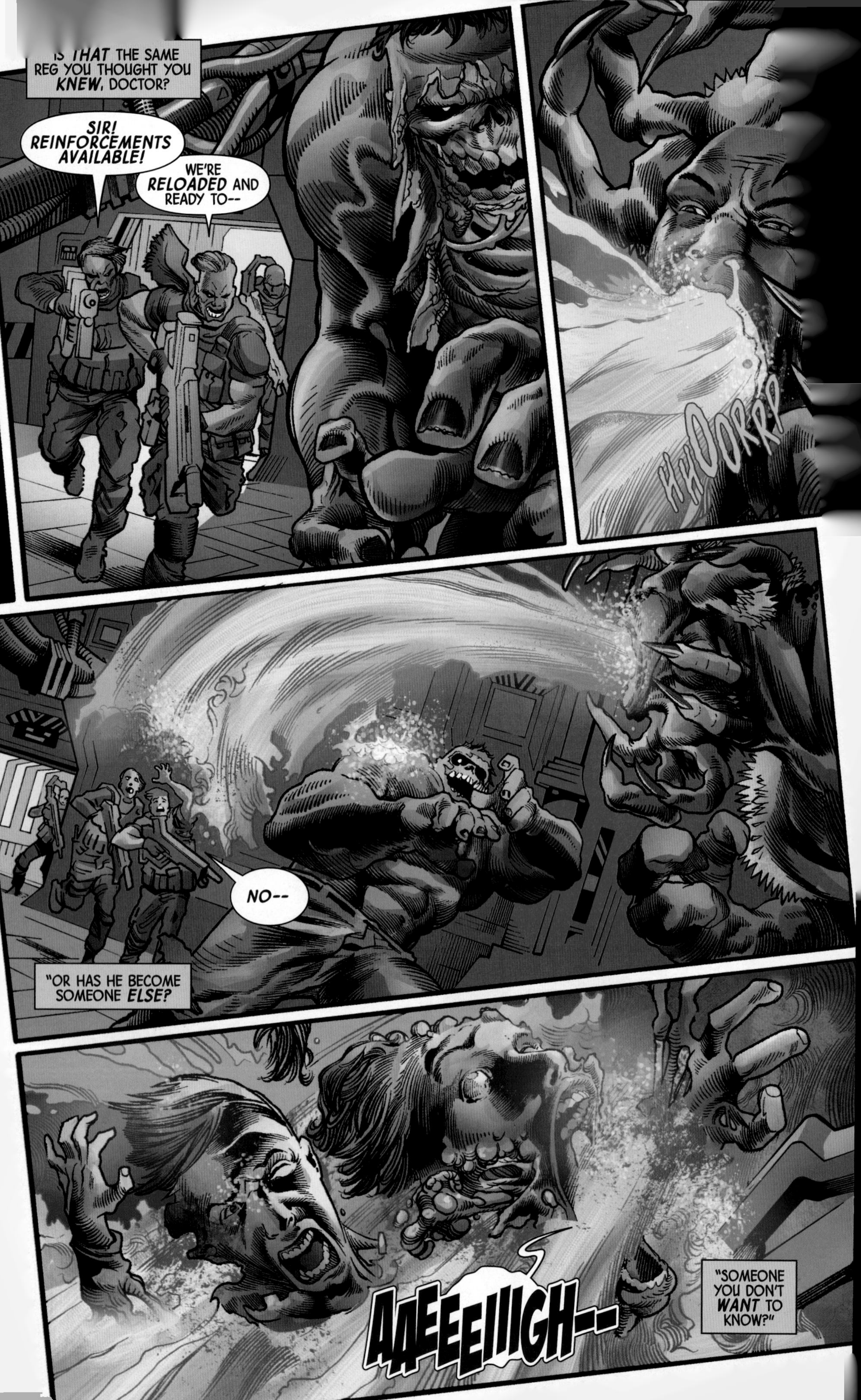
IS THAT THE SAME REG YOU THOUGHT YOU KNEW, DOCTOR?
SIR! REINFORCEMENTS AVAILABLE!
WE'RE RELOADED AND READY TO--
HHOORRP
NO--
"OR HAS HE BECOME SOMEONE ELSE?
AAEEEIIIGH--
"SOMEONE YOU DON'T WANT TO KNOW?"

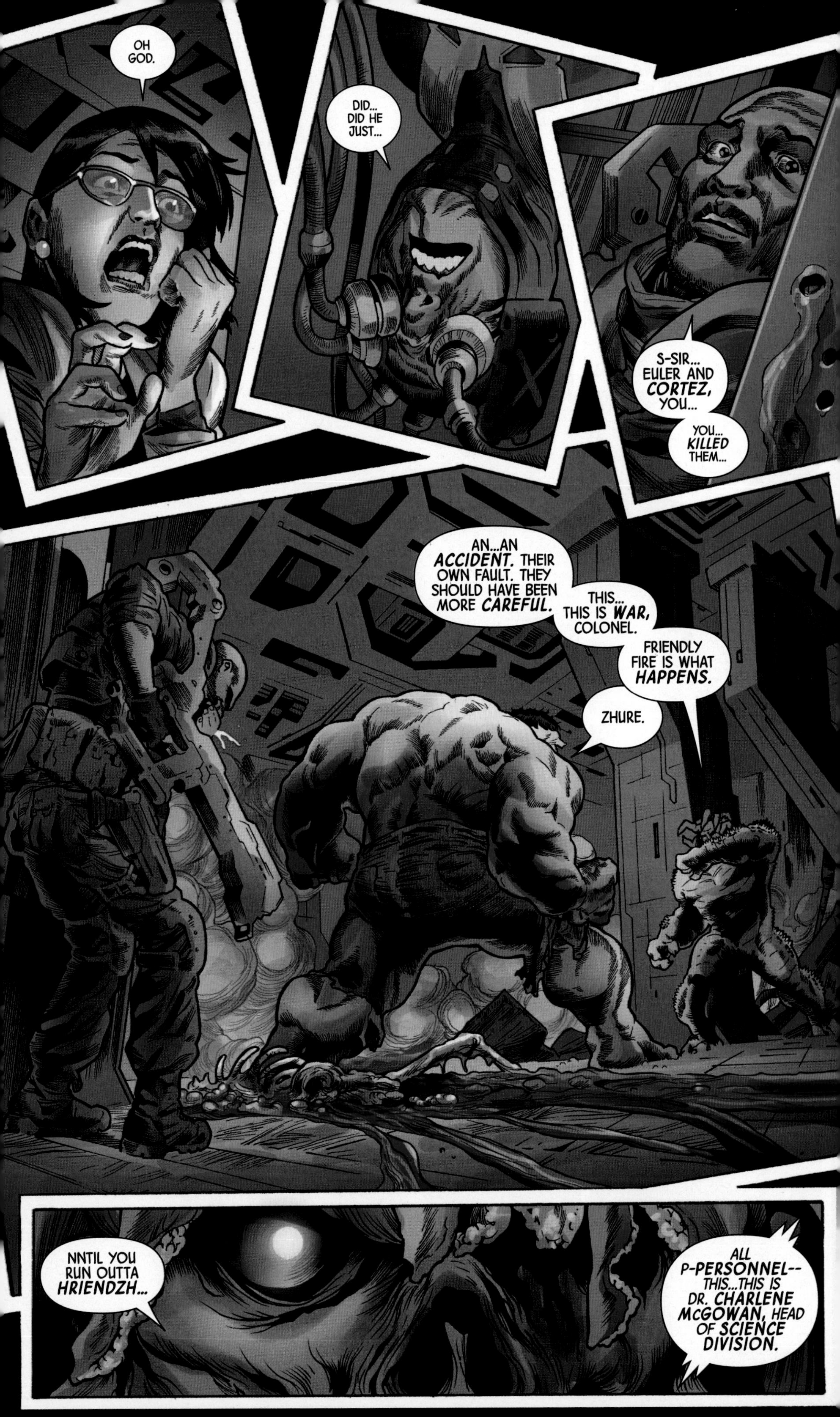
OH GOD.
DID... DID HE JUST...
S-SIR... EULER AND CORTEZ, YOU...
YOU... KILLED THEM...
AN...AN ACCIDENT. THEIR OWN FAULT. THEY SHOULD HAVE BEEN MORE CAREFUL.
THIS... THIS IS WAR, COLONEL.
FRIENDLY FIRE IS WHAT HAPPENS.
ZHURE.
NNTIL YOU RUN OUTTA HRIENDZH...
ALL P-PERSONNEL-- THIS...THIS IS DR. CHARLENE McGOWAN, HEAD OF SCIENCE DIVISION.

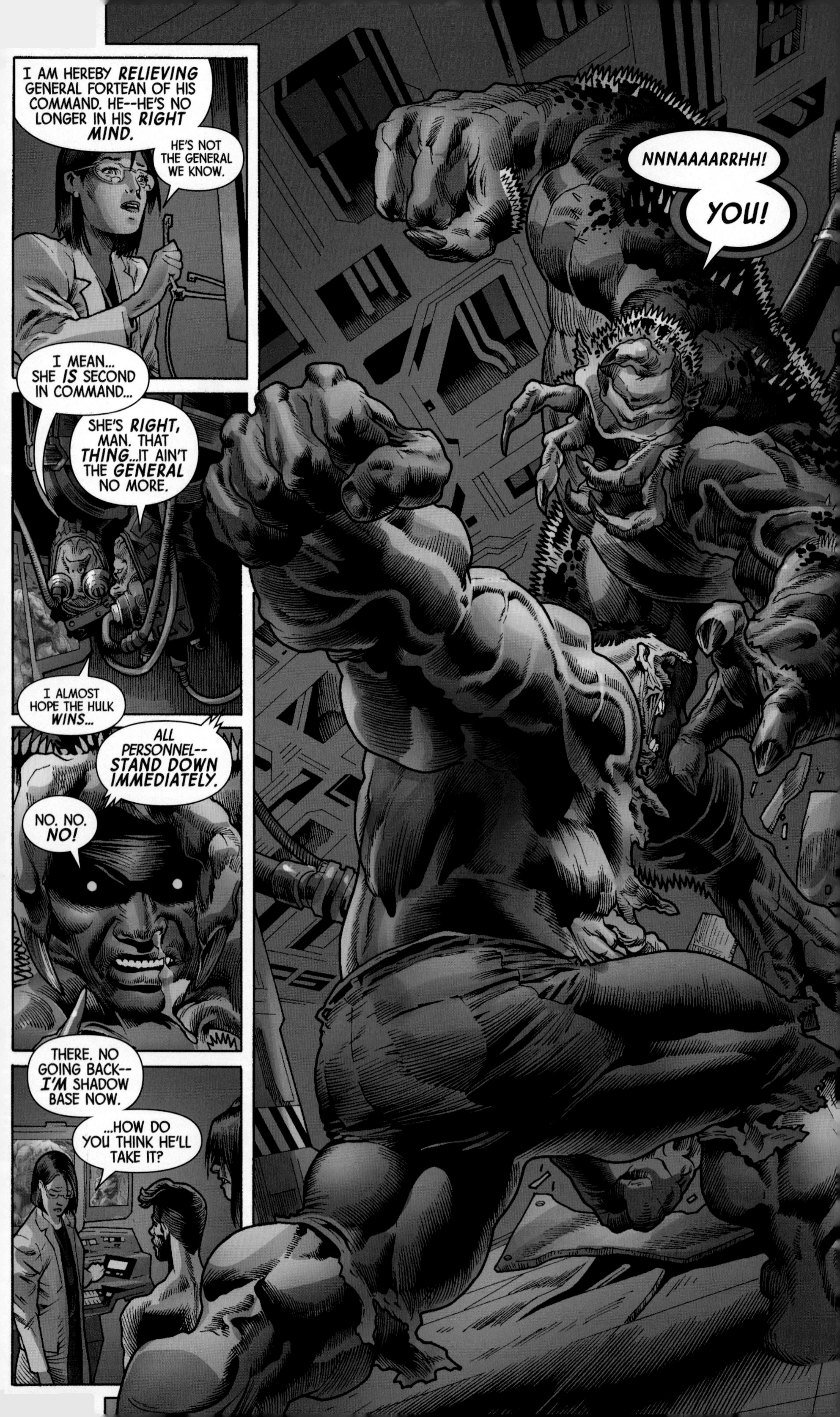
I AM HEREBY RELIEVING GENERAL FORTEAN OF HIS COMMAND. HE--HE'S NO LONGER IN HIS RIGHT MIND.
HE'S NOT THE GENERAL WE KNOW.
I MEAN... SHE IS SECOND IN COMMAND...
SHE'S RIGHT, MAN. THAT THING...IT AIN'T THE GENERAL NO MORE.
I ALMOST HOPE THE HULK WINS...
ALL PERSONNEL-- STAND DOWN IMMEDIATELY.
NO. NO. NO!
THERE. NO GOING BACK-- I'M SHADOW BASE NOW.
...HOW DO YOU THINK HE'LL TAKE IT?
NNNAAAARRHH!
YOU!

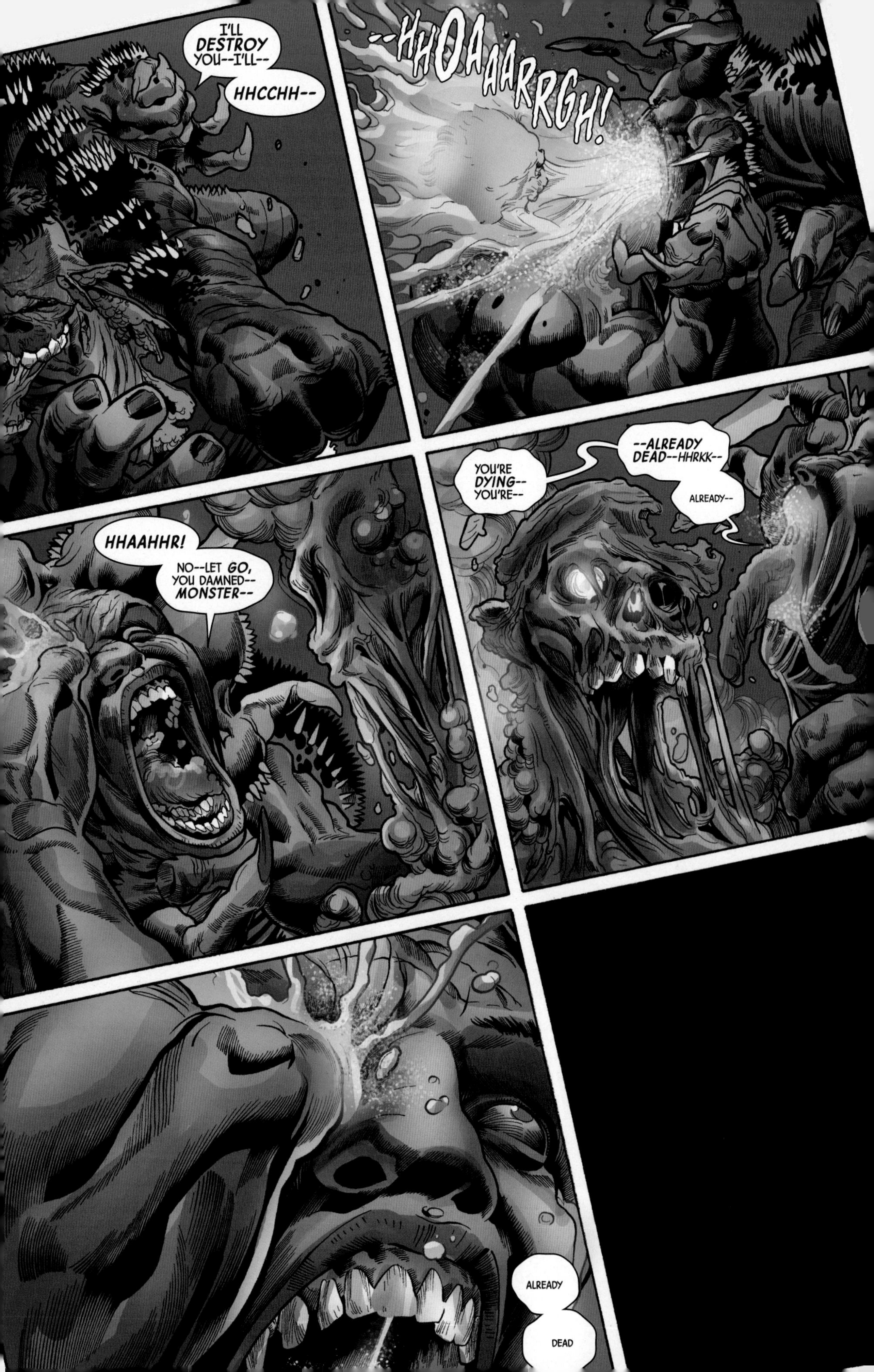
I'LL DESTROY YOU--I'LL--
HHCCHH--
--HHOAAARRGH!
YOU'RE DYING--YOU'RE--
--ALREADY DEAD--HHRKK--
ALREADY--
HHAAHHR!
NO--LET GO, YOU DAMNED--MONSTER--
ALREADY
DEAD

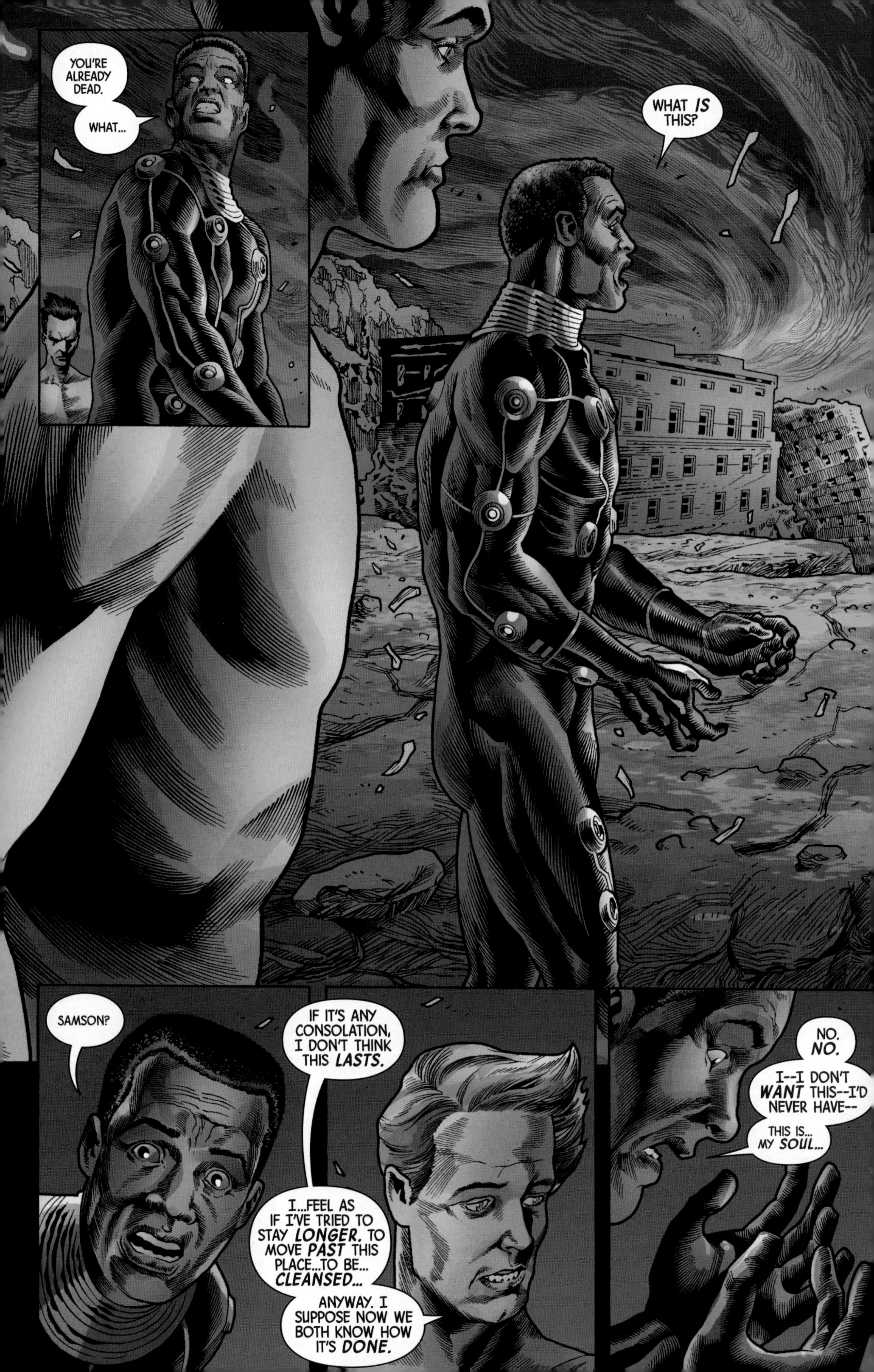
YOU'RE ALREADY DEAD.
WHAT...
WHAT *IS* THIS?
SAMSON?
IF IT'S ANY CONSOLATION, I DON'T THINK THIS *LASTS.*
I...FEEL AS IF I'VE TRIED TO STAY *LONGER.* TO MOVE *PAST* THIS PLACE...TO BE... *CLEANSED...*
ANYWAY. I SUPPOSE NOW WE BOTH KNOW HOW IT'S *DONE.*
NO. *NO.*
I--I DON'T *WANT* THIS--I'D NEVER HAVE--
THIS IS... MY *SOUL...*

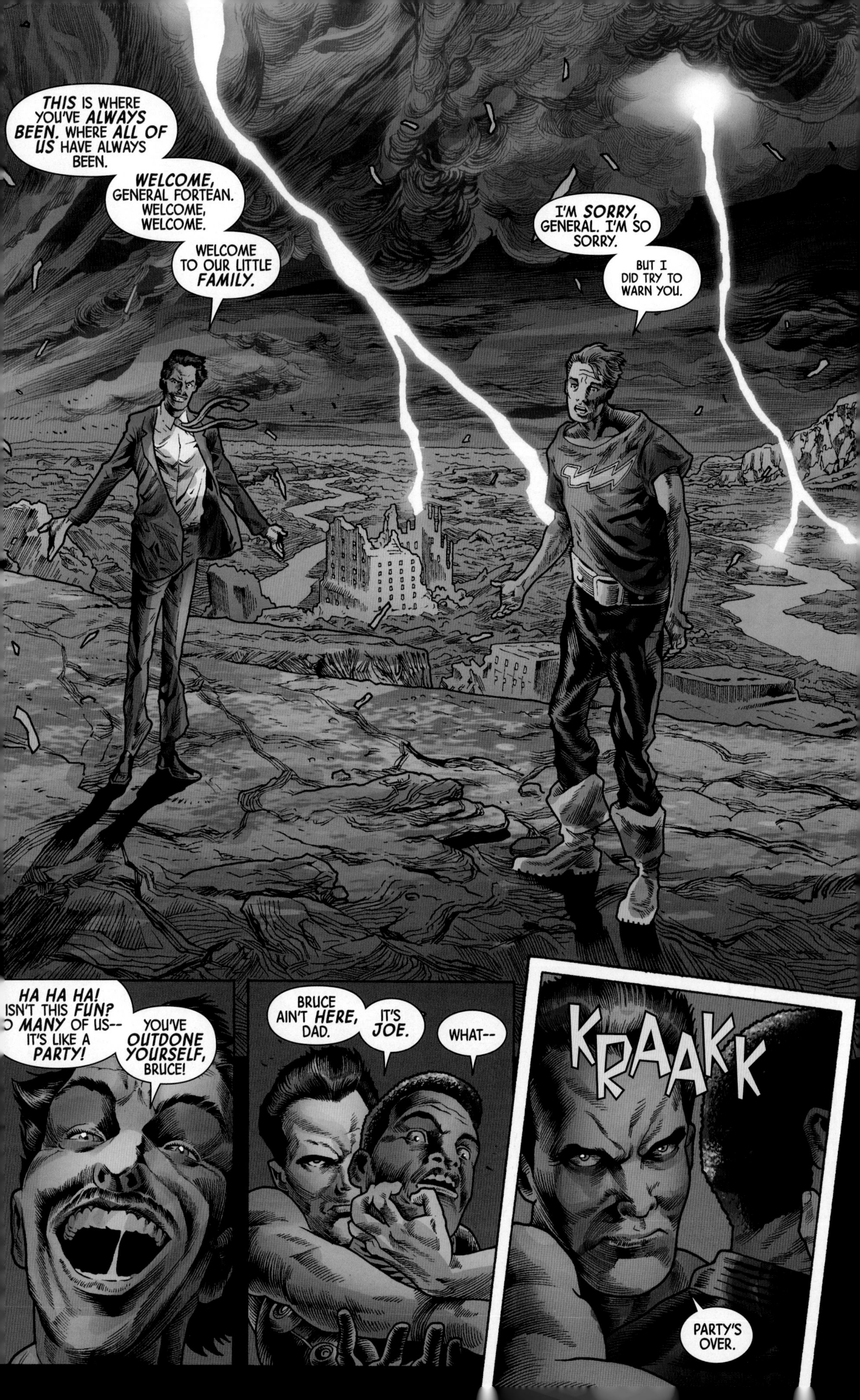
THIS IS WHERE YOU'VE ALWAYS BEEN. WHERE ALL OF US HAVE ALWAYS BEEN.
WELCOME, GENERAL FORTEAN. WELCOME, WELCOME.
WELCOME TO OUR LITTLE FAMILY.
I'M SORRY, GENERAL. I'M SO SORRY.
BUT I DID TRY TO WARN YOU.
HA HA HA! ISN'T THIS FUN? SO MANY OF US-- IT'S LIKE A PARTY!
YOU'VE OUTDONE YOURSELF, BRUCE!
BRUCE AIN'T HERE, DAD.
IT'S JOE.
WHAT--
KRAAKK
PARTY'S OVER.

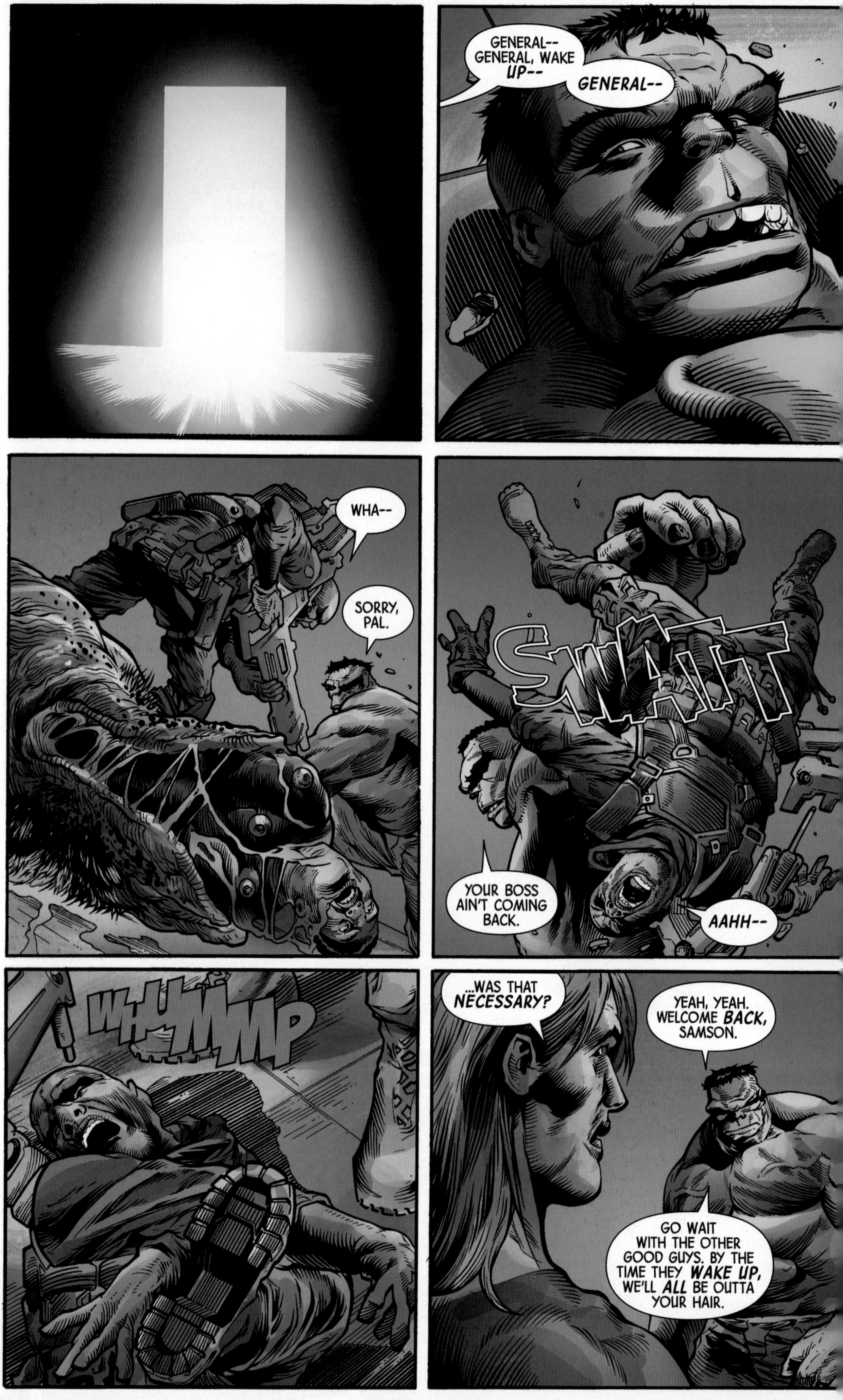
GENERAL-- GENERAL, WAKE UP--
GENERAL--
WHA--
SORRY, PAL.
SWAT
YOUR BOSS AIN'T COMING BACK.
AAHH--
WHUMMMP
...WAS THAT NECESSARY?
YEAH, YEAH. WELCOME BACK, SAMSON.
GO WAIT WITH THE OTHER GOOD GUYS. BY THE TIME THEY WAKE UP, WE'LL ALL BE OUTTA YOUR HAIR.

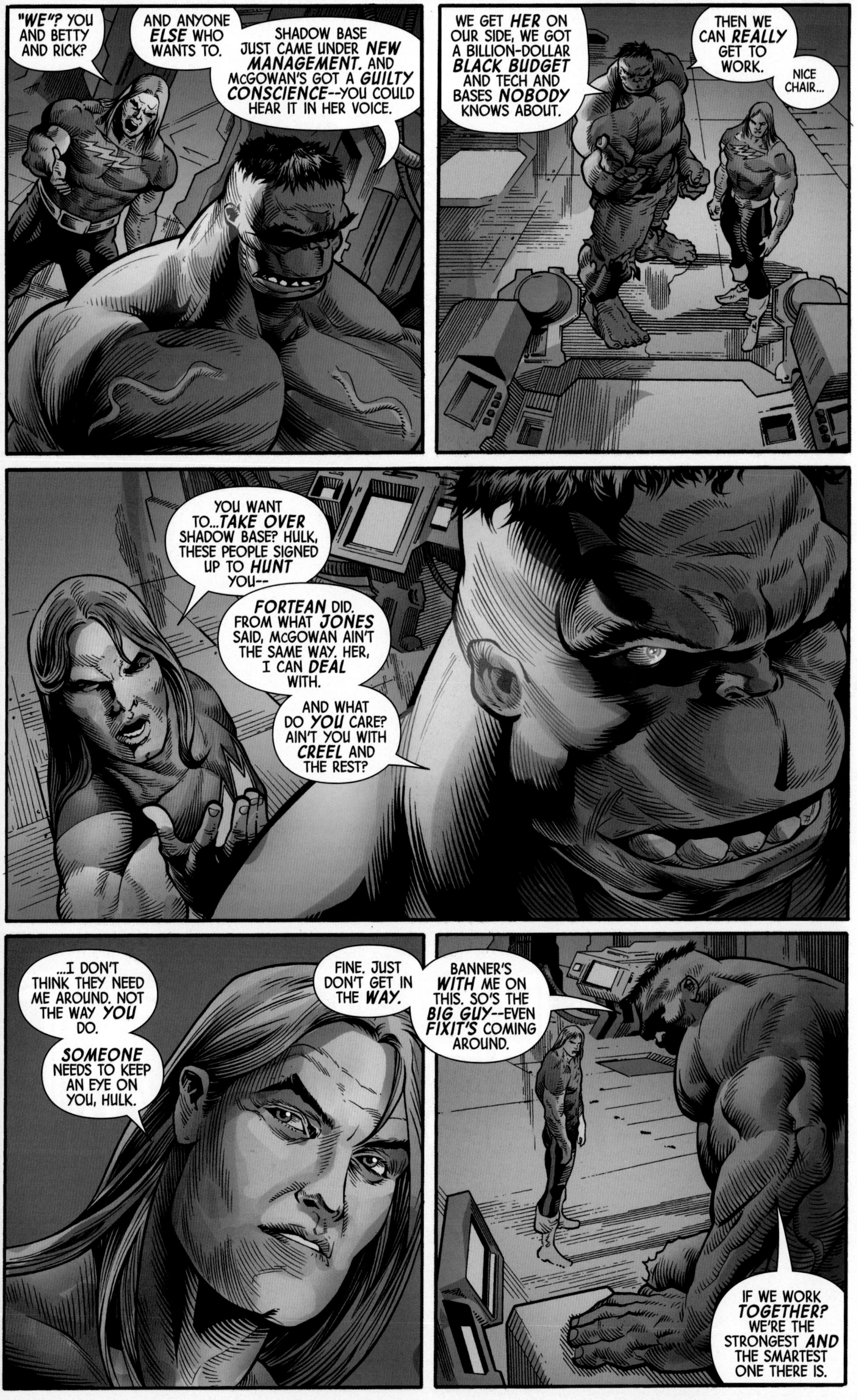
"WE"? YOU AND BETTY AND RICK?
AND ANYONE ELSE WHO WANTS TO.
SHADOW BASE JUST CAME UNDER NEW MANAGEMENT. AND McGOWAN'S GOT A GUILTY CONSCIENCE--YOU COULD HEAR IT IN HER VOICE.
WE GET HER ON OUR SIDE, WE GOT A BILLION-DOLLAR BLACK BUDGET AND TECH AND BASES NOBODY KNOWS ABOUT.
THEN WE CAN REALLY GET TO WORK.
NICE CHAIR...
YOU WANT TO...TAKE OVER SHADOW BASE? HULK, THESE PEOPLE SIGNED UP TO HUNT YOU--
FORTEAN DID. FROM WHAT JONES SAID, McGOWAN AIN'T THE SAME WAY. HER, I CAN DEAL WITH.
AND WHAT DO YOU CARE? AIN'T YOU WITH CREEL AND THE REST?
...I DON'T THINK THEY NEED ME AROUND. NOT THE WAY YOU DO.
SOMEONE NEEDS TO KEEP AN EYE ON YOU, HULK.
FINE. JUST DON'T GET IN THE WAY.
BANNER'S WITH ME ON THIS. SO'S THE BIG GUY--EVEN FIXIT'S COMING AROUND.
IF WE WORK TOGETHER? WE'RE THE STRONGEST AND THE SMARTEST ONE THERE IS.

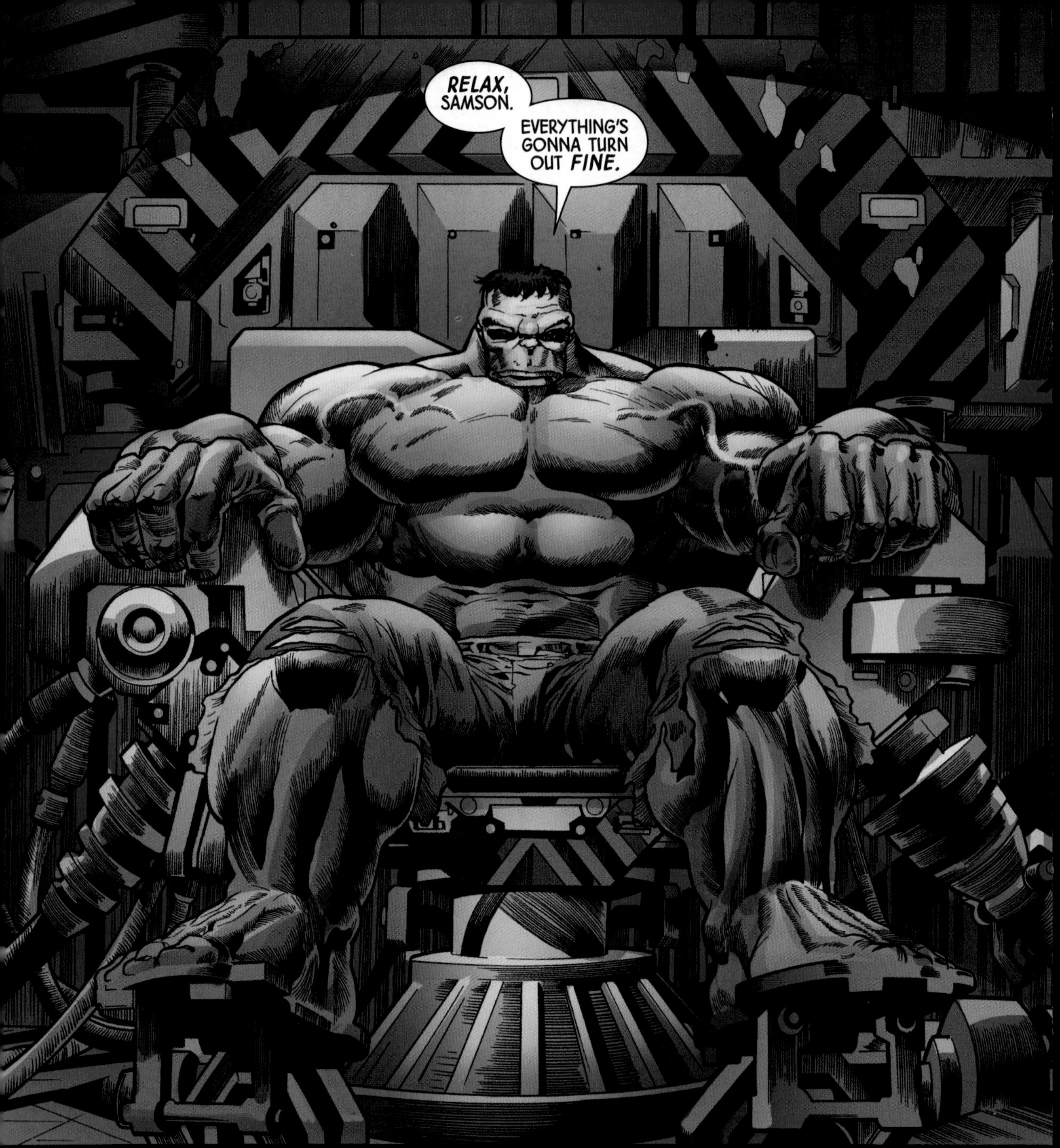
RELAX, SAMSON.
EVERYTHING'S GONNA TURN OUT FINE.

THE STEEL THRONE

EONS FROM NOW.

AT THE END OF ALL THINGS.

Bruce Banner
of Earth.

I am the
Sentience of the Cosmos...

...and you are its
last survivor.

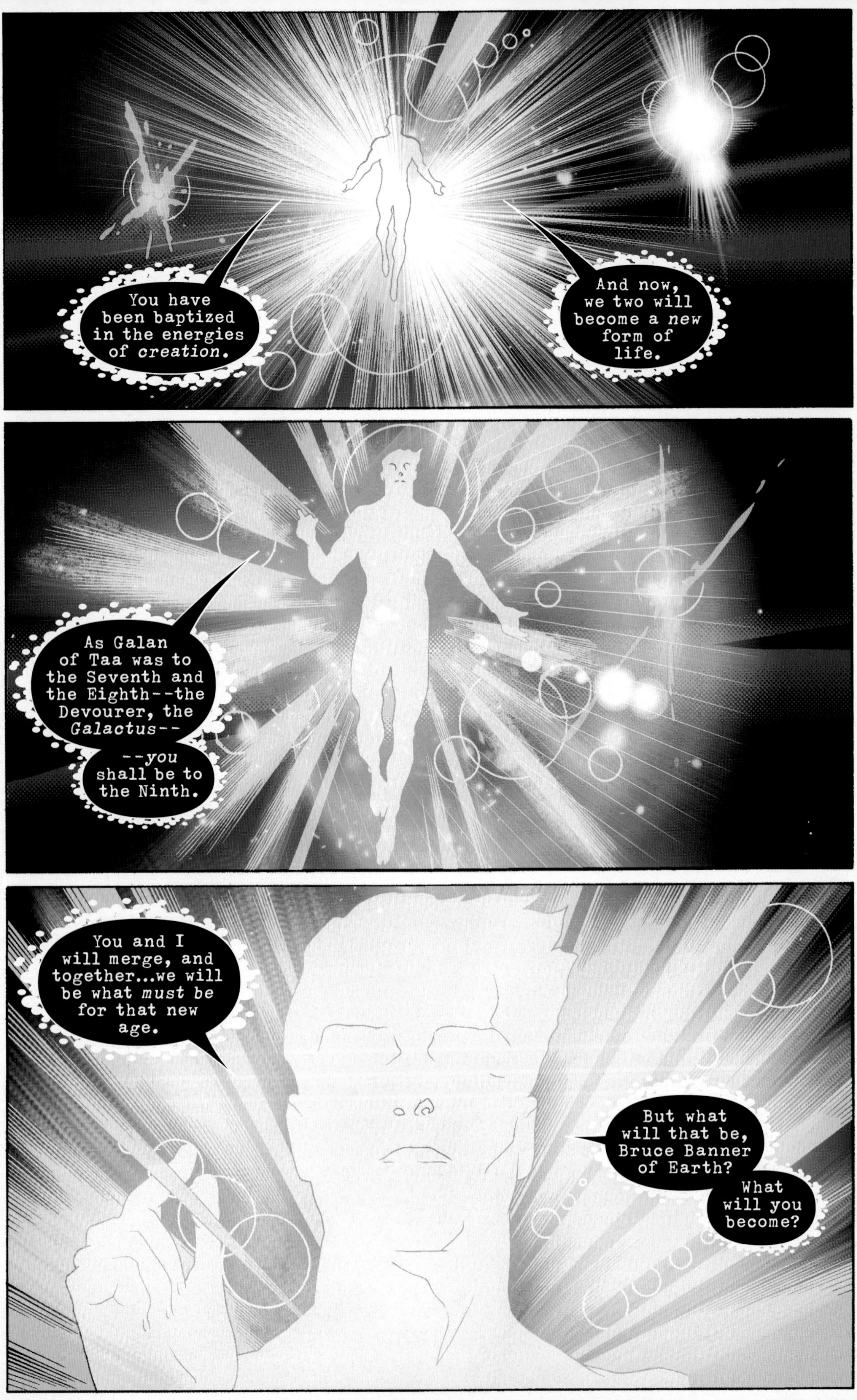
You have been baptized in the energies of *creation*.
And now, we two will become a *new* form of life.
As Galan of Taa was to the Seventh and the Eighth--the Devourer, the *Galactus*--
--*you* shall be to the Ninth.
You and I will merge, and together...we will be what *must be* for that new age.
But what will that be, Bruce Banner of Earth?
What will you become?

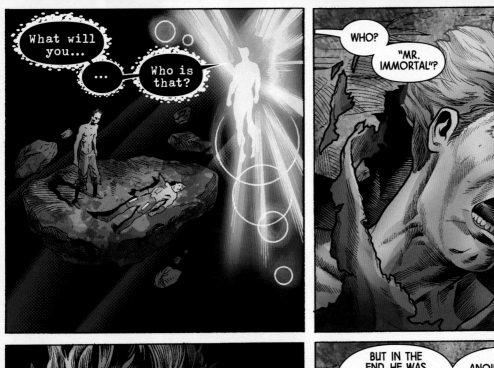

What will you...

...

Who is that?

WHO? "MR. IMMORTAL"?

HIS REAL NAME WAS CRAIG.

HE WAS... HOMO SUPREME. THE ULTIMATE EVOLUTION OF MUTANT POWER.

HE THOUGHT THAT MADE HIM SPECIAL.

BUT IN THE END, HE WAS JUST A BACKUP. SOMEONE TO STAND HERE, MEET YOU, DO...THIS...

...IF THE ANOINTED PRINCE, FRANKLIN RICHARDS, COULDN'T MAKE IT.

I KILLED FRANKLIN RICHARDS TWO BILLION YEARS AGO.

THE SAME WAY I KILLED CRAIG. AND YOUR GALACTUS.

AND ALL THE REST OF THEM...

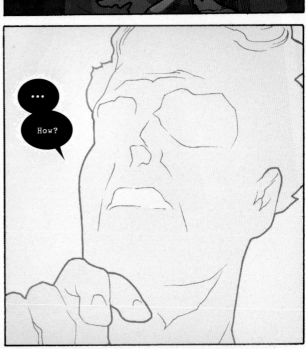

...

How?

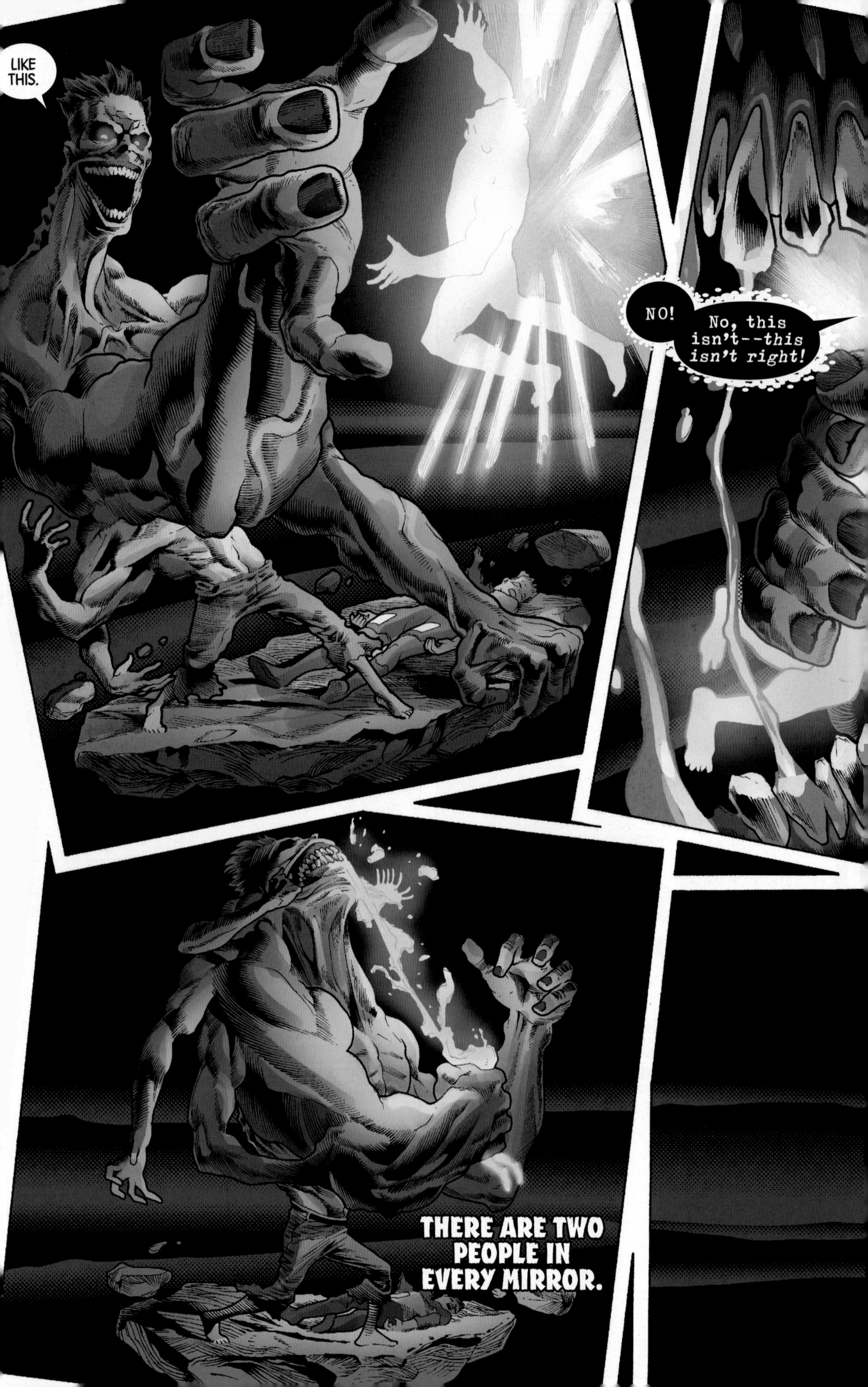
LIKE THIS.
NO!
No, this isn't--this isn't right!
THERE ARE TWO PEOPLE IN EVERY MIRROR.

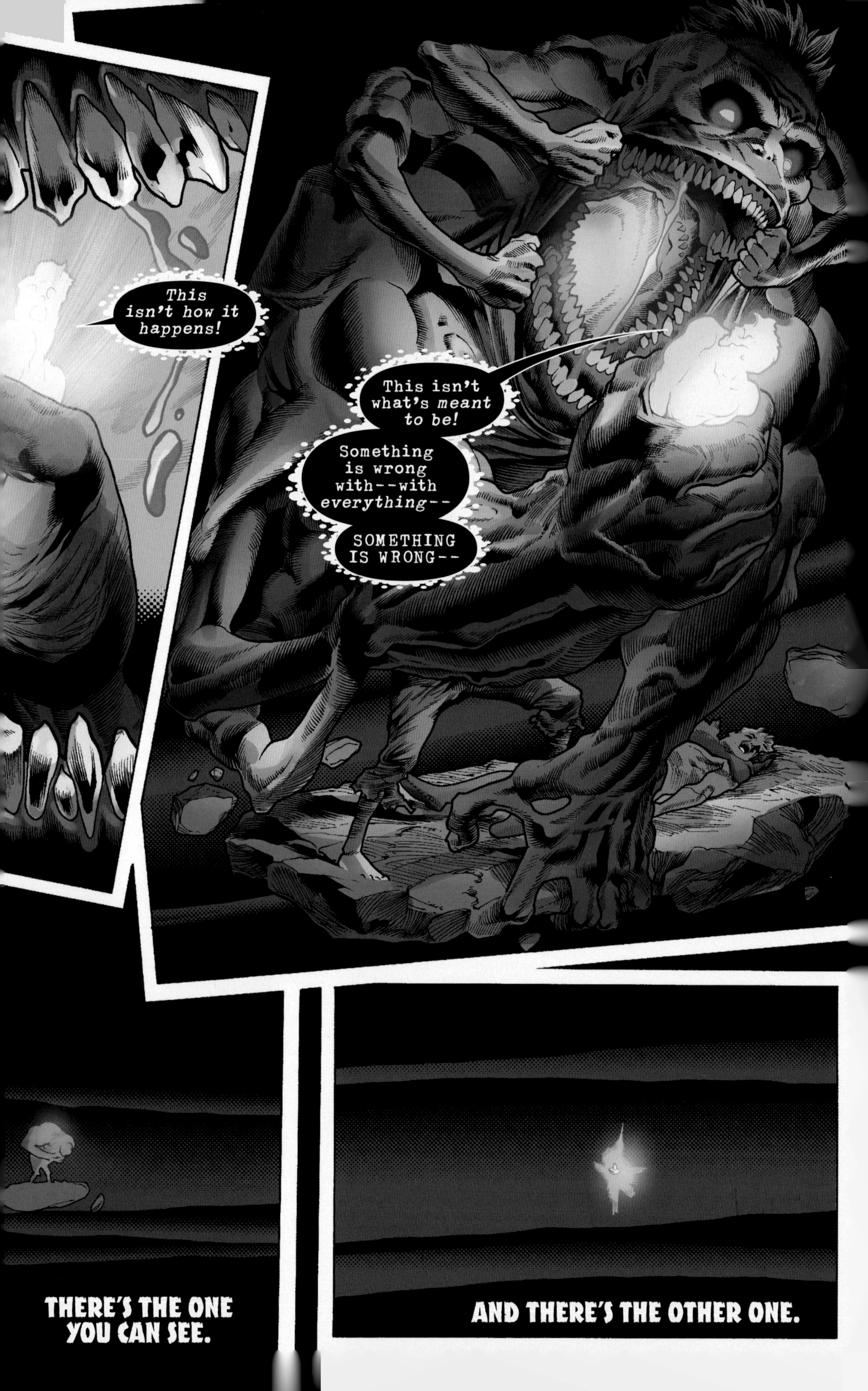
This isn't how it happens!
This isn't what's *meant* to be!
Something is wrong with--with *everything*--
SOMETHING IS WRONG--
THERE'S THE ONE YOU CAN SEE.
AND THERE'S THE OTHER ONE.

THE ONE YOU DON'T WANT TO.

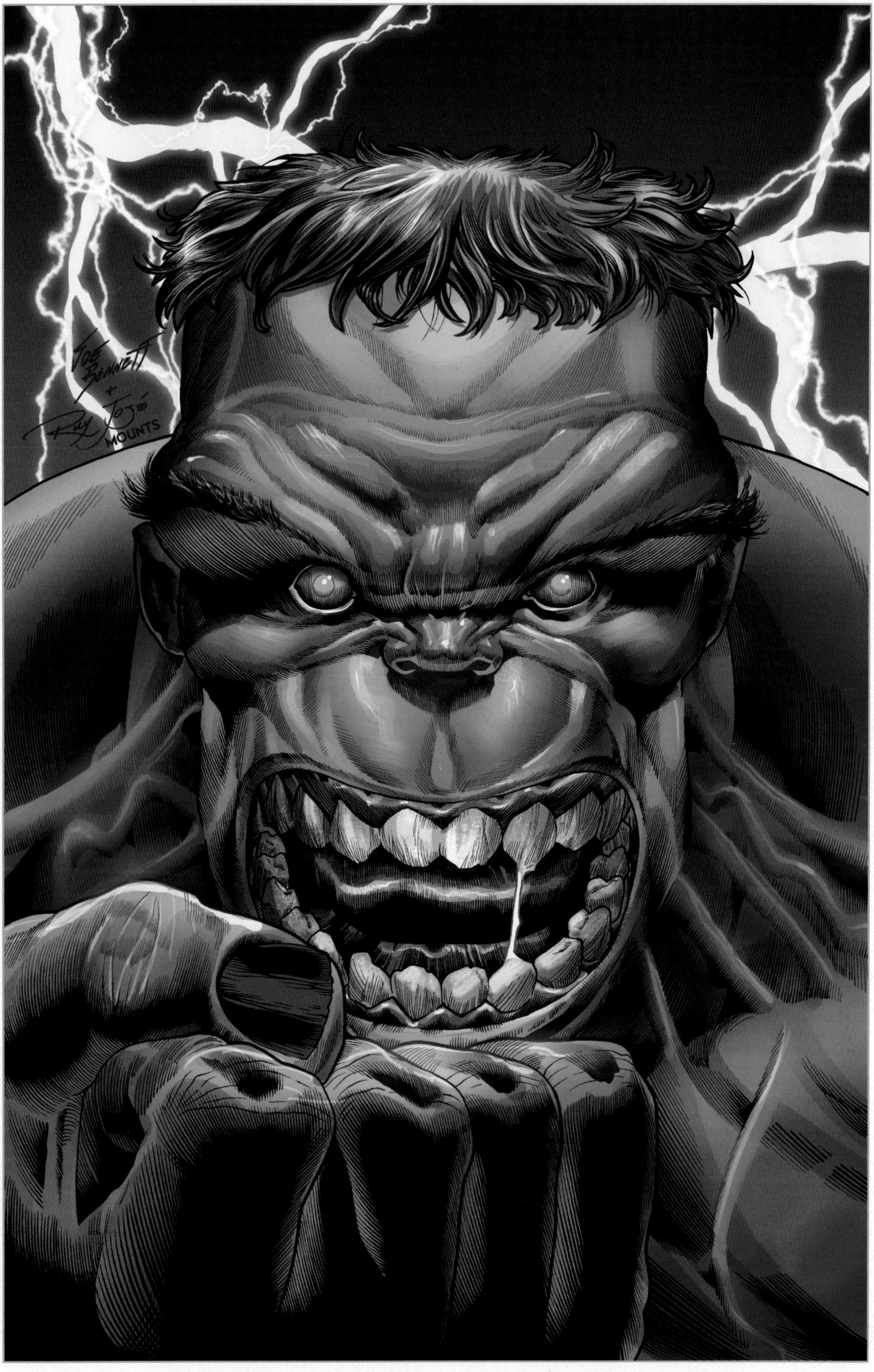
MOUNTS

#25 VARIANT BY JOE BENNETT, RUY JOSÉ & PAUL MOUNTS

25

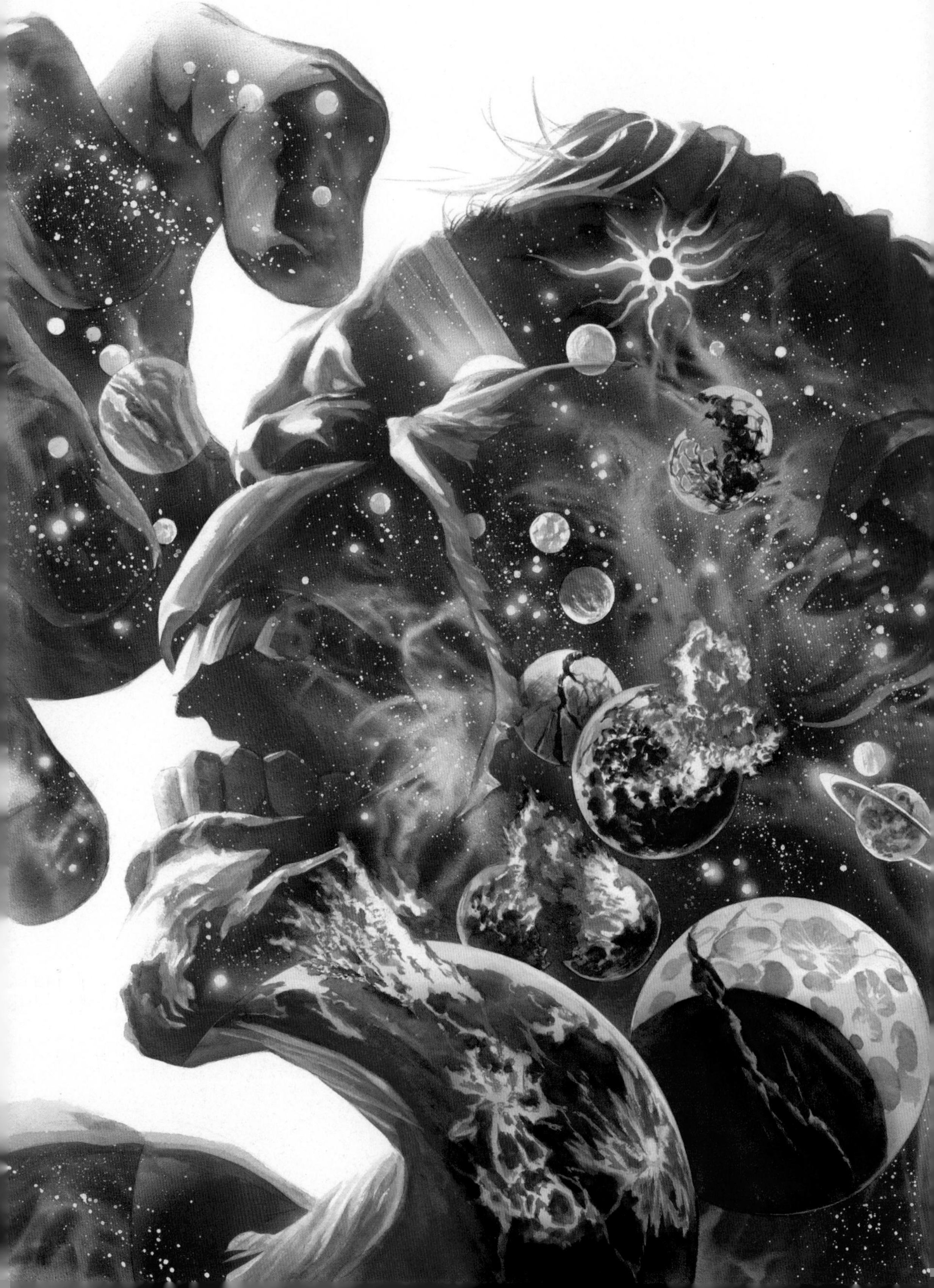

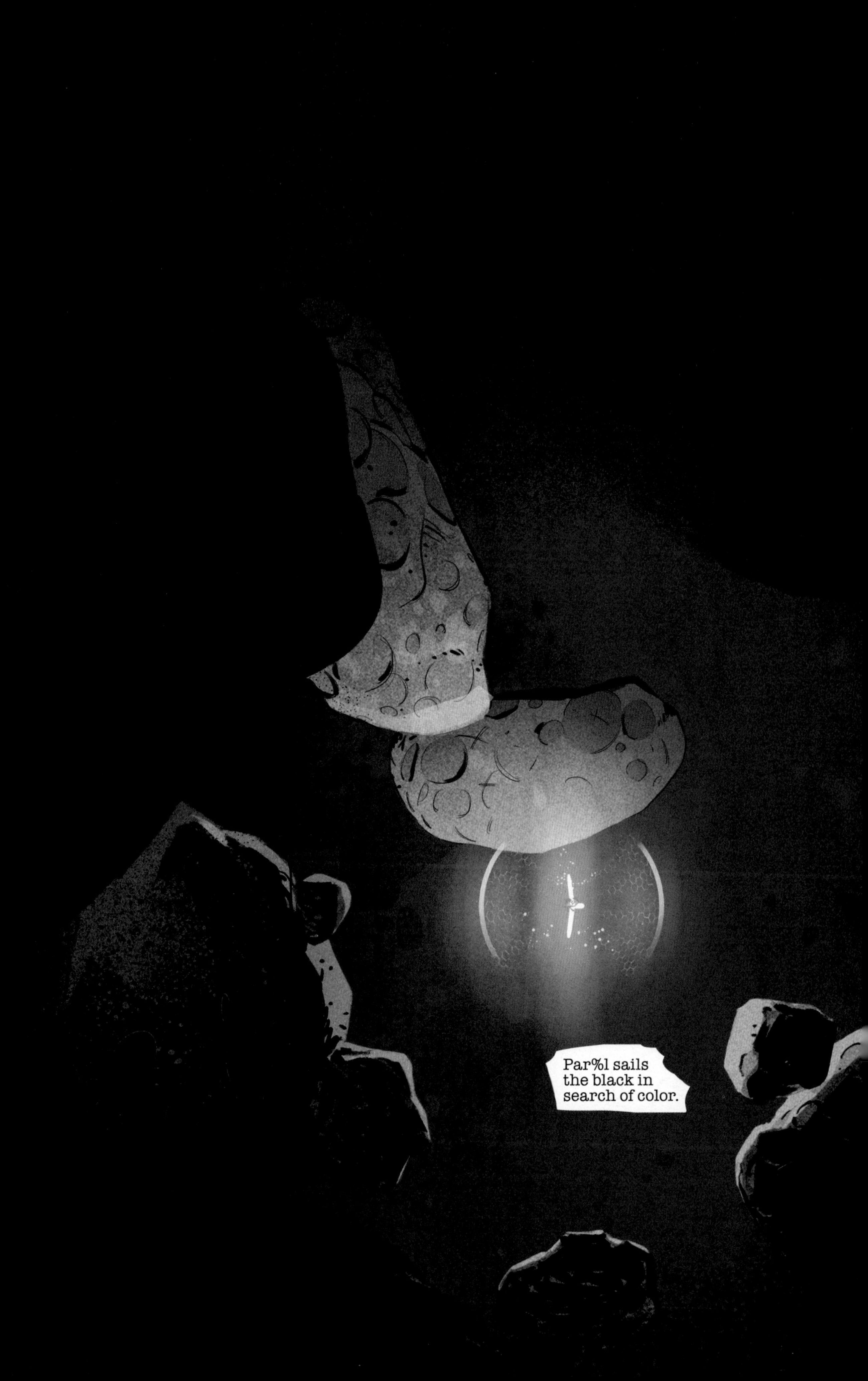
Par%l sails the black in search of color.

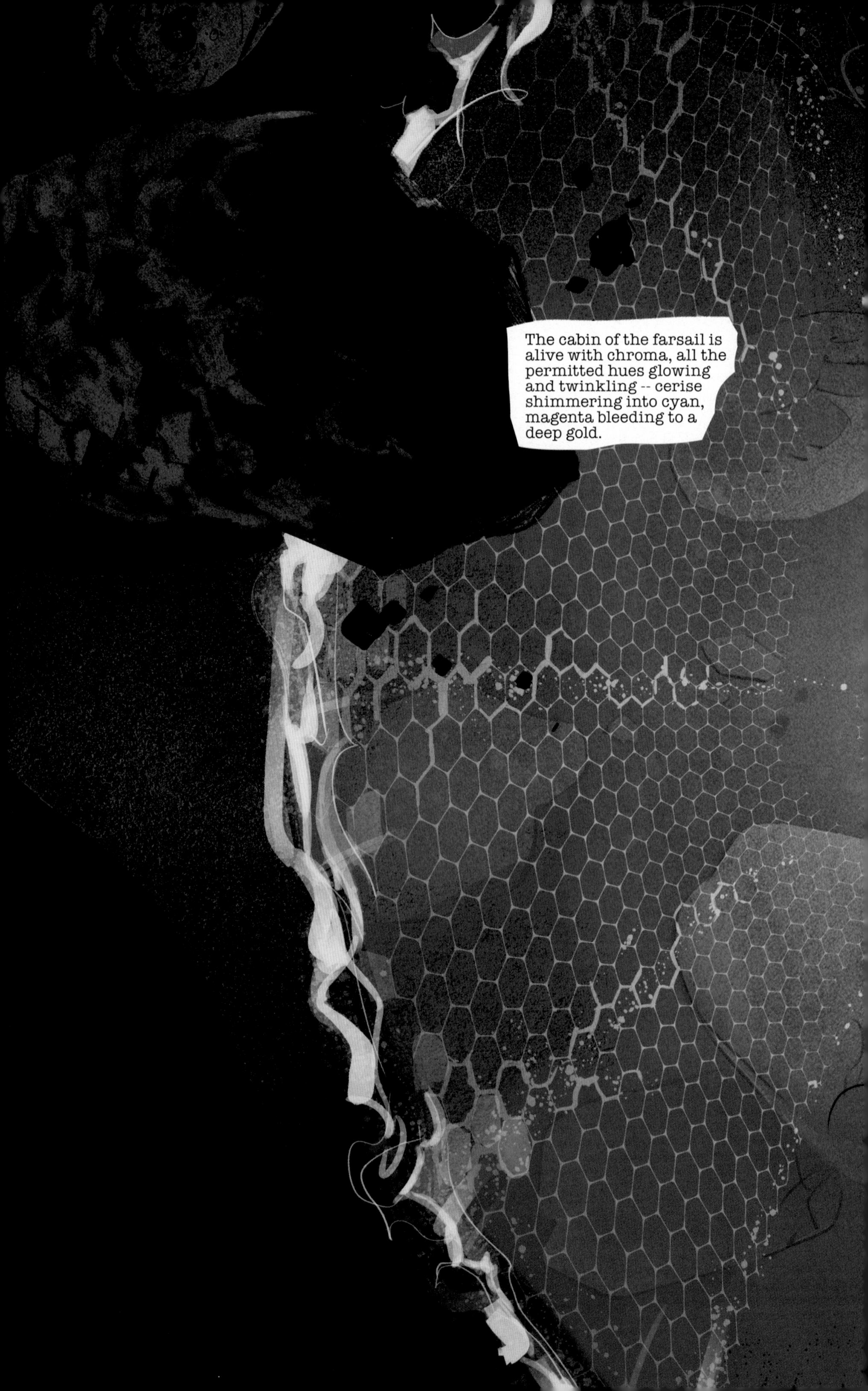
The cabin of the farsail is alive with chroma, all the permitted hues glowing and twinkling -- cerise shimmering into cyan, magenta bleeding to a deep gold.

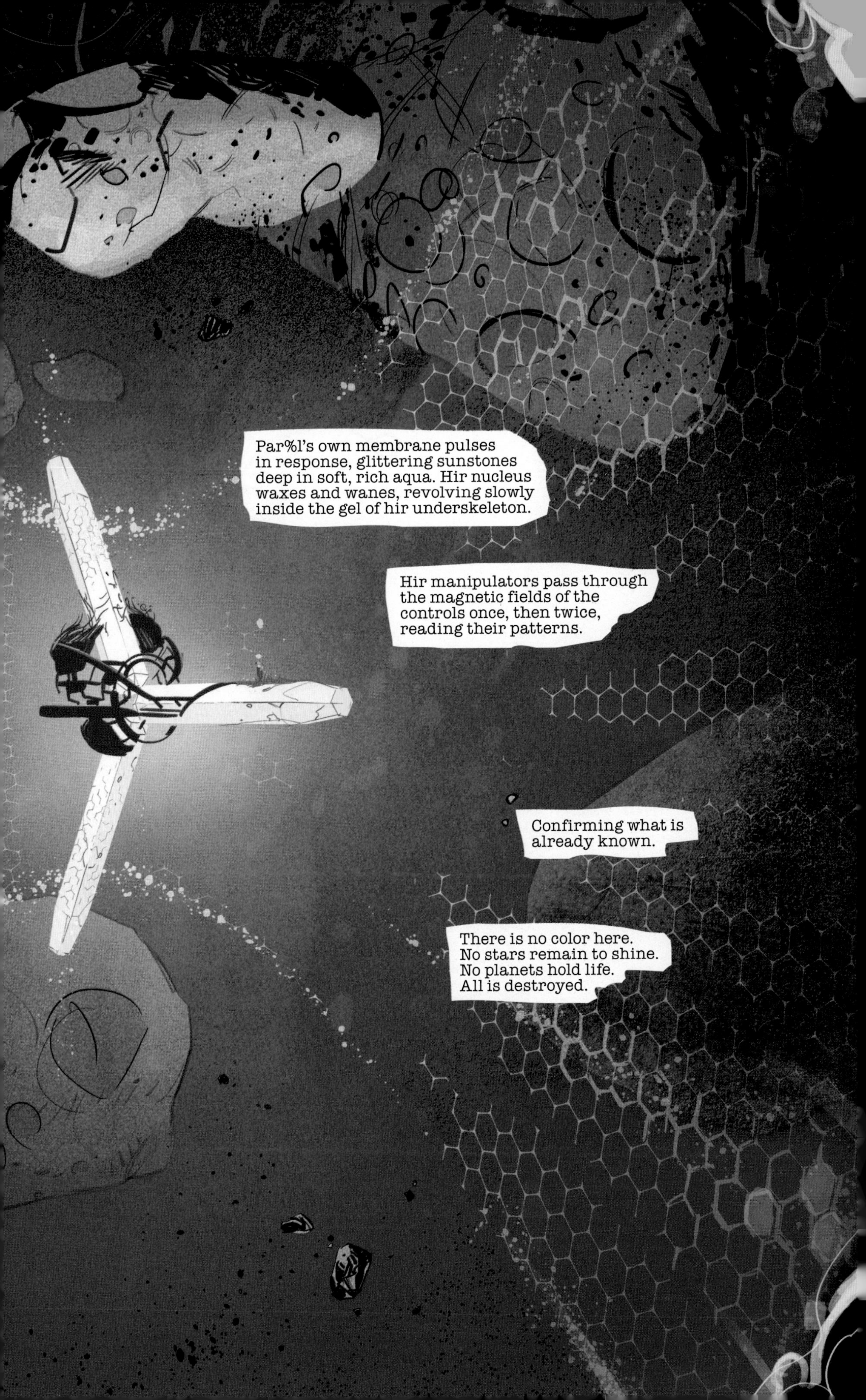
Par%l's own membrane pulses in response, glittering sunstones deep in soft, rich aqua. Hir nucleus waxes and wanes, revolving slowly inside the gel of hir underskeleton.
Hir manipulators pass through the magnetic fields of the controls once, then twice, reading their patterns.
Confirming what is already known.
There is no color here. No stars remain to shine. No planets hold life. All is destroyed.

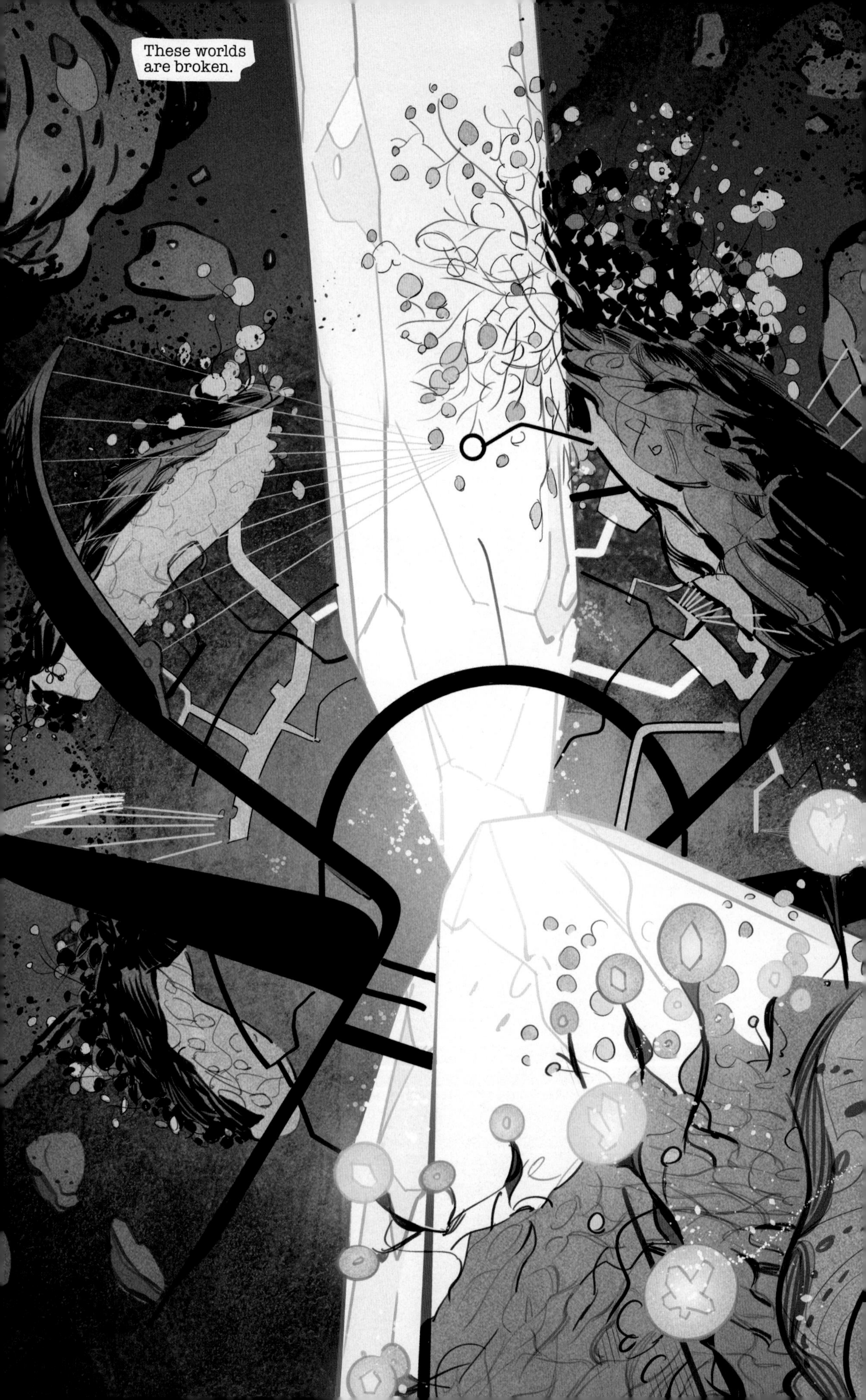
These worlds are broken.

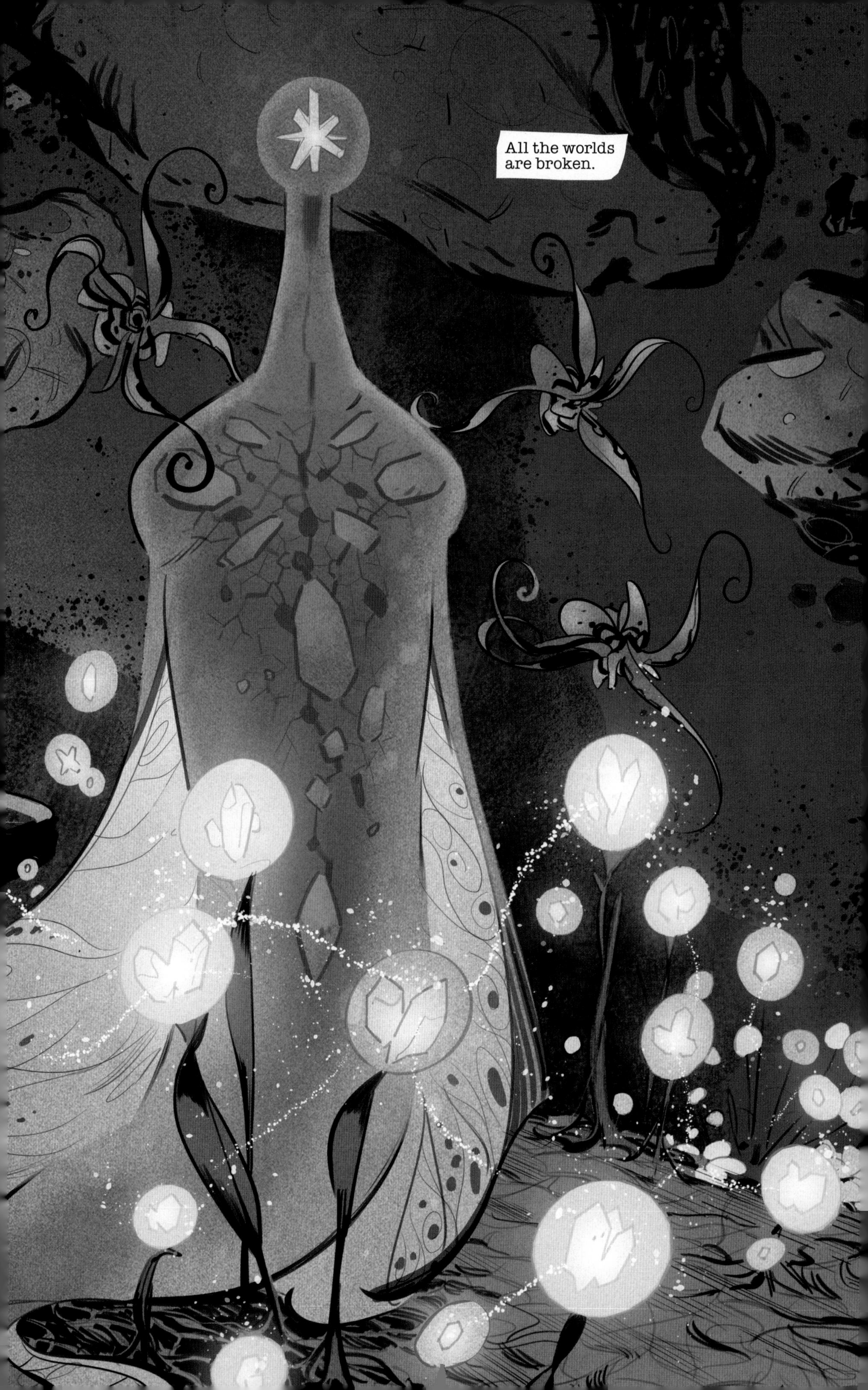
All the worlds are broken.

BREAKER

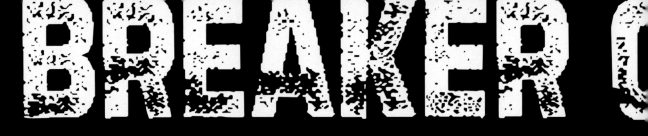

F WORLDS

"IT IS A FEARFUL THING TO FALL INTO THE HANDS OF THE LIVING GOD."

– HEBREWS 10:31

Once, the Observer's Berth tacked to the starlight, intricate pseudo-minds choreographing its motions as it danced through the orbits of planets.

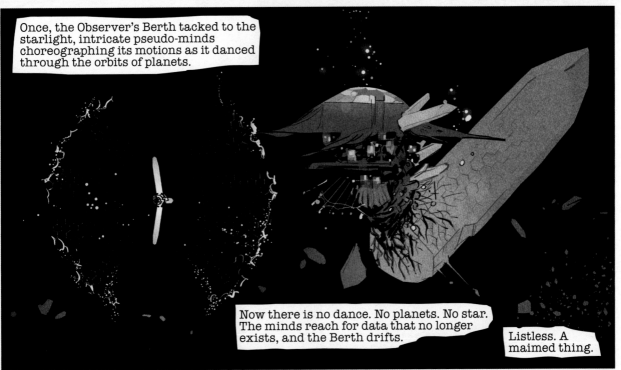

Now there is no dance. No planets. No star. The minds reach for data that no longer exists, and the Berth drifts.

Listless. A maimed thing.

It makes docking easier, but still, Par%l is careful. Should the lamina suffer damage during the linking process, there can be no repair.

Not anymore.

Par%l telepathically summons hir manipulators, carefully arranging them in the configuration for polite greeting to a superior.

The etiquette is very important.

It is all they have left.

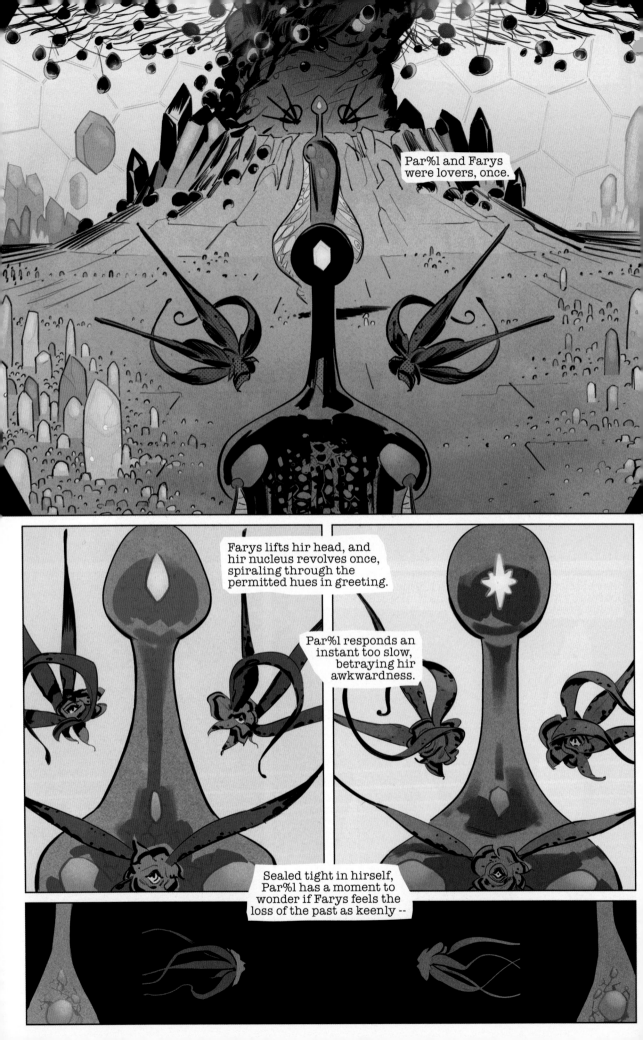

Par%l and Farys were lovers, once.

Farys lifts hir head, and hir nucleus revolves once, spiraling through the permitted hues in greeting.

Par%l responds an instant too slow, betraying hir awkwardness.

Sealed tight in hirself, Par%l has a moment to wonder if Farys feels the loss of the past as keenly --

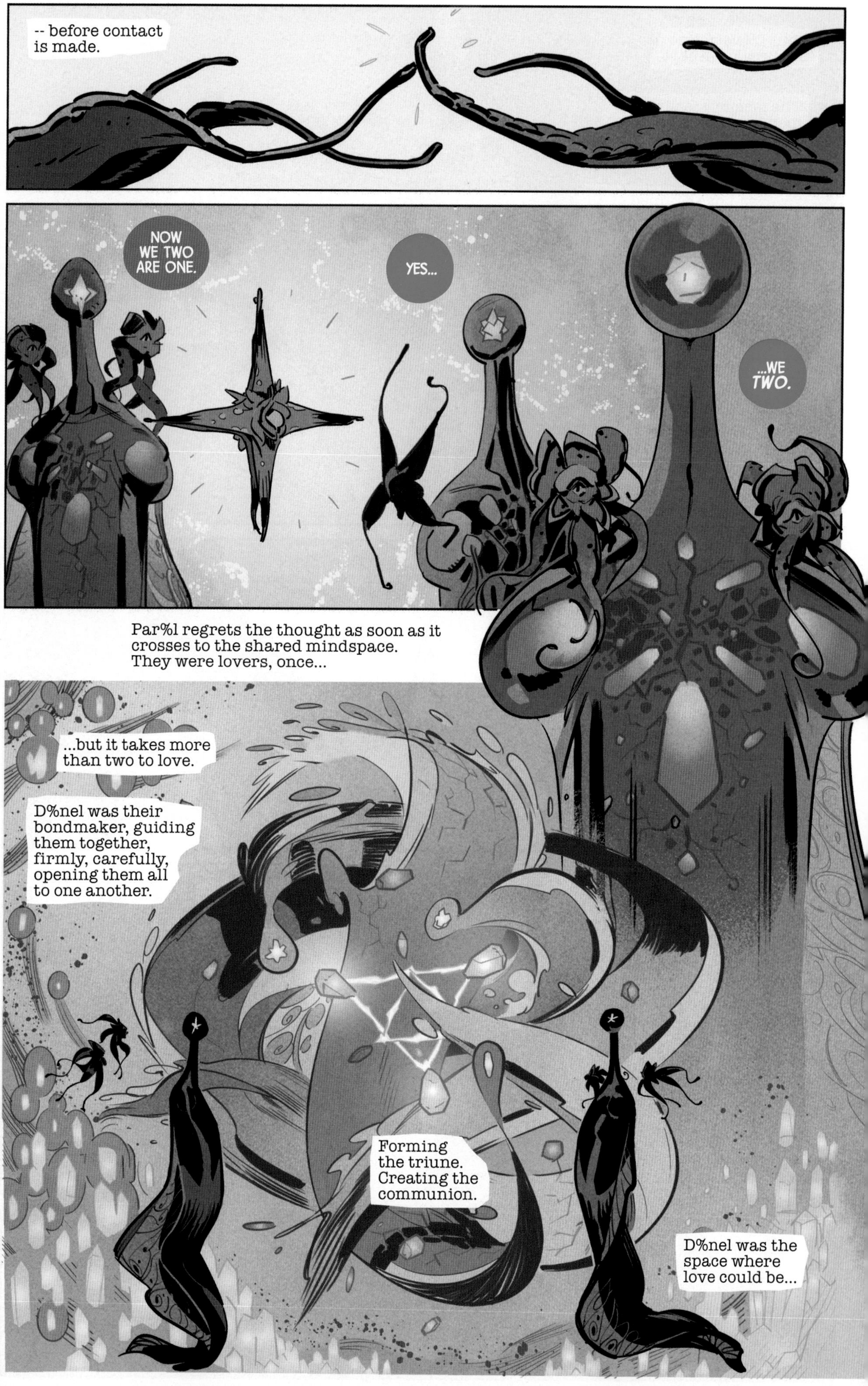

-- before contact is made.
NOW WE TWO ARE ONE.
YES...
...WE TWO.
Par%l regrets the thought as soon as it crosses to the shared mindspace. They were lovers, once...
...but it takes more than two to love.
D%nel was their bondmaker, guiding them together, firmly, carefully, opening them all to one another.
Forming the triune. Creating the communion.
D%nel was the space where love could be...

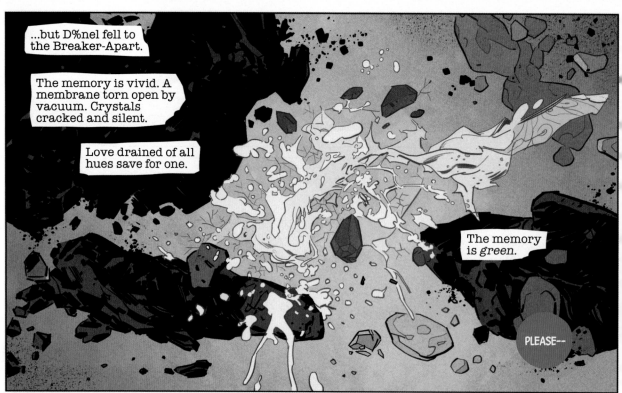

...but D%nel fell to the Breaker-Apart.

The memory is vivid. A membrane torn open by vacuum. Crystals cracked and silent.

Love drained of all hues save for one.

The memory is *green*.

PLEASE--

PLEASE. MY *OWN* PAIN IS TOO MUCH AS IT IS.

WE MUST THINK OF OUR *DUTIES*...

Par%l shrinks from the reflected sorrow. Regret becomes shame.

YES... OUR DUTIES.

WHAT HAVE YOU OBSERVED OUT HERE? I KNOW WE CAN'T GET CLOSE TO IT, BUT...DID YOU *SEE* IT?

IS THERE... CAN THE CREATURE BE *STOPPED?*

NO, PAR%L. NO, IT CANNOT BE STOPPED.

IT WILL NEVER STOP MAKING US *PAY.*

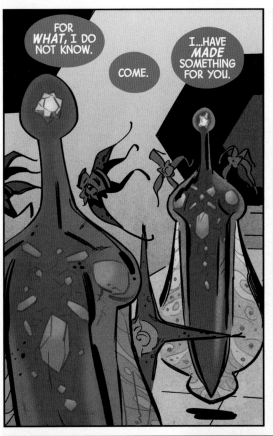

FOR *WHAT*, I DO NOT KNOW.

COME.

I...HAVE *MADE* SOMETHING FOR YOU.

The tiding-eggs pulse erratically in their creche.

As the energies of the Berth flicker and fail, growing the larvae inside to maturity has become all but impossible.

That even one remains viable is a tribute to Farys' skill.

Par%l directs the thought outward. An attempt to breach the gulf between them.

A failure.

"*VIABLE*" IS NO LONGER ADEQUATE.

WHAT USE ARE *TIDINGS* IN THE BROKEN AGE? WE KNOW THE TIDINGS *ALREADY.*

THIS...IS A *WARNING.*

FOR THOSE WHO DO NOT.

The ovum seems to shudder as Farys gently tears it free.

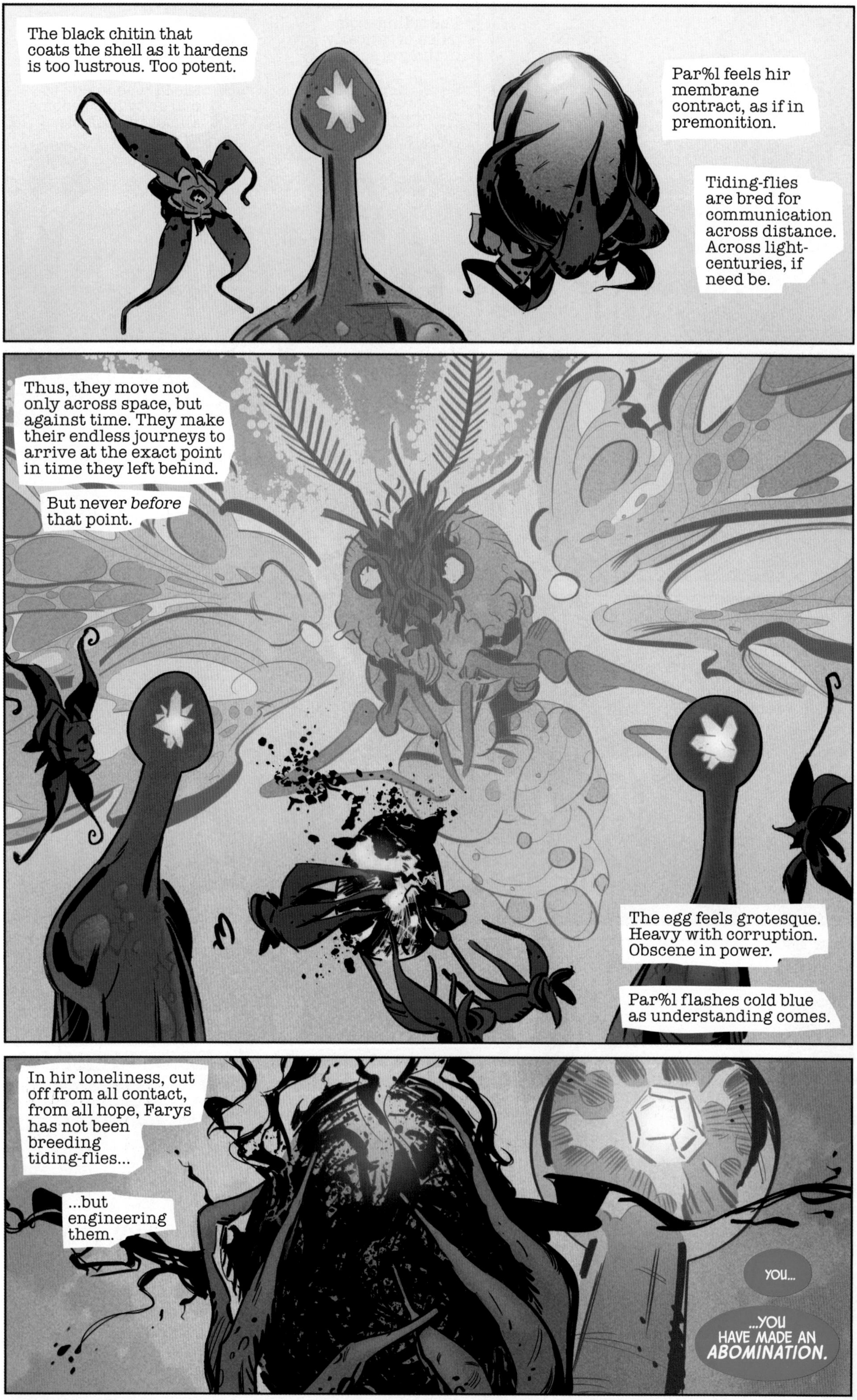
The black chitin that coats the shell as it hardens is too lustrous. Too potent.
Par%l feels hir membrane contract, as if in premonition.
Tiding-flies are bred for communication across distance. Across light-centuries, if need be.
Thus, they move not only across space, but against time. They make their endless journeys to arrive at the exact point in time they left behind.
But never *before* that point.
The egg feels grotesque. Heavy with corruption. Obscene in power.
Par%l flashes cold blue as understanding comes.
In hir loneliness, cut off from all contact, from all hope, Farys has not been breeding tiding-flies...
...but engineering them.
YOU...
...YOU HAVE MADE AN ***ABOMINATION.***

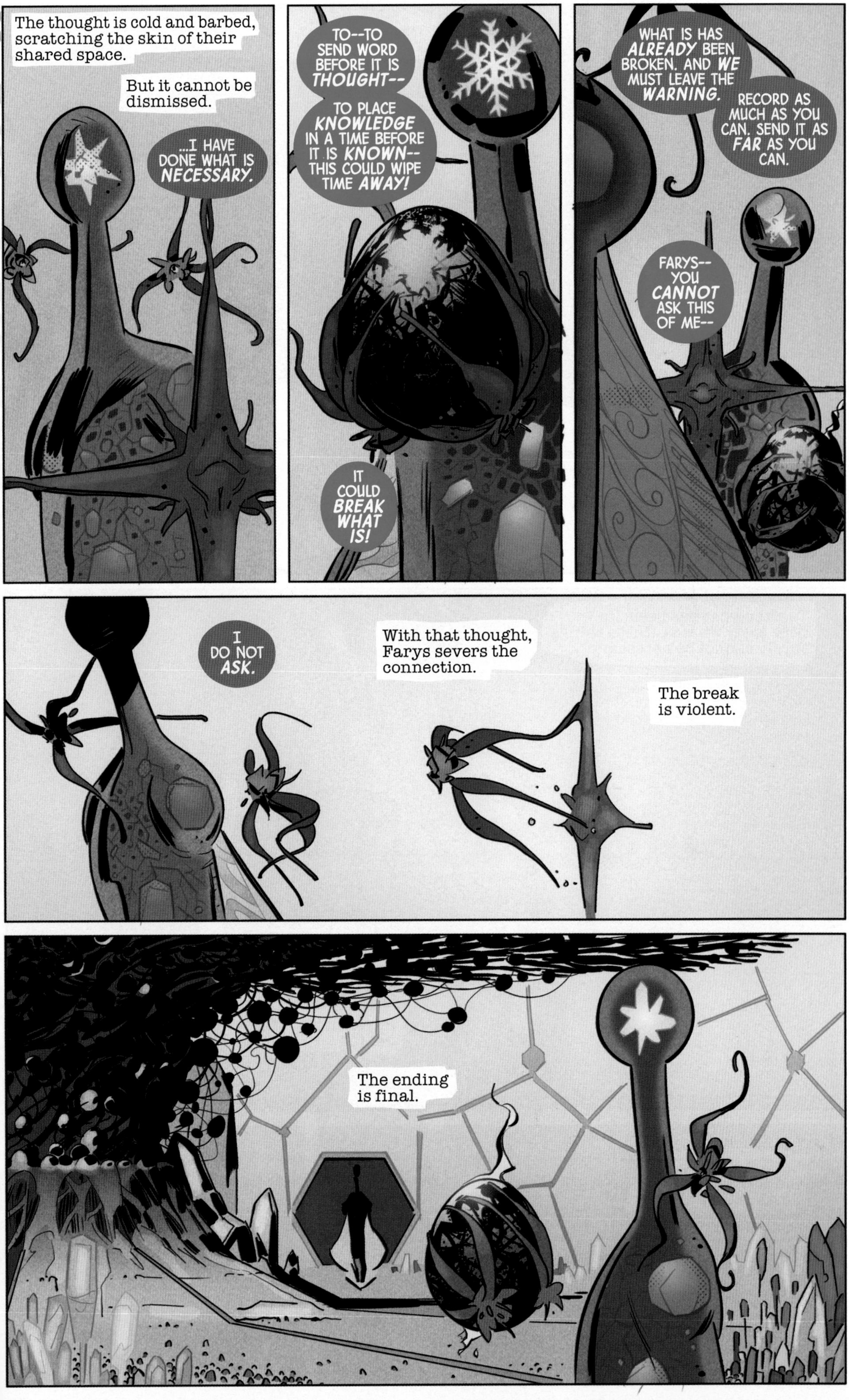
The thought is cold and barbed, scratching the skin of their shared space.
But it cannot be dismissed.
...I HAVE DONE WHAT IS NECESSARY.
TO--TO SEND WORD BEFORE IT IS THOUGHT--
TO PLACE KNOWLEDGE IN A TIME BEFORE IT IS KNOWN-- THIS COULD WIPE TIME AWAY!
IT COULD BREAK WHAT IS!
WHAT IS HAS ALREADY BEEN BROKEN. AND WE MUST LEAVE THE WARNING.
RECORD AS MUCH AS YOU CAN. SEND IT AS FAR AS YOU CAN.
FARYS-- YOU CANNOT ASK THIS OF ME--
I DO NOT ASK.
With that thought, Farys severs the connection.
The break is violent.
The ending is final.

As the farsail slips free from the Berth, Par%l examines the dark egg in hir grip, nervous at the weight of it.

"Necessary," Farys called it.

Par%l must return to the birth-world. Report what has been done. This warning -- this weapon -- cannot be kept hidden.

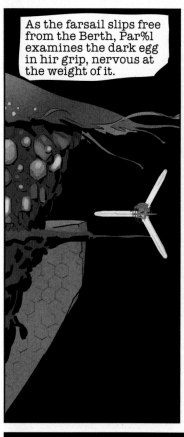

To alter what has been...to wipe away what is...these things surely cannot be necessary.

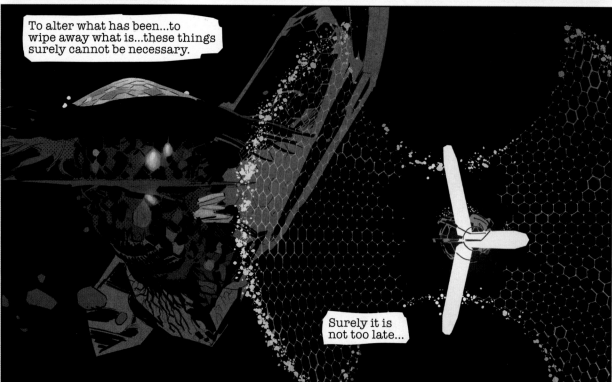

Surely it is not too late...

Behind the farsail, the colors of the Berth flicker and die.

One by one.

Final.

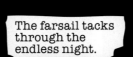

The farsail tacks through the endless night.

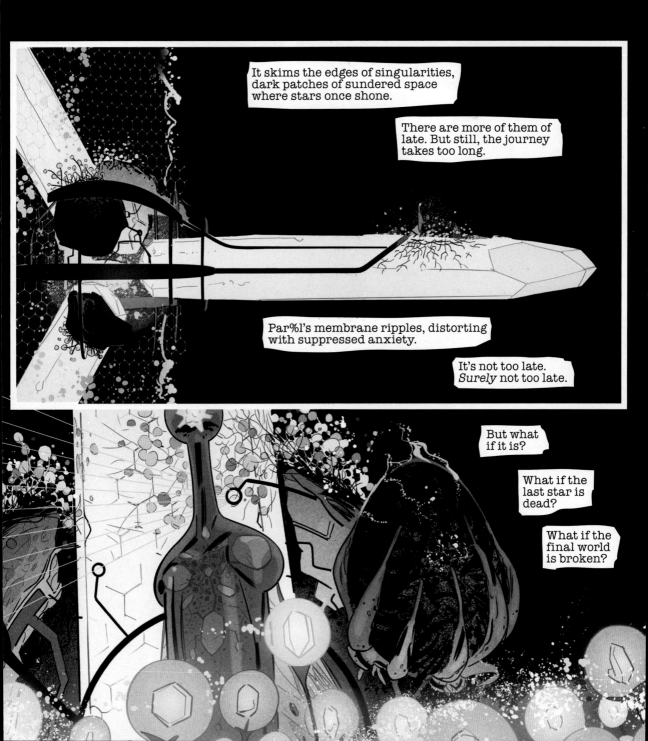

It skims the edges of singularities, dark patches of sundered space where stars once shone.

There are more of them of late. But still, the journey takes too long.

Par%l's membrane ripples, distorting with suppressed anxiety.

It's not too late. *Surely* not too late.

But what if it is?

What if the last star is dead?

What if the final world is broken?

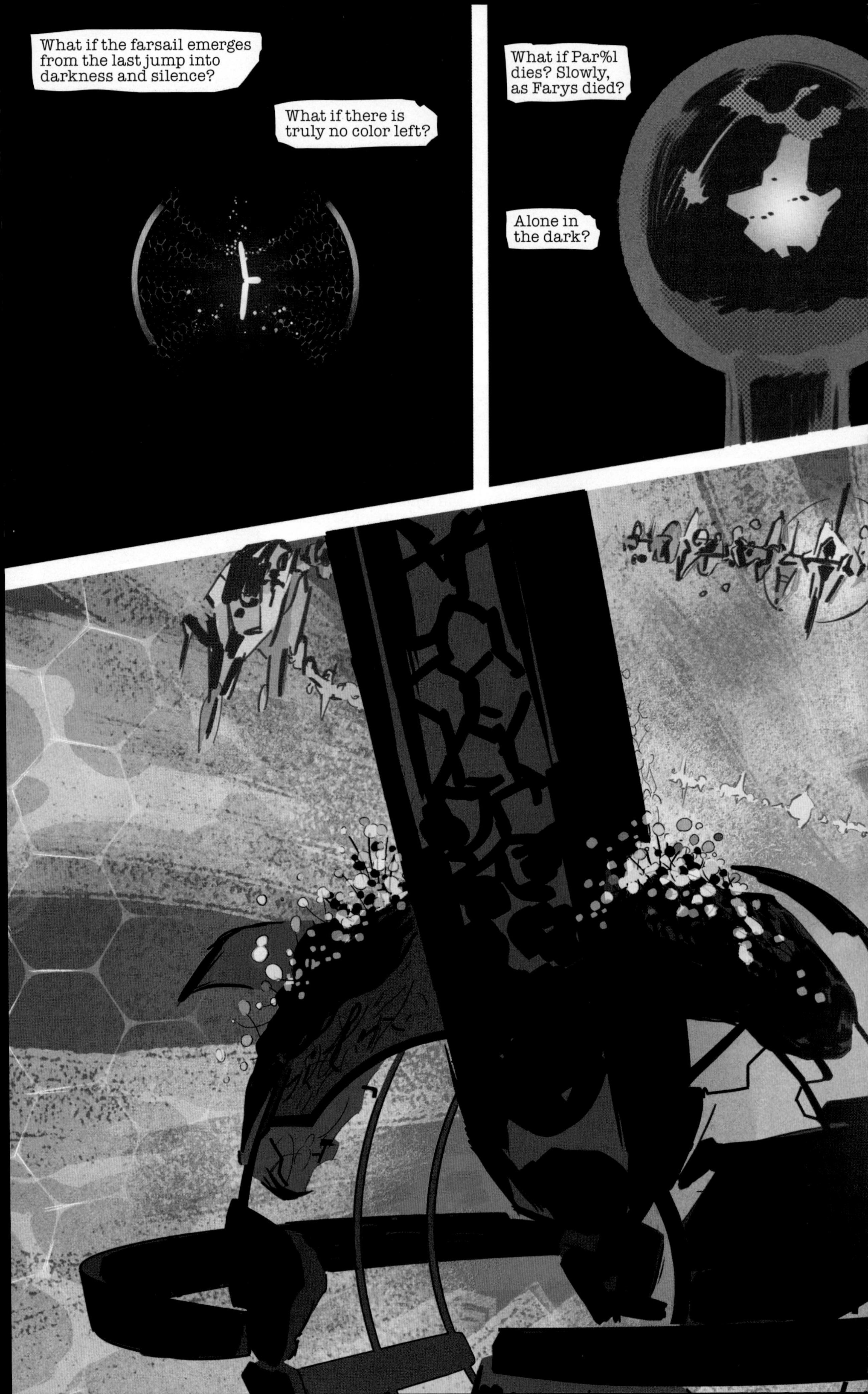
What if the farsail emerges from the last jump into darkness and silence?
What if there is truly no color left?
What if Par%l dies? Slowly, as Farys died?
Alone in the dark?

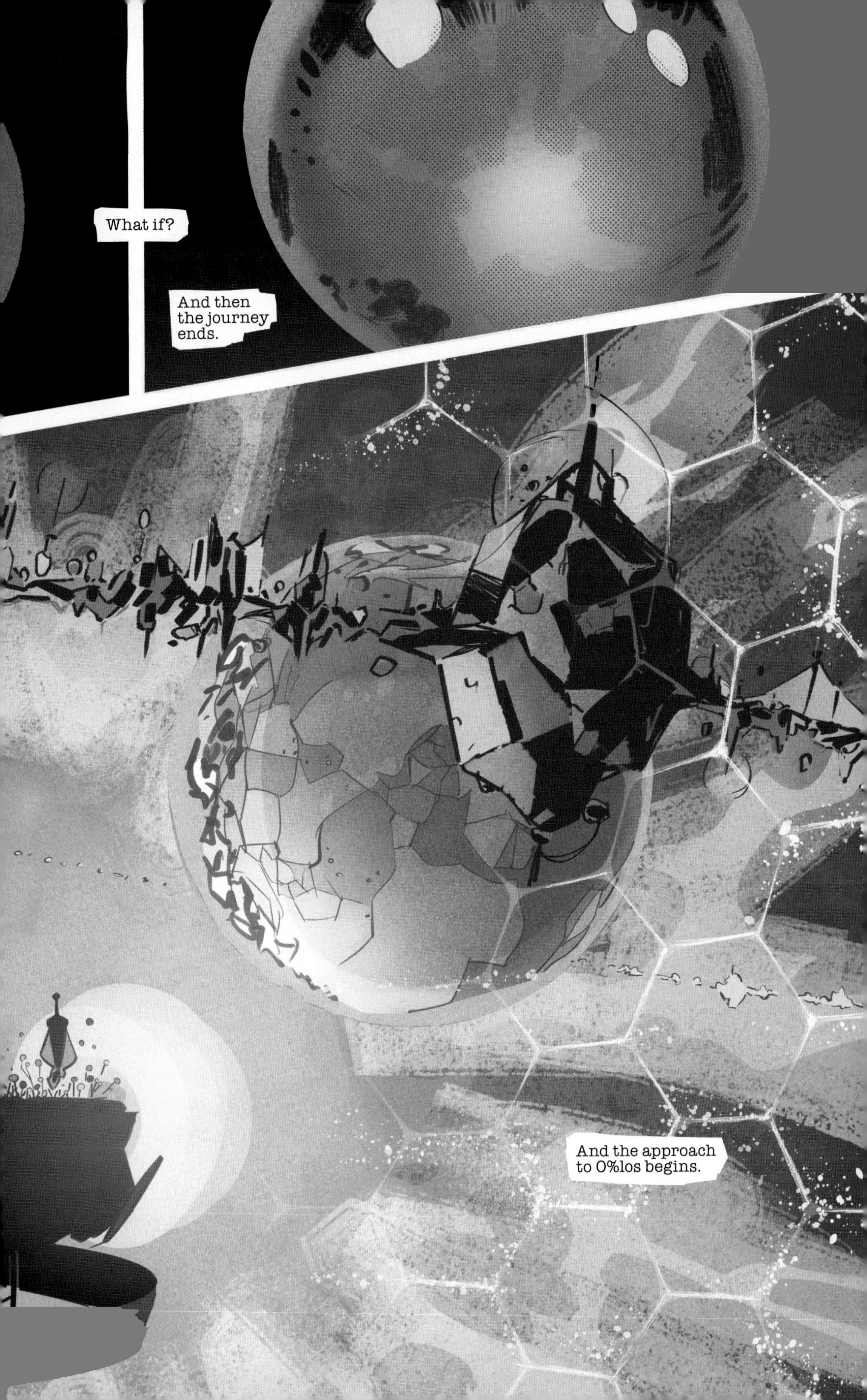
What if?
And then the journey ends.
And the approach to O%los begins.

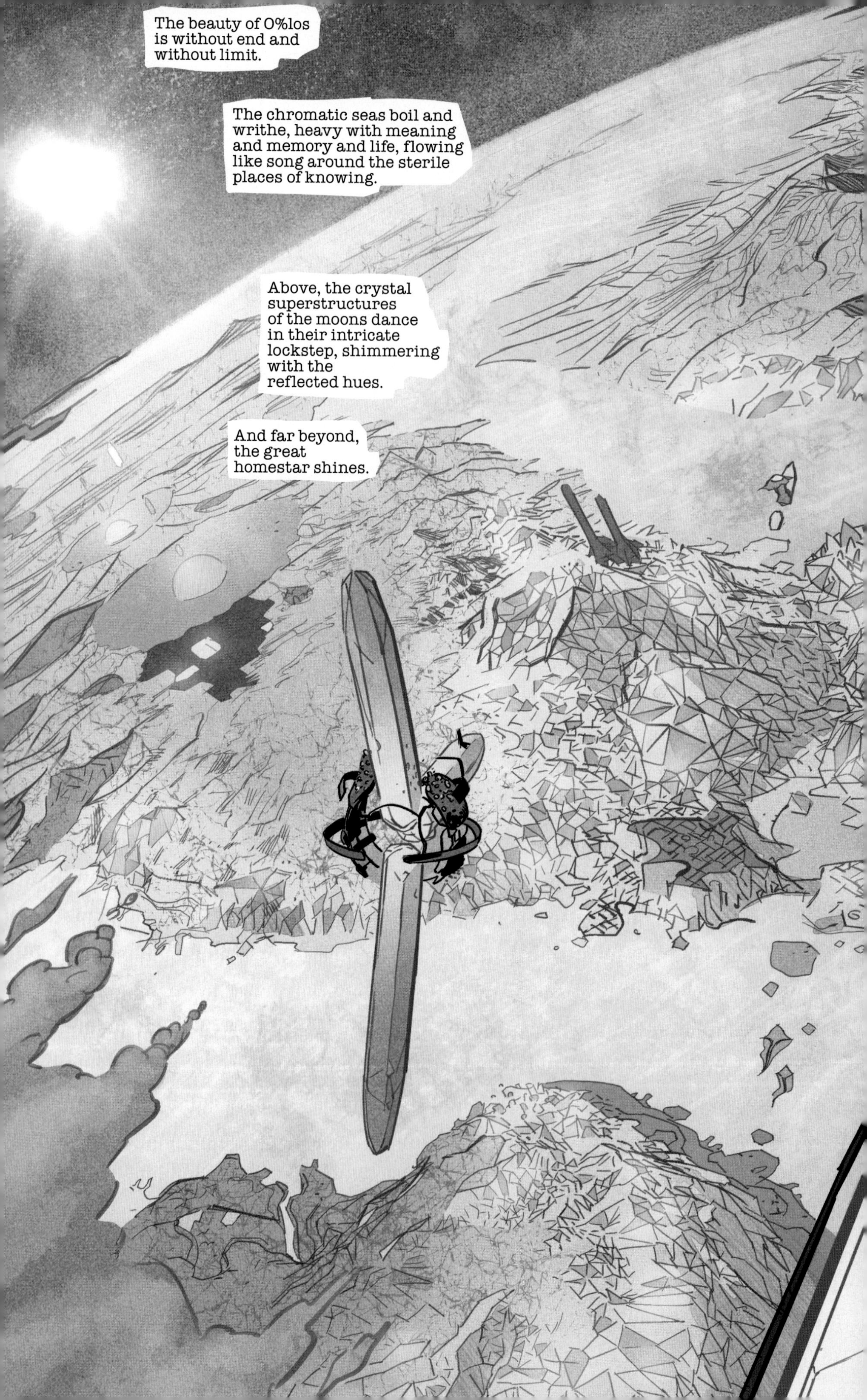
The beauty of O%los is without end and without limit.
The chromatic seas boil and writhe, heavy with meaning and memory and life, flowing like song around the sterile places of knowing.
Above, the crystal superstructures of the moons dance in their intricate lockstep, shimmering with the reflected hues.
And far beyond, the great homestar shines.

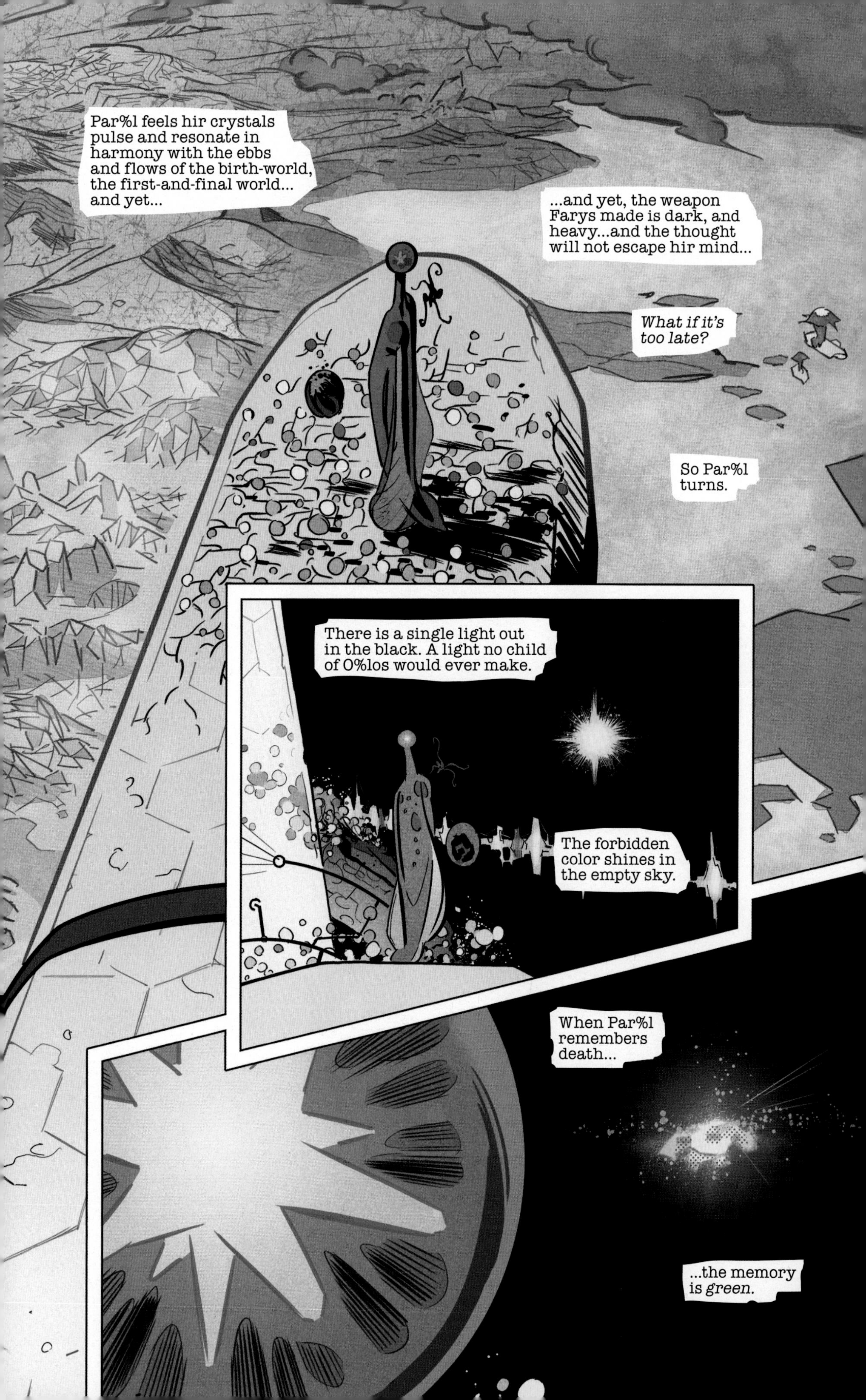
Par%l feels hir crystals pulse and resonate in harmony with the ebbs and flows of the birth-world, the first-and-final world... and yet...
...and yet, the weapon Farys made is dark, and heavy...and the thought will not escape hir mind...
What if it's too late?
So Par%l turns.
There is a single light out in the black. A light no child of O%los would ever make.
The forbidden color shines in the empty sky.
When Par%l remembers death...
...the memory is *green.*

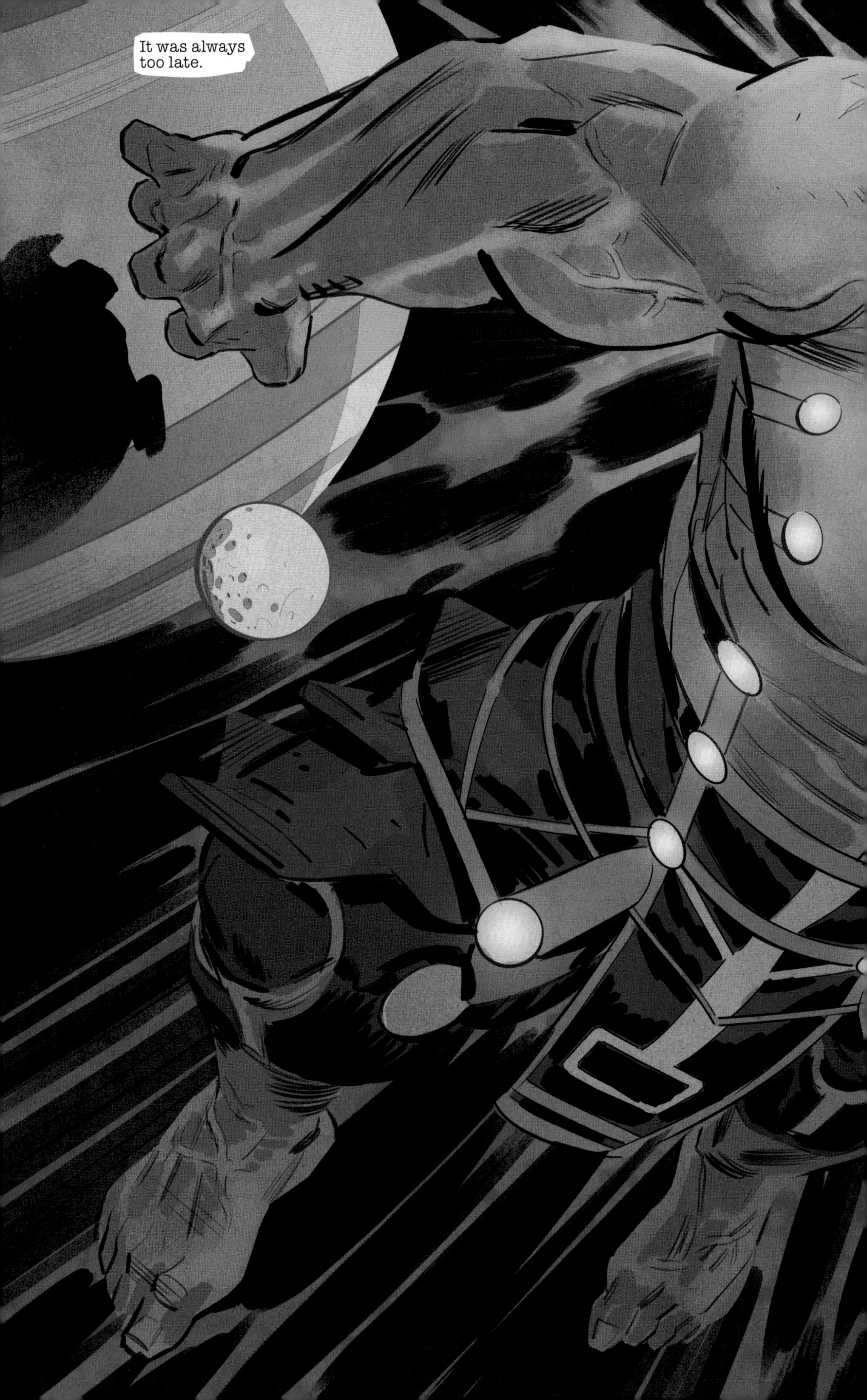
It was always too late.

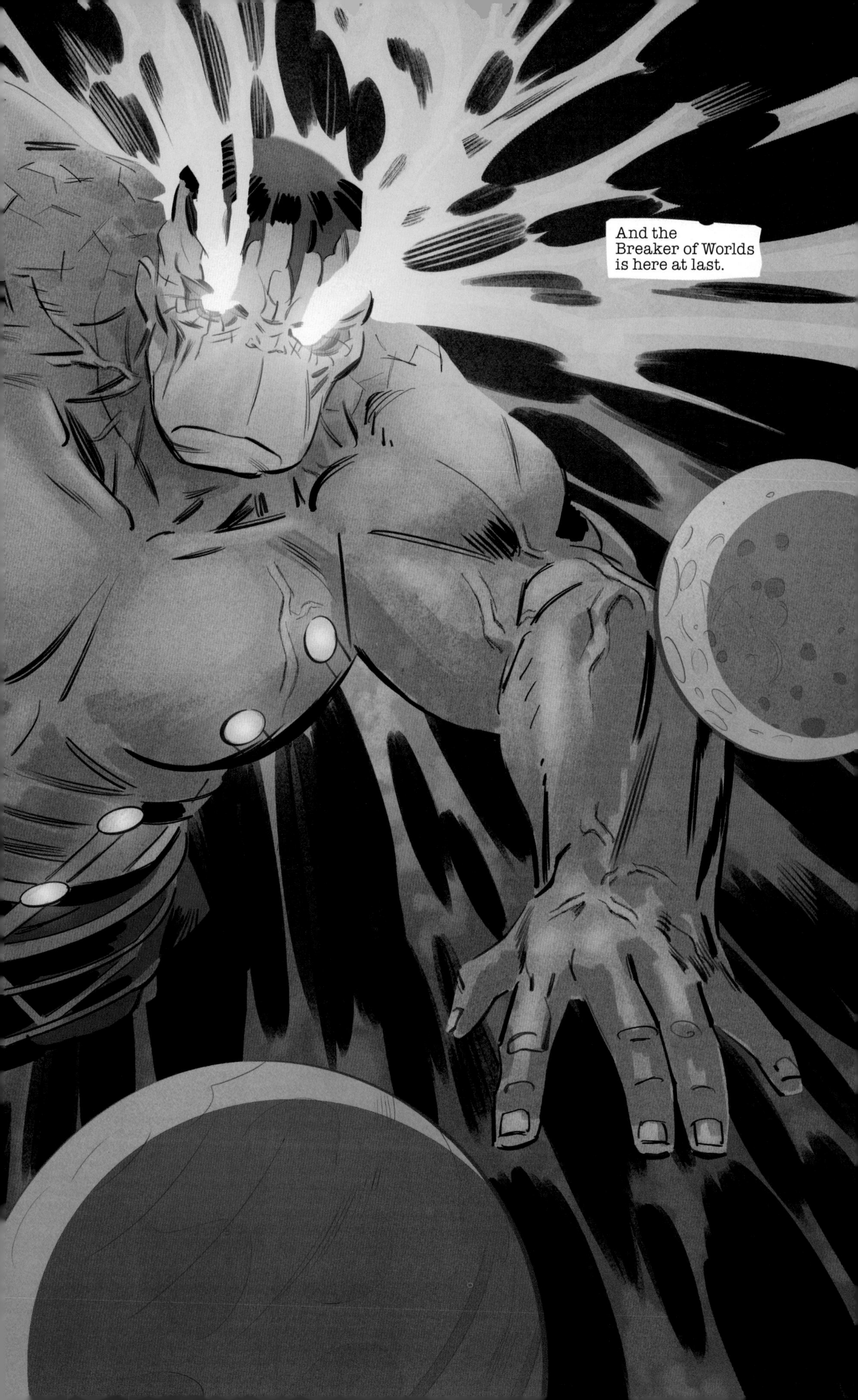
And the Breaker of Worlds is here at last.

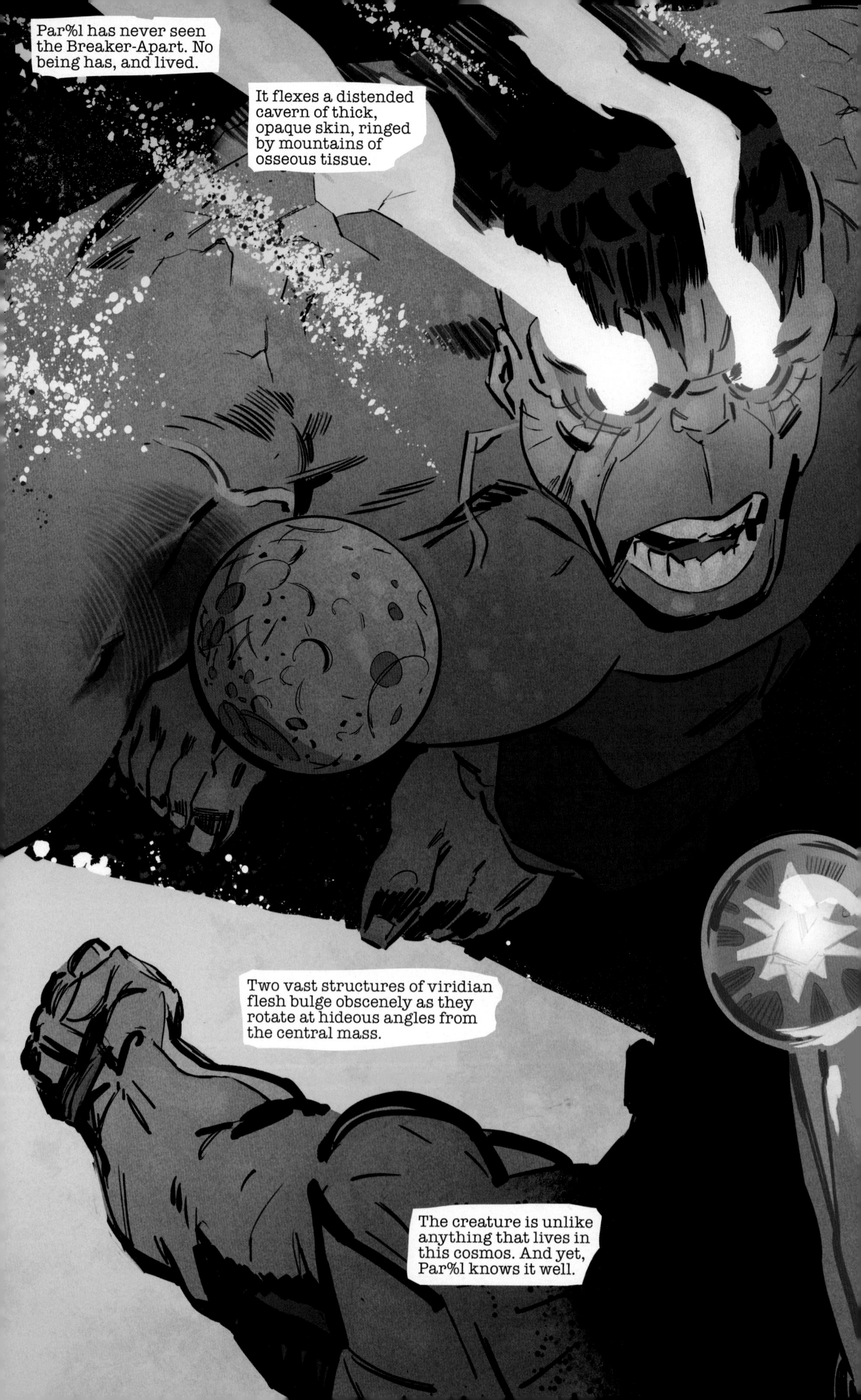
Par%l has never seen the Breaker-Apart. No being has, and lived.
It flexes a distended cavern of thick, opaque skin, ringed by mountains of osseous tissue.
Two vast structures of viridian flesh bulge obscenely as they rotate at hideous angles from the central mass.
The creature is unlike anything that lives in this cosmos. And yet, Par%l knows it well.

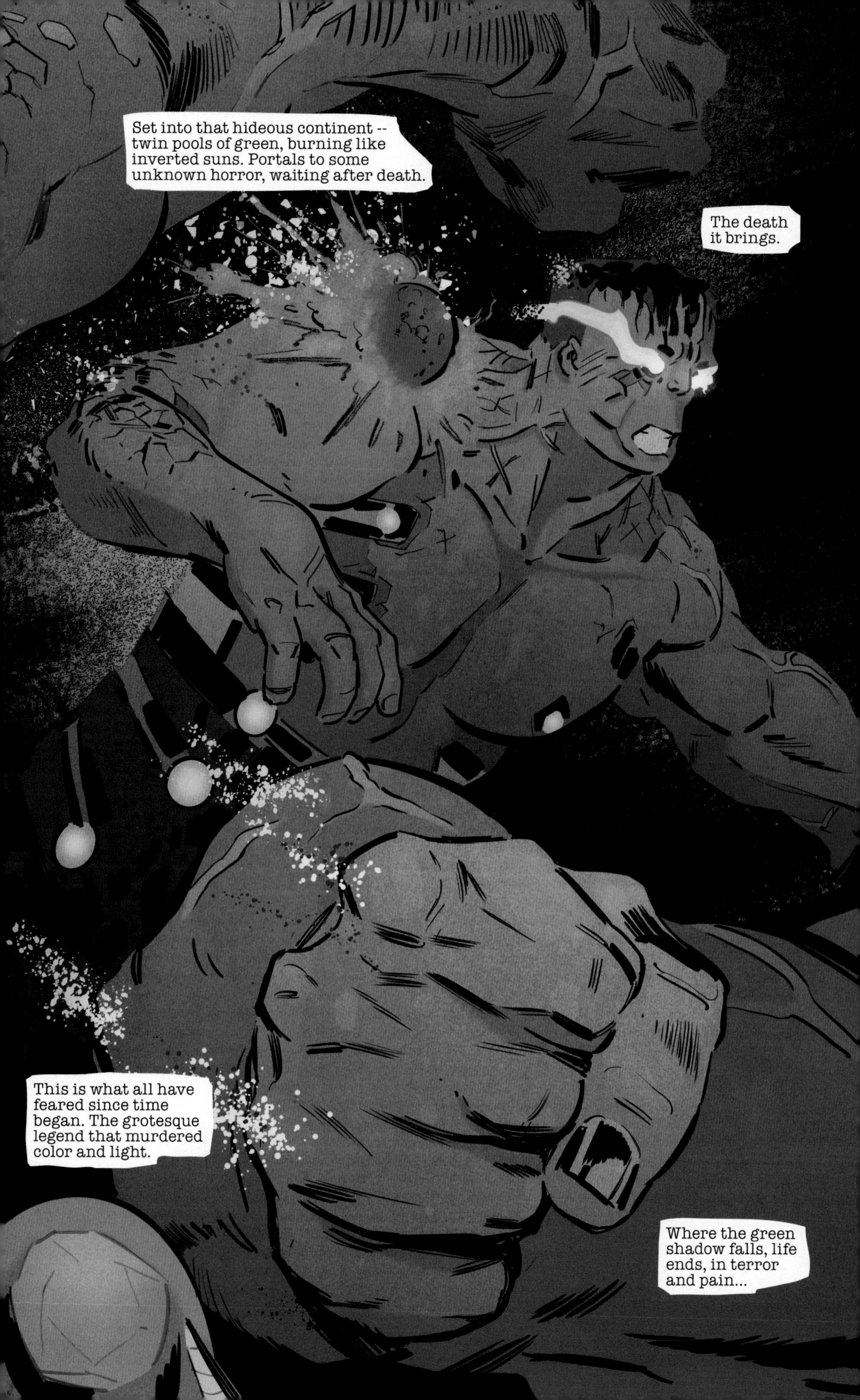
Set into that hideous continent -- twin pools of green, burning like inverted suns. Portals to some unknown horror, waiting after death.
The death it brings.
This is what all have feared since time began. The grotesque legend that murdered color and light.
Where the green shadow falls, life ends, in terror and pain...

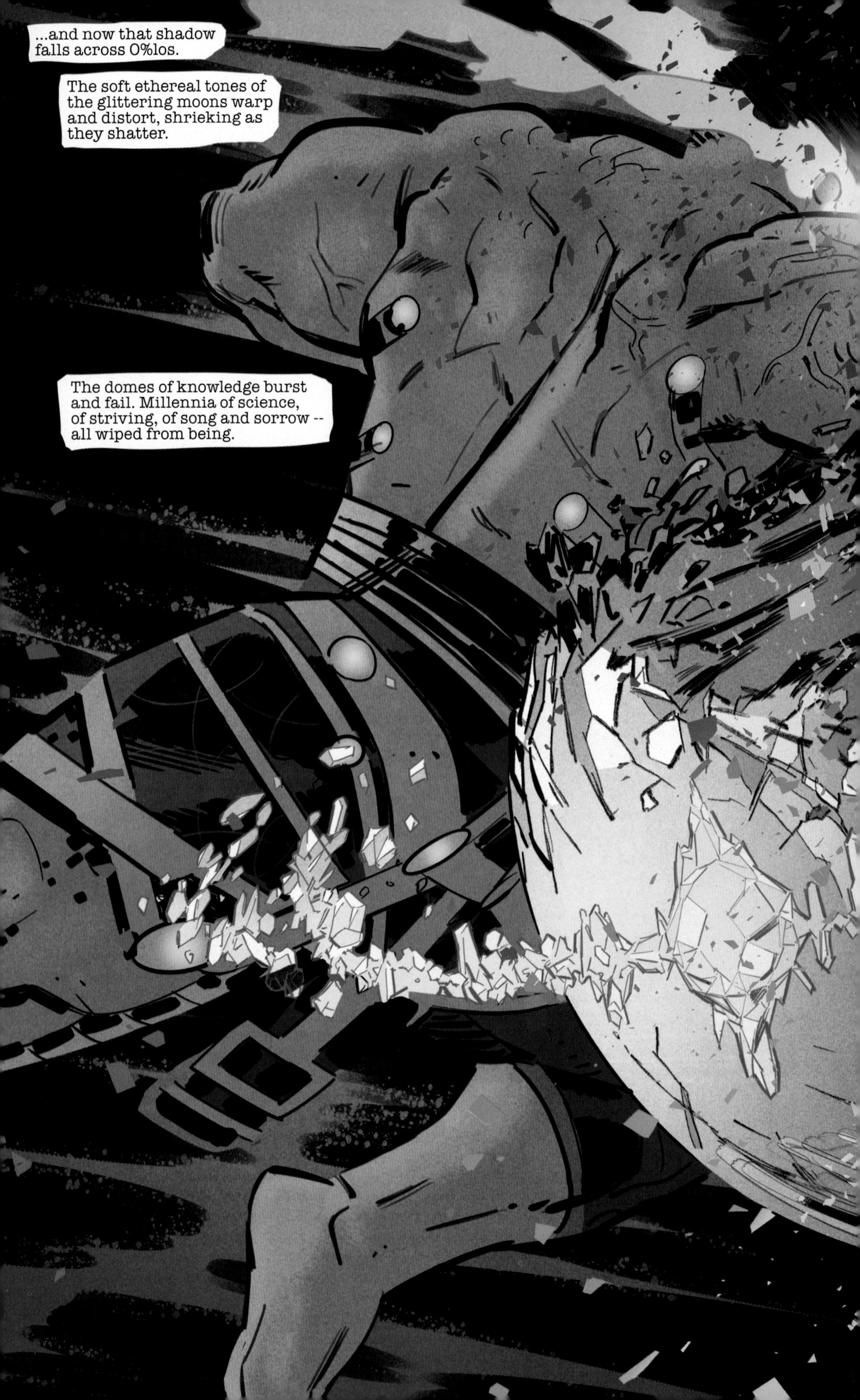
...and now that shadow falls across O%los.
The soft ethereal tones of the glittering moons warp and distort, shrieking as they shatter.
The domes of knowledge burst and fail. Millennia of science, of striving, of song and sorrow -- all wiped from being.

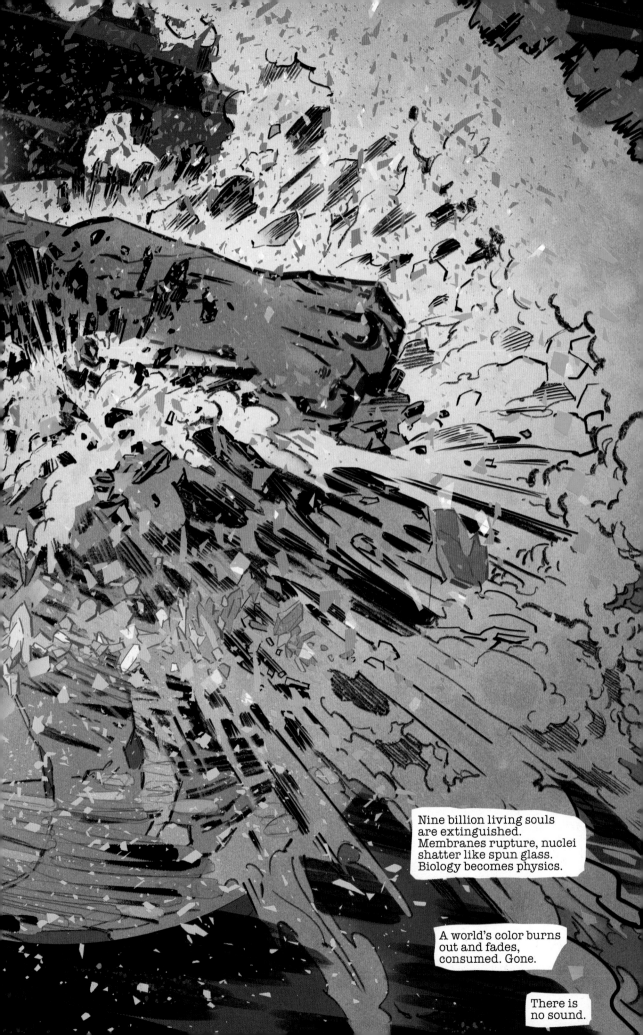

Nine billion living souls
are extinguished.
Membranes rupture, nuclei
shatter like spun glass.
Biology becomes physics.

A world's color burns
out and fades,
consumed. Gone.

There is
no sound.

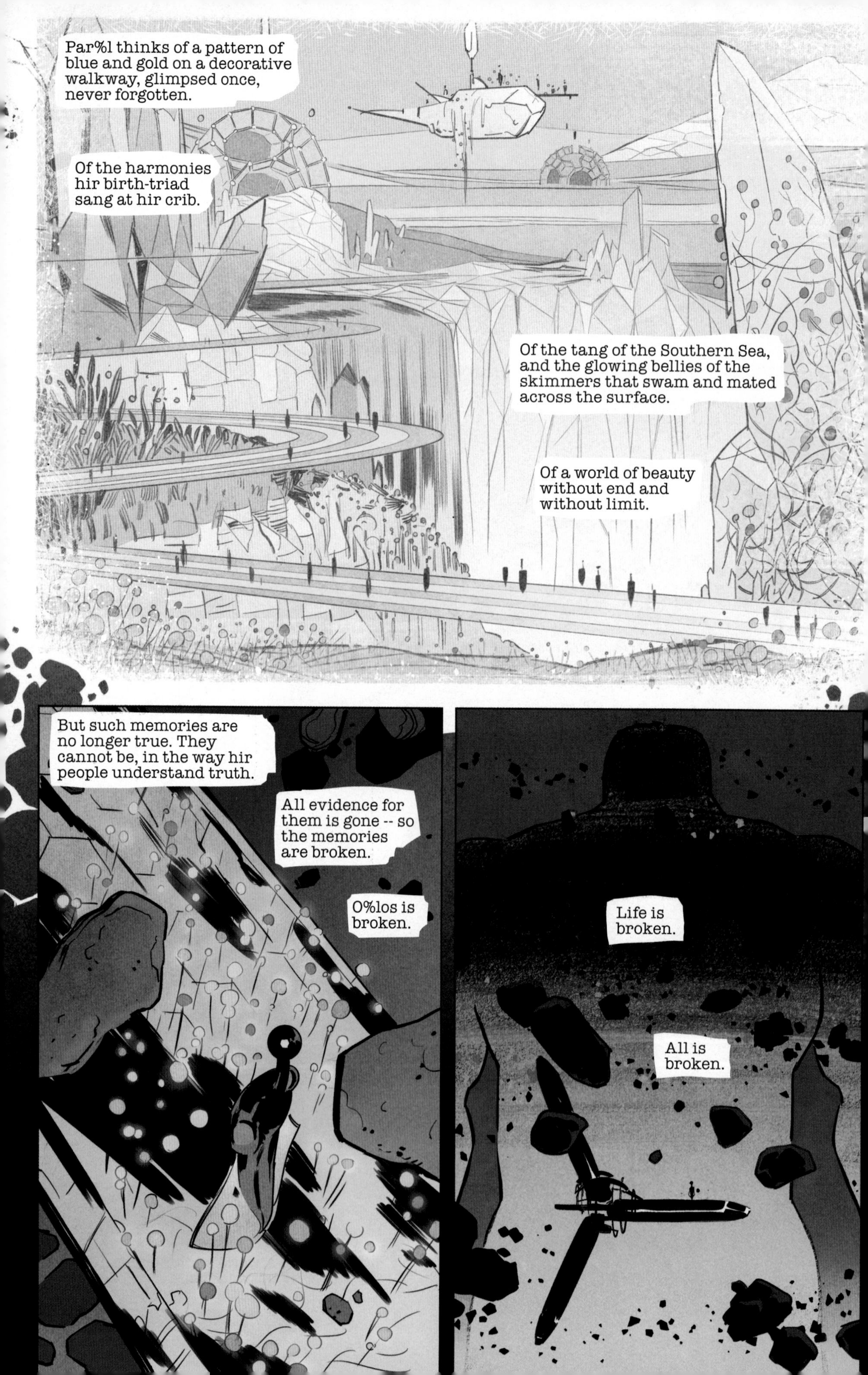
Par%l thinks of a pattern of blue and gold on a decorative walkway, glimpsed once, never forgotten.
Of the harmonies hir birth-triad sang at hir crib.
Of the tang of the Southern Sea, and the glowing bellies of the skimmers that swam and mated across the surface.
Of a world of beauty without end and without limit.
But such memories are no longer true. They cannot be, in the way hir people understand truth.
All evidence for them is gone -- so the memories are broken.
O%los is broken.
Life is broken.
All is broken.

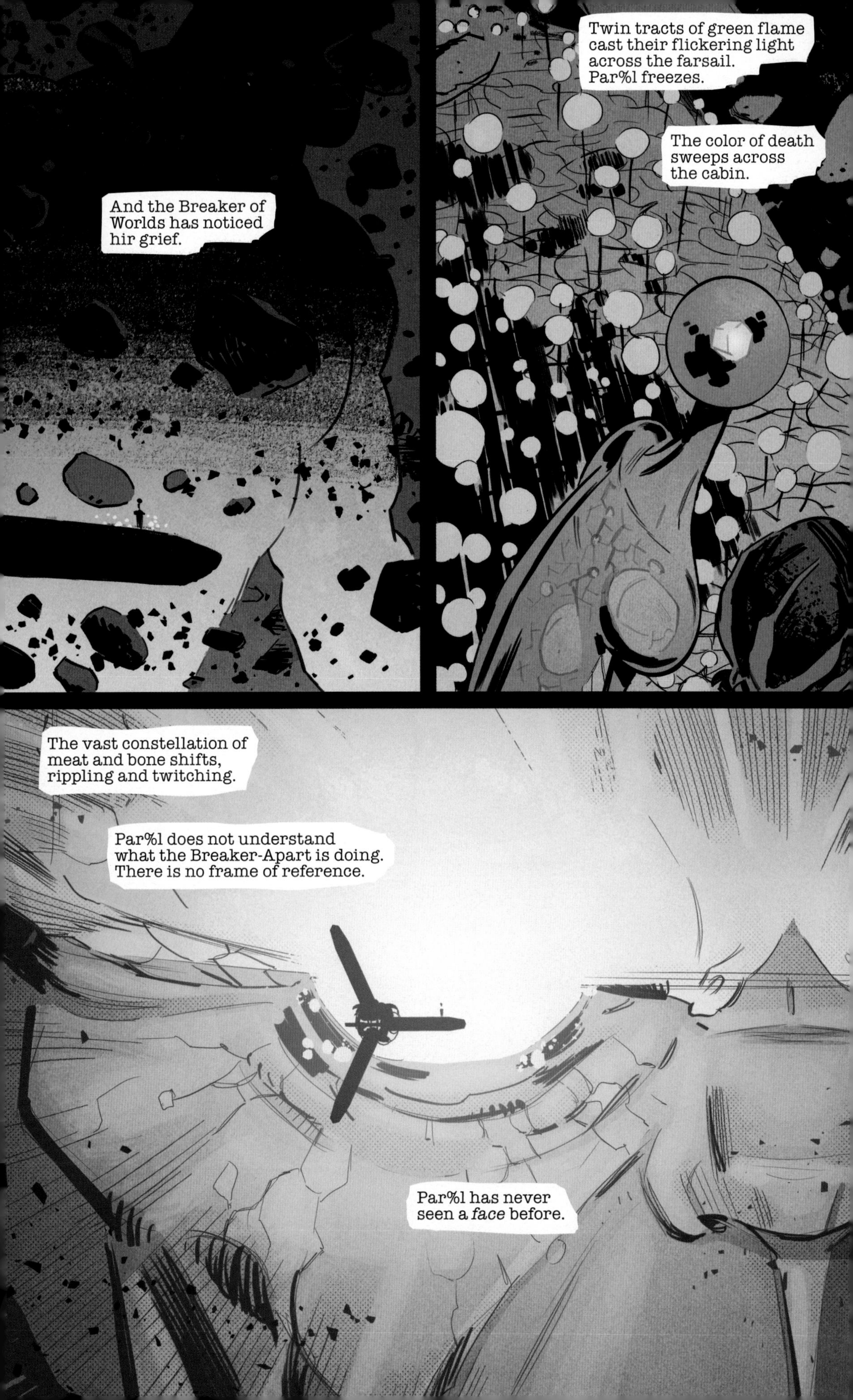
And the Breaker of Worlds has noticed hir grief.
Twin tracts of green flame cast their flickering light across the farsail. Par%l freezes.
The color of death sweeps across the cabin.
The vast constellation of meat and bone shifts, rippling and twitching.
Par%l does not understand what the Breaker-Apart is doing. There is no frame of reference.
Par%l has never seen a *face* before.

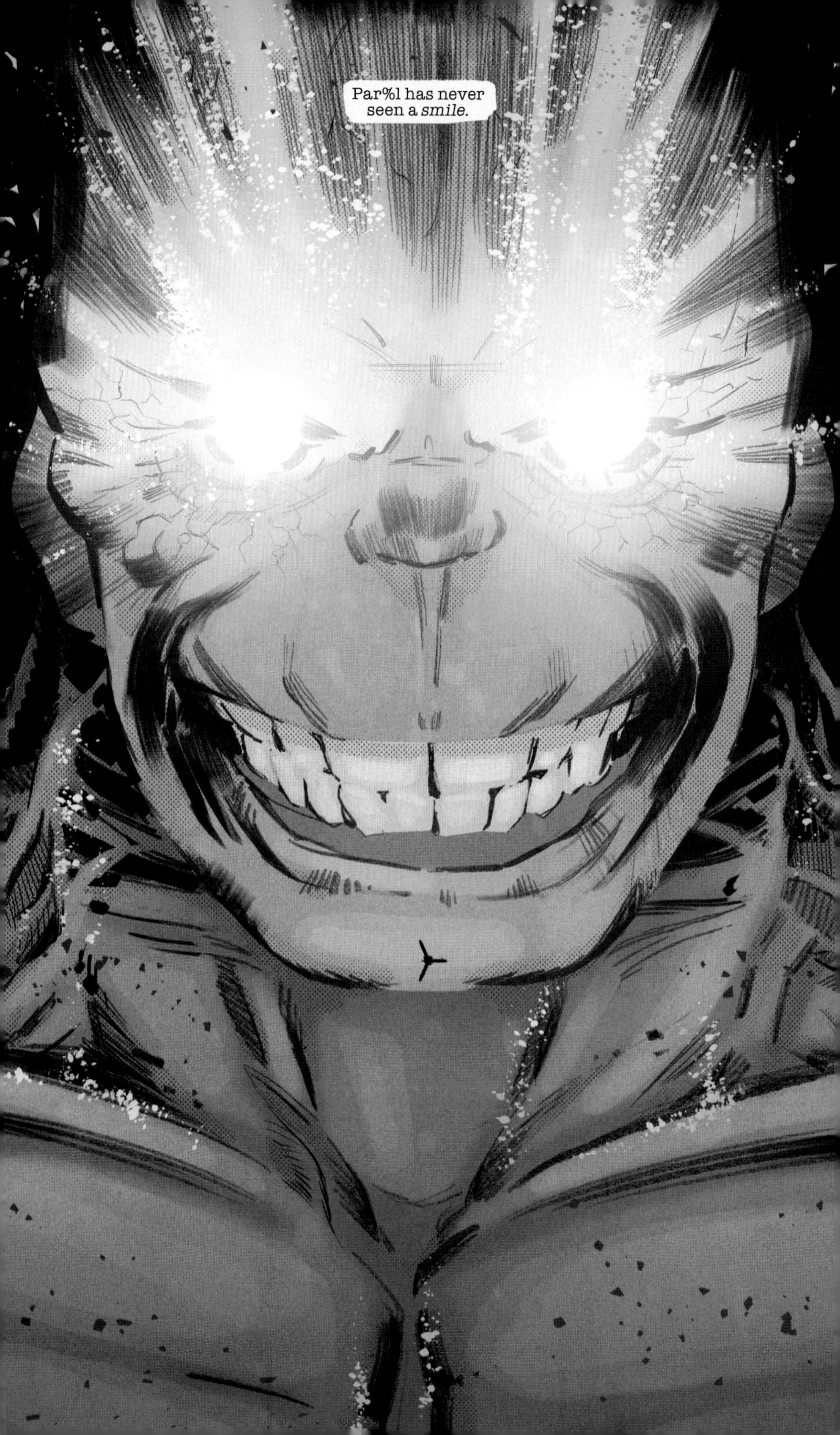
Par%l has never seen a *smile.*

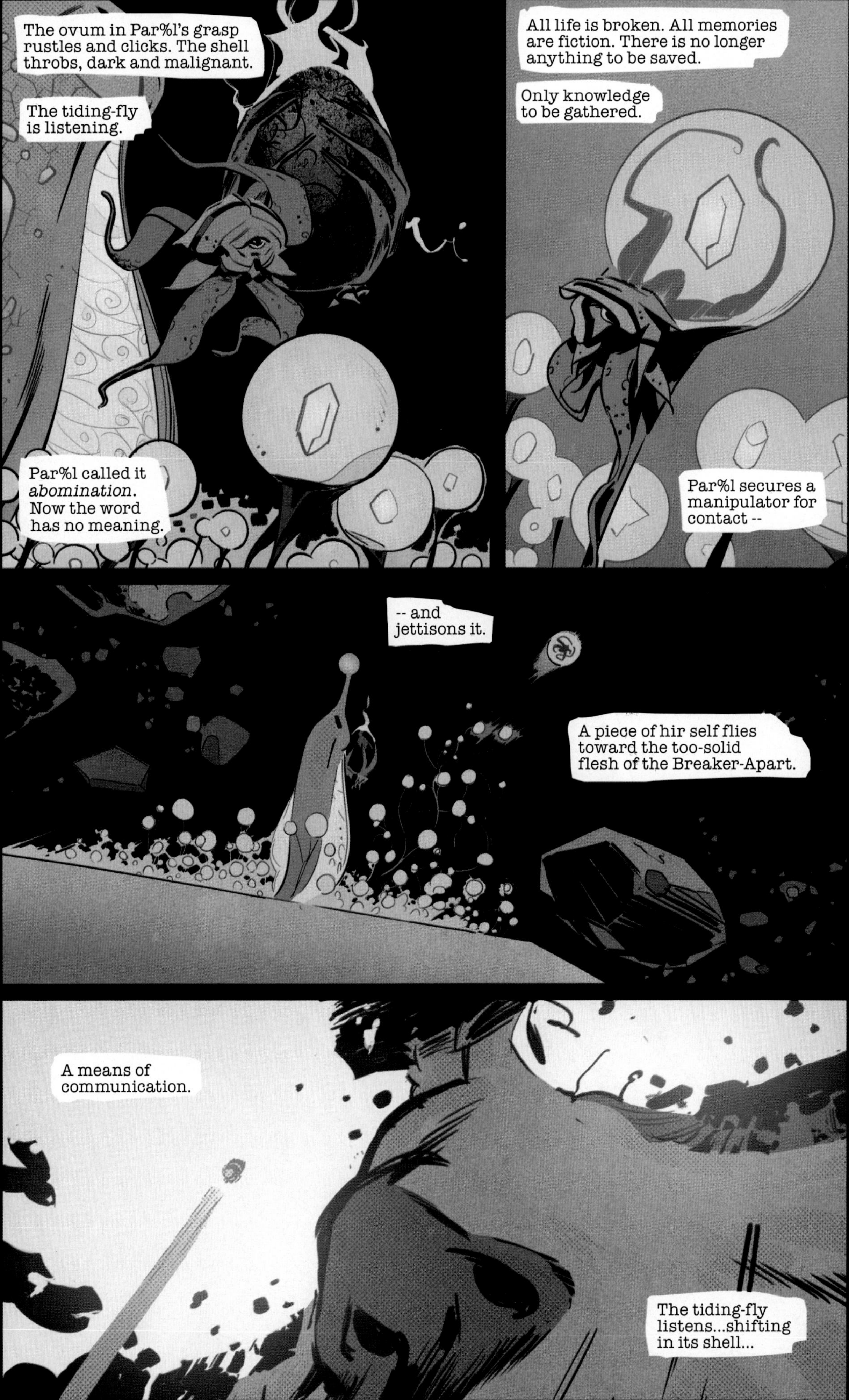
The ovum in Par%l's grasp rustles and clicks. The shell throbs, dark and malignant.
The tiding-fly is listening.
Par%l called it *abomination*. Now the word has no meaning.
All life is broken. All memories are fiction. There is no longer anything to be saved.
Only knowledge to be gathered.
Par%l secures a manipulator for contact --
-- and jettisons it.
A piece of hir self flies toward the too-solid flesh of the Breaker-Apart.
A means of communication.
The tiding-fly listens...shifting in its shell...

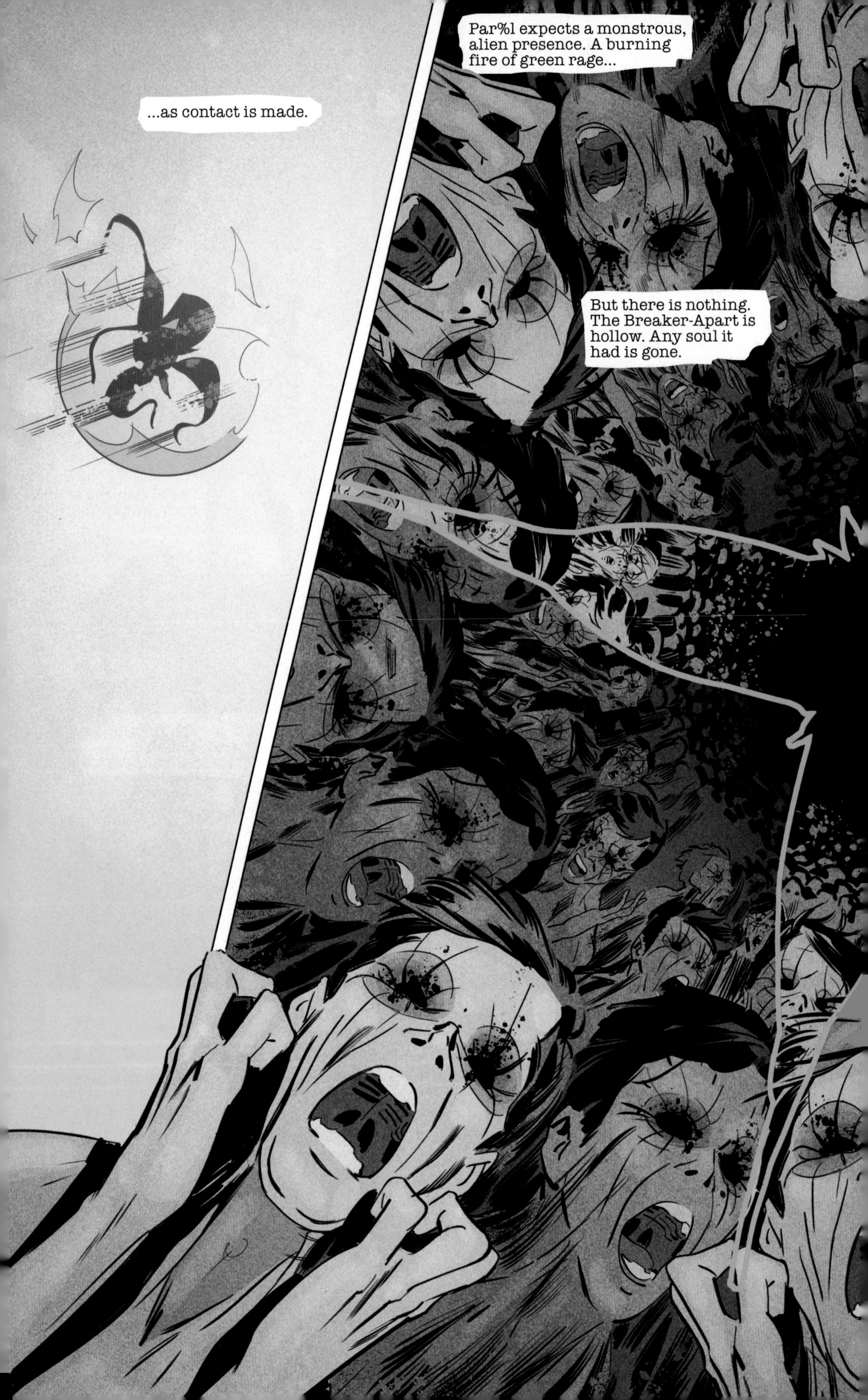
...as contact is made.
Par%l expects a monstrous, alien presence. A burning fire of green rage...
But there is nothing. The Breaker-Apart is hollow. Any soul it had is gone.

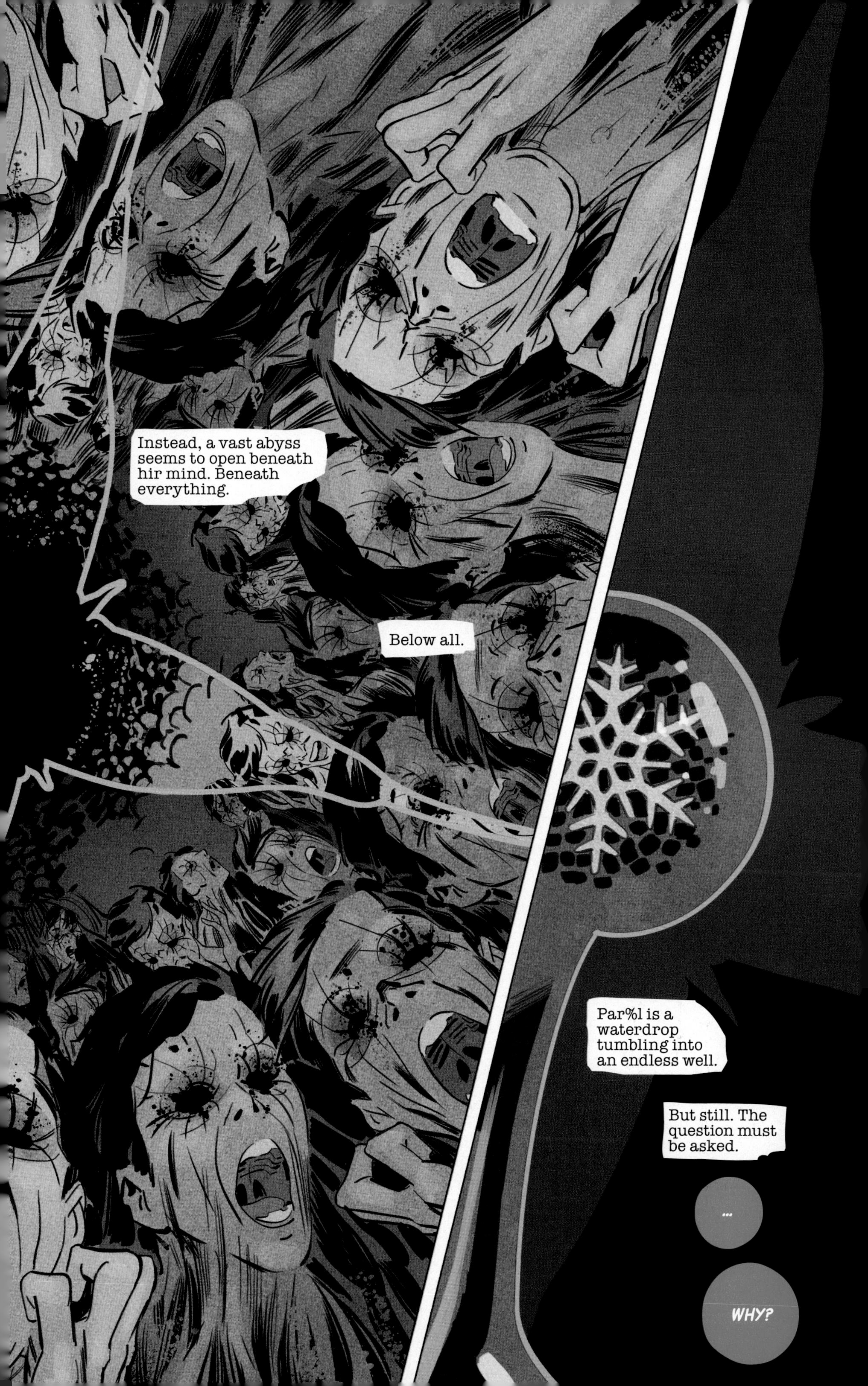

Instead, a vast abyss seems to open beneath hir mind. Beneath everything.
Below all.
Par%l is a waterdrop tumbling into an endless well.
But still. The question must be asked.
...
WHY?

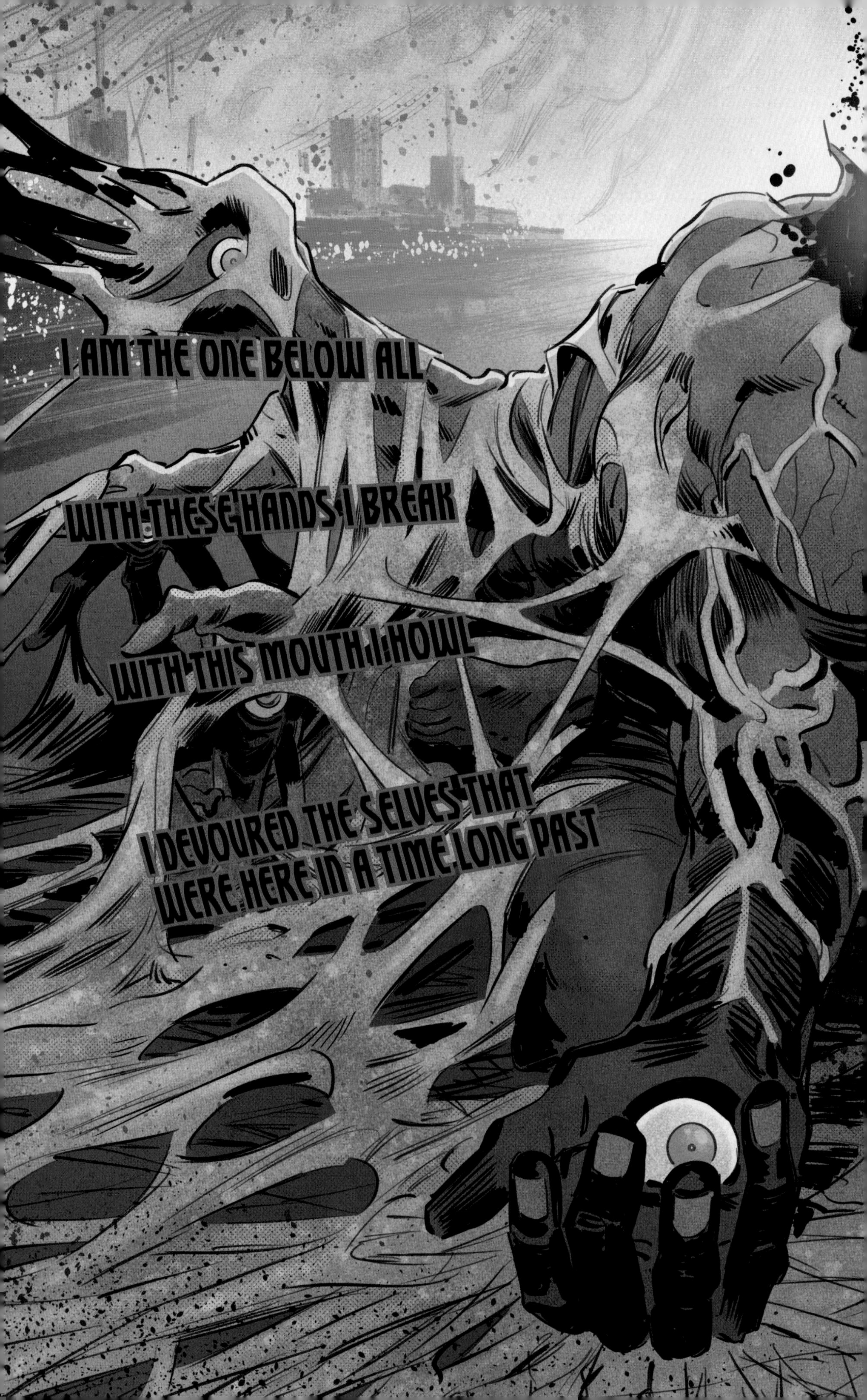
I AM THE ONE BELOW ALL
WITH THESE HANDS I BREAK
WITH THIS MOUTH I HOWL
I DEVOURED THE SELVES THAT WERE HERE IN A TIME LONG PAST

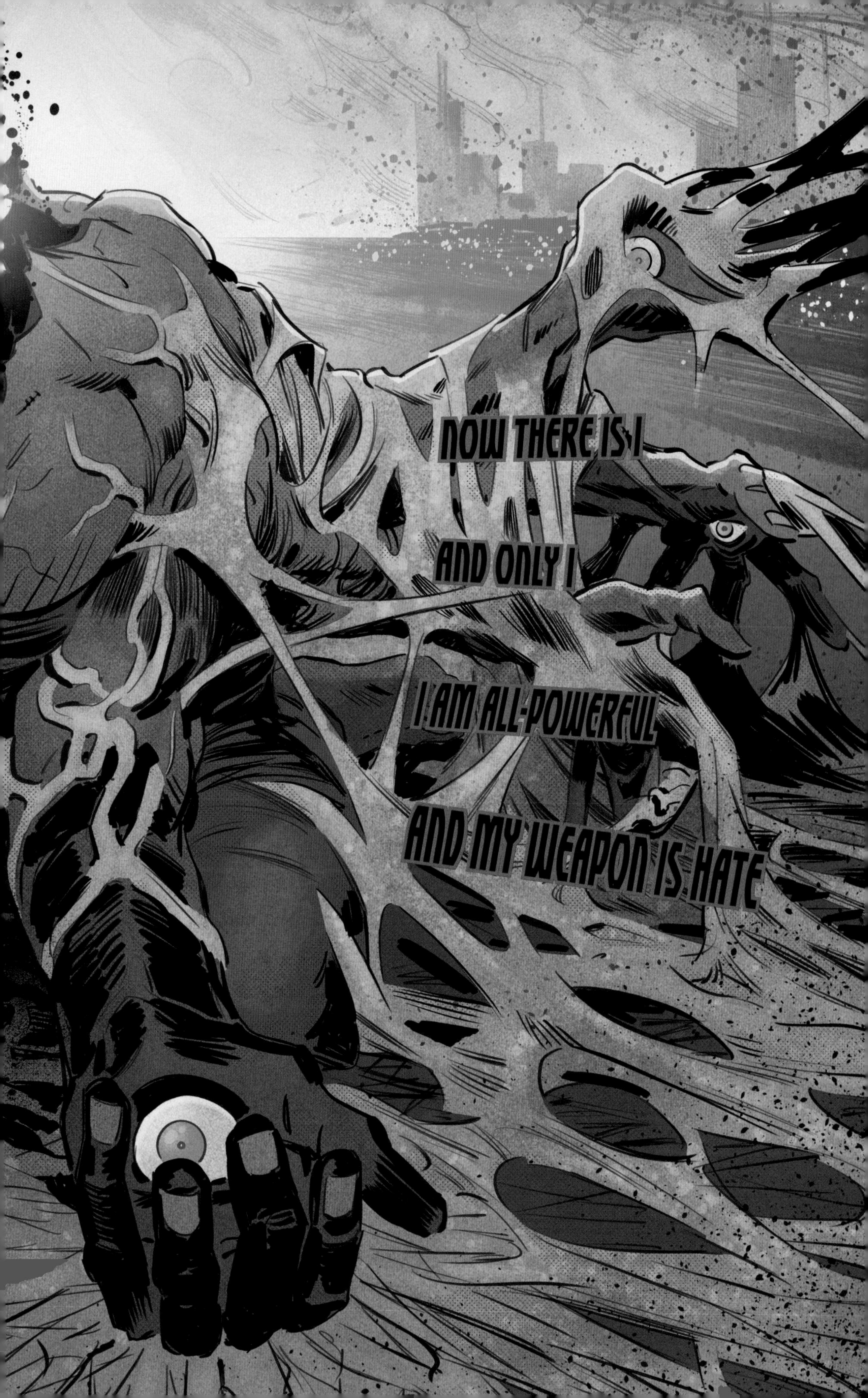
NOW THERE IS I
AND ONLY I
I AM ALL-POWERFUL
AND MY WEAPON IS HATE

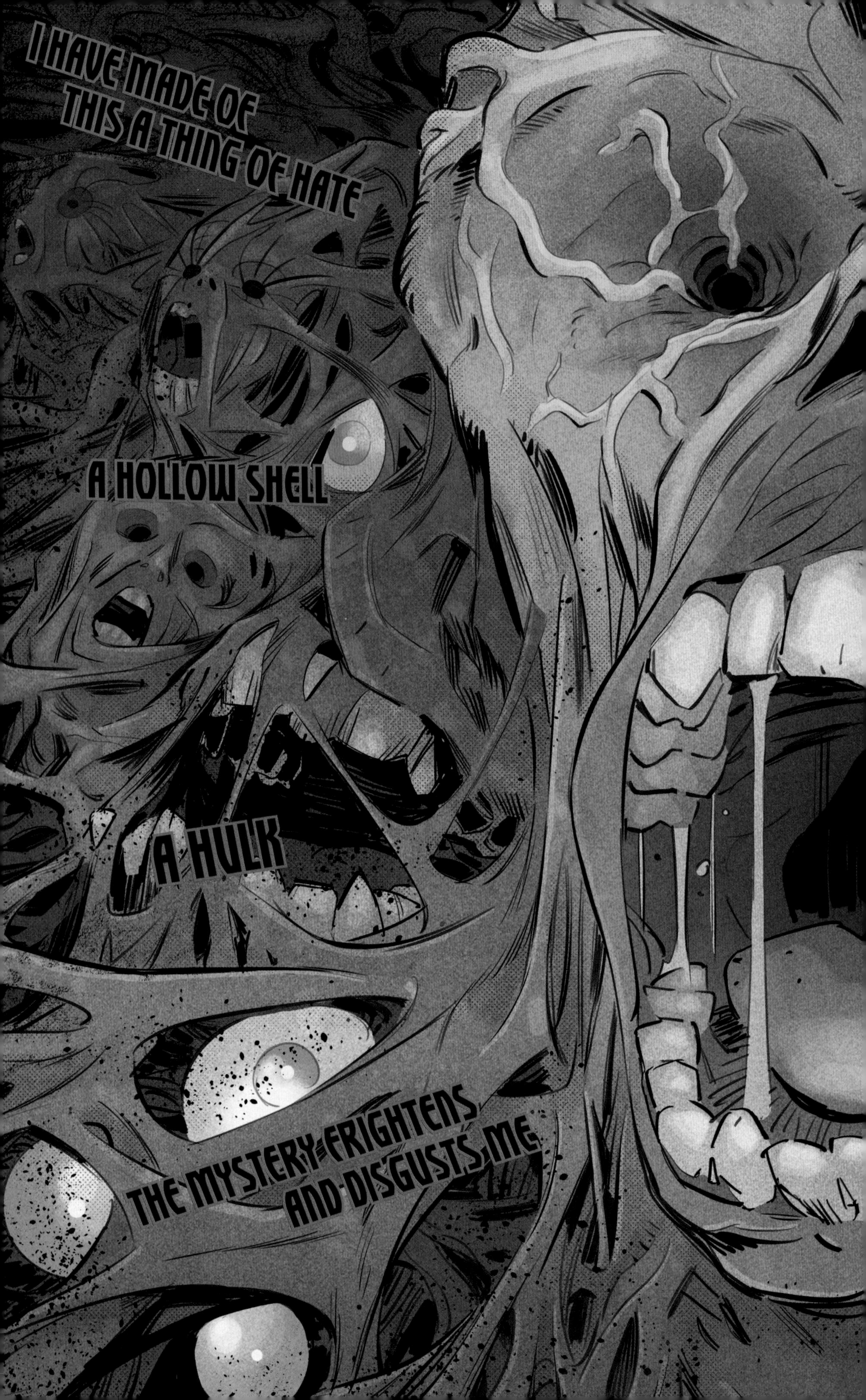
I HAVE MADE OF THIS A THING OF HATE
A HOLLOW SHELL
A HULK
THE MYSTERY FRIGHTENS AND DISGUSTS ME

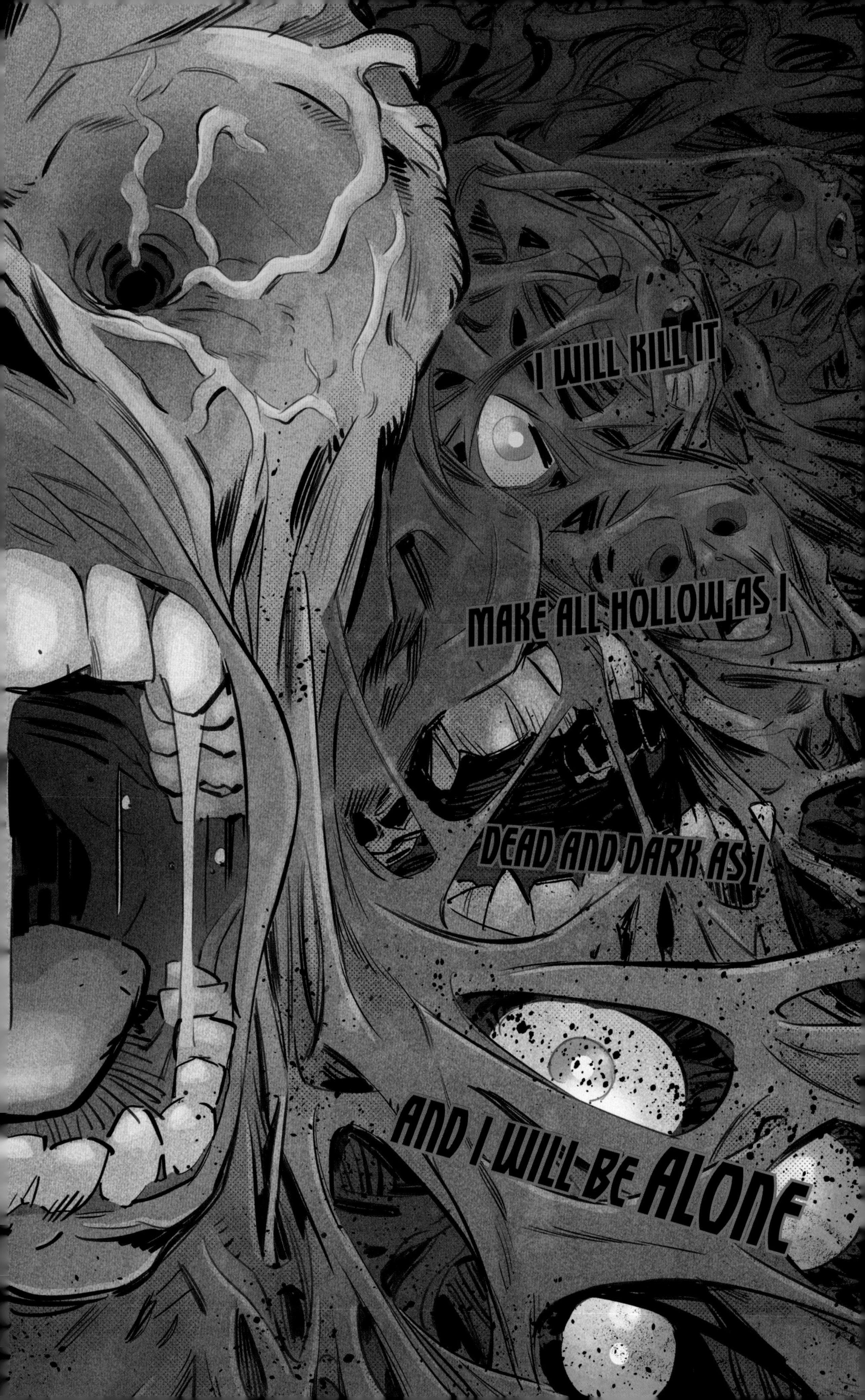

I WILL KILL IT
MAKE ALL HOLLOW AS I
DEAD AND DARK AS I
AND I WILL BE ALONE

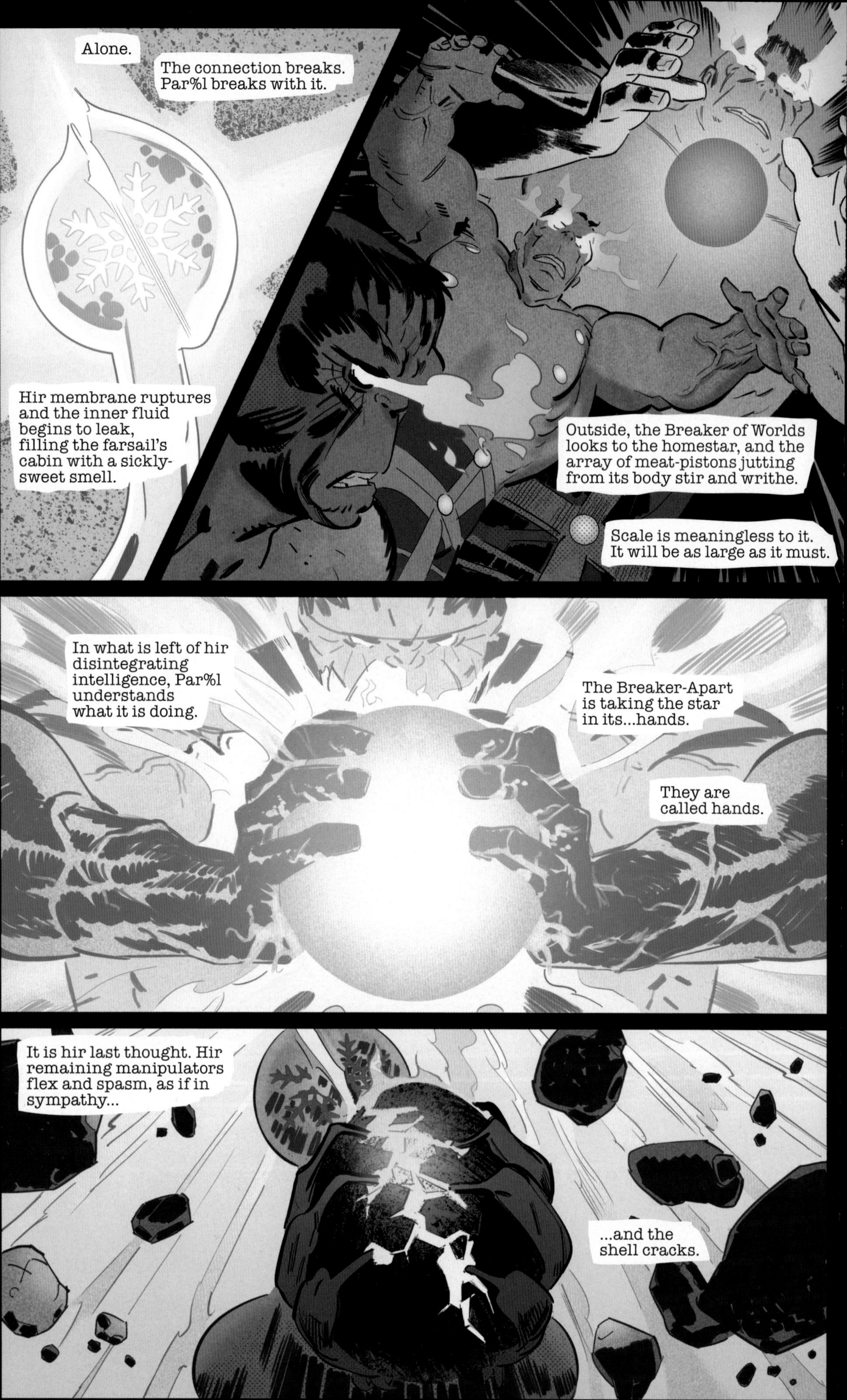
Alone.
The connection breaks. Par%l breaks with it.
Hir membrane ruptures and the inner fluid begins to leak, filling the farsail's cabin with a sickly-sweet smell.
Outside, the Breaker of Worlds looks to the homestar, and the array of meat-pistons jutting from its body stir and writhe.
Scale is meaningless to it. It will be as large as it must.
In what is left of hir disintegrating intelligence, Par%l understands what it is doing.
The Breaker-Apart is taking the star in its...hands.
They are called hands.
It is hir last thought. Hir remaining manipulators flex and spasm, as if in sympathy...
...and the shell cracks.

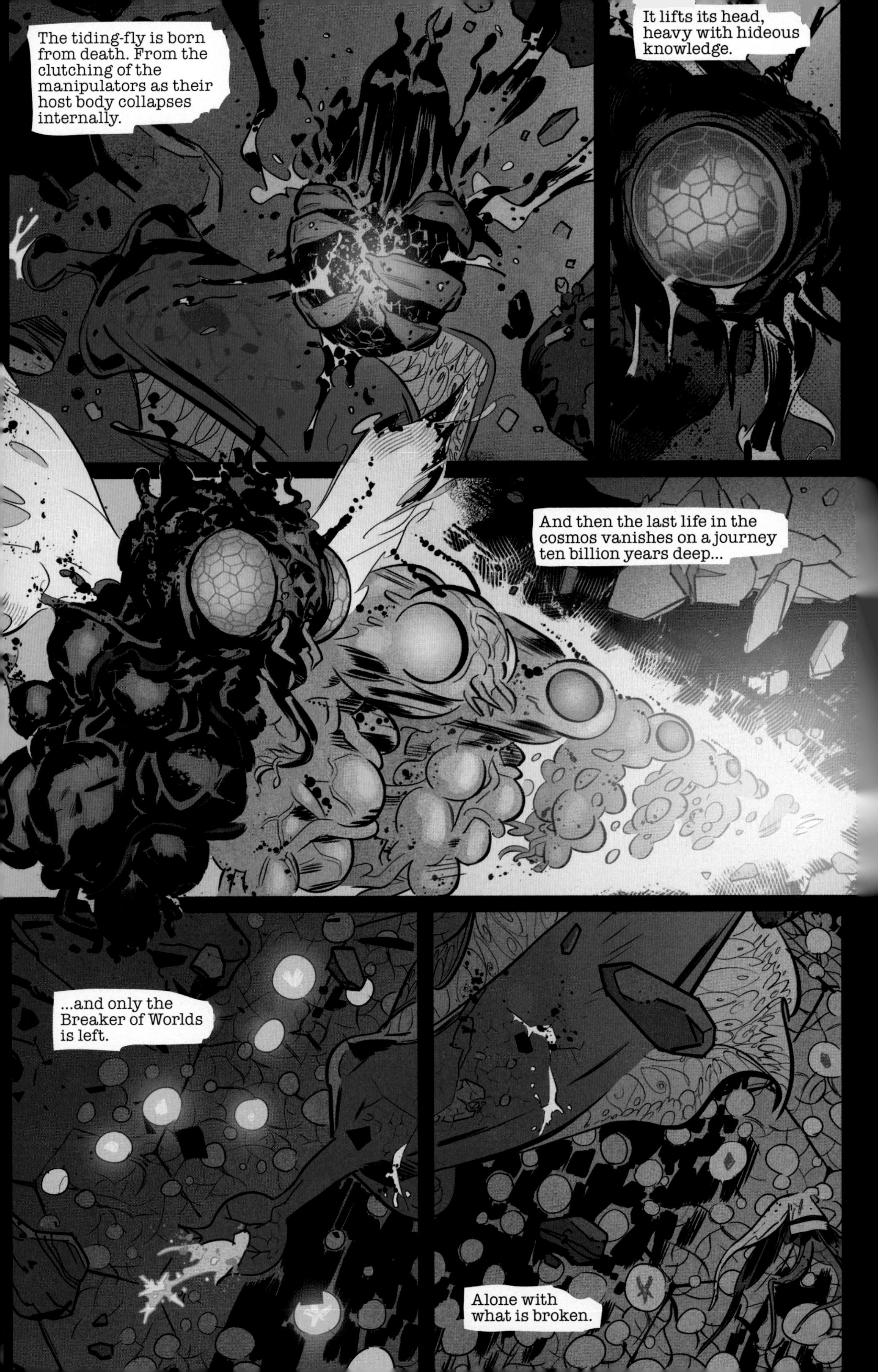
The tiding-fly is born from death. From the clutching of the manipulators as their host body collapses internally.
It lifts its head, heavy with hideous knowledge.
And then the last life in the cosmos vanishes on a journey ten billion years deep...
...and only the Breaker of Worlds is left.
Alone with what is broken.

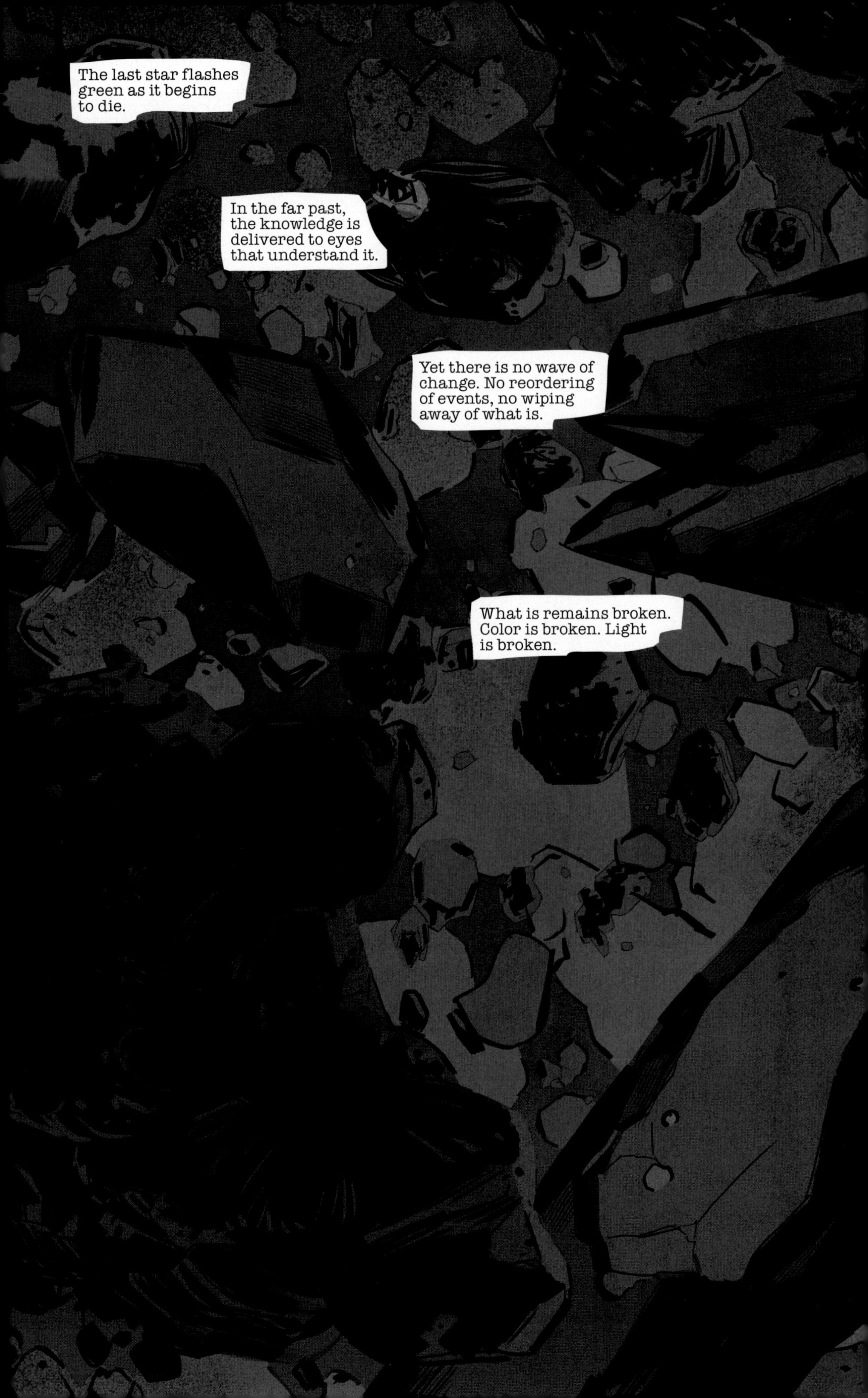
The last star flashes green as it begins to die.
In the far past, the knowledge is delivered to eyes that understand it.
Yet there is no wave of change. No reordering of events, no wiping away of what is.
What is remains broken. Color is broken. Light is broken.

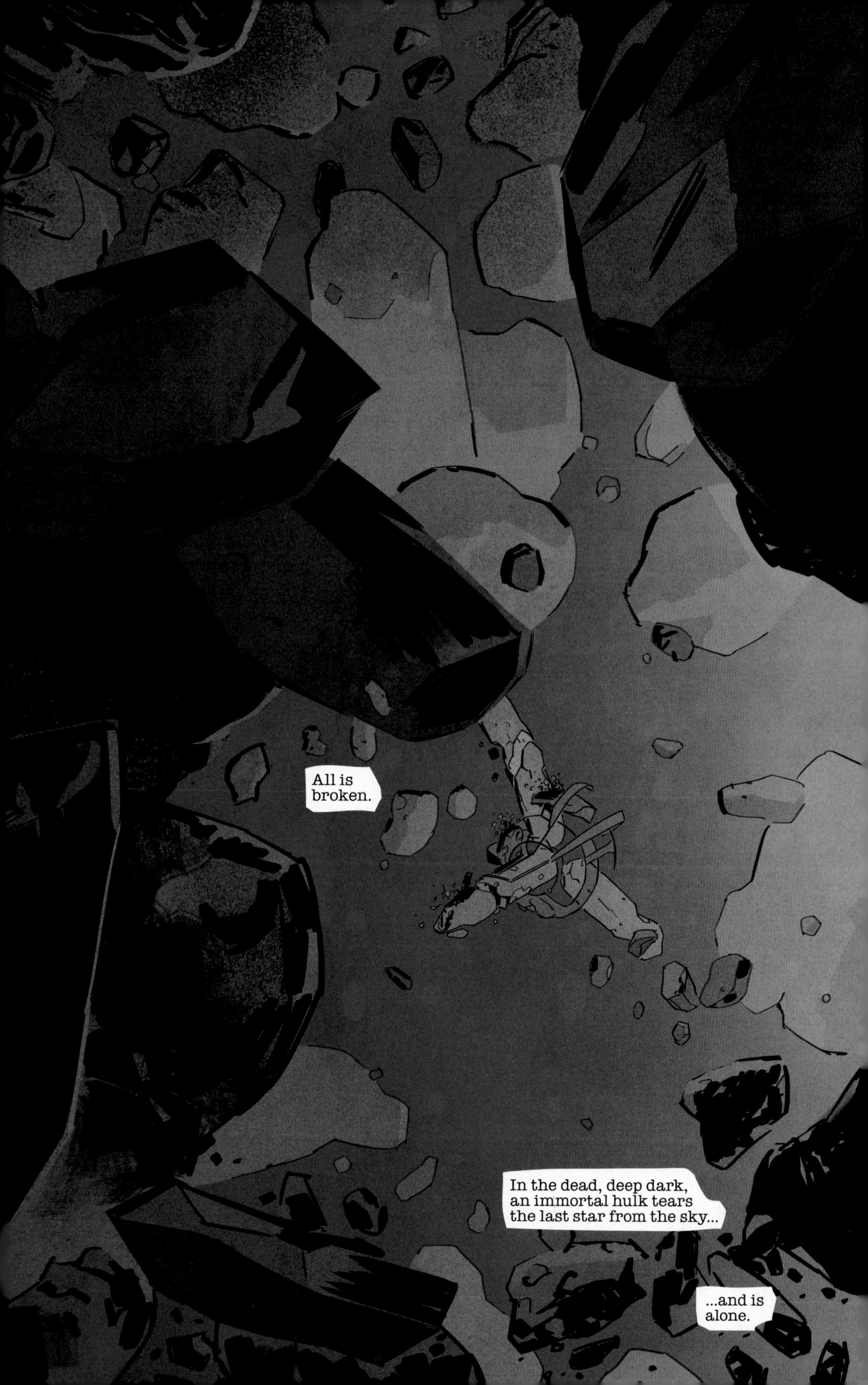
All is broken.
In the dead, deep dark, an immortal hulk tears the last star from the sky...
...and is alone.

"JOE?

IS THAT YOU? ARE YOU THERE?
I NEED HELP, JOE. I CAN'T SEE.

SOMETHING'S EATING ME.

I THINK...

I THINK IT KILLED THE HULK."

AND I'LL BE BACK.

WHEN THE MORN IS NEW.

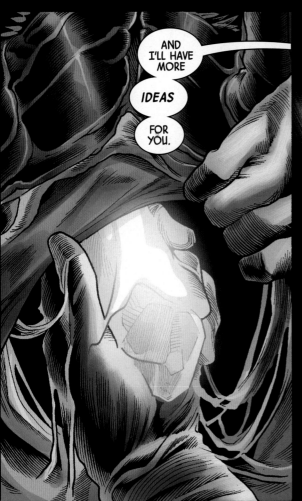

AND I'LL HAVE MORE

IDEAS

FOR YOU.

AND YOU'LL HAVE THINGS YOU'D LIKE TO *DO...*

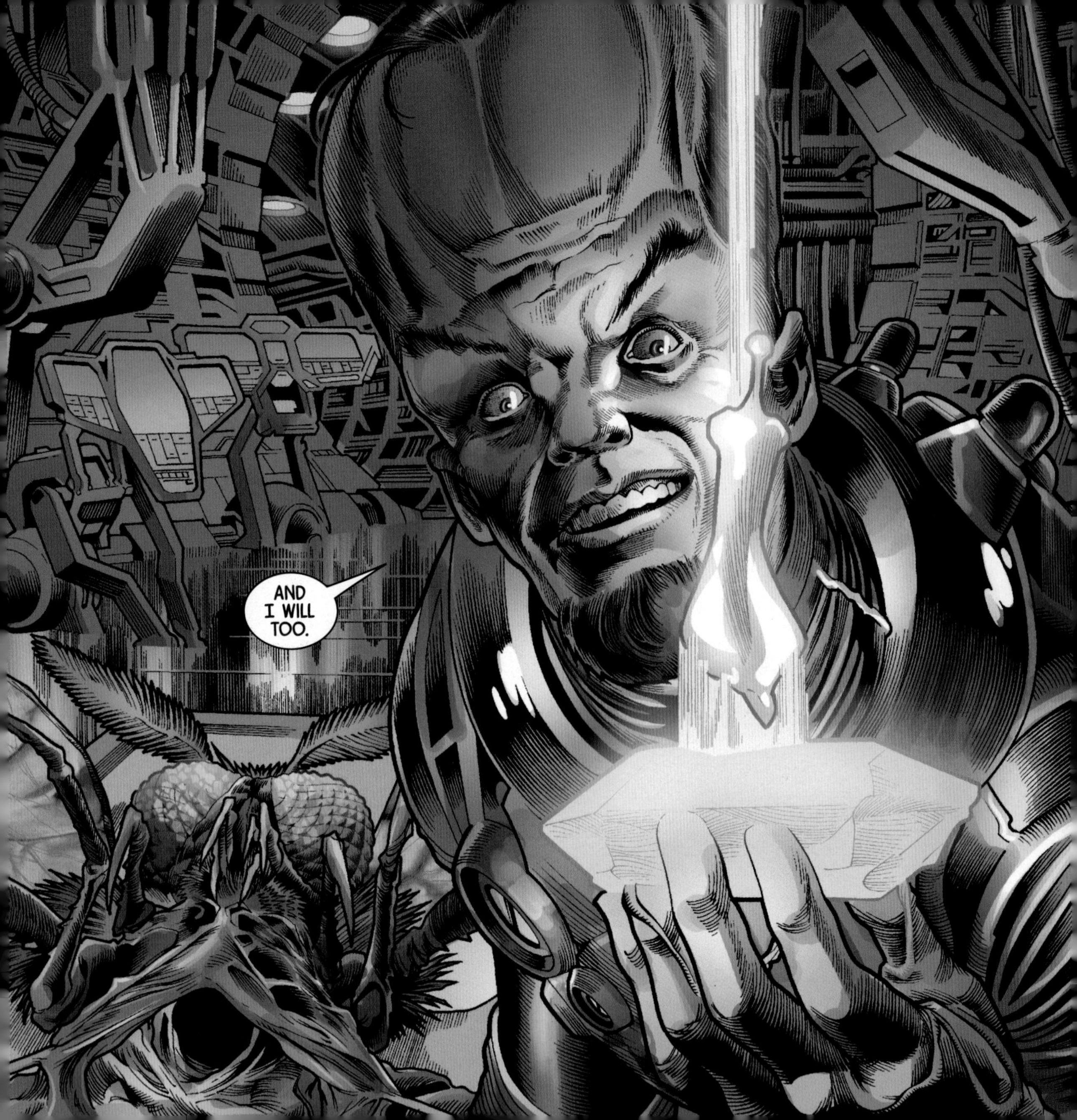
AND I WILL TOO.

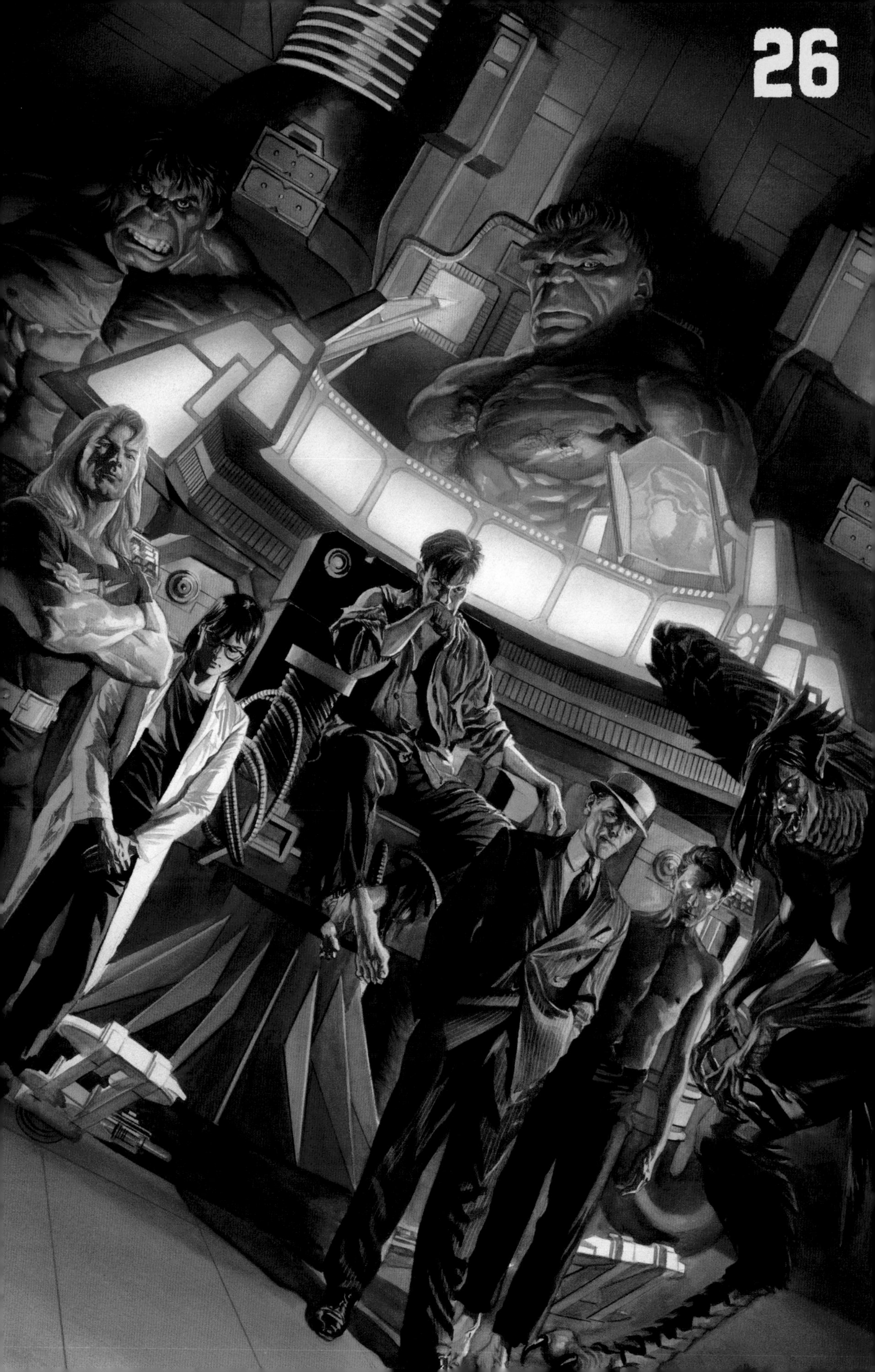
26

" **THAT STONY LAW I STAMP TO DUST; AND SCATTER RELIGION ABROAD TO THE FOUR WINDS AS A TORN BOOK, & NONE SHALL GATHER THE LEAVES...** "

– WILLIAM BLAKE
AMERICA: A PROPHECY

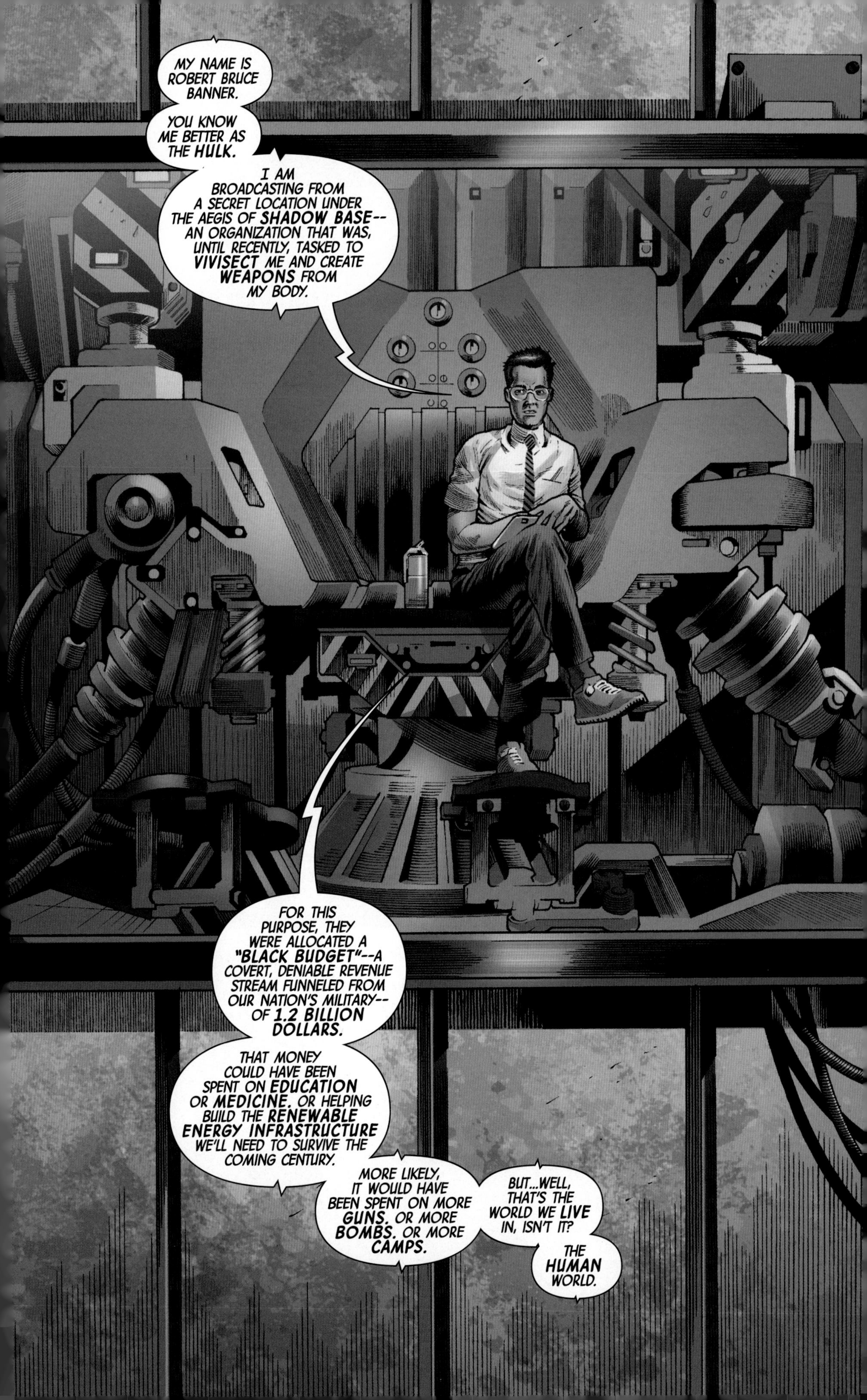
MY NAME IS ROBERT BRUCE BANNER.
YOU KNOW ME BETTER AS THE HULK.
I AM BROADCASTING FROM A SECRET LOCATION UNDER THE AEGIS OF SHADOW BASE--AN ORGANIZATION THAT WAS, UNTIL RECENTLY, TASKED TO VIVISECT ME AND CREATE WEAPONS FROM MY BODY.
FOR THIS PURPOSE, THEY WERE ALLOCATED A "BLACK BUDGET"--A COVERT, DENIABLE REVENUE STREAM FUNNELED FROM OUR NATION'S MILITARY--OF 1.2 BILLION DOLLARS.
THAT MONEY COULD HAVE BEEN SPENT ON EDUCATION OR MEDICINE. OR HELPING BUILD THE RENEWABLE ENERGY INFRASTRUCTURE WE'LL NEED TO SURVIVE THE COMING CENTURY.
MORE LIKELY, IT WOULD HAVE BEEN SPENT ON MORE GUNS. OR MORE BOMBS. OR MORE CAMPS.
BUT...WELL, THAT'S THE WORLD WE LIVE IN, ISN'T IT?
THE HUMAN WORLD.

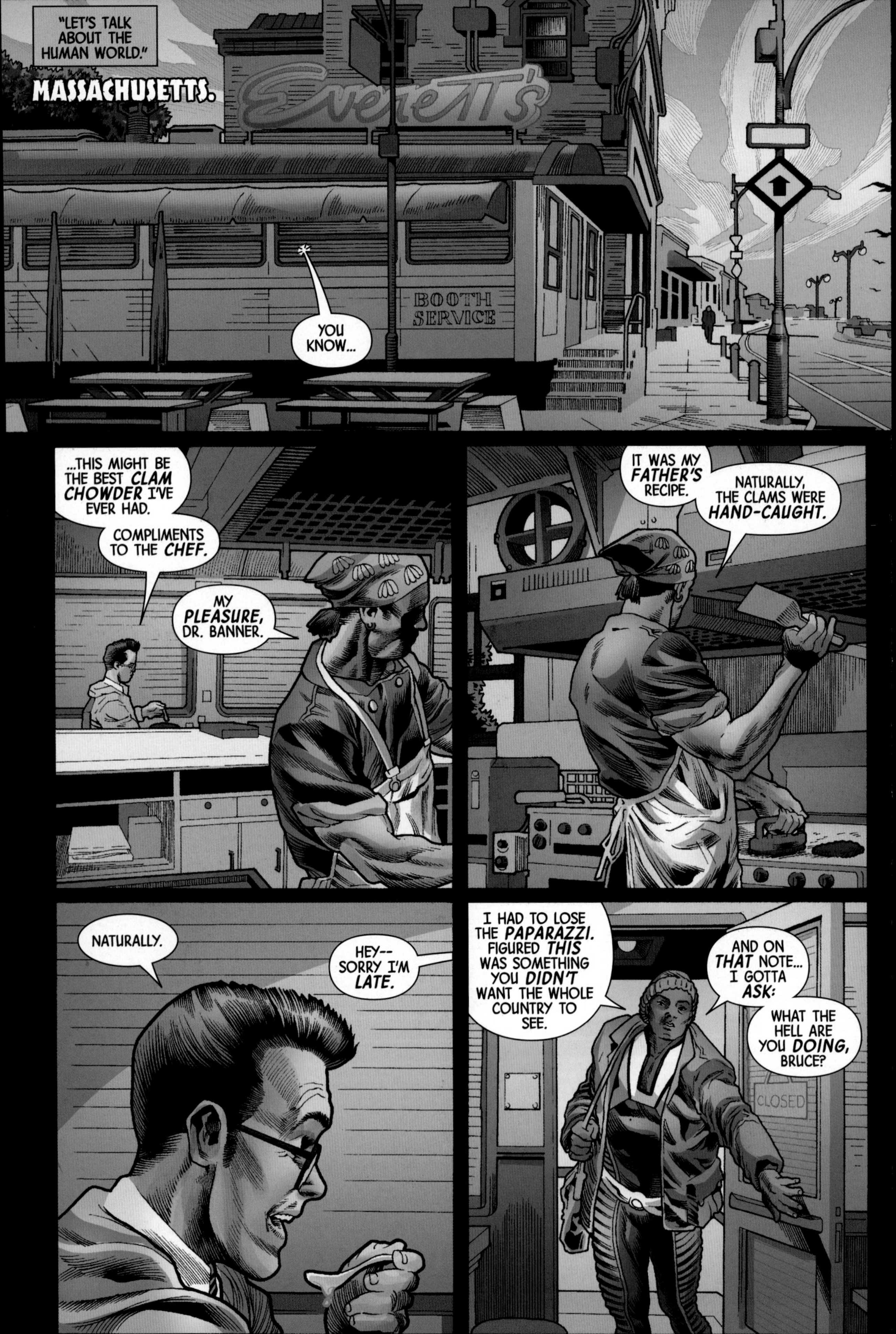
"LET'S TALK ABOUT THE HUMAN WORLD."
MASSACHUSETTS.
Everett's
BOOTH SERVICE
YOU KNOW...
...THIS MIGHT BE THE BEST CLAM CHOWDER I'VE EVER HAD.
COMPLIMENTS TO THE CHEF.
MY PLEASURE, DR. BANNER.
IT WAS MY FATHER'S RECIPE.
NATURALLY, THE CLAMS WERE HAND-CAUGHT.
NATURALLY.
HEY-- SORRY I'M LATE.
I HAD TO LOSE THE PAPARAZZI. FIGURED THIS WAS SOMETHING YOU DIDN'T WANT THE WHOLE COUNTRY TO SEE.
AND ON THAT NOTE... I GOTTA ASK:
WHAT THE HELL ARE YOU DOING, BRUCE?
CLOSED

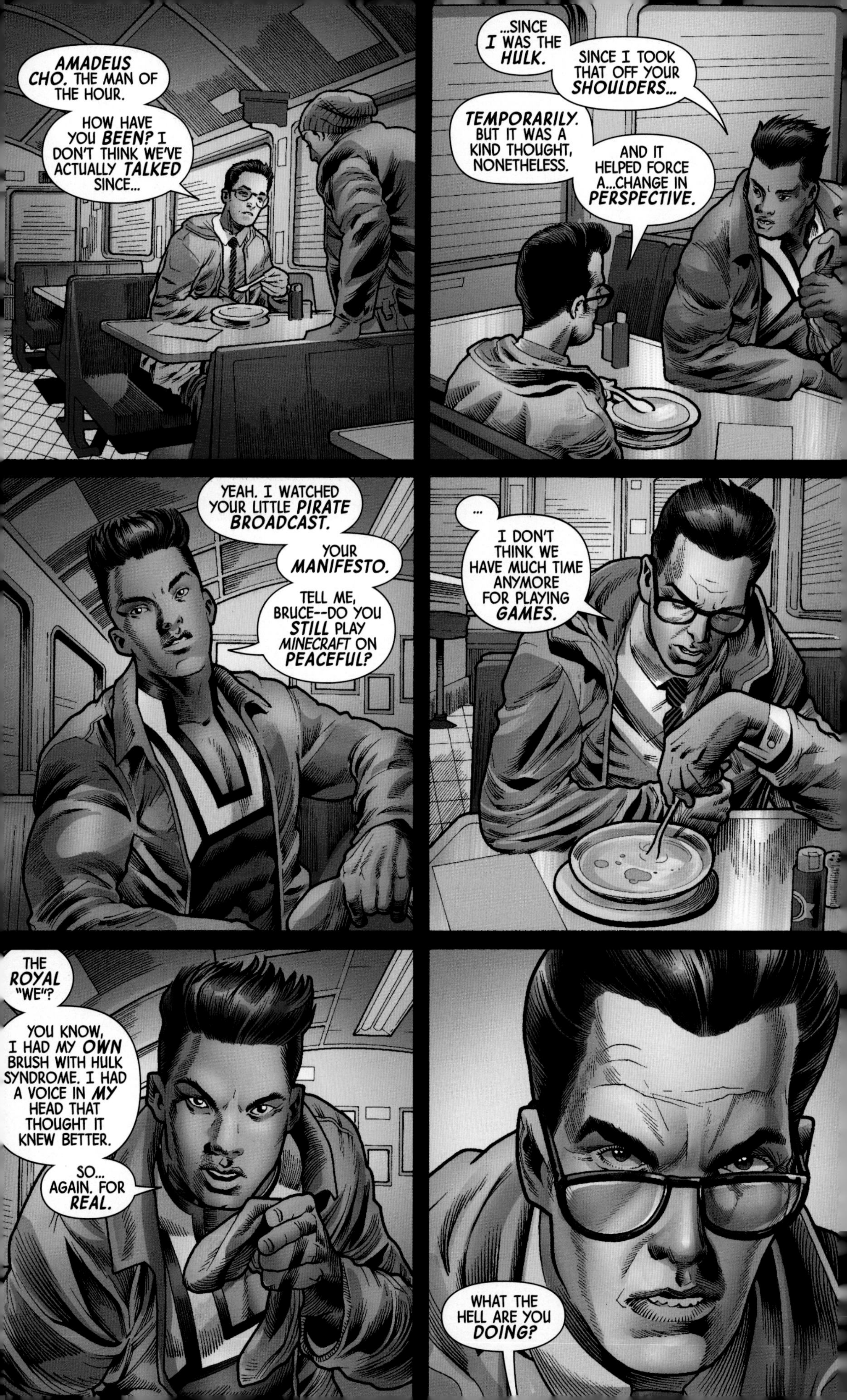
AMADEUS CHO. THE MAN OF THE HOUR.
HOW HAVE YOU BEEN? I DON'T THINK WE'VE ACTUALLY TALKED SINCE...
...SINCE I WAS THE HULK.
SINCE I TOOK THAT OFF YOUR SHOULDERS...
TEMPORARILY. BUT IT WAS A KIND THOUGHT, NONETHELESS.
AND IT HELPED FORCE A...CHANGE IN PERSPECTIVE.
YEAH. I WATCHED YOUR LITTLE PIRATE BROADCAST.
YOUR MANIFESTO.
TELL ME, BRUCE--DO YOU STILL PLAY MINECRAFT ON PEACEFUL?
...
I DON'T THINK WE HAVE MUCH TIME ANYMORE FOR PLAYING GAMES.
THE ROYAL "WE"?
YOU KNOW, I HAD MY OWN BRUSH WITH HULK SYNDROME. I HAD A VOICE IN MY HEAD THAT THOUGHT IT KNEW BETTER.
SO... AGAIN. FOR REAL.
WHAT THE HELL ARE YOU DOING?

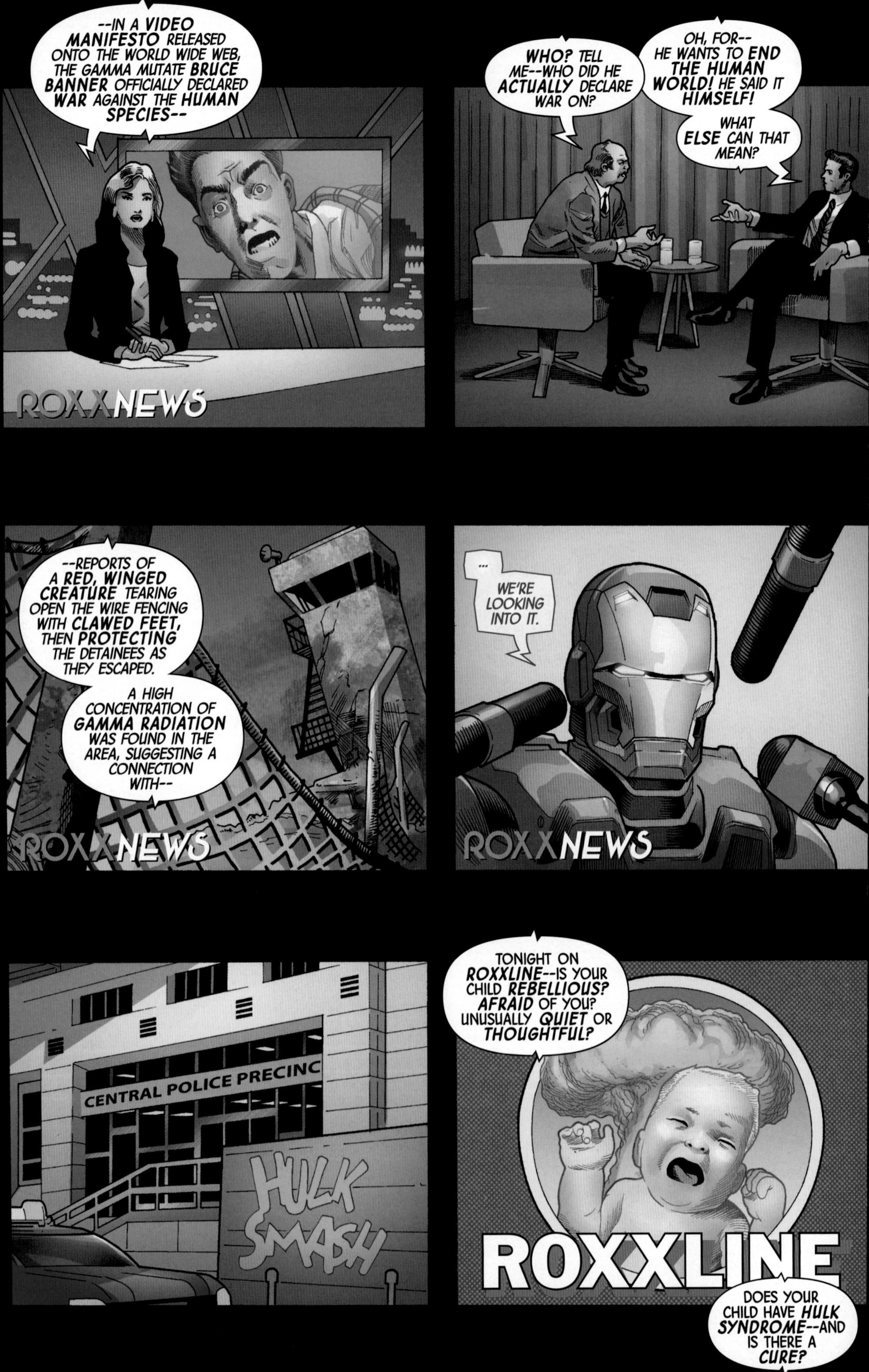
--IN A VIDEO MANIFESTO RELEASED ONTO THE WORLD WIDE WEB, THE GAMMA MUTATE BRUCE BANNER OFFICIALLY DECLARED WAR AGAINST THE HUMAN SPECIES--
ROXXNEWS
WHO? TELL ME--WHO DID HE ACTUALLY DECLARE WAR ON?
OH, FOR-- HE WANTS TO END THE HUMAN WORLD! HE SAID IT HIMSELF!
WHAT ELSE CAN THAT MEAN?
--REPORTS OF A RED, WINGED CREATURE TEARING OPEN THE WIRE FENCING WITH CLAWED FEET, THEN PROTECTING THE DETAINEES AS THEY ESCAPED.
A HIGH CONCENTRATION OF GAMMA RADIATION WAS FOUND IN THE AREA, SUGGESTING A CONNECTION WITH--
ROXXNEWS
...
WE'RE LOOKING INTO IT.
ROXXNEWS
CENTRAL POLICE PRECINC
HULK SMASH
TONIGHT ON ROXXLINE--IS YOUR CHILD REBELLIOUS? AFRAID OF YOU? UNUSUALLY QUIET OR THOUGHTFUL?
ROXXLINE
DOES YOUR CHILD HAVE HULK SYNDROME--AND IS THERE A CURE?

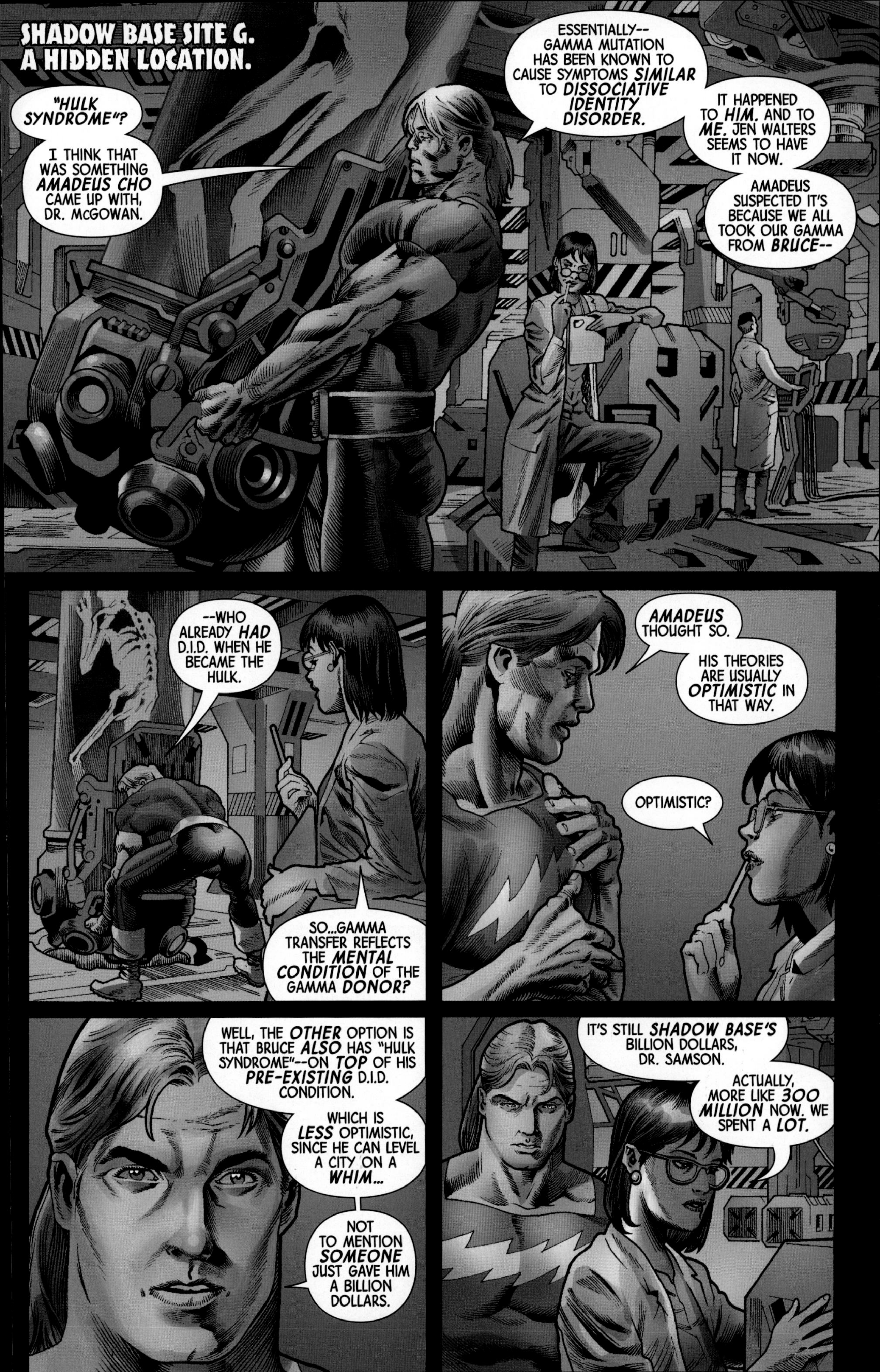
SHADOW BASE SITE G. A HIDDEN LOCATION.
"HULK SYNDROME"?
I THINK THAT WAS SOMETHING AMADEUS CHO CAME UP WITH, DR. McGOWAN.
ESSENTIALLY-- GAMMA MUTATION HAS BEEN KNOWN TO CAUSE SYMPTOMS SIMILAR TO DISSOCIATIVE IDENTITY DISORDER.
IT HAPPENED TO HIM. AND TO ME. JEN WALTERS SEEMS TO HAVE IT NOW.
AMADEUS SUSPECTED IT'S BECAUSE WE ALL TOOK OUR GAMMA FROM BRUCE--
--WHO ALREADY HAD D.I.D. WHEN HE BECAME THE HULK.
SO...GAMMA TRANSFER REFLECTS THE MENTAL CONDITION OF THE GAMMA DONOR?
AMADEUS THOUGHT SO.
HIS THEORIES ARE USUALLY OPTIMISTIC IN THAT WAY.
OPTIMISTIC?
WELL, THE OTHER OPTION IS THAT BRUCE ALSO HAS "HULK SYNDROME"--ON TOP OF HIS PRE-EXISTING D.I.D. CONDITION.
WHICH IS LESS OPTIMISTIC, SINCE HE CAN LEVEL A CITY ON A WHIM...
NOT TO MENTION SOMEONE JUST GAVE HIM A BILLION DOLLARS.
IT'S STILL SHADOW BASE'S BILLION DOLLARS, DR. SAMSON.
ACTUALLY, MORE LIKE 300 MILLION NOW. WE SPENT A LOT.

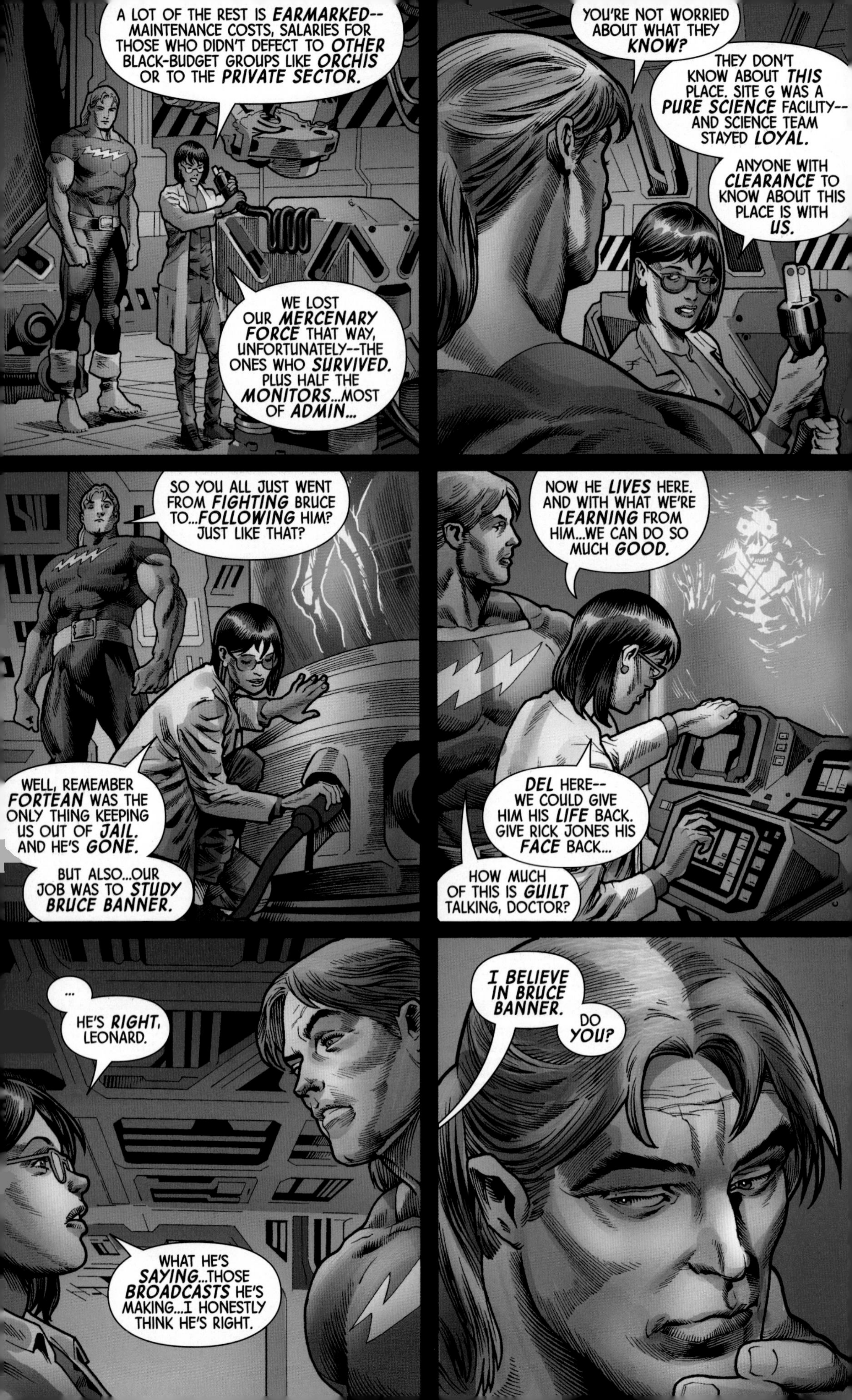
A LOT OF THE REST IS EARMARKED--MAINTENANCE COSTS, SALARIES FOR THOSE WHO DIDN'T DEFECT TO OTHER BLACK-BUDGET GROUPS LIKE ORCHIS OR TO THE PRIVATE SECTOR.
WE LOST OUR MERCENARY FORCE THAT WAY, UNFORTUNATELY--THE ONES WHO SURVIVED. PLUS HALF THE MONITORS...MOST OF ADMIN...
YOU'RE NOT WORRIED ABOUT WHAT THEY KNOW?
THEY DON'T KNOW ABOUT THIS PLACE. SITE G WAS A PURE SCIENCE FACILITY--AND SCIENCE TEAM STAYED LOYAL.
ANYONE WITH CLEARANCE TO KNOW ABOUT THIS PLACE IS WITH US.
SO YOU ALL JUST WENT FROM FIGHTING BRUCE TO...FOLLOWING HIM? JUST LIKE THAT?
WELL, REMEMBER FORTEAN WAS THE ONLY THING KEEPING US OUT OF JAIL. AND HE'S GONE.
BUT ALSO...OUR JOB WAS TO STUDY BRUCE BANNER.
NOW HE LIVES HERE. AND WITH WHAT WE'RE LEARNING FROM HIM...WE CAN DO SO MUCH GOOD.
DEL HERE--WE COULD GIVE HIM HIS LIFE BACK. GIVE RICK JONES HIS FACE BACK...
HOW MUCH OF THIS IS GUILT TALKING, DOCTOR?
...
HE'S RIGHT, LEONARD.
WHAT HE'S SAYING...THOSE BROADCASTS HE'S MAKING...I HONESTLY THINK HE'S RIGHT.
I BELIEVE IN BRUCE BANNER.
DO YOU?

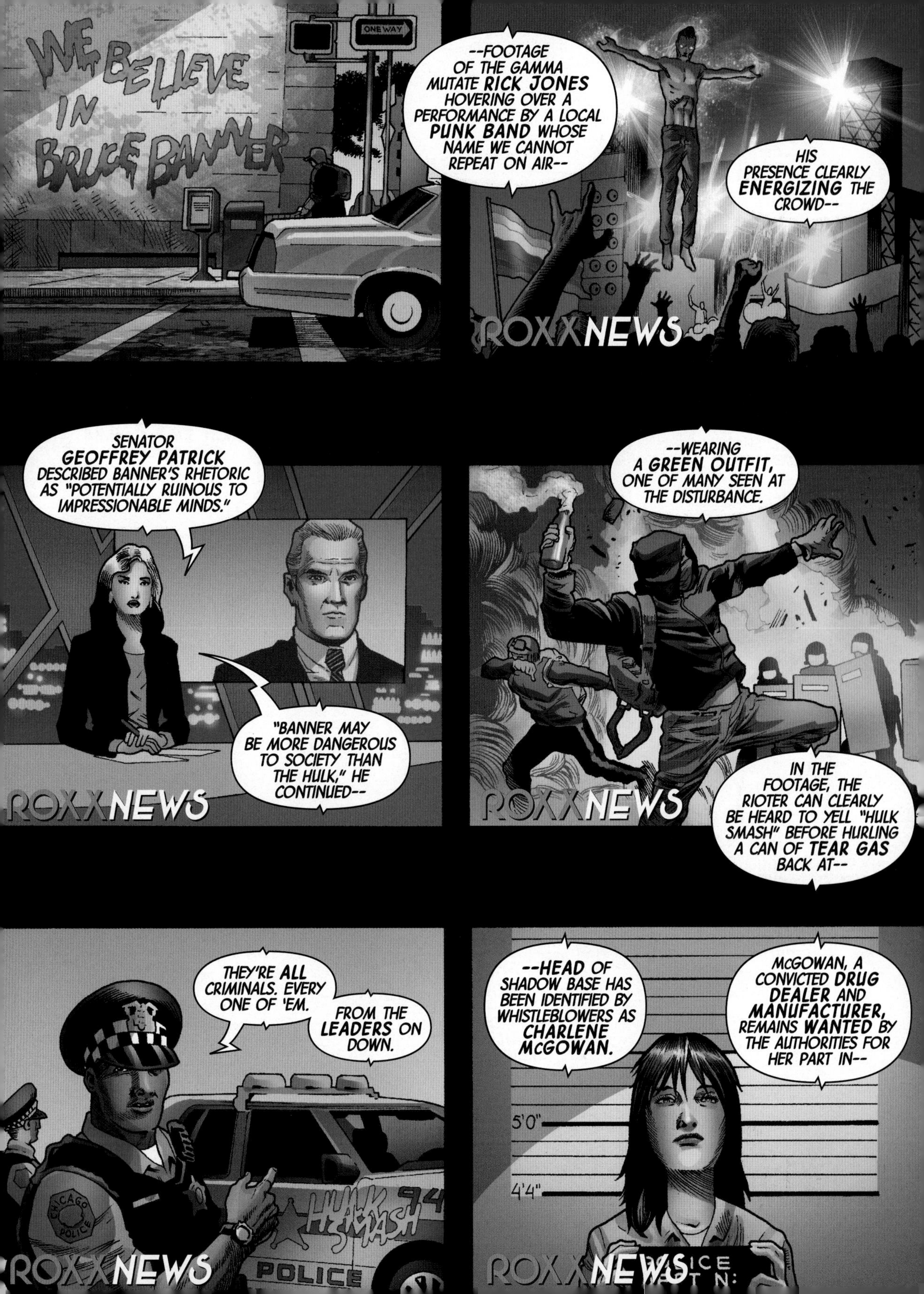
WE BELIEVE IN BRUCE BANNER
ONE WAY
--FOOTAGE OF THE GAMMA MUTATE RICK JONES HOVERING OVER A PERFORMANCE BY A LOCAL PUNK BAND WHOSE NAME WE CANNOT REPEAT ON AIR--
HIS PRESENCE CLEARLY ENERGIZING THE CROWD--
ROXX NEWS
SENATOR GEOFFREY PATRICK DESCRIBED BANNER'S RHETORIC AS "POTENTIALLY RUINOUS TO IMPRESSIONABLE MINDS."
"BANNER MAY BE MORE DANGEROUS TO SOCIETY THAN THE HULK," HE CONTINUED--
ROXX NEWS
--WEARING A GREEN OUTFIT, ONE OF MANY SEEN AT THE DISTURBANCE.
IN THE FOOTAGE, THE RIOTER CAN CLEARLY BE HEARD TO YELL "HULK SMASH" BEFORE HURLING A CAN OF TEAR GAS BACK AT--
ROXX NEWS
THEY'RE ALL CRIMINALS. EVERY ONE OF 'EM.
FROM THE LEADERS ON DOWN.
CHICAGO POLICE
HULK SMASH
POLICE
ROXX NEWS
--HEAD OF SHADOW BASE HAS BEEN IDENTIFIED BY WHISTLEBLOWERS AS CHARLENE McGOWAN.
McGOWAN, A CONVICTED DRUG DEALER AND MANUFACTURER, REMAINS WANTED BY THE AUTHORITIES FOR HER PART IN--
5'0"
4'4"
ROXX NEWS

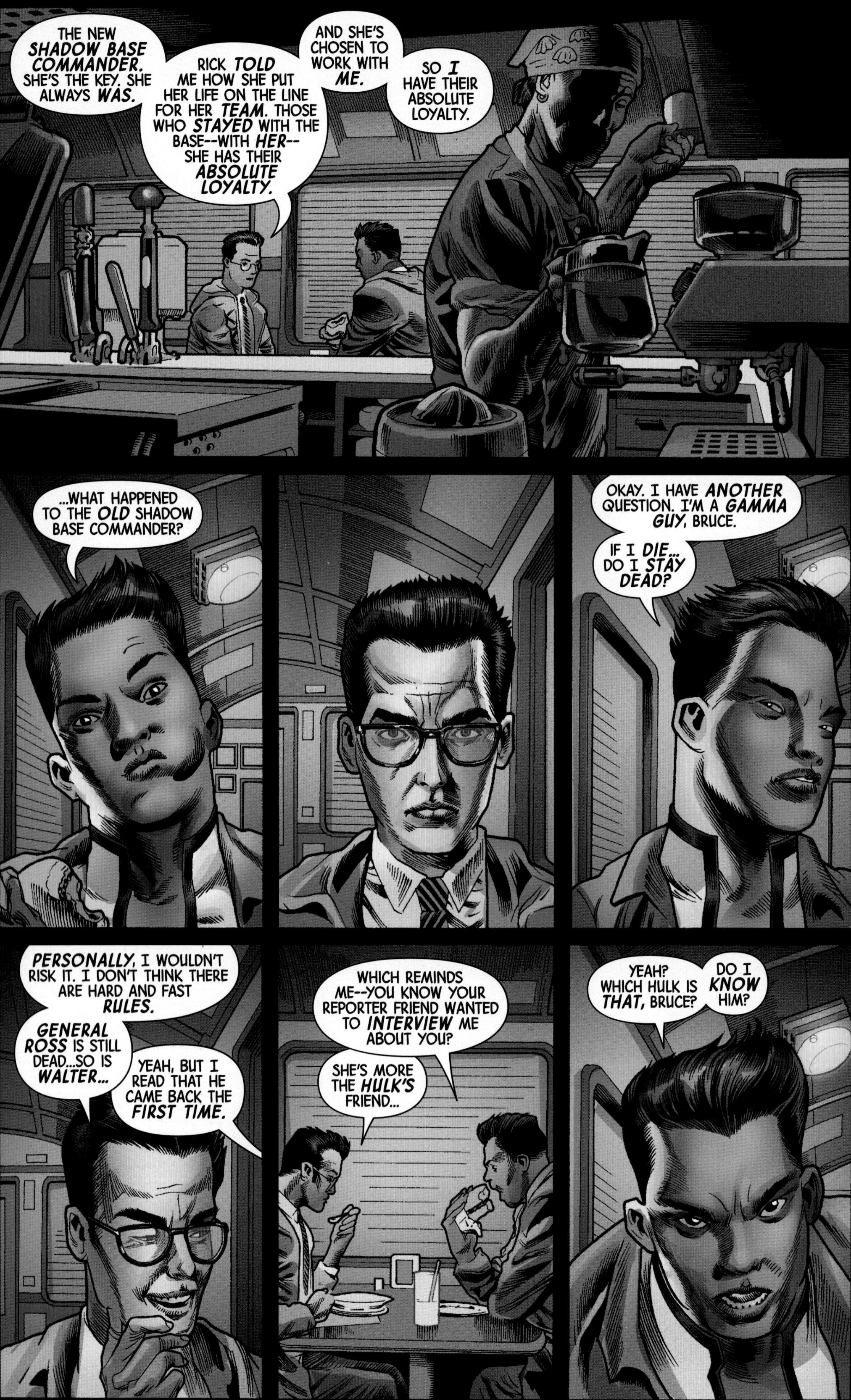
THE NEW SHADOW BASE COMMANDER. SHE'S THE KEY. SHE ALWAYS WAS.
RICK TOLD ME HOW SHE PUT HER LIFE ON THE LINE FOR HER TEAM. THOSE WHO STAYED WITH THE BASE--WITH HER--SHE HAS THEIR ABSOLUTE LOYALTY.
AND SHE'S CHOSEN TO WORK WITH ME.
SO I HAVE THEIR ABSOLUTE LOYALTY.
...WHAT HAPPENED TO THE OLD SHADOW BASE COMMANDER?
OKAY. I HAVE ANOTHER QUESTION. I'M A GAMMA GUY, BRUCE.
IF I DIE... DO I STAY DEAD?
PERSONALLY, I WOULDN'T RISK IT. I DON'T THINK THERE ARE HARD AND FAST RULES.
GENERAL ROSS IS STILL DEAD...SO IS WALTER...
YEAH, BUT I READ THAT HE CAME BACK THE FIRST TIME.
WHICH REMINDS ME--YOU KNOW YOUR REPORTER FRIEND WANTED TO INTERVIEW ME ABOUT YOU?
SHE'S MORE THE HULK'S FRIEND...
YEAH? WHICH HULK IS THAT, BRUCE?
DO I KNOW HIM?

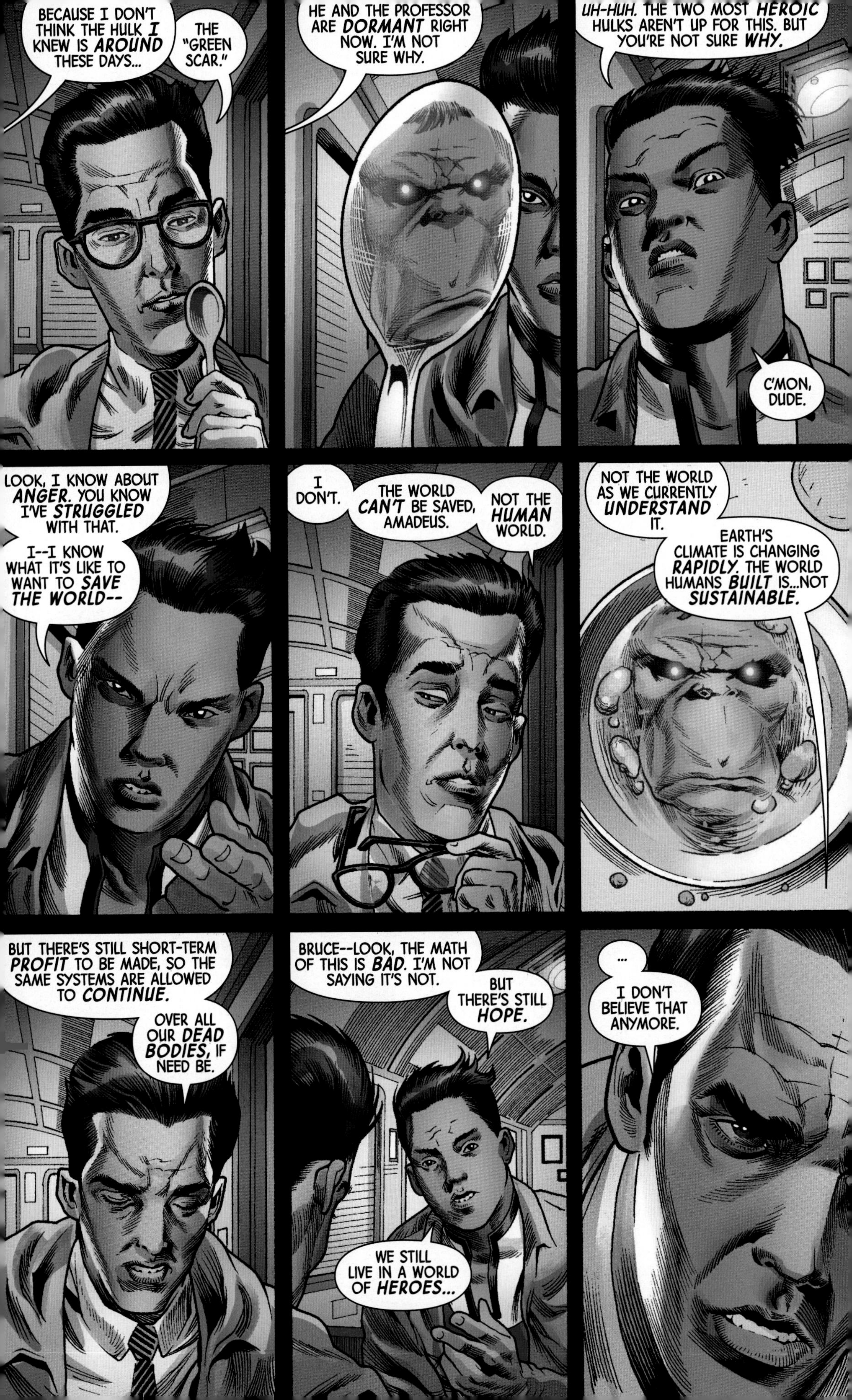
BECAUSE I DON'T THINK THE HULK I KNEW IS AROUND THESE DAYS...
THE "GREEN SCAR."
HE AND THE PROFESSOR ARE DORMANT RIGHT NOW. I'M NOT SURE WHY.
UH-HUH. THE TWO MOST HEROIC HULKS AREN'T UP FOR THIS. BUT YOU'RE NOT SURE WHY.
C'MON, DUDE.
LOOK, I KNOW ABOUT ANGER. YOU KNOW I'VE STRUGGLED WITH THAT.
I--I KNOW WHAT IT'S LIKE TO WANT TO SAVE THE WORLD--
I DON'T.
THE WORLD CAN'T BE SAVED, AMADEUS.
NOT THE HUMAN WORLD.
NOT THE WORLD AS WE CURRENTLY UNDERSTAND IT.
EARTH'S CLIMATE IS CHANGING RAPIDLY. THE WORLD HUMANS BUILT IS...NOT SUSTAINABLE.
BUT THERE'S STILL SHORT-TERM PROFIT TO BE MADE, SO THE SAME SYSTEMS ARE ALLOWED TO CONTINUE.
OVER ALL OUR DEAD BODIES, IF NEED BE.
BRUCE--LOOK, THE MATH OF THIS IS BAD. I'M NOT SAYING IT'S NOT.
BUT THERE'S STILL HOPE.
WE STILL LIVE IN A WORLD OF HEROES...
...
I DON'T BELIEVE THAT ANYMORE.

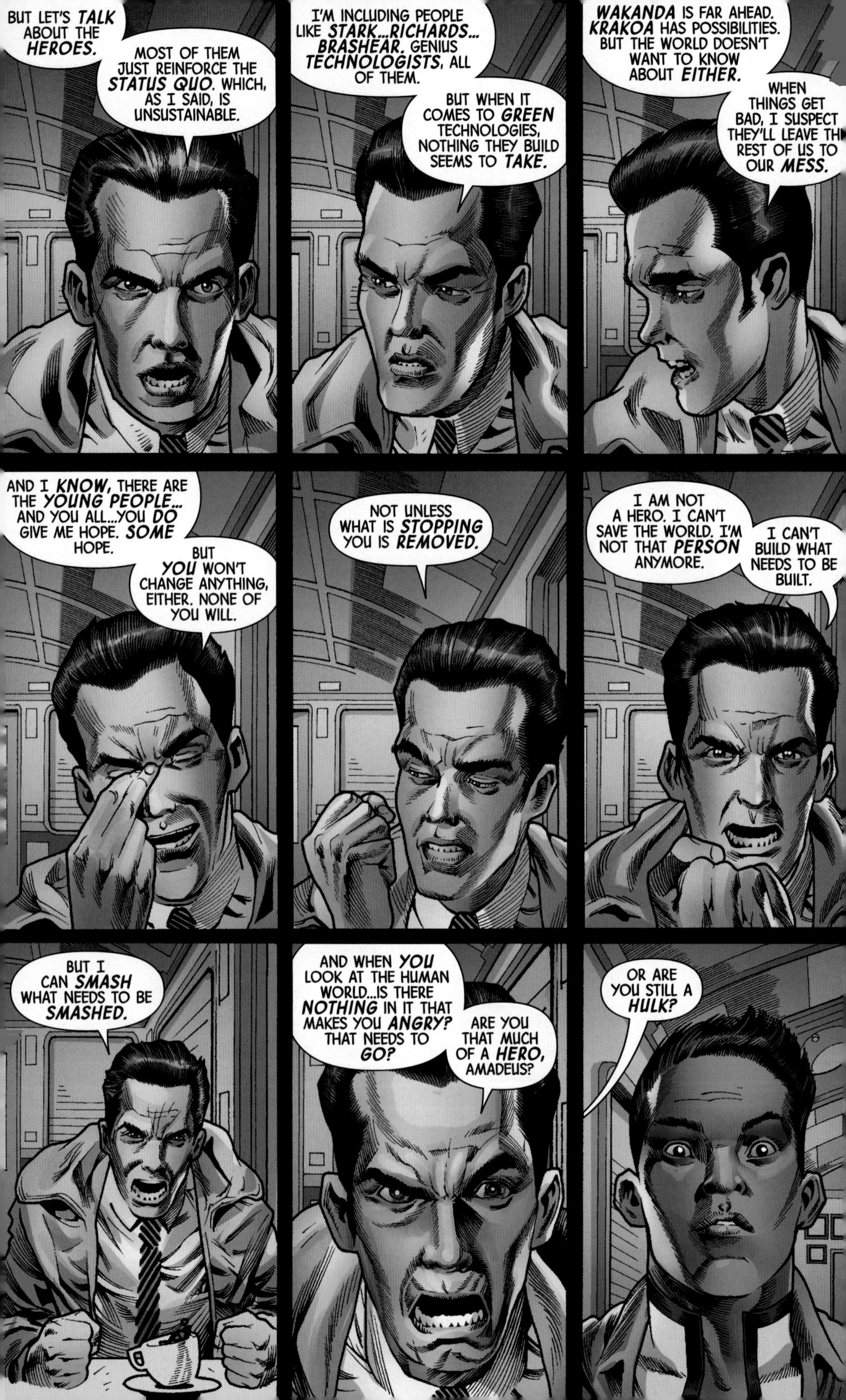
BUT LET'S TALK ABOUT THE HEROES.
MOST OF THEM JUST REINFORCE THE STATUS QUO. WHICH, AS I SAID, IS UNSUSTAINABLE.
I'M INCLUDING PEOPLE LIKE STARK...RICHARDS... BRASHEAR. GENIUS TECHNOLOGISTS, ALL OF THEM.
BUT WHEN IT COMES TO GREEN TECHNOLOGIES, NOTHING THEY BUILD SEEMS TO TAKE.
WAKANDA IS FAR AHEAD. KRAKOA HAS POSSIBILITIES. BUT THE WORLD DOESN'T WANT TO KNOW ABOUT EITHER.
WHEN THINGS GET BAD, I SUSPECT THEY'LL LEAVE THE REST OF US TO OUR MESS.
AND I KNOW, THERE ARE THE YOUNG PEOPLE... AND YOU ALL...YOU DO GIVE ME HOPE. SOME HOPE.
BUT YOU WON'T CHANGE ANYTHING, EITHER. NONE OF YOU WILL.
NOT UNLESS WHAT IS STOPPING YOU IS REMOVED.
I AM NOT A HERO. I CAN'T SAVE THE WORLD. I'M NOT THAT PERSON ANYMORE.
I CAN'T BUILD WHAT NEEDS TO BE BUILT.
BUT I CAN SMASH WHAT NEEDS TO BE SMASHED.
AND WHEN YOU LOOK AT THE HUMAN WORLD...IS THERE NOTHING IN IT THAT MAKES YOU ANGRY? THAT NEEDS TO GO?
ARE YOU THAT MUCH OF A HERO, AMADEUS?
OR ARE YOU STILL A HULK?

BECAUSE WE *DO NOT NEED* ANOTHER *HULK!* AND YET *THAT* IS WHAT THEY WANTED TO *DO!* THE CREEPS IN THE *DEEP STATE!*

MAKE *MORE* OF HIM! USING *YOUR MONEY* TO DO IT! ONE BILLION DOLLARS OF TAXPAYER MONEY--HANDED TO *CRIMINALS* AND *JUNKIES!*

--SECRETARY OF *SUPER HUMAN AFFAIRS,* SENATOR *KEVIN KRASK,* PUBLICALLY *DENIED* REPORTS OF SO-CALLED *"HULK FUNDING"* GOING TO-- I'M SORRY, EXCUSE ME--

--I'M GETTING WORD THE SENATOR HAS JUST *RESIGNED--*

ROXX NEWS

"I THOUGHT THAT GUY WAS DEAD!"

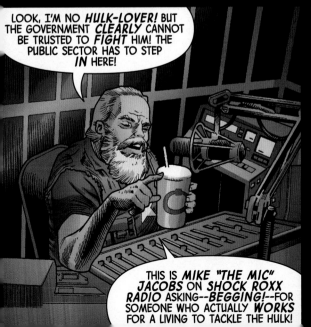

LOOK, I'M NO *HULK-LOVER!* BUT THE GOVERNMENT *CLEARLY* CANNOT BE TRUSTED TO *FIGHT* HIM! THE PUBLIC SECTOR HAS TO STEP *IN* HERE!

THIS IS *MIKE "THE MIC" JACOBS* ON *SHOCK ROXX RADIO* ASKING--*BEGGING!*--FOR SOMEONE WHO ACTUALLY *WORKS* FOR A LIVING TO TACKLE THE HULK!

AND NOW, A WORD FROM OUR SPONSORS.

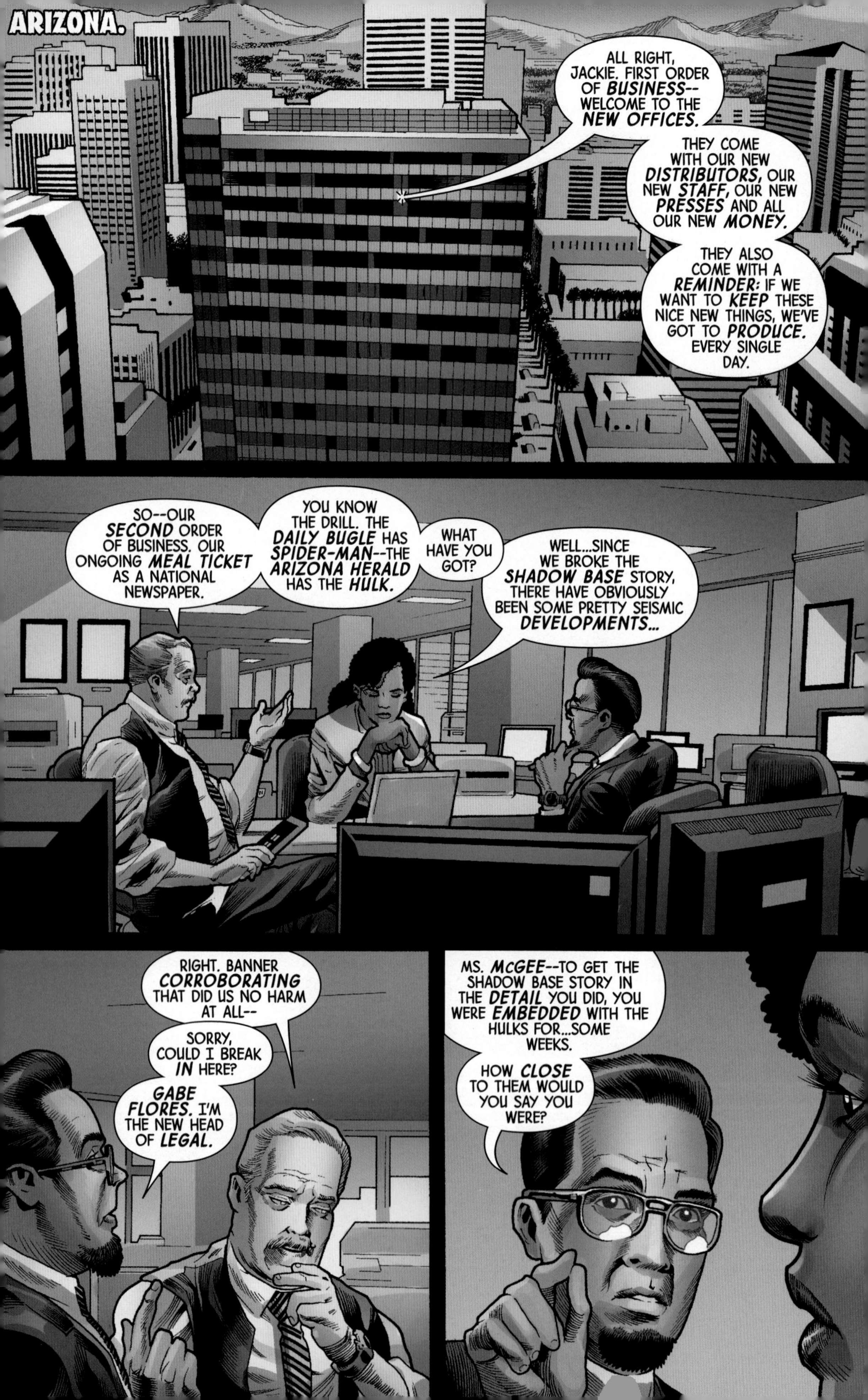
ARIZONA.
ALL RIGHT, JACKIE. FIRST ORDER OF BUSINESS-- WELCOME TO THE NEW OFFICES.
THEY COME WITH OUR NEW DISTRIBUTORS, OUR NEW STAFF, OUR NEW PRESSES AND ALL OUR NEW MONEY.
THEY ALSO COME WITH A REMINDER: IF WE WANT TO KEEP THESE NICE NEW THINGS, WE'VE GOT TO PRODUCE. EVERY SINGLE DAY.
SO--OUR SECOND ORDER OF BUSINESS. OUR ONGOING MEAL TICKET AS A NATIONAL NEWSPAPER.
YOU KNOW THE DRILL. THE DAILY BUGLE HAS SPIDER-MAN--THE ARIZONA HERALD HAS THE HULK.
WHAT HAVE YOU GOT?
WELL...SINCE WE BROKE THE SHADOW BASE STORY, THERE HAVE OBVIOUSLY BEEN SOME PRETTY SEISMIC DEVELOPMENTS...
RIGHT. BANNER CORROBORATING THAT DID US NO HARM AT ALL--
SORRY, COULD I BREAK IN HERE?
GABE FLORES. I'M THE NEW HEAD OF LEGAL.
MS. MCGEE--TO GET THE SHADOW BASE STORY IN THE DETAIL YOU DID, YOU WERE EMBEDDED WITH THE HULKS FOR...SOME WEEKS.
HOW CLOSE TO THEM WOULD YOU SAY YOU WERE?

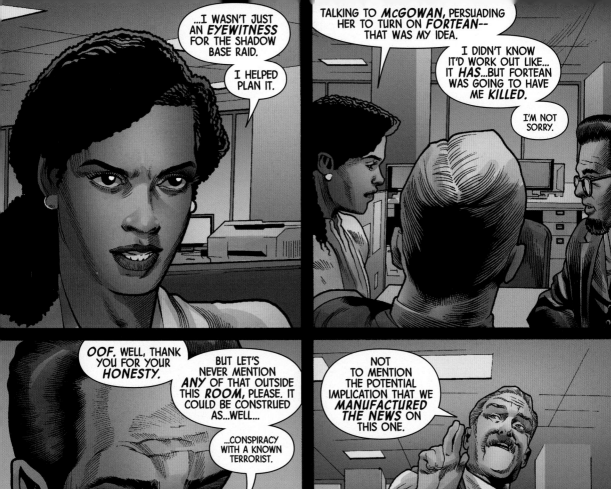

...I WASN'T JUST AN *EYEWITNESS* FOR THE SHADOW BASE RAID.

I HELPED PLAN IT.

TALKING TO *McGOWAN*, PERSUADING HER TO TURN ON *FORTEAN*-- THAT WAS MY IDEA.

I DIDN'T KNOW IT'D WORK OUT LIKE... IT *HAS*...BUT FORTEAN WAS GOING TO HAVE ME *KILLED*.

I'M NOT SORRY.

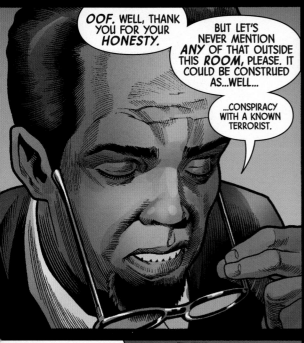

OOF. WELL, THANK YOU FOR YOUR *HONESTY.*

BUT LET'S NEVER MENTION *ANY* OF THAT OUTSIDE THIS *ROOM*, PLEASE. IT COULD BE CONSTRUED AS...WELL...

...CONSPIRACY WITH A KNOWN TERRORIST.

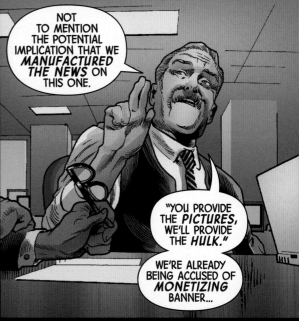

NOT TO MENTION THE POTENTIAL IMPLICATION THAT WE *MANUFACTURED THE NEWS* ON THIS ONE.

"YOU PROVIDE THE *PICTURES*, WE'LL PROVIDE THE *HULK.*"

WE'RE ALREADY BEING ACCUSED OF *MONETIZING* BANNER...

WELL...THE GOOD NEWS IS THAT AFTER *TODAY*, WE WON'T BE THE ONLY ONES.

THAT'S *TOMORROW'S* FRONT PAGE. MY SOURCES SAY THE GOVERNMENT IS READY TO ANNOUNCE THEY'RE *SUBCONTRACTING* ANTI-HULK OPERATIONS.

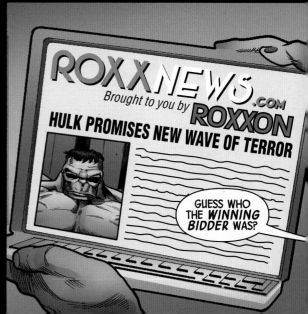

ROXX NEWS.com
Brought to you by ROXXON

HULK PROMISES NEW WAVE OF TERROR

GUESS WHO THE *WINNING BIDDER* WAS?

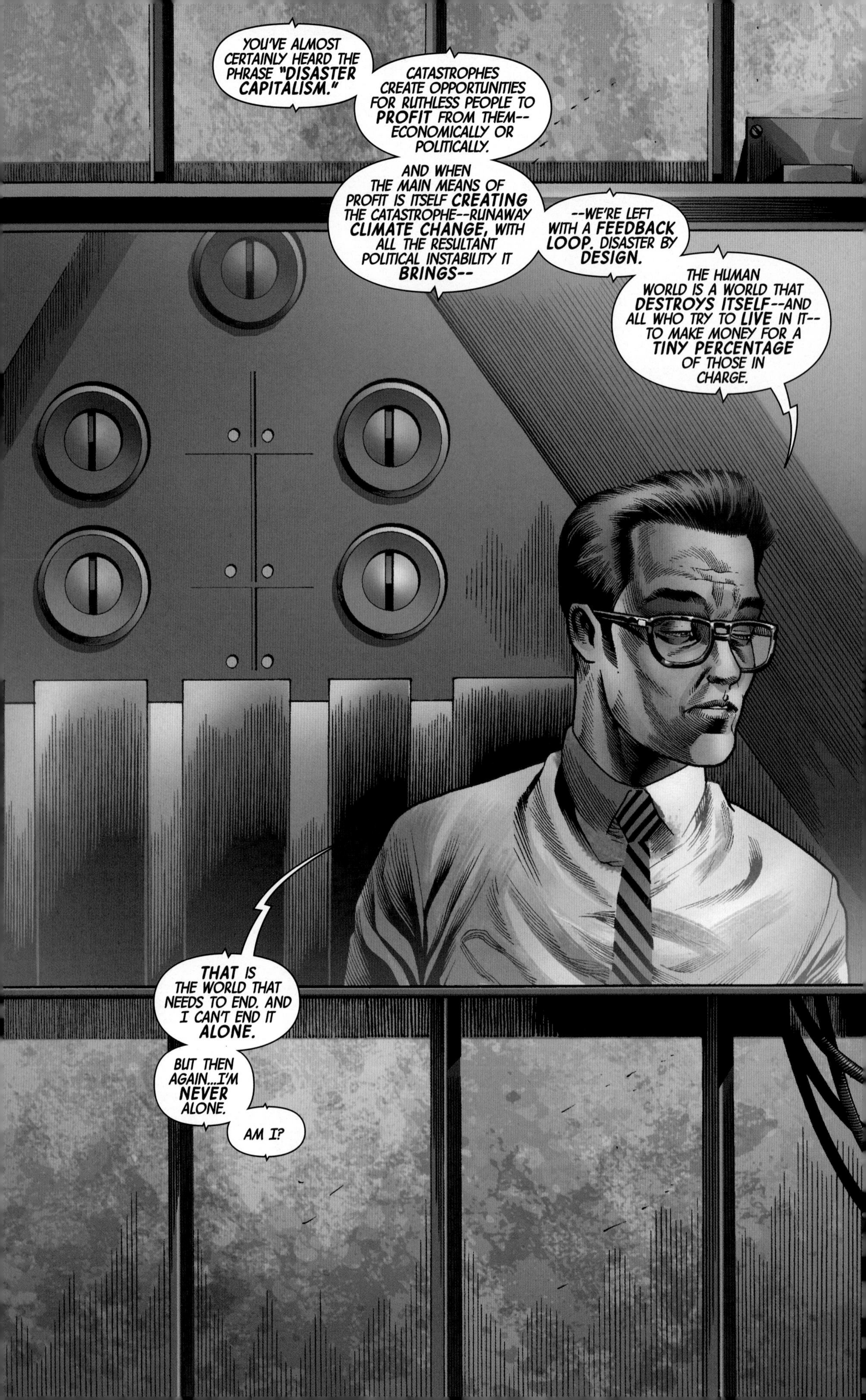
YOU'VE ALMOST CERTAINLY HEARD THE PHRASE "DISASTER CAPITALISM."
CATASTROPHES CREATE OPPORTUNITIES FOR RUTHLESS PEOPLE TO PROFIT FROM THEM-- ECONOMICALLY OR POLITICALLY.
AND WHEN THE MAIN MEANS OF PROFIT IS ITSELF CREATING THE CATASTROPHE--RUNAWAY CLIMATE CHANGE, WITH ALL THE RESULTANT POLITICAL INSTABILITY IT BRINGS--
--WE'RE LEFT WITH A FEEDBACK LOOP. DISASTER BY DESIGN.
THE HUMAN WORLD IS A WORLD THAT DESTROYS ITSELF--AND ALL WHO TRY TO LIVE IN IT-- TO MAKE MONEY FOR A TINY PERCENTAGE OF THOSE IN CHARGE.
THAT IS THE WORLD THAT NEEDS TO END. AND I CAN'T END IT ALONE.
BUT THEN AGAIN...I'M NEVER ALONE.
AM I?

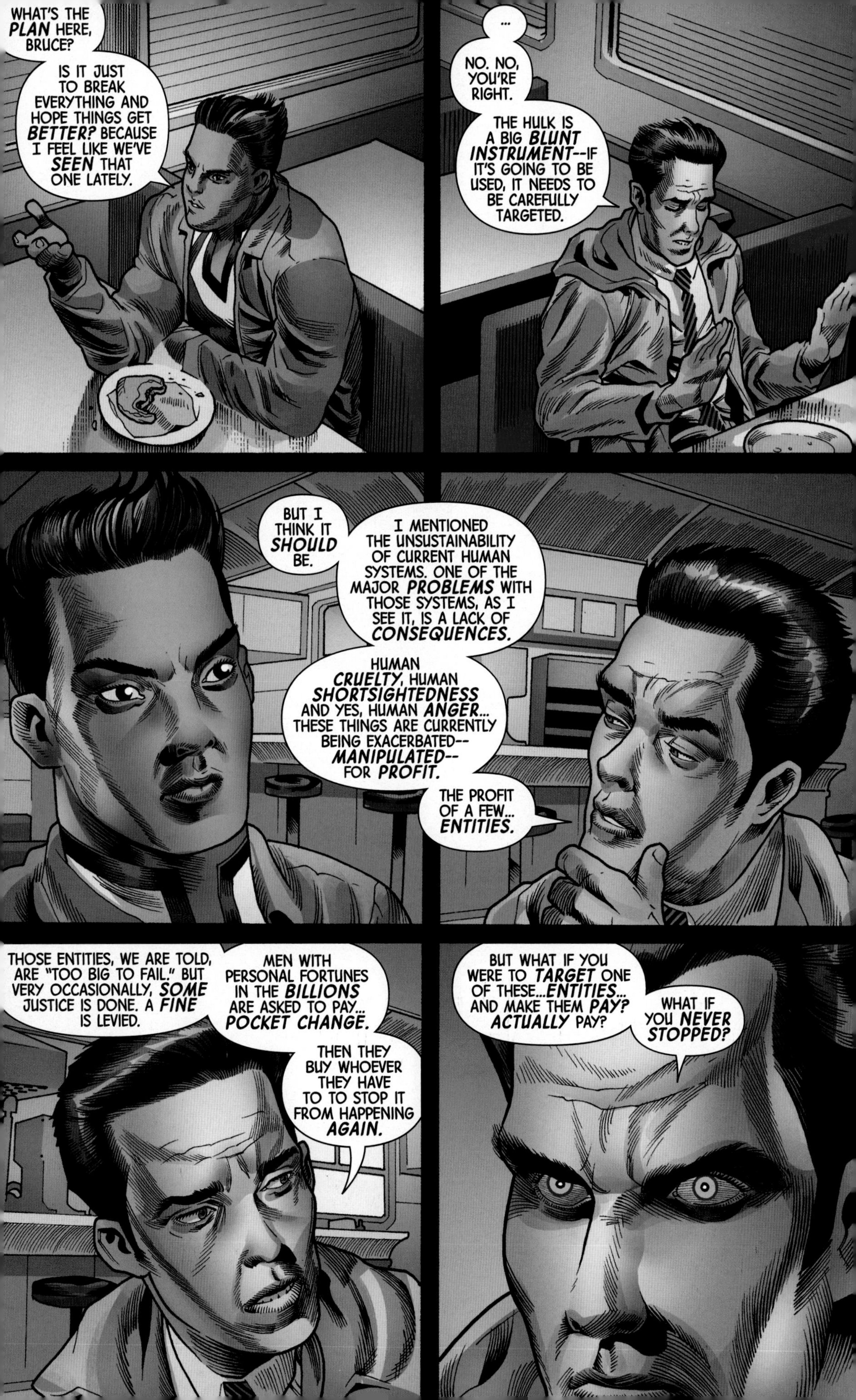
WHAT'S THE PLAN HERE, BRUCE?
IS IT JUST TO BREAK EVERYTHING AND HOPE THINGS GET BETTER? BECAUSE I FEEL LIKE WE'VE SEEN THAT ONE LATELY.
...
NO. NO, YOU'RE RIGHT.
THE HULK IS A BIG BLUNT INSTRUMENT--IF IT'S GOING TO BE USED, IT NEEDS TO BE CAREFULLY TARGETED.
BUT I THINK IT SHOULD BE.
I MENTIONED THE UNSUSTAINABILITY OF CURRENT HUMAN SYSTEMS. ONE OF THE MAJOR PROBLEMS WITH THOSE SYSTEMS, AS I SEE IT, IS A LACK OF CONSEQUENCES.
HUMAN CRUELTY, HUMAN SHORTSIGHTEDNESS AND YES, HUMAN ANGER... THESE THINGS ARE CURRENTLY BEING EXACERBATED-- MANIPULATED-- FOR PROFIT.
THE PROFIT OF A FEW... ENTITIES.
THOSE ENTITIES, WE ARE TOLD, ARE "TOO BIG TO FAIL." BUT VERY OCCASIONALLY, SOME JUSTICE IS DONE. A FINE IS LEVIED.
MEN WITH PERSONAL FORTUNES IN THE BILLIONS ARE ASKED TO PAY... POCKET CHANGE.
THEN THEY BUY WHOEVER THEY HAVE TO TO STOP IT FROM HAPPENING AGAIN.
BUT WHAT IF YOU WERE TO TARGET ONE OF THESE...ENTITIES... AND MAKE THEM PAY? ACTUALLY PAY?
WHAT IF YOU NEVER STOPPED?

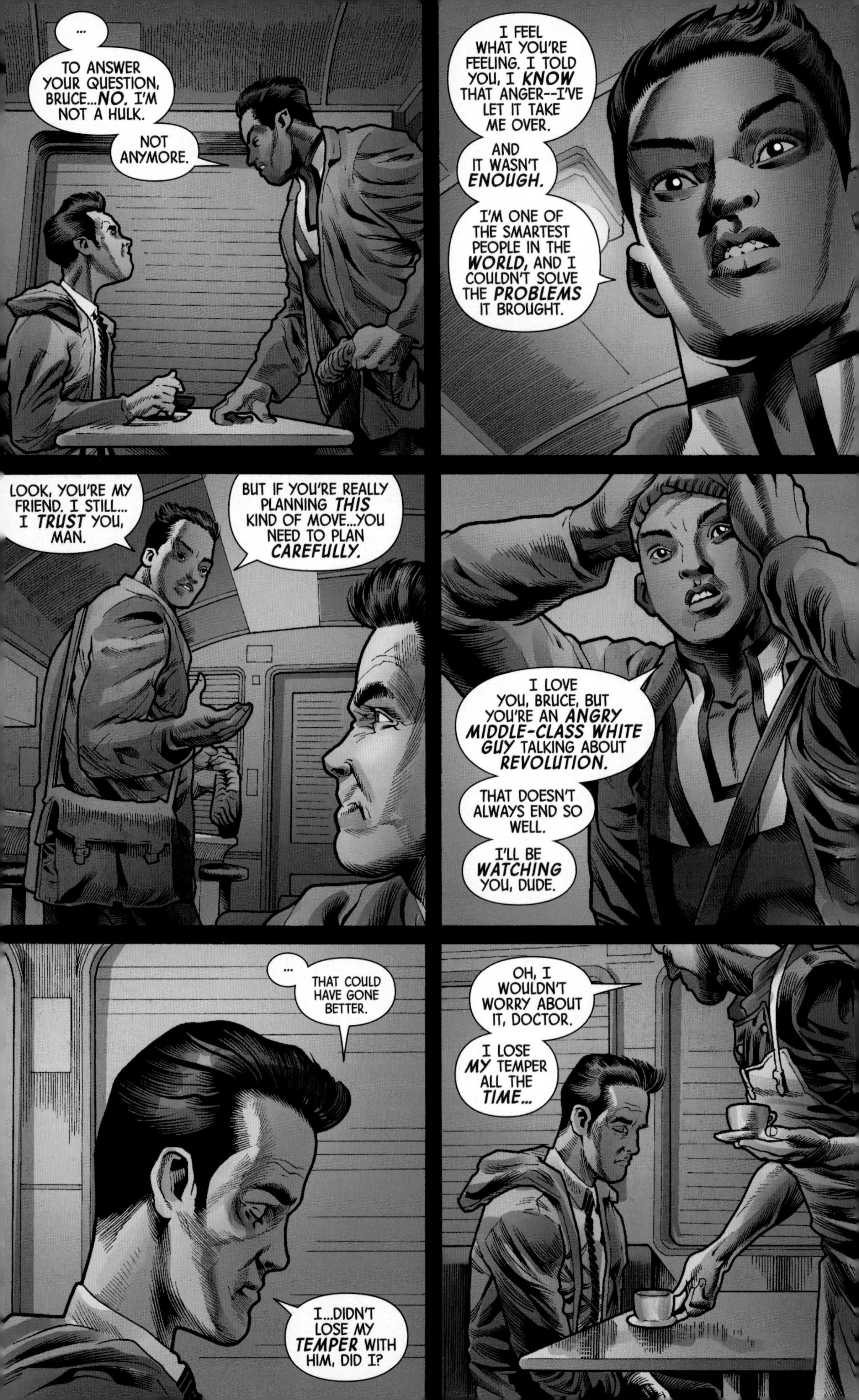
...
TO ANSWER YOUR QUESTION, BRUCE...NO. I'M NOT A HULK.
NOT ANYMORE.
I FEEL WHAT YOU'RE FEELING. I TOLD YOU, I KNOW THAT ANGER--I'VE LET IT TAKE ME OVER.
AND IT WASN'T ENOUGH.
I'M ONE OF THE SMARTEST PEOPLE IN THE WORLD, AND I COULDN'T SOLVE THE PROBLEMS IT BROUGHT.
LOOK, YOU'RE MY FRIEND. I STILL... I TRUST YOU, MAN.
BUT IF YOU'RE REALLY PLANNING THIS KIND OF MOVE...YOU NEED TO PLAN CAREFULLY.
I LOVE YOU, BRUCE, BUT YOU'RE AN ANGRY MIDDLE-CLASS WHITE GUY TALKING ABOUT REVOLUTION.
THAT DOESN'T ALWAYS END SO WELL.
I'LL BE WATCHING YOU, DUDE.
...
THAT COULD HAVE GONE BETTER.
I...DIDN'T LOSE MY TEMPER WITH HIM, DID I?
OH, I WOULDN'T WORRY ABOUT IT, DOCTOR.
I LOSE MY TEMPER ALL THE TIME...

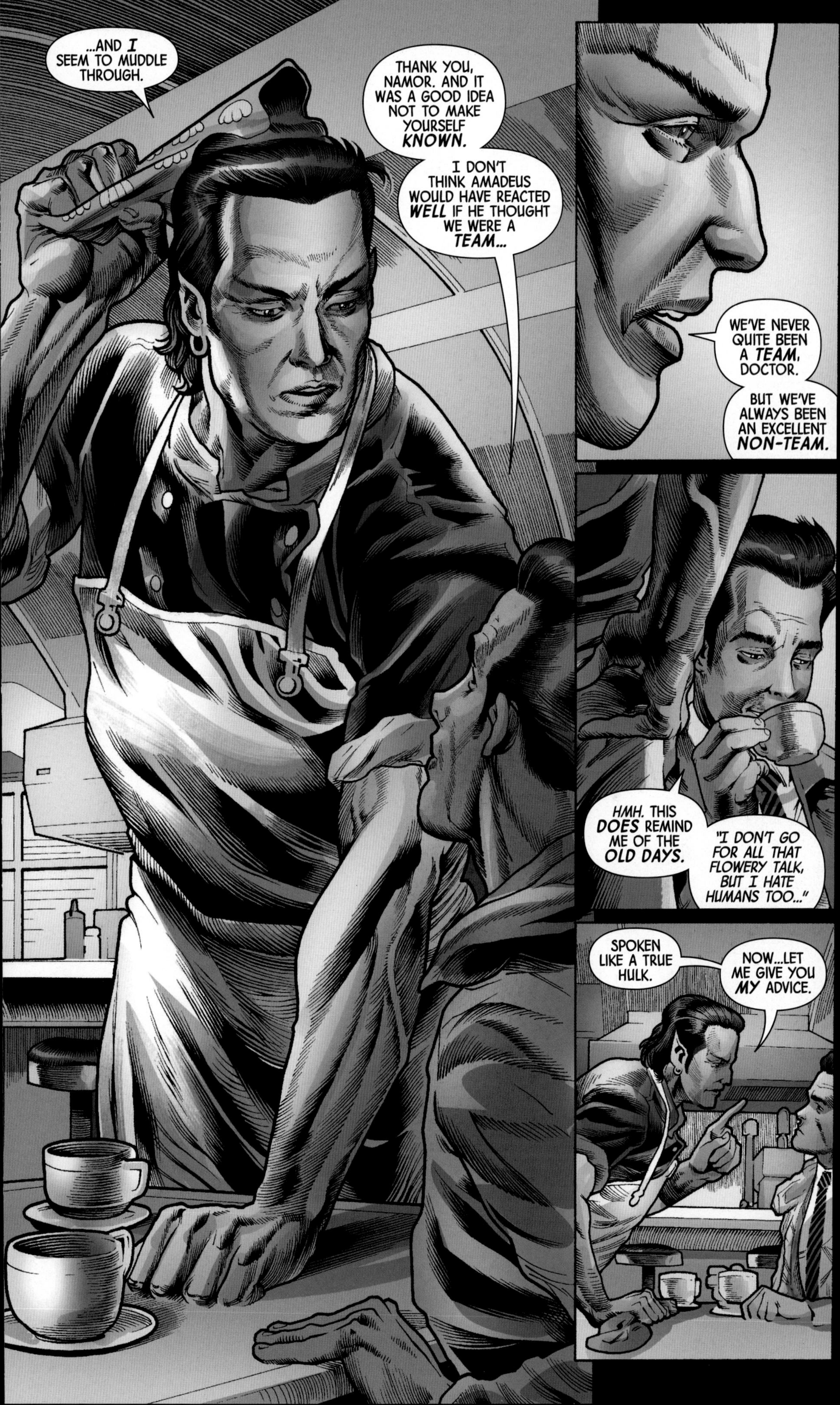

...AND *I* SEEM TO MUDDLE THROUGH.
THANK YOU, NAMOR. AND IT WAS A GOOD IDEA NOT TO MAKE YOURSELF *KNOWN.*
I DON'T THINK AMADEUS WOULD HAVE REACTED *WELL* IF HE THOUGHT WE WERE A *TEAM...*
WE'VE NEVER QUITE BEEN A *TEAM*, DOCTOR.
BUT WE'VE ALWAYS BEEN AN EXCELLENT *NON-TEAM.*
HMH. THIS *DOES* REMIND ME OF THE *OLD DAYS.*
"I DON'T GO FOR ALL THAT FLOWERY TALK, BUT I HATE HUMANS TOO..."
SPOKEN LIKE A TRUE HULK.
NOW...LET ME GIVE YOU *MY* ADVICE.

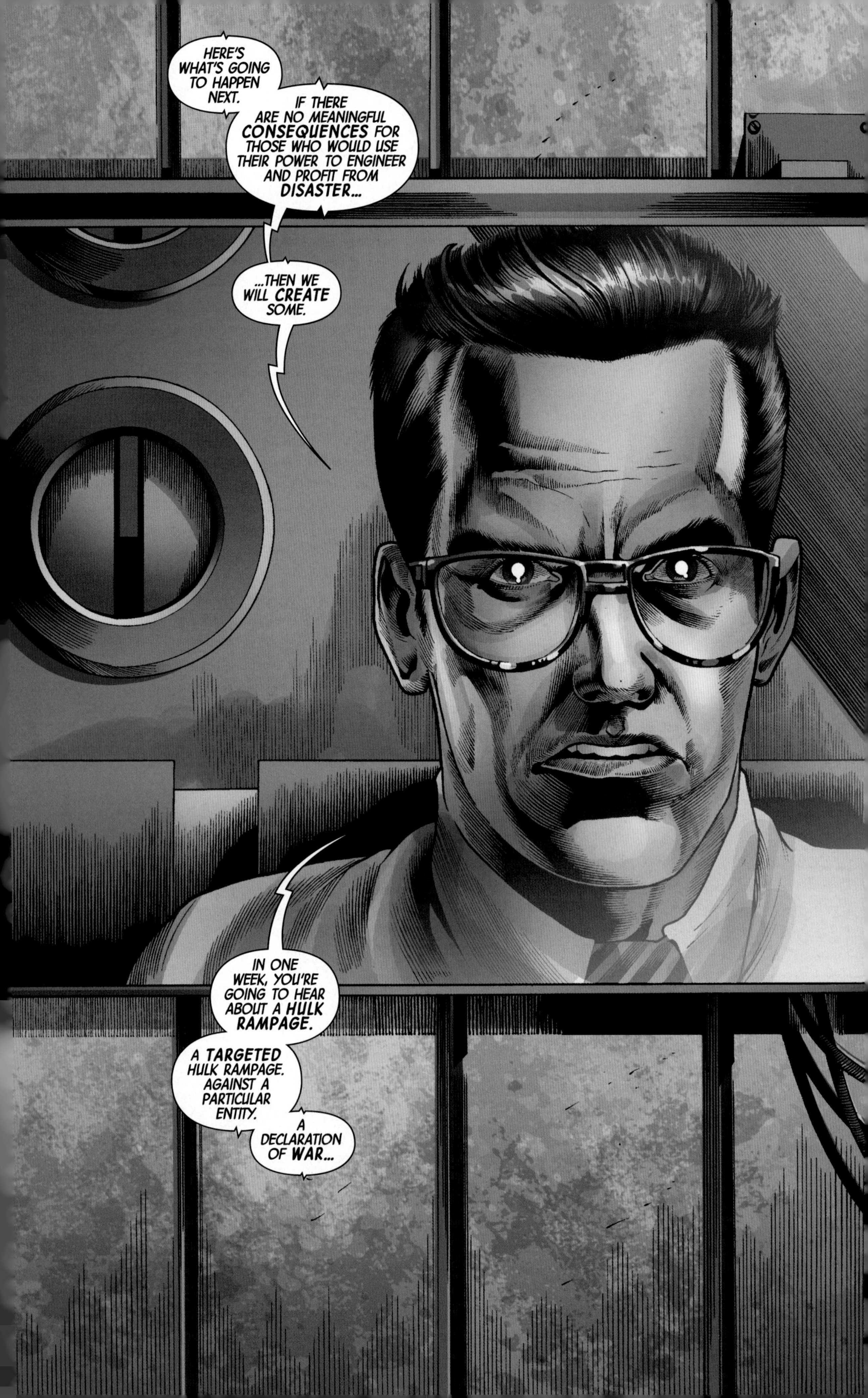
HERE'S WHAT'S GOING TO HAPPEN NEXT.
IF THERE ARE NO MEANINGFUL CONSEQUENCES FOR THOSE WHO WOULD USE THEIR POWER TO ENGINEER AND PROFIT FROM DISASTER...
...THEN WE WILL CREATE SOME.
IN ONE WEEK, YOU'RE GOING TO HEAR ABOUT A HULK RAMPAGE.
A TARGETED HULK RAMPAGE. AGAINST A PARTICULAR ENTITY.
A DECLARATION OF WAR...

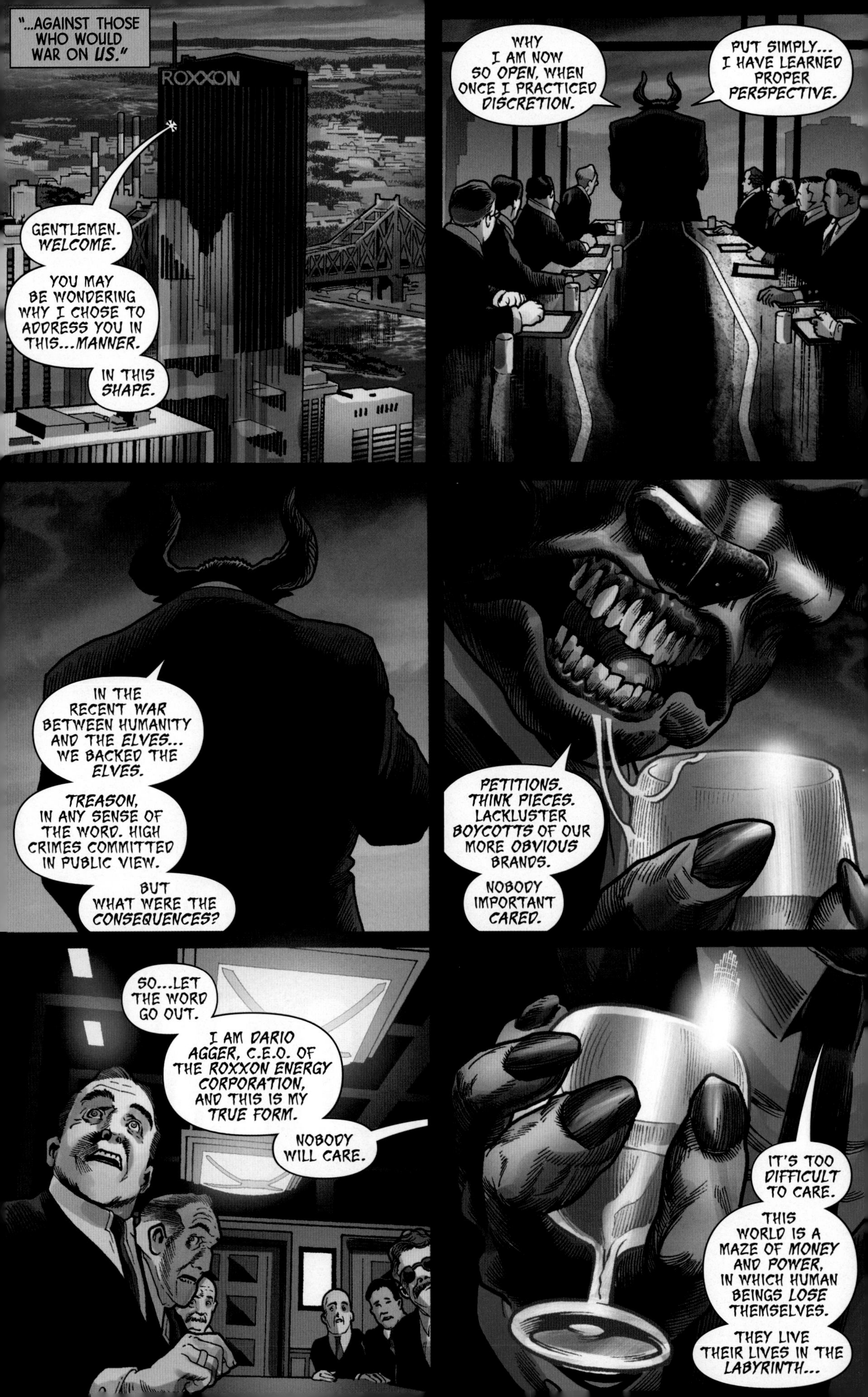
"...AGAINST THOSE WHO WOULD WAR ON US."
GENTLEMEN. WELCOME.
YOU MAY BE WONDERING WHY I CHOSE TO ADDRESS YOU IN THIS...MANNER.
IN THIS SHAPE.
ROXXON
WHY I AM NOW SO OPEN, WHEN ONCE I PRACTICED DISCRETION.
PUT SIMPLY... I HAVE LEARNED PROPER PERSPECTIVE.
IN THE RECENT WAR BETWEEN HUMANITY AND THE ELVES... WE BACKED THE ELVES.
TREASON, IN ANY SENSE OF THE WORD. HIGH CRIMES COMMITTED IN PUBLIC VIEW.
BUT WHAT WERE THE CONSEQUENCES?
PETITIONS. THINK PIECES. LACKLUSTER BOYCOTTS OF OUR MORE OBVIOUS BRANDS.
NOBODY IMPORTANT CARED.
SO...LET THE WORD GO OUT.
I AM DARIO AGGER, C.E.O. OF THE ROXXON ENERGY CORPORATION, AND THIS IS MY TRUE FORM.
NOBODY WILL CARE.
IT'S TOO DIFFICULT TO CARE.
THIS WORLD IS A MAZE OF MONEY AND POWER, IN WHICH HUMAN BEINGS LOSE THEMSELVES.
THEY LIVE THEIR LIVES IN THE LABYRINTH...

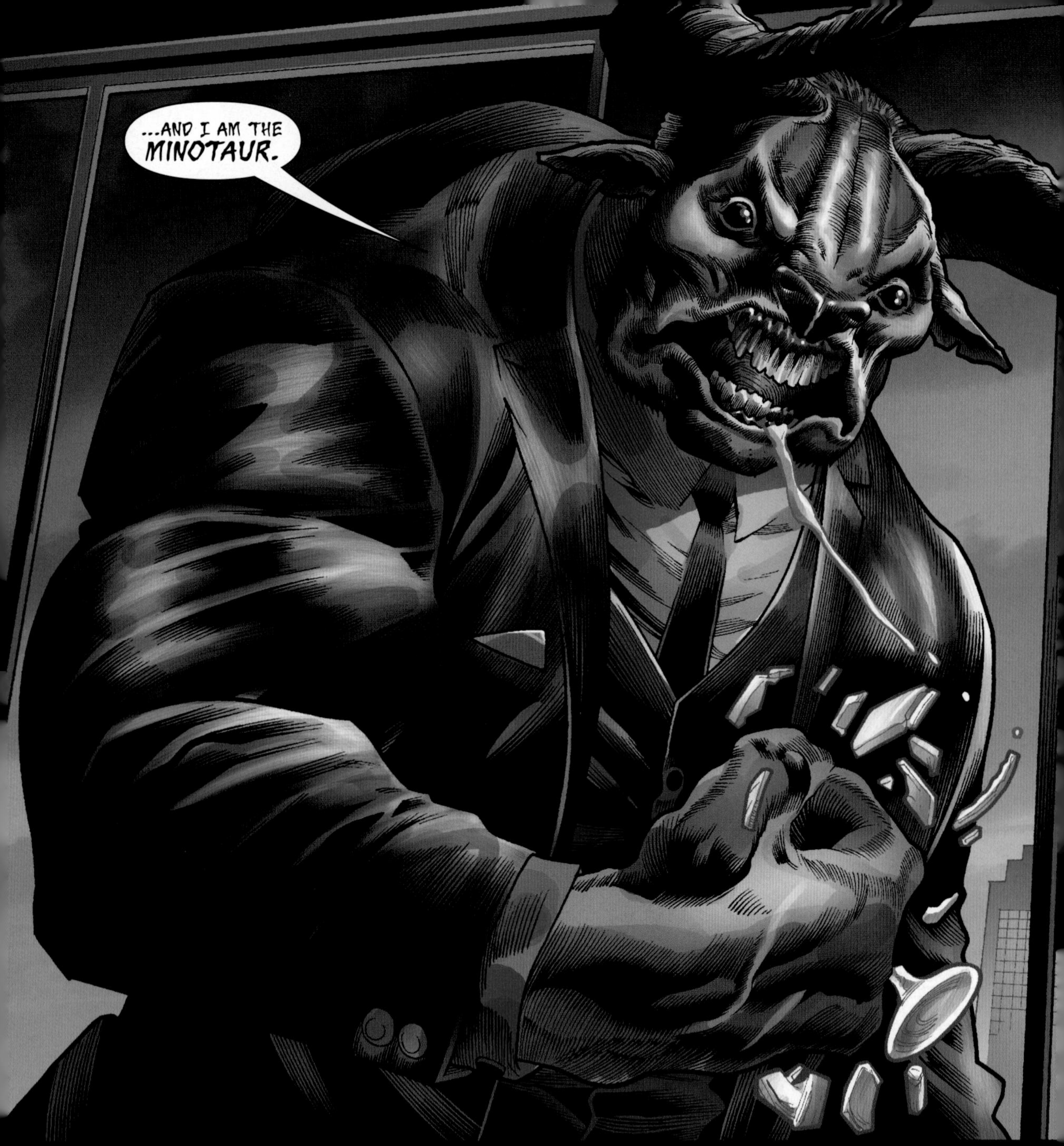
...AND I AM THE MINOTAUR.

STATUS QUO ANTE

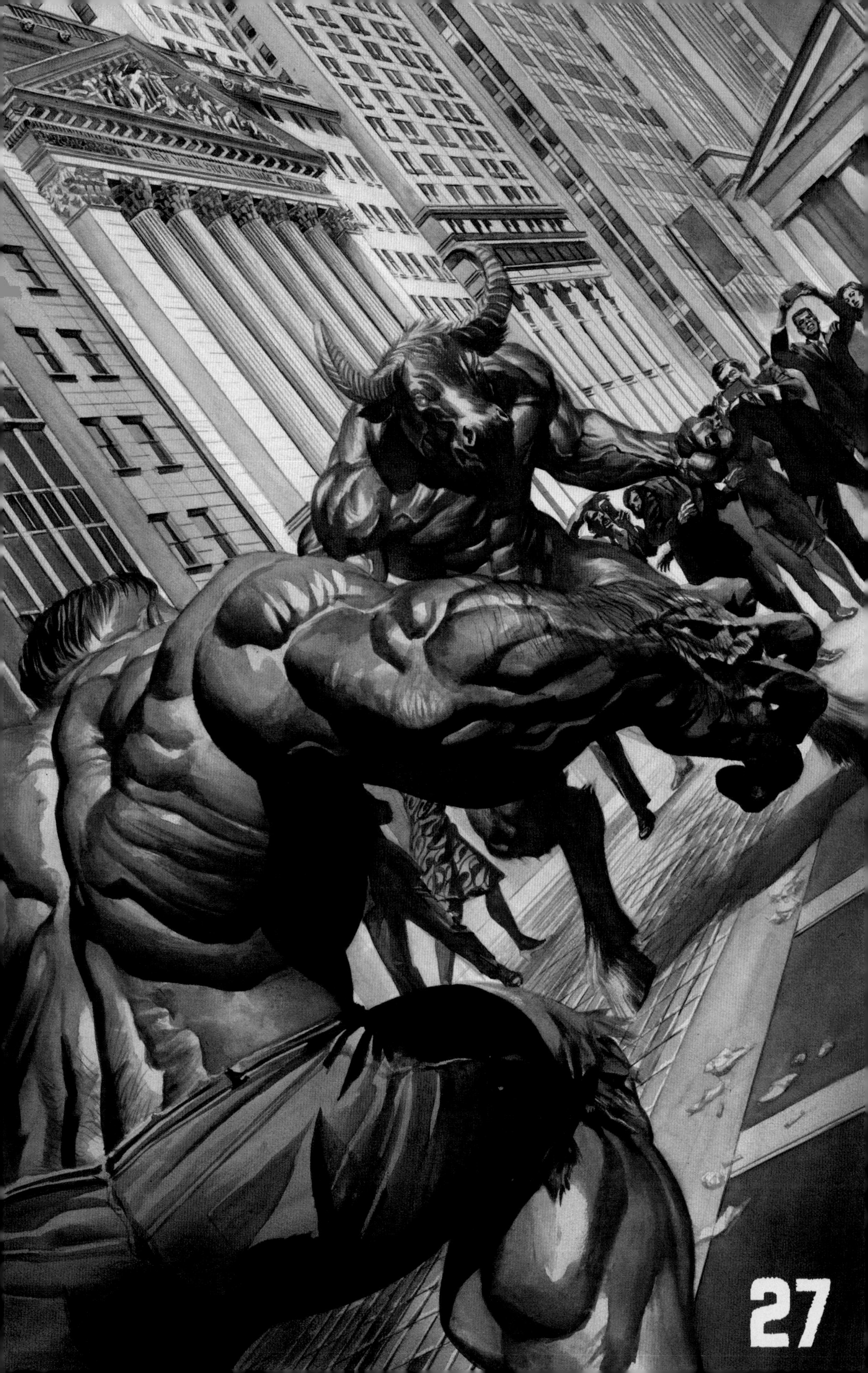
27

"He is finite, though he is powerful to do much harm and suffers not as we do. But we are strong, each in our purpose; and we are all more strong together."

– BRAM STOKER
DRACULA

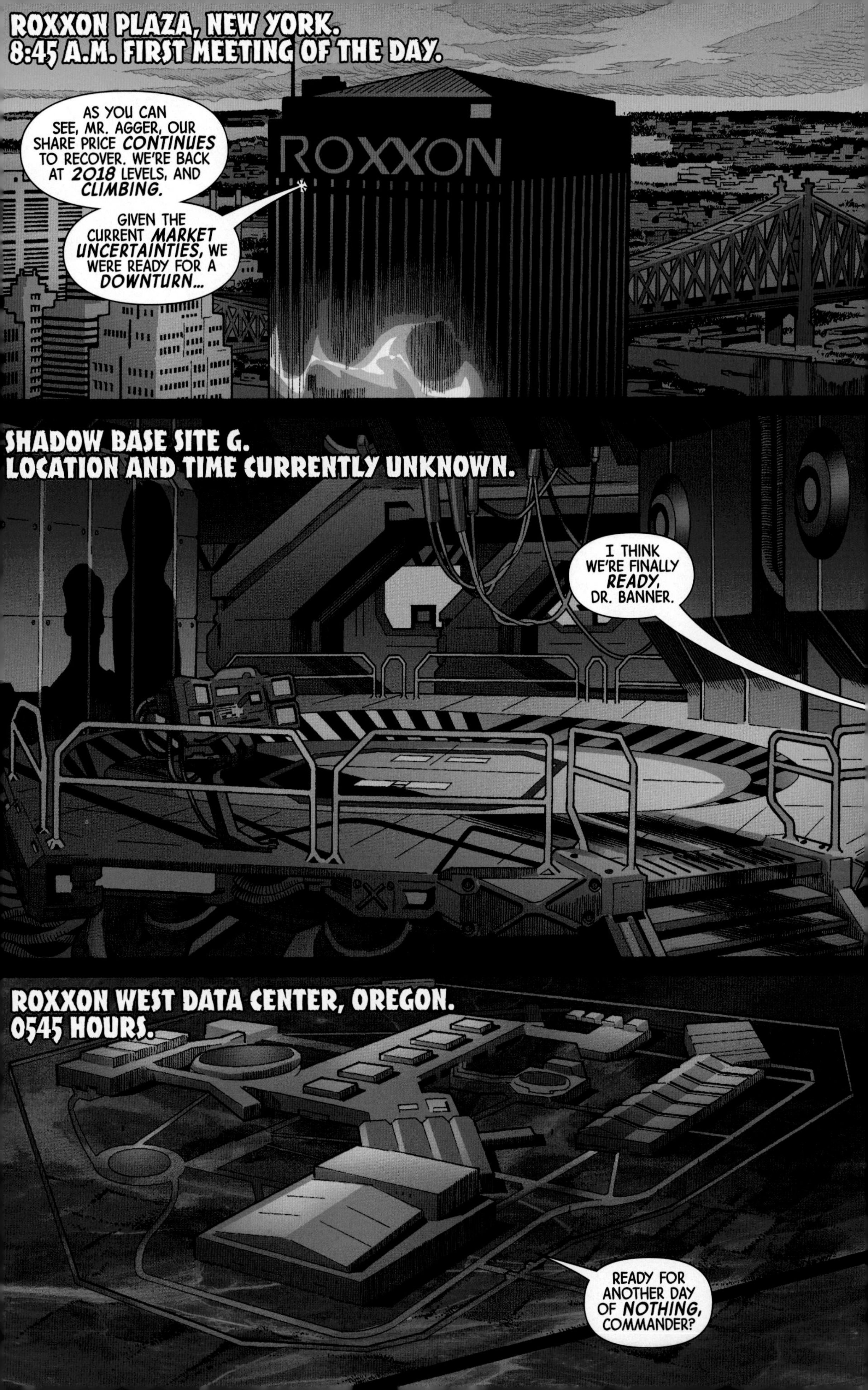
ROXXON PLAZA, NEW YORK.
8:45 A.M. FIRST MEETING OF THE DAY.
AS YOU CAN SEE, MR. AGGER, OUR SHARE PRICE CONTINUES TO RECOVER. WE'RE BACK AT 2018 LEVELS, AND CLIMBING.
GIVEN THE CURRENT MARKET UNCERTAINTIES, WE WERE READY FOR A DOWNTURN...
ROXXON
SHADOW BASE SITE G.
LOCATION AND TIME CURRENTLY UNKNOWN.
I THINK WE'RE FINALLY READY, DR. BANNER.
ROXXON WEST DATA CENTER, OREGON.
0545 HOURS.
READY FOR ANOTHER DAY OF NOTHING, COMMANDER?

...BUT NOTHING TO REPORT ON *THAT* FRONT AS YET. STILL, I'D SUGGEST AVOIDING *RISKY VENTURES*--

DON'T BE A *COWARD,* HIGGINS.

ROXXON

SHARE PRICE

THE MINOTAUR.

WE'RE NOT SOME MOM-AND-POP STORE THAT CLOSES DOWN IN A STRONG WIND. WE...ARE THE *HURRICANE.*

UNCERTAINTY IS WHAT WE WANT.

I'M *STILL* NOT CERTAIN ABOUT THIS.

I DON'T CARE *HOW* EASY *REED RICHARDS* MAKES IT LOOK-- TRANSLOCATION IS *BEYOND* DANGEROUS.

THE HULK.

IF IT WERE UP TO *ME,* YOU WOULDN'T BE DOING THIS AT *ALL.*

BUT AT LEAST *YOU* GIVE ME TIME TO RUN THE NECESSARY *CHECKS...*

YOU HAD BEST CHECK YOUR *ATTITUDE,* AGENT PALICKI.

SIR--

YOUR *JOB* IS TO GUARD THIS FACILITY-- UNTIL YOU *DROP,* IF NEED BE-- WITH *ZERO* BACKCHAT.

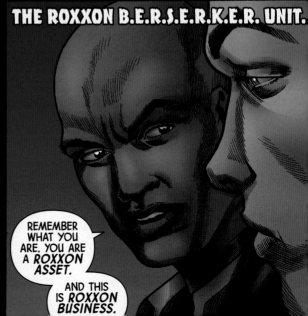

THE ROXXON B.E.R.S.E.R.K.E.R. UNIT.

REMEMBER WHAT YOU ARE. YOU ARE A *ROXXON ASSET.*

AND THIS IS *ROXXON BUSINESS.*

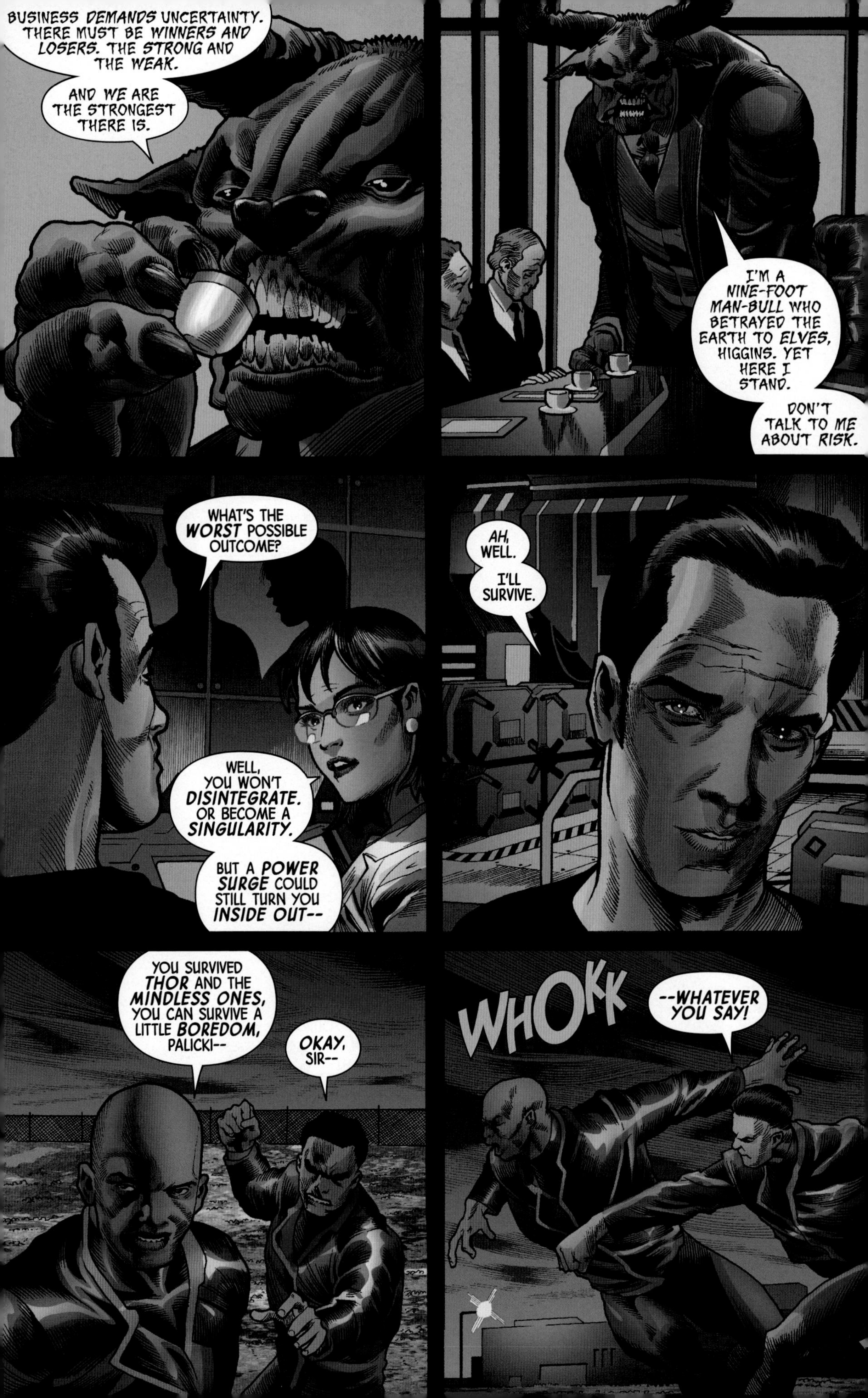
BUSINESS DEMANDS UNCERTAINTY. THERE MUST BE WINNERS AND LOSERS. THE STRONG AND THE WEAK.
AND WE ARE THE STRONGEST THERE IS.
I'M A NINE-FOOT MAN-BULL WHO BETRAYED THE EARTH TO ELVES, HIGGINS. YET HERE I STAND.
DON'T TALK TO ME ABOUT RISK.
WHAT'S THE WORST POSSIBLE OUTCOME?
WELL, YOU WON'T DISINTEGRATE. OR BECOME A SINGULARITY.
BUT A POWER SURGE COULD STILL TURN YOU INSIDE OUT--
AH, WELL.
I'LL SURVIVE.
YOU SURVIVED THOR AND THE MINDLESS ONES, YOU CAN SURVIVE A LITTLE BOREDOM, PALICKI--
OKAY, SIR--
WHOKK
--WHATEVER YOU SAY!

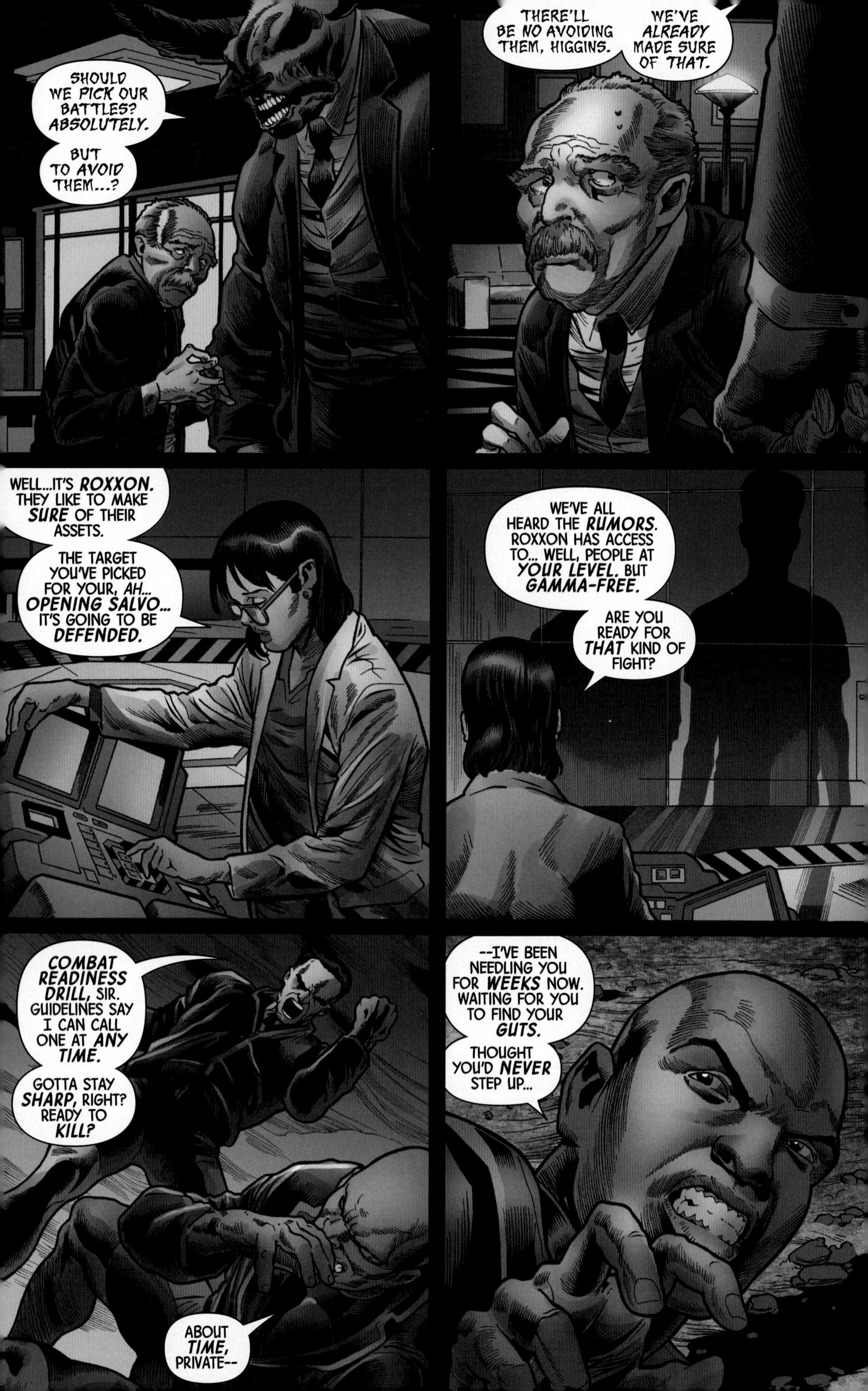
SHOULD WE PICK OUR BATTLES? ABSOLUTELY.
BUT TO AVOID THEM...?
THERE'LL BE NO AVOIDING THEM, HIGGINS.
WE'VE ALREADY MADE SURE OF THAT.
WELL...IT'S ROXXON. THEY LIKE TO MAKE SURE OF THEIR ASSETS.
THE TARGET YOU'VE PICKED FOR YOUR, AH... OPENING SALVO... IT'S GOING TO BE DEFENDED.
WE'VE ALL HEARD THE RUMORS. ROXXON HAS ACCESS TO... WELL, PEOPLE AT YOUR LEVEL. BUT GAMMA-FREE.
ARE YOU READY FOR THAT KIND OF FIGHT?
COMBAT READINESS DRILL, SIR. GUIDELINES SAY I CAN CALL ONE AT ANY TIME.
GOTTA STAY SHARP, RIGHT? READY TO KILL?
ABOUT TIME, PRIVATE--
--I'VE BEEN NEEDLING YOU FOR WEEKS NOW. WAITING FOR YOU TO FIND YOUR GUTS.
THOUGHT YOU'D NEVER STEP UP...

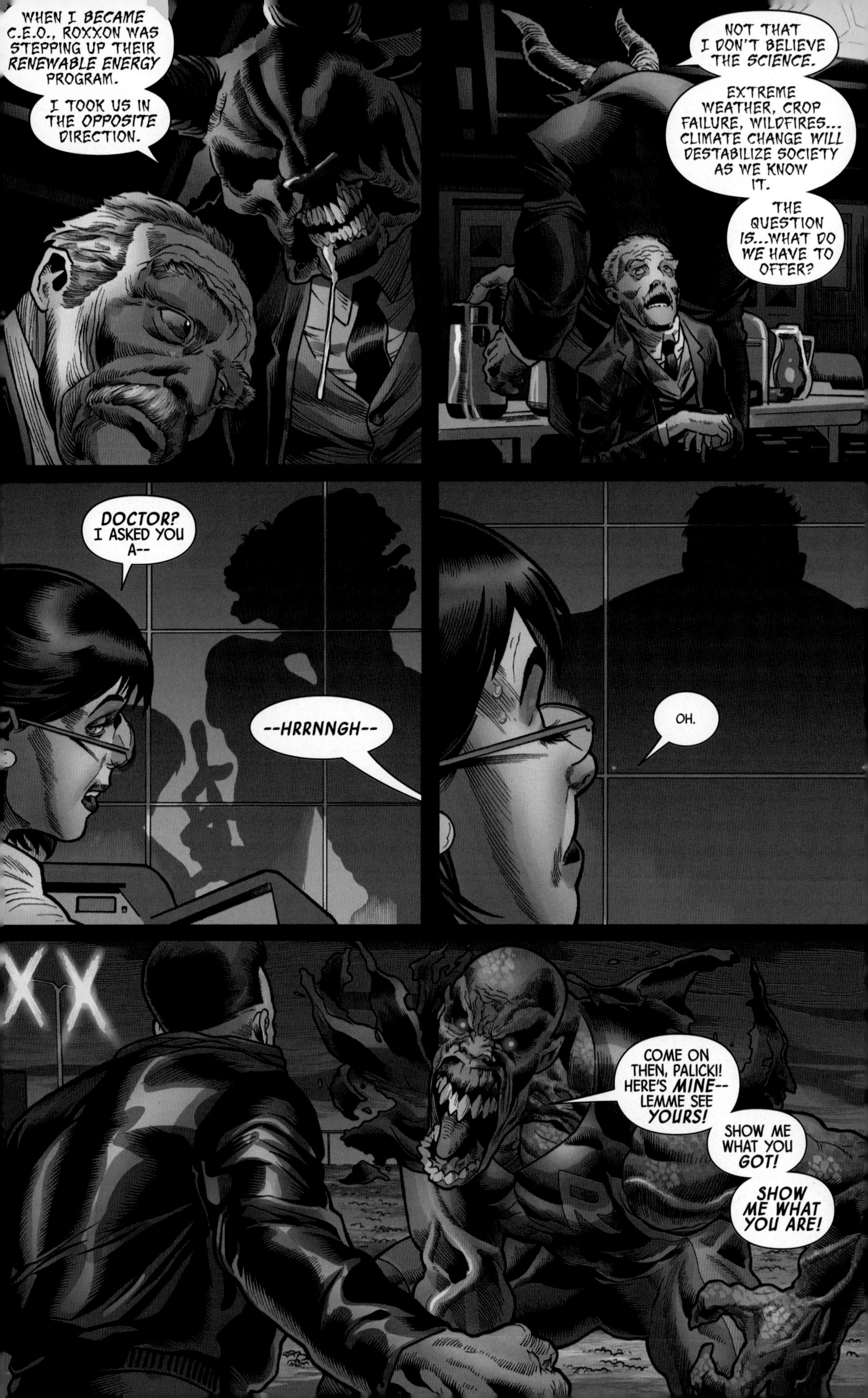
WHEN I BECAME C.E.O., ROXXON WAS STEPPING UP THEIR RENEWABLE ENERGY PROGRAM.
I TOOK US IN THE OPPOSITE DIRECTION.
NOT THAT I DON'T BELIEVE THE SCIENCE.
EXTREME WEATHER, CROP FAILURE, WILDFIRES... CLIMATE CHANGE WILL DESTABILIZE SOCIETY AS WE KNOW IT.
THE QUESTION IS...WHAT DO WE HAVE TO OFFER?
DOCTOR? I ASKED YOU A--
--HRRNNGH--
OH.
COME ON THEN, PALICKI! HERE'S MINE-- LEMME SEE YOURS!
SHOW ME WHAT YOU GOT!
SHOW ME WHAT YOU ARE!

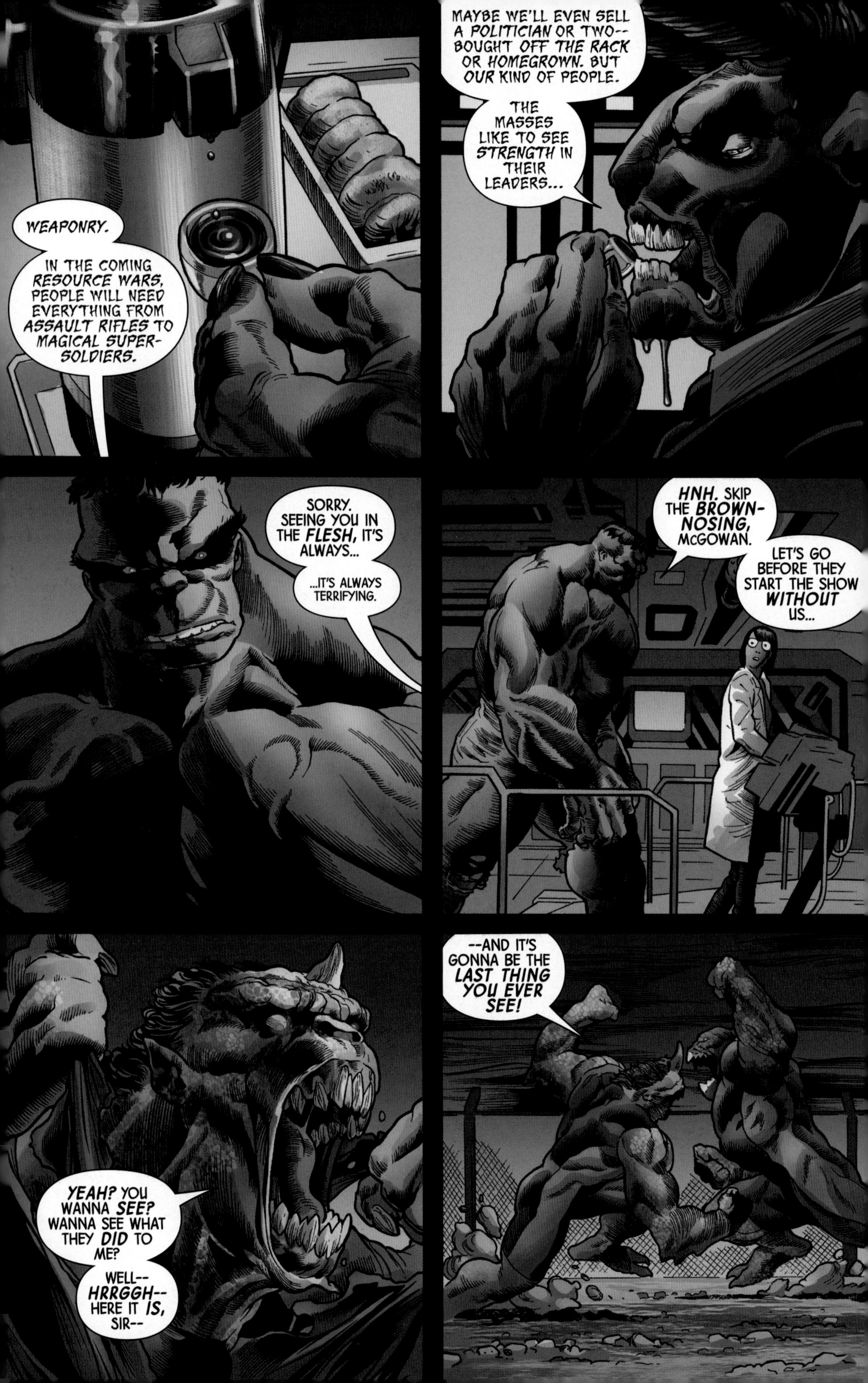
WEAPONRY.
IN THE COMING RESOURCE WARS, PEOPLE WILL NEED EVERYTHING FROM ASSAULT RIFLES TO MAGICAL SUPER-SOLDIERS.
MAYBE WE'LL EVEN SELL A POLITICIAN OR TWO-- BOUGHT OFF THE RACK OR HOMEGROWN. BUT OUR KIND OF PEOPLE.
THE MASSES LIKE TO SEE STRENGTH IN THEIR LEADERS...
SORRY. SEEING YOU IN THE FLESH, IT'S ALWAYS...
...IT'S ALWAYS TERRIFYING.
HNH. SKIP THE BROWN-NOSING, McGOWAN.
LET'S GO BEFORE THEY START THE SHOW WITHOUT US...
YEAH? YOU WANNA SEE? WANNA SEE WHAT THEY DID TO ME?
WELL-- HRRGGH-- HERE IT IS, SIR--
--AND IT'S GONNA BE THE LAST THING YOU EVER SEE!

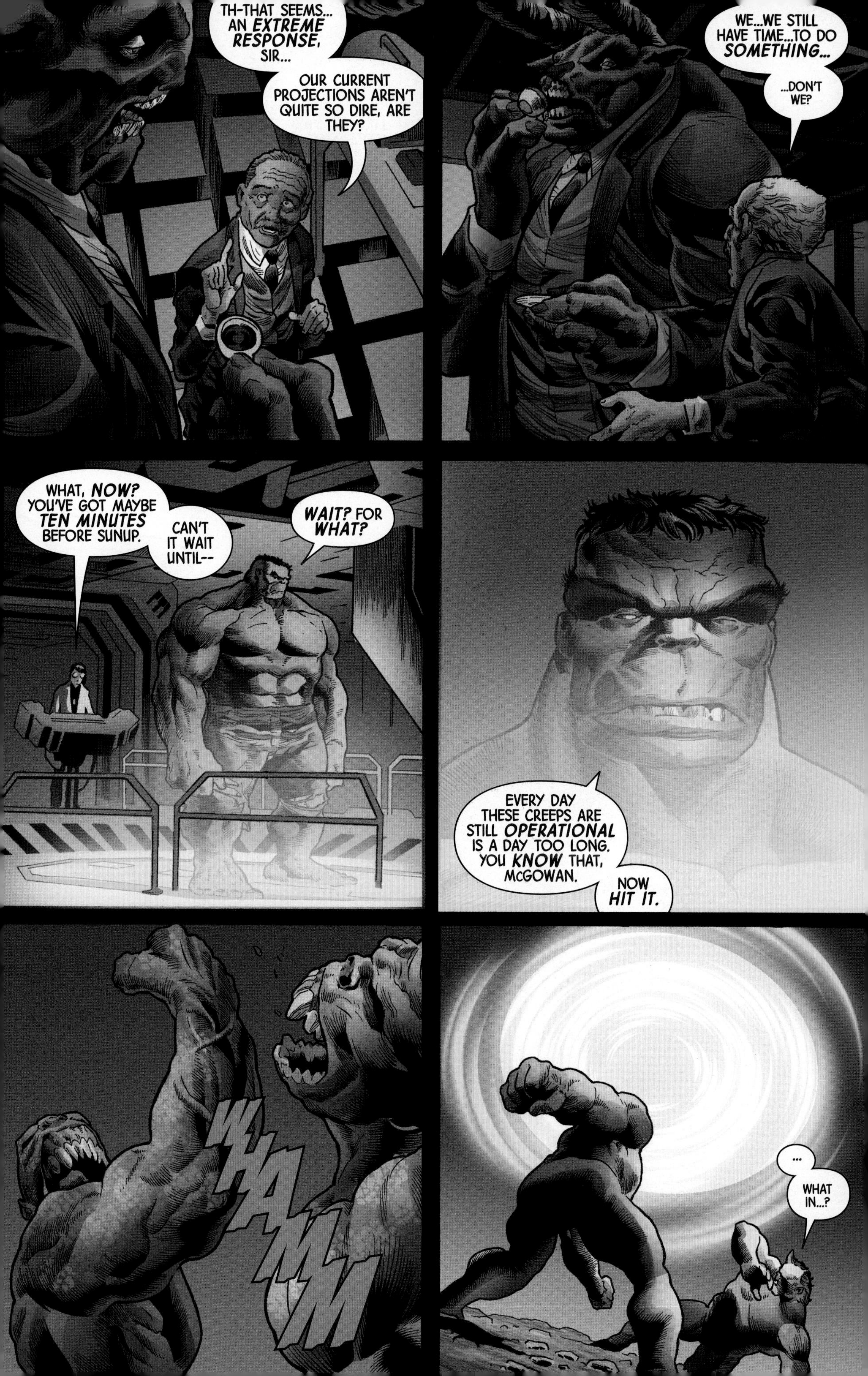
TH-THAT SEEMS... AN EXTREME RESPONSE, SIR...
OUR CURRENT PROJECTIONS AREN'T QUITE SO DIRE, ARE THEY?
WE...WE STILL HAVE TIME...TO DO SOMETHING...
...DON'T WE?
WHAT, NOW? YOU'VE GOT MAYBE TEN MINUTES BEFORE SUNUP.
CAN'T IT WAIT UNTIL--
WAIT? FOR WHAT?
EVERY DAY THESE CREEPS ARE STILL OPERATIONAL IS A DAY TOO LONG. YOU KNOW THAT, McGOWAN.
NOW HIT IT.
WHAM
...
WHAT IN...?

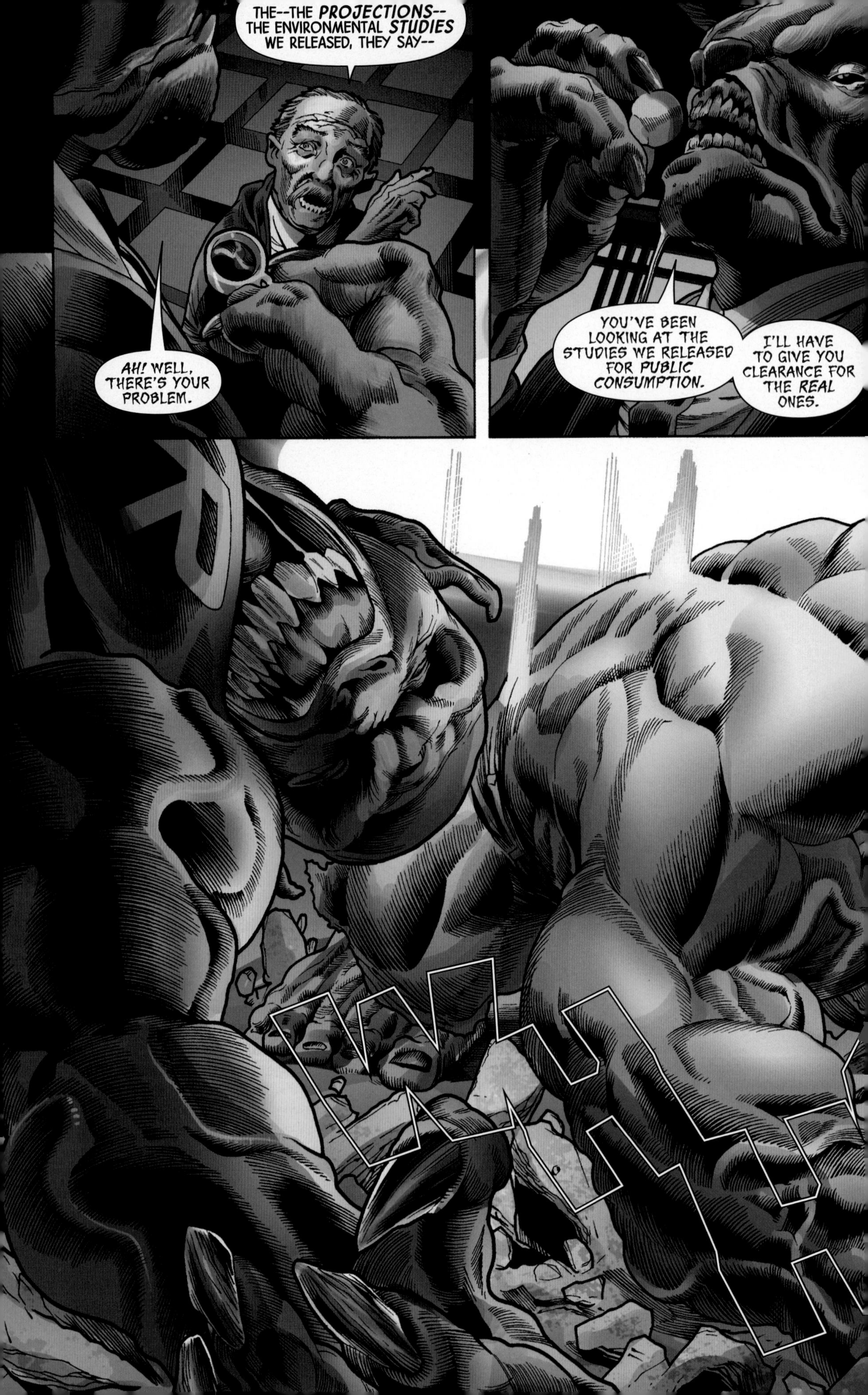
THE--THE PROJECTIONS-- THE ENVIRONMENTAL STUDIES WE RELEASED, THEY SAY--
AH! WELL, THERE'S YOUR PROBLEM.
YOU'VE BEEN LOOKING AT THE STUDIES WE RELEASED FOR PUBLIC CONSUMPTION.
I'LL HAVE TO GIVE YOU CLEARANCE FOR THE REAL ONES.

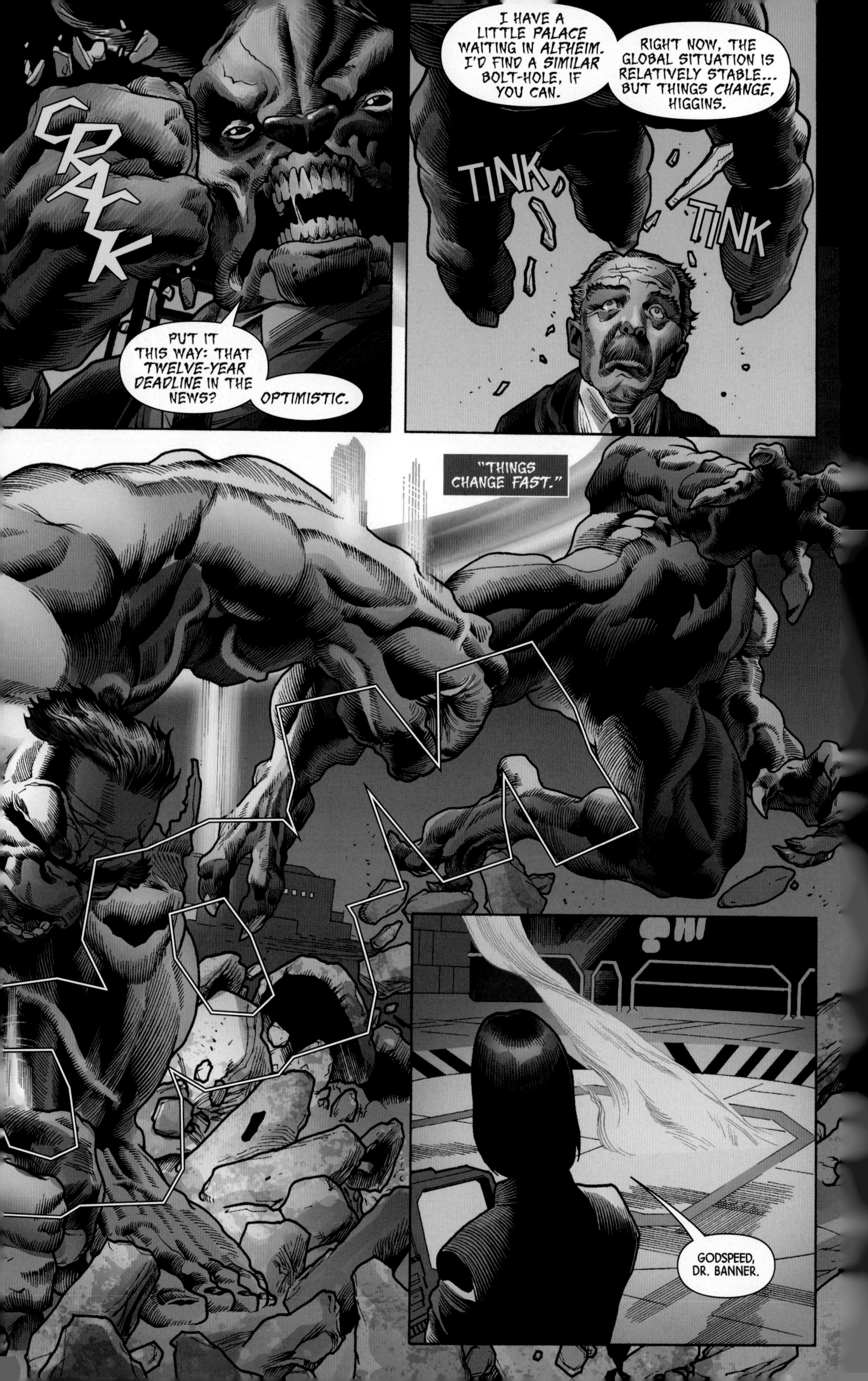
CRACK
PUT IT THIS WAY: THAT TWELVE-YEAR DEADLINE IN THE NEWS?
OPTIMISTIC.
I HAVE A LITTLE PALACE WAITING IN ALFHEIM. I'D FIND A SIMILAR BOLT-HOLE, IF YOU CAN.
RIGHT NOW, THE GLOBAL SITUATION IS RELATIVELY STABLE... BUT THINGS CHANGE, HIGGINS.
TINK
TINK
"THINGS CHANGE FAST."
GODSPEED, DR. BANNER.

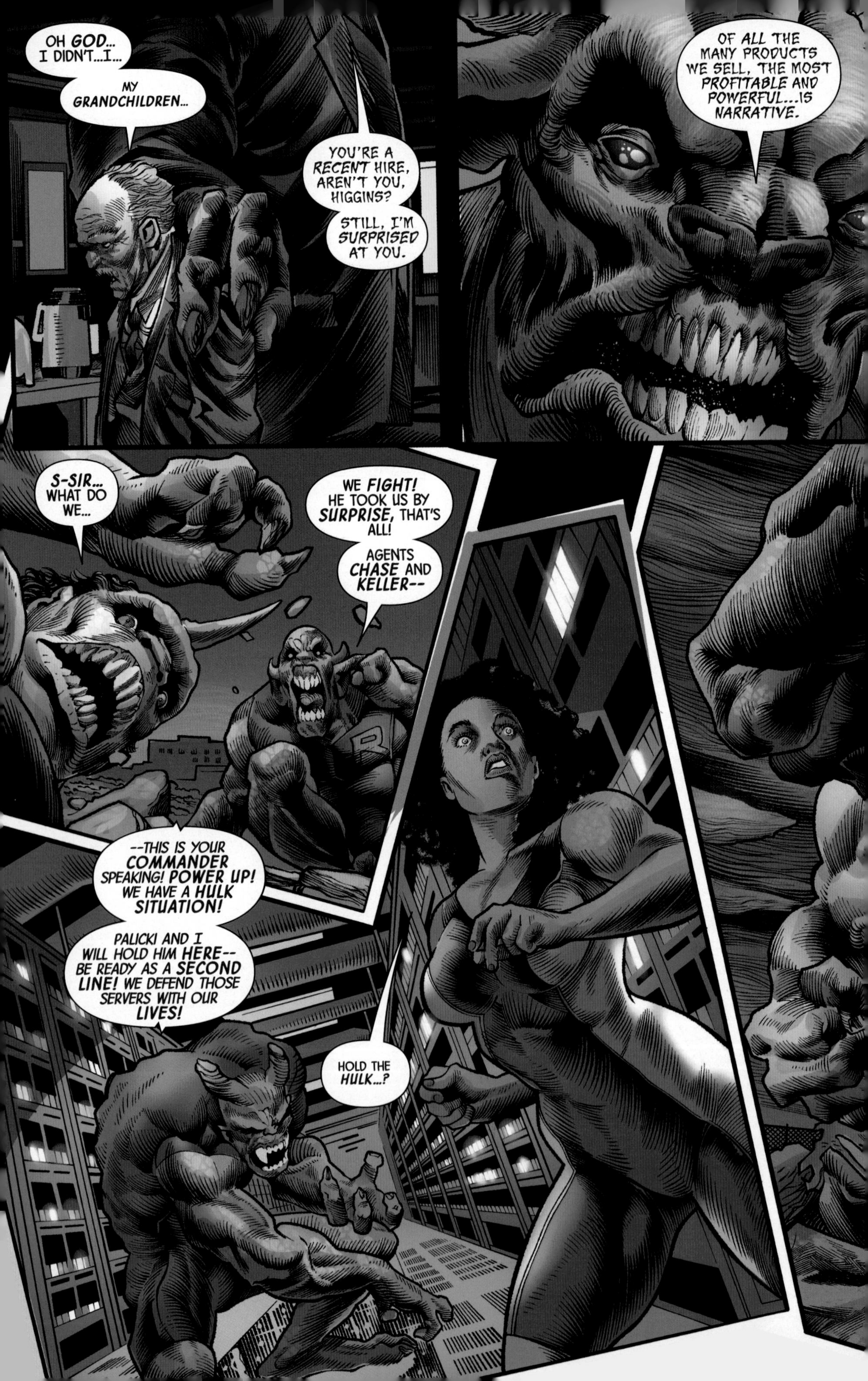
OH GOD... I DIDN'T...I...
MY GRANDCHILDREN...
YOU'RE A RECENT HIRE, AREN'T YOU, HIGGINS?
STILL, I'M SURPRISED AT YOU.
OF ALL THE MANY PRODUCTS WE SELL, THE MOST PROFITABLE AND POWERFUL...IS NARRATIVE.
S-SIR... WHAT DO WE...
WE FIGHT! HE TOOK US BY SURPRISE, THAT'S ALL!
AGENTS CHASE AND KELLER--
--THIS IS YOUR COMMANDER SPEAKING! POWER UP! WE HAVE A HULK SITUATION!
PALICKI AND I WILL HOLD HIM HERE--BE READY AS A SECOND LINE! WE DEFEND THOSE SERVERS WITH OUR LIVES!
HOLD THE HULK...?

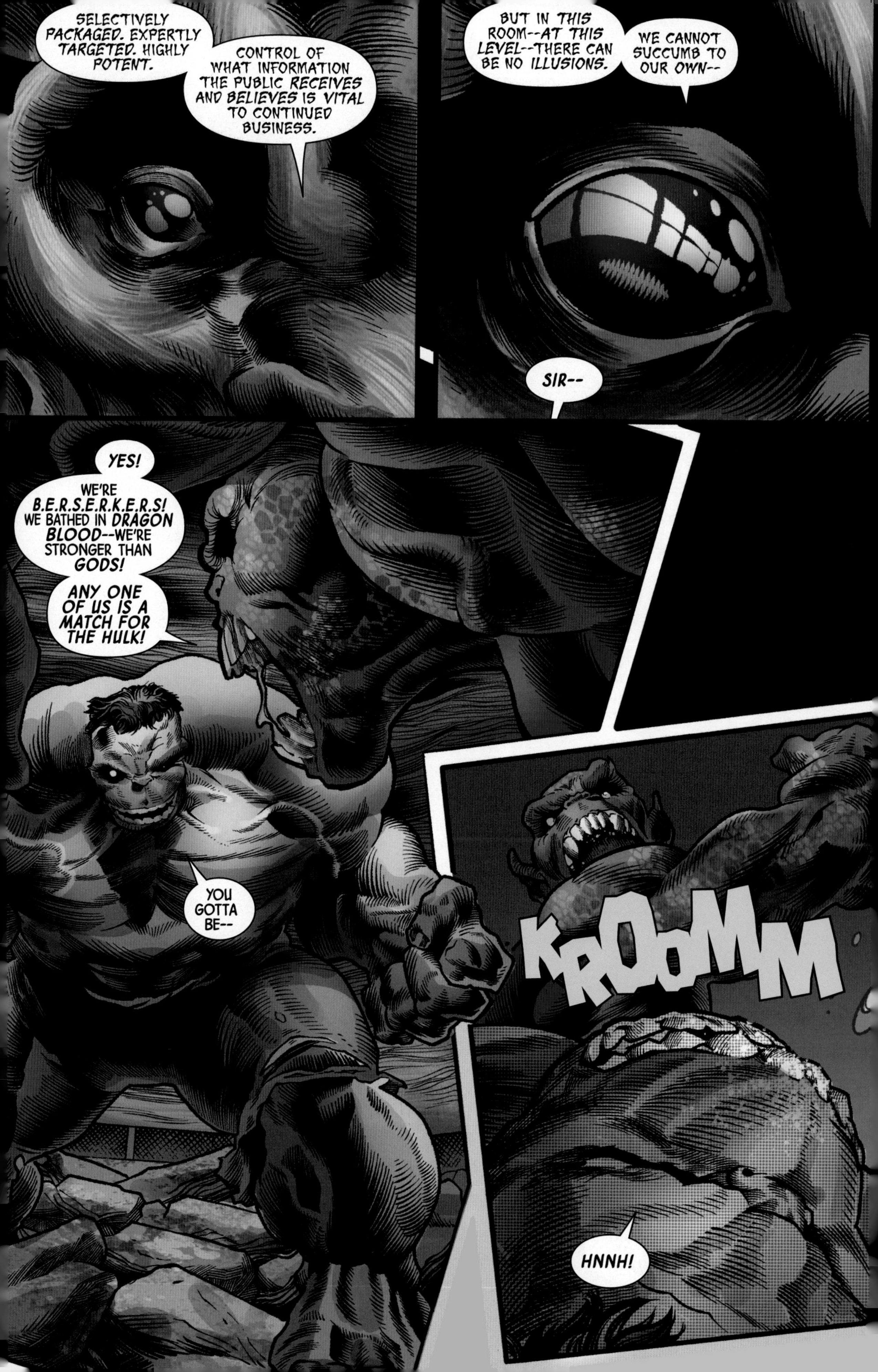
SELECTIVELY PACKAGED. EXPERTLY TARGETED. HIGHLY POTENT.
CONTROL OF WHAT INFORMATION THE PUBLIC RECEIVES AND BELIEVES IS VITAL TO CONTINUED BUSINESS.
BUT IN THIS ROOM--AT THIS LEVEL--THERE CAN BE NO ILLUSIONS.
WE CANNOT SUCCUMB TO OUR OWN--
SIR--
YES!
WE'RE B.E.R.S.E.R.K.E.R.S! WE BATHED IN DRAGON BLOOD--WE'RE STRONGER THAN GODS!
ANY ONE OF US IS A MATCH FOR THE HULK!
YOU GOTTA BE--
KROOMM
HNNH!

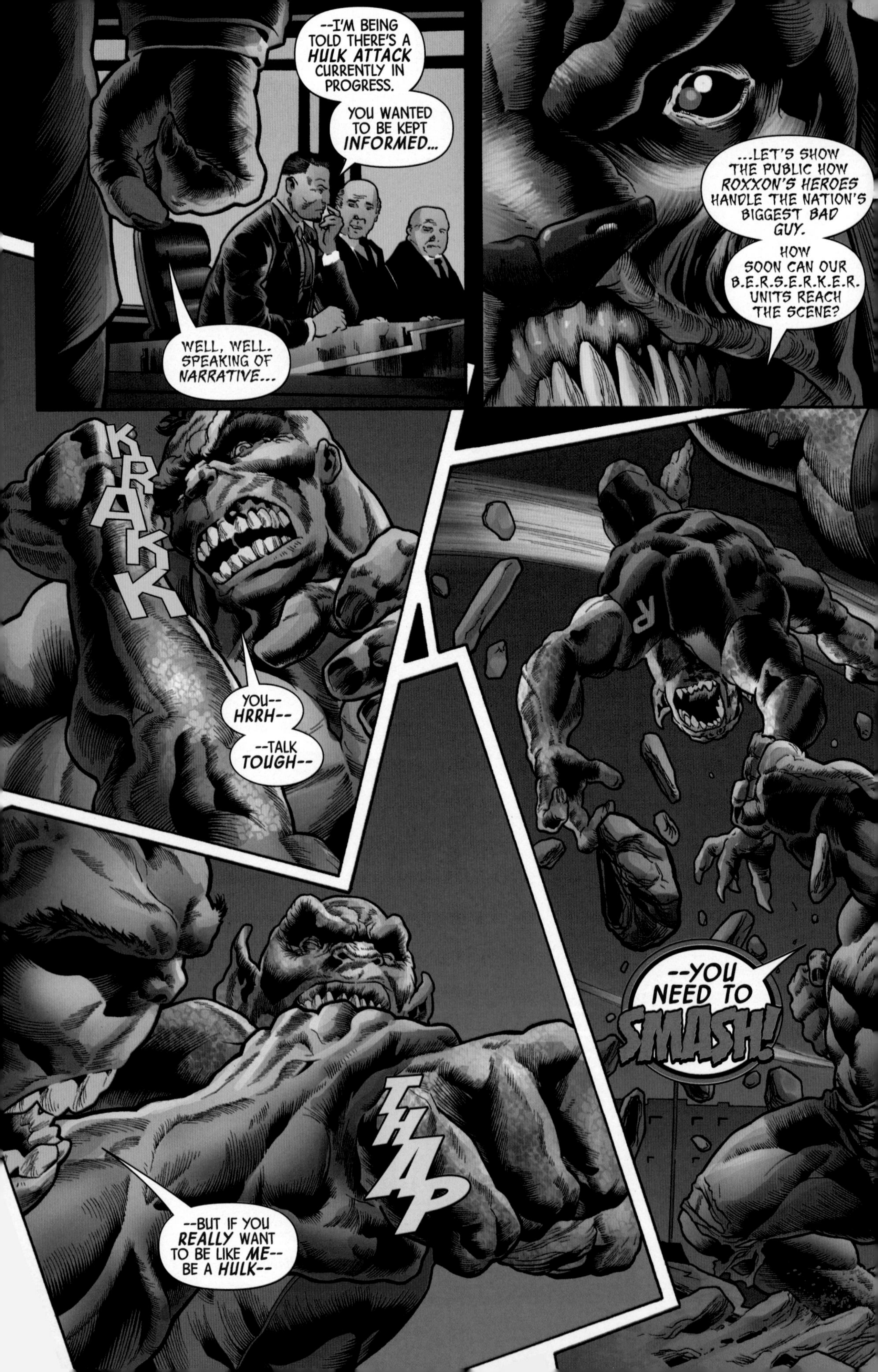
--I'M BEING TOLD THERE'S A HULK ATTACK CURRENTLY IN PROGRESS.
YOU WANTED TO BE KEPT INFORMED...
WELL, WELL. SPEAKING OF NARRATIVE...
...LET'S SHOW THE PUBLIC HOW ROXXON'S HEROES HANDLE THE NATION'S BIGGEST BAD GUY.
HOW SOON CAN OUR B.E.R.S.E.R.K.E.R. UNITS REACH THE SCENE?
KRAKK
YOU-- HRRH--
--TALK TOUGH--
--BUT IF YOU REALLY WANT TO BE LIKE ME-- BE A HULK--
THAP
--YOU NEED TO SMASH!

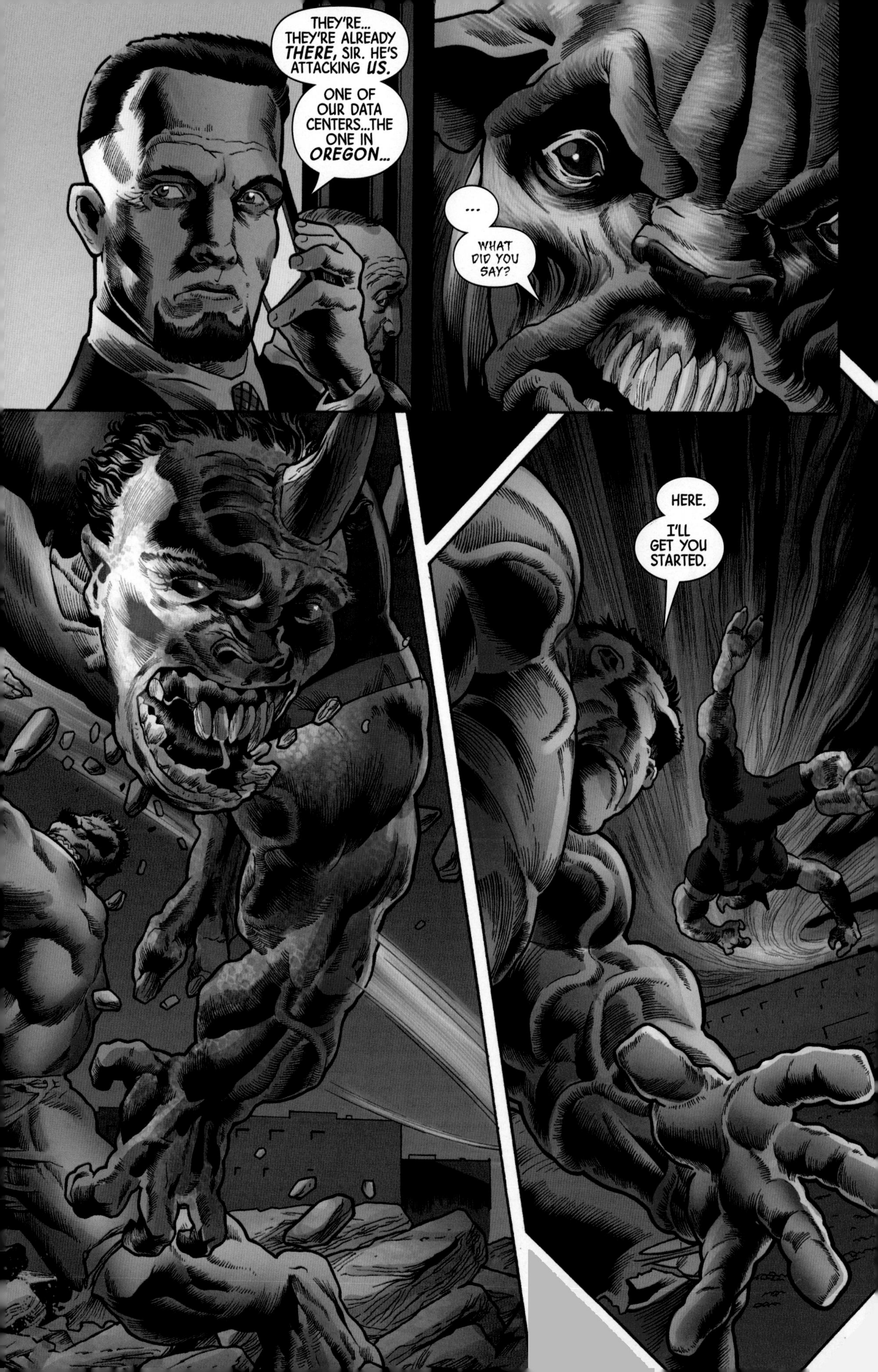
THEY'RE... THEY'RE ALREADY THERE, SIR. HE'S ATTACKING US.
ONE OF OUR DATA CENTERS...THE ONE IN OREGON...
...
WHAT DID YOU SAY?
HERE.
I'LL GET YOU STARTED.

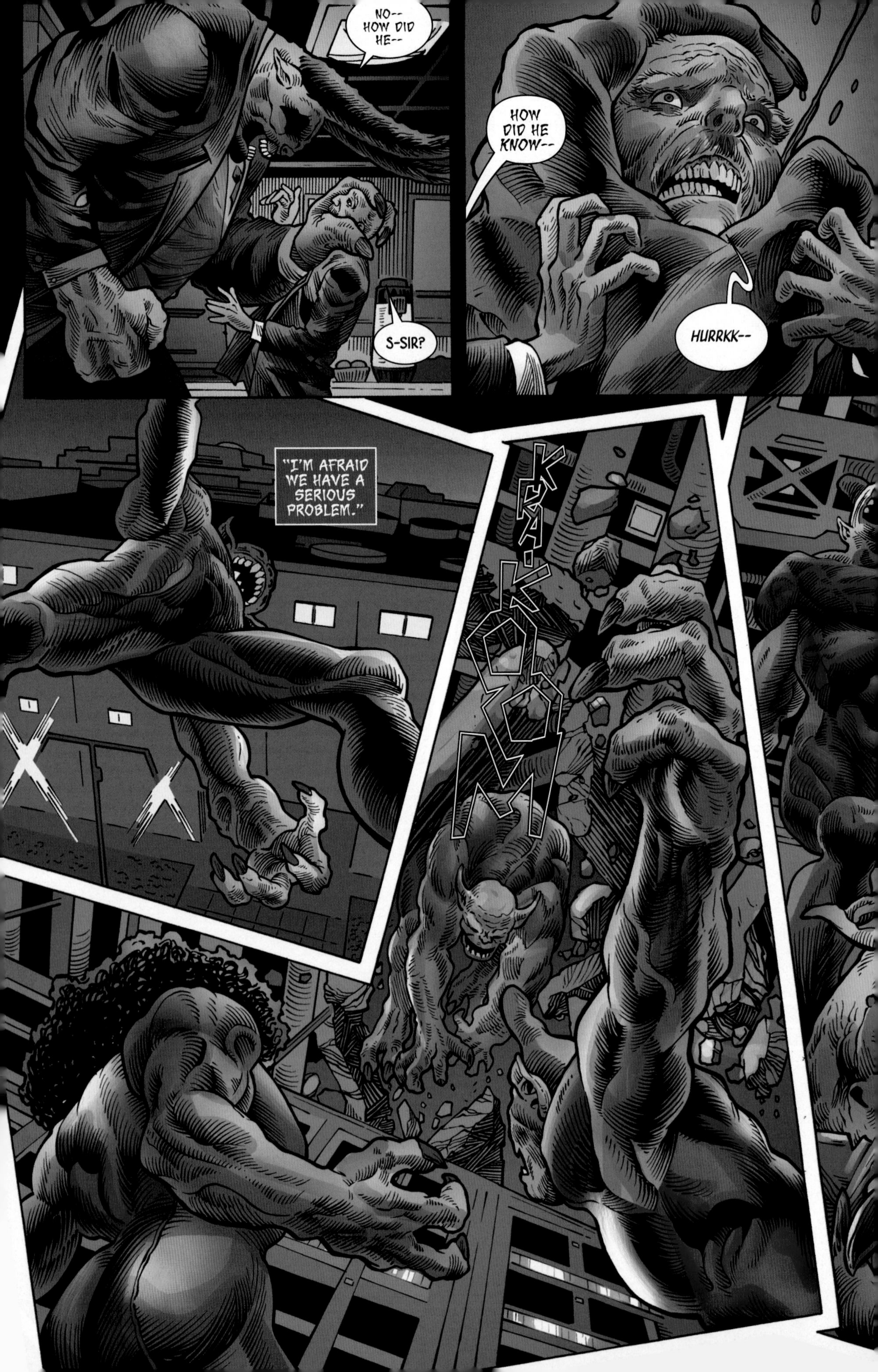
NO-- HOW DID HE--
S-SIR?
HOW DID HE KNOW--
HURRKK--
"I'M AFRAID WE HAVE A SERIOUS PROBLEM."
KRA-KOOM

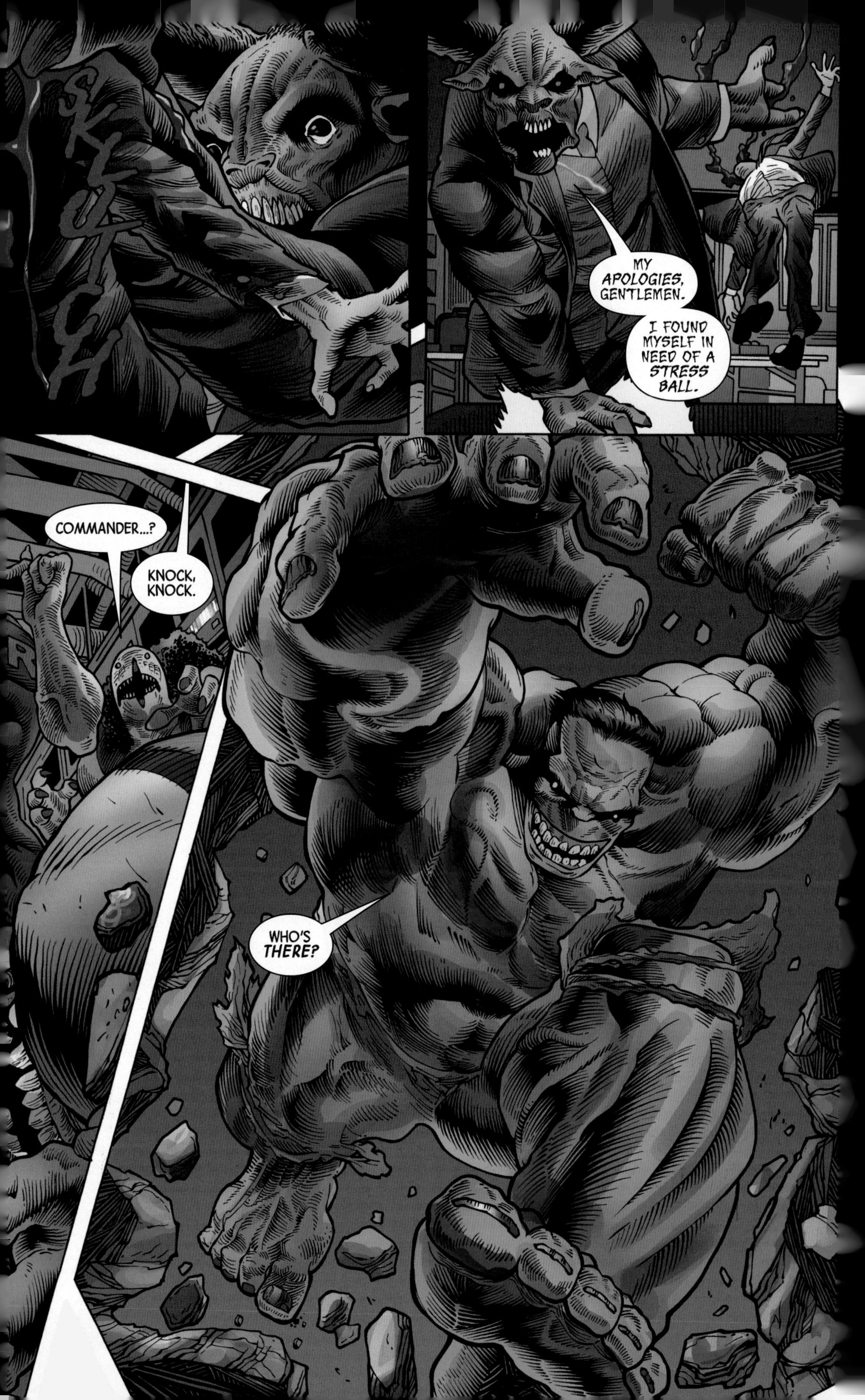
MY APOLOGIES, GENTLEMEN.
I FOUND MYSELF IN NEED OF A STRESS BALL.
COMMANDER...?
KNOCK, KNOCK.
WHO'S THERE?

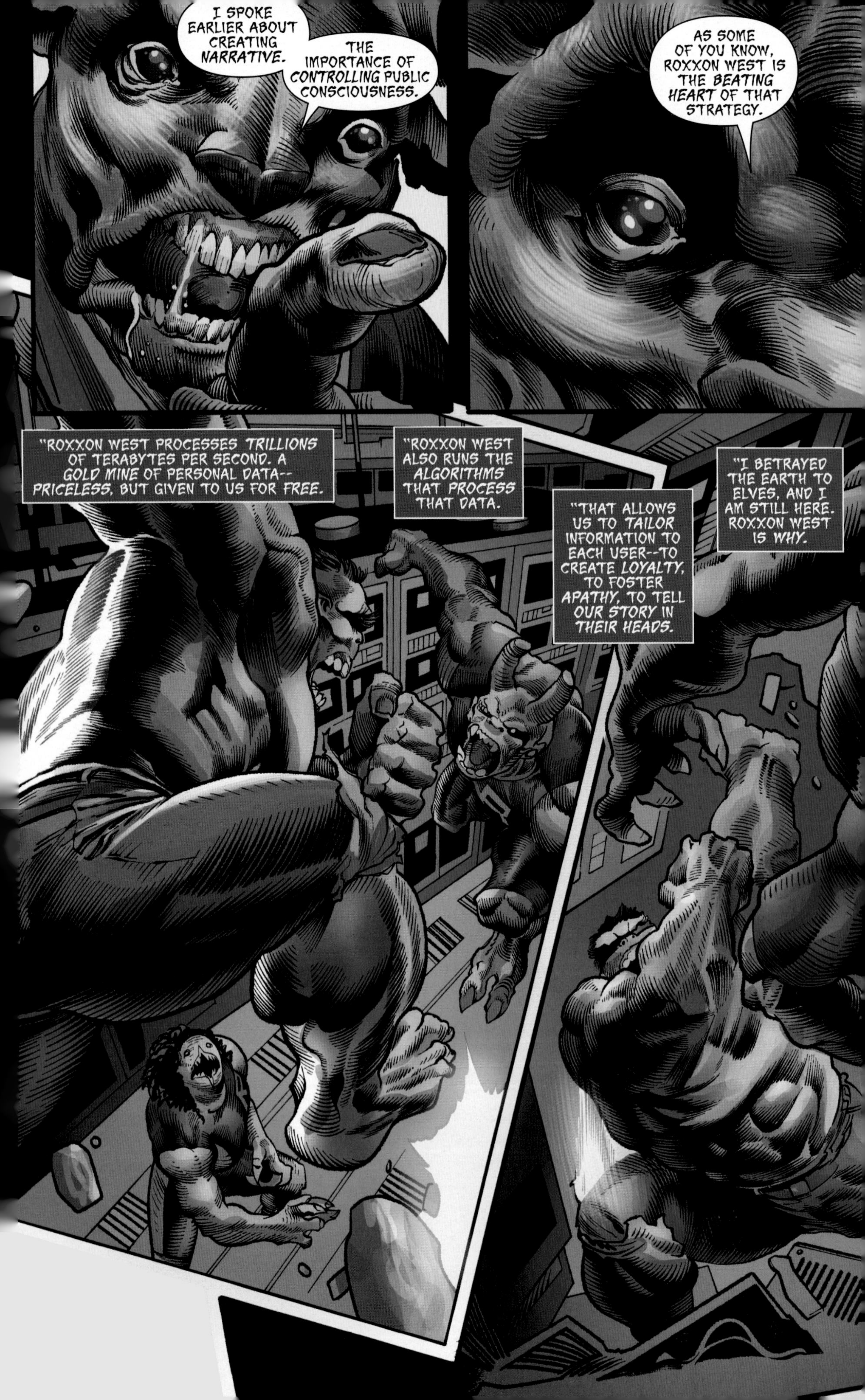
I SPOKE EARLIER ABOUT CREATING NARRATIVE.
THE IMPORTANCE OF CONTROLLING PUBLIC CONSCIOUSNESS.
AS SOME OF YOU KNOW, ROXXON WEST IS THE BEATING HEART OF THAT STRATEGY.
"ROXXON WEST PROCESSES TRILLIONS OF TERABYTES PER SECOND. A GOLD MINE OF PERSONAL DATA--PRICELESS, BUT GIVEN TO US FOR FREE.
"ROXXON WEST ALSO RUNS THE ALGORITHMS THAT PROCESS THAT DATA.
"THAT ALLOWS US TO TAILOR INFORMATION TO EACH USER--TO CREATE LOYALTY, TO FOSTER APATHY, TO TELL OUR STORY IN THEIR HEADS.
"I BETRAYED THE EARTH TO ELVES, AND I AM STILL HERE. ROXXON WEST IS WHY.

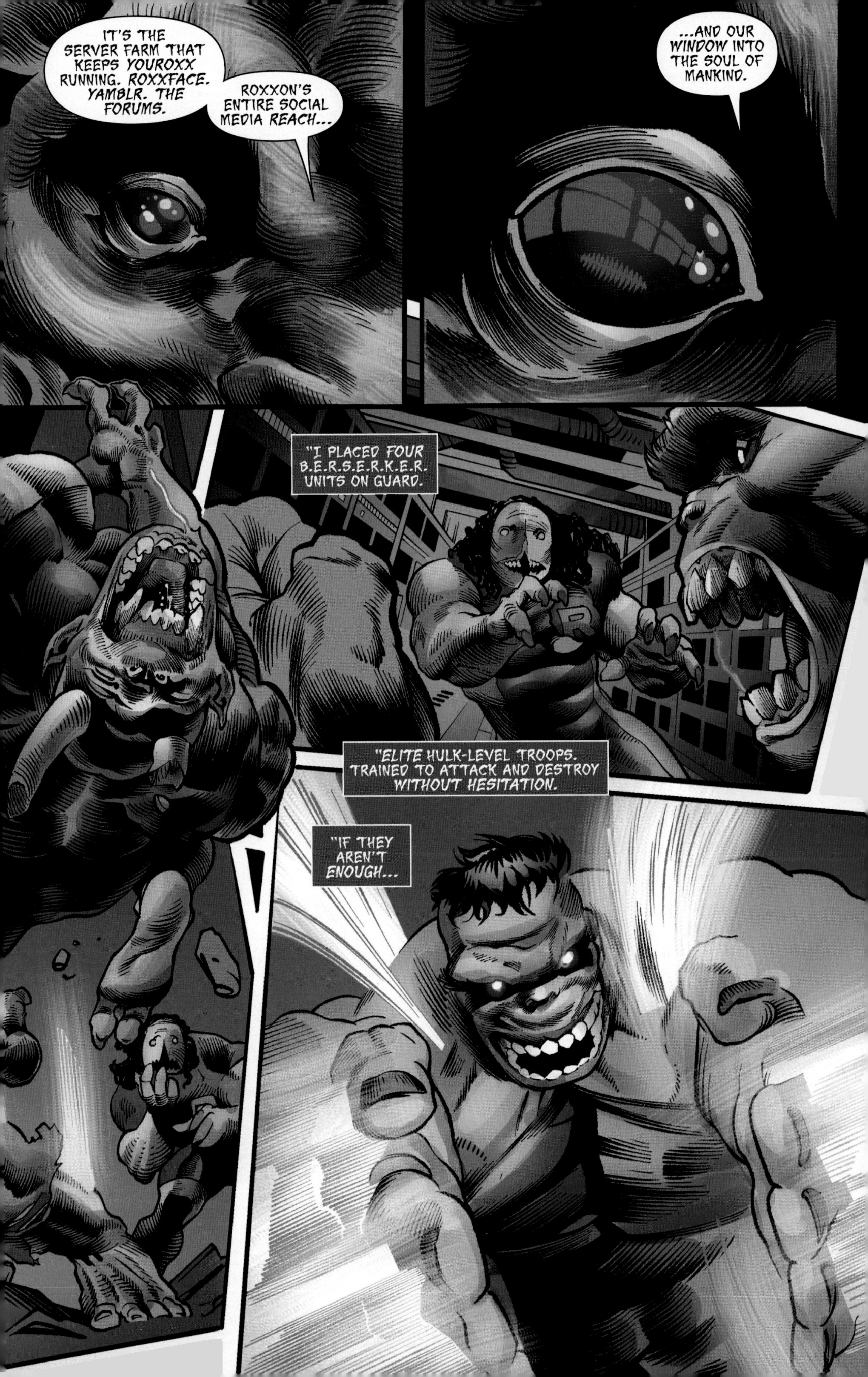
IT'S THE SERVER FARM THAT KEEPS YOUROXX RUNNING. ROXXFACE. YAMBLR. THE FORUMS.
ROXXON'S ENTIRE SOCIAL MEDIA REACH...
...AND OUR WINDOW INTO THE SOUL OF MANKIND.
"I PLACED FOUR B.E.R.S.E.R.K.E.R. UNITS ON GUARD.
"ELITE HULK-LEVEL TROOPS. TRAINED TO ATTACK AND DESTROY WITHOUT HESITATION.
"IF THEY AREN'T ENOUGH...

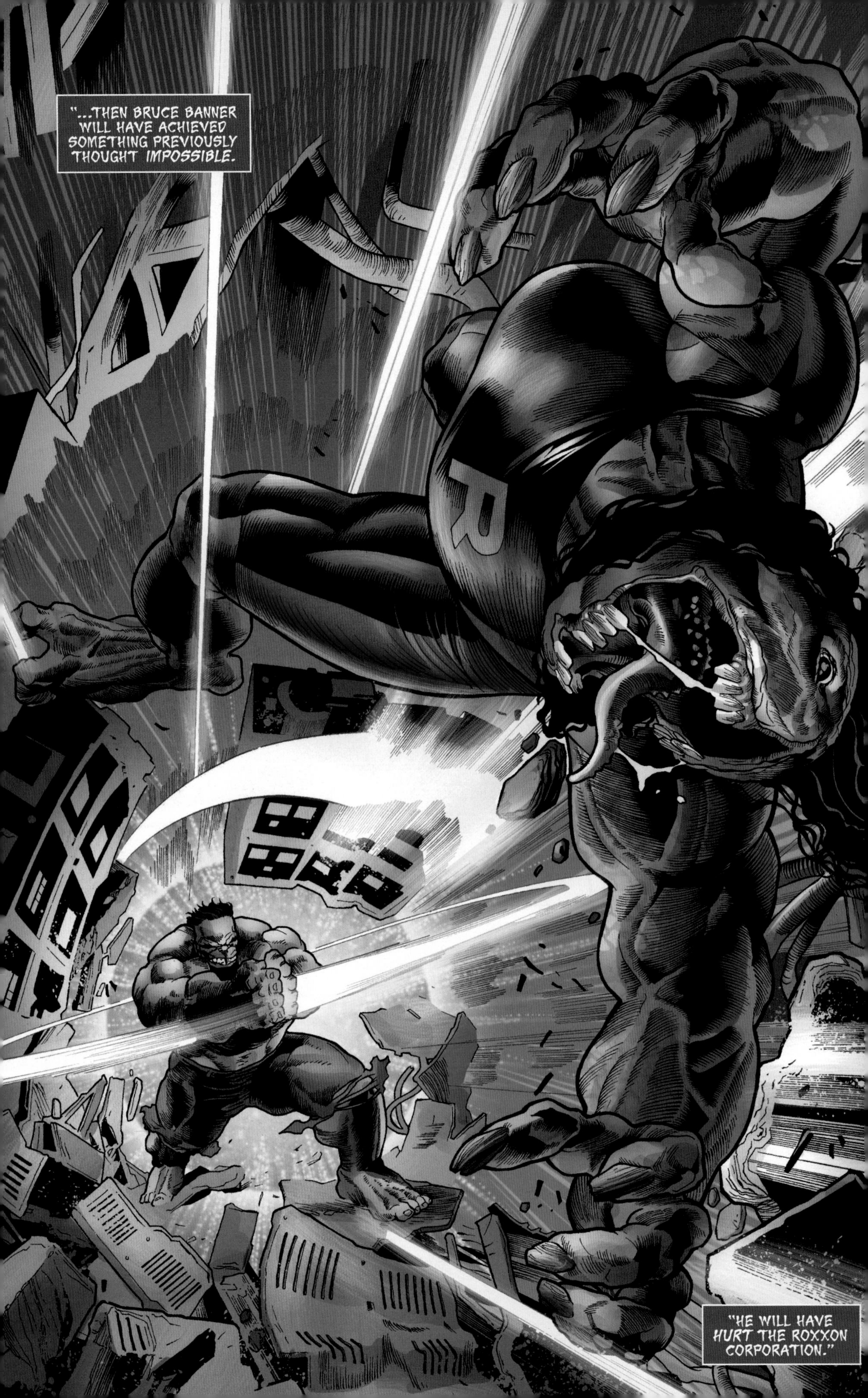
"...THEN BRUCE BANNER WILL HAVE ACHIEVED SOMETHING PREVIOUSLY THOUGHT IMPOSSIBLE.
"HE WILL HAVE HURT THE ROXXON CORPORATION."

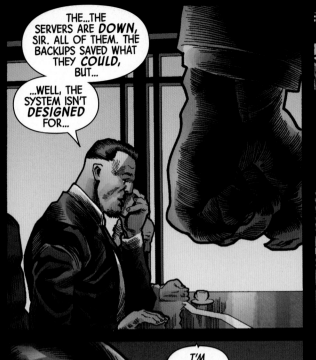

THE...THE SERVERS ARE *DOWN*, SIR. ALL OF THEM. THE BACKUPS SAVED WHAT THEY *COULD*, BUT...

...WELL, THE SYSTEM ISN'T *DESIGNED* FOR...

NO. AND NEITHER ARE WE.

NOT *YET*.

MEETING ADJOURNED.

I'M ALL DONE HERE.

WHAT'S THE *WORD*, McGOWAN?

WELL, *ROXXFACE* STOPPED WORKING, AND I CAN'T GET ANYTHING ELSE TO *LOAD*, SO...

ROXXFACE
ERROR
PAGE NOT FOUND

...I GUESS DR. BANNER WAS *RIGHT*. THAT'S HOW YOU HURT THEM.

WE SHOULD TRANSLOCATE YOU *BACK*--IT'S ALMOST *SUNRISE*--

YEAH. FIGURED I'D *WATCH* IT.

WHAT?

I--I THOUGHT--THE SUNLIGHT--

YEAH. THE DAY AIN'T *MY* TIME. BUT BANNER SHOWED ME I... HRRHH...I COULD *FIGHT* THAT.

WE CAN FIGHT THAT. WE WORK *TOGETHER*, McGOWAN.

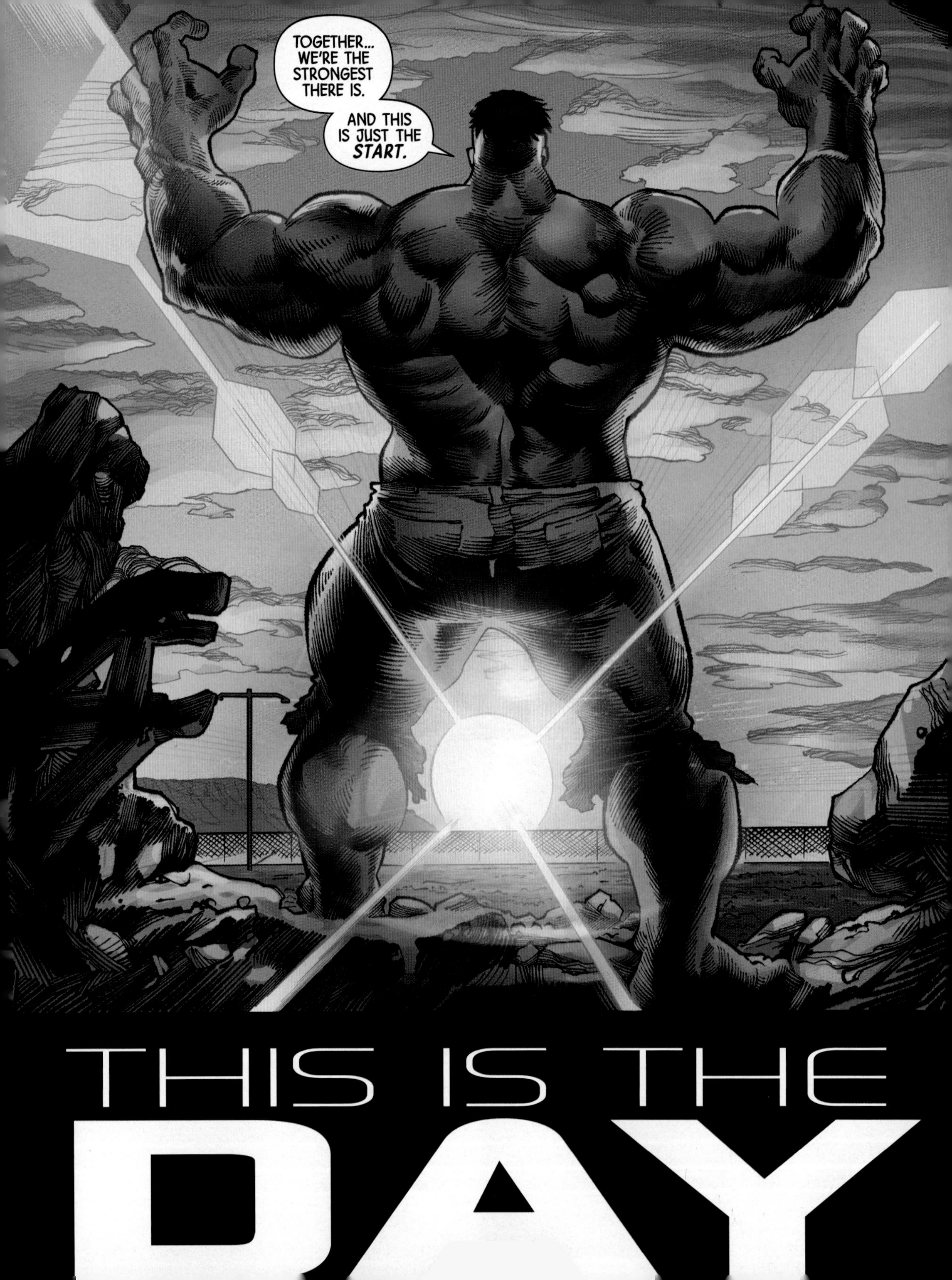
TOGETHER... WE'RE THE STRONGEST THERE IS.
AND THIS IS JUST THE START.

THIS IS THE DAY

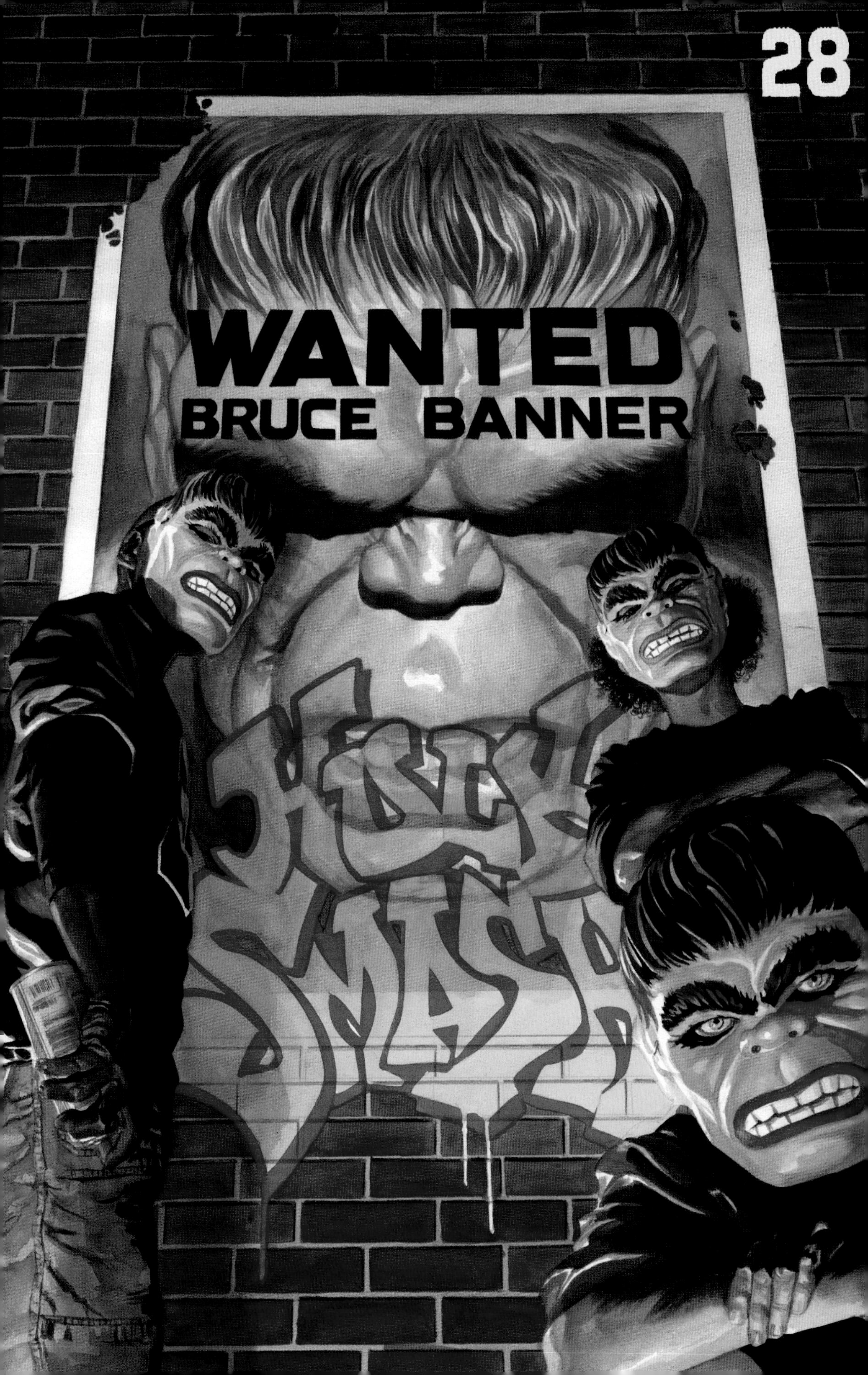
28
WANTED
BRUCE BANNER

"WE CONSIDERED OURSELVES TO BE A POWERFUL CULTURE."

– U.S. DEPARTMENT OF ENERGY

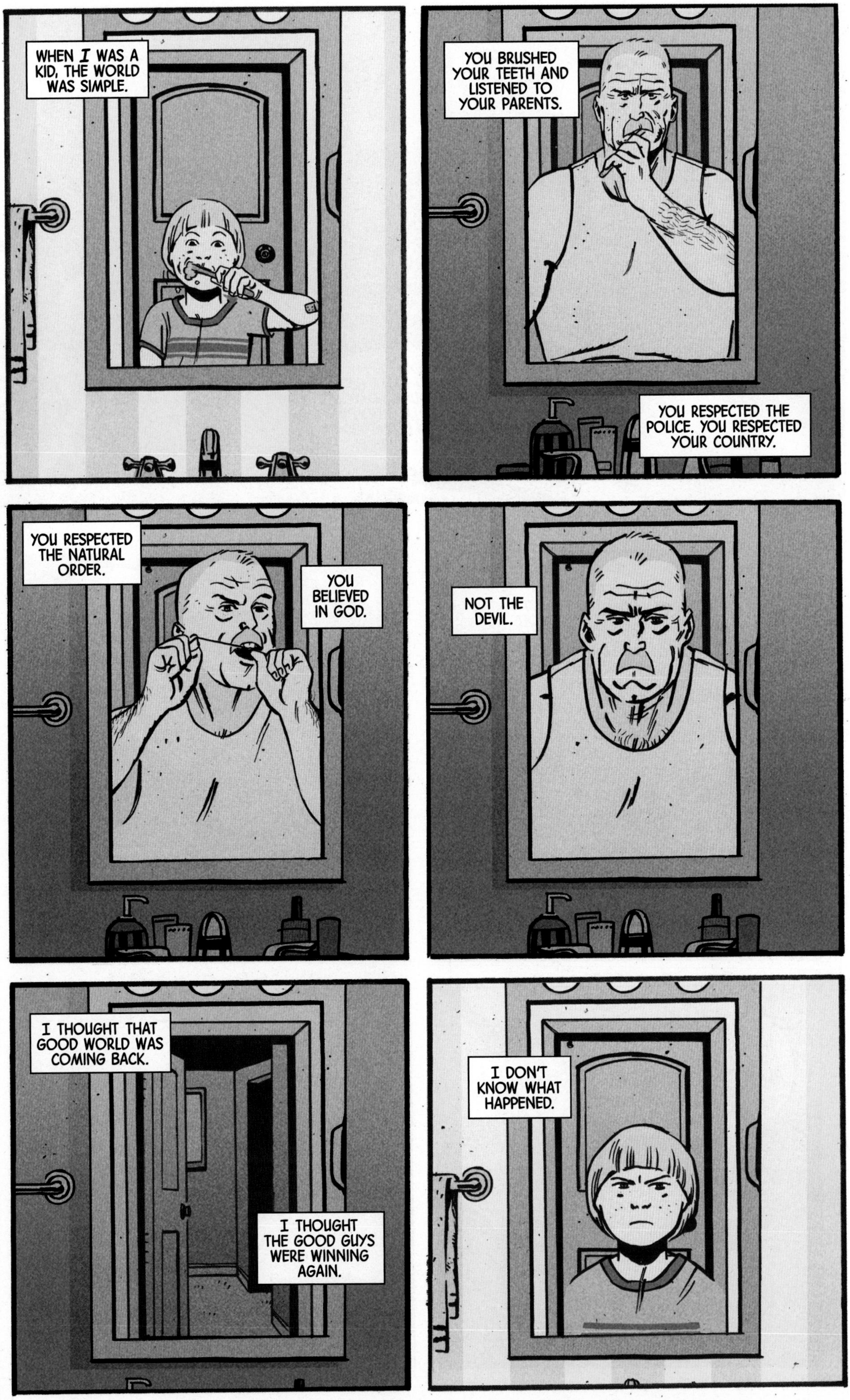
WHEN I WAS A KID, THE WORLD WAS SIMPLE.
YOU BRUSHED YOUR TEETH AND LISTENED TO YOUR PARENTS.
YOU RESPECTED THE POLICE. YOU RESPECTED YOUR COUNTRY.
YOU RESPECTED THE NATURAL ORDER.
YOU BELIEVED IN GOD.
NOT THE DEVIL.
I THOUGHT THAT GOOD WORLD WAS COMING BACK.
I THOUGHT THE GOOD GUYS WERE WINNING AGAIN.
I DON'T KNOW WHAT HAPPENED.

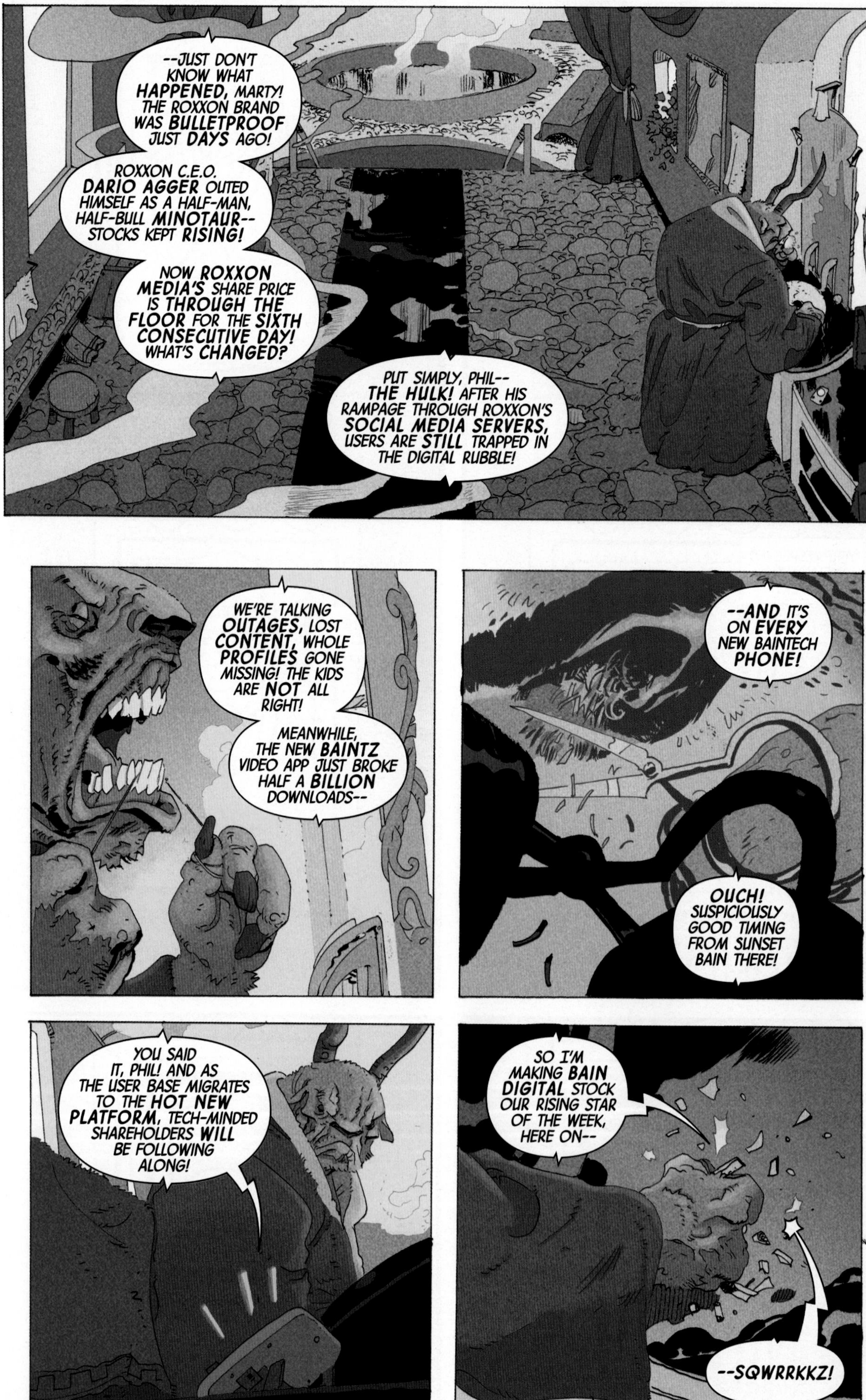
--JUST DON'T KNOW WHAT HAPPENED, MARTY! THE ROXXON BRAND WAS BULLETPROOF JUST DAYS AGO!
ROXXON C.E.O. DARIO AGGER OUTED HIMSELF AS A HALF-MAN, HALF-BULL MINOTAUR--STOCKS KEPT RISING!
NOW ROXXON MEDIA'S SHARE PRICE IS THROUGH THE FLOOR FOR THE SIXTH CONSECUTIVE DAY! WHAT'S CHANGED?
PUT SIMPLY, PHIL--THE HULK! AFTER HIS RAMPAGE THROUGH ROXXON'S SOCIAL MEDIA SERVERS, USERS ARE STILL TRAPPED IN THE DIGITAL RUBBLE!
WE'RE TALKING OUTAGES, LOST CONTENT, WHOLE PROFILES GONE MISSING! THE KIDS ARE NOT ALL RIGHT!
MEANWHILE, THE NEW BAINTZ VIDEO APP JUST BROKE HALF A BILLION DOWNLOADS--
--AND IT'S ON EVERY NEW BAINTECH PHONE!
OUCH! SUSPICIOUSLY GOOD TIMING FROM SUNSET BAIN THERE!
YOU SAID IT, PHIL! AND AS THE USER BASE MIGRATES TO THE HOT NEW PLATFORM, TECH-MINDED SHAREHOLDERS WILL BE FOLLOWING ALONG!
SO I'M MAKING BAIN DIGITAL STOCK OUR RISING STAR OF THE WEEK, HERE ON--
--SQWRRKKZ!

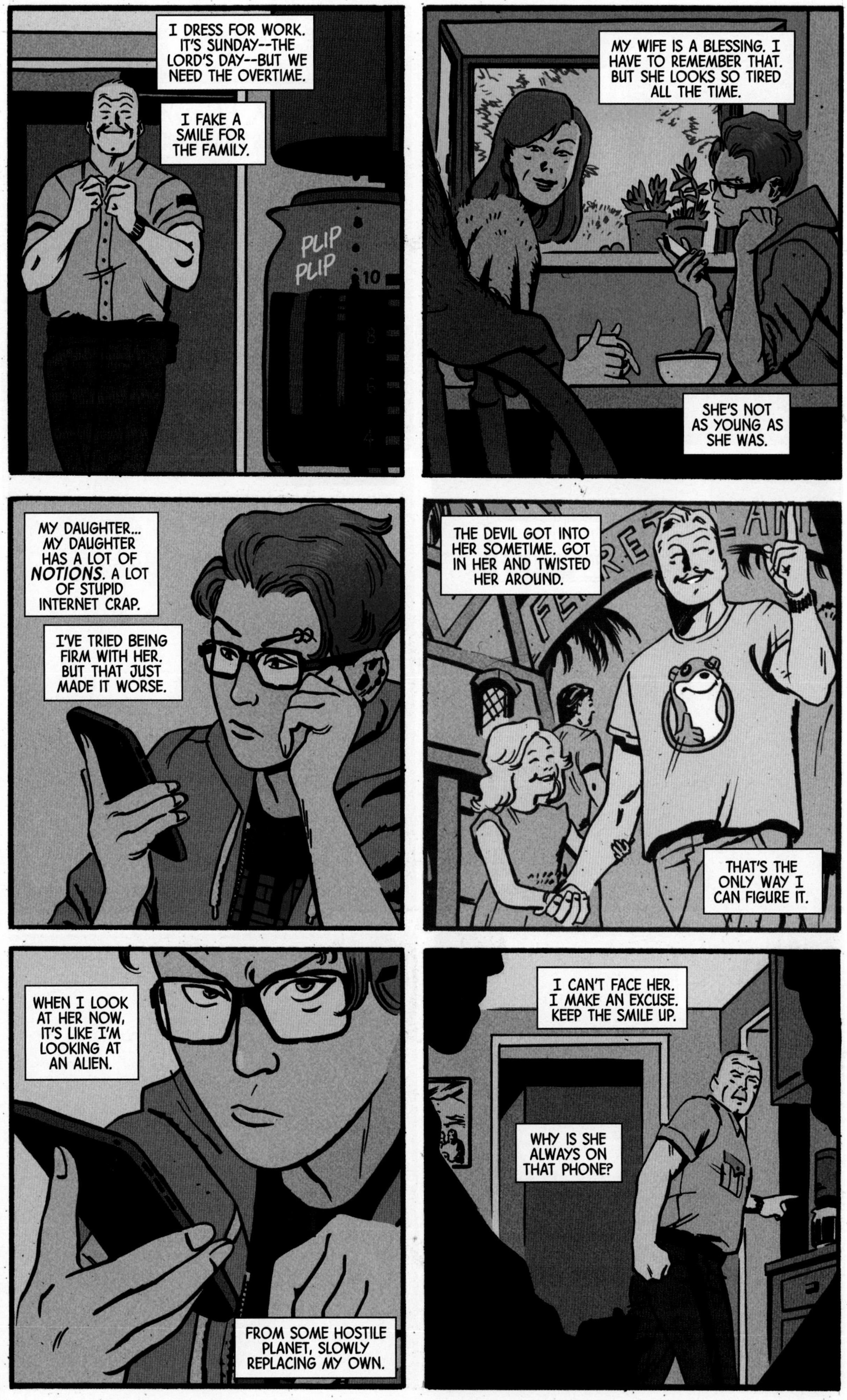
I DRESS FOR WORK. IT'S SUNDAY--THE LORD'S DAY--BUT WE NEED THE OVERTIME.
I FAKE A SMILE FOR THE FAMILY.
PLIP PLIP
MY WIFE IS A BLESSING. I HAVE TO REMEMBER THAT. BUT SHE LOOKS SO TIRED ALL THE TIME.
SHE'S NOT AS YOUNG AS SHE WAS.
MY DAUGHTER... MY DAUGHTER HAS A LOT OF NOTIONS. A LOT OF STUPID INTERNET CRAP.
I'VE TRIED BEING FIRM WITH HER. BUT THAT JUST MADE IT WORSE.
THE DEVIL GOT INTO HER SOMETIME. GOT IN HER AND TWISTED HER AROUND.
THAT'S THE ONLY WAY I CAN FIGURE IT.
WHEN I LOOK AT HER NOW, IT'S LIKE I'M LOOKING AT AN ALIEN.
FROM SOME HOSTILE PLANET, SLOWLY REPLACING MY OWN.
I CAN'T FACE HER. I MAKE AN EXCUSE. KEEP THE SMILE UP.
WHY IS SHE ALWAYS ON THAT PHONE?

IT'S BETTER DOWN HERE.

I CAN BREATHE.

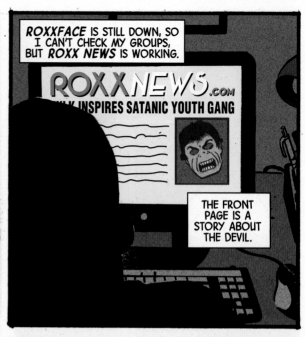

ROXXFACE IS STILL DOWN, SO I CAN'T CHECK MY GROUPS, BUT ROXX NEWS IS WORKING.

ROXXNEWS.com

ULK INSPIRES SATANIC YOUTH GANG

THE FRONT PAGE IS A STORY ABOUT THE DEVIL.

OXXNEWS.com

SPIRES SATANIC YOUTH GANG

YOUTH GANGS. RIOTING AND PROTESTING, WEARING HIS FACE, HIS COLORS. IN THRALL TO HIM.

THE "TEEN BRIGADE," THEY CALL THEMSELVES.

CHK!

I'M NOT AFRAID OF THEM. I'VE NEVER SHOWN FEAR IN MY LIFE.

BUT WHEN I'M OUT ON THE STREETS, I LIKE TO BE PREPARED.

PEOPLE LIKE ME-- WE MADE THIS COUNTRY.

9MM

THIS WHOLE DAMN WORLD-- WE MADE IT. FOR OUR CHILDREN.

WE CAN STILL TAKE IT BACK.

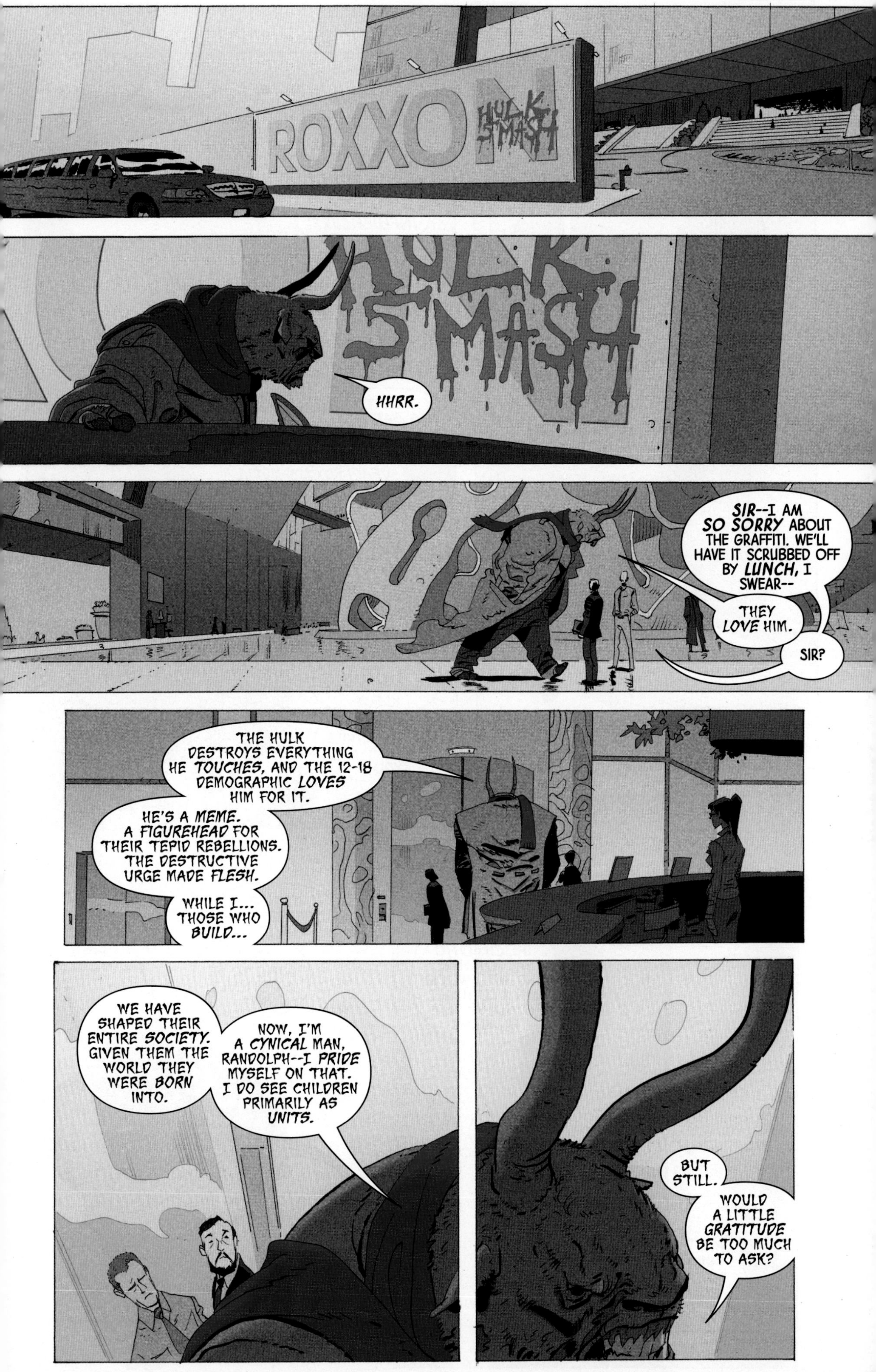
ROXXON
HULK SMASH
HULK SMASH
HHRR.
SIR--I AM SO SORRY ABOUT THE GRAFFITI. WE'LL HAVE IT SCRUBBED OFF BY LUNCH, I SWEAR--
THEY LOVE HIM.
SIR?
THE HULK DESTROYS EVERYTHING HE TOUCHES, AND THE 12-18 DEMOGRAPHIC LOVES HIM FOR IT.
HE'S A MEME. A FIGUREHEAD FOR THEIR TEPID REBELLIONS. THE DESTRUCTIVE URGE MADE FLESH.
WHILE I... THOSE WHO BUILD...
WE HAVE SHAPED THEIR ENTIRE SOCIETY. GIVEN THEM THE WORLD THEY WERE BORN INTO.
NOW, I'M A CYNICAL MAN, RANDOLPH--I PRIDE MYSELF ON THAT. I DO SEE CHILDREN PRIMARILY AS UNITS.
BUT STILL.
WOULD A LITTLE GRATITUDE BE TOO MUCH TO ASK?

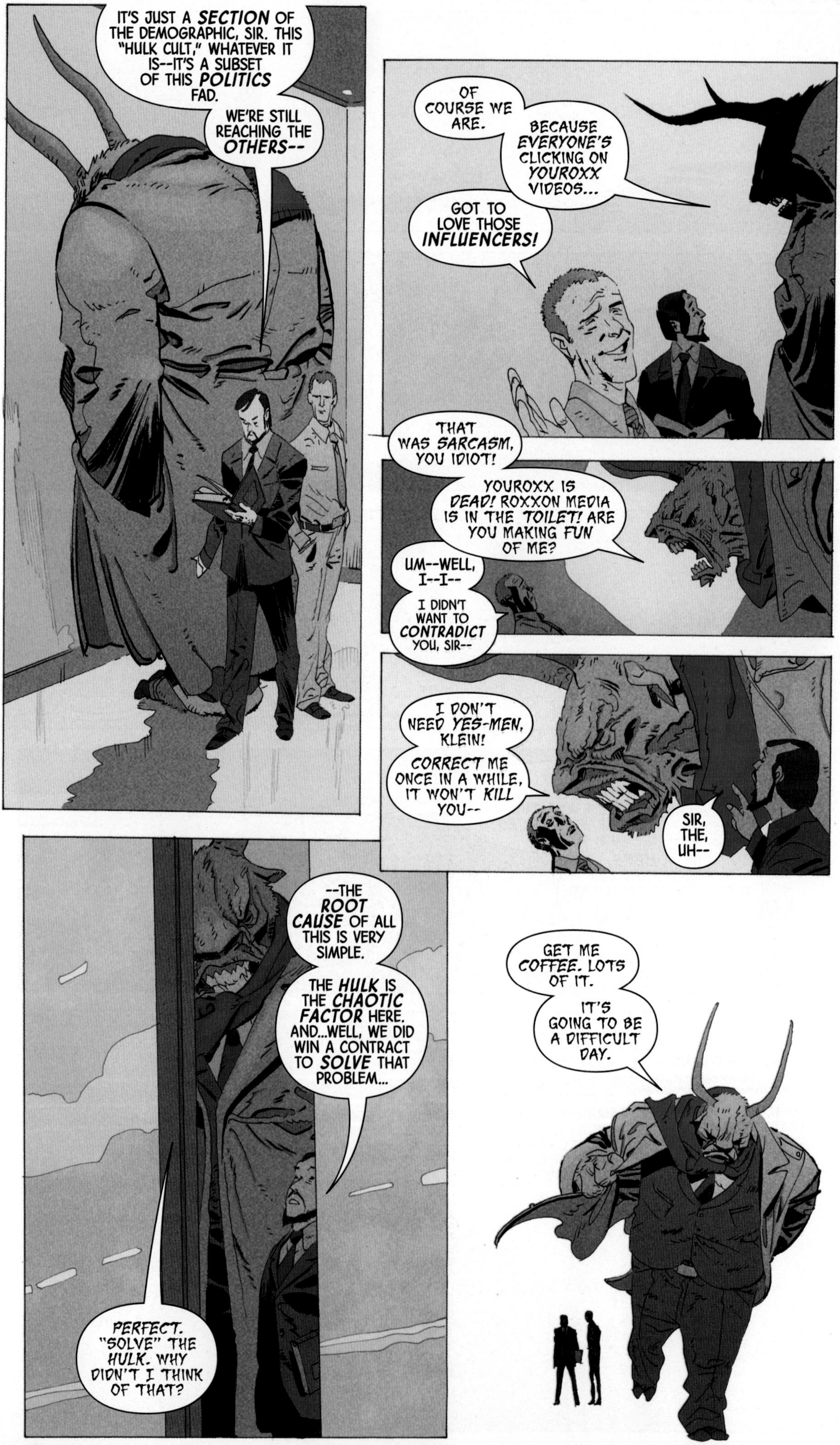
IT'S JUST A SECTION OF THE DEMOGRAPHIC, SIR. THIS "HULK CULT," WHATEVER IT IS--IT'S A SUBSET OF THIS POLITICS FAD.
WE'RE STILL REACHING THE OTHERS--
OF COURSE WE ARE.
BECAUSE EVERYONE'S CLICKING ON YOUROXX VIDEOS...
GOT TO LOVE THOSE INFLUENCERS!
THAT WAS SARCASM, YOU IDIOT!
YOUROXX IS DEAD! ROXXON MEDIA IS IN THE TOILET! ARE YOU MAKING FUN OF ME?
UM--WELL, I--I--
I DIDN'T WANT TO CONTRADICT YOU, SIR--
I DON'T NEED YES-MEN, KLEIN!
CORRECT ME ONCE IN A WHILE, IT WON'T KILL YOU--
SIR, THE, UH--
--THE ROOT CAUSE OF ALL THIS IS VERY SIMPLE.
THE HULK IS THE CHAOTIC FACTOR HERE. AND...WELL, WE DID WIN A CONTRACT TO SOLVE THAT PROBLEM...
PERFECT. "SOLVE" THE HULK. WHY DIDN'T I THINK OF THAT?
GET ME COFFEE. LOTS OF IT.
IT'S GOING TO BE A DIFFICULT DAY.

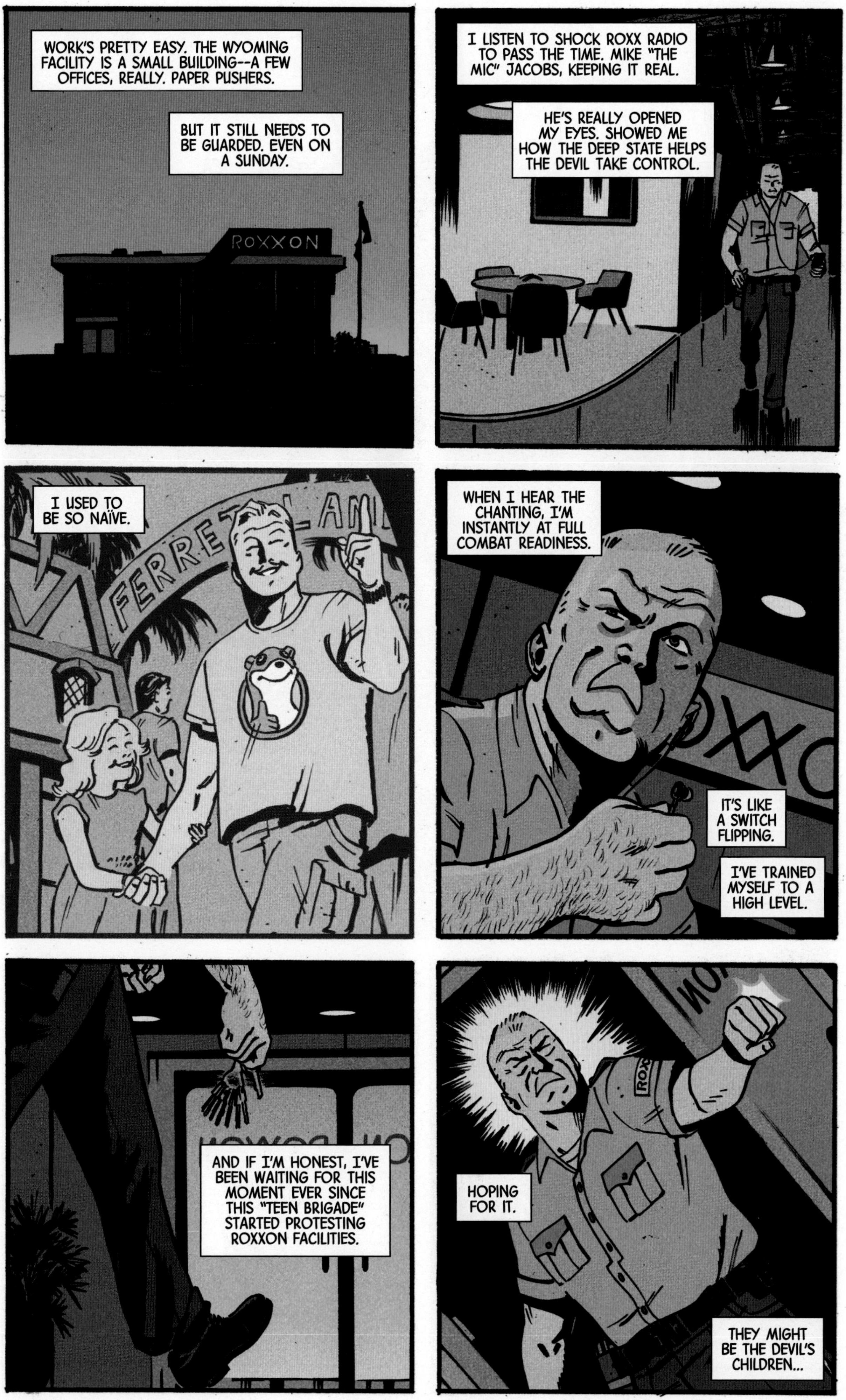
WORK'S PRETTY EASY. THE WYOMING FACILITY IS A SMALL BUILDING--A FEW OFFICES, REALLY. PAPER PUSHERS.
BUT IT STILL NEEDS TO BE GUARDED. EVEN ON A SUNDAY.
ROXXON
I LISTEN TO SHOCK ROXX RADIO TO PASS THE TIME. MIKE "THE MIC" JACOBS, KEEPING IT REAL.
HE'S REALLY OPENED MY EYES. SHOWED ME HOW THE DEEP STATE HELPS THE DEVIL TAKE CONTROL.
I USED TO BE SO NAÏVE.
WHEN I HEAR THE CHANTING, I'M INSTANTLY AT FULL COMBAT READINESS.
IT'S LIKE A SWITCH FLIPPING.
I'VE TRAINED MYSELF TO A HIGH LEVEL.
AND IF I'M HONEST, I'VE BEEN WAITING FOR THIS MOMENT EVER SINCE THIS "TEEN BRIGADE" STARTED PROTESTING ROXXON FACILITIES.
HOPING FOR IT.
THEY MIGHT BE THE DEVIL'S CHILDREN...

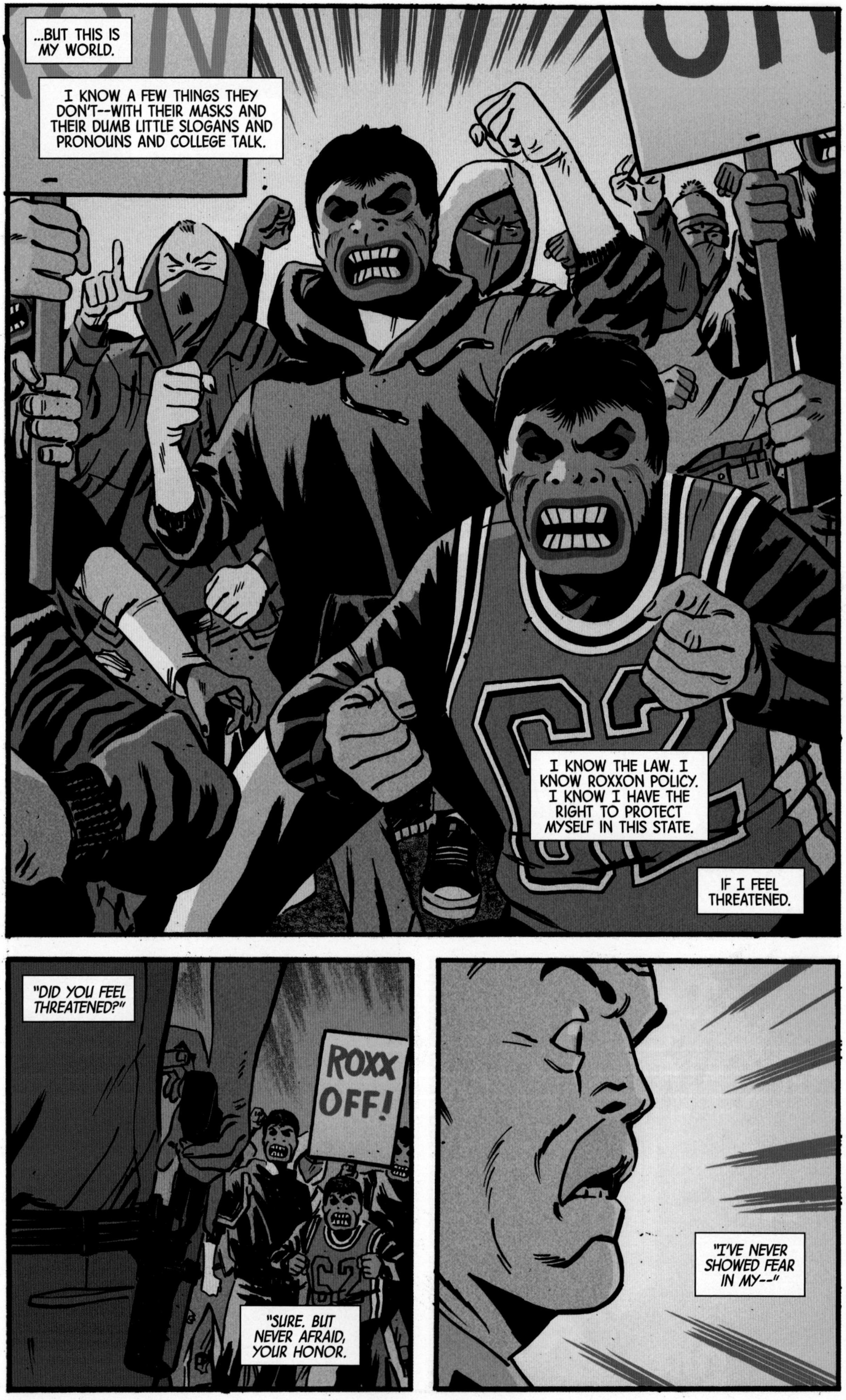
...BUT THIS IS MY WORLD.
I KNOW A FEW THINGS THEY DON'T--WITH THEIR MASKS AND THEIR DUMB LITTLE SLOGANS AND PRONOUNS AND COLLEGE TALK.
I KNOW THE LAW. I KNOW ROXXON POLICY. I KNOW I HAVE THE RIGHT TO PROTECT MYSELF IN THIS STATE.
IF I FEEL THREATENED.
"DID YOU FEEL THREATENED?"
ROXX OFF!
"SURE. BUT NEVER AFRAID, YOUR HONOR.
"I'VE NEVER SHOWED FEAR IN MY--"

THAT ONE.

I KNOW HER.

IT'S NOT YOUR FAULT, HONEY.

THE DEVIL WAS IN HER.

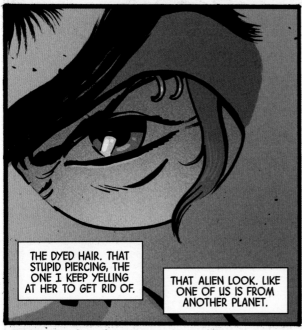

THE DYED HAIR. THAT STUPID PIERCING, THE ONE I KEEP YELLING AT HER TO GET RID OF.

THAT ALIEN LOOK. LIKE ONE OF US IS FROM ANOTHER PLANET.

THE DEVIL WAS IN HER, SIR.

YOU FELT THREATENED.

YES.

I KNOW HER. BUT...SHE'S WEARING HIS FACE. SHE MIGHT AS WELL BE A STRANGER.

SHE MIGHT AS WELL BE A STRANGER... AND...

AND...IF I DIDN'T KNOW IT WAS HER...

...I COULD FEEL THREATENED.

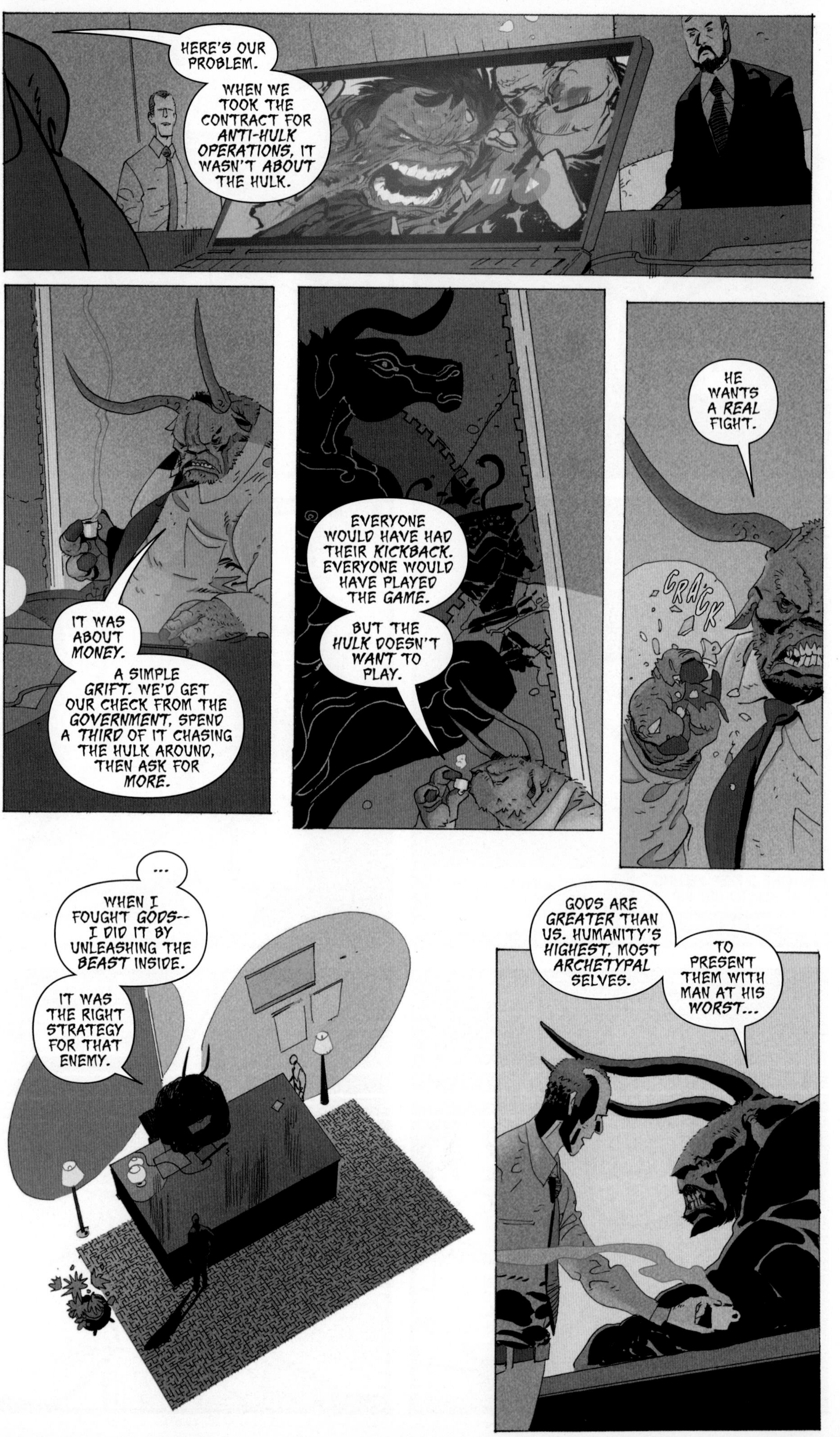
HERE'S OUR PROBLEM.
WHEN WE TOOK THE CONTRACT FOR ANTI-HULK OPERATIONS, IT WASN'T ABOUT THE HULK.
IT WAS ABOUT MONEY.
A SIMPLE GRIFT. WE'D GET OUR CHECK FROM THE GOVERNMENT, SPEND A THIRD OF IT CHASING THE HULK AROUND, THEN ASK FOR MORE.
EVERYONE WOULD HAVE HAD THEIR KICKBACK. EVERYONE WOULD HAVE PLAYED THE GAME.
BUT THE HULK DOESN'T WANT TO PLAY.
HE WANTS A REAL FIGHT.
CRACK
...
WHEN I FOUGHT GODS-- I DID IT BY UNLEASHING THE BEAST INSIDE.
IT WAS THE RIGHT STRATEGY FOR THAT ENEMY.
GODS ARE GREATER THAN US. HUMANITY'S HIGHEST, MOST ARCHETYPAL SELVES.
TO PRESENT THEM WITH MAN AT HIS WORST...

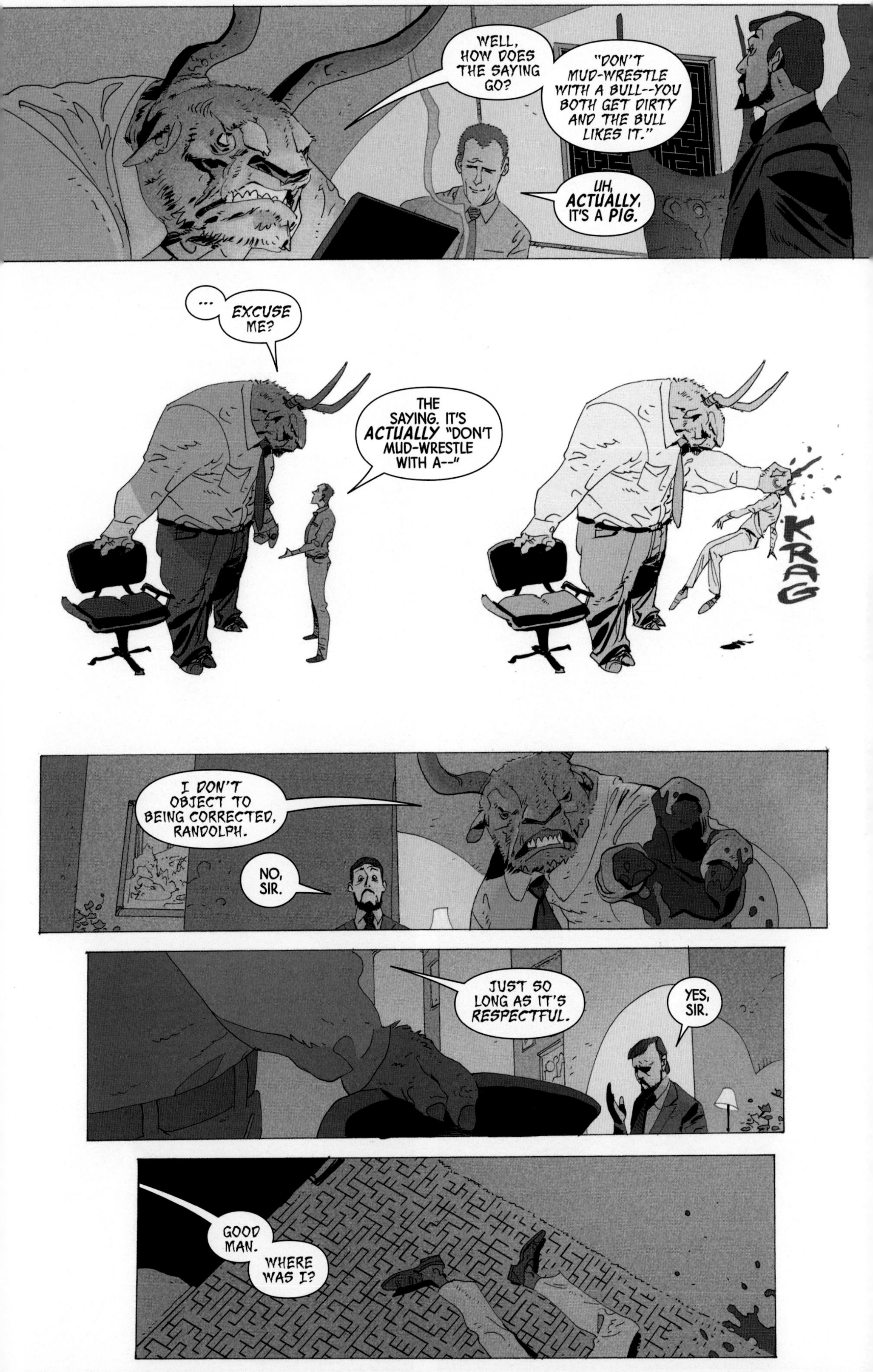
WELL, HOW DOES THE SAYING GO?
"DON'T MUD-WRESTLE WITH A BULL--YOU BOTH GET DIRTY AND THE BULL LIKES IT."
UH, ACTUALLY, IT'S A PIG.
... EXCUSE ME?
THE SAYING. IT'S ACTUALLY "DON'T MUD-WRESTLE WITH A--"
KRAG
I DON'T OBJECT TO BEING CORRECTED, RANDOLPH.
NO, SIR.
JUST SO LONG AS IT'S RESPECTFUL.
YES, SIR.
GOOD MAN.
WHERE WAS I?

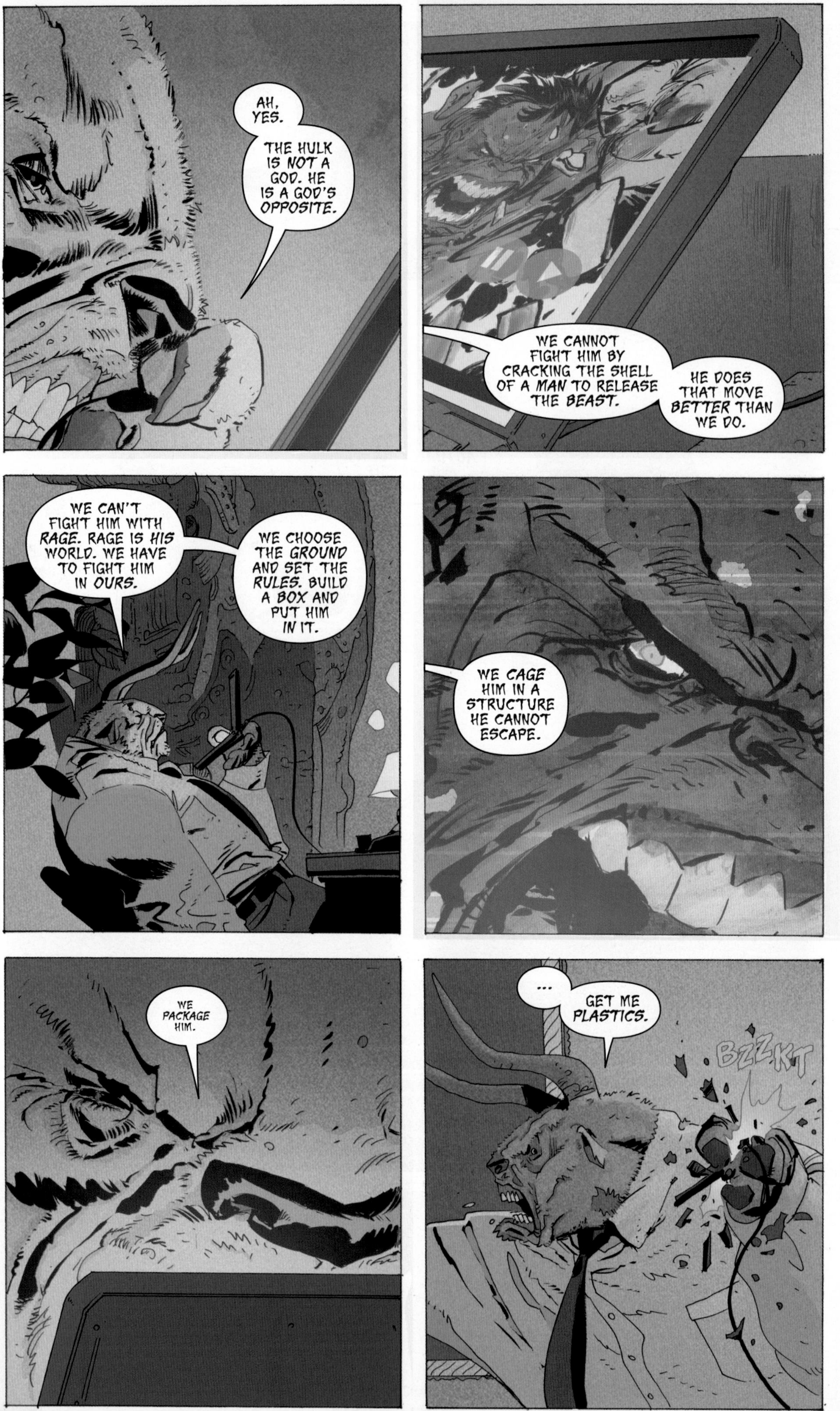
AH, YES.
THE HULK IS NOT A GOD. HE IS A GOD'S OPPOSITE.
WE CANNOT FIGHT HIM BY CRACKING THE SHELL OF A MAN TO RELEASE THE BEAST.
HE DOES THAT MOVE BETTER THAN WE DO.
WE CAN'T FIGHT HIM WITH RAGE. RAGE IS HIS WORLD. WE HAVE TO FIGHT HIM IN OURS.
WE CHOOSE THE GROUND AND SET THE RULES. BUILD A BOX AND PUT HIM IN IT.
WE CAGE HIM IN A STRUCTURE HE CANNOT ESCAPE.
WE PACKAGE HIM.
...
GET ME PLASTICS.
BZZKT

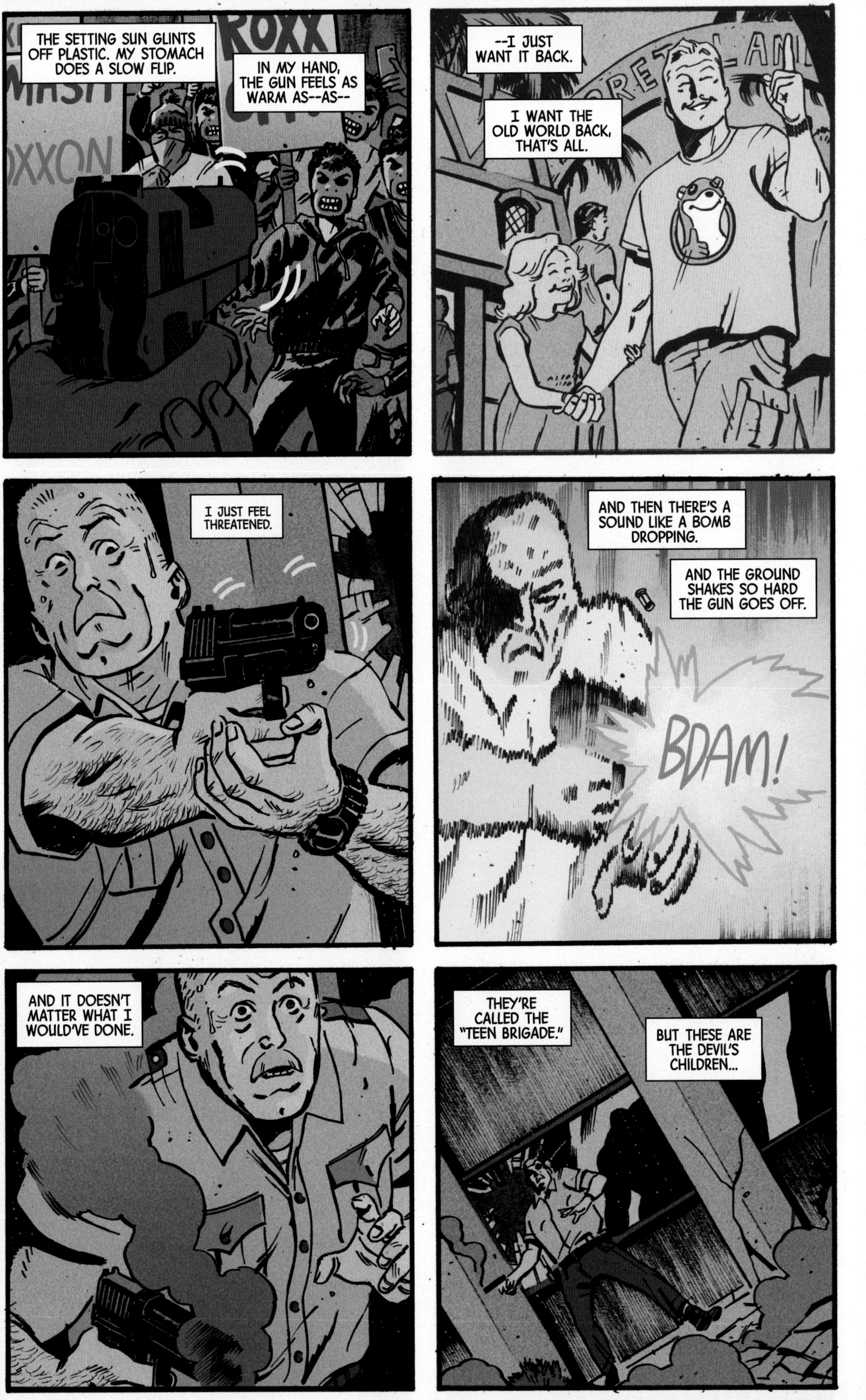
ROXX
MASH
OXXON
THE SETTING SUN GLINTS OFF PLASTIC. MY STOMACH DOES A SLOW FLIP.
IN MY HAND, THE GUN FEELS AS WARM AS--AS--
--I JUST WANT IT BACK.
I WANT THE OLD WORLD BACK, THAT'S ALL.
I JUST FEEL THREATENED.
AND THEN THERE'S A SOUND LIKE A BOMB DROPPING.
AND THE GROUND SHAKES SO HARD THE GUN GOES OFF.
BDAM!
AND IT DOESN'T MATTER WHAT I WOULD'VE DONE.
THEY'RE CALLED THE "TEEN BRIGADE."
BUT THESE ARE THE DEVIL'S CHILDREN...

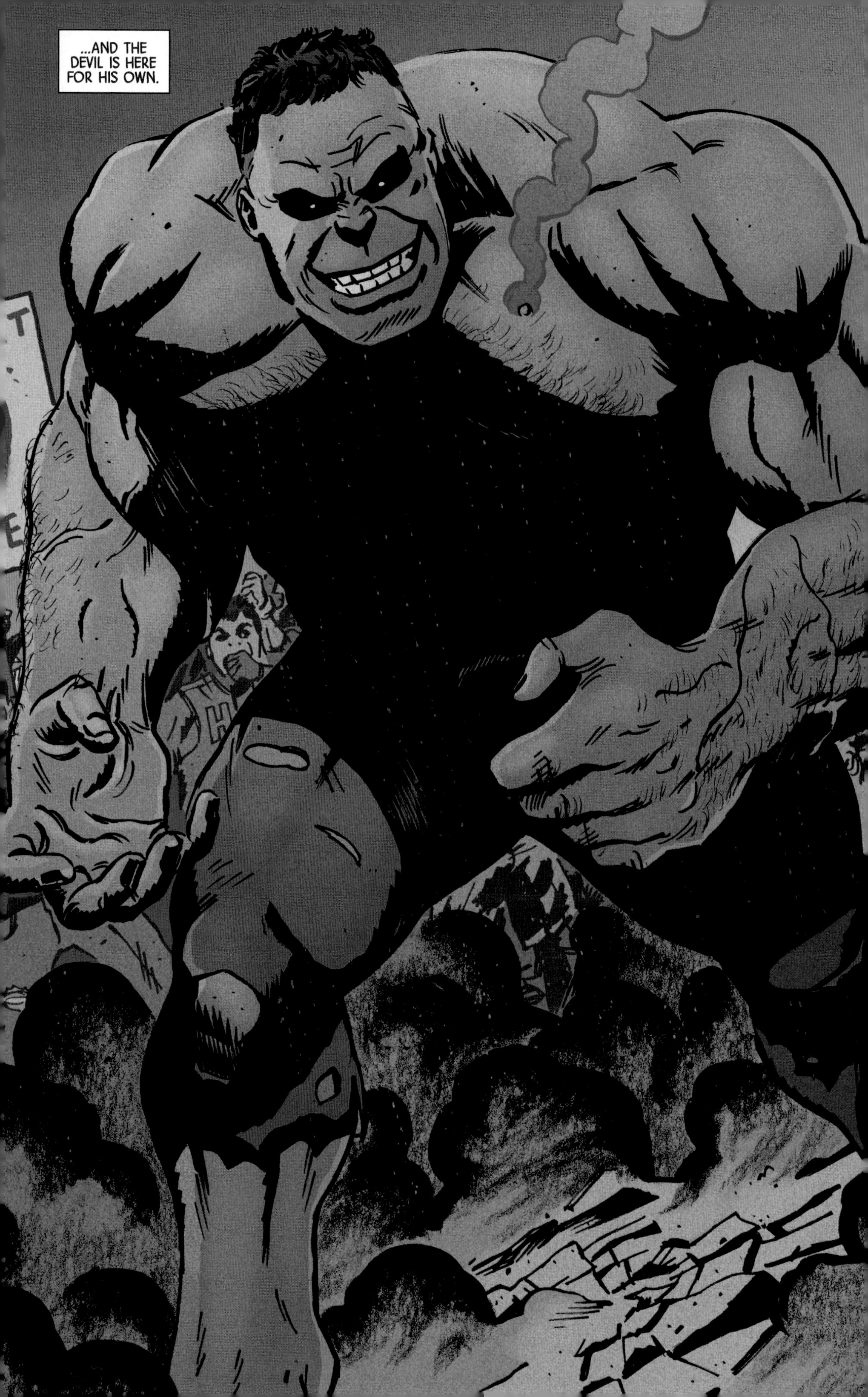
...AND THE DEVIL IS HERE FOR HIS OWN.

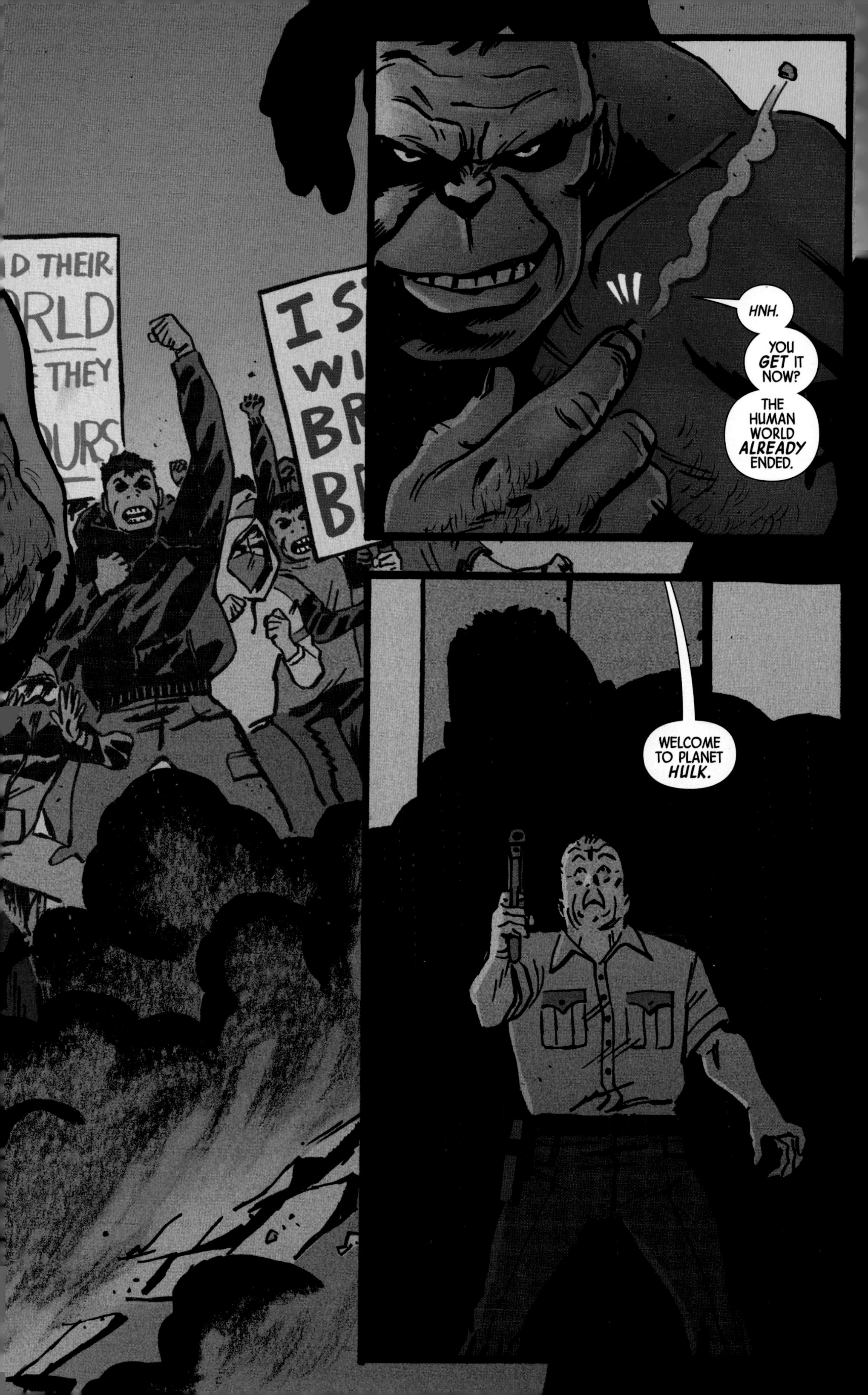
HNH.
YOU GET IT NOW?
THE HUMAN WORLD ALREADY ENDED.
WELCOME TO PLANET HULK.

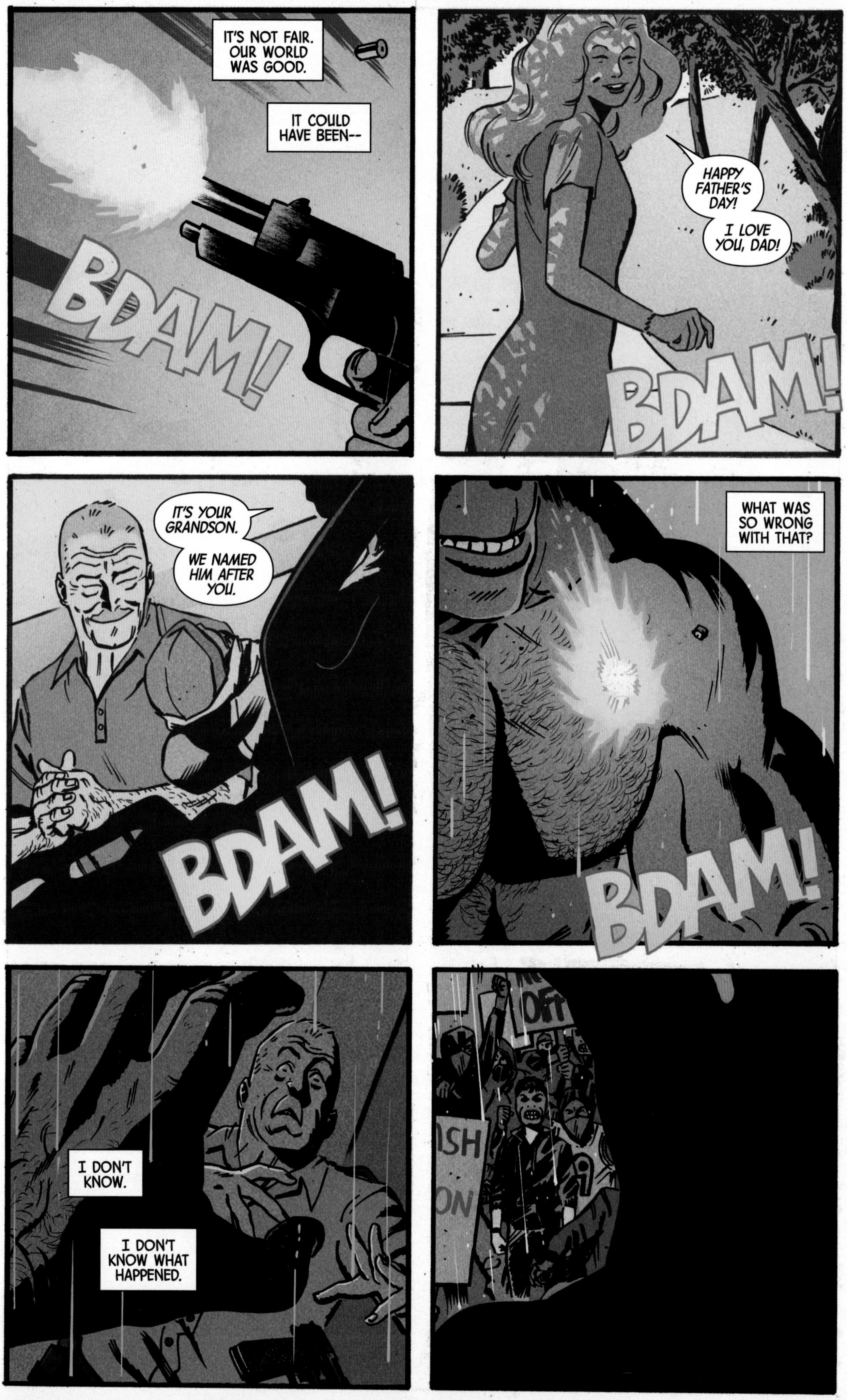
IT'S NOT FAIR. OUR WORLD WAS GOOD.
IT COULD HAVE BEEN--
BDAM!
HAPPY FATHER'S DAY!
I LOVE YOU, DAD!
BDAM!
IT'S YOUR GRANDSON.
WE NAMED HIM AFTER YOU.
BDAM!
WHAT WAS SO WRONG WITH THAT?
BDAM!
I DON'T KNOW.
I DON'T KNOW WHAT HAPPENED.

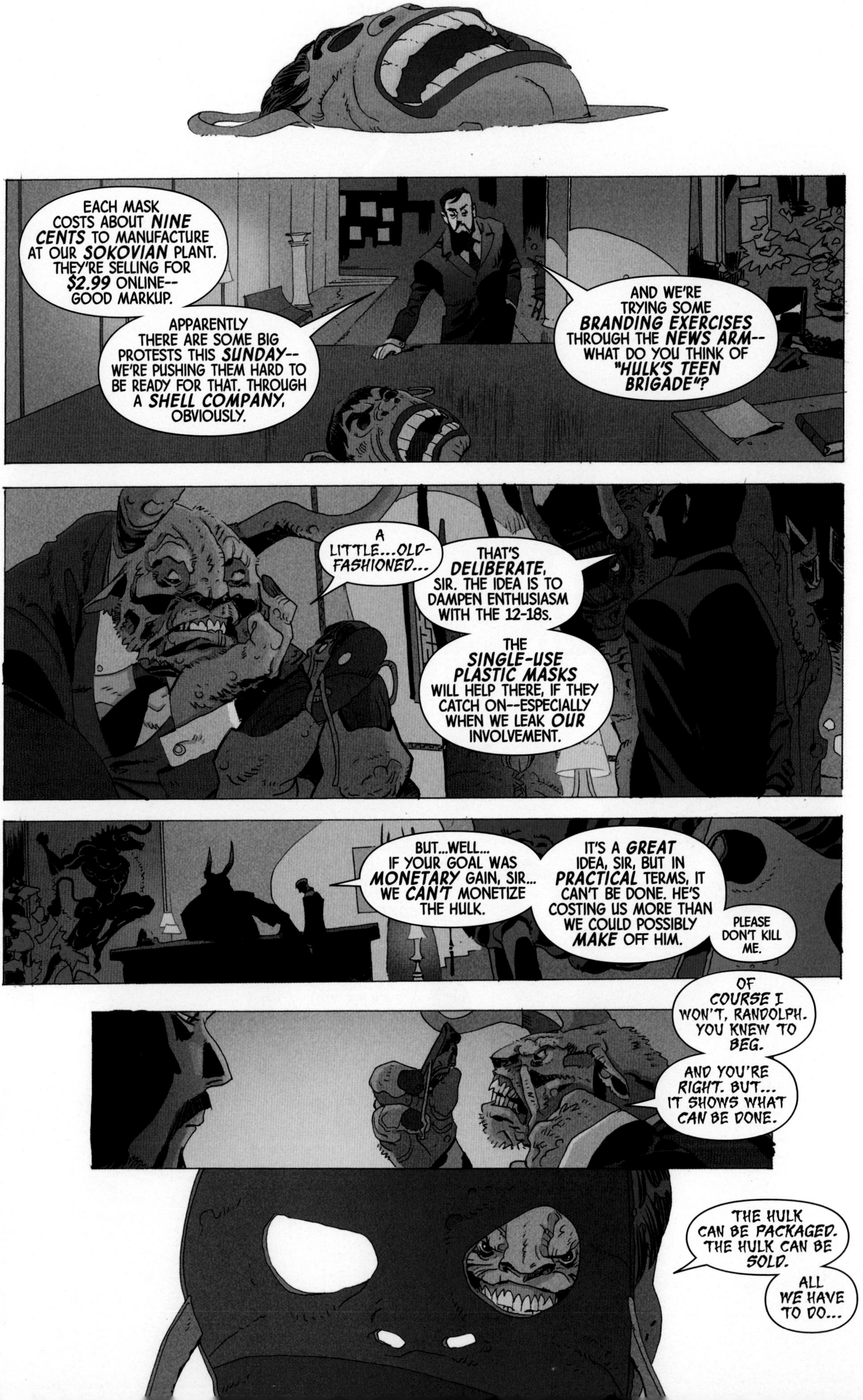
EACH MASK COSTS ABOUT NINE CENTS TO MANUFACTURE AT OUR SOKOVIAN PLANT. THEY'RE SELLING FOR $2.99 ONLINE-- GOOD MARKUP.
APPARENTLY THERE ARE SOME BIG PROTESTS THIS SUNDAY-- WE'RE PUSHING THEM HARD TO BE READY FOR THAT. THROUGH A SHELL COMPANY, OBVIOUSLY.
AND WE'RE TRYING SOME BRANDING EXERCISES THROUGH THE NEWS ARM-- WHAT DO YOU THINK OF "HULK'S TEEN BRIGADE"?
A LITTLE...OLD-FASHIONED...
THAT'S DELIBERATE, SIR. THE IDEA IS TO DAMPEN ENTHUSIASM WITH THE 12-18S.
THE SINGLE-USE PLASTIC MASKS WILL HELP THERE, IF THEY CATCH ON--ESPECIALLY WHEN WE LEAK OUR INVOLVEMENT.
BUT...WELL... IF YOUR GOAL WAS MONETARY GAIN, SIR... WE CAN'T MONETIZE THE HULK.
IT'S A GREAT IDEA, SIR, BUT IN PRACTICAL TERMS, IT CAN'T BE DONE. HE'S COSTING US MORE THAN WE COULD POSSIBLY MAKE OFF HIM.
PLEASE DON'T KILL ME.
OF COURSE I WON'T, RANDOLPH. YOU KNEW TO BEG.
AND YOU'RE RIGHT. BUT... IT SHOWS WHAT CAN BE DONE.
THE HULK CAN BE PACKAGED. THE HULK CAN BE SOLD.
ALL WE HAVE TO DO...

"...IS CREATE OUR OWN."
ROXXON
WE'RE HERE, SIR.
MONSTER ISLE.
SIR, PLEASE-- IT'S NOT SAFE--
IT'S DESERTED.
MOST OF THE MONSTERS LEFT TO FOUND SOME RIDICULOUS KINGDOM.
I'M THE WORST THING AROUND FOR MILES, YOU MORON.
WAIT THERE.

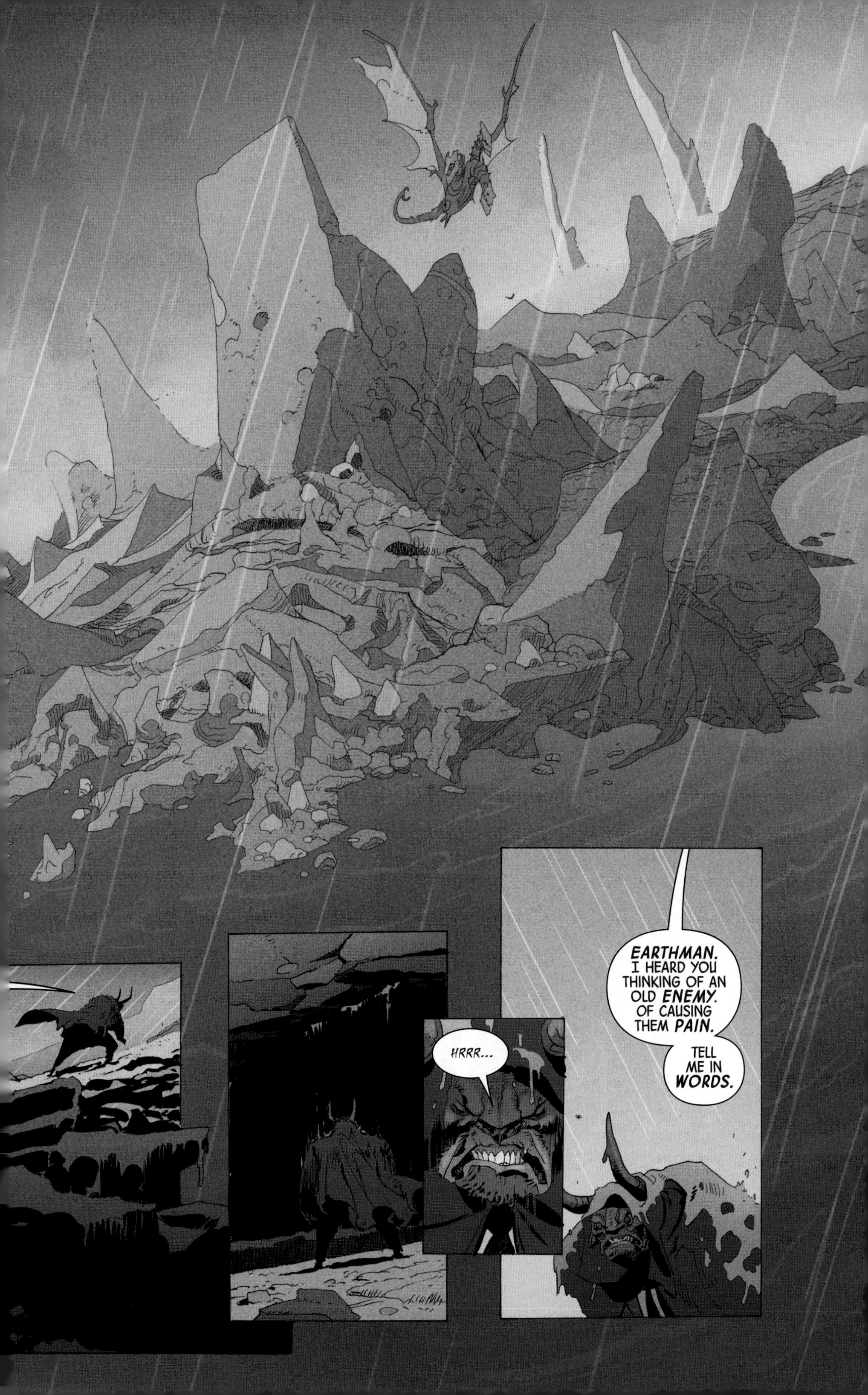
EARTHMAN. I HEARD YOU THINKING OF AN OLD ENEMY. OF CAUSING THEM PAIN.
HRRR...
TELL ME IN WORDS.

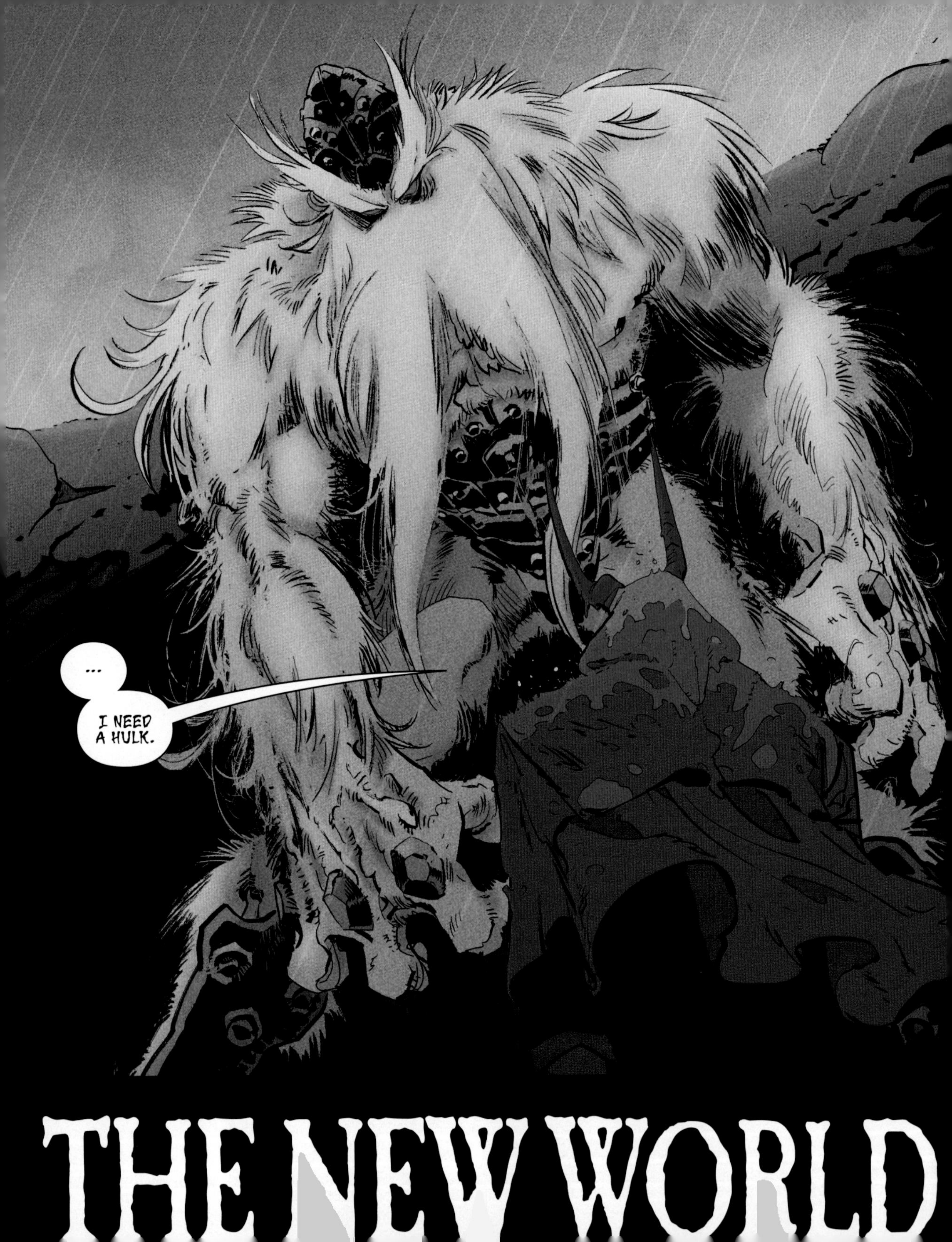
...
I NEED A HULK.

THE NEW WORLD

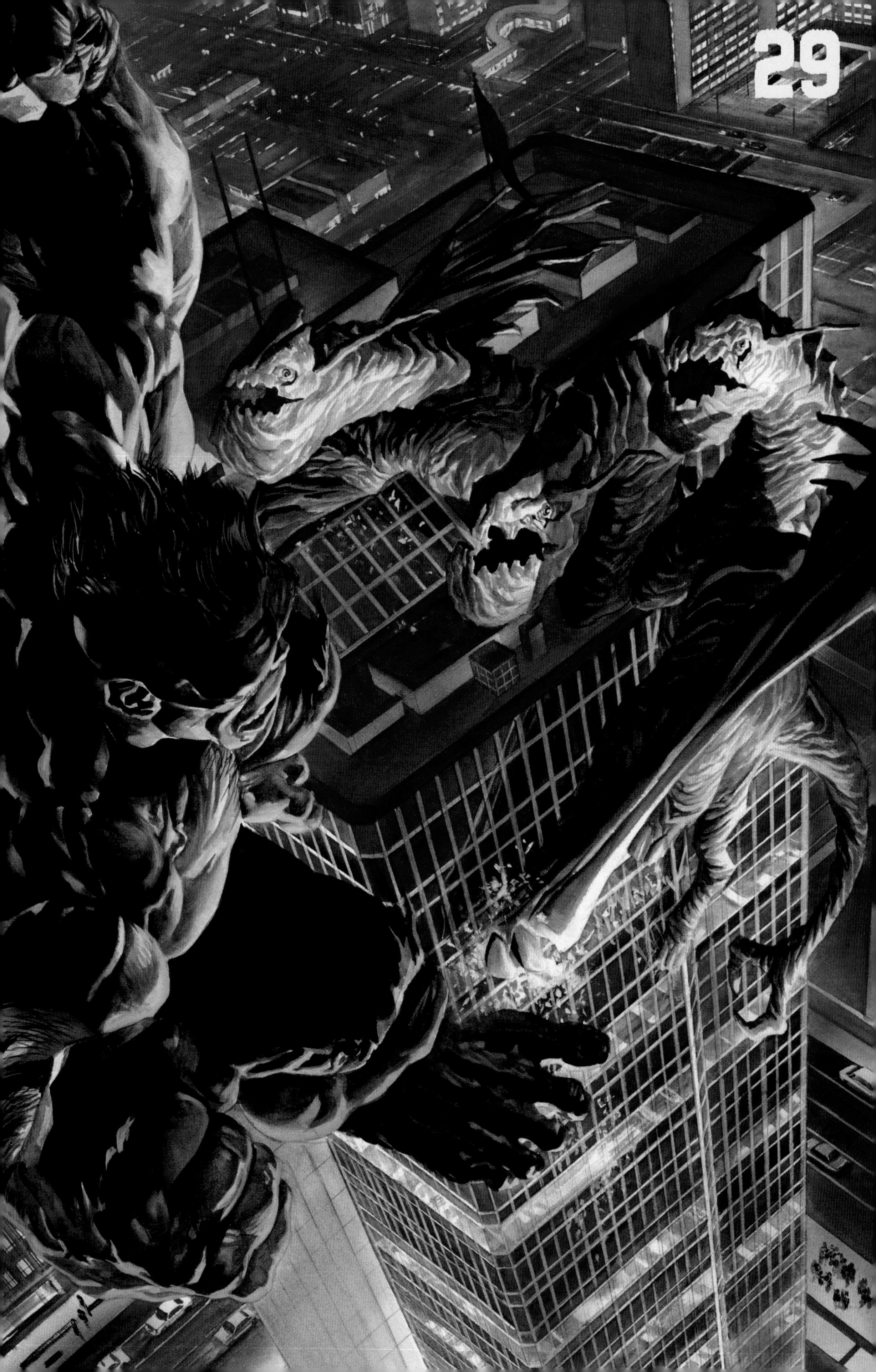
29

" SUCH IS THE CONDITION OF ORGANIC NATURE! WHOSE FIRST LAW MIGHT BE EXPRESSED IN THE WORDS 'EAT OR BE EATEN!' AND WHICH WOULD SEEM TO BE ONE GREAT SLAUGHTER-HOUSE, ONE UNIVERSAL SCENE OF RAPACITY AND INJUSTICE!"

– ERASMUS DARWIN
PHYTOLOGIA

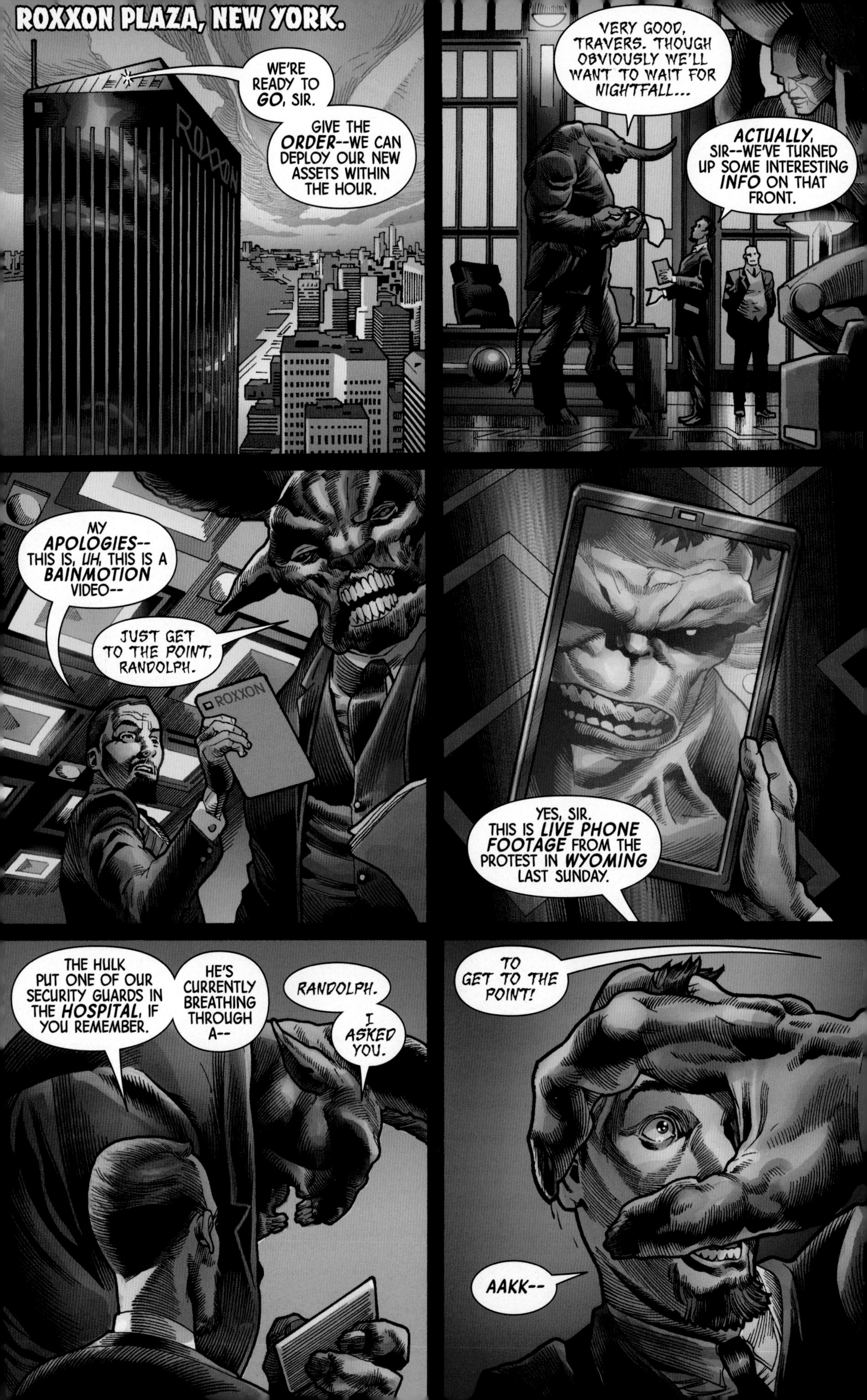
ROXXON PLAZA, NEW YORK.
WE'RE READY TO GO, SIR.
GIVE THE ORDER--WE CAN DEPLOY OUR NEW ASSETS WITHIN THE HOUR.
VERY GOOD, TRAVERS. THOUGH OBVIOUSLY WE'LL WANT TO WAIT FOR NIGHTFALL...
ACTUALLY, SIR--WE'VE TURNED UP SOME INTERESTING INFO ON THAT FRONT.
MY APOLOGIES-- THIS IS, UH, THIS IS A BAINMOTION VIDEO--
JUST GET TO THE POINT, RANDOLPH.
ROXXON
YES, SIR. THIS IS LIVE PHONE FOOTAGE FROM THE PROTEST IN WYOMING LAST SUNDAY.
THE HULK PUT ONE OF OUR SECURITY GUARDS IN THE HOSPITAL, IF YOU REMEMBER.
HE'S CURRENTLY BREATHING THROUGH A--
RANDOLPH.
I ASKED YOU.
TO GET TO THE POINT!
AAKK--

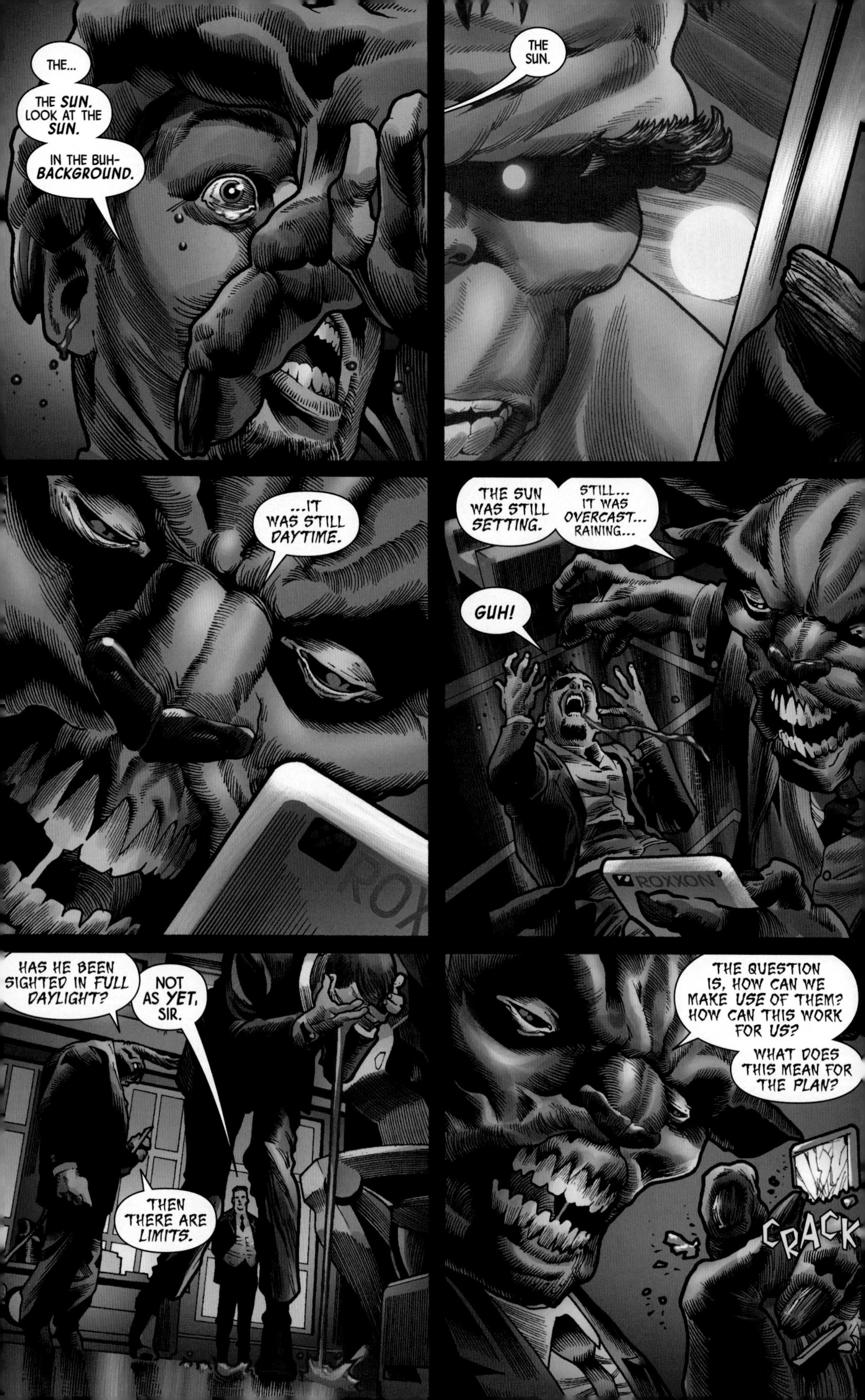
THE...
THE SUN. LOOK AT THE SUN.
IN THE BUH-BACKGROUND.
THE SUN.
...IT WAS STILL DAYTIME.
ROX
THE SUN WAS STILL SETTING.
STILL... IT WAS OVERCAST... RAINING...
GUH!
ROXXON
HAS HE BEEN SIGHTED IN FULL DAYLIGHT?
NOT AS YET, SIR.
THEN THERE ARE LIMITS.
THE QUESTION IS, HOW CAN WE MAKE USE OF THEM? HOW CAN THIS WORK FOR US?
WHAT DOES THIS MEAN FOR THE PLAN?
CRACK

I DON'T KNOW, LEONARD. WHAT *DOES* HULK BEING OUT IN THE DAYLIGHT MEAN?

I KNOW YOU'RE DYING TO TELL *SOMEONE*...

HONESTLY? I THINK WE'VE SEEN SOMETHING LIKE THIS *BEFORE*.

BRUCE MAY HAVE CEDED *OPERATIONAL CONTROL*, SO TO SPEAK, TO THIS *DEVIL HULK* ALTER--BUT HE RETAINS A DEGREE OF *AUTHORITY*.

IF YOU REMEMBER, WHEN *JOE*-- JOE FIXIT, THE *GRAY* HULK--

I KNOW WHO JOE IS, LEONARD.

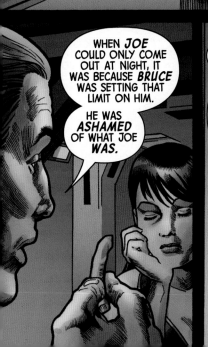

WHEN *JOE* COULD ONLY COME OUT AT NIGHT, IT WAS BECAUSE *BRUCE* WAS SETTING THAT LIMIT ON HIM.

HE WAS *ASHAMED* OF WHAT JOE *WAS*.

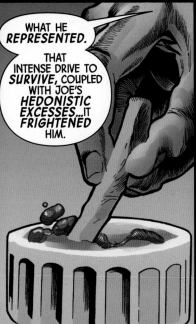

WHAT HE *REPRESENTED*.

THAT INTENSE DRIVE TO *SURVIVE*, COUPLED WITH JOE'S *HEDONISTIC EXCESSES*...IT *FRIGHTENED* HIM.

IT WAS ONLY WHEN BRUCE *ACCEPTED* THAT PART OF HIMSELF *AS* PART OF HIMSELF THAT JOE BEGAN TO EXIST DURING THE *DAY*--

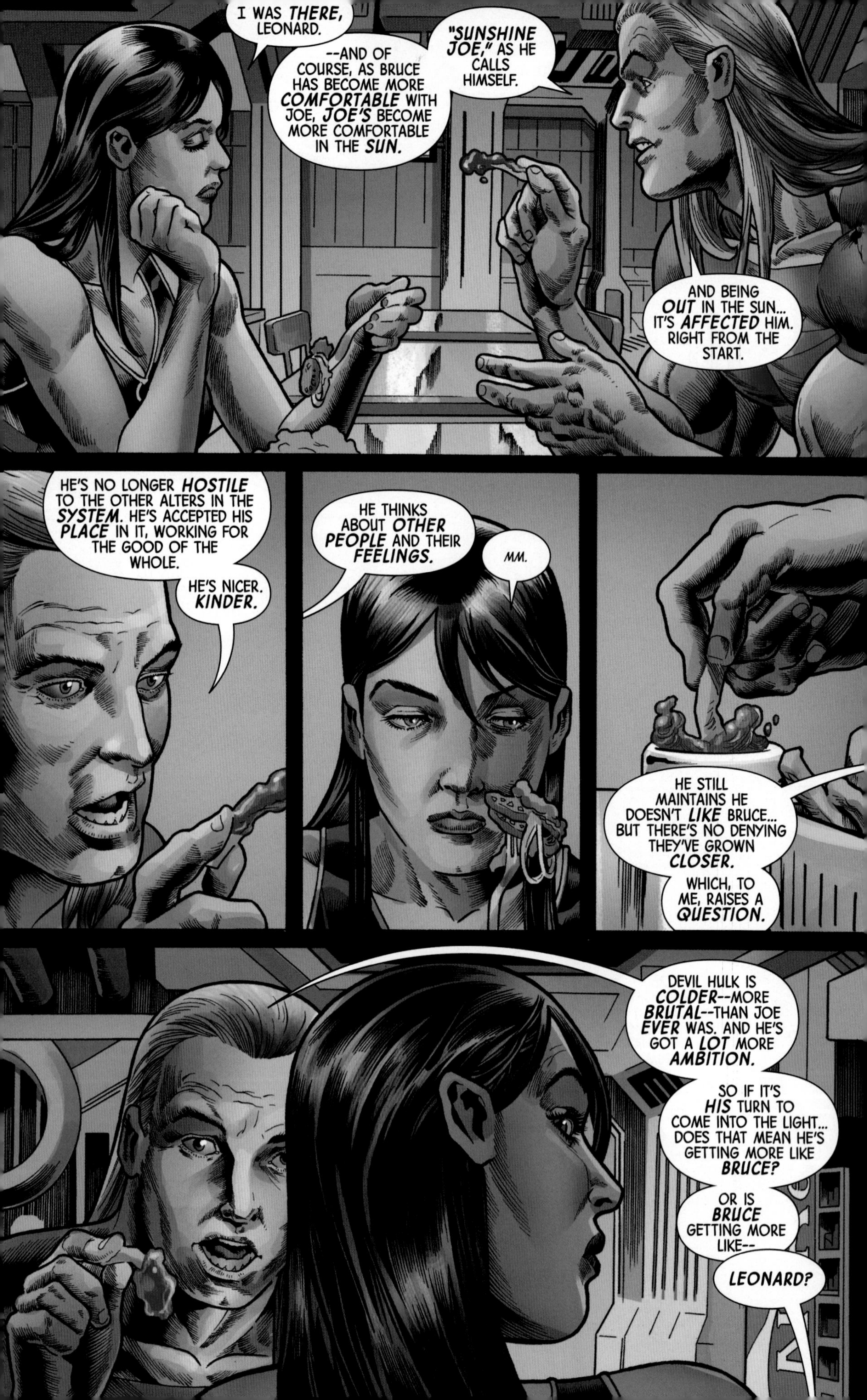

I WAS THERE, LEONARD.
--AND OF COURSE, AS BRUCE HAS BECOME MORE COMFORTABLE WITH JOE, JOE'S BECOME MORE COMFORTABLE IN THE SUN.
"SUNSHINE JOE," AS HE CALLS HIMSELF.
AND BEING OUT IN THE SUN... IT'S AFFECTED HIM. RIGHT FROM THE START.
HE'S NO LONGER HOSTILE TO THE OTHER ALTERS IN THE SYSTEM. HE'S ACCEPTED HIS PLACE IN IT, WORKING FOR THE GOOD OF THE WHOLE.
HE'S NICER. KINDER.
HE THINKS ABOUT OTHER PEOPLE AND THEIR FEELINGS.
MM.
HE STILL MAINTAINS HE DOESN'T LIKE BRUCE... BUT THERE'S NO DENYING THEY'VE GROWN CLOSER.
WHICH, TO ME, RAISES A QUESTION.
DEVIL HULK IS COLDER--MORE BRUTAL--THAN JOE EVER WAS. AND HE'S GOT A LOT MORE AMBITION.
SO IF IT'S HIS TURN TO COME INTO THE LIGHT... DOES THAT MEAN HE'S GETTING MORE LIKE BRUCE?
OR IS BRUCE GETTING MORE LIKE--
LEONARD?

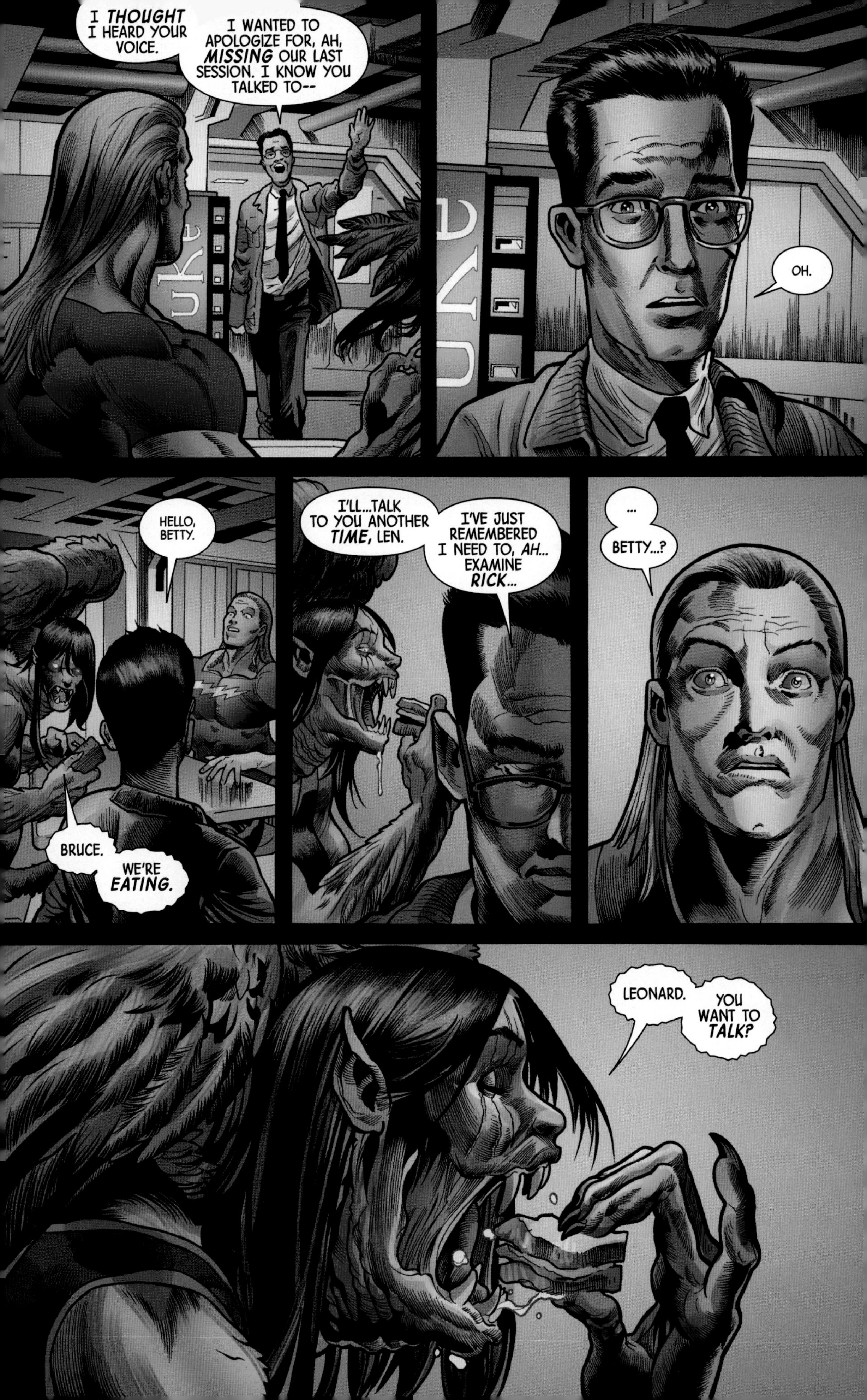
I THOUGHT I HEARD YOUR VOICE.
I WANTED TO APOLOGIZE FOR, AH, MISSING OUR LAST SESSION. I KNOW YOU TALKED TO--
OH.
HELLO, BETTY.
BRUCE.
WE'RE EATING.
I'LL...TALK TO YOU ANOTHER TIME, LEN.
I'VE JUST REMEMBERED I NEED TO, AH... EXAMINE RICK...
...
BETTY...?
LEONARD.
YOU WANT TO TALK?

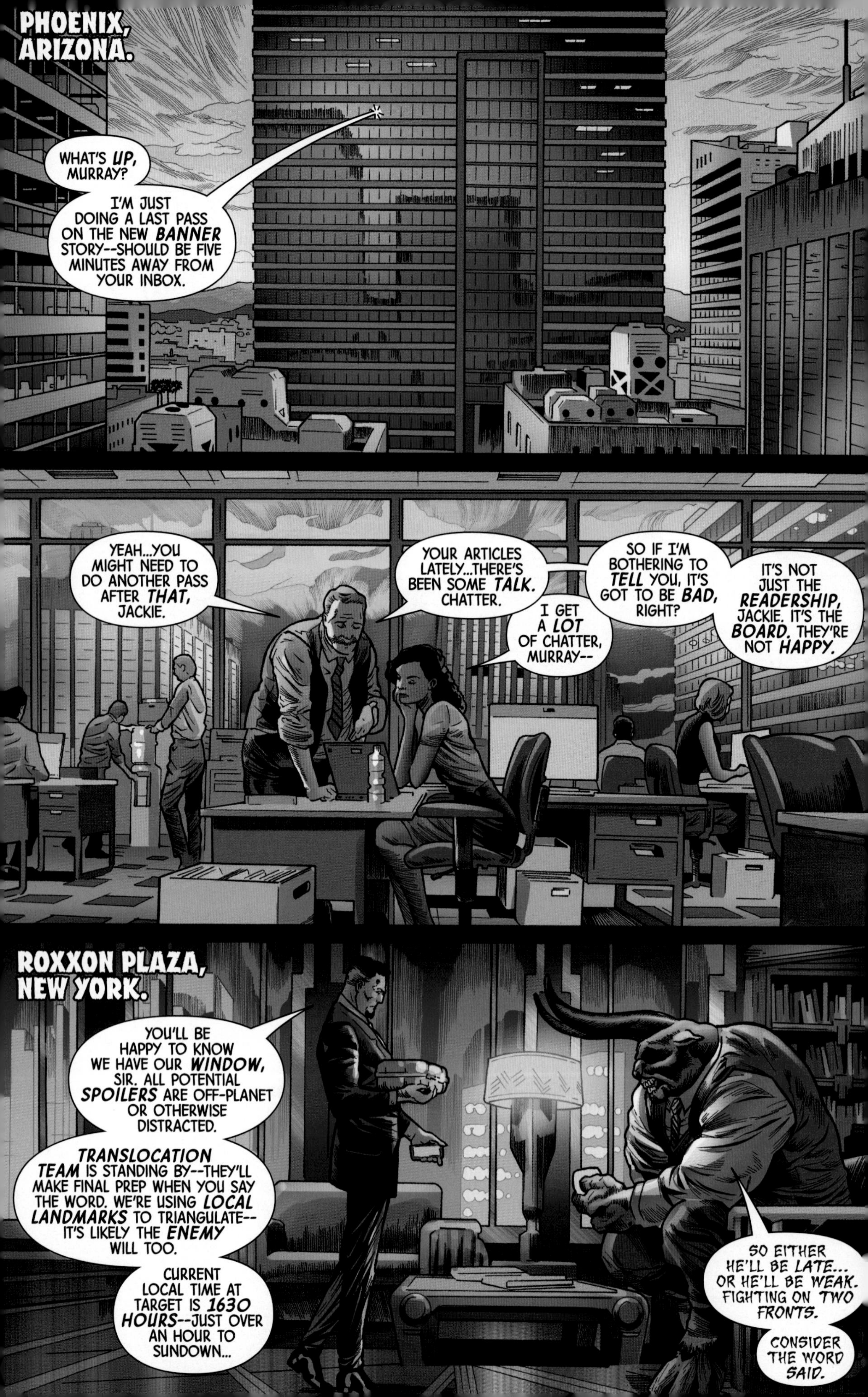
PHOENIX, ARIZONA.
WHAT'S UP, MURRAY?
I'M JUST DOING A LAST PASS ON THE NEW BANNER STORY--SHOULD BE FIVE MINUTES AWAY FROM YOUR INBOX.
YEAH...YOU MIGHT NEED TO DO ANOTHER PASS AFTER THAT, JACKIE.
YOUR ARTICLES LATELY...THERE'S BEEN SOME TALK. CHATTER.
I GET A LOT OF CHATTER, MURRAY--
SO IF I'M BOTHERING TO TELL YOU, IT'S GOT TO BE BAD, RIGHT?
IT'S NOT JUST THE READERSHIP, JACKIE. IT'S THE BOARD. THEY'RE NOT HAPPY.
ROXXON PLAZA, NEW YORK.
YOU'LL BE HAPPY TO KNOW WE HAVE OUR WINDOW, SIR. ALL POTENTIAL SPOILERS ARE OFF-PLANET OR OTHERWISE DISTRACTED.
TRANSLOCATION TEAM IS STANDING BY--THEY'LL MAKE FINAL PREP WHEN YOU SAY THE WORD. WE'RE USING LOCAL LANDMARKS TO TRIANGULATE-- IT'S LIKELY THE ENEMY WILL TOO.
CURRENT LOCAL TIME AT TARGET IS 1630 HOURS--JUST OVER AN HOUR TO SUNDOWN...
SO EITHER HE'LL BE LATE... OR HE'LL BE WEAK. FIGHTING ON TWO FRONTS.
CONSIDER THE WORD SAID.

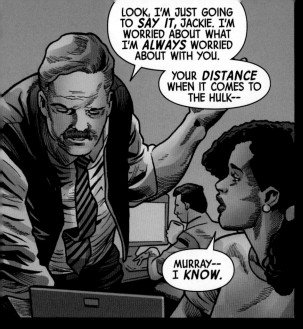

LOOK, I'M JUST GOING TO *SAY IT*, JACKIE. I'M WORRIED ABOUT WHAT I'M *ALWAYS* WORRIED ABOUT WITH YOU.

YOUR *DISTANCE* WHEN IT COMES TO THE HULK--

MURRAY-- I *KNOW*.

I KNOW YOU HAD TO PUSH ME BACK *INTO* THIS. I...I WAS *SCARED*, I ADMIT IT. OF THEM, OF THEIR *WORLD*.

BUT...I'M NOT *AFRAID* ANYMORE.

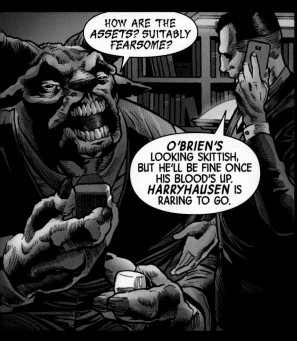

HOW ARE THE *ASSETS?* SUITABLY *FEARSOME?*

O'BRIEN'S LOOKING SKITTISH, BUT HE'LL BE FINE ONCE HIS BLOOD'S UP. *HARRYHAUSEN* IS RARING TO GO.

OH--AND THEY DIDN'T FEED *LOVECRAFT* TODAY...

SO HE'S HUNGRY.

I LIKE THAT.

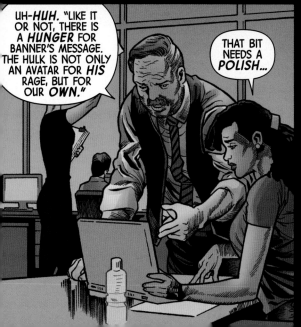

UH-*HUH*. "LIKE IT OR NOT, THERE IS A *HUNGER* FOR BANNER'S MESSAGE. THE HULK IS NOT ONLY AN AVATAR FOR *HIS* RAGE, BUT FOR OUR *OWN*."

THAT BIT NEEDS A *POLISH*...

"OUR" RAGE, THOUGH. YOU'RE EXPLICITLY *IDENTIFYING* WITH HIM IN THE PIECE.

THAT'S WHAT I MEAN ABOUT *DISTANCE*.

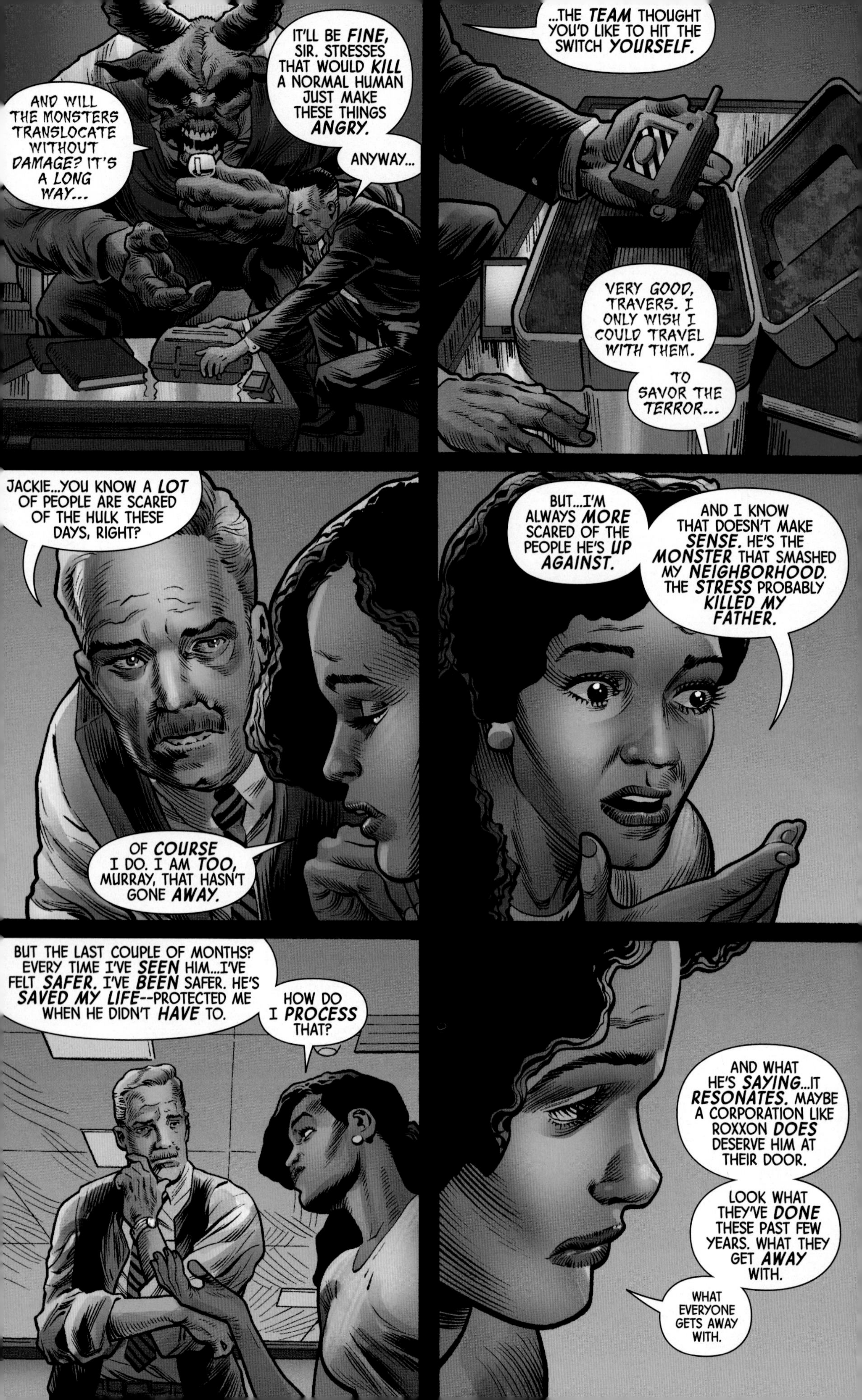
AND WILL THE MONSTERS TRANSLOCATE WITHOUT DAMAGE? IT'S A LONG WAY...
IT'LL BE FINE, SIR. STRESSES THAT WOULD KILL A NORMAL HUMAN JUST MAKE THESE THINGS ANGRY.
ANYWAY...
...THE TEAM THOUGHT YOU'D LIKE TO HIT THE SWITCH YOURSELF.
VERY GOOD, TRAVERS. I ONLY WISH I COULD TRAVEL WITH THEM.
TO SAVOR THE TERROR...
JACKIE...YOU KNOW A LOT OF PEOPLE ARE SCARED OF THE HULK THESE DAYS, RIGHT?
OF COURSE I DO. I AM TOO, MURRAY, THAT HASN'T GONE AWAY.
BUT...I'M ALWAYS MORE SCARED OF THE PEOPLE HE'S UP AGAINST.
AND I KNOW THAT DOESN'T MAKE SENSE. HE'S THE MONSTER THAT SMASHED MY NEIGHBORHOOD. THE STRESS PROBABLY KILLED MY FATHER.
BUT THE LAST COUPLE OF MONTHS? EVERY TIME I'VE SEEN HIM...I'VE FELT SAFER. I'VE BEEN SAFER. HE'S SAVED MY LIFE--PROTECTED ME WHEN HE DIDN'T HAVE TO.
HOW DO I PROCESS THAT?
AND WHAT HE'S SAYING...IT RESONATES. MAYBE A CORPORATION LIKE ROXXON DOES DESERVE HIM AT THEIR DOOR.
LOOK WHAT THEY'VE DONE THESE PAST FEW YEARS. WHAT THEY GET AWAY WITH.
WHAT EVERYONE GETS AWAY WITH.

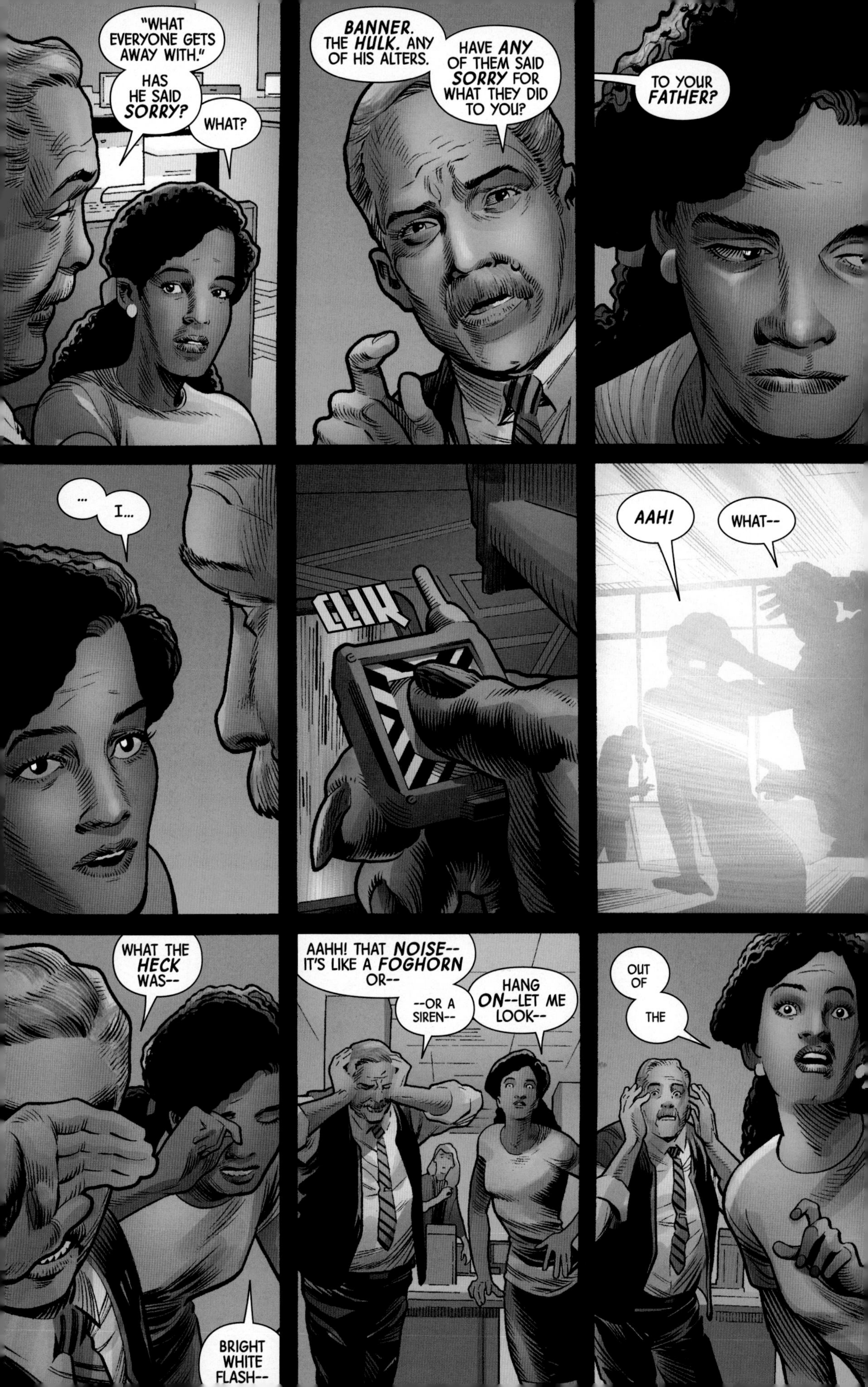
"WHAT EVERYONE GETS AWAY WITH."
HAS HE SAID SORRY?
WHAT?
BANNER. THE HULK. ANY OF HIS ALTERS.
HAVE ANY OF THEM SAID SORRY FOR WHAT THEY DID TO YOU?
TO YOUR FATHER?
...
I...
CLIK
AAH!
WHAT--
WHAT THE HECK WAS--
BRIGHT WHITE FLASH--
AAHH! THAT NOISE-- IT'S LIKE A FOGHORN OR--
--OR A SIREN--
HANG ON--LET ME LOOK--
OUT OF
THE

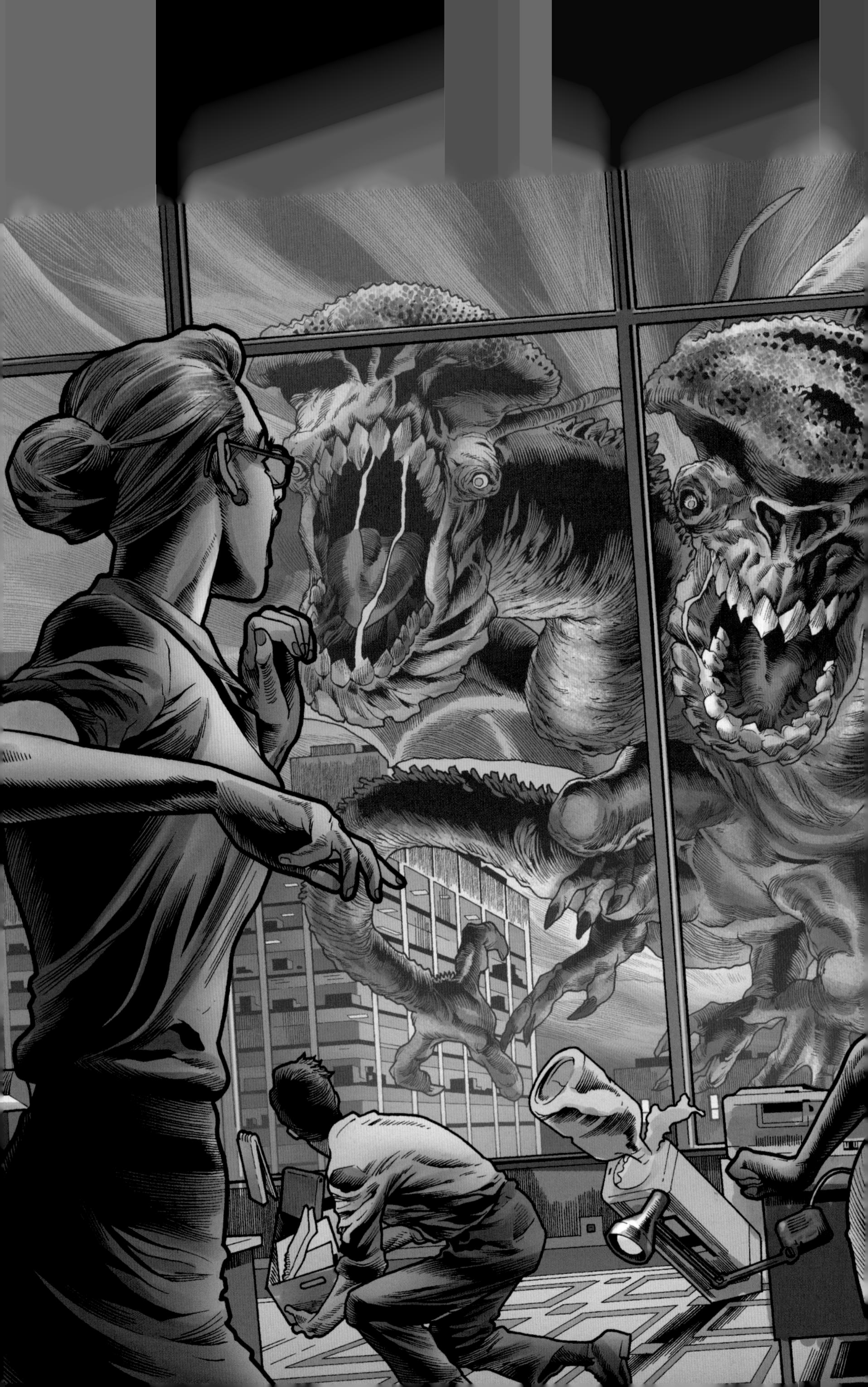

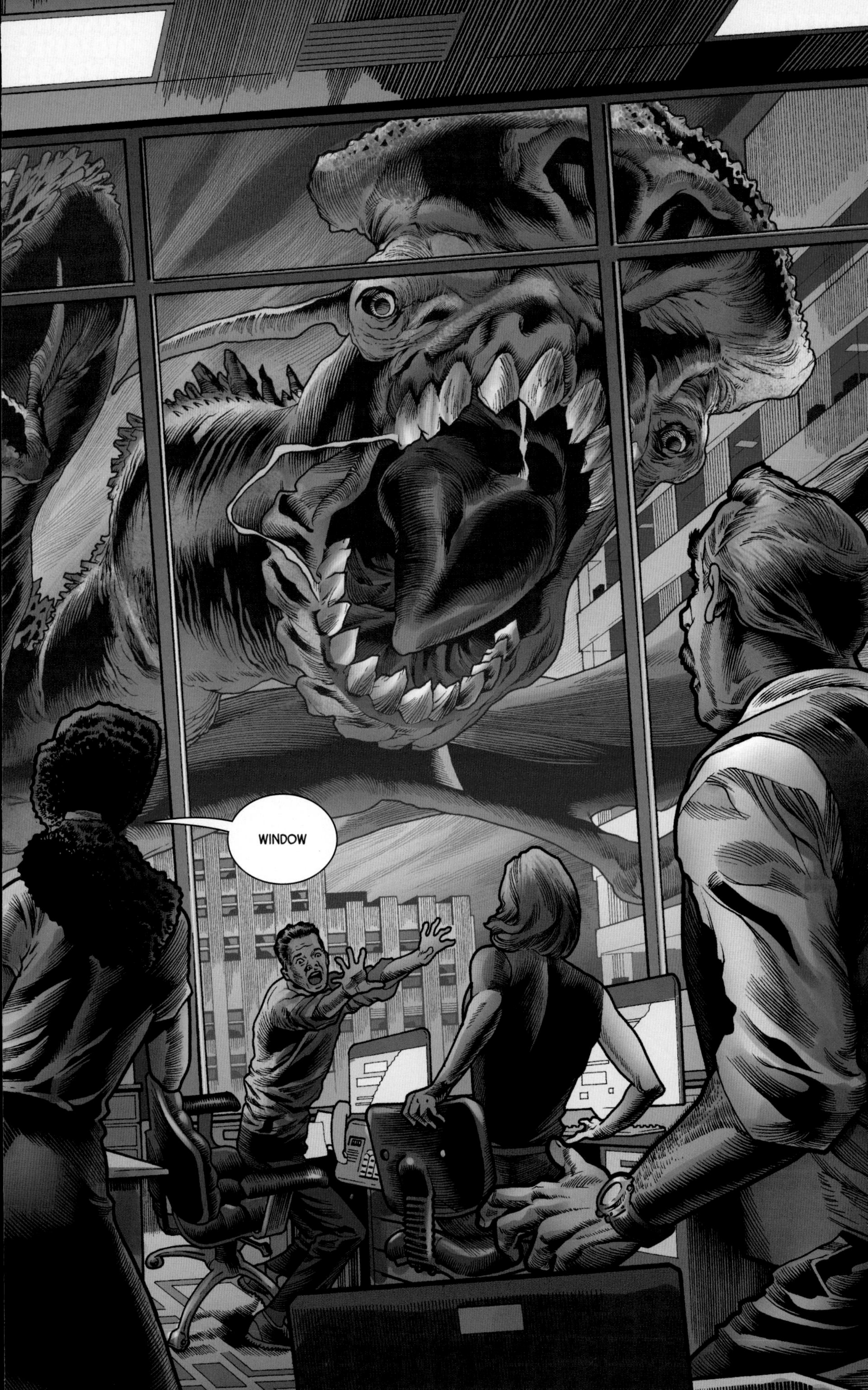
WINDOW

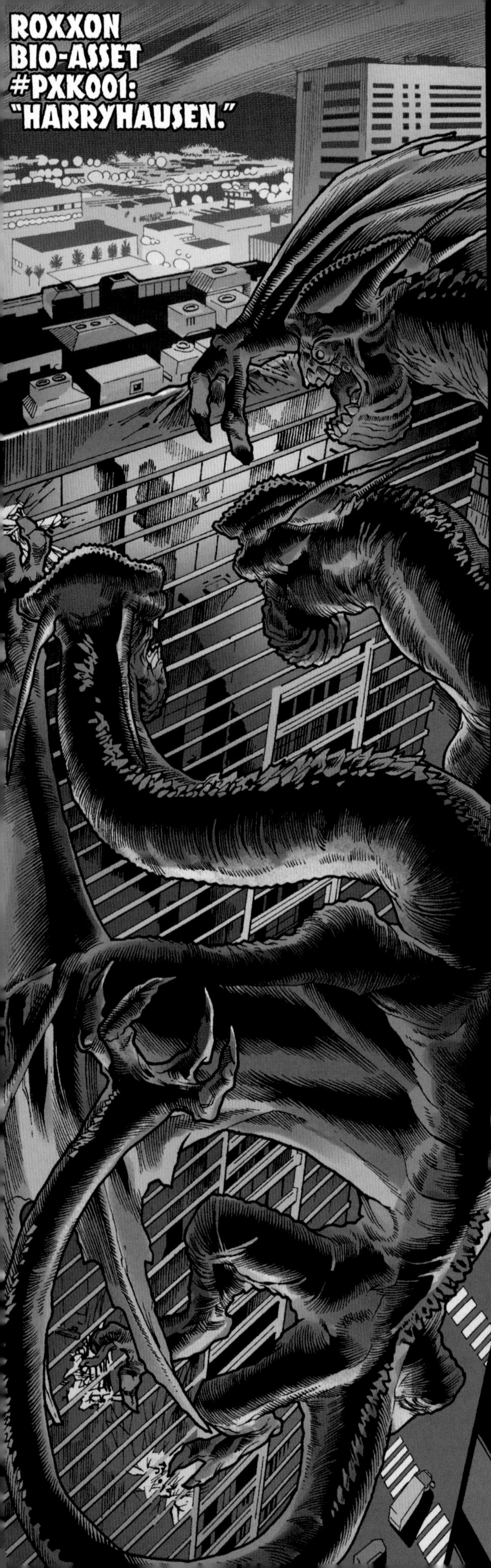
ROXXON BIO-ASSET #PXK001: "HARRYHAUSEN."

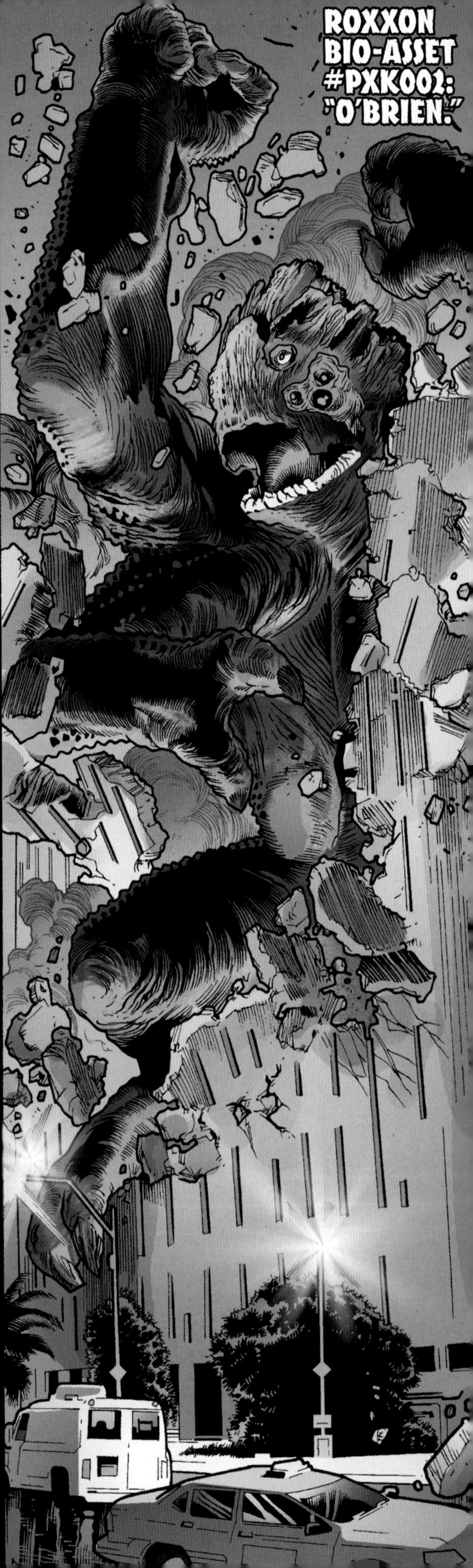
ROXXON BIO-ASSET #PXK002: "O'BRIEN."

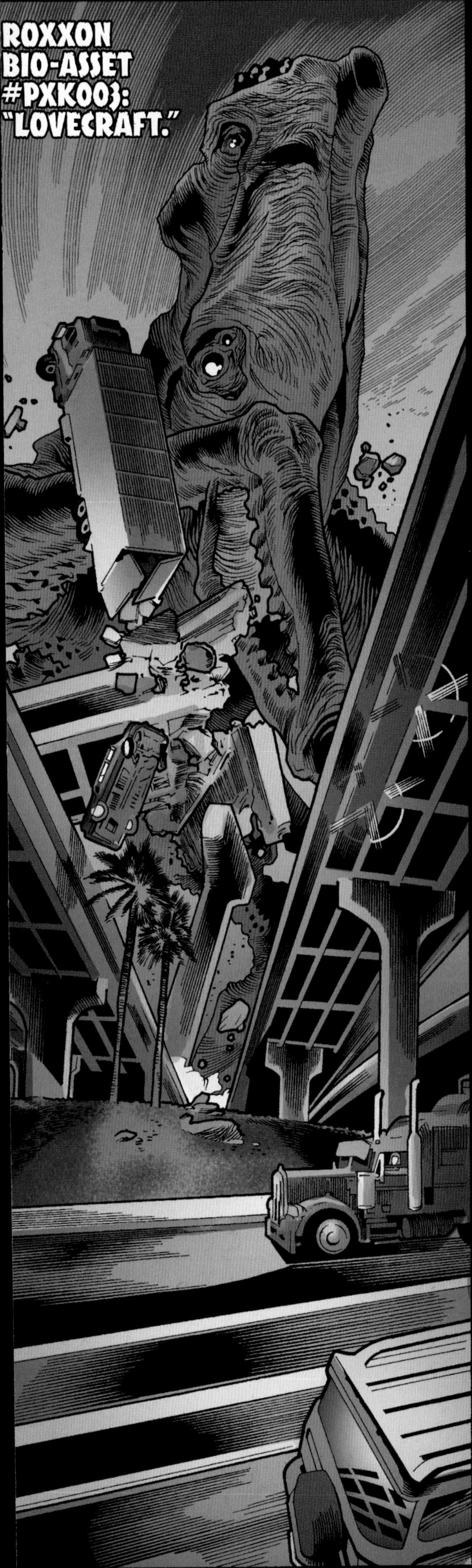
ROXXON
BIO-ASSET
#PXK003:
"LOVECRAFT."

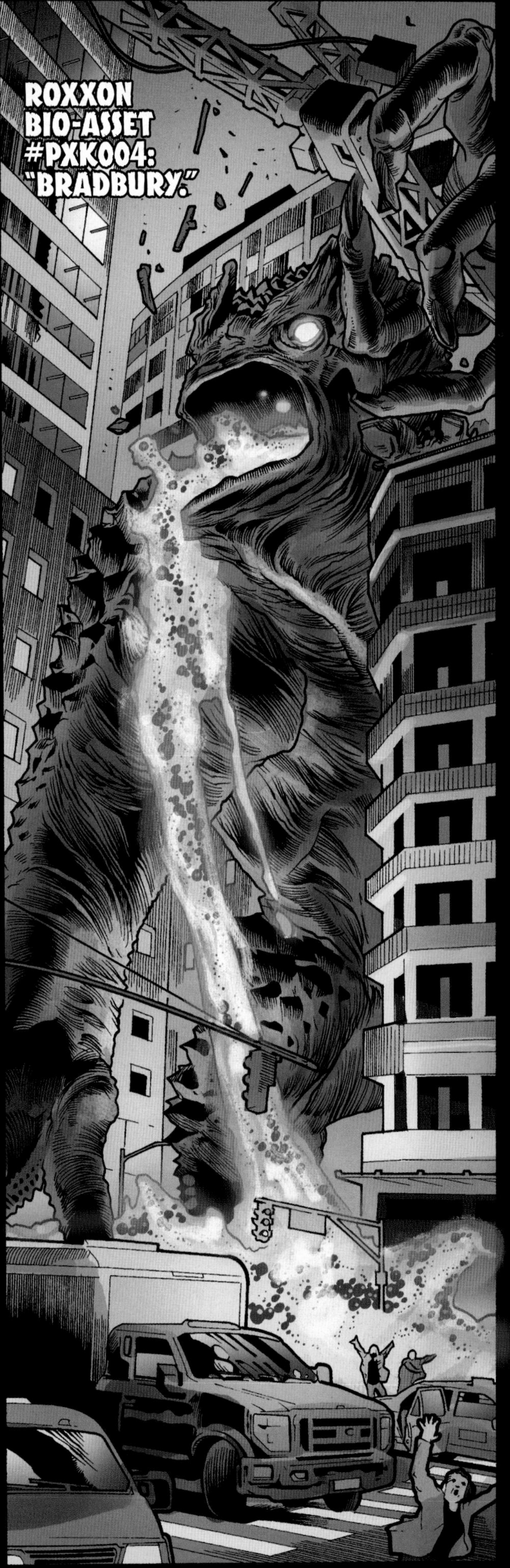
ROXXON
BIO-ASSET
#PXK004:
"BRADBURY."

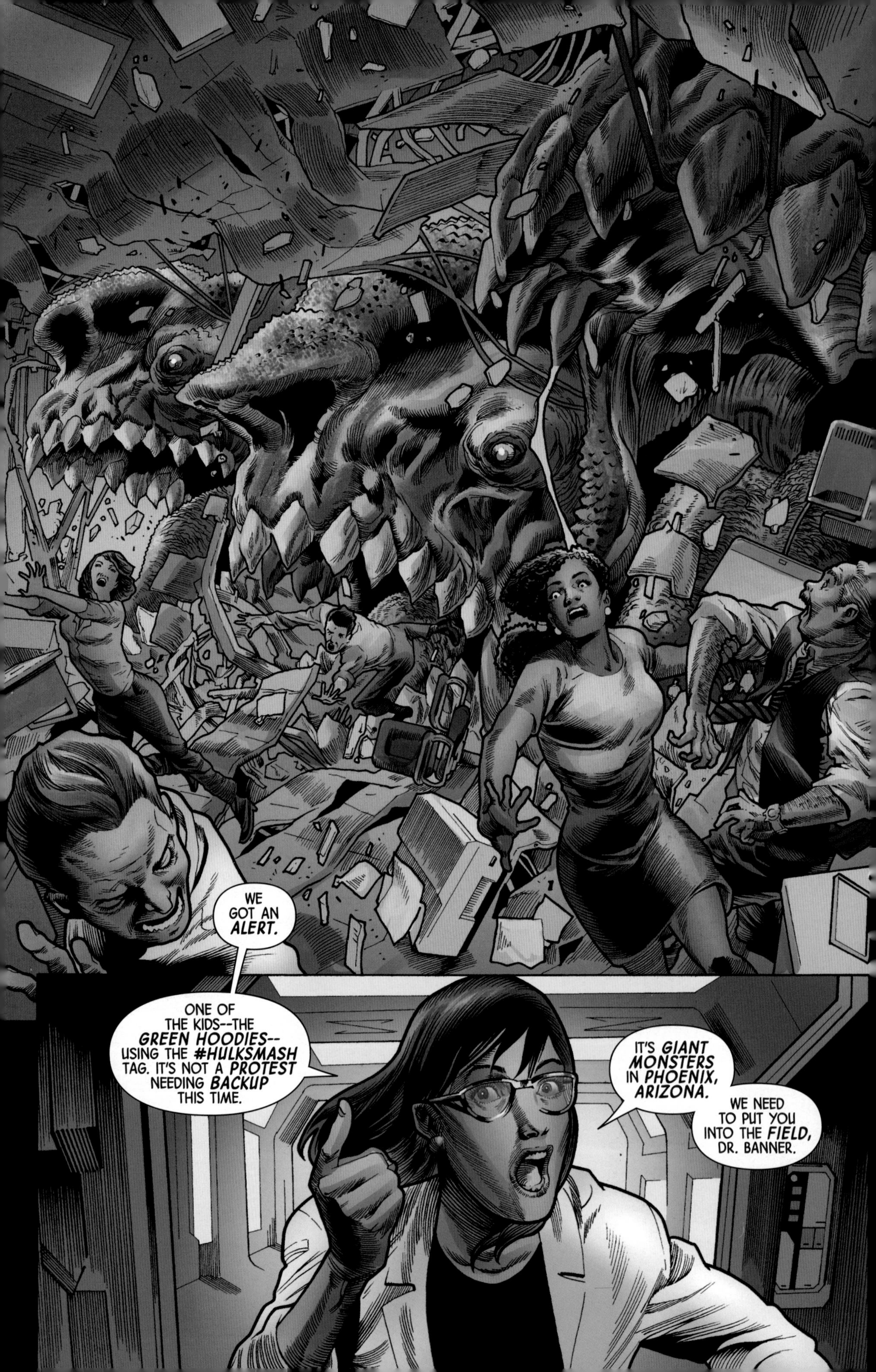
WE GOT AN ALERT.
ONE OF THE KIDS--THE GREEN HOODIES--USING THE #HULKSMASH TAG. IT'S NOT A PROTEST NEEDING BACKUP THIS TIME.
IT'S GIANT MONSTERS IN PHOENIX, ARIZONA.
WE NEED TO PUT YOU INTO THE FIELD, DR. BANNER.

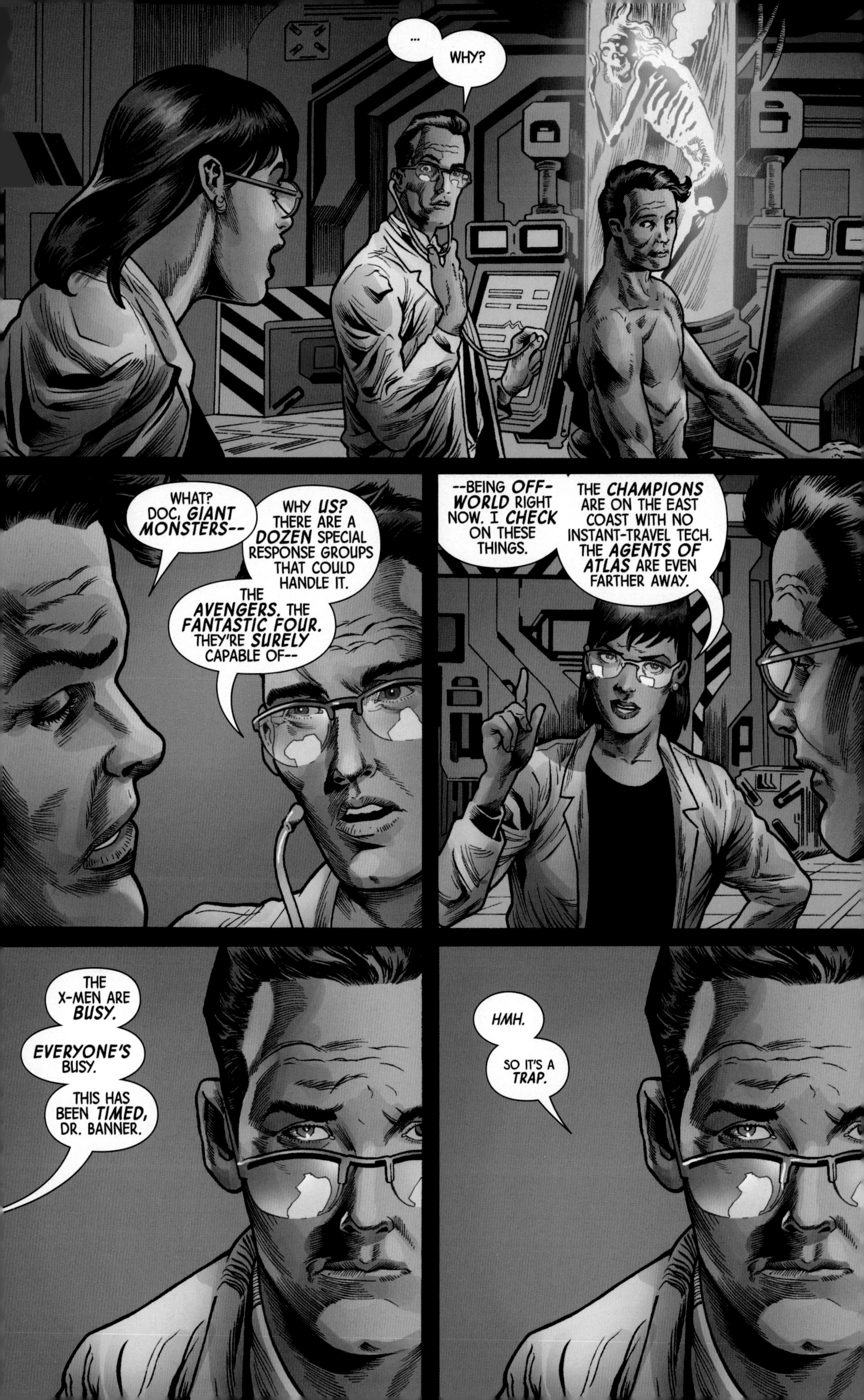
...
WHY?
WHAT? DOC, GIANT MONSTERS--
WHY US? THERE ARE A DOZEN SPECIAL RESPONSE GROUPS THAT COULD HANDLE IT.
THE AVENGERS. THE FANTASTIC FOUR. THEY'RE SURELY CAPABLE OF--
THE CHAMPIONS ARE ON THE EAST COAST WITH NO INSTANT-TRAVEL TECH. THE AGENTS OF ATLAS ARE EVEN FARTHER AWAY.
--BEING OFF-WORLD RIGHT NOW. I CHECK ON THESE THINGS.
THE X-MEN ARE BUSY.
EVERYONE'S BUSY.
THIS HAS BEEN TIMED, DR. BANNER.
HMH.
SO IT'S A TRAP.

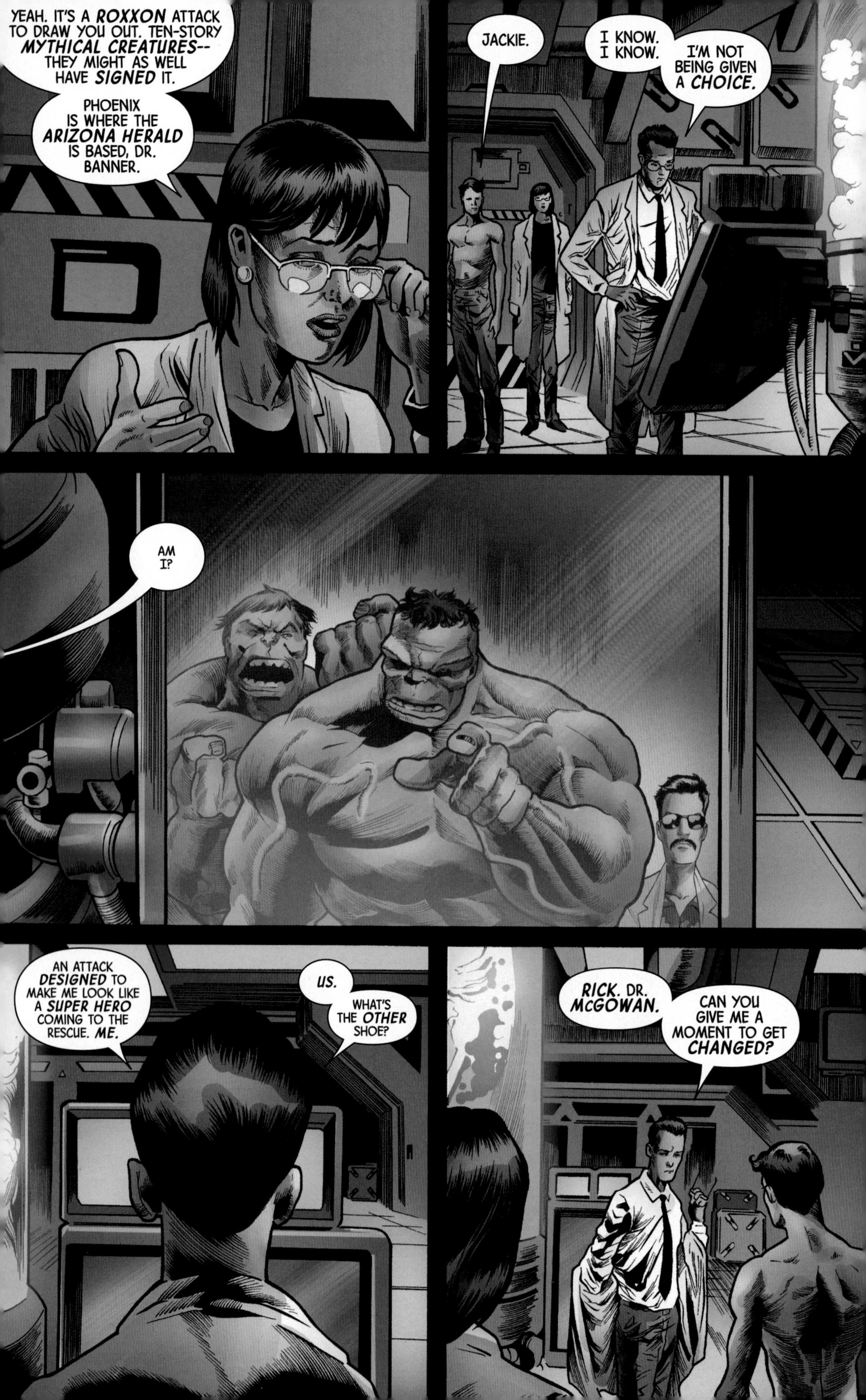
YEAH. IT'S A ROXXON ATTACK TO DRAW YOU OUT. TEN-STORY MYTHICAL CREATURES-- THEY MIGHT AS WELL HAVE SIGNED IT.
PHOENIX IS WHERE THE ARIZONA HERALD IS BASED, DR. BANNER.
JACKIE.
I KNOW. I KNOW.
I'M NOT BEING GIVEN A CHOICE.
AM I?
AN ATTACK DESIGNED TO MAKE ME LOOK LIKE A SUPER HERO COMING TO THE RESCUE. ME.
US.
WHAT'S THE OTHER SHOE?
RICK. DR. MCGOWAN.
CAN YOU GIVE ME A MOMENT TO GET CHANGED?

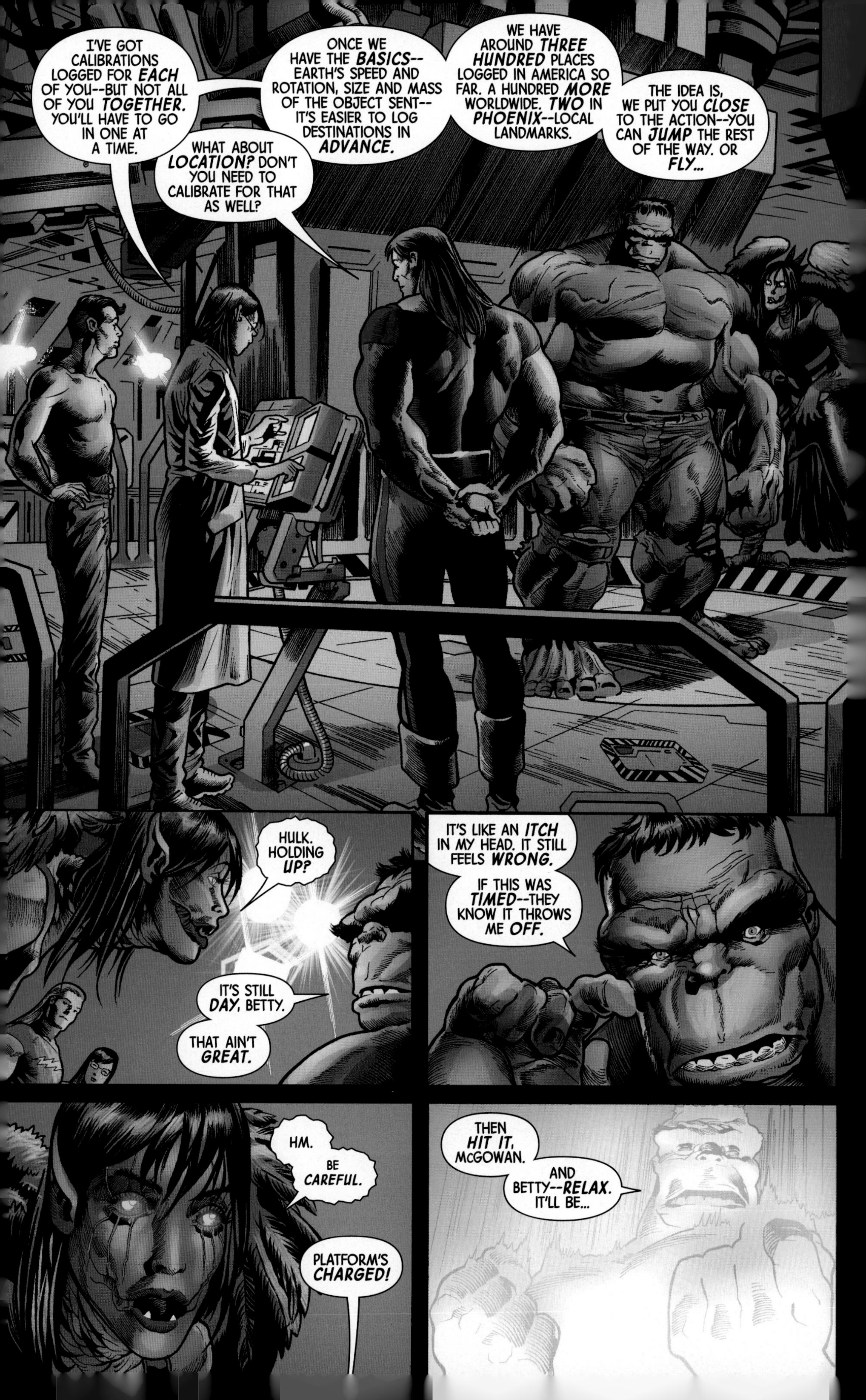

I'VE GOT CALIBRATIONS LOGGED FOR EACH OF YOU--BUT NOT ALL OF YOU TOGETHER. YOU'LL HAVE TO GO IN ONE AT A TIME.
WHAT ABOUT LOCATION? DON'T YOU NEED TO CALIBRATE FOR THAT AS WELL?
ONCE WE HAVE THE BASICS-- EARTH'S SPEED AND ROTATION, SIZE AND MASS OF THE OBJECT SENT-- IT'S EASIER TO LOG DESTINATIONS IN ADVANCE.
WE HAVE AROUND THREE HUNDRED PLACES LOGGED IN AMERICA SO FAR. A HUNDRED MORE WORLDWIDE. TWO IN PHOENIX--LOCAL LANDMARKS.
THE IDEA IS, WE PUT YOU CLOSE TO THE ACTION--YOU CAN JUMP THE REST OF THE WAY. OR FLY...
HULK. HOLDING UP?
IT'S STILL DAY, BETTY.
THAT AIN'T GREAT.
IT'S LIKE AN ITCH IN MY HEAD. IT STILL FEELS WRONG.
IF THIS WAS TIMED--THEY KNOW IT THROWS ME OFF.
HM.
BE CAREFUL.
PLATFORM'S CHARGED!
THEN HIT IT, McGOWAN.
AND BETTY--RELAX. IT'LL BE...

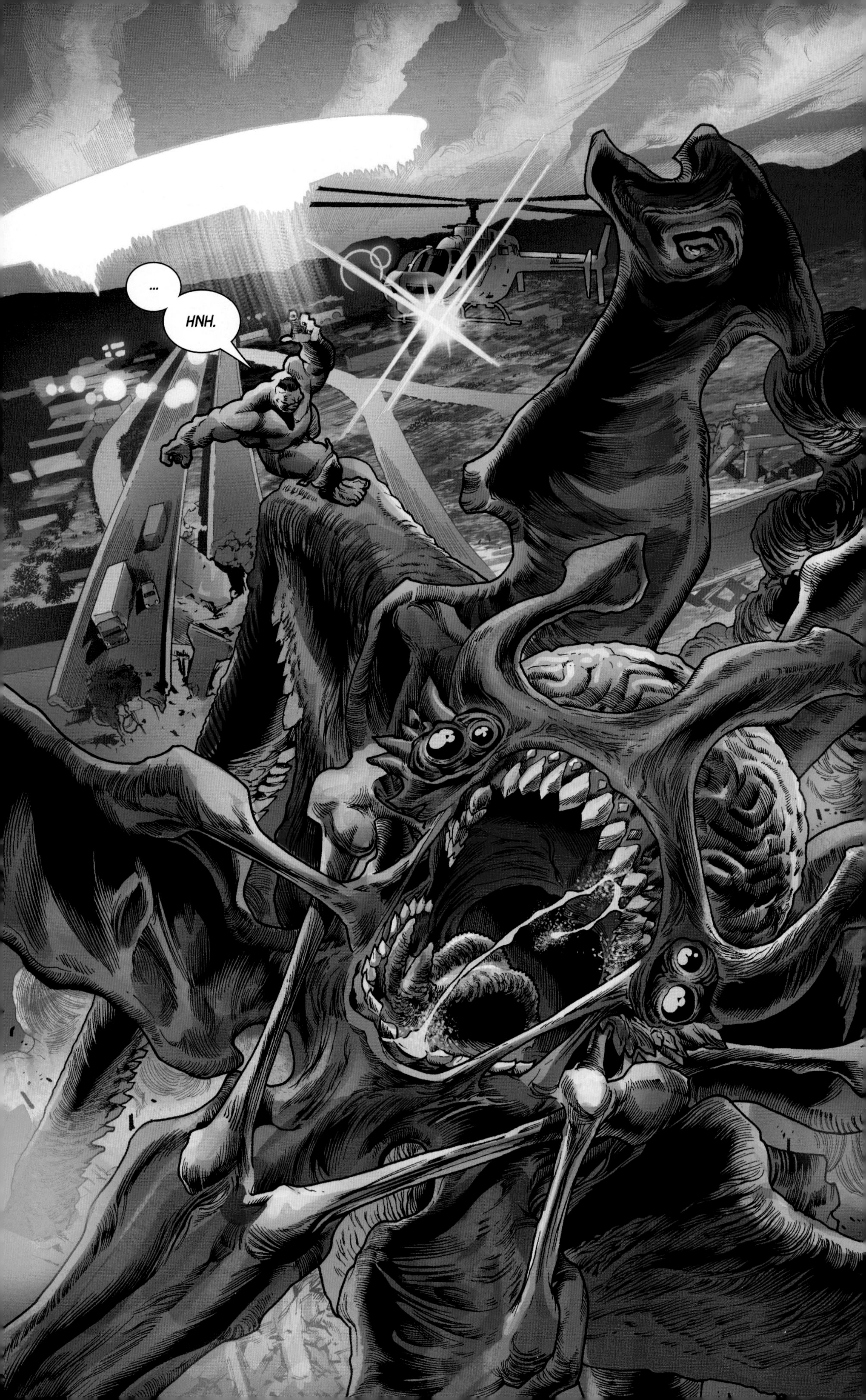
...
HNH.

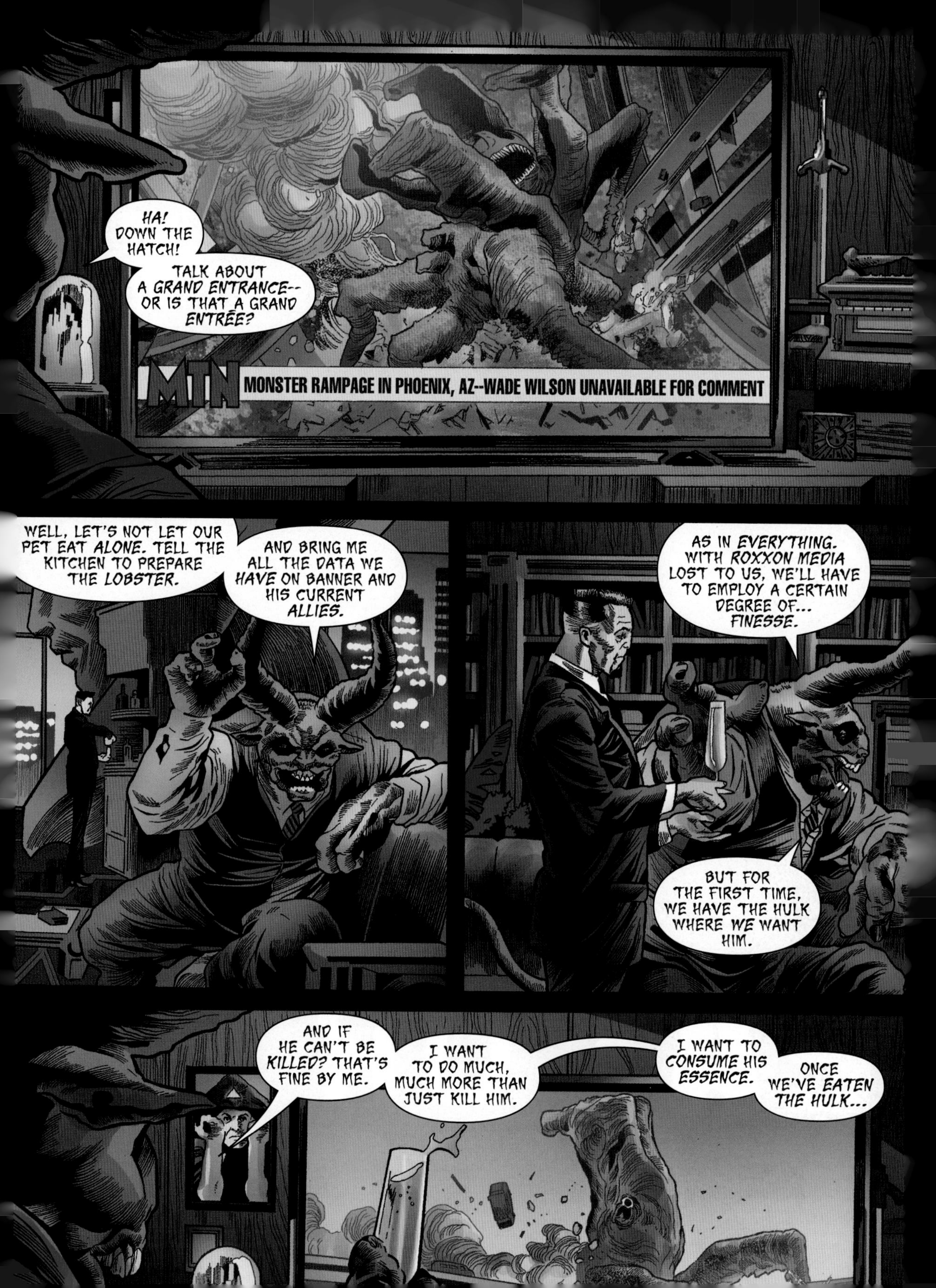
HA! DOWN THE HATCH!
TALK ABOUT A GRAND ENTRANCE--OR IS THAT A GRAND ENTRÉE?
MTN
MONSTER RAMPAGE IN PHOENIX, AZ--WADE WILSON UNAVAILABLE FOR COMMENT
WELL, LET'S NOT LET OUR PET EAT ALONE. TELL THE KITCHEN TO PREPARE THE LOBSTER.
AND BRING ME ALL THE DATA WE HAVE ON BANNER AND HIS CURRENT ALLIES.
AS IN EVERYTHING. WITH ROXXON MEDIA LOST TO US, WE'LL HAVE TO EMPLOY A CERTAIN DEGREE OF... FINESSE.
BUT FOR THE FIRST TIME, WE HAVE THE HULK WHERE WE WANT HIM.
AND IF HE CAN'T BE KILLED? THAT'S FINE BY ME.
I WANT TO DO MUCH, MUCH MORE THAN JUST KILL HIM.
I WANT TO CONSUME HIS ESSENCE.
ONCE WE'VE EATEN THE HULK...

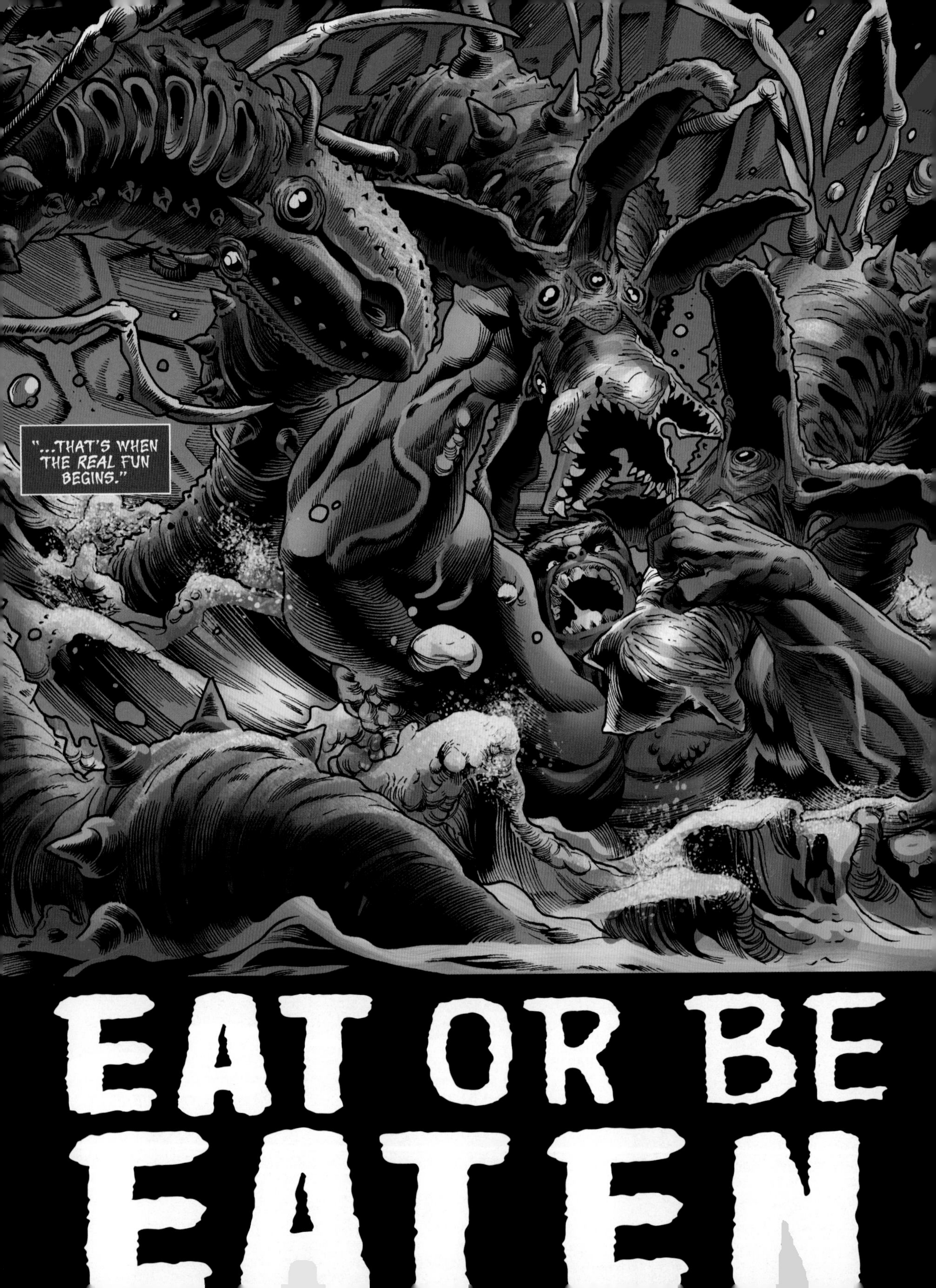
"...THAT'S WHEN THE REAL FUN BEGINS."
EAT OR BE EATEN

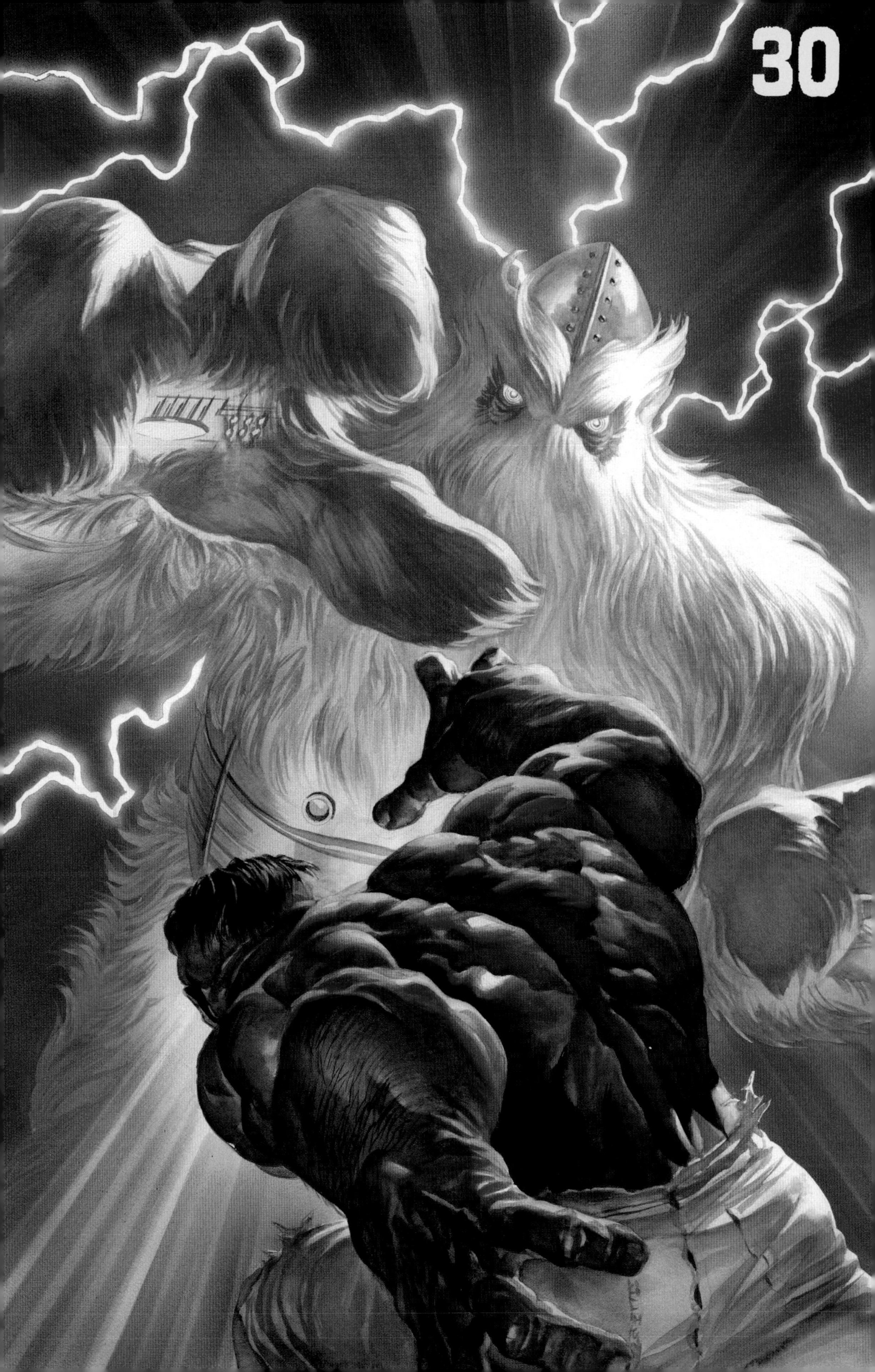
30

"**Watch therefore: for ye know not what hour your lord doth come.**"

– MATTHEW 24:42

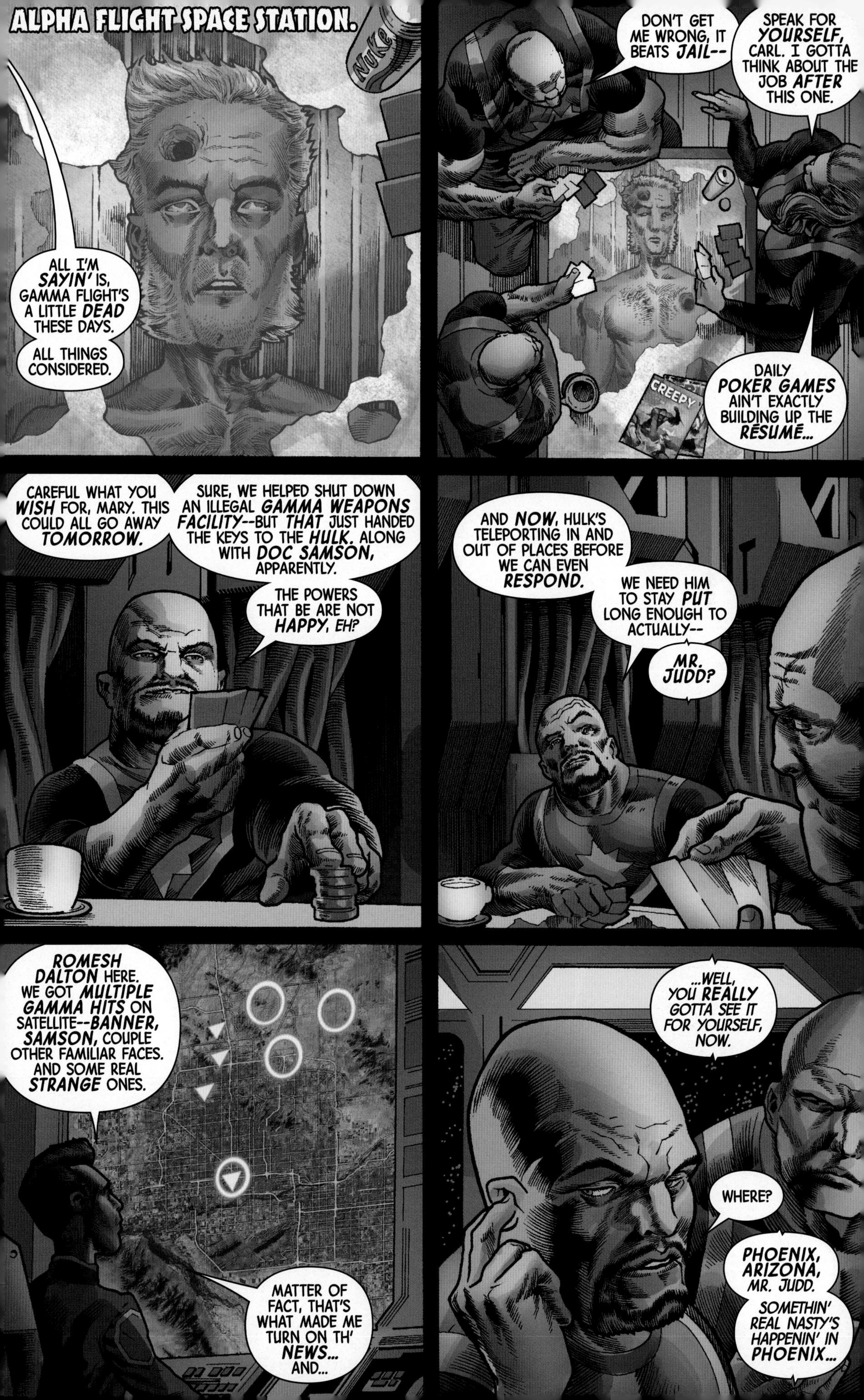
ALPHA FLIGHT SPACE STATION.
ALL I'M SAYIN' IS, GAMMA FLIGHT'S A LITTLE DEAD THESE DAYS.
ALL THINGS CONSIDERED.
DON'T GET ME WRONG, IT BEATS JAIL--
SPEAK FOR YOURSELF, CARL. I GOTTA THINK ABOUT THE JOB AFTER THIS ONE.
DAILY POKER GAMES AIN'T EXACTLY BUILDING UP THE RÉSUMÉ...
CAREFUL WHAT YOU WISH FOR, MARY. THIS COULD ALL GO AWAY TOMORROW.
SURE, WE HELPED SHUT DOWN AN ILLEGAL GAMMA WEAPONS FACILITY--BUT THAT JUST HANDED THE KEYS TO THE HULK. ALONG WITH DOC SAMSON, APPARENTLY.
THE POWERS THAT BE ARE NOT HAPPY, EH?
AND NOW, HULK'S TELEPORTING IN AND OUT OF PLACES BEFORE WE CAN EVEN RESPOND.
WE NEED HIM TO STAY PUT LONG ENOUGH TO ACTUALLY--
MR. JUDD?
ROMESH DALTON HERE. WE GOT MULTIPLE GAMMA HITS ON SATELLITE--BANNER, SAMSON, COUPLE OTHER FAMILIAR FACES. AND SOME REAL STRANGE ONES.
MATTER OF FACT, THAT'S WHAT MADE ME TURN ON TH' NEWS... AND...
...WELL, YOU REALLY GOTTA SEE IT FOR YOURSELF, NOW.
WHERE?
PHOENIX, ARIZONA, MR. JUDD.
SOMETHIN' REAL NASTY'S HAPPENIN' IN PHOENIX...

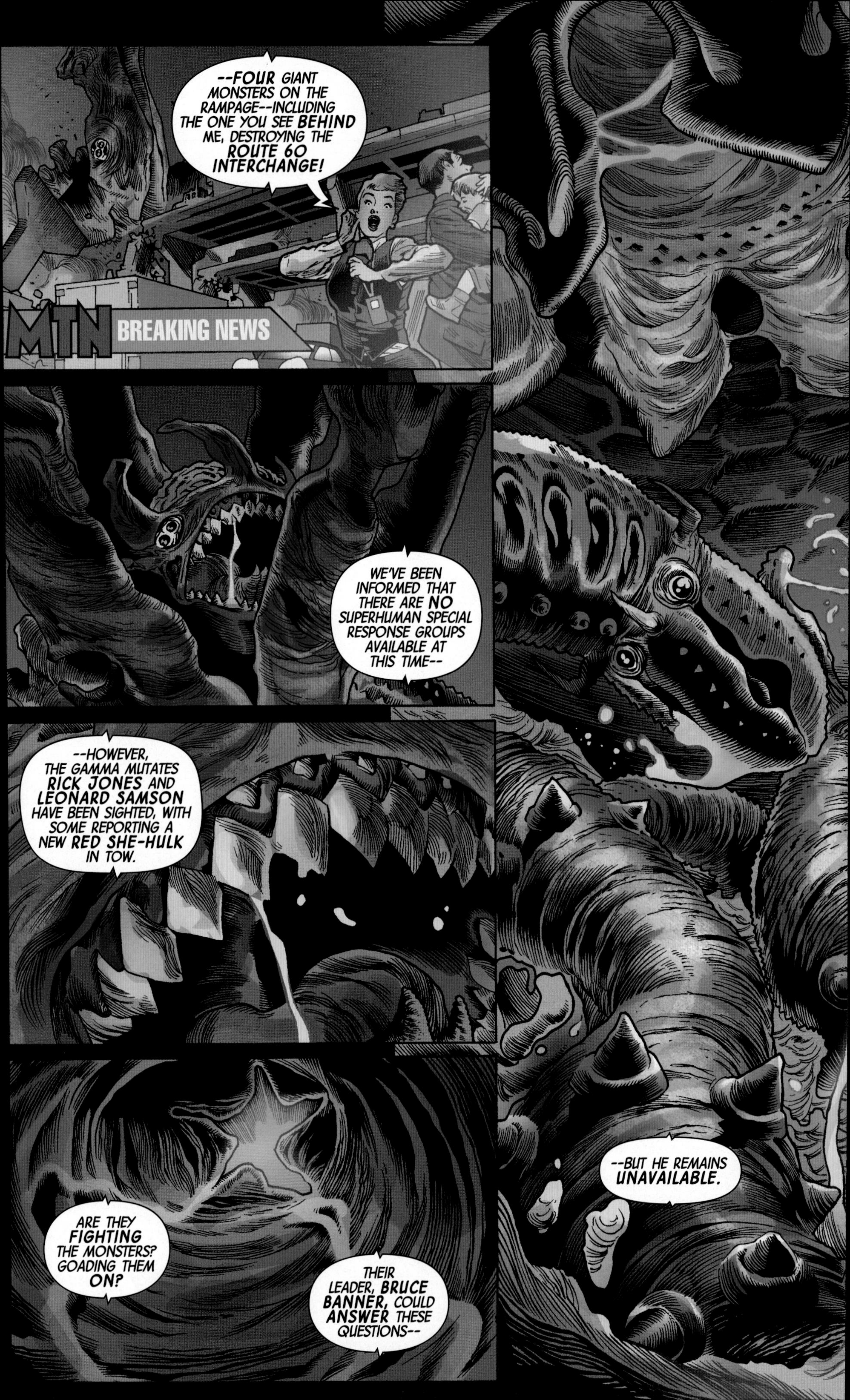
--FOUR GIANT MONSTERS ON THE RAMPAGE--INCLUDING THE ONE YOU SEE BEHIND ME, DESTROYING THE ROUTE 60 INTERCHANGE!
MTN BREAKING NEWS
WE'VE BEEN INFORMED THAT THERE ARE NO SUPERHUMAN SPECIAL RESPONSE GROUPS AVAILABLE AT THIS TIME--
--HOWEVER, THE GAMMA MUTATES RICK JONES AND LEONARD SAMSON HAVE BEEN SIGHTED, WITH SOME REPORTING A NEW RED SHE-HULK IN TOW.
ARE THEY FIGHTING THE MONSTERS? GOADING THEM ON?
THEIR LEADER, BRUCE BANNER, COULD ANSWER THESE QUESTIONS--
--BUT HE REMAINS UNAVAILABLE.

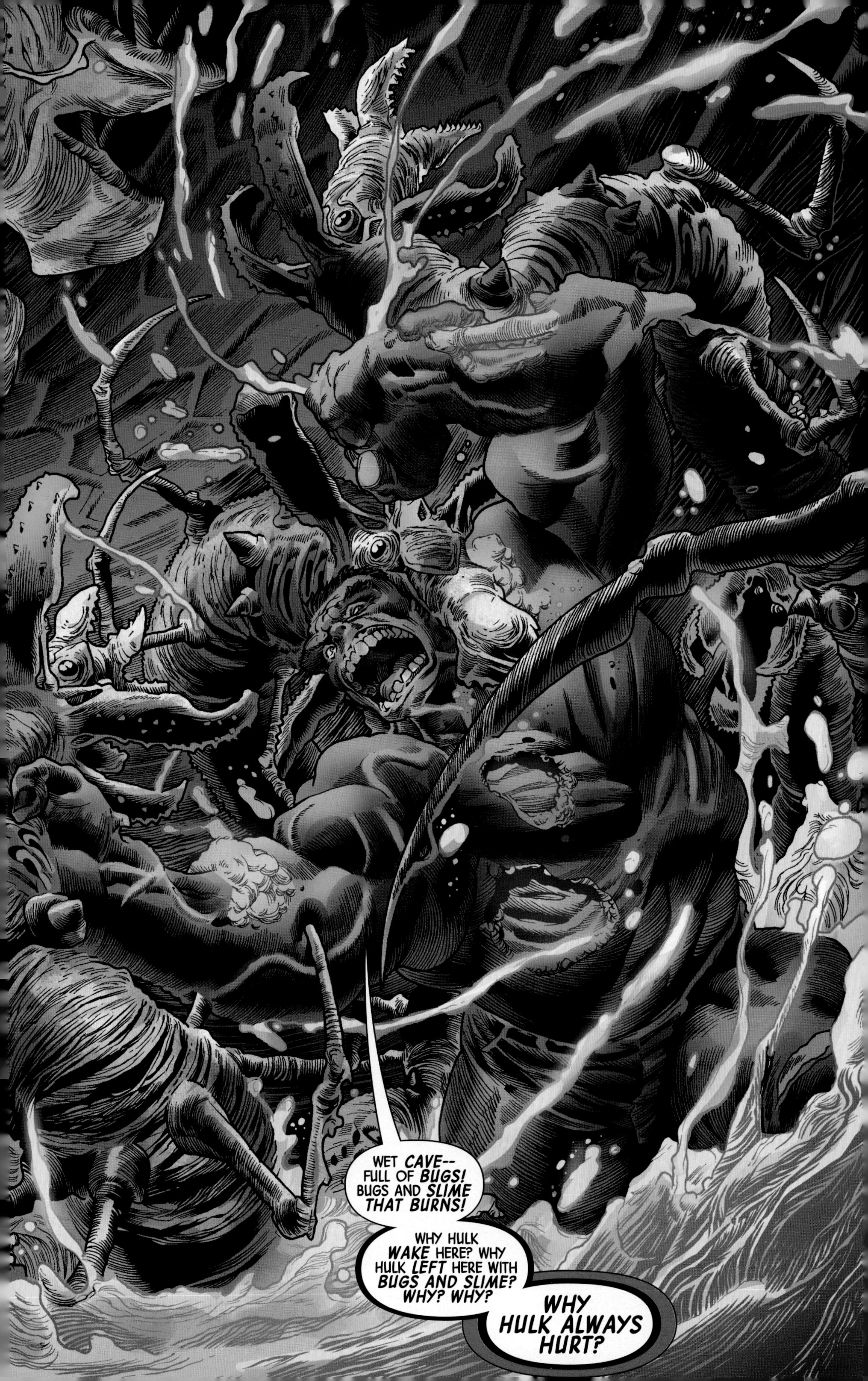
WET CAVE-- FULL OF BUGS! BUGS AND SLIME THAT BURNS!
WHY HULK WAKE HERE? WHY HULK LEFT HERE WITH BUGS AND SLIME? WHY? WHY?
WHY HULK ALWAYS HURT?

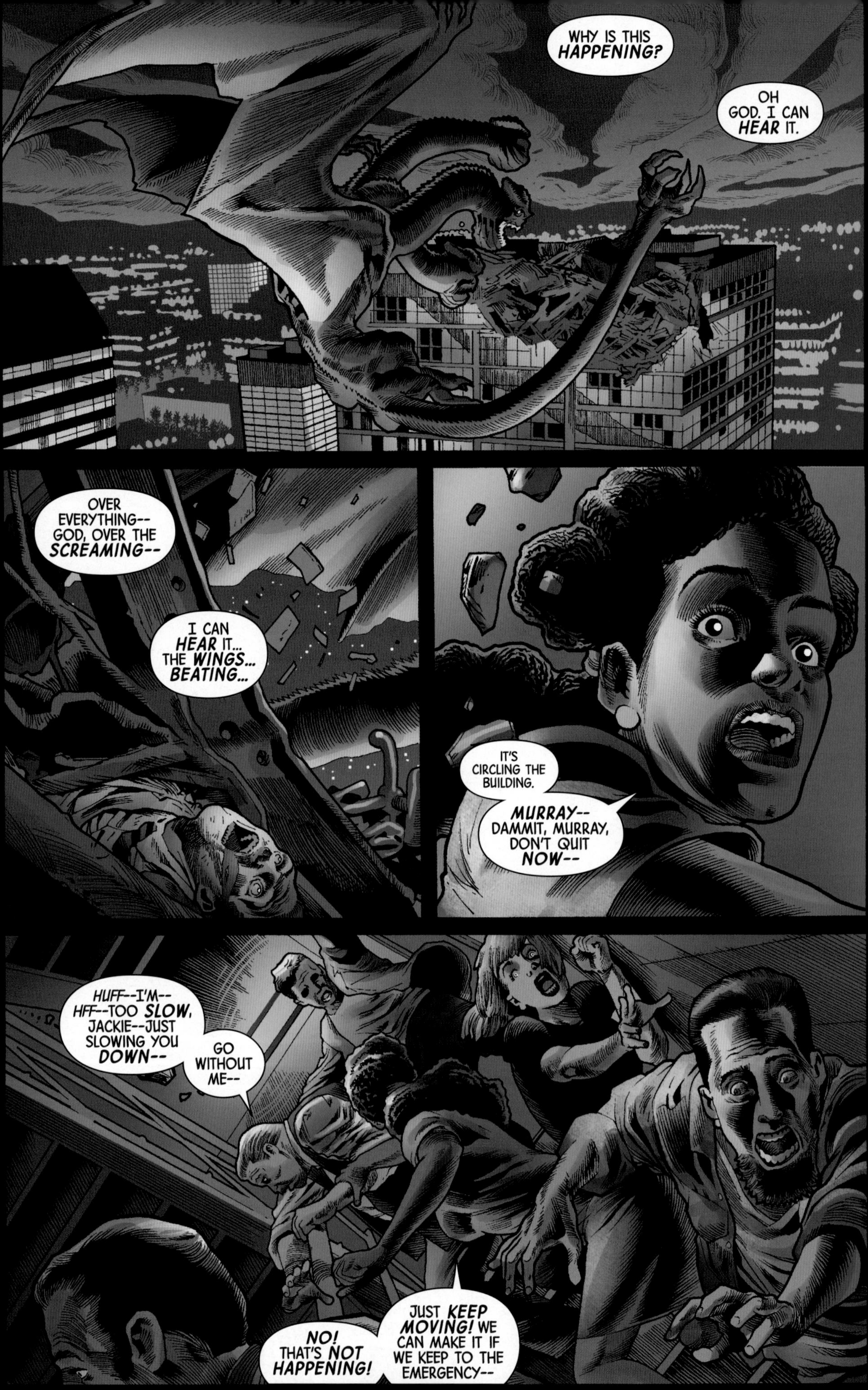
WHY IS THIS HAPPENING?
OH GOD. I CAN HEAR IT.
OVER EVERYTHING-- GOD, OVER THE SCREAMING--
I CAN HEAR IT... THE WINGS... BEATING...
IT'S CIRCLING THE BUILDING.
MURRAY-- DAMMIT, MURRAY, DON'T QUIT NOW--
HUFF--I'M-- HFF--TOO SLOW, JACKIE--JUST SLOWING YOU DOWN--
GO WITHOUT ME--
NO! THAT'S NOT HAPPENING!
JUST KEEP MOVING! WE CAN MAKE IT IF WE KEEP TO THE EMERGENCY--

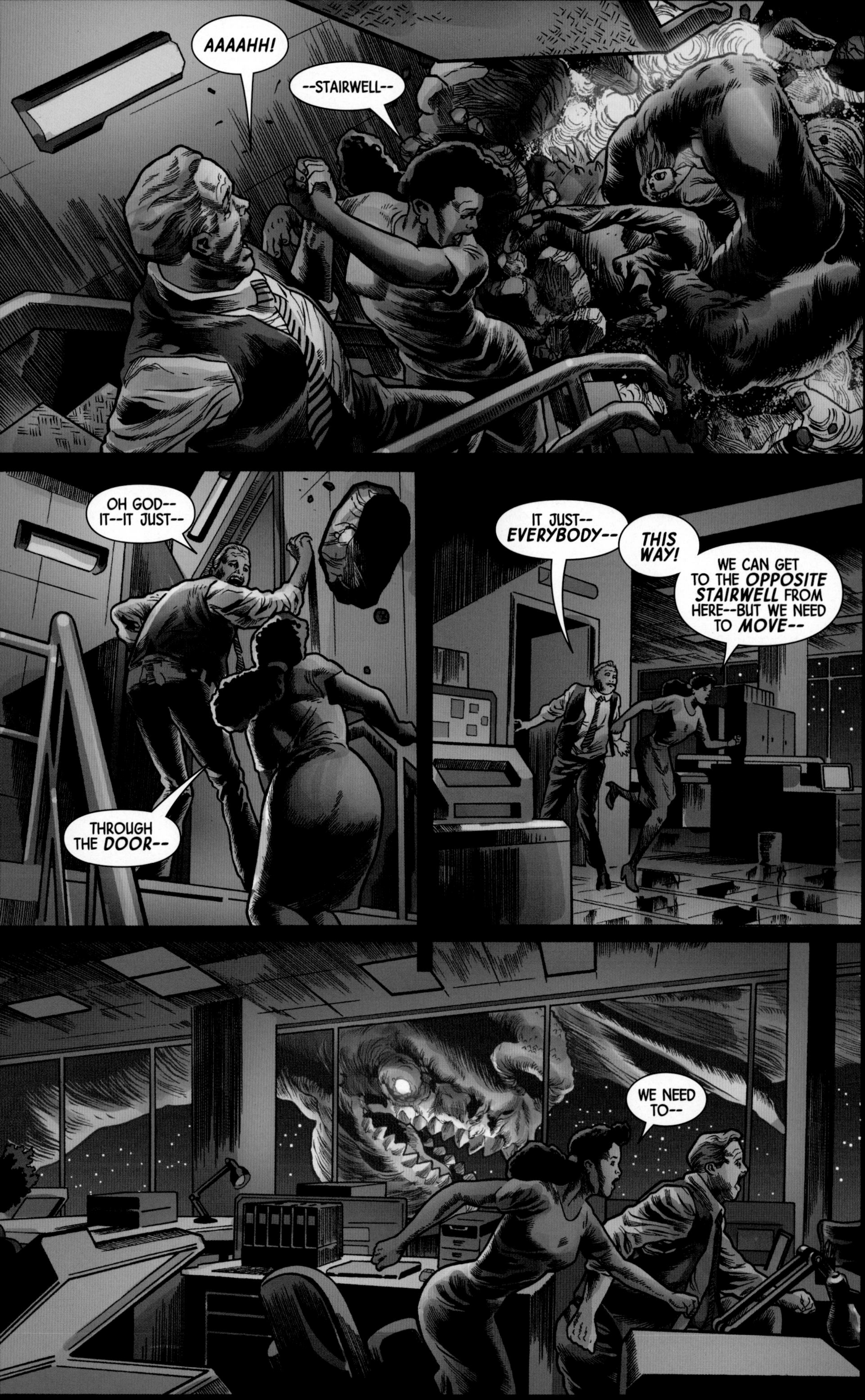
AAAAHH!
--STAIRWELL--
OH GOD-- IT--IT JUST--
THROUGH THE DOOR--
IT JUST-- EVERYBODY--
THIS WAY!
WE CAN GET TO THE OPPOSITE STAIRWELL FROM HERE--BUT WE NEED TO MOVE--
WE NEED TO--

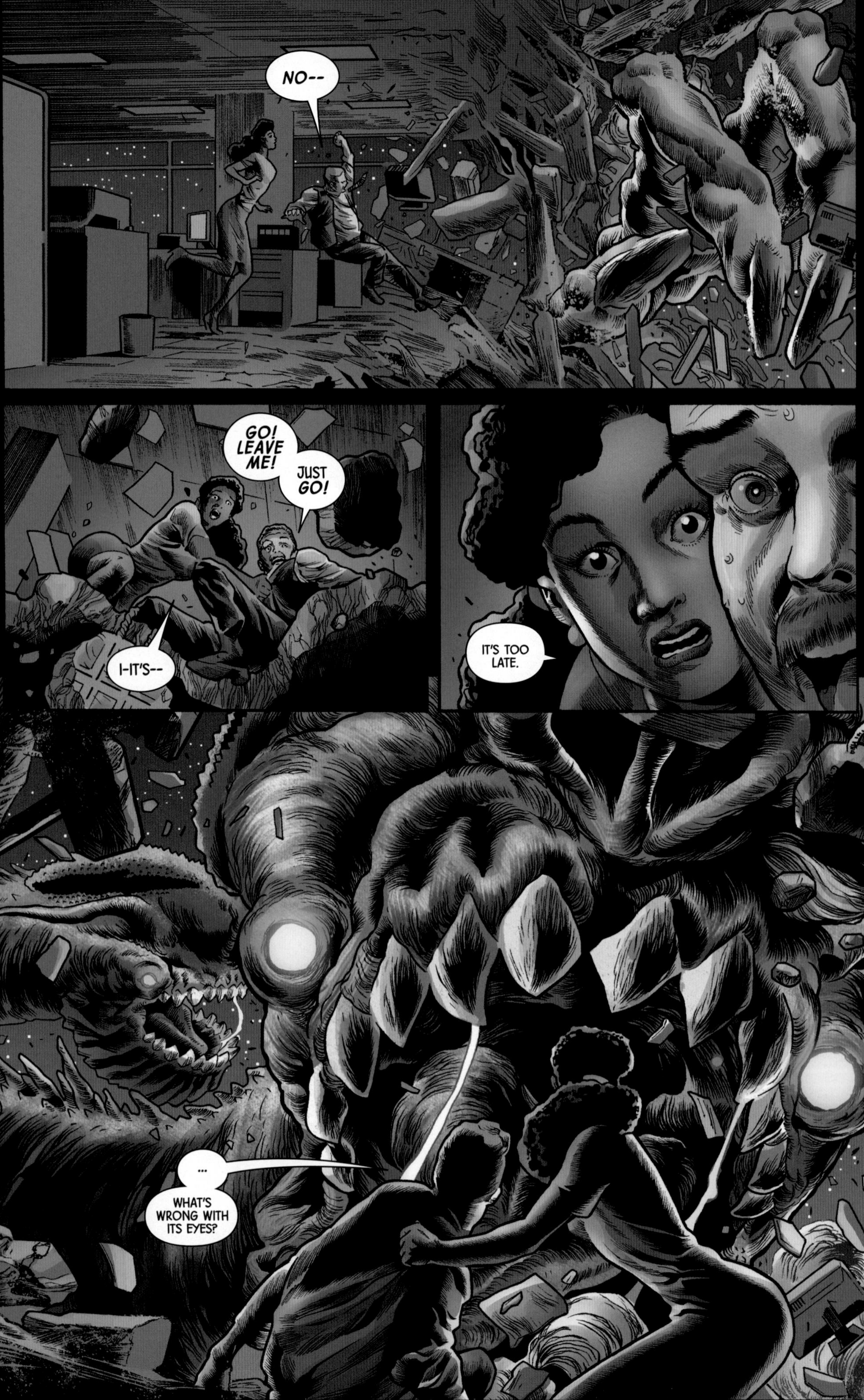
NO--
GO! LEAVE ME!
JUST GO!
I-IT'S--
IT'S TOO LATE.
...
WHAT'S WRONG WITH ITS EYES?

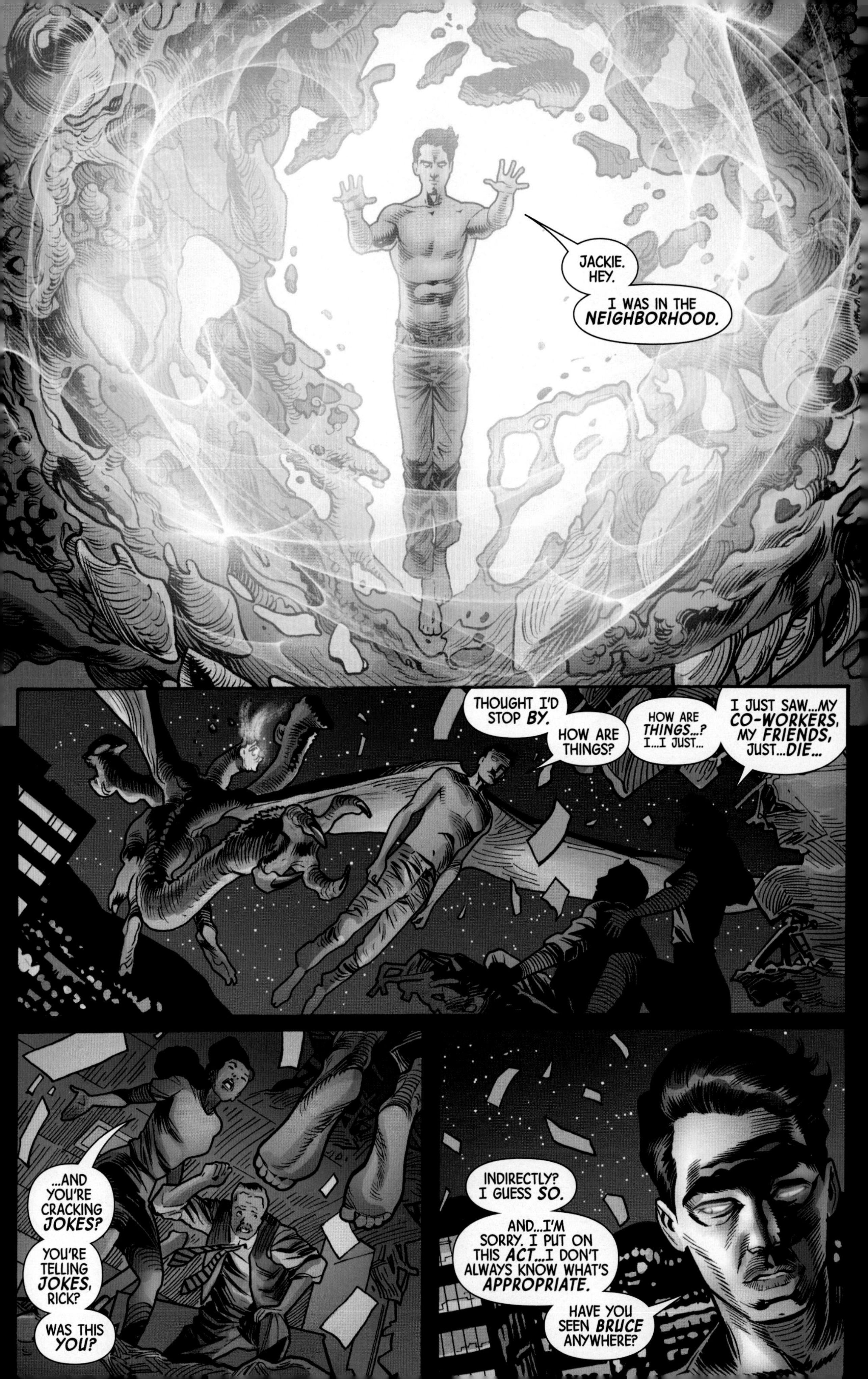
JACKIE. HEY.
I WAS IN THE NEIGHBORHOOD.
THOUGHT I'D STOP BY.
HOW ARE THINGS?
HOW ARE THINGS...? I...I JUST...
I JUST SAW...MY CO-WORKERS, MY FRIENDS, JUST...DIE...
...AND YOU'RE CRACKING JOKES?
YOU'RE TELLING JOKES, RICK?
WAS THIS YOU?
INDIRECTLY? I GUESS SO.
AND...I'M SORRY. I PUT ON THIS ACT...I DON'T ALWAYS KNOW WHAT'S APPROPRIATE.
HAVE YOU SEEN BRUCE ANYWHERE?

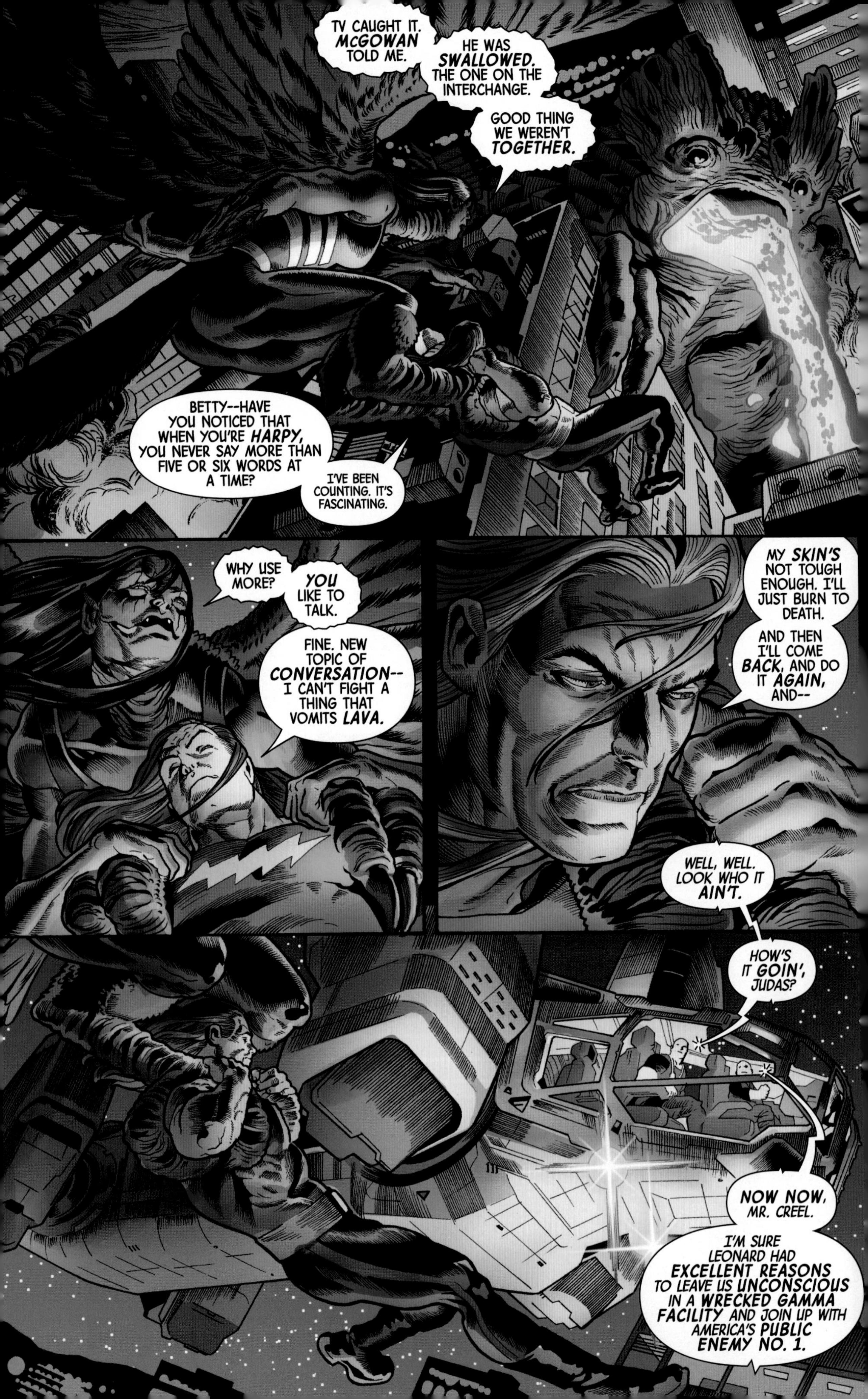
TV CAUGHT IT. McGOWAN TOLD ME.
HE WAS SWALLOWED. THE ONE ON THE INTERCHANGE.
GOOD THING WE WEREN'T TOGETHER.
BETTY--HAVE YOU NOTICED THAT WHEN YOU'RE HARPY, YOU NEVER SAY MORE THAN FIVE OR SIX WORDS AT A TIME?
I'VE BEEN COUNTING. IT'S FASCINATING.
WHY USE MORE?
YOU LIKE TO TALK.
FINE. NEW TOPIC OF CONVERSATION-- I CAN'T FIGHT A THING THAT VOMITS LAVA.
MY SKIN'S NOT TOUGH ENOUGH. I'LL JUST BURN TO DEATH.
AND THEN I'LL COME BACK, AND DO IT AGAIN, AND--
WELL, WELL. LOOK WHO IT AIN'T.
HOW'S IT GOIN', JUDAS?
NOW NOW, MR. CREEL.
I'M SURE LEONARD HAD EXCELLENT REASONS TO LEAVE US UNCONSCIOUS IN A WRECKED GAMMA FACILITY AND JOIN UP WITH AMERICA'S PUBLIC ENEMY NO. 1.

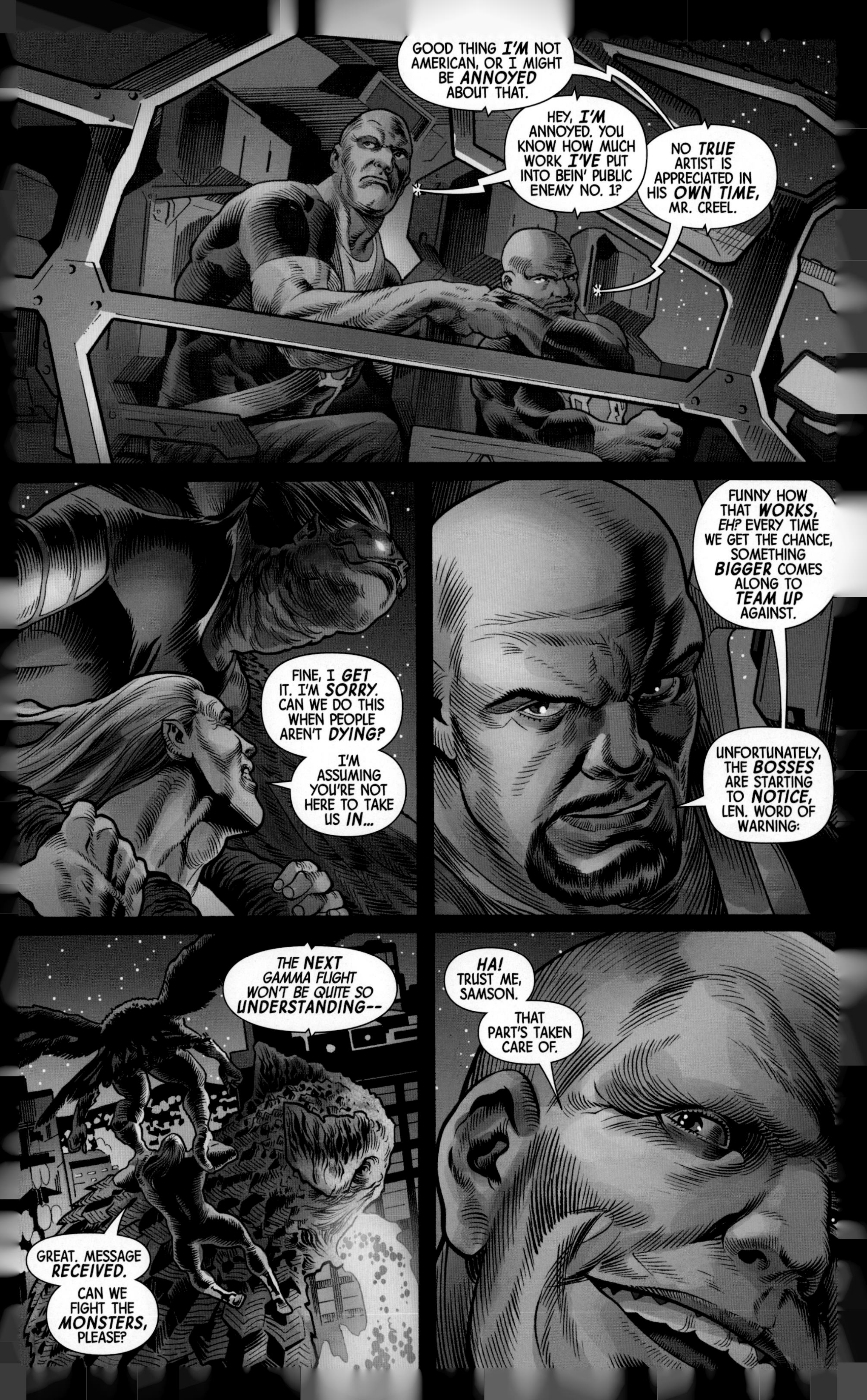
GOOD THING I'M NOT AMERICAN, OR I MIGHT BE ANNOYED ABOUT THAT.
HEY, I'M ANNOYED. YOU KNOW HOW MUCH WORK I'VE PUT INTO BEIN' PUBLIC ENEMY NO. 1?
NO TRUE ARTIST IS APPRECIATED IN HIS OWN TIME, MR. CREEL.
FINE, I GET IT. I'M SORRY. CAN WE DO THIS WHEN PEOPLE AREN'T DYING?
I'M ASSUMING YOU'RE NOT HERE TO TAKE US IN...
FUNNY HOW THAT WORKS, EH? EVERY TIME WE GET THE CHANCE, SOMETHING BIGGER COMES ALONG TO TEAM UP AGAINST.
UNFORTUNATELY, THE BOSSES ARE STARTING TO NOTICE, LEN. WORD OF WARNING:
THE NEXT GAMMA FLIGHT WON'T BE QUITE SO UNDERSTANDING--
GREAT. MESSAGE RECEIVED.
CAN WE FIGHT THE MONSTERS, PLEASE?
HA! TRUST ME, SAMSON.
THAT PART'S TAKEN CARE OF.

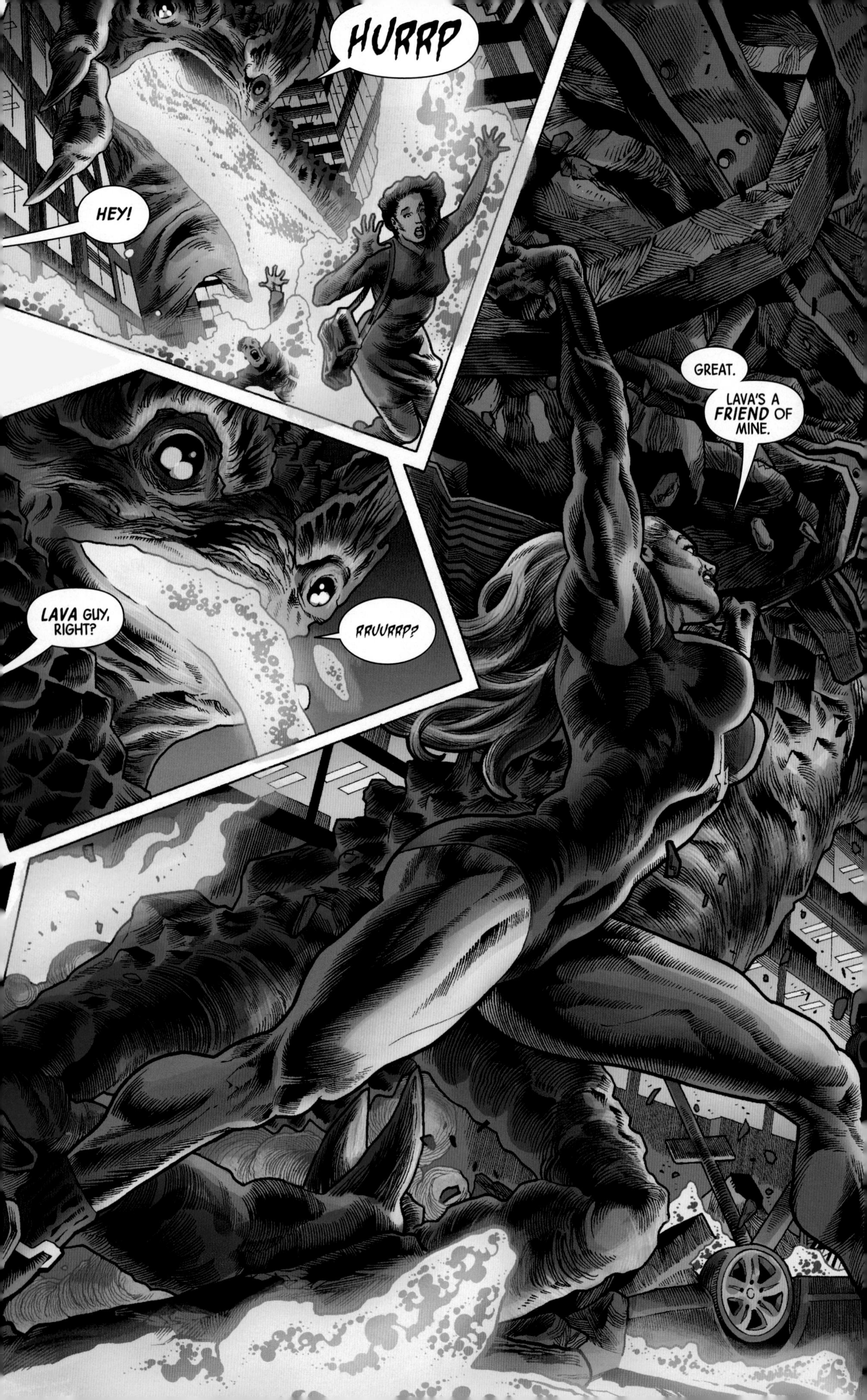
HURRP
HEY!
GREAT.
LAVA'S A FRIEND OF MINE.
LAVA GUY, RIGHT?
RRUURRP?

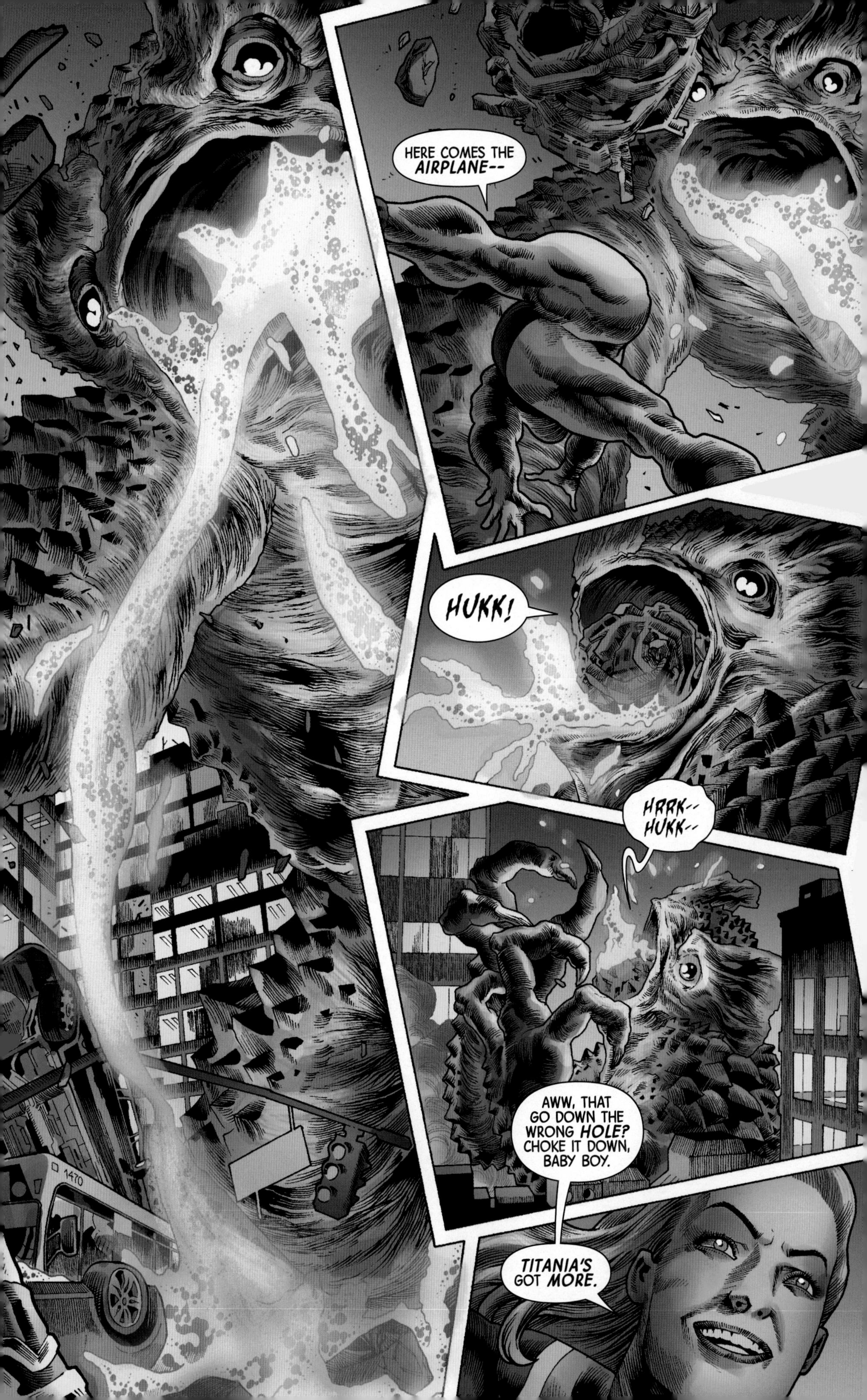
HERE COMES THE AIRPLANE--
HUKK!
HRRK-- HUKK--
AWW, THAT GO DOWN THE WRONG HOLE? CHOKE IT DOWN, BABY BOY.
TITANIA'S GOT MORE.
1470

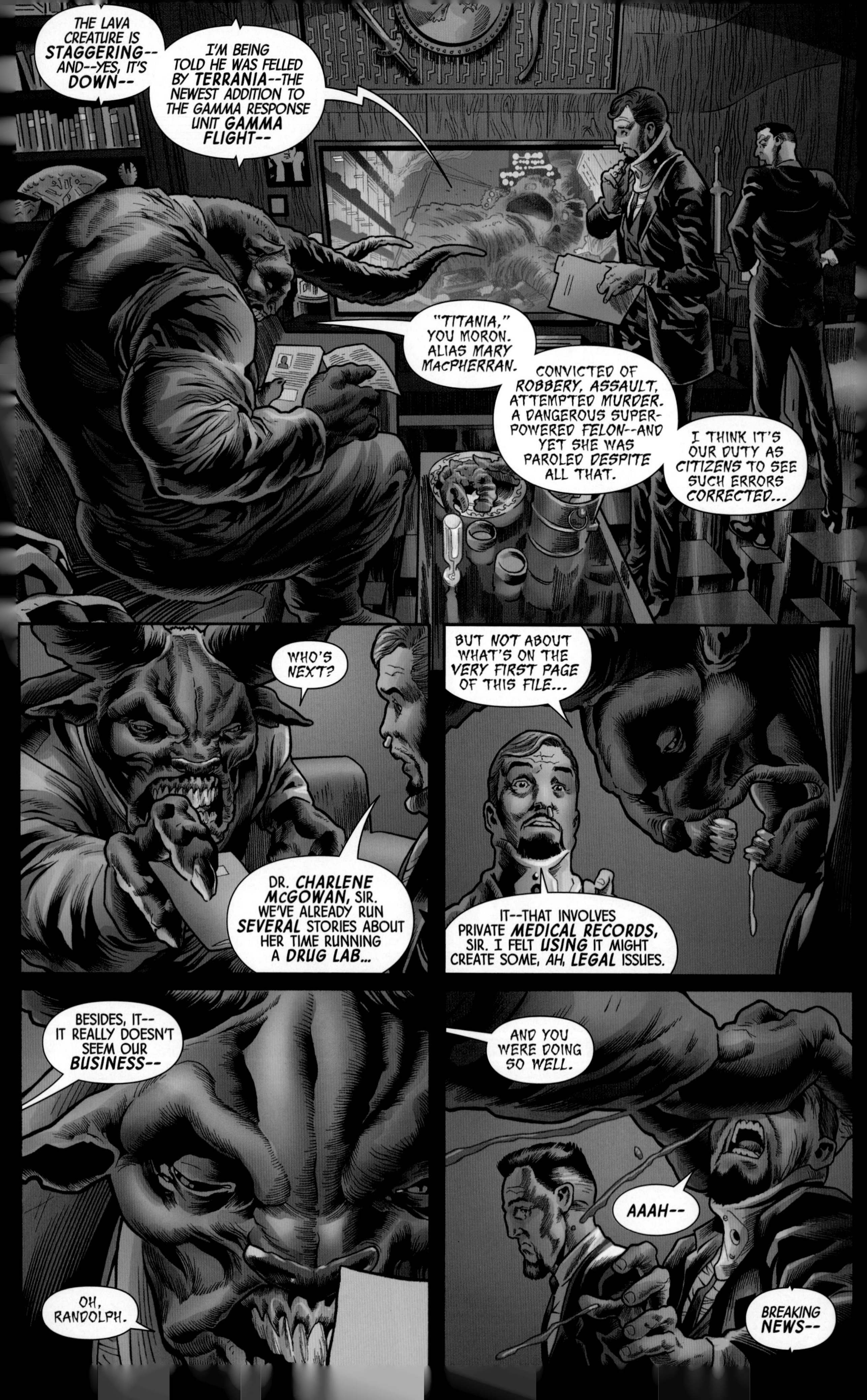

THE LAVA CREATURE IS STAGGERING--AND--YES, IT'S DOWN--
I'M BEING TOLD HE WAS FELLED BY TERRANIA--THE NEWEST ADDITION TO THE GAMMA RESPONSE UNIT GAMMA FLIGHT--
"TITANIA," YOU MORON. ALIAS MARY MACPHERRAN.
CONVICTED OF ROBBERY, ASSAULT, ATTEMPTED MURDER. A DANGEROUS SUPER-POWERED FELON--AND YET SHE WAS PAROLED DESPITE ALL THAT.
I THINK IT'S OUR DUTY AS CITIZENS TO SEE SUCH ERRORS CORRECTED...
WHO'S NEXT?
DR. CHARLENE McGOWAN, SIR. WE'VE ALREADY RUN SEVERAL STORIES ABOUT HER TIME RUNNING A DRUG LAB...
BUT NOT ABOUT WHAT'S ON THE VERY FIRST PAGE OF THIS FILE...
IT--THAT INVOLVES PRIVATE MEDICAL RECORDS, SIR. I FELT USING IT MIGHT CREATE SOME, AH, LEGAL ISSUES.
BESIDES, IT--IT REALLY DOESN'T SEEM OUR BUSINESS--
OH, RANDOLPH.
AND YOU WERE DOING SO WELL.
AAAH--
BREAKING NEWS--

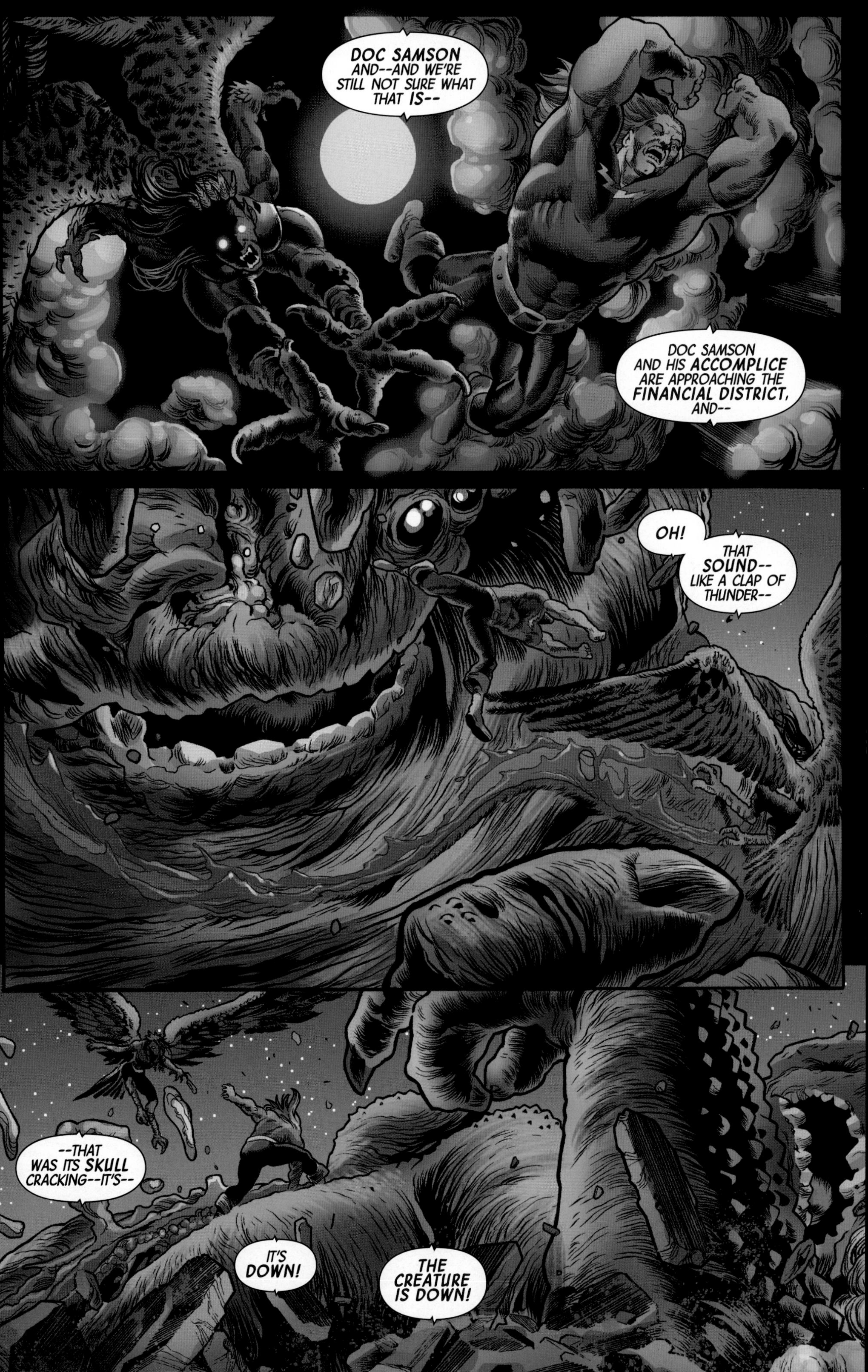
DOC SAMSON AND--AND WE'RE STILL NOT SURE WHAT THAT IS--
DOC SAMSON AND HIS ACCOMPLICE ARE APPROACHING THE FINANCIAL DISTRICT, AND--
OH!
THAT SOUND-- LIKE A CLAP OF THUNDER--
--THAT WAS ITS SKULL CRACKING--IT'S--
IT'S DOWN!
THE CREATURE IS DOWN!

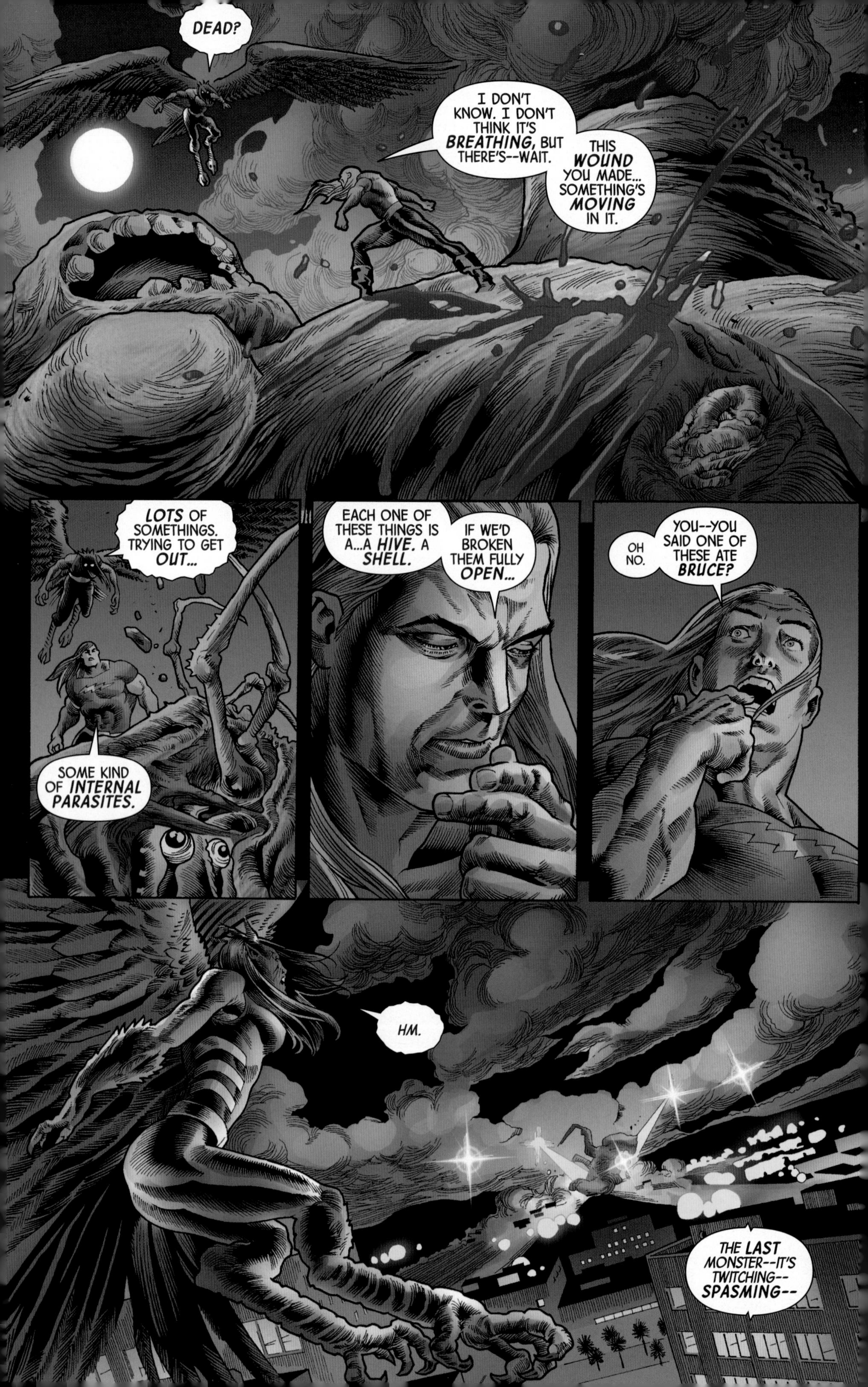
DEAD?
I DON'T KNOW. I DON'T THINK IT'S BREATHING, BUT THERE'S--WAIT.
THIS WOUND YOU MADE... SOMETHING'S MOVING IN IT.
LOTS OF SOMETHINGS. TRYING TO GET OUT...
SOME KIND OF INTERNAL PARASITES.
EACH ONE OF THESE THINGS IS A...A HIVE. A SHELL.
IF WE'D BROKEN THEM FULLY OPEN...
OH NO.
YOU--YOU SAID ONE OF THESE ATE BRUCE?
HM.
THE LAST MONSTER--IT'S TWITCHING--SPASMING--

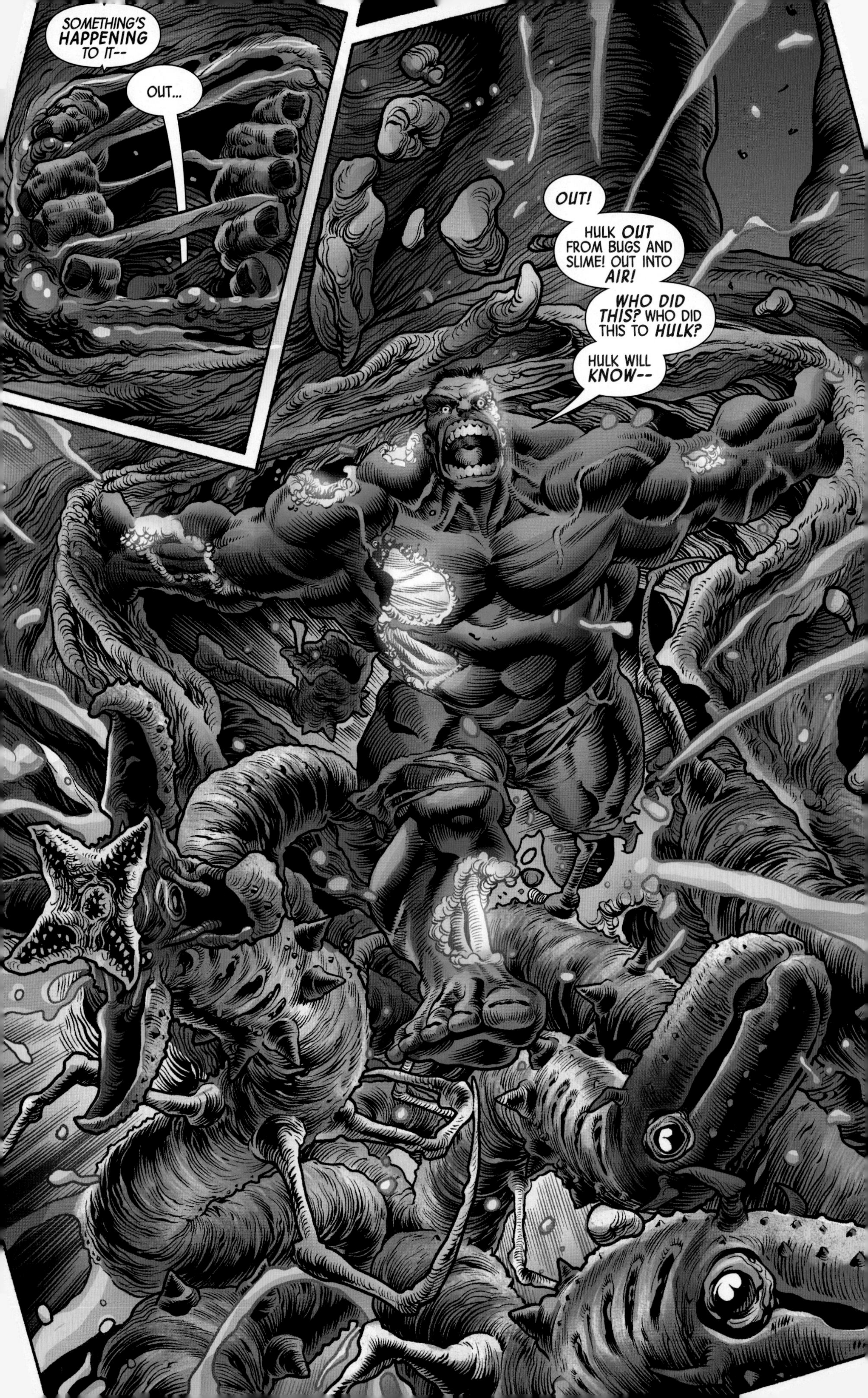
SOMETHING'S HAPPENING TO IT--
OUT...
OUT!
HULK OUT FROM BUGS AND SLIME! OUT INTO AIR!
WHO DID THIS? WHO DID THIS TO HULK?
HULK WILL KNOW--

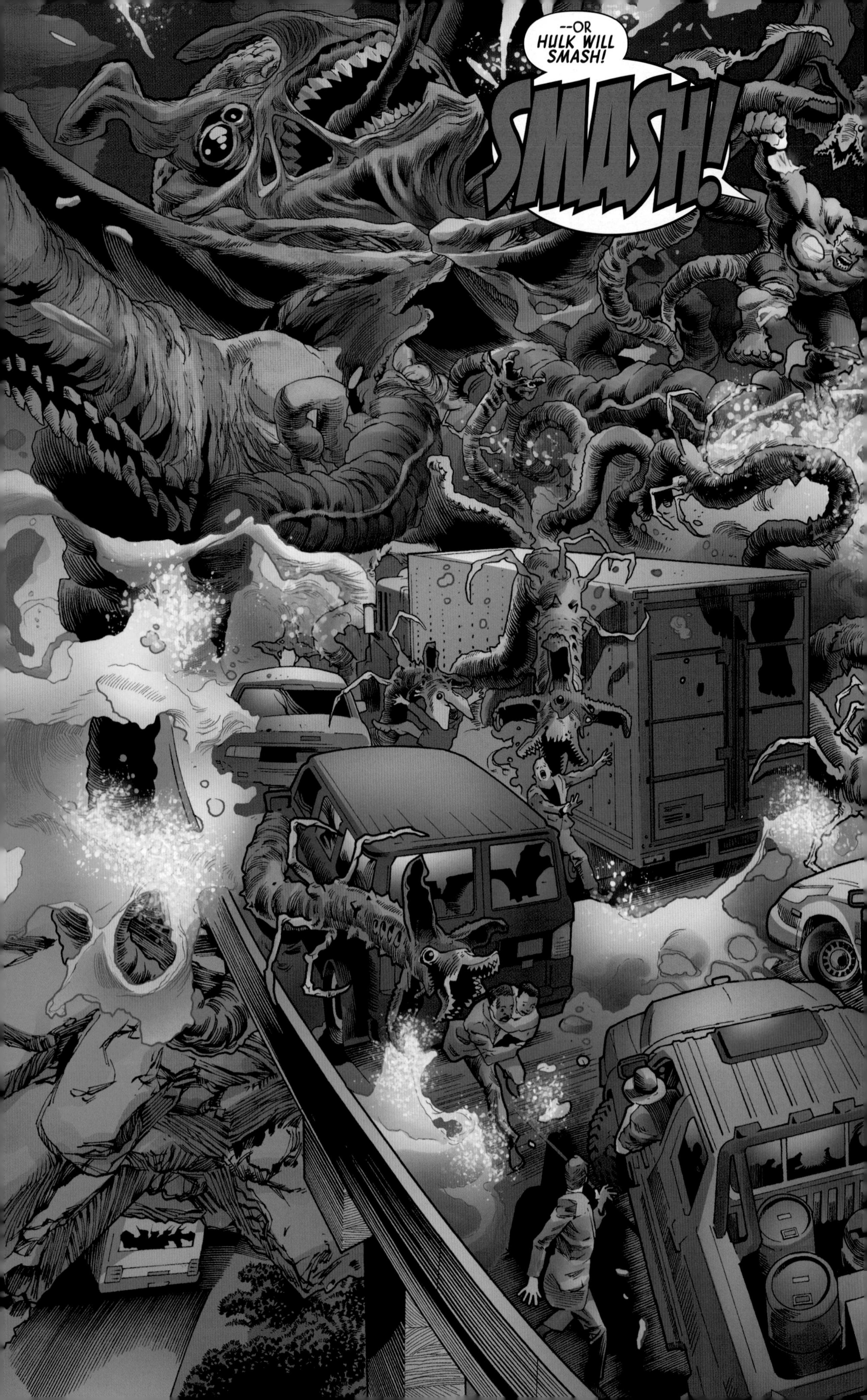
--OR HULK WILL SMASH!
SMASH!

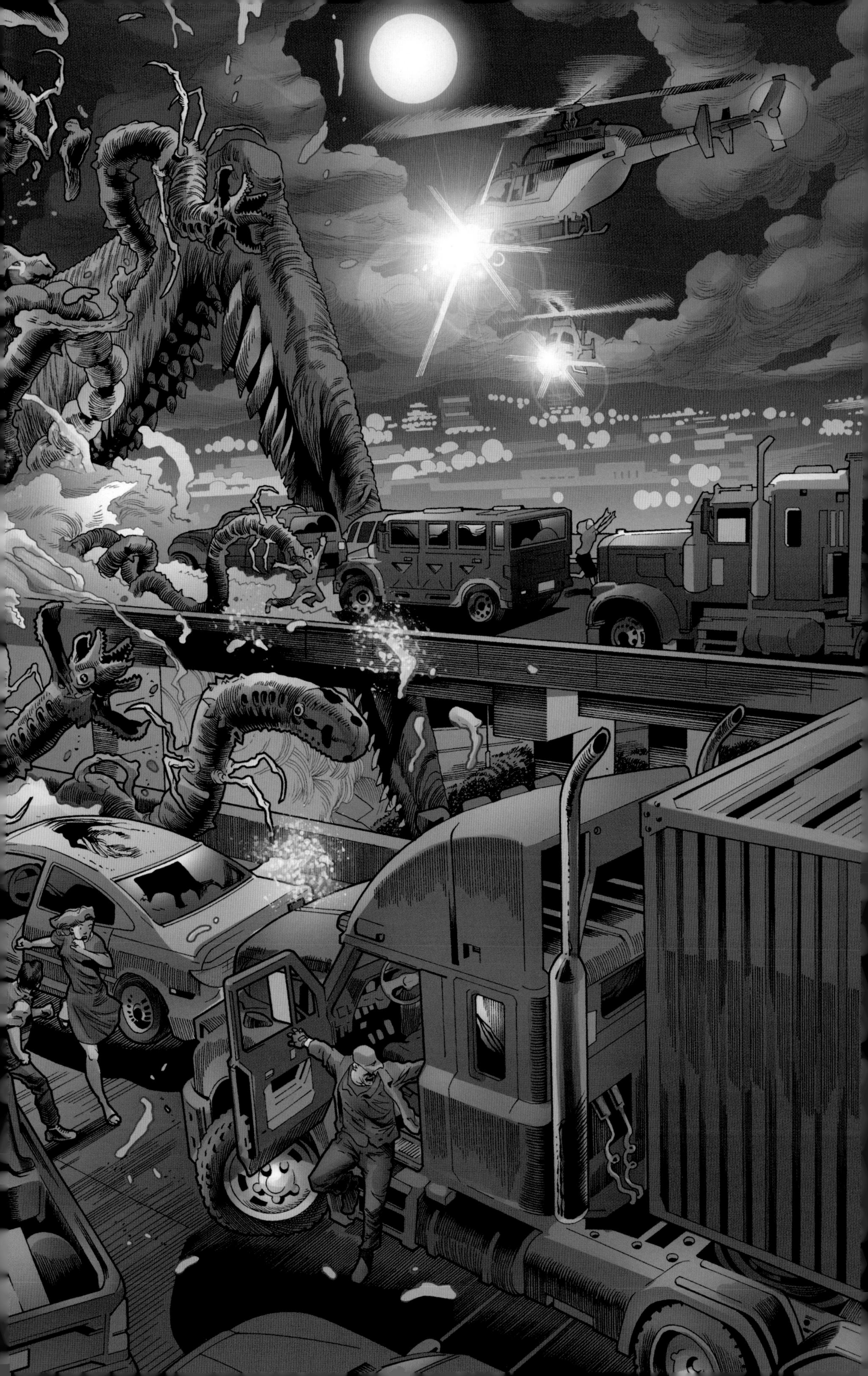

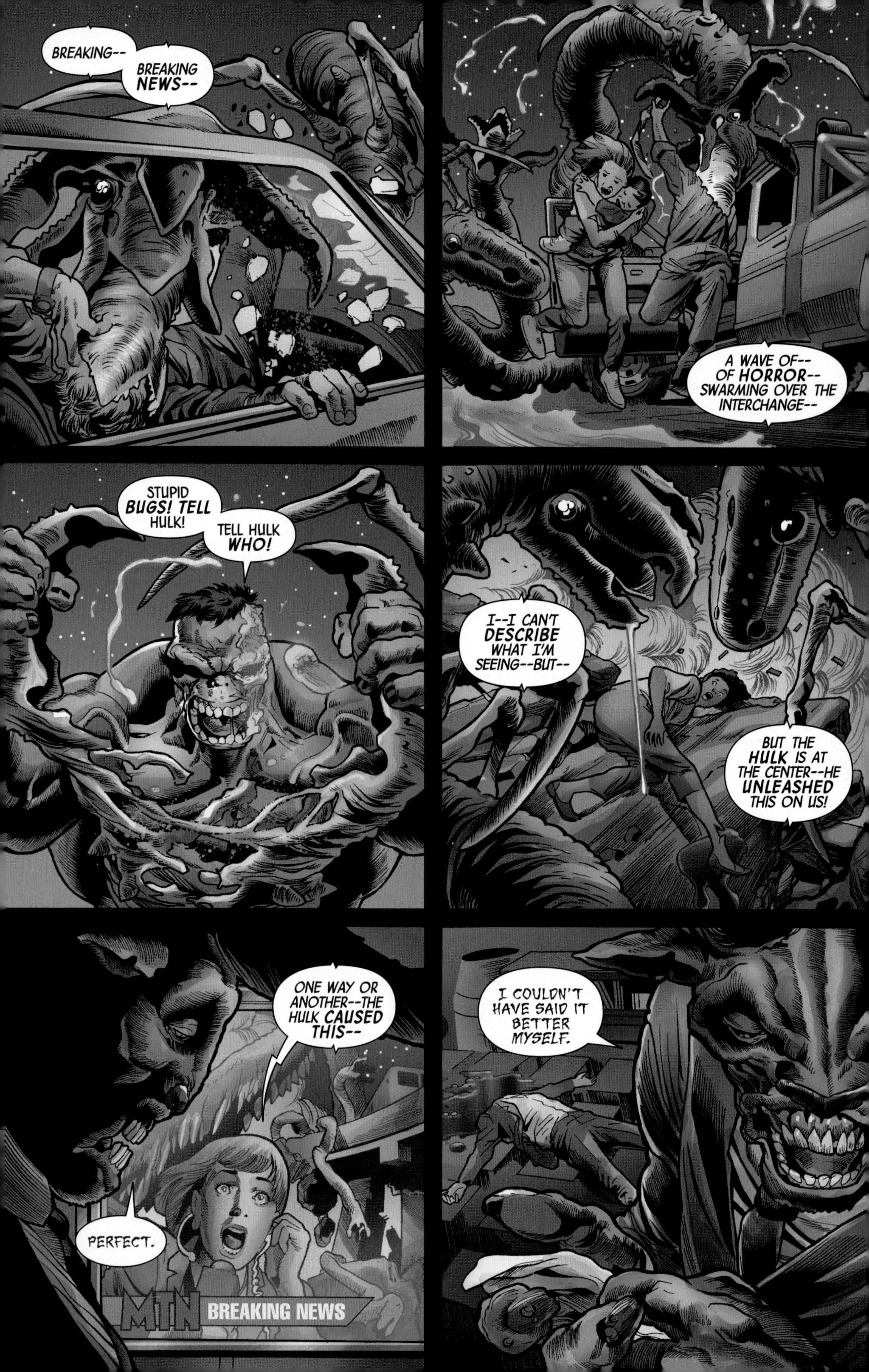

BREAKING--
BREAKING NEWS--
A WAVE OF-- OF HORROR-- SWARMING OVER THE INTERCHANGE--
STUPID BUGS! TELL HULK!
TELL HULK WHO!
I--I CAN'T DESCRIBE WHAT I'M SEEING--BUT--
BUT THE HULK IS AT THE CENTER--HE UNLEASHED THIS ON US!
ONE WAY OR ANOTHER--THE HULK CAUSED THIS--
PERFECT.
MTN
BREAKING NEWS
I COULDN'T HAVE SAID IT BETTER MYSELF.

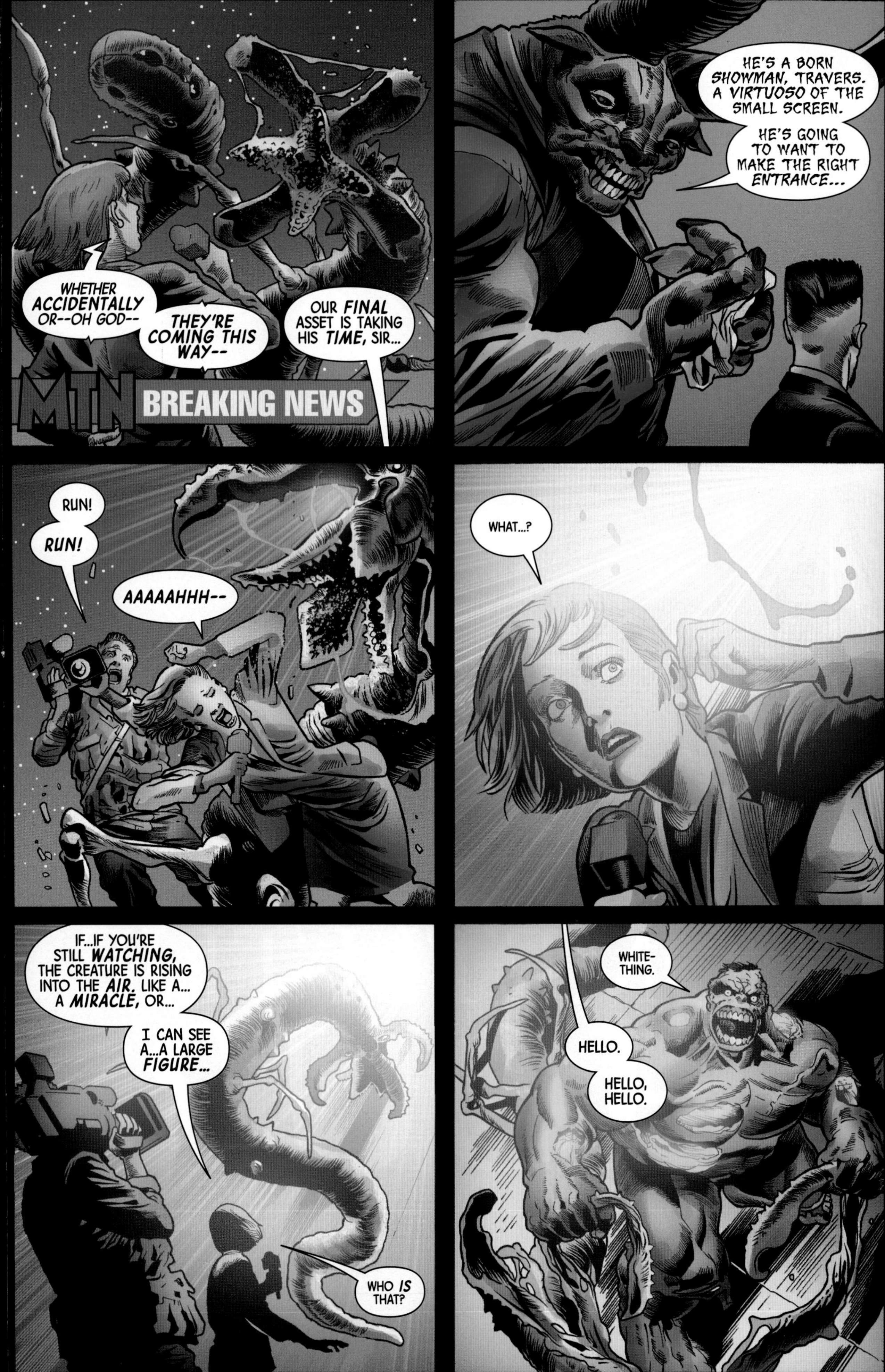

WHETHER ACCIDENTALLY OR--OH GOD--
THEY'RE COMING THIS WAY--
OUR FINAL ASSET IS TAKING HIS TIME, SIR...
MTN BREAKING NEWS
HE'S A BORN SHOWMAN, TRAVERS. A VIRTUOSO OF THE SMALL SCREEN.
HE'S GOING TO WANT TO MAKE THE RIGHT ENTRANCE...
RUN!
RUN!
AAAAAHHH--
WHAT...?
IF...IF YOU'RE STILL WATCHING, THE CREATURE IS RISING INTO THE AIR. LIKE A... A MIRACLE, OR...
I CAN SEE A...A LARGE FIGURE...
WHO IS THAT?
WHITE-THING.
HELLO.
HELLO, HELLO.

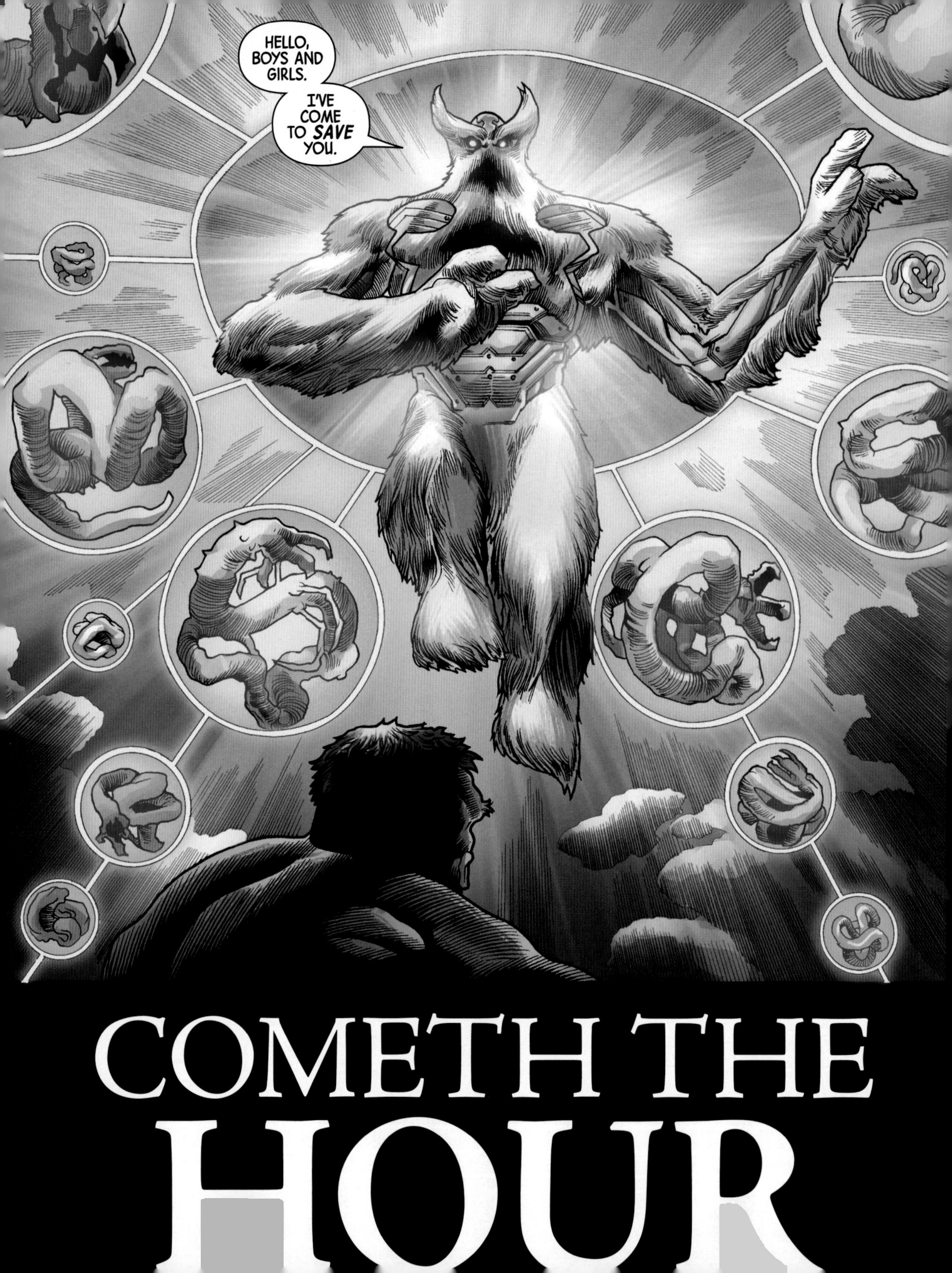
HELLO, BOYS AND GIRLS.
I'VE COME TO SAVE YOU.

COMETH THE HOUR

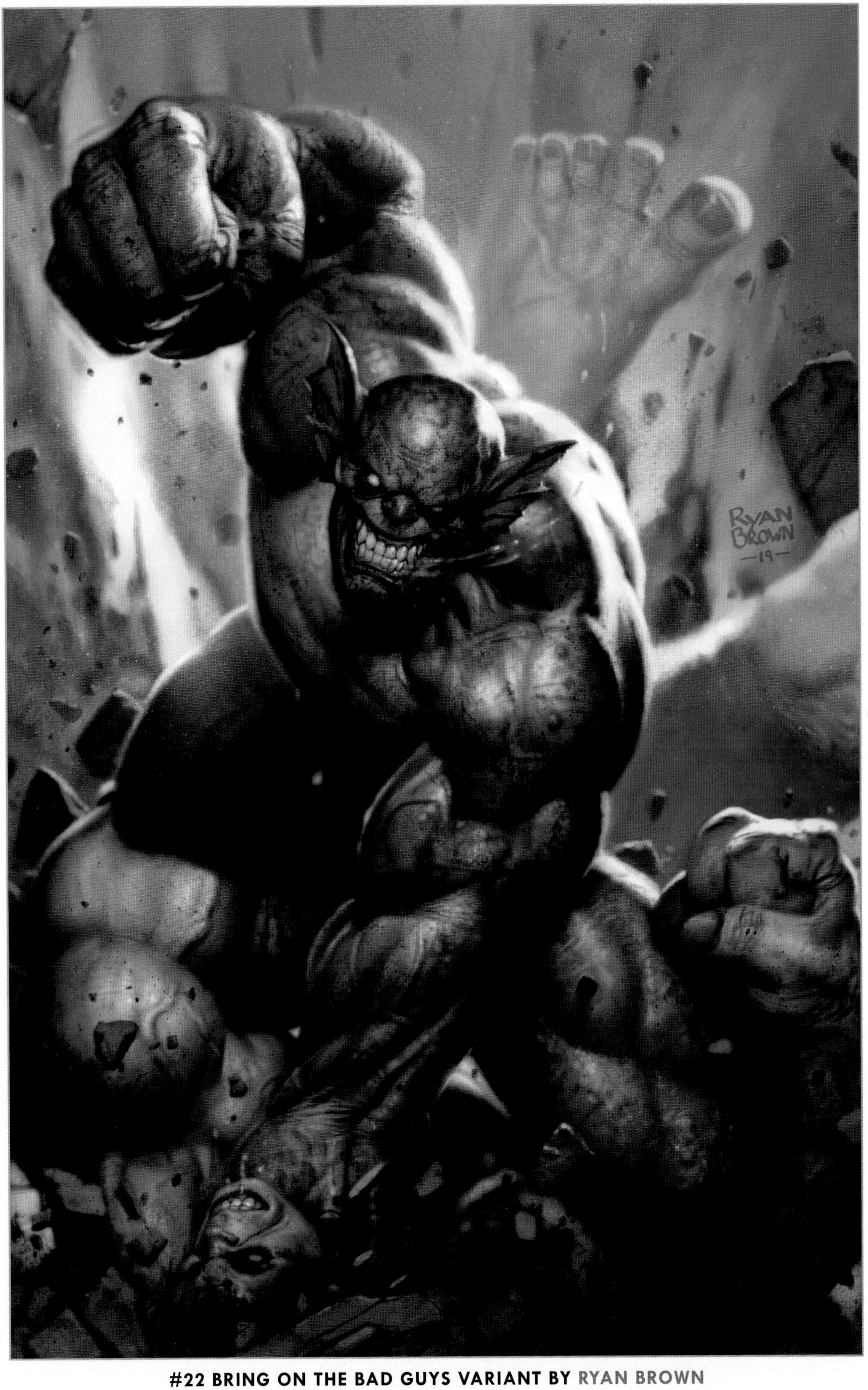
RYAN BROWN -19-

#22 BRING ON THE BAD GUYS VARIANT BY RYAN BROWN

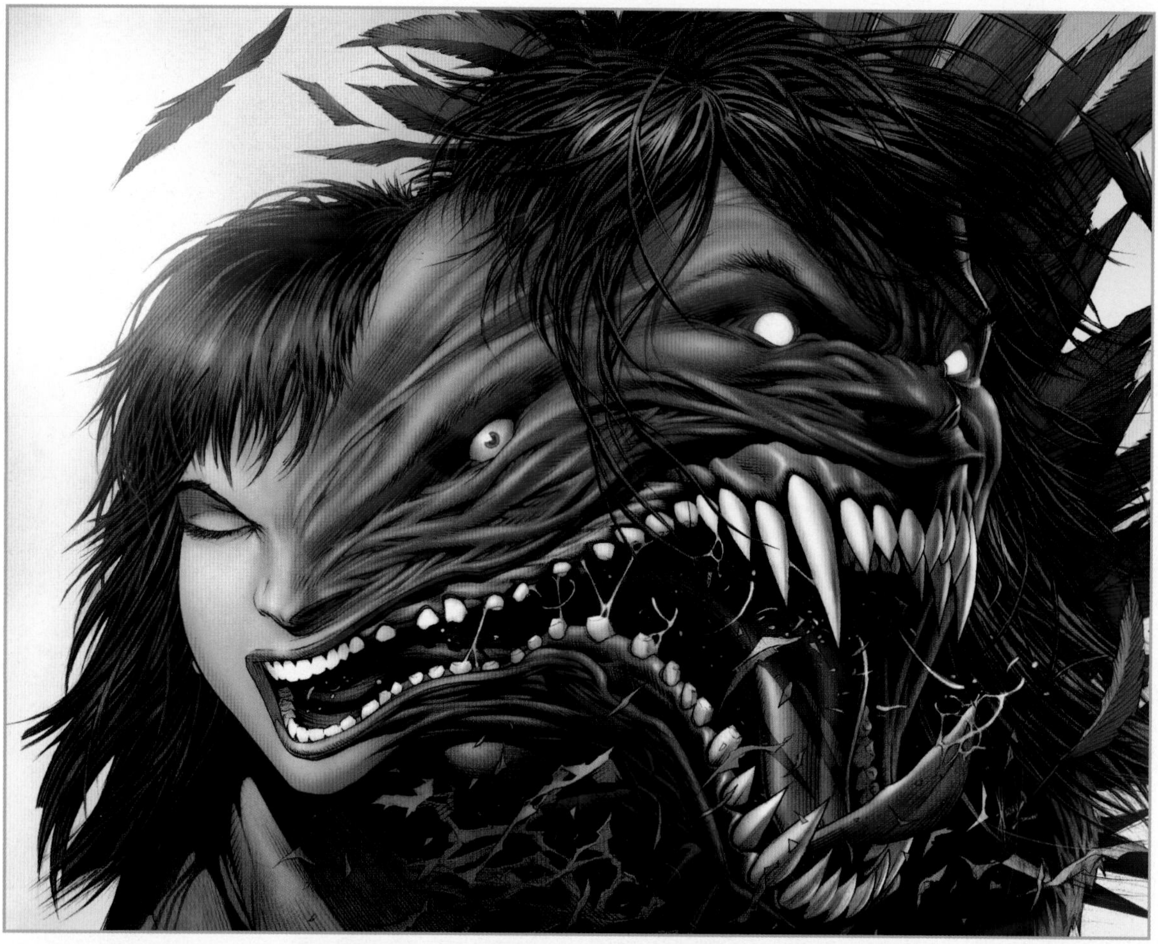

#23 IMMORTAL VARIANT BY DALE KEOWN & JASON KEITH

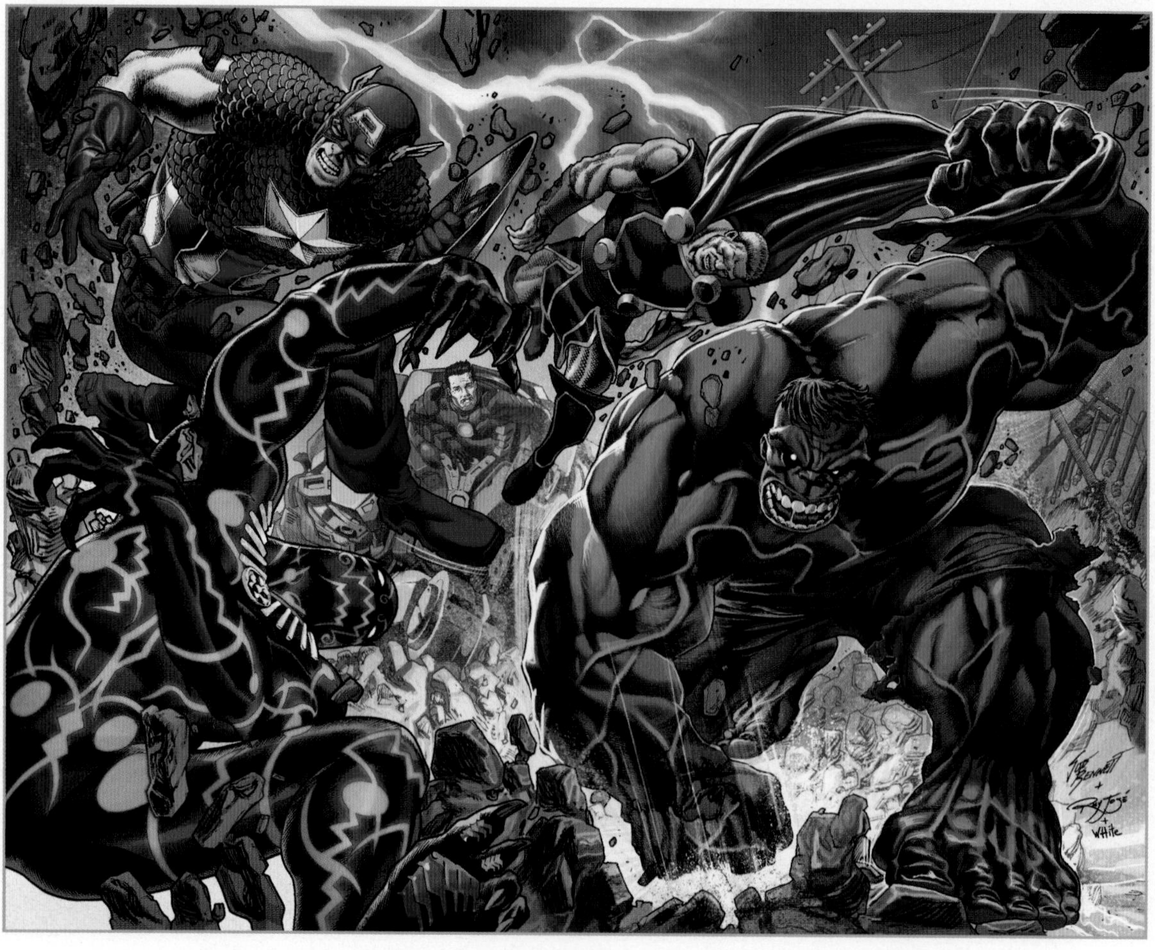

#24 VARIANT BY JOE BENNETT, RUY JOSÉ & DEAN WHITE

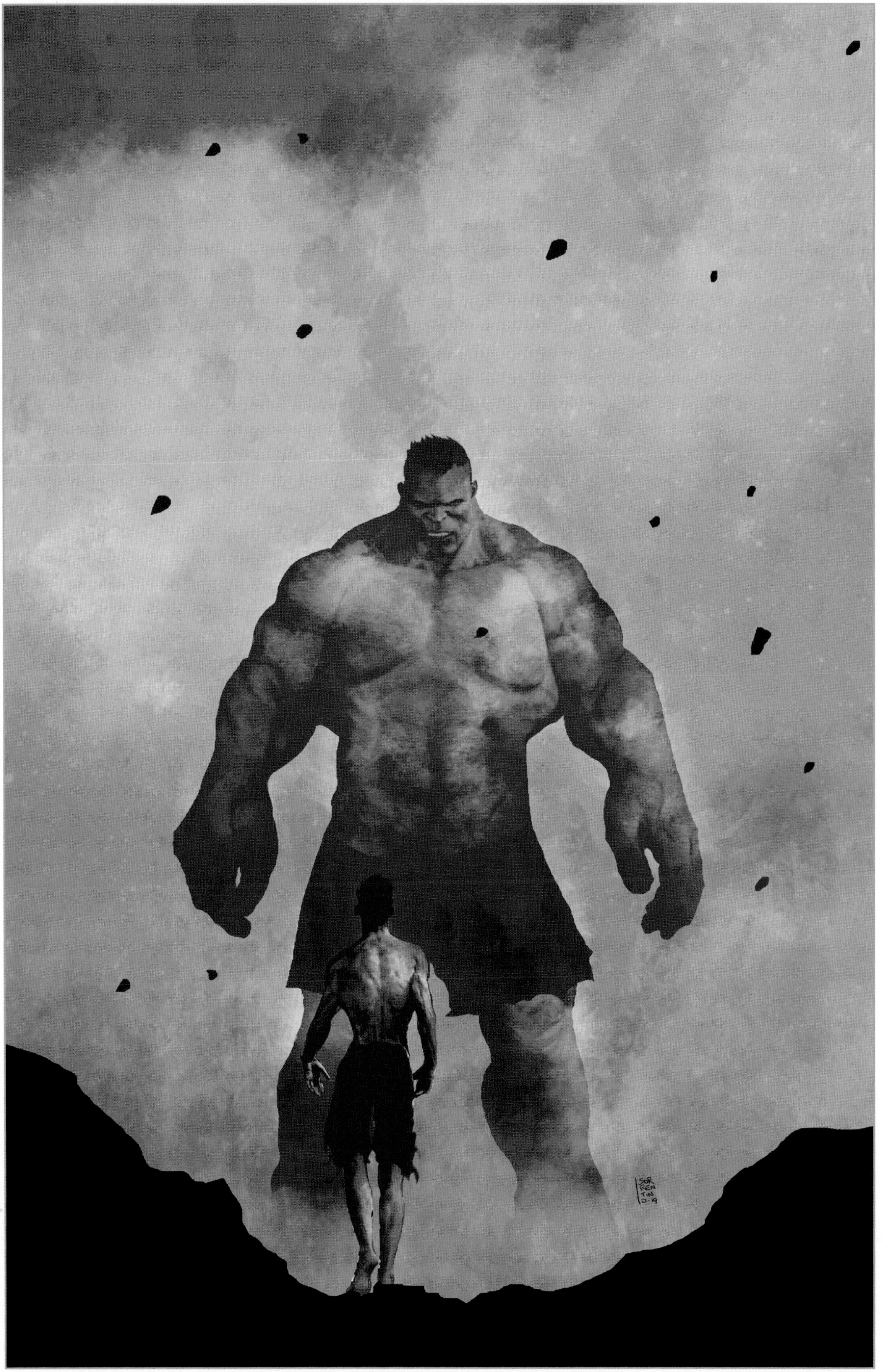

#25 VARIANT BY ANDREA SORRENTINO

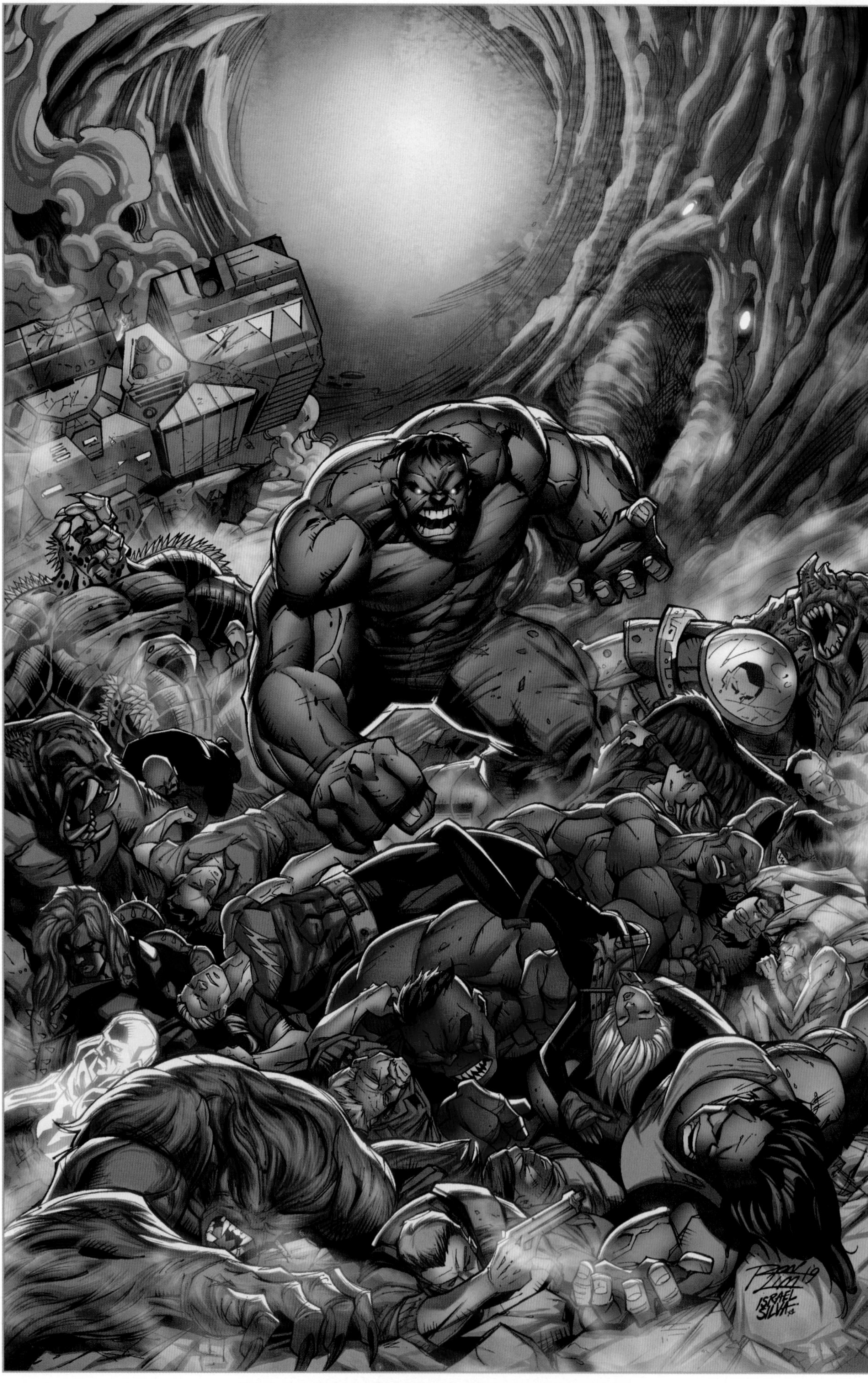

#25 VARIANT BY RON LIM **&** ISRAEL SILVA

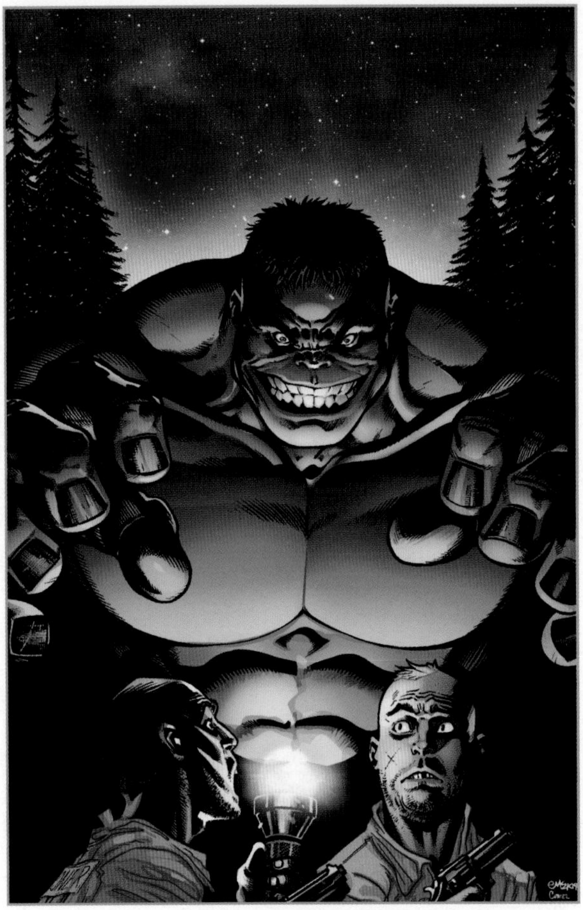

#25 VARIANT BY
ED McGUINNESS & DAVID CURIEL

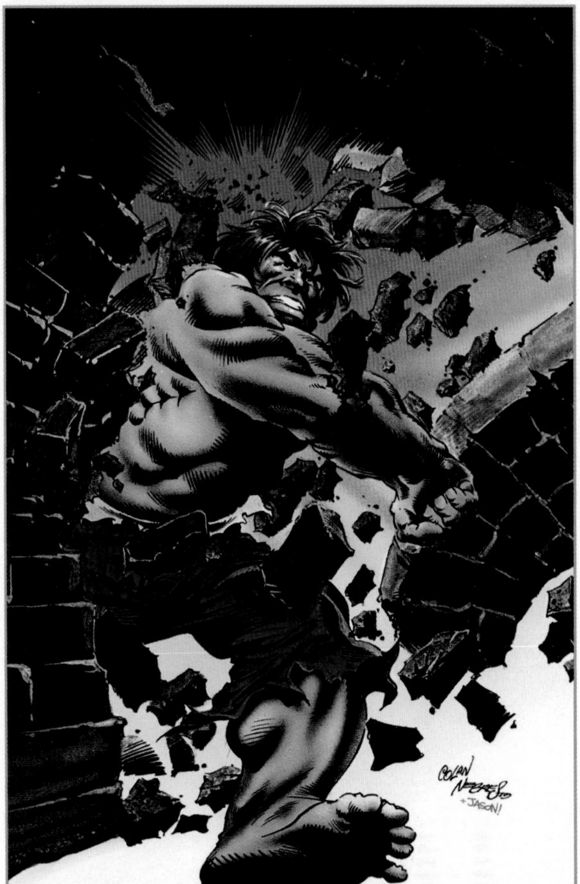

#25 HIDDEN GEM VARIANT BY
GENE COLAN, RUDY NEBRES & JASON KEITH

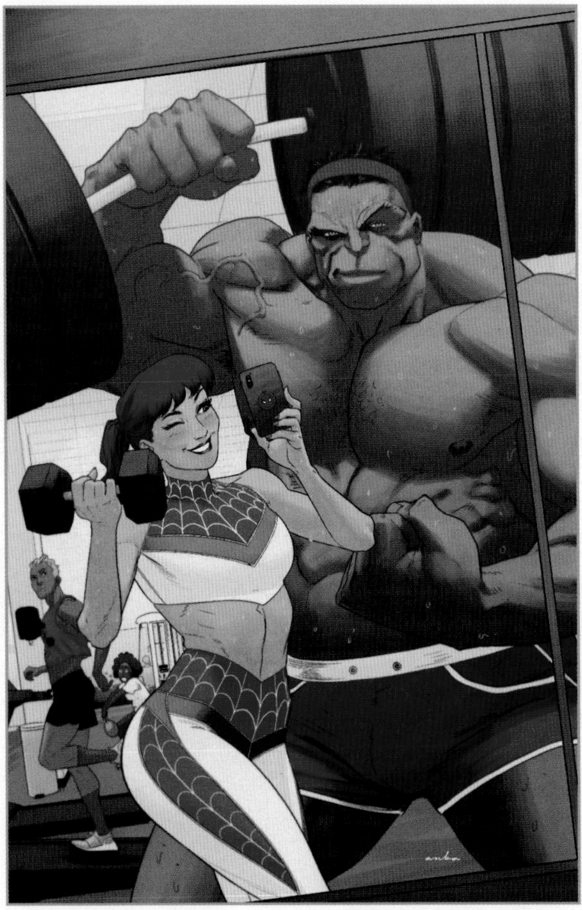

#25 AMAZING MARY JANE VARIANT BY KRIS ANKA

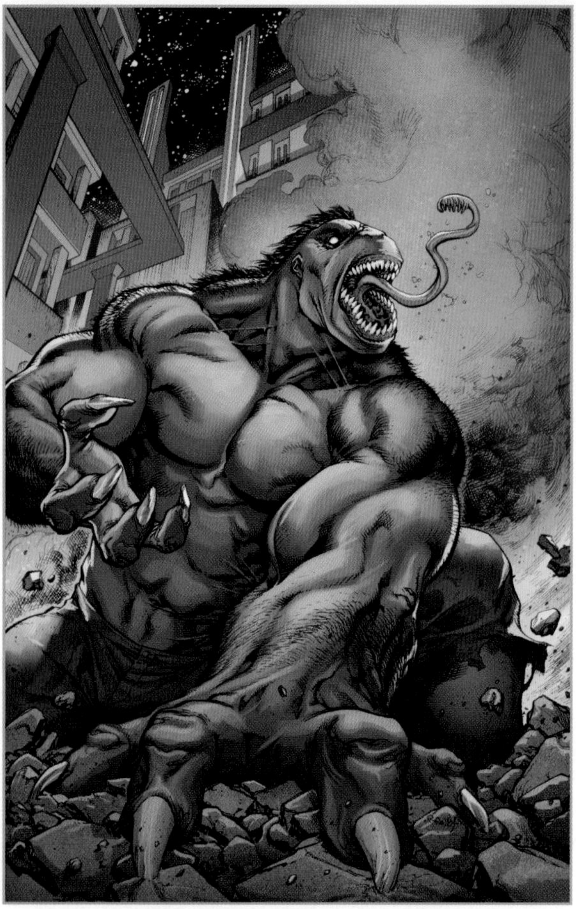

#27 2099 VARIANT BY
TOM RANEY & RACHELLE ROSENBERG

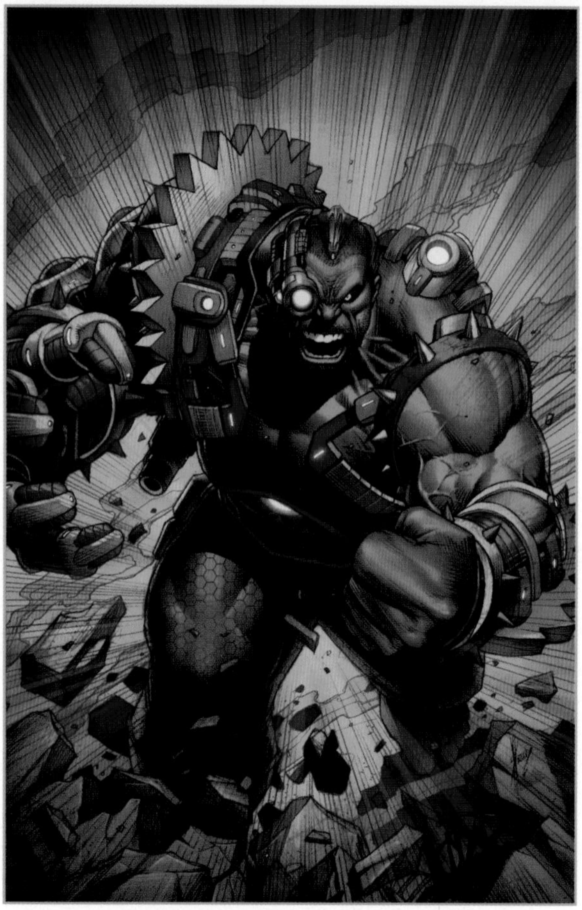

#28 2020 VARIANT BY
DALE KEOWN & JASON KEITH

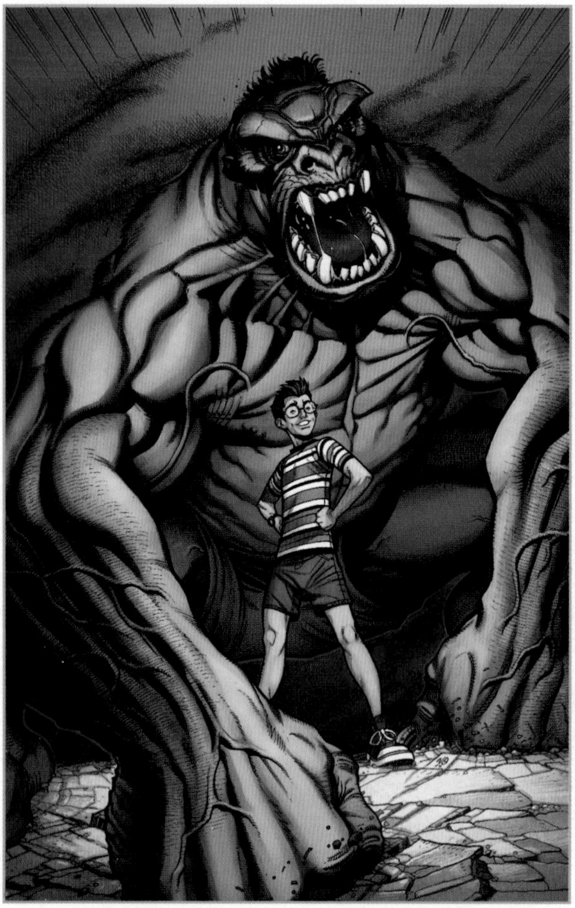

#29 MARVELS X VARIANT BY
NICK BRADSHAW & JASON KEITH

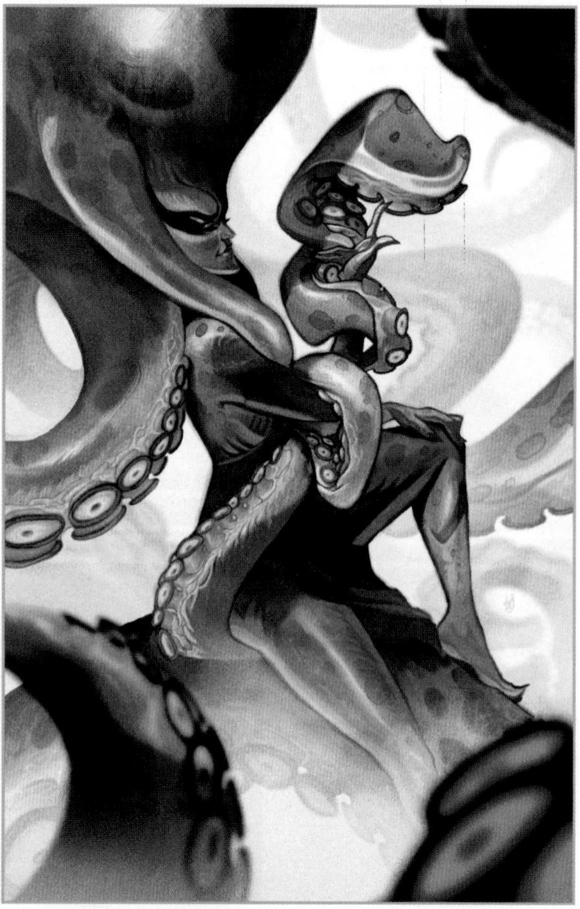

#30 MARVELS X VARIANT BY
MIKE DEL MUNDO